Wandering in Darkness

Wandering in Darkness

Narrative and the Problem of Suffering

ELEONORE STUMP

CLARENDON PRESS · OXFORD

OXFORD

UNIVERSITY PRESS

Great Clarendon Street, Oxford OX2 6DP

Oxford University Press is a department of the University of Oxford.
It furthers the University's objective of excellence in research, scholarship,
and education by publishing worldwide in

Oxford New York

Auckland Cape Town Dar es Salaam Hong Kong Karachi
Kuala Lumpur Madrid Melbourne Mexico City Nairobi
New Delhi Shanghai Taipei Toronto

With offices in

Argentina Austria Brazil Chile Czech Republic France Greece
Guatemala Hungary Italy Japan Poland Portugal Singapore
South Korea Switzerland Thailand Turkey Ukraine Vietnam

Oxford is a registered trade mark of Oxford University Press
in the UK and in certain other countries

Published in the United States
by Oxford University Press Inc., New York

British Library Cataloguing in Publication Data

Data available

Library of Congress Cataloging in Publication Data

Library of Congress Control Number: 2010927167

Typeset by Laserwords Private Limited, Chennai, India
Printed in Great Britain
on acid-free paper by
MPG Biddles Ltd., King's Lynn, Norfolk

ISBN 978–0–19–927742–1

1 3 5 7 9 10 8 6 4 2

For Ted
In fletu solacium

PREFACE

All my adult life, I have wanted to write what has turned into this book, but only in these latter years have I had any idea how to do so. I made a first try in my Stob Lectures at Calvin College. My Gifford Lectures at the University of Aberdeen incorporated and developed that material; they were a precursor to what has become Part 3 of this book. My Wilde Lectures at Oxford University were the predecessor of what is now Part 2. And my Stewart Lectures at Princeton University were an earlier version of Part 1. I am grateful to the schools and committees whose invitations to me gave me the opportunity to work on what, for a long time, has been my heart's desire to write.

Part 1 of this book is given over to explaining and justifying some of the characteristics of this book that run counter to more than one academic discipline's culture; but, even so, there are still a few things that need some word of explanation.

First, there is the matter of the poems. I suppose that, when I take up the books of other authors, I am not unusual in my practice of happily failing to read the ornaments of epigraphs and poetry that some authors like to put at the start of their chapters. If I had to put into words what motivates that practice on my part, it would be a sense that such epigraphs are basically just autobiographical expression on the part of the author and therefore not of much interest except to those people to whom the author is dear. But, in the case of this book, the poems interspersed throughout are meant not as autobiographical decorations but as part of the work of the volume. In my view, the poems give a different sort of access (a Franciscan access, as Chapter 4 explains) to the thought of the book. It is my hope that readers will not follow my own jaundiced reading practice but will instead read these poems reflectively in conjunction with the parts or chapters to which they are appended.

A special word needs to be said about the poem appended to Chapter 7. I found it in the texts for Osvaldo Golijov's *Passion According to St Mark*, and I have used it here by Golijov's kind permission. Golijov's prize-winning *Passion* is a stunning musical accomplishment, but it is also the best contemporary theological reflection on the passion and death of Christ of any that I know. I am grateful to Golijov for allowing me to include this one poem from the texts of his music in this book.

All but two of the poems introduce chapters; the two exceptions are the poems headed 'Incipit' (it begins) and 'Desinit' (it ceases). Medieval logic thought that there is something philosophically perplexing and worth investigating about beginning and ceasing. If, for example, the last instant (the ceasing) of a person's life is identified, it is not possible to identify the first instant (the beginning) of his death. Medieval work on beginning and ceasing and the theory of limits of continua that developed from it gave rise to something resembling a precursor to calculus. From the medieval point of view, *incipit* and *desinit* are an entangled pair, so to speak. It seems to me that something similar can be said as regards deep and abiding philosophical problems. The ending point is not independent of the starting point. And so this project is bounded at each end by poems that mark the beginning and the ceasing of the process of redemption whose exposition and defense are the heart of this book.

The poem headed 'Desinit' is taken from the Song of Songs, a collection of love poems between a bridegroom and a bride in the Hebrew Bible. In Jewish and Christian tradition, this biblical book has been interpreted allegorically as a love song between God and the soul, or between God and his people. In the passage given as the 'Desinit' poem, the voice of the bridegroom calls to the bride when the time of the wedding is at hand and when the terribly troubled times that preceded it are finally over. By contrast, the poem headed 'Incipit' is a passage taken from a longer poem found after the war among the remains at Auschwitz. I have not dealt directly with the Holocaust in this book, for reasons I give in the first chapter. But the power of the Auschwitz poem, the witness it gives even in a hell on earth, is always with me. I have taken the book's beginning, and its name, from that witness.

Secondly, philosophers are accustomed to clarify claims with examples they themselves construct, which typically involve faceless characters baptized with common names—'Smith' and 'Jones,' for example. But because this book emphasizes the importance of persons and personal relations, I wanted the names of real persons to figure in my examples; and so I picked the names of historical figures in the Patristic period: 'Jerome' and 'Paula,' and occasionally 'Julia' (another name for Paula's daughter Eustochium). Sometimes we get very lucky; we find among the people we love someone who has an unusual power to fortify us, to ease what hurts, support what is broken, and strengthen what is weak. Some of the biblical stories in the book have such a relationship at their center, but every age has notable examples, too. The Patristic period is full of them—Rufinus and Melania, for example, or John Chrysostom and Olympias. The Patristic Jerome and Paula are a particularly moving pair. Irascible, self-willed Jerome was afraid of nothing and deferred to no one; plenty of people were afraid of him, however, and with good reason, because he could be venomous. But he loved Paula, and she loved him. For twenty years or more, she was his companion in an ascetic, self-sacrificial monasticism. When Paula finally died, Jerome was crushed. For months he was unable to do anything at all. "I have lost her who was my consolation," he said.[1] He pulled himself together eventually, in part because Paula's daughter Julia loved him in her mother's place; and with her he reformed his life, centered then as before in companionship. I have learned something from Paula and Jerome of the possibilities of real companionship to give birth to the best in human lives, and so I wove their names into this project. My examples involve not 'Smith' and 'Jones' but 'Paula' and 'Jerome,' and sometimes 'Julia' as well.

Finally, although in my view the first part of this book had to be dedicated to an exposition and defense of the book's methodology, John Foley persuaded me that the methodology being defended required the book to begin with a story. The very short story sketched in the Prologue therefore stands in for an abstract of the book. In the circumstances, I thought I should say that this Prologue has its source in my own companionship with him.

This book has benefited immensely from the help of others, as would be clear just from the long list of acknowledgments given below, but there are specific debts that need to be acknowledged here.

To begin with what is essential, I have been fortunate in having outstanding administrative help. Various research assistants have contributed good work to this project, including Timothy Pawl, Fiona Grooms, and John Putz. My research assistant for the last three years, Stephen Chanderbhan, has been invaluable in helping to shepherd this manuscript through its various stages. He has been a superb proofreader for the entire project, too. My secretary Barbara Manning has been the fairy godmother of the operation. That various disasters have *not* befallen this project are due to her intelligent, energetic, gracious labor and initiative. I am also grateful to Peter Momtchiloff, editor at Oxford University Press, for his superb judgment and generous care not only with regard to this project but also with regard to many other things over the years I have known him. I owe a debt of thanks to the staff at Oxford University Press, too, for their excellent work in the production of the book and their graciousness in working with me in the process. I am very grateful for all this help.

I am indebted to Mike Gale and Dan Schutte for finding the image on the cover of this book. In my view, the image they came up with is a tribute to their own sensitivity and insight into the problem of suffering. I am grateful to them for the gift of their time and labor in finding it.[2]

I did some work for this project as a Lilly Fellow at the National Humanities Center; I am grateful for the help of the able administrators at the Center and for the good fellowship of the other scholars who were in residence with me. I wrote much of the material that I presented at the University of Aberdeen as a Fellow of the Collegeville Institute for Ecumenical and Cultural Research at St John's University, surrounded by the warm hospitality of the Benedictine monks and their abbot. Some of the material was also worked out during the term I spent at Baylor University as a recipient of the very generous Robert Foster Cherry Award for Great Teaching. I am grateful to these communities for their graciousness to me while I was with them. I also owe a debt to Tantur Ecumenical Institute in Jerusalem and its Rector Michael McGarry. Tantur is a magnificent place to work. Its setting is beautiful and quiet, and its library is excellent. I wrote various parts of this book there, during different visits; and I finished the book there as well. I am indebted to Tantur for its welcome, and I am grateful for the friendship of the people visiting or at home there, especially Michael McGarry, whose kindness over the years has made a difference to me.

At one point in the process of writing this book, I imagined that it would consist just in a revised version of my Gifford Lectures. At that point, a small group of scholars spent some months carefully working through that revised version and then assembled for a week at the Collegeville Institute to discuss the manuscript chapter by chapter. I am grateful to the Collegeville Institute and its Director Don Ottenhoff for making available to us the facilities of the Institute, which are lovely, and for the support of the Institute while we were there. I am particularly grateful to the very generous scholars, representing more than one discipline, who came together at the Institute to discuss the revised Gifford Lectures: Jeffrey Brower, Frank Burch Brown, John Foley, Scott MacDonald, Michael Murray, Michael Rea, and Theodore Vitali. This book is immeasurably better because of their contributions; and that week of intense conversation around the topic of the problem of evil, important to everyone present, is one of the most precious and memorable experiences of my academic career.

I also need to express a debt of gratitude to the community around me in St Louis. In one seminar or another, I have taught parts of this book to graduate students, whose challenging questions have helped me in shaping the final manuscript. My colleagues and students also gave of their time to listen to all the Wilde Lectures and discuss them with me in the term before I gave them at Oxford. I was touched by their generosity, and I benefited from their many helpful criticisms and questions. The Dominican friars, whose support is a blessing to me, have worked through some of the ideas with me in reading groups and conversations; I am particularly indebted to Paul Philibert, who read much of the manuscript and gave me welcome encouragement as well as very helpful comments. I would be remiss if I did not add that I am also very grateful for the university at which I work and the administrators who have run it in the years I have been here, especially the school's president, Lawrence Biondi. His ability to combine the excellences of a successful university president with the virtues of a mendicant in a passionate, living commitment to Jesuit ideals has been a significant source of the nurture this community has given me.

Among my local community, however, I owe a special debt of gratitude to Michael Barber, John Foley, John Kavanaugh, William Rehg, and Theodore Vitali. They discussed the issues of this book with me as I was thinking about them; they read the chapters as I wrote them, and sometimes reread them as I rewrote them; and they were among a group of friends who came to Aberdeen, Scotland, to hear me deliver the lectures on which some of the chapters are based. The acknowledgments I have made to one or the other of them in the footnotes of this book are insufficient to express my debt to them or my gratitude for them. The good of their companionship is woven throughout this whole book. John Foley and Paul Philibert also each wrote for me a *vade mecum*, which I kept by me as I was working. Those pieces, and new music John Foley wrote during this time, have been a source of strength and consolation for me. I am intensely grateful for all the generous gifts of this community.

The period in which I wrote the Stob Lectures, which were the beginning of this project, was marked for me by a firestorm of grief. I owe more than I could possibly say to Theodore Vitali, whose wise counsel and great-hearted willingness to suffer with me walked me through the storm. The poem by Rabanus Maurus appended to Chapter 5 expresses something of my own gratitude for him in the intervening years between then and now. I have dedicated this book to him, as a small return for the gift his continuing companionship is to me. (The line in the dedication comes from the medieval Latin hymn, *Veni Sancte Spiritus*. It is reproduced in Latin and in my translation at the end of the acknowledgements section.)

Finally, I am grateful to my husband Donald and to my children, all of them, including those I have acquired as my biological children got married. Their love and care are the sine qua non of everything I do.

ACKNOWLEDGMENTS

The following people gave me comments on one or more of the chapters, and I am grateful for their help:

Marilyn McCord Adams, William Alston (+), Charity Anderson, Pia Antolic-Piper, James Alexander Arieti, Robert Audi, Annette Baier, Michael Barber, Ronald Belgau, Scott Berman, Lipman Bodoff, Jon Bowman, Kathleen Brennan, Berit Brogaard, Jeffrey Brower, Susan Brower-Toland, Frank Burch Brown, Brian Carl, J.W. Case, Stephen Chanderbhan, Kelly James Clark, Christopher Coope, John Cottingham, Thomas Crisp, Ingolf Dalferth, Rachel Douchant, Stephen Evans, Alicia Finch, John Martin Fischer, John Foley, Harry Frankfurt, Robert Gahl, Robyn Gaier, Yehuda Gellman, Matt Gilbertson, Carl Ginet, Lenn Goodman, Robert Gordon, John Greco, Adam Green, Monica Green, Fiona Grooms, Ishtiyaque Haji, David Hartmann, John Heil, Wayne Hellmann, Christopher Hill, Jonathan Jacobs, Anja Jauernig, Monte Johnson, Karen Jones, John Kavanaugh, Fergus Kerr, Norman Kretzmann (+), Brian Leftow, Minghe Li, Yong Li, Hilde Lindeman, Scott MacDonald, Jonathan Malino, Jonathan Marsh, Colleen McCluskey, Dave Meconi, Richard Moran, Jeffrie Murphy, Michael Murray, Jeremy Neill, Jonathan Nelson, William O'Brien, Courtney Oakes, Robert Pasnau, Faith Glavey Pawl, Timothy Pawl, Adam Peterson, Paul Philibert, Mark Piper, Alvin Plantinga, Alex Plato, Ksenija Puskaric, John Putz, Philip Quinn (+), Scott Ragland, Beth Rath, Michael Rea, Jason Reed, William Rehg, Jonathan Reibsamen, Michael Rogers, William Rowe, Christopher Ryan, Eric Silverman, Alan Soble, Krzysztof Sonak, Irem Steen, Mark Steen, Josef Stern, Richard Swinburne, Patrick Taylor, Matille Thebolt, Kevin Vallier, Bas van Fraassen, Jimmy Vaught, Theodore Vitali, Henry Weinfield, Paul Weithman, Howard Wettstein, Nicholas Wolterstorff, Tedla Woldeyohannes.

In addition to the universities mentioned above, some version of one or another of the chapters were presented as lectures at various schools, including Aquinas Institute / St. Louis, University of Auckland, Baylor University, University of Canterbury / Christchurch, University of Colorado / Boulder, Thomas Institute / University of Cologne, Columbia University, Cornell University, Dominican School of Theology / Berkeley, Edinburgh University, Franklin and Marshall College, Georgetown University, Goethe University / Frankfurt, Harvard University, Holy Trinity Monastery / Krakow, University of Innsbruck, Jagiellonian University / Krakow, Katholieke Universiteit / Leuven, Massey University, National University of Ireland / Maynooth, Otego University, Peking University / Beijing, Polish Academy of Sciences / Warsaw, the Pontifical College at the Josephinum, Providence College, University of Salzburg, St. Thomas University / St. Paul, Stanford University, Thomistic Institute / Warsaw, Victoria University / Wellington, and the University of Wuhan / Wuhan, China. Precursors to various chapters were also presented at the Association for Jewish Studies, the Australasian Association of Philosophy, and the Castelli Congress/Rome; a short version of Chapter 5 was my presidential address for the APA Central Division Meeting in 2006. I am grateful to the audiences whose questions and comments helped me to think more deeply about the issues.

I wish to thank the following publishers for permission to reprint some or all of the material in the works listed:

the American Philosophical Association, for "Love, By All Accounts,"

Eerdmans, for "Second Person Accounts and the Problem of Evil" and Evil and the Nature of Faith,"

Routledge, for Chapter 13 of my book *Aquinas*,

University of Maryland Press, for "Samson and Self-Destroying Evil,"

Notre Dame Press, for "Presence and Omnipresence,"

Faith and Philosophy, for "Modes of Knowing: Autism, Fiction, and Second-person Perspectives."

VENI SANCTE SPIRITUS

Veni, Sancte Spiritus,
Et emitte caelitus
Lucis tuae radium.
Veni, Pater pauperum,
Veni, Dator munerum,
Veni, Lumen cordium.

Consolator optime,
Dulcis hospes animae,
Dulce refrigerium,
In labore requies,
In aestu temperies,
In fletu solacium,

O lux beatissima,
Reple cordis intima
Tuorum fidelium.
Sine tuo nomine
Nihil est in homine,
Nihil est innoxium.

Lava quod est sordidum,
Riga quod est aridum,
Sana quod est saucium.
Flecte quod est rigidum,
Fove quod est frigidum,
Rege quod est devium.

Da tuis fidelibus,
In te confidentibus,
Sacrum septenarium.
Da virtutis meritum,
Da salutis exitum,
Da perenne gaudium.

Come, Holy Spirit,
and send forth from heaven
the stream of your light.
Come, Father of the poor,
come, Giver of gifts,
come, Light of the heart.

Best of comforters,
sweet guest of the soul,
sweet healer,
rest in hardship,
cool in stifling heat,
solace in sorrow,

O most blessed light,
fill the inmost hearts
of those who trust in you.
Apart from you
we are nothing,
and everything is toxic.

Wash what is filthy;
water what is dry;
heal what is unhealthy;
soften what is unyielding;
enflame what is cold;
govern what is bent.

To those who trust in you,
who put their confidence in you,
give your sevenfold gifts.
Give the merit of virtue;
give salvation in the final hour;
give unending joy.

CONTENTS

PROLOGUE

There is a special kind of pain in watching someone whom you love in agony and being helpless to help him. This must have been what Mary Magdalene suffered at the death of Jesus. The Gospels report that, when Jesus was crucified, she was there, watching.[1]

It is not really clear who Mary Magdalene was. Augustine is partly responsible for a tradition that identifies her with Mary of Bethany.[2] Mary of Bethany is the woman who washed the feet of Jesus with her tears and dried them with her hair. John Chrysostom is vehement in his rejection of that identification. That is because Mary Magdalene is a sinful woman, and Mary of Bethany is the friend of Jesus. Chrysostom, who knew how to be friends with a woman,[3] is sure that Jesus would never have been friends with a sinful woman.[4]

Whoever exactly she was, Mary Magdalene loved Jesus enough to brave being present at his crucifixion, when most of the others who had followed him had fled. His agony must have been an agony for her. The Gospel stories report her both as near him and also as at some distance from him. Maybe she was near enough to see him and hear him but far enough away not to be close to him. At any rate, the comfort of being able to give him any comfort at all was unavailable to her. It must have been heartbreaking for her.

In these circumstances, she forms a plan. She watches till he is taken down dead from the cross, and she marks where they put his dead body. She gathers the necessary things and waits, as she must, till the time is right and the coast is clear. Then she goes to the tomb to anoint him. If she could not comfort him in his dying, she can anoint his body after his death. It must have been her heart's desire to do so.

How much she had her heart in that plan is shown by her reaction to its failure. When she came to the tomb and found his body missing, she wept hard. In his harmony of the Gospel narratives, Augustine supposes that several angels came to her, on successive occasions, to try to stop her weeping, but without making any real impression on her.[5] Whatever we may think about Augustine's harmonizing, and however we are to understand the narratives about her experience of angels at the tomb, there is no other biblical story in which angelic visits have so little impact on the person being visited. In her heartbrokenness over not being able to anoint the body of Jesus, Mary Magdalene brushes off even angels.

And then Jesus appears to her, to her first of all the people close to him, before the apostles, before his family, before his mother. "Mary!," he says to her; and she recognizes him in the saying of her name.

In that electric moment, in that presence of each to the other, her weeping ends. Her heartbreak at his death is over, and her heart's desire to anoint him, so pain-filled in its formulation, falls away. What she had wanted is so small by comparison with what she has. She has him, and she has him gloriously. Who could fail to miss his love for her? Neither she nor anyone else in her community—that is the answer. The whole community—apostles, disciples, family—first learn that Jesus is still present among them from her report of her experience of him.

All the elements of the problem of evil are present in this story, and so are the elements of theodicy. Jesus suffers physical pain and death, and Mary Magdalene's helpless endurance of his suffering makes psychic suffering for her. The source of his pain is the moral evil of others. Her suffering has in it the pain of those who are powerless and the shame that comes to people unable to protect their beloved from the depredations of others. Suffering in all its variety is present here. Furthermore, the story also shows us that there is more than one kind of heartbrokenness that can afflict us. When Mary Magdalene weeps because she cannot find the dead body of Jesus, what matters to her matters only because she has her heart set on it. The loss of his dead body is not the loss of *him*. She lost *him* when he died. There is heartbreak when a person loses something of great value, the life of someone she loves, for example; but there is also heartbreak when she loses what matters only because she wants it so badly. In the world of the story, for Mary Magdalene, in the presence of the loving beloved, heartbreak of both kinds is redeemed in love.

It is—isn't it?

No!, someone may think. There is no redemption of her suffering in this story. Mary Magdalene is glad in her reunion with Jesus only because she has restored to her what caused her great suffering when it was taken away. But it would have been much better if it had never been taken away in the first place. *She* would have been better off if Jesus had never suffered and died. She gains nothing in consequence of her suffering that she did not have before. And so her life without that suffering would have been better. In the story, her suffering is for nothing.

What does it take to redeem suffering—to defeat evil, as philosophers say? It is not always easy to say in the abstract. How would we adjudicate an answer to this question? What would count as evidence for our answer? How are we to discuss the question? What looks perplexingly blank in the abstract has handholds for our thought when we think about the question in connection with a story. In the world of this story, perhaps it is not so difficult. If, in the end, Mary Magdalene herself would prefer her life with the suffering in it, if she would be unwilling to lose what the loss of the suffering would take from her, then, for her, the suffering is surely redeemed.

A blind man, telling the painful story of losing his sight, says that he came to see his blindness as a gift. In the end, what he says about his blindness is, "I accept the gift; I accept the gift."[6] How could anyone—anyone sane or reasonable, that is—receive suffering as a gift? How could anyone receive blindness as a gift? It takes the details of the narrative of a life to answer questions such as these. And so the difficult questions raised by the problem of suffering can be considered best in the context of narratives, especially biblical narratives.

Or so I will argue in this book. In my view, narrative makes a contribution to philosophical reflection that cannot be gotten as well, or at all, without the narrative.

And, contrary to trends still prevailing in biblical studies, I will argue that it is legitimate to examine biblical narratives philosophically, rather than historically as source material for the understanding of ancient civilization.

In the course of this book, I will explore and reflect philosophically on biblical stories of suffering in its manifold variety, from moral evil to psychic brokenness and shame. I will present a philosophical case for a certain response to the problem of suffering, but I will make that case through an examination of narratives. I will argue that suffering can be redeemed for the sufferer in personal relationship, that heartbreak can be woven into joy through the reciprocity of love.

INCIPIT

There is grace, though,
and wonder, on the way.
Only they are hard to see,
hard to embrace, for
those compelled to
wander in darkness.

—poem by an anonymous inmate at Auschwitz, found on a
wall there, from *Last Traces: The Lost Art of Auschwitz*,
Joseph Czarnecki (New York: Atheneum, 1989), p.11.

The text is in German, and a part of it is unrecoverable; the portion translated reads:

'Immer freilich sind für … die Gnade und das Wunder unterwegs, nur sind sie schwer
zu sehen und zu begreifen, für die, die im Dunkeln wandern müssen.'

PART 1

THE NATURE OF THE PROJECT

Chapter 1

Suffering, Theodicy, and Defense

No worst, there is none. Pitched past pitch of grief,
More pangs will, schooled at forepangs, wilder wring.
Comforter, where, where is your comforting?
. . . . .
O the mind, mind has mountains; cliffs of fall
Frightful, sheer, no-man-fathomed. Hold them cheap
May who ne'er hung there. . . .*

Introduction

My topic in this book is the problem of evil. Only the most naive or tendentious among us would deny the extent and intensity of suffering in the world. Can one hold, consistently with the common view of suffering in the world, that there is an omniscient, omnipotent, perfectly good God? Some philosophers who were influential in the earlier twentieth-century discussion of the problem of evil answered this question in the negative and went so far as to claim that the existence of evil is logically incompatible with the existence of God. But, as the subsequent philosophical discussion of the problem of evil has made clear, such a claim is much harder to support than its proponents originally supposed. The propositions

(1) there is suffering in the world

and

(2) there is an omniscient, omnipotent, perfectly good God

* Gerard Manley Hopkins, *The Poems of Gerard Manley Hopkins*, ed. W. H. Gardner and N. H. MacKenzie (4th edn., Oxford: Oxford University Press, 1967), poem 65.

are not by themselves logically incompatible. At the very least, for a sound argument from evil against the existence of God, we need to add this premiss:

(3) There is no morally sufficient reason for an omniscient, omnipotent, perfectly good God to allow suffering in the world.

But this premiss is eminently debatable. In fact, a theodicy can be thought of as an attempt to show this premiss false by providing a morally sufficient reason for God's allowing suffering.

I have formulated this expression of what is commonly called 'the argument from evil' in terms of suffering rather than evil, because suffering, not evil, seems to me the salient thing. It has become customary to divide evil into natural evil and moral evil and then to focus discussions of theodicy on one or another or both of these sorts of evil. But so-called natural evil would not raise the problem of evil if there were no sentient creatures who suffered from hurricanes, viruses, and the rest. It is the fact of suffering, not its origin, that raises the problem of evil in connection with so-called natural evil. As for moral evil, the phrase 'moral evil' is confusingly ambiguous as between 'moral wrongdoing' and 'suffering caused as a result of human agency.' But both of these referents for the phrase 'moral evil' raise the problem of evil only because of suffering. The second obviously does, and the first does so in only slightly more complicated ways. When Jesus says about the person who will betray him that it would have been good for the betrayer himself if he had never been born,[1] he gives voice to a commonly felt but less commonly expressed intuition. Even if a malefactor feels no pain over the moral evil he does, his life suffers because of it.[2] None of us (well, virtually none of us) would willingly trade lives with a moral monster such as Herman Goering, even if Goering had in fact been jovial or content, even if Goering had died before the Nazis lost the war. Just because Goering was a moral monster, we would not want to have had a life such as his. So, even if Goering felt no remorse over the moral evil he did, his life suffered because of it, as our virtually unanimous unwillingness to trade places with him testifies.

As regards the problem of evil, then, what is in need of justification is God's allowing suffering. This is a book about the problem of suffering.

In the chapters that follow, I will consider the suffering not of all sentient creatures, but only of adult human beings who are mentally fully functional.[3] There are two reasons for this restriction. In the first place, there is no a priori reason for thinking that there should be just one morally sufficient reason for God's allowing the whole panoply of sentient suffering or that a solution to the problem of suffering has to be based on only one kind of benefit defeating suffering. And so it need not be the case that a justification for God's allowing the suffering of mentally fully functional human adults applies to all other cases of suffering as well. In the second place, considering the suffering of animals, infants, or adult human beings who are not fully mentally functional requires looking closely at the nature of their suffering; and this, in turn, requires careful consideration of the kind of subjective experience of which they are capable. But such issues are complicated and cannot be dealt with adequately in passing, and considerations of space rule out addressing them at length here.[4] It seems to me not easy to rule out the possibility that the theodicy I discuss in this book might be extended to other sentient creatures.[5] Nonetheless, because it is not possible to do everything in one book, the discussion of this book is confined to the suffering of mentally fully functional adult human beings.[6]

Suffering and pain

Discussions of the problem of evil typically assume that suffering itself needs no philosophical consideration.[7] But this seems to me false. To understand the nature of the problem of evil, we also need to reflect on the nature of suffering. And so I want to ask a question that is apparently colossally stupid but that is in fact propaedeutically helpful. When we look for morally sufficient reasons that might justify an omniscient, omnipotent, perfectly good being in allowing the suffering of mentally fully functional adult human beings, what is it about suffering that requires such a justification? What is wrong with the evil human persons suffer? Why is it to be lamented and avoided? What is *bad* about it?

The first answer likely to occur to us is that the evil human beings suffer is painful and that pain is a prima facie bad thing. Now it is certainly true that there is a use of the term 'suffering' that equates suffering with pain. We say, for example, "she died without suffering"; and we mean by this that she did not experience pain in the process of death. On the other hand, however, we also say that death is one of the evils human beings suffer, and we do not mean by this claim to be commenting only on those instances of death that are painful for the people who die. And so the suffering at issue in the problem of evil cannot be equated simply with pain.

In fact, some of the evils human beings suffer bring with them little or no pain, either physical or psychological.[8] What seems to be sudden instantaneous death is an example. And so is the peculiar phenomenon of Anton's Syndrome.[9] As a result of some injury to the brain, a person with Anton's Syndrome becomes blind but cannot be brought to believe that he has gone blind. His condition is not physically painful, and he suffers no psychological pain either, in virtue of his inability to believe in his blindness. Nonetheless, it would obviously be a mistake to suppose that, because there is no associated pain, Anton's Syndrome is not an evil human beings suffer.

So, although it is surely right that pain is a prima facie bad thing, this claim is not enough to explain what is bad about all the variegated evils human beings suffer.

Furthermore, even pain is bad *only* prima facie, other things being equal; and other things are not always equal. To see this, consider that, for a variety of reasons, human beings voluntarily submit themselves to pain they could otherwise avoid—that is, pain that is not necessary for life or health. Perhaps the most obvious case in our culture has to do with athletics, where the best athletes put themselves through agonies in the interests of athletic excellence. We might suppose that in cases of this sort pain is only a necessary accompaniment to something that we would be glad enough to have without the pain if we could. But even if, contrary to appearances, this is true as regards athletics, not all cases in which people voluntarily accept pain they could forgo can be similarly explained away.[10] Many women refuse anesthetics in childbirth, for example, although the baby would be born without the mother's pain just as well as with it.[11]

We are not inclined to raise the problem of evil in connection with the voluntarily accepted pains of childbirth, not only because the sufferer has in some sense chosen the pain, but also because it seems that, at least in the view of the women who have chosen to forgo anesthetics, the experience of so-called natural childbirth (that is, childbirth with its attendant pain) is, somehow, a great good. Consider, for example, this quotation taken from a midwife's manual on natural childbirth:

With the availability of such beneficent medications [as anesthetics], why . . . would anyone choose to experience the pain of labor and birth? . . . labor pain is not a feedback mechanism telling the neocortex of the laboring mother that something is wrong, but rather a means of letting her know that a process is taking place that will lead to the birth of her baby. The laboring woman . . . must have the willingness and openness to dive deep within herself and find the stamina to endure, to focus, to trust. She may have to stretch beyond her own perceived limitations in order to experience this act of creation in the now . . . Pushing a baby out of her body with her own efforts [in natural childbirth] can be one of the most exhilarating and joyful accomplishments of a woman's life.[12]

It is not my intention to endorse the sentiments in the midwife's manual, but I do want to call attention to her attitude. As the midwife knows, childbirth can be very painful. Nonetheless, there are women who have experienced severe pain in a prior childbirth and who even so refuse anesthetics in subsequent births, which are similarly painful for them. Like the midwife, most of us would not suppose that their voluntary experiences of great pain in childbirth raise the problem of evil. We are not prone to wonder, with grief, why it is not possible for such women to have without the pain of the birth whatever good they think they find in natural childbirth. The voluntarily accepted pain of childbirth does not strike us as suffering in need of justification.[13]

What is there about the pains of voluntarily chosen natural childbirth that distinguishes those pains from the suffering that raises the problem of evil? Pain can be, pain too often is, shockingly, lamentably, heartbreakingly, unacceptably bad. And yet, as these brief considerations show, pain is not necessary for something to be an evil which human beings suffer, and even severe pain is not sufficient for it.

Suffering and heartbreak

What is it, then, about all the variegated awfulness of human evils that prompts grief and wonder in us? What is bad about human suffering if it is not just a matter of pain?

Reflection on the example of childbirth helps here. A woman who of her own accord chooses natural childbirth, even after having had some experience of pain in an earlier birth, apparently thinks that the pains of the process of childbirth do not take away from her something that she wants. On the contrary, in her view, there is something about the process, with the pain, that she values as a good for herself. And so, in the painful experience of childbirth, such a woman has, somehow, what she herself cares about. By contrast, although she would endure much less pain of any sort, physical or psychological, if she were simply the victim of a purse-snatching, nonetheless she would feel that the purse-snatcher had in some sense undermined her, even if there were nothing in her purse worth stealing. She did not want him to have her purse and he got it anyway. So her will was not efficacious in the distribution of her own possessions; his will was.

The stronger the human willing is that is violated in the evil a person endures, the worse the evil seems. Evils that (as we say) break the will of their victim, such as rape, are horrifying to us. It is clear that, like pain, breaking the will of a human being is a prima facie bad thing.[14] So if the badness of suffering is not just a function of pain, then we might try thinking of it as a matter of violating a person's will.

It is important to be clear that not every contravention of a person's will counts as a violation of his will. Violating a person's will is more nearly a contravention of something at the core of a person's volitional structure. For want of a better term, I will call this core 'the desires of the heart,' borrowing a phrase from the Psalmist. In later chapters, I will say much more about the notion of the desires of the heart; here I want just to call attention to it. When the Psalmist says, "Delight yourself in the Lord, and he will give you the desires of your heart,"[15] we all have some idea what the Psalmist is promising. We are clear, for example, that some abstract theological good that a person does not care much about does not count as one of the desires of that person's heart. Suffering can arise when a human being fails to get a desire of her heart or has and then loses a desire of her heart.[16]

I do not know how to make the notion of a desire of the heart precise; but we have some intuitive grasp of the idea, and we commonly use expressions related to it in ordinary discourse. We say, for example, that a person is heartsick because he has lost his heart's desire. He is filled with heartache because his heart's desire is kept from him. He loses heart, because something he had put his heart into is taken from him. It would have been different for him if he had wanted it only half-heartedly; but, since it was what he had at heart, he is likely to be heartsore a long time over the loss of it, unless, of course, he has a change of heart about it—and so on.

Perhaps we could say that a person's heart's desire is a particular kind of commitment on her part to something—a person or a project—that has great value for her in virtue of her care for it but that need not be essential to her flourishing; it could be that, for her, human flourishing is possible without it. So, for example, Coretta Scott King's life arguably exemplifies flourishing, on any ordinary measure of human flourishing; and yet her husband's assassination was undoubtedly heartbreaking for her. If there is such a thing as a web of belief, with some beliefs peripheral and others central to a person's set of beliefs, maybe there is also a web of desire. A desire of a person's heart is a desire that is at or near the center of the web of desire for her. If she loses what she wants when her desire is at or near the center of the web, then other things that she had wanted begin to lose their ability to attract her because what she had most centrally wanted is gone. The web of desire starts to fall apart when the center does not hold, we might say. That is why the ordinary good things of life, like food and work, fail to draw a person who has lost the desires of her heart. She is heartbroken, we say, and that is why she has no heart for anything else now.

We might then try to understand suffering and the badness of suffering as a matter of violating a person's will.

Suffering and flourishing

But this is not quite right either. Not all evils, not even all horrifying evils, violate the will of the person who suffers them. Reporters attempting to elicit from a Mauritanian woman rescued from enslavement the story of her suffering at the hands of her master asked her whether he had raped her; but she had a hard time understanding the question. *Rape?*, she asked; *you mean what he did when he came in the night? Yes*, she said, *he did that often.* And she seemed almost indifferent to it. It is part of the horror of her story that she consents to what is in fact non-consensual sex.[17] In this case, the evil suffered does not violate the will of the sufferer. It diminishes her and makes her less than the flourishing self she would be if she were to flourish. It makes her less than she ought to be—that is, less than she would be if the world were what it ought to be.[18] But part of the way the evil she endures diminishes her is that it makes her acquiesce in her own diminishing.

And so, although violating a person's will is sufficient for suffering, it is not necessary for it. As this example shows, it is not even the case that all the evil human persons suffer is so much as contrary to the will of the person who suffers it. In the history of the world, there are many cases of human beings who have not had their wills opposed to the evils they suffered. The usual examples given to illustrate this point involve women or slaves, as the preceding example does; but we can also think of those working-class men in seventeenth-century Britain who supported the absolute right of kings, or those corporate leaders in our own times whose whole lives are given to the pursuit of money and material success. The lack of participation in the government of one's country is one kind of evil suffered by human beings, and a life stunted in its human relationships by a demeaning obsession with wealth is another. And yet these are things that are not only not against the wills of some people, but are in fact eagerly embraced by them.

Even if an evil suffered by some person does not go against his will, however, it is nonetheless the case that the evil he suffers undermines him and keeps him from the well-being that, without the evil, he could and should have had. And so something can be an evil a person suffers in virtue of its making him less than he ought to be[19]—that is, less than he would have been if he had flourished and had as much well-being as he was capable of, even if it does not violate his will that he suffers in this way. So the undermining of a person's flourishing, regardless of a person's will, is also a source of suffering.

What we care about

These reflections regarding suffering rely on notions that are themselves evidently in need of further clarification. Later in this book, I will discuss the scale of values that gives some specific content to the notion of a person's flourishing or being what she ought to be. Here I want to say something briefly about the notion of what a person cares about.[20] This notion is susceptible of at least two different interpretations.

To see the ambiguity in it, consider, for example, a college athlete who is a runner at some undistinguished small college and who wants very badly to be the best runner his school has ever had. If we ask him whether he wants to be a mediocre runner, he will surely not say 'yes.' Although many people settle happily enough for what is in effect mediocrity, hardly anyone sets out with mediocrity as his aim for himself and his life. And yet it might well be that, if the athlete in my example were the best runner his school had ever had, he would still be a mediocre runner. So, on the one hand, there is what a person cares about and is conscious of caring about. It is in this sense that the athlete in my example wants to be the best runner his school has ever had. And, on the other hand, there is a person's flourishing as the best he can be. Being in a flourishing condition is also what a person cares about, even if he does not know what exactly flourishing is for him, even if he does not know that he does not know, even if he thinks he knows but is mistaken. *Ceteris paribus*, if a magic genie conferred on the college athlete the gifts and abilities that made him the best runner his school had ever had and also a competitive runner in his event at the Olympic Games, the runner would not suppose that he had been given something he did not care about.[21]

Another way to think about the distinction at issue here is to see it as a variant of the distinction that needs to be made as regards the Aristotelian claim that every human being wants to be happy. On Aristotle's view, there is an objective fact of the matter about what happiness is—namely, a life lived in accordance with reason. But although it is the case, on Aristotle's view, that every human being wants happiness, Aristotle does not suppose it is the case that every human being consciously desires a life lived in accordance with reason. Still, if (as Aristotle thought) happiness is in fact a life lived in accordance with reason, and every person wants happiness, then there is a sense in which it is true to say that what every person wants, objectively speaking, is a life lived in accordance with reason. But to the extent to which a person does not think that happiness consists in that life, there will also be a sense in which it is true to say of some person who wants happiness that, subjectively considered, she does not want a life lived according to reason.

Accordingly, there are two different elements in what a person cares about, a subjective element and an objective element.

On the one hand, what a person cares about is equivalent to that person's well-being, objectively understood, to her flourishing and being the best she can be. Understood in this way, what a person cares about is what she ought to be. I do not mean that a person has a moral obligation to flourish, although that might be true. The force of the 'ought' in the expression 'what one ought to be' indicates a normativity about the world and not a duty on the part of the person. It should be the case and in an optimal world would be the case that a person is the best she can be.

On the other hand, what a person cares about is what has great value for her in virtue of her commitment to it. The great English poet John Milton strongly desired to be politically active in the Puritan government of his day. This desire of his kept him for years away from writing poetry; and, in fact, if Milton had died before Cromwell did, Milton's life would have been the life of a minor government official, not the life of a great poet. Arguably, what Milton should have been was the great poet he was capable of being. The best Milton could be was something much better than a minor Puritan administrator, and being a minor Puritan administrator kept Milton from the flourishing he was capable of. Nonetheless, even though Milton knew his gifts were for poetry and thought he had a vocation to write poetry, during the Puritan reign what Milton himself wanted to be was a member of that government. So there is also a sense of what one cares about that is *not*, or not necessarily, equivalent to what one ought to be. Instead, it picks out something a person is deeply committed to, whether or not that is what would constitute his flourishing or even be compatible with it. We care about our own flourishing, but that is not all we care about.

Suffering and what we care about

And so we can understand suffering in terms of what we care about. Because there is both an objective and a subjective element to what we care about, there are two sides to the nature of suffering, too. Every human person has some care about what kind of person she is and about her flourishing as that kind of person. For that reason, part of what it is for her to suffer is for her to be kept, to one degree or another, from flourishing. We can think of this as the objective side of suffering, since there is an objective fact of the matter about what will make a human person flourish. On the other hand, there is a subjective element to what we care about, too; there are the desires of a person's heart.[22] Although a thing that is a heart's desire for some person may (or may not) have considerable intrinsic value, the very great value it has for that person is a function of her commitment to it. Like the value a child has for its parents, the value of a heart's desire for a particular person is derivative from her caring for it, her love of it, and not the other way around. The suffering stemming from the loss of these things is the subjective side of suffering.

A loving philosopher-father, trying to deal gently with his small daughter's childish tantrums, finally said to her with exasperated adult feeling: "It isn't reasonable to cry about these things!" Presumably, the father meant that the things for which his little daughter was weeping did not have much value on the scale that measures the intrinsic value of good things important for human flourishing; and, no doubt, he was right in that assessment. But there is another scale by which to measure, too, and that is the scale that measures the value a thing has for a particular person because of the love she has for it. The second scale cannot be reduced to the first.[23] We care about those things that are the desires of our hearts, and we suffer when we are denied them.[24] For my part, I would say that it is not reasonable to say to a weeping child that it is not reasonable for her to weep about the loss of something she had her heart set on.

And so, on the basis of these considerations regarding suffering and what we care about, we can formulate what is bad about suffering in this way:

What is bad about the evil a human being suffers is that it undermines (partly or entirely) her flourishing, or it deprives her (in part or in whole) of the desires of her heart, or both.

Theories of morality that make a connection between morality and God tend to tie goodness either to God's nature or to God's will. Moral evil then becomes either what is contrary to God's nature or what is contrary to God's will (or both).[25] Given the preceding reflections on suffering, a roughly analogous point can be made about human suffering. The evil human beings endure constitutes suffering for them because it goes contrary to human flourishing or contrary to the core desires of the will of the sufferer or both.[26]

Most pain, of course, is bad in both these modes, sometimes in ways that leave a person permanently broken, as in some cases of torture, for example. But there are also cases where pain is bad in neither mode, as in the example of voluntarily chosen natural childbirth. The connection between suffering and what we care about helps explain why the pains of childbirth do not count as suffering in need of justification.[27] In ordinary cases of normal birth, the pains of childbirth do not undermine the mother's flourishing; and, if she chooses voluntarily, of her own accord, to have these pains, enduring them does not take away from her what she cares about in this respect either.

We might suppose that, on this view, all pain that is not voluntarily accepted would count as suffering; but this supposition is mistaken or at least in need of careful nuance. People sometimes return later in life to a teacher or coach whom, at an earlier time, they hated as stern and heartless in order to thank her for her efforts on their behalf. In this way, they show that the pain they endured through the agency of that teacher or coach is not *ultimately* against their wills or contrary to their flourishing as they perceive it.

What is bad about suffering, then, is that it undermines or destroys what the sufferer centrally cares about, her own flourishing or the desires of her heart or both. In my view, suffering so understood is what is in need of explanation in the problem of evil.[28]

Suffering and transparency

This understanding of suffering has implications for what we might call 'the transparency of suffering.' Nothing guarantees that a person will be consciously aware of what constitutes his own flourishing or of what the desires of his heart are. For that matter, nothing guarantees that a person will know when he is flourishing or when he has the desires of his heart.[29]

To see this point, consider first flourishing. Our social evils make it obvious that people can be confused about what constitutes their flourishing. But it is also evident that even a person who is clear about the nature of his flourishing can think that he has it when he does not and, conversely, that he can have it when he thinks he does not. Take health, for example. Many people take health to be an essential component of their flourishing. And yet, as we all know, it is possible for someone who feels perfectly healthy to have a cancer that will kill him in a matter of weeks. On the other hand, someone who has had cancer might well have been cured by the treatments for the disease but believe that she is still cancer-ridden. She might not be aware that she is cured until, at some later date, she receives the results of lab tests done to determine the success of the treatments. In the period after the end of the treatment that cured her and before the test results are in, she will be healthy; but she may not know that she is.

Mutatis mutandis, the same point applies to the matter of the desires of one's heart. Nothing guarantees that a person will be introspective enough or insightful enough to be clear about what the desires of his heart are; repression, self-deception, obtuseness, simple-mindedness, and no doubt other things as well can rob a person of self-understanding. But, even if a person knows himself well enough to be clear on this score, nothing guarantees that he will know whether or not he has the desires of his heart.

To see this last point, consider the case of Victor Klemperer. Klemperer was an assimilated German Jew who was a noted scholar of eighteenth-century French literature in Dresden before the Nazis came to power. His heart's desire was to write a great book, which would be his legacy to the intellectual world; he wanted to write a book in his area of expertise that would show eighteenth-century French literature in a significant new light. But the Nazi rise to power quickly stripped him of any chance of doing scholarly work. Instead, at great risk to himself and his wife, he wrote and preserved a diary. This diary has only recently been discovered in the Dresden archives. It turns out to be not just an invaluable historical resource but in fact a magnificent literary work. It has met with overwhelming praise from reviewers everywhere. One reviewer, for example, has called it one of the greatest works of confessional literature in the German language.[30] And yet, in that very diary, Klemperer records his despair over what he took to be the Nazi success at keeping him from writing a great book.[31]

It is therefore possible that a person be in ignorance about whether or not he is flourishing and also about whether or not he has his heart's desires. Since this is so, the account of suffering I have argued for here implies that a human being can suffer without knowing that she is suffering, and that she can think that she suffers when she does not. The counter-intuitive appearance of this claim stems from equating all suffering with pain; but this is a confusion, as I have tried to show. It may be true that, if a person thinks he is in pain, then he is; and if he does not think he is in pain, then he is not.[32] But even if, as many philosophers still think, it is not possible to be mistaken about whether or not one is in pain, pain is neither necessary nor sufficient for suffering, as I argued above; and suffering does not share with pain the characteristic of always being transparent to the person who has it or to observers of the sufferer either.

To say this is not to say that a person *never* knows when he is suffering. It is only to say that a person's views on the matter of his own suffering are not infallible. And so suffering is more nearly like ill health than like pain. Unlike pain, the state of our bodily health is not a matter that is invariably known to us by introspection or to those around us by ordinary observation. In the same way, neither introspection nor observation is invariably sufficient to recognize suffering. Suffering can have an opacity that pain typically does not.

What we care about and the benefits defeating suffering

A morally sufficient reason for God's allowing suffering has generally been supposed to consist of a benefit, to some group or to the sufferer in particular, that could not be gotten without the suffering and that outweighs the suffering. Such a benefit is sometimes said to defeat the suffering.[33] If what is bad about suffering is that it undermines a person's flourishing or that it deprives her of the desires of her heart or both, then a benefit that constitutes a morally sufficient reason for God's allowing suffering must be something that somehow defeats the badness of suffering so understood.

Such a benefit must presumably also be something we care about. Who would be willing to accept as a benefit that defeats his suffering something that he did not care about? But then the benefit must, in a sense, overturn the suffering. That is, if the benefit is something one cares about, then it must somehow enhance flourishing or contribute to one's having one's heart's desires.

If, however, suffering is a matter of one's having one's flourishing undermined or of being deprived of the desires of one's heart, then it may seem as if, in principle, there could not be a benefit that defeats suffering for the sufferer. If one did not care more about what one gained in the benefit than about what one lost in the suffering, how could the benefit defeat one's suffering? And what could one care about more than one's flourishing or the desires of one's heart? But these are just what are lost or undermined in suffering. How, then, could it be the case that they cannot be gotten without suffering, and how could one gain more of either one through losing it? But unless the benefit is such that it could not be gotten without the suffering and such that it outweighs the suffering, the benefit does not defeat the suffering for the sufferer. I raise these problems here, however, only to put them to one side; in the chapters of Part 4, I will return to them to see what can be said by way of resolution.

Finally, it is important to see that, since benefits are also a matter of what we care about, the opacity of suffering attaches to the benefits that could defeat suffering, too. Since there is no transparency as regards flourishing or one's heart's desires, then, contrary to a conviction commonly found among philosophers,[34] it is not the case that one has a benefit that defeats suffering if and only if one knows that one has it. A fortiori, others may fail to see it also.

Visible invisibility: what theodicy is not

In recent years, a substantial literature has developed which contends on the basis of epistemological considerations that a theodicy is not needed in order to rebut the argument from evil. This response to the problem of evil has come to be called 'skeptical theism,' and it is centered on the limitedness of human cognitive capacities. On the view of skeptical theism, we can know that we are not in an epistemic position to recognize morally sufficient reasons for God's allowing suffering,[35] because we can see that finite human minds cannot comprehend the infinite mind of God or cannot evaluate the intricacies of probabilistic reasoning or cannot calculate complicated modal claims or something else along these lines.[36] Since we can know that our minds are limited in one or more of these ways, the response of skeptical theism goes, then the argument from evil is deprived of its crucial premiss (3).[37]

But what the preceding reflections on suffering show is that there is a much more mundane reason for being doubtful about our ability to discern the morally sufficient reason justifying any particular case of human suffering: neither the suffering nor the benefits that could defeat it are transparent to us. For this reason, the inference in any particular instance of suffering to the absence of a benefit defeating suffering from the appearance of the absence of such a benefit is not valid. Reason can see that the nature of a benefit able to defeat suffering is such that reason is not always able to see it in particular cases.

Unlike the agnosticism of skeptical theism, however, this is not an agnosticism about the general nature of the morally sufficient reasons for God's allowing suffering. Consequently, this agnosticism does not militate against the possibility of theodicy in general, as skeptical theism does. Rather, these reflections about the nature of suffering and the benefits that could defeat it constitute an argument only against our confidence in our ability to evaluate the application of the general claims of theodicy to any particular case of suffering. If in some particular case we can see no particular benefit which justifies that particular suffering, we are not thereby entitled to claim that in that case there is none.

It is important to see, therefore, that the project of theodicy is different from the project of explaining the suffering of any particular person. In this respect, theodicy resembles clinical psychology or embryology or any other body of knowledge in which the possession of a general theory is not the same as the ability to apply that theory in any given particular case. Why *this* person should have become sick in *this* way, given her genetics and environment, may be mysterious to us, not because we lack the relevant theory, but because the information about this particular person that is necessary in order to apply the general theory to her case is lacking to us. Analogously, it is possible to have a general theory about the justification for God's allowing human suffering in general without being able to understand why any given person suffered as he did. Theodicy is therefore not the project of proposing to explain God's particular reasons for his dealings with any particular person or group of persons.

As for skeptical theism, even if human cognitive capacities are in fact limited in the way skeptical theists claim, so that human reason by itself is insufficient to discover the morally sufficient reasons justifying God's allowing suffering, the major monotheisms suppose that there is an additional source of information available to human beings besides the deliverances of unaided human cognitive capacities. That is God's revelation of himself, of his actions and purposes, especially in the texts of the Bible taken to constitute divine revelation.[38] And so, on the view of the major monotheisms themselves, it is possible that the claims of skeptical theism about unaided human reason be entirely correct, and yet that there nonetheless be a successful theodicy available to human beings.[39]

As far as that goes, even if we discount the possibility of revelation as a source for theodicy, we can think of attempted theodicies as thought experiments designed to test the skeptical theist's assessment of human cognitive capacities. If, in fact, all attempted theodicies should turn out to be demonstrable failures, then the skeptical theist may consider that the demonstrated lack of success of theodicies is grist for his mill. In that case, theodicy and skeptical theism would be useful to each other, because skeptical theism would be a fallback position for theodicists, whose manifested failure would lend skeptical theism some support, at least in the eyes of its adherents.

And so, in what follows, I will not address skeptical theism and the literature on it.[40] Although I have no quarrel with its claims about unaided human reason, my focus in this book obviates the need to enter into the debate over it.

Theodicy in the medieval world

The medieval tradition from Augustine onwards took God's providential governing of the world to be perplexing in certain respects, but it certainly supposed itself to have a religiously deep and morally satisfying account of God's reasons for allowing suffering. Unlike those in our own age who find it hard to understand how an omniscient, omnipotent, perfectly good deity could let bad things happen to good people, the medievals, who were confident of the correctness of their theodicy, puzzled over those cases in which bad things do *not* happen to good people.[41] There is a passage in Gregory the Great's commentary on the book of Job that illustrates that medieval view vividly. The ways of Providence are often hard to understand, Gregory says, but they are

still more mysterious when things go well with good people here, and ill with bad people . . . since the human mind is hemmed in by the thick fog of its uncertainty among the divine judgments, when holy people see the prosperity of this world coming to them, they are troubled with a frightening suspicion. For they are afraid that they might receive the fruits of their labors here; they are afraid that divine justice detects a secret wound in them and, heaping external rewards on them, drives them away from internal ones . . . Consequently, holy people are more fearful of prosperity in this world than of adversity.[42]

(This position no doubt also helps explain why the medievals are less likely to worry over the biblical line, attributed to God: Jacob have I loved; Esau have I hated.[43] Jacob suffered famine and went into exile in a foreign country, where his descendants were enslaved and suffered dreadfully; Esau and his descendants just lived pretty quietly in their own country.[44])

Whatever we are to make of this medieval attitude, so alien to contemporary philosophical sensibilities, it is clear that there is a long tradition of philosophically sophisticated, biblically based theodicies in the West—and, of course, an equally long tradition of counter-arguments designed to rebut them.

My project falls within this genus of philosophical discussion about the problem of evil, and it is indebted to the Christian and Jewish medieval traditions for its approach.[45] The focus of this book is on theodicy, broadly construed, understood in the way outlined here.

Animadversions against theodicy

Because my project falls within the genre, broadly construed, of theodicy, it is worthwhile looking briefly at two different sorts of vituperation often directed against the whole enterprise of theodicy.

In a recent indictment of all attempted theodicies, Terrence Tilley[46] argues that theodicies are immoral because they blind us to the horror of evil, and they make us comfortable with suffering we might otherwise strive against. Although I think Tilley's claim is false, I have a great deal of sympathy with his attitude. Philosophical analyses of the problem of evil can border on the obscene unless the pattern-processing of the intellectual exercise is coupled with a clear recognition of the awfulness of suffering and of our obligation to do what we can to alleviate it. Furthermore, it would be obtuse to fail to see that, no matter how successful a theodicy is, it cannot possibly alter the fact of suffering. Whatever justification for suffering theodicy finds, it remains a justification for *suffering*. To explain suffering is not to explain it away; the suffering remains and the grief over it ought also to remain, no matter how successful the justification.

In fact, for some evils, the grief and the pain are so great that, in my view, those evils are not fit subjects for the academic exploration of the problem of evil. For me, the Holocaust is an evil of this sort. Although it is vitally important for us to remember the Holocaust and to reflect deeply on it, taking it simply as one more example or counter-example in academic disputation on the problem of evil strikes me as unspeakably awful. It is enough for me that I am a member of the species that propagated this evil. Stricken awe in the face of it seems to me the only response bearable.

And so I share something of Tilley's attitude, although I disagree with his claim.

On the other hand, there are attacks on the project of theodicy with which I have considerably less sympathy. Some philosophers write as if the mere attempt at theodicy were in the same league as child-beating, the sort of thing only the heartless and uneducated would do in public.[47] In a scathingly derisive review of John Polkinghorne's defense of Christianity, Simon Blackburn begins by quoting with approval Hume's remark that, when he heard a man was religious, he concluded he was a rascal.[48] And he finishes with this black-spirited sarcasm: his reading of Polkinghorne's work has left him, he says, "in despair about humanity's desperate self-deceptions and vanities and illusions. Everything will be all right in the end, we are washed in the blood of the lamb, we are blessed, and above all God is on our side . . . Fantasy beats reason every time."[49]

In response, I would say that every theodicy, and likewise every attack on theodicy, is embedded in a larger picture of the world, and everything depends on the adequacy of that larger picture. Blackburn's own scientific description of what the world is like is remarkably blind to the things that seem to me most important in it.[50] He says:

the cosmos is some fifteen billion years old, almost unimaginably huge, and governed by natural laws that will compel its extinction in some billions more years, although long before that the Earth and the solar system will have been destroyed by the heat death of the sun. Human beings occupy an infinitesimally small fraction of space and time, on the edge of one galaxy among a hundred thousand million or so galaxies. We evolved only because of a number of cosmic accidents . . . Nature shows us no particular favors: we get parasites and diseases and we die, and we are not all that nice to each other. True, we are moderately clever, but our efforts to use our intelligence . . . quite often backfire . . . That, more or less, is the scientific picture of the world. [51]

But I would say that the immensity of the universe does not trivialize the human response of awe to its beauty or the yearning desire to share that sensed beauty with someone else. There is sickness and death, but there is also the fear of being abandoned to loneliness in sickness and the wish for tender care in dying. Moderate cleverness and moral mediocrity are part of reality; but so is the heart-melting genius of Mozart's music and the overwhelming self-sacrifice of Maximilian Kolbe. The very bleakness of Blackburn's picture testifies to its inadequacy. The dreariness of it would not affect us if our own experience of love and beauty did not make us feel forlorn at a picture of a world without them.

To me, such scornful disparagers of theodicy seem a bit like avuncular Martians whose sole knowledge of human life on earth comes just from videotape footage of medical treatments taking place within a large city hospital. Imagine how the doctors who run the hospital must look to such a Martian. The Martian sees patients being given drugs that make them sick and wretched. He sees patients having their limbs amputated or their internal organs cut out, and he hears the groans of those recovering from surgery. He sees patients dying in the hospital, including those dying as medical teams are doing things to them, and he observes the grief of their families and friends. This litany of miseries could continue ad nauseam. The Martian seeing all this will be filled with horror and with moral indignation at the doctors who plainly allow the suffering when they are not in fact actively causing it.

Any suggestion that the doctors are actually benevolent toward their patients will be met by the Martian with scorn and with incredulity that we would have the face to try advancing such a claim. The Martian knows what he has seen. We can try telling him that the patients are in the hospital in the first place only because they are sick, and he will reply indignantly that in very many cases there was no sign of sickness in them that he could see when they came into the hospital; the signs of sickness appeared only after the doctors went to work on them. We can explain to him that the sicknesses in question often take specialized skills, which only the doctors have, to diagnose; and he will dismiss our explanation with disdain as special pleading. We can tell him that without the treatments the patients would be sicker or would even die, and he will point out that many of the patients he saw died apparently just because of the doctors' treatments. We can respond that, on the contrary, many of the patients are in fact cured and live a long time outside the hospital, and then the Martian will turn on us with withering moral disgust at such pie-in-the-sky nonsense as the notion of life outside the hospital. And so on and on.

Clearly, the right of things between the Martian and his human interlocutors depends entirely on who has the correct version of the whole story in which the suffering of the patients is embedded; but, of course, that is a question which is not decidable by any amount of self-righteous scorn.

Theodicy and defense

A theodicy and a rejection of theodicy thus in effect each offer or presuppose a view about what the world is like. The picture theodicy paints is meant to show us God and human beings in such a light that we can begin to see the compatibility of God and human suffering in our world. The picture offered by opponents of theodicy, on the other hand, presents the world in such a way that some defect of mind or character (or both) would be required to believe that the world included God as well as suffering.

Sometimes the thing to do with such a divergence of views is to try to adjudicate the truth or falsity of the claims particularly important to it. In the hospital example, for instance, we could begin by presenting the Martian with biological information about some diseases to show him that a person who looks healthy can nonetheless be seriously sick, and then we could go on to other claims significant to the disagreement. In other words, we could argue through each claim that divides the Martian's view of the hospital from our own, in order to try to establish the truth of our position.

But another thing we could do would be to describe for the Martian in great detail our own worldview and then let the Martian re-consider what he sees in the hospital in the light of this worldview. We could, for example, describe to him our understanding of the prevalence of sickness and injury in our world and the way in which that prevalence is exacerbated by pollution and unhealthy lifestyles. We could then explain to him our understanding of the advances and powers of contemporary biology and medicine and of the role hospitals play in delivering the benefits of medical expertise. We could lay out for him our understanding of the social role of medicine, including the role of government in supporting the huge expenses of medical research and the role of the private sector in underwriting the enormous costs of medical practices, in order to convey to the Martian the trust our society has in the restorative power of the medical arts. And so on. In presenting these views to the Martian, we would not be arguing for the truth of our own claims about the hospital but rather showing the Martian the worldview within which those claims are embedded.

It is this second sort of strategy that I will pursue in this book. Strictly speaking, this makes my project a defense, rather than a theodicy, as these terms have come to be used.[52]

The nature of a defense

The word 'defense' has by now become a term of art in philosophy of religion, and various people have contributed to the development of the distinction between a defense and a theodicy since Alvin Plantinga first introduced it. Plantinga described the theodicies then known to him as tepid, shallow, and frivolous; in his view, the actual reason for God's allowing evil is and will remain mysterious.[53] The best we can do, Plantinga claimed, is to provide just a *possible* morally sufficient reason why an omniscient, omnipotent, perfectly good God might allow evil. In his terminology, this is a defense, not a theodicy. That is, a defense describes a possible world that contains God and suffering and that is similar to the actual world, at least in the sense that it contains human beings, natural laws, and evils much like those in our world; and then the defense proposes a morally sufficient reason for God's allowing evil in such a possible world.

What distinguishes a defense from a theodicy is that a defense does not claim that the possible world it describes is the actual world. It does not claim either that the morally sufficient reasons for God's allowing suffering which the defense proposes should be taken to be those (if there are any) which in the actual world do in fact justify God's actions in permitting suffering (if in the actual world there is a God). A defense, then, makes no claims about the way the actual world is or about any actual intentions and reasons for allowing evil on the part of God.

On the other hand, however, although a defense does not require that the morally sufficient reasons for God's allowing suffering which it presents are the actual reasons of a God in the actual world, it does not rule out that they are either. Nothing in a defense rules out someone's accepting the defense as a theodicy. And so Peter van Inwagen describes a defense as "a story according to which God and suffering of the sort contained in the actual world both exist, and which is such that (given the existence of God) there is no reason to think it false . . . "[54] On Van Inwagen's view, then, nothing about what we currently know demonstrates that the possible world of the defense is not the actual world.

In effect, then, the point of a defense is to undermine confidence in the crucial third premiss of the argument from evil. If, for all we know, the story told by a defense might be true, then, for all we know, there might also be a morally sufficient reason in the actual world for an omniscient, omnipotent, perfectly good God to allow suffering. Van Inwagen puts the point this way:

What does the defender of theism accomplish by constructing a defense? Well, it's like this. Suppose that Jane wishes to defend the character of Richard III and that she must contend with evidence that has convinced many people that Richard murdered the two princes in the Tower.

Suppose that she proceeds by telling a story—which she does not claim to be true or even more probable than not—that accounts for the evidence that has come down to us, a story according to which Richard did not murder the princes. If my reaction to her story is "For all I know, that's true . . . ," I shall be less willing to accept a negative evaluation of Richard's character than I might otherwise have been.[55]

Understood in this way, the notion of a defense is widely employed in philosophy, although not always in the self-conscious way in which it has been used in philosophy of religion in discussions of the problem of evil. So, for example, in arguing for a particular position regarding mental causation, E. J. Lowe remarks,

a correlation [between the mental and the neural] is consistent with various different relationships between the mental event and the brain events concerned: identity and 'realization' are two such possible relationships, but causation is another . . . [in certain] complicated situations, it . . . [would] be easy to confuse different possible sources of 'correlation' between mental and physical events. And, of course, we have no particular reason to suppose that this sort of situation is purely hypothetical; it may, for all we presently know, be the sort of situation that actually obtains with human minds and brains.[56]

Lowe is dismissive of those who object to this line of argument on the grounds that the postulated and possible correlation between the mental and the neural strikes them as implausible. He says: "plausibility is very much in the eye of the beholder."[57]

So a defense, in Van Inwagen's sense, is a common kind of argument in philosophical discussions. Of course, in some cases objectors may not be willing to grant that the defense is plausible to any degree, however small. That is, not everyone in a position to hear Jane's story might feel that that story could be true for all anyone knows; some people might feel certain that Jane's story is false, because, for example, for other reasons they are already committed to a negative evaluation of Richard's character. Even for such people, however, Jane's story will have the salutary effect of showing what the basis of the disagreement is between Richard's detractors and his defenders. In the same way, even for those people who are not inclined to judge a particular defense true "for all anyone knows," the defense will deepen the discussion between the proponents of the argument from evil and the presenters of that defense, because the defense will show the difference in worldview between the two groups, so that the discussion can be more fruitfully focused on the underlying sources of disagreement.

Defense and medieval theodicies

A defense can be constructed by sketching some possible morally sufficient reason for God to allow evil, together with just a few other metaphysical or theological claims. Plantinga's celebrated free-will defense proceeds in this way. But a great many philosophical and theological positions are relevant to a defense, and these can make a significant difference to the construction and assessment of a defense. For all its virtues, Plantinga's free-will defense, for example, has very little to say about the nature of morality and ethics, although these are significant for the argument from evil, which includes an attribution of goodness to God and a claim about reasons that count as *morally* sufficient for God's allowing suffering. And so, in this book, I want to go about the presentation of a defense in a different and more indirect way.

In the course of this book, I will explicate the worldview within which a typical medieval theodicy is embedded. In particular, I will examine at length both one medieval account of the good for human beings, especially the nature of loving relations between persons and the character of the things that impede such relations; and I will present one theodicy built on that worldview. My aim will not be to argue for the truth of the medieval account but only to show what it is. That is because, from our vantage point, we can take the medieval account as constituting a rich, sophisticated description of a possible world in which God and suffering coexist. For us, then, the medieval worldview and the theodicy embedded in it can be considered, in effect, as a particularly full and elaborate defense.

Within the medieval period, there is, naturally, a divergence of philosophical and theological opinions. Although, as regards theodicy, there is remarkable similarity among the views of such medievals as Augustine, Gregory the Great, Saadya Gaon, and others, nonetheless, the medieval period certainly does not speak with one voice. For my purposes, then, it will be necessary to focus on a particular medieval thinker; and, since Aquinas is the philosopher I know best among the medievals, I will present his thought as a representative medieval account of the world and God's reasons for allowing suffering in it.

I will begin by explicating Aquinas's general view of what we care about (in both its objective and subjective elements). Everything Aquinas believes about God's reasons for allowing suffering depends on that general view. For Aquinas, the best things and the worst things for human beings are a function of relations of love among persons, so that for Aquinas love is at the heart of what we care about. In subsequent chapters, I will, therefore, examine Aquinas's account of love, together with the understanding it gives us of the ancillary notion of forgiveness, which also needs to be considered in connection with the problem of evil. Then I will work at unfolding a part of Aquinas's account that he himself leaves undeveloped—namely, the nature of the union desired in love. I will go on to explicate Aquinas's view of the impediments to union between loving persons, and I will also use recent developments in neurobiology and developmental psychology to illuminate the nature of such union. Finally, I will show that, for Aquinas, the worst thing for human beings is a kind of willed loneliness, and I will explain the things that Aquinas sees as necessary for overcoming such willed loneliness.

With this exposition, I will have sketched the world as Aquinas believed it to be, at least as far as the basic nature of what we care about is concerned. Against this background, I will then shift course and turn to an examination of narratives. In my view—a view I defend in the next chapters—narrative has a role to play in the discussion of certain philosophical issues, and what it contributes is not reducible to non-narrative philosophical explanation or expressible in non-narrative philosophical prose.

The narratives I will explore are biblical narratives about human suffering and God's relationship to it. They include the book of Job, the story of Samson, the narrative of Abraham and Isaac, and the Gospel accounts of Mary of Bethany. On my view, these biblical narratives, taken together, constitute a larger story, a meta-narrative, as it were, of a world that contains both God and suffering.

In the context of this larger story, I will then present Aquinas's own theodicy. Put very roughly, Aquinas takes God's allowing suffering to be morally justified either as an antidote to permanent willed loneliness or else as therapeutic for deepened union among persons. Understood in the context of the narratives, I will argue, Aquinas's theodicy explains in a consistent and cogent way why God would allow suffering.

Powerful as it is, Aquinas's theodicy is nonetheless relatively silent about one element central to what we care about, as I will try to show. This element is what in this chapter I have called 'the desires of the heart.' Although Aquinas largely ignores the notion of the desires of the heart, I will suggest one way in which this missing element might be incorporated into Aquinas's theodicy. With this incorporation, the defense I want to offer will be complete and will extend to the whole problem of suffering for mentally fully functional adult human beings.

Because it is a defense and not a theodicy, the larger story composed of Aquinas's theodicy and the world of the narratives does not purport to give actual morally sufficient reasons for God's allowing suffering.[58] Nonetheless, this should also be said: the larger story is lovely, or so it seems to me at any rate; and beauty is also a road to truth.[59]

Chapter 2

Philosophy and Narrative

Lord, where shall I find You?
Your place is lofty and secret.
And where shall I not find You?
The whole earth is full of your glory.*

Introduction

The contemporary philosophical debate in Anglo-American philosophy over the problem of evil has become complicated and technical; for example, intricate questions of probability have played an important role in some of the philosophical literature on the subject. The analytic precision in such debate is a good thing; and I, along with many others, welcome it. But this turn in the discussion also has the vices of its virtues. In its focus on such philosophical technicalities as the appropriate patterns of probabilistic reasoning, it seems simply to sidestep much that has been at the heart of the problem of evil for many reflective thinkers. And so, to many people, there has also been something heartily unsatisfying about the direction of this contemporary debate.

This vague, unfocused complaint is reminiscent of the sort of criticism often leveled against the whole field of Anglo-American philosophy by its opponents, within philosophy and in other disciplines as well. Philosophy as it is commonly practiced in the Anglo-American tradition (a tradition to which I count myself an adherent) prizes lucidity, analysis, careful distinction, and rigorous argument—all unquestionably worth prizing. Nonetheless, those more sympathetic to other traditions in philosophy have regularly complained about what they call 'the aridity' or 'the narrowness' of Anglo-American philosophy; and, in my view, this reproach is not altogether unjustified.

---

* Judah Halevi, "Lord, Where Shall I Find You?," from *The Penguin Book of Hebrew Verse*, ed. T. Carmi (Philadelphia: Penguin Books and the Jewish Publication Society of America, 1981), 338.

To the extent to which one prizes rigor, one will eschew or even disdain breadth, since it is obviously easier to achieve rigor if one limits one's focus. And so Anglo-American philosophy sometimes looks like a species of the lapidary's art.

But simply encouraging philosophers in this tradition to broaden their focus would not yield satisfactory results. This trouble with the gauge of vision is, I think, a symptom of something deeper, which is both the strength and the weakness of this style of philosophizing.

Anglo-American philosophy has typically been concerned with analysis, to such an extent that its other common name is 'analytic philosophy.' It has been preoccupied with precise definitions of terms, fine distinctions among concepts, and complex arguments for philosophical claims. It is in consequence also marked by a hunt for counter-examples to someone else's definition, further distinctions lying between things someone else has already distinguished, and even more complex arguments showing the invalidity of someone else's complex arguments.

These practices of Anglo-American philosophy, characterized by an attention to analytic detail and a predilection for precision, can be conveniently thought of as mediated by left-brain skills (to use amateur but accurate neurobiological concepts). Such practices and skills are certainly important to any careful thinking in general and to philosophy in particular. Without them, philosophy is in some danger of turning into what can be (and often is) practiced by anyone at all over a couple of beers. But there is also no reason to suppose that left-brain skills alone will reveal to us all that is philosophically interesting about the world. The narrowness for which Anglo-American philosophy is reproached is thus a concomitant of the analytic strengths that characterize it. Breadth of focus is a right-brain skill. So are many abilities useful in interpersonal relations. As one contemporary neurobiological text puts it, those who are impaired with respect to right-hemisphere functions have an "inability to give an overview or extract a moral from a story . . . or to assess properly social situations."[1]

In his recent book *The Empirical Stance*, that exemplary analytic philosopher Bas van Fraassen frames a related charge that he levels against a part of his own discipline, namely, analytic metaphysics. He says, "[analytic] metaphysicians interpret what we initially understand into something hardly anyone understands, and then insist that we cannot do without that. To any incredulous listener they'll say: Construct a better alternative! But that just signals their invincible presumption that [analytic] metaphysics is the sine qua non of understanding."[2]

I would put the point, or my version of what I take his point to be, in this way. At its best, the style of philosophy practiced by analytic philosophy can be very good even at large and important problems. Aquinas's analytic analysis of the freedom of the will is an example. Alvin Plantinga's work on the nature of necessity (or any of a host of other issues) is another. (Van Fraassen's own analysis of the shortcomings of analytic philosophy is, ironically enough, yet another.) But left to itself, because it values intricate, technically expert argument, the analytic approach has a tendency to focus more and more on less and less; and so, at its worst, it can become plodding, pedestrian, sterile, and inadequate to its task.

In particular, in its emphasis on left-brain mediated pattern-processing, philosophy in the Anglo-American tradition has tended to leave to one side the messy and complicated issues involved in relations among persons. When analytic philosophers need to think about human interactions, they tend not to turn to complex cases drawn from real life or from the world's great literature; rather they make up short, thin stories of their own, involving the philosophical crash-dummies Smith and Jones. Bernard Williams, himself an analytic philosopher, considers the question why philosophers should not simply attempt to make up their own examples, drawn from life, as philosophers see it; and he says "what philosophers will lay before themselves and their readers as an alternative to literature will not be life, but bad literature [in the form of their own philosophical examples]."[3]

It is therefore misleadingly imprecise, I think, to diagnose the weakness of analytic philosophy as its narrowness. Its cognitive *hemianopia* is its problem. Its intellectual vision is occluded or obscured for the right half of the cognitive field,[4] especially for the part of reality that includes the complex, nuanced thought, behavior, and relations of persons. The deficit will perhaps be undetectable in work on modal logic or philosophy of mathematics, but in any issues where the interactions of persons make a difference it is more likely to be in evidence.[5]

Personal relations, however, are at the heart of certain philosophical problems. Central to the problem of suffering in all its forms, for example, is a question to which a consideration of interpersonal relations is maximally relevant: could a person who is omnipotent, omniscient, and perfectly good allow human persons to suffer as they do?

Analytic philosophy and narrative

Expertise regarding personal relations can be found with psychologists and anthropologists, among many others, but it seems to me to manifest itself especially helpfully among the creators of literature, especially the storytellers.[6] One idea, then, for addressing the shortcomings of analytic philosophy while preserving its characteristic excellences is to marry it to the study of narrative.[7] As this discussion itself shows, analytic philosophy can use its strengths to diagnose its own weaknesses. Analytic reason can see what analytic reason cannot see; and, having seen it, it can correct for its defects and limitations by bolstering itself with the cognitive virtues embodied in other intellectual endeavors. So one way to compensate for the limitations of analytic philosophy as regards philosophical problems such as the problem of suffering is to reflect on these problems by drawing on the insights of narratives as well as the results of contemporary analytic discussions.

In this book, then, I am going to consider the problem of suffering by reflection on narratives as well as contemporary analytic discussions of the problem. It is my hope that the result will be a true marriage, generating something newly good, and not just a forcible joining-together of reluctant bedfellows. I do not know if Isak Dinesen was right when she said, "All sorrows can be borne if you . . . tell a story about them";[8] but I hope to show that philosophical reflection on suffering is better with the help of a story.

I am hardly the first philosopher to whom it has occurred to think that analytic philosophy would benefit by some attention to literature. Others have also advocated this approach. Different proponents of the approach explain it in different ways;[9] but the person who has perhaps done the most to make it familiar is Martha Nussbaum. (The occasional acidulous complaints by critics that Nussbaum's work involving literature is not really philosophy seem to me an indictment of analytic philosophy, revealing the very defects I have just canvassed, rather than a criticism of the methods Nussbaum employs.[10]) To take just one example from her work, in examining Aeschylus's *Agamemnon*, Nussbaum focuses on the way circumstances trap Agamemnon in a moral dilemma and on the emotions with which Agamemnon confronts that dilemma; and she also calls our attention to the repugnance we feel for the attitude Agamemnon adopts in making the choice he does. These considerations then illuminate her examination of the role of luck in moral choice and in the formation of moral character.[11]

My own reasons for valuing a turn to literature, however, are somewhat different from those that have been given by Nussbaum and others; in the next two chapters, I will discuss those reasons at length. In those chapters, I will argue that there are things to know which can be known through narrative but which cannot be known as well, if at all, through the methods of analytic philosophy. For now, however, I want to try to allay some concerns which are bound to crop up here both from the melding of narrative and philosophy and from the particular narratives I am picking to examine.[12]

Narratives and the precision of analytic philosophy

One general concern which a proposal to include narrative in philosophical discussion will raise in some people has to do with order and structure.

Philosophical work in the analytic tradition commonly has a certain sort of tight order to it because it is typically structured around arguments. There is a thesis that is the conclusion of an argument, and that argument consists of premises, which themselves are argued for or at least elucidated. And so the discussion proceeds in an orderly way designed to try to command agreement. For philosophers, the structure of the argument is a kind of exoskeleton for the discussion, immediately visible and effective for defense.

One might suppose that this sort of structure can be preserved even with the inclusion of narrative in the discussion. One just has to let a narrative be brought in at the appropriate point where it supports or illustrates a premise. But to weave narrative into philosophy in this way is to demean the role of narrative, so that the narrative becomes little more than a picture put next to the text for those who find books without pictures boring. If we use literary texts in this way, just to illustrate premises in a philosophical argument, we are in effect dragging the literature in gratuitously, like anecdotes in an after-dinner speech, added to give entertainment to the proceedings without advancing the thought. But a real story cannot be reduced to an illustration for a premiss or two. Unless the literary texts in question are like Aesop's fables, designed on purpose to teach one philosophical lesson, what is philosophically interesting about a text will illustrate or illuminate philosophical reflection in a much messier way.

How, then, is narrative to be brought into philosophical discussion? Antiphonally, I think. A narrative has to be considered in its disorderly richness. But once it has been allowed into the discussion on its own terms, philosophical reflection enlightened by the narrative can proceed in its customary way.

In this choice of methodology, there is therefore some sacrifice of sharp and visible orderliness. By comparison with a philosophical work which moves in a disciplined way through arguments to the demonstration of a thesis, philosophical examination including narratives will look—will tend to be—softer and more rambling, with the bones of the thought beneath the surface. Something is lost as well as gained in right-brain approaches. Furthermore, there will ineluctably be some loss of the crisp, clean order of thought favored in philosophy even in the section on the exposition of the narratives themselves. Interpretations of texts—for that matter, interpretations of people and their actions—do not admit of rigorous argument. We can definitively rule some interpretations out, but it is hard to make a compelling argument that only *this* interpretation is right. Even a carefully supported interpretation of narratives is, in effect, only a recommendation to look at a text in a certain way. It invites readers to consider that text and ask themselves whether after all they do not see the text in the way the interpretation recommends. Interpretations present, suggest, offer, and invite; unlike philosophical arguments, they cannot attempt to compel.

On the other hand, part of what is useful about the methodology which includes narrative is that it helps us to remember that precise, compelling arguments are not everything. If we insist on rigor above everything else, we are in danger of getting it above everything else: a fossilized view of the world, unable to account for the richness of the reality in which we live our lives. Van Fraassen seems to me right when he says: "The world we live in is a precious thing; the world of the philosophers is well lost for love of it."[13]

Philosophical examination of narratives

Yet another problem with the methodology I mean to adopt stems from the fact that, while I want to consider narratives as narratives, I also intend to look at them as a philosopher. Some people may feel inspired to respond to this approach by adapting Samuel Johnson's dictum: the wonder is not how well it is done; the wonder is that a philosopher examines literature at all.[14] I am inclined, sensibly enough, to suppose that the best way to explain and defend a methodology for interpreting narratives is to show it in action. Nonetheless, here I want to try to allay skepticism by describing in broad terms the methodology involved in a philosopher's examination of literary texts. I am not here attempting to engage the extensive, contentious literature on the relationship between philosophy and literature; I mean only to say something about the particular method of bringing philosophy to bear on narratives that I will make use of in the chapters which follow.

Any attempt to characterize a methodology (and especially an interdisciplinary one) in a few lines invites trouble, of course, but I can begin cautiously enough by describing the approach at issue here as a method that involves asking philosophical questions of literary texts. This method will necessarily involve techniques used in literary criticism, in order first to avail ourselves of the narrative at all, but those techniques will also incorporate philosophical concerns and interests. So, for example, while both literary and philosophical examinations of a narrative might engage in character analysis, a philosophical study is more likely to ask whether the character in the narrative is violating moral standards in doing what she does or whether the worldview ascribed to her is coherent. Similarly, while both literary and philosophical examinations may look for philosophical or theological themes in a literary work—providence in *Hamlet* or nature in *Lear*—focused consideration of the concept of providence or the concept of nature is more likely to be found in the philosophical examination.

Some literary critics will not accept either this division of labor between philosophy and literary criticism or the presupposition that there is any salient difference between philosophical and literary texts. In reply to a similar objection, Bernard Williams says:

Some recent critics, in poststructuralist spirit, have attacked [philosophers] . . . for treating 'philosophical' and 'literary' texts as quite different from each other, and have at the same time scorned the idea that a determinate or privileged meaning can be extracted from any text. But, taken far enough, the second of these ideas undermines the first. If all that we can do with any text of the past is to play with it, then one satisfying style of play may be to force it into the regimentation demanded by . . . philosophy.[15]

I am inclined to think that there is something right about Williams's view.

On the other hand, if the methodology involved in a philosopher's examination of a literary text comes to no more than asking philosophical questions of literary texts, then philosophical examination of narratives would hardly count as new and should not need to be argued for. Many of the influential figures in the history of Christianity, for example, brought philosophical skill to bear on biblical narratives; and there is still much of philosophical interest to be learned from, for example, Chrysostom and Augustine on John, Jerome on Daniel, Aquinas on Job, Luther on Galatians, Calvin on Romans, Kierkegaard on Genesis, and hosts of other authors and biblical stories. (I know just enough of the history of Judaism to be sure that a similar list could be compiled for that tradition, including, for example, Saadya Gaon and Moses Maimonides on Job.) And, of course, philosophy has its own literary texts, such as Plato's dialogues, Augustine's *Confessions*, and Boethius's *Consolation of Philosophy*, in which philosophers present their positions through the literary devices of the literary texts they themselves construct, rather than expound.

It is clearly possible, however, to ask philosophical questions of literary texts in blissful disregard of their literary character, as some scholarship on Plato's dialogues, for example, makes clear.[16] The Patristic, medieval, and Reformation thinkers who asked philosophical questions of biblical narratives often had as their purpose just the analysis, as directly as possible, of the philosophical or theological lesson in the text. Sometimes that approach prompted a deep, sensitive interpretation of the texts, as is often the case in Augustine's *De Genesi ad litteram*, for example. On other occasions, however, it yielded a superficial reading of a biblical narrative precisely because it was ignoring the story's literary character, and in particular the human interplay in the story. Narratives presenting some human drama worth reflecting on were sometimes treated as if the human details were disposable wrapping around the far more interesting philosophical or theological lesson. Augustine, for example, uses the biblical text describing the exchange between Jesus and Mary at the wedding at Cana as an occasion to give a theology lesson on the nature of the incarnate Christ, but he leaves the human side of that exchange and all that it implies virtually unexplored.

And so the approach I use in this book has more to it than simply bringing philosophical concerns to bear on literary texts. Rather, it is an attempt to combine the techniques of philosophy and literary criticism in order to achieve something neither set of techniques would accomplish on its own. Its purpose is thus to give us access to a side of reality that can be captured better in narratives than in non-narrative prose but to give us access to it as philosophers. As such, it is different from simply asking philosophical questions of narratives.

This, then, is roughly how I understand the methodology at issue in the combination of narrative and philosophy in this book. In the end, though, the test of a method lies not in the apology for it but in its application

Philosophy and biblical narratives

Those philosophers willing to engage narratives have tended to consider literary works devised by single authors who were the creators of that literature. But narrative comes in many forms, from the highly self-conscious artistry of Aeschylean tragedy to the communally produced narratives of folklore. In this book, I am going to work at a part of the spectrum different from that typically focused on by philosophers looking at literature. The narratives I want to think about in connection with the problem of suffering are biblical. In subsequent chapters, in philosophical rather than historical or biblical order, I will examine the stories of Job, Samson, Abraham, and Mary of Bethany.

There are many other biblical narratives I might have used, including some that I had initially intended to explore in this volume. But considerations of space constrain ambition, and the narratives I do examine are sufficient to set forth the larger story requisite for my purposes. Among the narratives I had originally planned to examine and in the end was forced to omit are narratives about the temptations of Christ, the passion and death of Christ, and the resurrection of Christ. Some readers will find those omissions particularly disappointing. But it is not possible to do everything in one book, and so the part of the story of the problem of suffering involving the life and atoning work of Christ, as Christians understand it, will not be included here.[17]

To my mind, there is a certain commonsensical obviousness about the choice to use biblical stories in this project. Biblical narratives embody the reflections of communities signally concerned with both the insights and the problems of religion, and the narratives are also at least partially constitutive of the religions under attack in arguments from evil. So it is appropriate to incorporate biblical narratives in any attempt to meld literature and philosophy in reflection on the problem of evil. Furthermore, in virtually all of the narratives I will look at, not only is God a character in the narrative but he is also the character who manifestly allows or even brings about the suffering highlighted in the story. The stories are therefore specially pertinent to my purposes.

Nonetheless, my decision to employ biblical narratives will raise special resistance among some readers.[18]

One kind of objection regarding the methodology I am employing will arise not because of what the methodology is but because of what it is not. It is not a historical methodology.

Although multiple species of biblical exegesis can currently be found in the academy,[19] the sort of biblical criticism that has been dominant for a long time *is* historical. Historical biblical scholarship is an attempt to understand biblical texts by exploring and reconstructing the circumstances within which those texts were generated. That methodology is concerned, among other things, with the historical validity of the texts it examines, and it uses its historical expertise to determine the way in which biblical texts are related to the events they purport to describe.

Insofar as the point of my examination of the biblical texts is not to elucidate a period in history or a historical culture, but rather to shed light on a philosophical position through reflection informed by narratives, the historical approach is manifestly not so much as germane to my project. While it makes a great deal of difference to some issues in philosophical theology whether or not a particular biblical text is veridical, evaluation of the veridicality of the texts is not relevant to my work in this volume. Whether or not Job was a real person, for example, does not affect my interpretation of the story of Job or the use I make of it. My interpretation is equally compatible with the supposition that the entire narrative is historically accurate in every detail and with the supposition that it is a complete fiction. And so the results of historical biblical scholarship are not to the point for my purposes.

Nonetheless, because of the place historical biblical scholarship has had in the academy, it is probably necessary to say something in defense of my failure to employ that methodology here.

Historical biblical scholarship

Historical biblical scholarship has unquestionably been a valuable aid to our under-standing of biblical texts. It has yielded, for example, useful philological tools and illuminating archaeological research; it has opened up for us periods of history that were otherwise hidden or obscure. On the other hand, what is interesting about any text is not exhausted by a historical examination of it or the circumstances in which it arose, and one lamentable feature of the dominance of the historical approach is that other approaches to the texts did not grow well in its shade. For example, in W. Neil's detailed survey of the history of biblical studies in the *Cambridge History of the Bible*, biblical exegesis in the first half of the twentieth century is represented entirely by the historical approach, with no indication that any other approach might be desirable or even possible.[20]

The dominance of the historical approach has faltered in recent years, and other kinds of biblical exegesis have garnered attention in consequence.[21] Disciplines other than history have been brought to bear on the texts, and the results have been biblical exegesis informed primarily by feminist theory or by literary criticism, for example.[22] These new sorts of textual interpretation have not always been received enthusiastically by historical biblical critics, and those who practice the new methodologies have in turn raised some strenuous criticisms against the historical approach. For example, Robert Alter,[23] who has been influential in promoting literary exegesis of biblical narratives, has argued that historical biblical studies are a blunt instrument for examining some features of biblical texts. As Alter says in attempting to defend his own preferred methodology, "excavative scholarship," by which he means the historical approach generally, "demonstrably has its place as a necessary first step to the understanding of the Bible, but until the last few years there was little evidence that much more than excavation was going on. . . . "[24]

In Alter's view, when historical biblical scholars pay attention to literary texts, they can do so in uninformed and inadequate ways. Discussing Otto Eissfeldt's influential introduction to the Old Testament, Alter says:

when the nature of the biblical materials confronts [Eissfeldt] with literary categories, his apparent authoritativeness begins to look shaky. Thus, he divides biblical narrative into myths, fairy tales, sagas, legends, anecdotes, and tales, using these problematic terms with a casualness and a seeming indifference to their treatment in other fields that are quite dismaying. Or again, his eight-page summary of conflicting scholarly theories on biblical prosody painfully illustrates how scholars have read biblical poetry with roughly the intellectual apparatus appropriate to the decipherment of cuneiform inscriptions, multiplying confusion by the invention of elaborate pseudo-mathematical systems of scansion or the wholesale importation of terms and concepts from Greek prosody.[25]

Alter is not the only one leveling criticisms of this nature. In his literary study *Samuel and the Deuteronomist*, for example, Robert Polzin says:

the kind of close attention to the text that many biblical scholars' criticism represents turns out to be little more than textual in the narrow sense; the almost exclusive attention to *real texts* exhibited in their writings is attention to establishing a kind of *physical* text as a starting point for getting beyond it historically . . . Take Kyle McCarter's commentaries on 1 and 2 Samuel in the Anchor Bible. No one would deny his contribution to the text criticism and textual history of 1 and 2 Samuel or the judicious way he establishes a specific ancient text as the basis for his translation and interpretation. But having accomplished his task of translation, McCarter spends the rest of the over one thousand pages at his disposal mostly attending to matters of literary or cultural history. That is to say, the text that he establishes and translates so competently simply becomes a pretext for reconstructing either the prior stages in the formation of that text, or else those stages in the history of the religion of Israel that are exemplified in the textual strata he has 'discovered'. Anyone wanting to know how specific parts of 1 or 2 Samuel fit together or cohere in their final form finds amazingly little that does justice to the very text that McCarter so long and arduously establishes . . . A commentary like McCarter's—and his is typical—moves from establishing the text to translation to matters of literary and cultural history, proceeding with a profound lack of attention to what the entire text might mean in its final shape. This is simply not an important interest of biblical scholarship since the nineteenth century.[26]

In my view, there is something worth taking seriously in such complaints.

Scholars have also raised concerns about historical biblical criticism based on philosophical and theological considerations. So, for example, Jon Levenson contrasts the insistence of the historical critical method on trying to find the meaning a biblical passage had for its original author or audience with the interest of some readers in the meaning a passage has when its setting is the text of the Bible taken as a whole. He says:

we must be skeptical of the efforts of [historical biblical scholars] . . . to equate the *signal* that the canon (in whatever form) sends with the *intention* of the canonizers. We should be better advised to concede . . . that 'the text has meanings that no one ever meant' [footnotes omitted]. But how can the classic historicocritical method, with its concentration on 'one meaning' (the author's), do justice to a text that, as it stands, has no author, so that its meanings are ones 'that no one ever meant?' How can a method that distinguishes itself by its insistence on locating the text historically do justice to literature that conflates historical situations and thus repels all efforts to define it temporally, locally, and socially? My point is that the authorless text presupposed by a synchronic, or holistic, mode of analysis has certain affinities with the divinely authored text of pre-modern Jewish tradition . . . The affinities . . . become clear when the modes of interpretation of the two are seen against the author-centered interpretation championed by modern biblical criticism.[27]

And Levenson goes on to say:

in modern biblical criticism there will continue to be a broad basis for agreement on the meaning of textual units in their most limited literary or historical settings. But when we come to 'the final literary setting' and even more so 'the context of the canon,' we must part company, for *there is no public, nonparticularistic access to these larger contexts*, and no decision on these issues, even when made for secular purposes, can be neutral as between Christianity and Judaism.[28]

So there are also philosophical and theological concerns as regards the practices of historical biblical criticism.

The unity of a biblical text

For all the objections that have been leveled against it, however, the historical approach to biblical studies is still very much in the ascendancy, and those who practice it are likely to suppose that philosophical approaches to biblical texts are unacceptable in virtue of being ahistorical—or, as biblical scholars are accustomed to complain, in virtue of being historically naive. In fact, some proponents of the historical approach to biblical studies will be inclined to think that their discipline has demonstrated the inadvisability or even the impossibility of employing on biblical texts the interdisciplinary method of philosophy and literature as I describe and use it in this book. This method, they will object, might be suitable for an examination of a novel or some other product of an individual mind operating at a high level of artistry.[29] But the biblical texts, they will claim, are a melange of smaller bits put together by anonymous editors for various religious or polemical purposes.[30] It makes no sense, on this view, to ask philosophical and literary questions suitable to a single artist's work of a text that is a crazy-quilt of bits and pieces stitched together at various times by various people whose governing concerns were religious or political, not artistic or philosophical.

The issues raised by this sort of objection are important and complex and cannot be adequately dealt with in passing here; elsewhere I have discussed them at some length.[31] Nonetheless, something needs to be said here about it.[32] In my view, the force of this objection can be significantly diminished by a complementary pair of considerations.

In the first place, there is some reason for wondering whether every biblical text is such a melange as many historical scholars have supposed those texts to be. Traditional commentators, such as Augustine and Aquinas, often harmonized by multiplying. So, for example, a tension among the Gospel narratives as regards the number of angels at Jesus' tomb was resolved by multiplying episodes: first an episode with one angel (as in one Gospel) and then another episode with two angels (as in another Gospel), and so on. Historically oriented scholarship has tended to reject such traditional harmonizing interpretations because they solve textual difficulties by looking for ways in which apparently conflicting details might be part of one larger, consistent story. Historical biblical scholars tend to disapprove of such harmonizing because they think it does violence to the texts.[33]

But a little reflection shows that historical biblical scholarship is itself a certain kind of harmonizing.[34] Like the traditional harmonizing method it rejects, the historical approach tends to look for tensions or discrepancies in the biblical texts and to propose ways of resolving them.[35] Unlike the traditional harmonizing method, however, the historical approach resolves these tensions by separating the apparently discrepant bits of a text into separate layers or textual precursors. When they find tensions in the text, historical biblical scholars postulate different underlying stories or traditions, rather than different episodes of a larger and coherent narrative, as the medieval harmonizers did. And so historical biblical scholars get rid of the tensions they think they find in the texts by segregating the apparently incompatible elements into discrete sources, which they suppose to have been combined only later, often crudely, into one narrative. Historical biblical scholarship is thus a harmonization by division.[36]

The result of applying harmonization by multiplication to a narrative or set of narratives is a longer and often complicated story. The result of historical scholarship's harmonization by division is a series of short, relatively simple stories, each of them stripped of tensions and complexities. If historical accuracy is the aim of the historical biblical method, there is some reason for wondering whether harmonizing by division really is more likely to give historically accurate results than is harmonizing by multiplication. Is the reality of human history more likely to be simple than complex? There is an analogous question even as regards the texts and traditions. Paraphrasing another scholar with approval, Alter says:

the fact that the text is ancient and that its characteristic narrative procedures may differ in many respects from those of modern texts should not lead us to any condescending preconception that the text is therefore bound to be crude or simple . . . It is only by imposing a naive and unexamined aesthetic of their own . . . that modern scholars are able to declare so confidently that certain parts of the ancient text could not belong with others: the supposedly primitive narrative is subjected by scholars to tacit laws like the law of stylistic unity, of noncontradiction, of nondigression, of nonrepetition, and by these dim but purportedly universal lights is found to be composite, deficient, or incoherent . . . Attention to the ancient narrative's consciousness of its own operations . . . will reveal how irrelevant these complacently assumed criteria generally are.[37]

If historical naiveté is the Scylla in this case, then tone deafness to the literary complexities in a text is the Charybdis.

And so, without attempting to adjudicate the complicated conflict over hermeneutical principles at issue here, I think that this much can safely be said. Even if the historically oriented approach to biblical studies is entirely warranted in preferring its style of harmonizing by division, we will sensitize ourselves to possible excesses in the use of that historical methodology if we begin by trying to approach a biblical narrative as a unity. We may in the end have to give up our working hypothesis, finding the text intractably inconsistent, but at least we will have done what we can to avoid the sort of charge brought by Alter, of an ill-informed and insensitive parochialism, blind to the artistry of the text.

There is a second consideration that is also important to take into account in this regard. Even if we assume for the sake of argument that the picture the historical approach paints of biblical texts is altogether correct and that biblical texts do tend to be composites of simpler bits assembled by editors with varying concerns and interests, it does not follow that we cannot treat a biblical text as a unified whole. On the historical approach, a text will have the form it does because there was a *last* redactor or redactors who brought the earlier sources or stories together into that final form. But there is no reason for rejecting a priori the supposition that such redactors may have had literary or philosophical skills that were employed in the compilation of the final form of the text, even if the redactors' primary motivation was political or ideological, rather than literary and philosophical.

Alter puts a related point this way: "biblical critics frequently assume, out of some dim preconception about the transmission of texts in 'primitive' cultures, that the redactors were in the grip of a kind of manic tribal compulsion, driven again and again to include units of traditional material that made no connective sense, for reasons they themselves could not have explained."[38]

Whether or not this is an appropriate characterization of historically oriented biblical scholarship, it is clear that there is nothing in the historical approach itself that rules out the possibility that the final redactor had literary sensitivity or philosophical ability. And, of course, one way for us to decide whether a final redactor was artistically or philosophically competent is to see if the text can be read as the product of such a mind.

So, for all these reasons, I think there is nothing in the results of historical research on biblical texts which rules out approaching a biblical text as a unity or using on a biblical text the methods that have proved fruitful in other philosophical examinations of literature.

Biblical narratives and revelation

It should be clear that, for my purposes in this book, it does not matter whether or not the narratives I examine are revealed. A defense is a story that accounts for the existence of God and the existence of the suffering in our world and that is not demonstrably false; a defense does not need to claim that the reasons it ascribes to God for allowing suffering are God's actual reasons, only that they might be God's reasons, for all we know. And so fictional narratives can also undergird a defense, if those narratives are capable of providing an adequate story for the defense. On the other hand, of course, if the narratives in question are in fact divinely revealed truth, then the defense based on those narratives will also be a theodicy. There is nothing to keep readers committed to the belief that biblical texts are God's revelation from taking the defense I construct as a theodicy.

Nonetheless, for some readers who take the biblical texts to be revealed, my examination of biblical narratives will raise a special problem because those readers will suppose that revealed biblical texts *require* historical exegesis. Such readers will side with historical biblical scholars in supposing both that there is a single early state (or set of states) of the narrative in question and that that early state (or states) must be retrieved for any adequate exegesis of the text. The revelation God put into history is available to us now, such readers will think, only in case we are able to retrieve the preceding layers of the text. And so, from the point of view of such readers, the narratives are not treated adequately, or respectfully, without recourse to historical scholarship.

Elsewhere I have examined in detail the claim that there cannot be any religiously acceptable exegesis of revealed texts that is not historical.[39] There I showed that this claim has a Deistic cast, in virtue of supposing that God providentially put into history a message needed for salvation and intended for all people but that God then neglected to exercise any care for the subsequent transmission of that message. By contrast, medieval exegetes, who also took these texts to be revealed, accorded no special value to the early state of biblical texts because they supposed that not only the initial communication of the biblical message but also its transmission through the ages was under the control of a benevolent providence. For this reason, on the view of the medievals, however important historical exegesis may be for some purposes, it is not necessary in order to gain access to revelation.

Because readers troubled by this issue can consult the detailed discussion of it in that earlier work of mine, I will leave further consideration of it to one side here.[40]

Biblical narratives and character analysis

There is one last general point about methodology that probably needs to be made here. An important part of the examination of a narrative consists in reflection on the underlying thoughts or motivations of characters in the narrative, but some scholars will be uncomfortable with such an approach to biblical narratives. They will see such considerations as a matter of trying to see into the mind of characters in a historically conditioned text; they will tend to suppose that the whole process consists of eisegesis, rather than exegesis.[41]

In my view, such complaints are misplaced.[42] Literary criticism unfolds many features of texts, ranging from patterns of phraseology to political biases on the part of the text's author. One staple of literary criticism just is careful consideration of the thoughts, emotions, and motives that may underlie the behavior of the characters in a narrative. There is no cogent reason, as far as I can see, why biblical narratives should be exempt from this standard practice of literary criticism. As far as that goes, even biblical scholars whose primary interests are not literary but historical find themselves forced to consider the underlying thoughts of characters in the biblical narratives. So, for example, the historical biblical scholar Raymond Brown finds it necessary to try to explain why Jesus weeps in the story of the raising of Lazarus. As part of his exegesis of the text, he attempts to describe what the thoughts and emotions underlying the weeping of Jesus are in that narrative.[43]

In a philosophically interesting article on narratives entitled "The Truth of Fiction," the noted Nigerian novelist Chinua Achebe argues that one of the most important functions of fiction is precisely to require us to engage in character interpretation of this sort. Achebe asks: "Why does Amos Tutuola's *The Palm-Wine Drinkard* offer us a better, stronger, and more memorable insight into the problem of excess than all the sermons and editorials we have heard and read, or will hear and read, on the same subject?"[44] His answer to this question consists just in pointing out that fiction requires us to exercise our minds on the characters in the text and on their actions and circumstances. In coming to understand the author's characters by ferreting out as best we can their thoughts and motives, Achebe thinks, we learn vicariously the sorts of things we otherwise would have had to learn by experience. Achebe says: "without having to undergo personally the ordeals which the Drinkard has to suffer in atonement for his idleness and lack of self-control we become, through an act of our imagination, beneficiaries of his regenerative adventure."[45] On Achebe's view, then, it is our having to probe into the psyches of the characters to understand a narrative that gives fiction an edge over "sermons and editorials," or over philosophical prose in its other guises as well.[46]

I will have much more to say in the next two chapters about the contribution of narrative to philosophy, but for now I want only to comment that Achebe seems to me in general right. Reflecting on the thoughts and emotions of characters in biblical narratives is not a peculiar or illegitimate approach to the texts. It is part of a literary study of narratives, and it is necessary for unpacking what is philosophically interesting about them.

A last caveat

As I know from experience, the fact that the examination of the biblical narratives in subsequent chapters contains so much easy talk about God's actions, thoughts, and motives can give some readers the impression that this book is intended only for an audience which is committed to religious belief. The smallest amount of attention will show that this impression is entirely false.

As I have been at pains to explain, for my purposes here I am treating the biblical narratives only as stories, not as history or as revelation; and nothing in this project presupposes the truth of belief in God. Insofar as I am here engaged in the construction of a defense, my project is a matter of describing—describing vividly and in detail by means of the narratives—a possible world in which suffering and a perfectly good, omniscient, omnipotent God coexist. But the existence of a possible world of this sort does not entail or presuppose that there is a God in the actual world. Those people who think there is no God in the actual world can thus accept my conclusions without giving up their atheism.

A successful defense or theodicy does not prove the existence of God, any more than it presupposes it. To think that it does or should is to confuse the dialectic of the discussion. A defense or theodicy is a rebuttal of a charge made against religious belief, a charge of being somehow epistemically defective in virtue of believing both in the existence of God and the existence of suffering. A defense or theodicy thus provides support for theism by warding off an attack on it, not by trying to provide arguments that theism is true.

On the other hand, of course, insofar as the supposed success of this attack on theism is one of the main arguments in favor of atheism, the basis of atheistic belief is undermined by a successful theodicy or defense.

Conclusion

In his objections to analytical metaphysics, Van Fraassen says: "The metaphysical enterprise . . . subverts our understanding both of our own humanity and of the divine—be it real or unreal—by its development of a detailed intricate understanding of simulacra under the same names."[47] The problem with analytical metaphysics, as Van Fraassen sees it, is that it tends to "give absolute primacy to demands for explanation, and . . . [to be] satisfied with explanations-by-postulate."[48] If I understand Van Fraassen's thought correctly, then he seems to me right not only about analytical metaphysics but about all of analytic philosophy, for the sorts of reasons I have given here. Insofar as analytic philosophy is one of the pattern-processing arts, it will be incomplete at best when it comes to describing the parts of reality including persons. For this reason, if analytic philosophy insists on trying to produce by itself a complete explanation of the world in which we live, it will be mistaken; there will be features of reality that the pattern-processing arts alone cannot understand or explain.

In this chapter, I have claimed that help in accessing what is missing in analytic philosophy can be gotten from narratives. In particular, as regards the problem of suffering, biblical narratives are useful; and I have argued that such use of those narratives is not ruled out by historical biblical studies. In the next two chapters, I will try to argue further for this methodology by considering the kind of knowledge provided by narratives and the role of that knowledge in philosophy.

Chapter 3

Narrative as a Means of Knowledge:
Francis and Dominic

Most high, omnipotent, good Lord,
praise, glory and honor, and all blessing are yours!
They are right for you alone, Most High;
no man is worthy to have your names on his lips.

May you be praised, my Lord, with every one of your creatures,
and, most of all, with the lord, Brother Sun,
who is day, and you shine on us through him.
And he is beautiful and radiant in great splendor.
He offers us a sign of you, Most High.

May you be praised, my Lord, for Sister Moon and Stars,
which you have created in the heavens,
clear and precious and lovely.

May you be praised, my Lord, for Brother Wind,
and for air and clouds and fair weather and every season,
by which you give your creatures food.

May you be praised, my Lord, for Sister Water,
who is very useful and humble and precious and chaste.

May you be praised, my Lord, for Brother Fire,
by whom you light up the night,
and he is beautiful and cheerful and vigorous and strong.

May you be praised, my Lord, for our Sister Mother Earth,
who supports and guides us
and brings forth all sorts of plants
and fruits with flowers of every hue.

May you be praised, my Lord, for all those who let go for love of you
and who endure debility and affliction.

Blessed are they who endure them with peacefulness
Because you, Most High, will crown them with victory.

May you be praised, my Lord, for Sister Bodily Death,
whom no living person can escape.
Alas for those who die in mortal sins!
Blessed are they whom death will find settled in your most holy will!
The second death will do them no harm.

Praise and bless my Lord!
Give him thanks and serve him with great humility!*

Introduction

In the preceding chapter, I explained and defended the methodology I mean to employ in this book, but my argument for that methodology rested on a claim that will no doubt seem implausible to some readers—namely, that there are things we can know that are philosophically significant but that are difficult or impossible to know and express apart from stories. In this chapter, I want to spell out that claim in detail and do something more by way of defending it.

Because this claim is at odds with the general tenor of epistemology in analytic philosophy,[1] I will need to say something briefly about that contemporary current of thought. Analytic epistemology has spawned an enormous, highly diverse literature, however; and so any very general characterization of it is bound to be rough-hewn. It is also bound to irritate philosophers familiar with this literature and prompt them to the kind of activity for which the discipline of analytic philosophy is widely known: obstreperous focus on the inadequacy of the details of someone else's account. Perhaps it will help breed patience in such philosophers if I concede at the outset that my characterization of this part of analytic philosophy is constructed with an axe, not a scalpel. Furthermore, as I hope will become clear, I mean not so much to comment on analytic epistemology as to prompt reflection on a complement to it.

It is helpful to have some short names for the analytic theorizing about knowledge at issue and the alternative to it to which I want to call attention. For reasons that will emerge more clearly below, I will refer to the relevant analytic approach as Dominican and to the alternative as Franciscan. My aim in doing so is to illustrate as well as to describe the alternative I want to present here.

Analytic philosophy is in the habit of categorizing by means of sets of abstract properties, and the labels it uses in categorizing are designations summarizing those properties. So, for example, Descartes's theory of knowledge shares with various

---

* Francis of Assisi, *Canticle of the Creatures*. (The translation is my reworked version of the translation found in *Francis of Assisi: Early Documents*, ed. Regis Armstrong, J. A. Wayne Hellmann, and William J. Short (New York: New City Press, 1999), 113–14.)

contemporary theories of knowledge the properties of taking knowledge to be built up on a foundation, of supposing the foundation to be basic beliefs, and of imposing certain restrictions on the beliefs that can properly count as basic. Philosophers classify these contemporary and early modern theories together on the basis of such shared properties and refer to all of them with the designation 'foundationalist.'

But there is also another way of categorizing. It is based not so much on abstract properties as on stories, and the labels used for classification are the proper names of the stories' figures, not sets of abstract properties and general designations that call them to mind. This sort of categorization can be thought of as a kind of typology. The medieval period was fond of typology. For example, medieval thinkers recognized a difference between the contemplative life and the active life, and they liked to express their understanding of the difference typologically. Because they were steeped in biblical stories, medievals thought of the contemplative life in terms of Rachel and the active life in terms of Leah, in such a way that each woman was taken as a type of the life in question. In referring to analytic epistemology (and analytic philosophy generally) as Dominican and the alternative as Franciscan, I am engaging in a typological categorization of this sort, letting Dominic and Francis stand in as types of the different approaches, rather than classifying the different approaches on the basis of sets of abstract properties.

The difference in the two ways of categorizing is itself part of what I want to call attention to in this chapter. Categorizing on the basis of sets of abstract properties and abstract designations can itself be thought of as Dominican; categorizing on the basis of typology, which requires acquaintance with stories and persons, can be taken as Franciscan. The Dominican system is helpful for making clear distinctions, especially distinctions focused on details, about which argument is possible and often frequent. The Franciscan approach is not much help with definitory details or crisp distinctions, but it can be evocative, memorable, and illuminating. In case the thing being characterized is not amenable to crisp definition and precision, then, paradoxically, the vague but intuitive Franciscan approach will be more accurate than the Dominican approach, whose search for an unavailable accuracy will result in carefully patterned mischaracterization.[2]

Because I am going to engage in typology and use Dominic and Francis as my types, I also need to add a caveat about my description of these two men. The historical record contains many early stories about Francis and several early lives of Francis; the record is comparatively poor as regards early stories and lives of Dominic. (At the risk of being tiresome, I would say that the historical record about Francis is itself typically Franciscan, and that the comparative absence of stories about Dominic is typically Dominican.) I will avail myself of this early material, especially about Francis but also about Dominic, without concern for its authenticity. Determining the authenticity of these stories is about as relevant to my purposes as determining the accuracy of the biblical account of Rachel and Leah would have been to medieval thinkers taking them as types of the contemplative and the active life. What I do know of contemporary historical scholarship on the lives of Francis and Dominic, however, persuades me that the impression garnered from the stories that have come down to us gives a generally faithful portrayal of the temper and disposition of each man, whether or not any of the details of the stories are true.

Furthermore, for ease of exposition, and to avoid the clumsy locutions needed to signal my own epistemic distance from the world of these stories, I will generally write as if every one of the details of the stories is true, including the supernatural and miraculous details. But readers should make no inferences about my own views concerning the historical accuracy of the stories from the way in which I present and use them.

Additionally, many of the primary sources regarding Francis and Dominic are hagiographical. But, from our point of view, the primary sources can reveal not only those things about Francis and Dominic that are examples of human excellences (or things considered to be excellences in the medieval period) but also some of the worst features of human beings in medieval culture. So, for example, in his early *Rule* for his religious community, Francis reminds the brothers that they are to love and serve others; but when it comes to women, he says, "let all the brothers avoid evil glances and association with women. No one [of the brothers] may counsel them, travel alone with them or eat out of the same dish with them."[3] Because I mean to engage in typology, for which hagiography is more useful than history, I will not comment on the historically conditioned shortcomings of Francis and Dominic any more than I will concern myself with the accuracy of the hagiographical record.

As a final caveat, I want to ward off a possible misconception about my goal in this chapter. My aim is to show certain inadequacies in the approach to knowledge common in the analytic tradition and to stress the merits of what I am calling 'Franciscan knowledge' by pointing out the ways in which that alternative kind of knowledge remedies some of the inadequacies in the analytic approach. But it is *not* part of my aim to try to persuade readers to give up on analytic philosophy or, more generally, to repudiate the Dominican (typologically speaking) in favor of the Franciscan. I want only to reflect on an approach that is different from that of analytic philosophy and that can be used to strengthen and complement it, in order to provide support for my claim about the importance of narratives to philosophy.

I will begin (Franciscanly) with the stories of Francis and Dominic and the suggestive differences between them. Then, with the help of the stories, I will argue (Dominicanly) for my claim about the role of narrative in philosophy. I will first give reasons for thinking that there are things we can know where the (Franciscan) knowledge cannot be analyzed as (Dominican) knowledge *that* something or other is the case. Then I will show the way in which that alternative (Franciscan) knowledge can be conveyed by narratives. And, finally, I will argue that Franciscan knowledge, conveyed by narratives, is significant for philosophy. In the end, however, I will return (Franciscanly) to the stories, to let them finish the argument for my central claim about the role of narratives in philosophy.

Francis and Dominic

The story told of the beginning of the founding of the Dominican order makes clear that Dominic's gifts were for philosophical and theological argument. When he was over 30, Dominic set out from Spain for Denmark with his bishop on an embassy for the king. As they were passing through Toulouse, Dominic discovered that his landlord there was an Albigensian, an adherent to a dualistic sect highly critical of the official Church. Dominic sat up all night arguing with him, and in the morning the landlord decided to return to the Catholic Church. That was the beginning for Dominic of a devotion to preaching as a means of bringing heretics and unbelievers into the fold. He was apparently very good at producing arguments for his side, and the stories told about him stress his skill at argumentation. After one disputation, one of the heretics present expressed wonder at Dominic's ability. "We should never have thought," he said, "that the Catholics had so many powerful arguments."[4]

Such hagiographical stories as we have about Dominic include the usual miracles attributed to saints, but there are also some that highlight his gift for philosophical and theological argument. In one such story, for purposes of an official disputation between heretics and Catholics, the heretics appointed a person to argue their case in a book, and Dominic was chosen to prepare a book arguing the case for the official Church. Both books were read out to the people, and the people thought Dominic's case was far the better. But to make sure that this judgment was right, both books were subjected to trial by fire. The heretic's book burned up at once, but Dominic's book would not burn at all, even though it was thrown into the fire three times.

As his ministry of preaching spread and others joined him in it, he sought and received papal approval to found a new order that would be, and would be called, 'an Order of Preachers.'[5]

At Dominic's canonization hearing in 1233, while his asceticism and devotion to prayer were stressed, it was also made clear that his primary love was preaching and argumentation. One witness, for example, said of him that "on a journey or wherever he was, he wanted to be always preaching or talking or arguing about God."[6]

His preaching was mostly oral, rather than written, and virtually nothing that he did write has survived. There is a corresponding paucity of material about him. We have a short life or two (depending on how broadly we construe 'life'), and various stories about him, including the stories told at his canonization hearing. But, on the whole, Dominic was of interest to others more in his preaching than in his person, and there is comparatively little early material about the man himself. Furthermore, not much of what we do have constitutes a real story, although now and again there are some human touches in this material that illuminate Dominic's personality. For example, at the end of his life he revealed to some of the brothers that he had managed to remain a virgin all his life, but he confessed that he had nonetheless always been more excited by the conversation of young women than by the company of old ones.[7] By and large, however, such revelations of Dominic's personality or of his personal relations with others are few in the early record.

By contrast, the early record about Francis is large enough to fill a fat volume or two, and it is packed with stories that bring his personality and his relations with other people to life for us.

The story about the beginning of his ministry sets the stage for many of the rest of the stories about him. He was a pampered young son of a well-to-do merchant, and he spent his time partying. But a long sickness made him reflective, and in that reflective time he had one religious vision after another. In the most impressive of these, the image of Christ in a crucifix spoke to him. "Francis," the image of the crucified Christ said to him, "go and rebuild my church, which is all being destroyed."[8] After some initial confusion, Francis came to believe that he had been called to call others to the knowledge and love of Christ; and he responded to his call with passion. The story goes on to record the vehement opposition of Francis's father to Francis's newfound religiosity and Francis's response to his father's opposition, which shows the temperament of the young man. His father hauled Francis before the bishop to complain that in his almsgiving Francis was divesting himself of things he did not own, because absolutely everything Francis possessed in fact belonged to his father. The bishop ruled in the father's favor and required Francis to return his father's property. "Fine," said Francis, "then I will go to the Lord naked." And he left not only his money but the very clothes he was wearing on the floor in front of the consternated bishop.[9]

Eventually Francis also received official approval for the founding of a new order. He called his order "the Order of the Lesser Brothers,"[10] and he himself wrote a Rule for the order. In fact, Francis wrote a great deal, and much of it is extant. It includes many letters, exhortations, and admonitions to others.

So many engaging stories about Francis remain from the early record that it is hard to pick just one or two as illustrative. But for my purposes, besides the story about the start of his ministry, perhaps the most revealing story is one told about an interaction between Francis and a learned Dominican, a Doctor of Spiritual Theology.

The Dominican wanted Francis to explain to him the passage in Ezekiel in which God says, "If you do not warn the wicked man about his wickedness, I will hold you responsible for his sins." The Dominican said to Francis, "I'm acquainted with many people, good father, who live in mortal sin, as I'm aware. But I don't always warn them about their wickedness. Will I then be held responsible for their souls?" At first, Francis refused to answer, on the grounds that he was not an educated man and therefore not in a position to offer so learned a Dominican a helpful exegesis of a biblical text; but the Dominican insisted. "Well," said Francis, when he at last acceded to the Dominican's request:

if that passage is supposed to be understood in a universal sense, then I understand it to mean that a servant of God should be burning with life and holiness so brightly that by the light of example and the tongue of his conduct, he will rebuke all the wicked. In that way, I say, the brightness of his life and the fragrance of his reputation will proclaim their wickedness to all of them.[11]

This story, told by a Franciscan, ends with the Dominican's going away very impressed.

The moral of the stories

The difference between Francis and Dominic (and between Franciscans and Dominicans, typologically understood[12]) revealed by my short presentation of these stories is striking, in my view.

The difference in the stories about the beginnings of their ministries is illustrative. Dominic's ministry begins with his belief that there is a great need for argumentation to rebut unbelief and with his recognition (and the recognition of his interlocutors) that he himself is excellent at such arguments. Francis's ministry begins with visions in which God speaks to him directly and addresses him by name. In the chief of these precipitating visions, he is (as he takes it) face to face with the crucified Christ, who is calling Francis to bring others to God. There is all the difference in the world between understanding one's mission as converting the unbelieving by good arguments and understanding it as answering Christ's personal call to help him call persons to himself.

The difference in question is underlined by the different ways in which their followers chose to remember Francis and Dominic. The paucity of stories about Dominic and the paucity of information about persons and personal relations even in the stories about him that we do have is in strong contrast with the record regarding Francis. If the point of the Dominican mission is overturning wrong philosophical and theological views, then the personality of the founder of that mission clearly is not very important, and neither are stories about him or his relations to others. The postulates of theology will remain the same, whatever Dominic himself was like, and the arguments built on those postulates will not depend on his person either. So from the point of view of the Dominican mission, stories about Dominic have the status of gossip—pleasant but not particularly important or useful.

Francis's ministry, however, is grounded in his personal response to a personal call from a suffering incarnate deity. The rebuilding of Christ's church that Francis was called to do is based on Francis's personal relationship to the person of Christ, and it consists in inviting others to imitate him by forming their own analogue of such a relationship. Those who were capable of it could imitate Francis by joining the Franciscans and trying to form a personal relationship of their own to Christ. Writing to Clare and other women trying to live the Franciscan ideal, Francis says,

you have made yourselves daughters and servants of the most High King, the Heavenly Father, and [you] have taken the Holy Spirit as your spouse.[13]

On the other hand, for those who were not able or willing to make profession in the Order, it was nonetheless possible to imitate Francis through a personal connection to Francis, either by personal experience of Francis or by the knowledge of Francis garnered from stories about him.

Stories about Francis are thus an integral part of the mission Francis took to be his, and that is no doubt at least part of the reason why stories about him are plentiful and popular. Without the mysticism accompanying the severe asceticism of Franciscan life, something roughly analogous to the mystical connection to God is still available through knowledge and love of Francis himself. If argument is the coin of the realm for Dominicans, stories fill an analogous role for Franciscans.

The names of the orders are therefore properly significant of the most salient differences between Francis and Dominic.

Dominic founded an order of preachers, whose purpose was to argue against unbelief. He and his followers thought that knowledge about God, and thus knowledge about the ultimate foundation of reality, could be gotten best through philosophical and theological argument. Insofar as the knowledge of the good life and of morality depends on a correct understanding of God and the ultimate foundation of reality, then on Dominican views this knowledge is also gained by discursive reasoning and arguments. Metaphysics and theology, ethics and morality,[14] can be understood and explained best, on Dominican views (*typologically understood*), by careful reasoning and argumentation.

Francis, on the other hand, founded an order of lesser brothers, where a personal relationship to Christ or to Christ through relationship to Francis is at the core of the order's mission. For Francis, God is personal, and the personal nature of God is most fully revealed by Christ. The ultimate foundation of reality for Francis (*typologically understood*) is thus also personal, and for that reason knowledge of it will be a knowledge of persons.

The differences between the Dominican and the Franciscan approaches are well illustrated in the Franciscan story about Franciscan and Dominican biblical exegesis. The text of Ezekiel contains a command of God's together with a great threat in case the command is violated. For the medievals, then, to understand that text is to understand something about the nature of the sovereignty that rules the world and also to understand the requirements for human beings to live well and morally in a world ruled in this way. The Dominican interprets the text as a command to preach moral truths to those people who violate serious moral prescriptions. Presumably, the Dominican would take himself to be fulfilling the command in the text if he were to say to every sinner who crossed his path something along these lines. "You engage in acts of type A, but type A acts are morally wrong. The reason type A acts are morally wrong is that they violate moral principles of sort P." And the Dominican might then go on to give reasons for these principles. Furthermore, on the Dominican's understanding of the text, an essential ingredient in the good life for human beings is just this sort of activity: arguing about morality with human beings who are doing what is morally wrong.

But Francis understands the text in a radically different way. For Francis, a person who wants to obey the command implied in the biblical text first has to be rightly related to God. He has to know God and love God and desire to live for God. And, if he is rightly related to God in these ways, then he himself will be on fire, not only with the moral virtues constitutive of holiness but, more importantly, with a sort of spiritual luminescence manifested in his life because of his love for the person who is God. Those acquainted with him will be able to measure themselves by seeing him. In the light of their knowledge of him, they will know themselves, and they will know their own shortcomings in consequence.

Furthermore, it is not necessary that the servant of God have a direct personal relationship with those whose sins he is rebuking in this way. If the servant of God is really on fire in his love of God and relationship to God, other people will tell stories about him; and evildoers will come to know the servant of God by reputation, through the stories told. That means is also efficacious for the rebuking of wrongdoing.

According to (*typologically understood*) Franciscan views, then, the good life for human beings has as an essential ingredient living a life in personal connection to a personal God and manifesting that life to others. On this view, knowledge of the ultimate foundation of reality, knowledge of morality, and knowledge of the good life are all best understood as knowledge of persons.

Contrasting Francis and Dominic in this way helps explain the point at the outset of this chapter about modes of categorization. There is something suitably called 'Dominican' about the way in which analytic philosophy characterizes things. It categorizes by means of designations summarizing a cluster of abstract properties. But reflection inspired by the stories of Francis should help us see that the Dominican approach is not the only way to categorize. We can also group things together on the basis of their relations to a person whose story has a striking feature or whose personality has a notable bent. This is categorization by typology.

So, for example, we can say that contemporary biblical exegesis, with its emphasis on historical scholarship, is in the Dominican mode, while the biblical exegesis of African-American slaves before the Civil War, with its typological use of Old Testament figures to shape political and theological reflection, is in the Franciscan mode.[15] For those familiar with Francis and Dominic, this kind of categorization also conveys a great deal of information in short space, but it does so by reference to persons rather than properties. For that very reason, it is evocative and illuminating, but difficult to turn into definitions or formulas for drawing distinctions.

Furthermore, as I explained above, in cases where necessary and sufficient conditions for something are hard to find or in the nature of things not available (for example, because what we are attempting to define is irreducibly vague), then Franciscan categorization or typology may in fact be more accurate, or at least more true to the phenomena, than Dominican categorization. A pretension to precision where none is available can also produce a clumsy, axe-hewn categorization, which misrepresents the thing it seeks to describe.

In the context of the subject of this chapter (and this book), Franciscan typology is more appropriate than Dominican definition. Although I will argue for the claim that there are clear cases of Franciscan knowledge, which is not reducible to knowledge *that*, I am not able to say what all these cases have in common (except for the one negative feature of irreducibility to knowledge *that*);[16] and so I do not know how to give a set of necessary and sufficient conditions that will capture all the kinds of Franciscan knowledge there might be, or even all the kinds that are discussed in this chapter. Vague, evocative Franciscan categorization of it will therefore be more accurate than procrustean Dominican definition.

Analytic theories of knowledge

With this much explanation of the typology and the characters whose stories are the source for the typology of this chapter, I want to turn to a brief (Dominican) characterization of analytic epistemology. Here the first thing to see is that analytic epistemology is definitely in the Dominican mode.

As a recent author puts it, "one virtually universal presupposition [of contemporary epistemology] is that knowledge is true belief, but not mere true belief."[17] The true beliefs in question are propositional beliefs appropriately related to facts;[18] belief itself is generally taken just as an attitude toward a proposition, or a propositional attitude, as philosophers say. And so it is axiomatic in analytic philosophy that all (or virtually all[19]) knowledge is knowledge *that* something or other is the case. Some philosophers have gone so far as to argue that even knowing how to do something is reducible to knowledge *that* of some sort.[20] There are, of course, sentences that contain verbs of believing but that do not apparently make ascriptions of propositional attitudes. 'I believe you' is one common example; 'I believe in God' is a more complicated and controversial example. But many philosophers think that even such sentences "can always be analyzed as propositional attitude ascriptions."[21] 'I believe you' can be analyzed as 'I believe *p* because you tell me that *p*.' 'I believe in God' can be analyzed as 'I believe that God exists' or perhaps 'I believe that God exists and is good and trustworthy.' On this view, then, whatever else knowledge may require, it is at least a matter of having a certain attitude toward a proposition.

It is not just attitudes toward propositions that are central to knowledge on the analytic approach; it is also the discerning of patterns among propositions. One genus of theories of knowledge that has been prominent in modern epistemology is foundationalism. Foundationalism comes in different species, but they all share a certain account of the structure of knowledge. Some propositions are known on the basis of appropriate inference from other propositions, but there are also propositions that are foundational or properly basic for a knower, which are known but not known on the basis of other propositions. Knowledge is, then, a matter of believing a proposition that is true and properly basic for a knower or a proposition derived by the knower in an appropriate way from a properly basic belief.

Clearly, on an account of knowledge of this sort, knowledge belongs to the pattern-processing arts. That is because, with the possible exception of properly basic beliefs, on this account of knowledge, it is a matter of discerning the appropriate relations among propositions, especially the inferential relations between properly basic beliefs and beliefs ultimately based on them. Rules expressing appropriateness in inferential relations are a sort of pattern for discerning acceptable relations among propositions; and so, on foundationalist theories of knowledge, a knower needs to differentiate the patterns among propositions in order to relate his basic and non-basic beliefs appropriately to one another.

There are, of course, other theories of knowledge in contemporary philosophy, but most of them share with foundationalism the features to which I am drawing attention here.[22] Coherentism, for example, takes as a requirement of knowledge that there be certain relations of coherence among propositions believed by a person. Reliabilism takes knowledge to be a function of a certain kind of psychological process that can be construed as an input/output device; it takes in information and processes it in reliable ways into appropriate attitudes toward propositions. Both coherence and reliable processing of information require at least that the propositions the knower accepts as true not be thought to be inconsistent by the knower, and so these theories of knowledge also take knowledge to require the appropriate pattern-processing of propositions.

On all these theories of the nature of knowledge, then, knowledge is a matter of having an attitude toward a proposition, of knowing *that*; and, with the possible exception of basic beliefs, knowledge also requires suitable pattern-processing of propositions. Furthermore, excellence in a knower will include the knower's ability to see subtle or hard to recognize patterns among propositions and to be quick in the processing of such patterns. Even when they suppose that most of a colleague's philosophical beliefs are mistaken, philosophers nonetheless often admire his philosophical views because of his expert knowledge of the logical relations among the propositions he believes and his cleverness at finding the logical errors in the pattern-processing of his opponents. When analytic philosophers say in praise of one of their colleagues, "He is *so* smart!", skill in pattern-recognition and speed of pattern-processing are what they almost invariably have in mind.

It is worth noticing that the account of knowledge as a matter of knowing *that* has an analogue in contemporary philosophical accounts of desire. Explaining what he takes to be the contemporary theory of desire common enough to be the standard in the field, Timothy Schroeder says:

The standard theory has two central features. First, it holds that all desires are desires that P, for some proposition P. One cannot desire sex, an apple, Darren, or peace *simpliciter*, but must desire that one have sexual intercourse with one's partner that very minute, or that one eat an apple sometime that day, or that Darren fall in love with one and commit himself to a lasting relationship, or that all wars cease on Earth. This is a consequence that standard theorists find congenial. They . . . hold that what is desired can always be expressed with a complete proposition in a 'that-clause.' It may be that Eve desires an apple, but this is always shorthand for Eve's desiring that some state of affairs obtain . . . and to express this state of affairs (that Eve eat the apple at once, or that Eve eventually obtain an apple) requires a complete proposition.[23]

Knowledge *that*

Analytic philosophy has sometimes remembered that knowledge *that* cannot be all there is to knowledge. So, for example, some analytic philosophers, most famously Bertrand

Russell, have contrasted knowing *that* with knowing by acquaintance.[24] Examples of what we are said to know by acquaintance have included colors, the contents of consciousness, and sense data. But philosophical discussion of what we are supposed to know by acquaintance is sparse and undeveloped, and the nature of knowledge by acquaintance has also not been well worked out. Sometimes it has just been taken as a primitive. The notion of knowledge by acquaintance therefore is useful mainly for prompting us to reflect on the claim that there is more to knowing than knowing *that*.

Suppose we begin those reflections by considering sensory knowledge. It is true, as most but not all analytic philosophers recognize, that there is something about certain kinds of sensory knowledge, such as the knowledge of redness or of what it is like to see red, which cannot be captured adequately or at all as knowledge *that*.[25] There is a much discussed thought experiment in philosophy of mind, devised to sort out a different philosophical puzzle,[26] that helps to make this point clear.[27]

The thought experiment involves a neuroscientist Mary who knows everything there is to know about the brain, including everything there is to know about the way in which the brain processes color, but who has had no perceptual experience of color of any sort because from birth she has been isolated (by some suitable villain) in a black-and-white environment. Now suppose that Mary is finally rescued from her imprisonment and perceives color for the first time. Although, in her imprisonment, she knew all there was to know about the neurobiology of color perception, it seems clear that she will come to know something new when she finally perceives color.

This thought experiment was originally intended to drive a wedge between mental states and neural states and to support the intuition that not all mental states are reducible to neural states. If a mental state just is a neural state, then in knowing the neural states of color perception Mary would also know the mental states of color perception; but it seems clear that she does not know (because she does not have) those mental states until she actually perceives colors.

Now if the thought experiment is successful, and I think it (or some suitably revised version of it) is, then it shows something beyond the original claim it was constructed to support.[28] Even though in her imprisoned state Mary has available to her a library containing a completed neuroscience, it seems clear that she comes to know something new when she first sees colors. But the problem is not just that no *neuroscience* books could give her the knowledge she acquires when she first sees red. *No* books could give her this knowledge. There are certain first-person knowledge states that cannot be adequately acquired or expressed by means of propositional attitudes. That is why, when Mary first knows redness in virtue of perceiving it, it is hard to express what she knows adequately in terms of knowing *that*.

Of course, some things that Mary knows when she knows redness can be expressed as knowledge *that*, but these things are not the things Mary comes to know with her first perception of color. For example, Mary knows that seeing red is a conscious experience involving qualia of a certain sort. But this is a fact she could know before she had the experience of perceiving colors, and so it cannot be what she comes to know when she first sees red. It is also true that when Mary has her first perception of redness, she knows that seeing red is like *this*. But the 'this' here simply gestures toward what she knows; it does not reduce it to propositional form.

So knowing a color is a candidate for a kind of knowledge which is not knowing *that*. And, clearly, there are various other first-person experiences that are equally difficult to capture as knowledge *that* or as the object of a propositional attitude. What it is like to be in pain, what it is like to feel lonely, what it is like to feel at home, and myriad other experiences involving qualia of some sort are further examples.[29]

In what follows, I will call knowledge which cannot be reduced to knowledge *that* 'Franciscan knowledge'; I will call the other, more philosophically ordinary kind of knowledge 'Dominican knowledge'.

The knowledge of persons: Mary again

There are also examples where what is known is something other than qualia, and yet the knowledge in question is not reducible to knowledge *that*.[30] "She knew the music immediately," for example, is not equivalent to "she knew immediately that the music she was hearing was — —" (where the blank is to be filled in by the name of the music and/or the name of its composer in the genitive case).[31] It is possible to know the music one is hearing without knowing the identity of the music, as one does when one hears something one knows well but without being able to recall the title of the work or the name of its composer.[32] And, conversely, it is possible to know the identity of the music one is listening to—because, say, the radio announcer has just given it—without knowing the music.[33] So knowing music (as distinct from knowing something about music) is another example of Franciscan knowledge.[34]

In my view, there is also Franciscan knowledge of persons.

These claims go athwart the current of thought in contemporary epistemology, which takes knowledge to be almost exclusively knowledge *that*. So, for example, conceding that knowledge of persons is not *completely* reducible to propositional knowledge, Ernest Sosa says: "Knowing someone or something, knowing some 'object' in the broadest sense of this term, seems at least sometimes to require having had some special causal interaction with that 'object' . . . " Nonetheless, he continues: "In all of these propositional knowledge plays a crucial role, sometimes even an exclusive and exhaustive role, although in certain cases a certain causal interaction is required as well."[35]

I want to claim, however, that there is a kind of knowledge of persons, a Franciscan knowledge, which is non-propositional and which is not reducible to knowledge *that*. What could that possibly be?, a skeptical objector may ask. But, of course, if I give an answer to the skeptic's question, I will have an incoherent position: in answering the question, I will be presenting in terms of knowledge *that* what I am claiming could not be presented that way.

So is there another way of responding to the skeptical objector and showing that we learn something in coming to know a person which is not just a matter of knowing *that*? One way to answer the skeptic is to revise the thought experiment involving Mary. Suitably revised, it can support the intuition that knowledge of persons is no more expressible as knowledge *that* than first-person knowledge of color gained through perception is.

Imagine then that Mary in her imprisonment has had access to any and all information about the world as long as that information is *only* in the form of third-person accounts giving her knowledge *that*. So, for example, Mary has available to her the best science texts for any of the sciences, from physics to sociology. She knows that there are other people in the world, and (*mirabile dictu*) she knows all that science can teach her about them. But she has never had any personal interactions of an unmediated and direct sort with another person. She has read descriptions of human faces, for example, but she has never been face-to-face with another conscious person. She has read books that describe the process of human communication, including the role of melody in speech and body language; but she has never had a conversation of any sort with anyone, and she has never participated in any way, even as a bystander, in anyone else's real or imagined conversation. In short, Mary has been kept from anything that could count as a second-person experience, in which one can say 'you' to another person.[36] And then suppose that Mary is finally rescued from her imprisonment and united for the first time with her mother, who loves her deeply.

When Mary is first united with her mother, it seems indisputable that Mary will know things she did not know before, even if she knew everything about her mother that could be made available to her in non-narrative propositional form, including her mother's psychological states.[37] Although Mary knew that her mother loved her before she met her, when she is united with her mother, Mary will learn what it is like to be loved. And this will be new for her, even if in her isolated state she had as complete a scientific description as possible of what a human being feels like when she senses that she is loved by someone else. Furthermore, it is clear that this is only the beginning. Mary will also come to know what it is like to be touched by someone else, to be surprised by someone else, to ascertain someone else's mood, to detect affect in the melody of someone else's voice, to match thought for thought in conversation, and so on. These will be things she learns, even if before she had access to excellent books on human psychology and communication.

The way in which I have formulated what Mary learns—what it is like to be touched by someone else, and so on—may suggest to someone that Mary learns things just about herself, and that she learns them in virtue of having new first-person experiences. It seems, then, that whatever Mary learns can be explained adequately in terms of a first-person account.[38] But this is clearly wrong-headed. Even if Mary does learn new things about herself, what will come as the major revelation to Mary is *her mother*. Even this way of putting what Mary learns is misleading, because it suggests that

Mary's new knowledge can be expressed in a third-person description of her mother. But neither first-person nor third-person accounts will be adequate for Mary to describe what is new for her. What is new for her, what she learns, has to do with her personal interaction with another person. What is new for Mary is a second-person experience.

In her first direct and immediate encounter with another human being, Mary's mind is opened to all that we learn and experience in face-to-face contact, the complex give-and-take of interpersonal interactions. Mary will be surprised by the nature of a second-person experience, no matter how good her science textbooks have been or how rich her isolated introspective experience may have been. And her surprise makes two things clear to us: first, that Mary is learning something she did not know before the personal interaction, and, second, that it is not possible to teach her by means of the science books she has what she comes to learn through personal interaction. This thought experiment thus shows that there are things we come to know from our experience of other persons and that these things are difficult or impossible to formulate in terms of knowing *that*.[39] This is a variety of Franciscan knowledge, too.

Finally, *pace* Sosa, it is not necessary for Franciscan knowledge of this sort that there be any direct causal contact between the knower and the person known. Suppose that, unbeknownst to Mary, she had a brother who has since died and that, when Mary is reunited with her mother, her mother gives Mary pictures of her brother and tells her stories about him. Through the pictures and stories, Mary may come to know her brother, with Franciscan knowledge, to one degree or another. But she will do so without having "special causal contact" with her brother. At the time Mary comes to know him, he is dead. For that matter, just as it is possible to know things *about* characters in fiction, so it is possible to have Franciscan knowledge *of* them as well. For example, people familiar with Trollope's Palliser novels may know *that* Glencora is married to the Duke of Omnium. But it is also appropriate to say that those who have read all the Palliser novels may come to know the Duchess. Such readers will have a sense of her as a person, similar to the sense they have of those persons to whom they are related in the actual world. So, although there does seem to be an experiential component of some sort in Franciscan knowledge of persons, it is not a matter of special causal contact with the person known.[40]

The varieties of knowledge of persons

The kind of case at issue in Mary's coming to know her mother is only the beginning of the examples of Franciscan knowledge of persons. Consider these sentences.

(1) Joseph saw his brothers in the crowd and knew them at once.

(2) The old nurse knew Odysseus when she saw the scar on his thigh.

(3) Oedipus knew the goodness of the gods only when he came to Colonus.

(4) Dorothea Casaubon did not know her husband until she was able to feel compassion for him after his death.

(5) Thomas Aquinas knew the presence of God in the Eucharist.

What is at issue in (1) is Joseph's knowledge of the men before him. And so someone might suppose that, contrary to what I am claiming, what is known in this case is paradigmatically expressible in propositional form, in terms of knowledge *that*. (1) is equivalent, someone might think, to

(1′) Joseph knew that the men he saw in front of him in the crowd were his brothers.

It is true that in the recognition scene in Genesis Joseph does know this, but (1) conveys something more than (1′). Joseph might have known the identity of the men in front of him in any number of ways, but the sense of (1) is that Joseph knew their identity in virtue of knowing *them*, by face recognition, among other things.

It is clear that the brain of a normally functioning human being has the capacity to know a face, and it is equally clear that it is extremely difficult, if not impossible, to translate the knowledge conveyed by the sight of a particular face into a propositional description of that face. Humpty-Dumpty's attempt to describe Alice's face was ludicrously too simple: "two eyes, two ears, a nose in the middle, and a mouth under"; but, however we improve on Humpty Dumpty's attempt, the resulting description will fit many more faces than Alice's. And yet Humpty Dumpty knew the face of Alice and he knew Alice from seeing her face.

As far as that goes, it is possible for one person Paula to see and describe appropriately the face of another person Jerome and yet *not* know Jerome in virtue of knowing his face, even though Jerome is a person otherwise familiar to Paula. In the neurological debility of prosopagnosia, a patient can see a face and describe it adequately, but on the basis of that perception alone the patient is unable to know the person whose face she is perceiving, however well acquainted she is with that person. We can imagine that Jerome might try to help Paula function with such a disability by putting a gold star on his forehead and telling Paula that his face will always be the one with the gold star on it. In that case, Paula will be able to describe Jerome's face and will also know that *that* face is Jerome's face. But, clearly, the knowledge Paula would have in that case is not equivalent to Paula's knowing Jerome's face. A prosopagnosic patient who can describe the face she is seeing and can reliably categorize it as her friend's face because of the gold star on it is far from the normal state of knowing the face of her friend. So it is possible that Paula have as much knowledge *that* as practically possible with regard to the identity and the facial features of Jerome and yet not know Jerome's face.

For these reasons, (1) is not equivalent to (1′). Knowledge of a person on the basis of face recognition is thus another example of knowledge which is difficult or impossible to translate into knowledge *that*. It is also Franciscan knowledge.

Similarly, the nurse bathing Odysseus comes all at once to know Odysseus. In this case, the knowledge is not a matter of face recognition, but something more complicated, which arises from her perceiving the scar on Odysseus's leg and combining that perception with what else the nurse knows about Odysseus.[41] She is not, however, simply making an inference from her other beliefs to a conclusion that the man in front of her is Odysseus. On the contrary, what she knows cannot be adequately expressed in terms of a propositional attitude. To see this, consider that, in the story, there are other servants in the household who never knew Odysseus but who do know about Odysseus's scar. They would undoubtedly be able to infer correctly from the presence of the scar and other information available to them to the conclusion that the stranger in their midst is Odysseus himself. But they would not know Odysseus as the nurse does when she feels the scar. She knows not just *that* this man is Odysseus. When she feels the scar, the penny drops for her, as it were; and all of a sudden, in a moment of shock and recognition, she knows *him,* as the other servants not previously acquainted with Odysseus could not do, even if they could correctly identify him. If they knew about Odysseus and the scar, those servants might be able to know that this man is Odysseus; but it would not be true to say of them, as it is true to say of the nurse, that they knew *him* on the basis of the scar.

Sentences (3) and (4) are worth looking at in more detail, too. What is at issue in these sentences is not bare knowledge of a person but a deepened knowledge[42] in virtue of a new experience.

Oedipus would have affirmed sincerely the goodness of the gods before he wandered into the shrine at Colonus. But when he reached the shrine, he recognized that an old prophecy of Apollo's about himself had begun to come true, and that recognition filled him with an understanding of the goodness of the gods in a new and different way. At the outset of the play, Oedipus described himself as more stricken with pain than any human being who ever lived before him, in consequence of Oedipus's divinely ordained destiny to the suffering afflicting him.[43] But when he understood that he had come to the prophesied shrine of the gods, he was deeply moved and said to those around him, "I come here as one endowed with grace by those who are over nature."[44] In the same spirit of wonder and gratitude toward the gods, he told Theseus: "In my beaten self, there is a grace better and more lasting than beauty."[45] Before he came to the shrine, in the world of the play Oedipus knew that the gods are good. When he understood that he had finally reached the shrine, with all that that shrine implied to him, in the world of the play Oedipus knew the goodness of the gods. The two are not equivalent.

The case in (4) is roughly analogous. Long before her husband's death, Dorothea had understood his pinched limitations, but that understanding had prompted in her only a desire to be at a distance from him and a sense of suffering when she was in his presence. After his death, when her heart had softened toward him and she felt compassion for him, she understood him as she did not before. This new knowledge of him was not a matter of knowing facts about him that she did not know before. Although it did bring new emotional states with it, it was also not simply a new affective response to facts she already knew about her husband; her new state as regards him was not a result of her having acquired new positive attitudes toward the things in him that she had disliked before. Rather, in her newfound compassion, what was true was that Dorothea knew *him* as she did not know him before.

As for (5), assume for the sake of the point at issue here that Aquinas's theological beliefs are true and also meet the other analytic conditions for knowledge, whatever exactly they might be. Then, on these suppositions, it is true that

(5′) Thomas Aquinas knew that God is present in the Eucharist.

Nonetheless, it is clear that (5′) is not equivalent to

(5) Thomas Aquinas knew the presence of God in the Eucharist.

Many Christians committed to the doctrine of omnipresence take themselves to know that God is always present everywhere, but considerably fewer would claim to know the presence of God in the Eucharist or elsewhere.

All these examples count as Franciscan knowledge, too.

In all these cases, and in many others like them, then, it is arguable that it is not possible to express adequately what is known in terms of knowing *that*. Rather what is at issue in all these cases is a certain kind of knowledge of persons, oneself or others.[46]

Furthermore, knowledge of this sort is most definitely not of the pattern-processing kind. Trying to figure out that this is Jerome's face by reasoning to that conclusion on the basis of the patterns of the face, for example, is highly unlikely to be successful. If Paula does not just know *Jerome* when she sees his face, she would not figure it out by reasoning from the patterns of his face's shapes and lines.[47] Similarly, reasoning to the conclusion that this is Jerome's face by inference from the knowledge that Jerome's face is the one with the gold star on it is not the same as knowing Jerome by face. Knowledge of the sort at issue here is more a matter of insight than of discursive reasoning.[48]

For somewhat the same reasons, speed and accuracy are less important for excellence at this sort of knowledge than the wisdom born of experience is. If speed and accuracy with regard to pattern-processing are the main excellences with regard to knowing *that*, then perhaps insight or intuitiveness (of the kind Odysseus's nurse had) and wisdom (of the kind Oedipus had at Colonus) are the main excellences with regard to this other sort of knowledge.[49]

So there is a broad array of knowledge commonly had by human beings that cannot be formulated adequately or at all as knowledge *that*, and all of it counts as Franciscan knowledge, in the usage adopted here. Such knowledge is provided by some first-person experiences, especially those in which the qualia of the experience are among the salient parts of the knowledge. It also encompasses some kinds of knowledge of persons, including certain sorts of knowledge of oneself as well as knowledge of other persons. Although such knowledge is not propositional, it can be combined with propositional knowledge to yield further knowledge, either further knowledge *that* or further knowledge of persons.[50] So, for example, in the story of Joseph and his brothers, Joseph knows *that* it has been a very long time since he last saw his brothers and that he has altered much more than they have since then. This knowledge *that* combined with the knowledge of persons he has with respect to them when he knows their faces helps him to see (with the knowledge of persons) that his brothers do not recognize him and to know *that* they will be very surprised when he explains to them who he is.

Analogous cases: The larger phenomenon

It should be clear that these points about knowledge also apply, *mutatis mutandis*, to desire. A desire for the demi-goddess Kalypso on the part of Odysseus, for example, cannot be appropriately translated without remainder into desire *that* something or other be the case. Odysseus can desire that Kalypso "fall in love with [him]" or that she "commit [herself] to a lasting relationship" with him without desiring Kalypso. He might, for example, be trying to manipulate Kalypso for purposes of his own (as is in fact the case in the story Homer tells about their relationship). Odysseus could even desire "that [he] have sexual intercourse with [Kalypso] that very minute" without desiring Kalypso—say, because he is desperate to convince Kalypso that he is not contriving a plan to leave her and only this means at this moment will allay her suspicions.

Someone might suppose that, if we simply spell out the *that*-clause specifically enough, it will after all be possible to translate a desire for Kalypso into a desire *that*. We might, for example, say that, if Odysseus did in fact have a desire for Kalypso, it would be a desire that there be a loving relationship between them, for the sake of the relationship, rather than for the sake of some other good. Or perhaps we could spell out a desire for Kalypso on Odysseus's part as an ordered pair of desires: a desire that there be a loving relationship between them and a desire that this state of affairs obtain whether or not any other good is achieved by it. But these translations are defective, too. Odysseus might have sworn a vow to the gods that, if they kept him from dying at sea, he would try to establish a relationship with Kalypso for the sake of that relationship alone, no matter what other good was achieved by the relationship. In that case, he could desire these things, in gratitude to the gods for his rescue from shipwreck, without having any desire for Kalypso.

So it is not the case for desire, any more than for knowledge, that it is always reducible to a propositional attitude.[51]

And this is only the beginning. There are many other cases analogous to knowledge and desire in this respect. Consider, for example, the locution 'G is good for S,' where 'G' designates some good and 'S' designates some human person. Richard Kraut argues that any such locution is reducible to a *that*-formulation: "it is good for S that . . . " He says:

all claims about what is good for someone can be recast in such a way that they take the form 'It is good for S that P.' Knowledge is good for us: that means that it is good for us that we have knowledge . . . Being loved is good for us: in other words, it is good for us that we are loved. What is good for someone, then, is a certain state of affairs.[52]

But we also say, "She is good for him," and this locution is not equivalent to a locution about a state of affairs. It is not, for example, equivalent to the claim that it is good for him that he have a relationship with her. Before the wild boy of Aveyron met Dr. Itard and was in relationship with him, Itard had interested himself in the boy's case and taken steps to see to it that the boy was transferred to his care.[53] At that stage, it was true that Itard was good for the boy, but it was not then true that the boy was in relationship with Itard. And when the boy was brought into Itard's care, what was good for the boy was not that he had a relationship with Itard. Putting the claim in that way eviscerates it. What was good for the boy was Itard, whom the boy loved. The boy did not love his relationship with Itard.

Once we are attuned to the point, we can see that there are many other analogous cases. For example, there is a difference between one's imagining oneself in a certain state and imagining *that* one is in that state. A person blind from birth might be able to imagine that he sees red without being able to imagine seeing red.[54] For emotions, too, a case can be made for a difference between an emotion understood as an attitude *that* and an emotion which is not so construable.[55] Even for remembering, such a distinction can be made. 'I remember that I was born in Frankfurt' can be true, while 'I remember being born in Frankfurt' is false.

Franciscan knowledge, then, is one example of a much larger phenomenon well worth investigating in its own right.[56] In this book, however, what is at issue is primarily Franciscan knowledge, although the ancillary case of desire will be helpful later on, in connection with the discussion of shame.

Philosophy and Franciscan knowledge

If I am right in the claims I have made about Franciscan knowledge, the notion of Franciscan knowledge raises a host of questions, some of them analogous to standard questions in analytic epistemology. For example, we could ask what characteristics of Franciscan knowledge distinguish it from simulacra of Franciscan knowledge—apparent but not genuine knowledge of any kind. When a bereaved husband mistakenly seems to see the face of his newly dead wife in the faces of strangers in the crowd, then, apart from the fact that the object which is acting causally on his sight is not his wife's face, is there anything that distinguishes the husband's mistaken impression from the genuine knowledge of her face that he had while she was living? Or we could ask what distinguishes Franciscan knowledge from fortuitously successful beliefs. If Odysseus's old nurse had felt with a thrill of shock and (apparent) recognition that *this* man is Odysseus for every man of the right age who entered the house, she would eventually have got it right when Odysseus arrived; but it does not seem correct to count her lucky hit as knowledge. There is also a question about the appropriate method for combining items of knowledge when the knowledge is Franciscan. Is there a Franciscan analogue to discursive reasoning? What would the rules be for the acceptable forms of combination of Franciscan knowledge? How is Franciscan knowledge appropriately combined with knowledge *that*? Are there rules for the acceptable forms of combination of Franciscan and non-Franciscan knowledge? There is also a question about the relevant faculties and their reliability. What cognitive faculties are involved in Franciscan knowledge, and what reason do we have for thinking them reliable?

These are all sensible and useful questions; and, no doubt, there are many others we could ask as well. But, apart from the last question in the preceding paragraph, which I will discuss in the next chapter, the pursuit of answers to these questions falls outside the scope of my project. I raise them only to note their importance and leave them to one side. What is more important for my purposes in this book is a question of a very different sort. I want to ask why we should think Franciscan knowledge is of any interest to philosophers. Can Franciscan knowledge play any important role in philosophical discussion? The answer to this question seems to me decidedly affirmative.

Suppose that we leave all other sorts of Franciscan knowledge to one side and concentrate only on the Franciscan knowledge of persons. Insofar as it cannot be reduced to knowledge *that,* without this Franciscan knowledge we miss something crucial in our understanding of persons. Therefore, to the extent to which knowledge of persons is important to us, to that extent Franciscan knowledge is important also. But to say this is not yet to say that it is important for philosophy. Knowledge of persons clearly matters to us for many things that we value as human beings. Whether or not it matters to philosophy is a different question. We might think that Franciscan knowledge would matter to any area of philosophy in which the understanding of persons is important.[57] But, an objector might ask, what reason is there for not supposing, contrary to my position, that all the *philosophically interesting* things about persons are captured by Dominican, rather than Franciscan, knowledge?

At this point, it is worth considering how this question could be answered. Here is how it could *not* be answered. It could not be answered by trying to spell out what exactly is known in the Franciscan knowledge of persons, contrasting it with knowledge *that,* and considering whether the distinctive elements of that Franciscan knowledge are philosophically significant. The objector's question could not be answered in this way because then the position being defended would be incoherent, as I explained at a similar juncture above. I would be trying to describe in the familiar terms of knowing *that* the Franciscan knowledge which I have claimed cannot be formulated in that way.

How else, then, can the objector's question be answered?

There is one obvious answer to it, but it is disappointing. Insofar as Franciscan knowledge cannot be captured in terms of knowing *that,* there is certainly something of interest for epistemology about Franciscan knowledge. Theories of knowledge that ignore or fail to account for whole varieties of knowledge are correspondingly incomplete. In this sense, Franciscan knowledge *is* of importance to philosophy—but not in a way that requires us to do anything other than Dominican, analytic philosophizing. Here it is only the bare fact that there is Franciscan knowledge that is of interest to philosophy, and that is something for which Franciscan knowledge itself is not needed.

Is there then any way to show that what one can learn by means of Franciscan knowledge of persons is significant for philosophy?[58]

One could point to the role that intuitions about persons play in many areas of philosophy, from ethics to thought experiments about autonomy and freedom in metaphysics. Intuitions are derived from our experiences, often enough our experiences of other people; and thought experiments are generally, in effect, odd kinds of stories, which make one or another appeal to our intuitions. To the extent to which the absence of the distinctly Franciscan knowledge of persons would impoverish our intuitions and thus diminish our capacity to form appropriate judgments about thought experiments, to that extent Franciscan knowledge is significant for philosophy.

The designation 'thought experiments' is itself suggestive.[59] We test our philosophical theories against thought experiments, in a way that bears at least some similarity to the way in which scientific theories are tested against scientific experiments. Experience conveyed by experiment is, of course, central to scientific knowledge. There is, therefore, some help with the question about the role of Franciscan knowledge in philosophy in considerations of the role of experience in philosophical knowledge, as it finds expression in thought experiments.

In his Terry lectures on the nature and importance of empiricism, Bas van Fraassen recommends what he calls 'the empirical stance,' as an alternative to the practice of analytic metaphysics, which he disparages.[60] The empirical stance, Van Fraassen says, rejects the value of the principled, theory-laden explanations of analytical philosophy, is skeptical about the truth of such explanations, and repudiates the analytical view that there is no understanding without them.[61] Instead, the empirical stance values experience and what is known through experience. If I understand Van Fraassen's position correctly, then his arguments against analytical metaphysics also give some support to the philosophical importance of Franciscan knowledge. Insofar as analytical metaphysics, or any part of analytic philosophy, is one of the pattern-processing arts, it will be incomplete at best in its descriptions of reality; those parts of reality made accessible to us in experience, especially the experience of persons and the knowledge of persons it generates, will be slighted. Insofar as reflections based on second-person experience gained in personal relationships and conveyed through stories of any sort, including thought experiments, inform philosophical reflection, then Franciscan knowledge has a role to play in philosophy.

So reflection on the importance of experience and thought experiments based on experience of other persons for philosophical reflection also supports the philosophical significance of Franciscan knowledge.

A Franciscan approach

Clearly, these remarks about the philosophical significance of Franciscan knowledge are more suggestive than compelling; nothing in what I have said so far constitutes a decisive argument for the claim that Franciscan knowledge is important for philosophy. We should not, however, miss the fact that the effort to find such an argument is an attempt to show the philosophical importance of Franciscan knowledge by Dominican means. It would not be entirely surprising if that enterprise fell short of complete success. And so it is worth considering whether there is a Franciscan way of supporting the same conclusion. It seems clear to me that there is.

It is worth considering what would have been lost in this chapter if I had eschewed not only the stories of Francis and Dominic, together with the typological categorization based on them, but also the various thought experiments about Mary (which are stories, even if thin, short ones) and the examples drawn from narratives of all sorts, from Greek tragedy to British literary texts. It would, of course, be inconsistent to try to spell out in non-narrative prose what would be lost in this chapter if the narrative elements were omitted. But this much can safely be said: it is hard to imagine how one would manage so much as to call attention to the alternative kind of knowledge at issue in this chapter without these narrative helps. And, of course, our ability to understand what the narratives teach us, as well as our ability to formulate and understand the thought experiments about Mary, stem from our own experiences with other persons and the knowledge of persons conveyed to us in them. If we were unable to draw on any knowledge of persons of our own, whether first hand or conveyed through stories, it is hard to believe that the thought experiments and stories in this chapter could serve the purpose they do.

And so the stories in this chapter also help to make the case that Franciscan knowledge is important to philosophy. That is because the question whether Franciscan knowledge is philosophically significant is itself a philosophical question, and we could not deal with that philosophical question nearly as well, not as accurately or as insightfully, without the help of the stories.

Finally, someone may want to know what specific help narratives can give us with the particular philosophical issue of the problem of suffering. This is a question that is better deferred till after the exploration of the narratives in the subsequent chapters. But, for now, this much can be said. The problem of suffering is, in a sense, a question about interpersonal relations, insofar as the problem has to do with possible morally sufficient reasons for God, an omnipotent, omniscient, perfectly good person, to allow human persons to suffer as they do. The narratives in the subsequent chapters present for us direct interaction between a loving God and suffering human beings. They are therefore, in effect, descriptions of (part of) a world in which God exists and has a morally sufficient reason for allowing human beings to suffer. If we can learn from the narratives the Franciscan knowledge they have to convey, we can then use that knowledge in the (Dominican) philosophical project of formulating a defense and spelling out the nature of a possible morally sufficient reason for God to allow human suffering.

Conclusion

Knowledge by acquaintance as philosophers have discussed it is thus just one species of knowledge in the Franciscan mode. Much, though not all, of what is generally given as examples of knowledge by acquaintance is a knower's intuitive grasp of one or another feature of his own conscious first-person experiences. The whole panoply of Franciscan knowledge, however, encompasses much more than this. It includes, for example, the knowledge of persons conveyed by second-person experiences of persons.

That knowledge can give us philosophical understanding important for various areas of philosophy, including philosophy of religion in particular, as the subsequent chapters will make clear. (And, manifestly, insofar as reflection on the Franciscan alternative gives us insight into a different sort of knowledge from the kind gained by reflection on argument and reasoning, Franciscan knowledge is of interest for epistemology as well.) So, in one way or another, Franciscan knowledge makes a significant contribution to at least some standard areas of philosophy, a contribution that is not translatable into the conclusions of standard analytic philosophy but rather complementary to them.

There are, then, more things in heaven and earth than are captured by analytic philosophy. The knowledge of persons conveyed to us through our own second-person experiences and narratives about such experiences can, however, help us to apprehend them. There is a story told about Aquinas that seems to me just right here. Aquinas is the quintessential Dominican, in the literal as well as the typological sense, and he was one of the greatest philosophers and theologians in the Western tradition. But after a religious vision he quit writing. He said that, by comparison with what he had seen of God, the theories and arguments in his work were nothing but straw.[62] This Dominican is contrasting (*typologically understood*) Dominican and Franciscan kinds of knowledge and decidedly privileging the Franciscan as regards the deity.

There are also debilities on the (*typologically understood*) Franciscan side, of course. Unchecked by reliance on principles and arguments, the Franciscan approach can disintegrate into superstition or fanaticism. There is also a story told about Francis that he fearfully called one of the brothers to stay by him in the night because he knew (as he thought) that there were devils in his pillow.[63] This is not Francis at his most admirable. In later years, what the Franciscans manifested in their lives was sometimes not incandescent holiness but the unedifying spectacle of fratricidal quarreling. The Franciscans, for example, fought bitterly among themselves over such trivial matters as the length of the Franciscan habit; and each side claimed to be the true imitators of Francis, either with regard to his poverty or with regard to his obedience to the Church.[64] Without some principled way of arguing about the relative merits of the opposing positions, disputes about the nature of the true (Franciscan) knowledge of, and fidelity to, Francis collapse into simple power struggles. Furthermore, since even on his own view Francis was still a post-Fall human being who got at least some things wrong, there is no guarantee that those who come to know him and try to imitate him will imitate only his excellences and not also his defects. But, without some principles and arguments to draw the line between what should and what should not be imitated, stories about Francis can promote the worst as well as the best of his character.

In the end, it is hard not to think that some Dominican reasoning of a careful Thomistic sort would have done the quarreling Franciscans a world of good.

It is therefore better to see the (*typologically understood*) Franciscan and Dominican approaches not as competitors but as allies, each with something to contribute to and correct in the other. Van Fraassen's strictures on analytic metaphysics apply to all of analytic philosophy when analytic philosophy presents itself with adolescent cockiness as providing the only, or the only complete, explanation of values, knowledge, and metaphysical reality. Chastened and willing to learn from the Franciscan approach, analytic metaphysics, as well as the rest of analytic philosophy, is as powerful as it is incisive. Both the Franciscan and the Dominican approaches are needed for understanding the world and the way we can best live in it.

In this project, I will begin Dominicanly, in Part 2, with an examination of the nature of love, in all its complexity. Then, in Part 3, I will shift into the Franciscan mode for the consideration of biblical narratives. Finally, in Part 4, I will see what can be done to marry the two approaches in the construction of the defense that is the object of this book.

Chapter 4

Narrative and the Knowledge of Persons

Methought I saw my late espoused saint
Brought to me like Alcestis from the grave,
Whom Jove's great son to her glad husband gave,
Rescued from Death by force, though pale and faint.
Mine, as whom washed from spot of childbed taint
Purification in the Old law did save,
And such as yet once more I trust to have
Full sight of her in heaven without restraint,
Came vested all in white, pure as her mind.
Her face was veiled; yet to my fancied sight
Love, sweetness, goodness, in her person shined
So clear as in no face with more delight.
But, O!, as to embrace me she inclined,
I waked, she fled, and day brought back my night.*

Introduction

In Chapter 2 I argued that narratives have a contribution to make to analytic philosophy, which is blind to some things without the help of narratives. In the third chapter, I argued that there are things we can know which are philosophically significant but which are difficult or impossible to translate into knowledge *that*. I called this kind of knowledge 'Franciscan knowledge,' and I argued that Franciscan knowledge includes much, if not all, of what has been subsumed under knowledge by acquaintance, and other things besides. In particular, I argued that a kind of knowledge of persons is philosophically significant Franciscan knowledge. But what exactly is the knowledge of persons and what does it have to do with narratives?

---

* John Milton, "On His Deceased Wife," in *John Milton*, ed. Stephen Orgel and Jonathan Goldberg (Oxford: Oxford University Press, 1990), Sonnet 19, p. 82.

In this chapter, I want to finish the *apologia pro methodologia mea* by trying to explain more clearly what the knowledge of persons is and what the role of narratives is in conveying it.

Autism

It is helpful to begin by considering autism.

The rapid, perplexing increase in the incidence of autism has led to a correlative increase in research on it (or on 'autism spectrum disorder,' as it is now often called, to indicate the variability of the disorder). One pair of researchers sums up the disorder by saying that "the chief diagnostic signs of autism are social isolation, lack of eye contact, poor language capacity and absence of empathy."[1] Trying to summarize his own understanding of autism, Peter Hobson, a developmental psychologist, says that these diagnostic signs of autism arise "because of a disruption in the system of child-in-relation-to-others."[2] He expresses himself in this deliberately unconventional and obscure way, because he is struggling to make a point that is at once scientific and philosophical. By way of explanation, he says:

my experience [as a researcher] of autism has convinced me that such a system [of child-in-relation-to-others] not only exists, but also takes charge of the intellectual growth of the infant. Central to mental development is a psychological system that is greater and more powerful than the sum of its parts. The parts are the caregiver and her infant; the system is what happens when they act and feel in concert. The combined operation of infant-in-relation-to-caregiver is a motive force in development, and it achieves wonderful things. When it does not exist, and the motive force is lacking, the whole of mental development is terribly compromised. At the extreme, autism results.[3]

Trying to capture what it was like for her to live with an autistic child, the mother of that child says that her daughter's "eerie imperviousness, her serene self-sufficiency, belonged to those who, like the fairies, can live somehow untouched by the human experience."[4]

Whatever ties together the different clinical signs of all the degrees of autism spectrum disorder, the most salient feature of the disorder is its "eerie imperviousness," its absence of acting in concert. The source of this characteristic symptom of autism, we now think, is a severe impairment in the cognitive capacities necessary for what some psychologists call 'social cognition' and some philosophers call 'mindreading.'[5] This is the knowledge of persons and their mental states.

Autism and typically developing children

Autism's deficits as regards social cognition or mind-reading have made researchers increasingly aware of what typically developing children can do effortlessly. So, for example, numerous studies[6] show that a pre-linguistic infant can know her primary care-giver as a person and can even, as it were, read the mind of her care-giver to some limited extent.[7] Attempting to describe what it is that typically developing infants can do, Hobson says:

To be emotionally connected with someone *is* to experience the someone else as a person. Such connectedness is what enables a baby. . . to differentiate people from things. I don't just mean that it is used to classify people as one type of thing and objects as other types of thing. A baby could do this on the basis of a number of physical features such as size, the presence of arms and legs, spontaneous motion, and so on. I mean something deeper. It is through emotional connectedness that a baby discovers the *kind* of thing a person is. A person is the kind of thing with which one can feel and share things, and the kind of thing with which one can communicate.[8]

In fact, it has become clear that a pre-linguistic infant's capacity for social cognition is foundational to the infant's ability to learn a language or to develop normal cognitive abilities in many other areas. The difficulty in learning language evinced by many autistic children seems to be a function of the fact that autism leaves a person severely impaired as regards the knowledge of persons.

The knowledge which is impaired for an autistic child, however, cannot be taken as knowledge *that* something or other is the case. A pre-linguistic infant is not capable of knowledge *that* a particular person is her mother; but she can know her mother, and to one extent or another she can also know some of her mother's mental states. Conversely, an autistic child can know *that* a particular macroscopic object is her mother or *that* the person who is her mother has a certain mental state. But the autistic child can know such things without the knowledge that comes with mind-reading. For example, an autistic child might know that his mother is sad, but in virtue of the impairment of autism he is unlikely to have this knowledge *that* because he knows the sadness of his mother. An autistic child can know that the person he is looking at is sad because, for example, someone who is a reliable authority for the child has told him so. This is clearly not the same as the child's knowing the sadness in the face of the person he is looking at.[9] What is impaired in the cognition of an autistic child is a direct knowledge of persons and their mental states.[10]

What sort of impairment is this? Hobson gives a psychologist's view of a philosophical controversy by commenting that

developmental psychologists [and, he might have added, philosophers] have taken to calling a [typically developing] child's growing understanding of people's mental life a 'theory of mind'. In many ways this is a daft expression because it suggests that a child theorizes about the nature of feelings, wishes, beliefs, intentions, and so on. This is not what happens at all. The child comes to know about such aspects of mental life, and the way the child comes to know is mostly very *un*like theorizing.[11]

Some neurobiologists working in the area share this sort of view. So, for example, Vilayanur Ramachandran and Lindsay Oberman put the point this way: "Saying that people with autism cannot interact socially because they lack a 'theory of other minds' does not go very far beyond restating the symptoms."[12]

For his part, Hobson quotes Wittgenstein to help him explain the kind of knowledge which typically developing infants do have and with regard to which autistic children are impaired. He says: " 'We *see* emotion'—As opposed to what?—We do not see facial contortions and *make the inference* that he is feeling joy, grief, boredom."[13] For Hobson, we know the mental states of others not as knowledge *that* but more nearly by direct awareness, in the manner of perception, as it were.

As far as that goes, knowledge of mental states is conveyed not only by facial expression, but also by, for example, gesture and inarticulate vocal sound. The knowledge conveyed by these means, however, is also not always, or not entirely, translatable into knowledge *that*. Trying to explain what gesture adds to speech, for example, one pair of researchers says: "because gesture is less codified than speech and has the potential to convey information imagistically . . . meanings not easily encoded into speech can be conveyed in the accompanying gestural stream."[14]

Congenitally blind children, who have never seen the gesture of another, tend themselves to develop patterns of gesture and to use them as a means of aiding communication by speech.[15] Presumably, what one knows which one communicates by gesture is not propositional knowledge either. If it were readily translatable into propositional knowledge, it is hard to imagine why congenitally blind children would avail themselves of communication by gesture rather than communication by speech.

It is also not surprising to learn from recent neurobiological studies that the production and interpretation of the affective elements of vocal sound are subserved by a brain system different from that which is responsible for the semantic and syntactic elements of language.[16] What is it that we know when we hear a person groan or giggle? What is the difference between what we know when we hear a groan and what we know when we hear a giggle? How would we translate what we know when we hear a person giggle into knowledge *that*? That the person giggling is amused? Is nervous? Is trying to be flirtatious? Or that the person has a conjunction of some but not all of these attitudes? And how would those attitudes have been different if the person had chuckled instead of giggling?

And so it has become apparent that fully functioning human beings have the capacity for a knowledge of persons and their mental states which is fundamentally different from knowledge *that*. Insofar as autistic children are deficient in their knowledge *that* something is the case as regards the mental states of other people, it is because they are first impaired in their capacity for a kind of knowledge which is not reducible, or not entirely reducible, to knowledge *that*.

But what is this cognitive capacity? How are we to understand it and the kind of knowledge it makes possible?

Mirror neurons

There is as yet no uncontested explanation of autism; but at present two lines of research seem particularly promising in their ability to illuminate it. Studies done by developmental psychologists and discussed also by philosophers highlight a deficiency among autistic children in their capacity for engaging in what researchers call 'attention sharing' or 'joint attention.' For purposes related to my larger project, I am reserving a consideration of this research for a later chapter.[17] Here I want to call attention only to the second line of research, that having to do with mirror neurons.[18] (It may be that the system of mirror neurons also explains the capacity of fully functioning human beings to participate in shared or joint attention, but consideration of the neural substrate of joint attention is outside the bounds of my project.)

Recent studies have demonstrated that

newborn infants less than an hour old can . . . imitate facial gestures . . . Even in circumstances of . . . delays (of 24 hours) infants clearly remember and imitate gestures . . . Furthermore, the data . . . indicate that neonate imitative behavior involves memory and representation, since imitation can happen even after a delay.[19]

Like an infant's ability to recognize persons as persons and to know (some of) the mental states of other persons,[20] an infant's ability to imitate facial expressions is a perplexing phenomenon. As Shaun Gallagher says: "It is clear . . . that newborns do not have a visual perception of their own face . . . "[21] It is also clear that a newborn is not able to know *that* the person whose facial expression she is imitating is a person, that that person shares with the infant the property of having a face, or any of the myriad other items of knowledge that seem necessary for a newborn to attempt to mimic the expression on someone else's face. How is it, then, that neonates can imitate facial expressions?

One hypothesis has to do with the recently discovered brain system of mirror neurons. In the 1990s, a team of Italian neuroscientists discovered that certain neurons—which they came to call 'mirror neurons'—fire in the brain both when one does some action oneself *and also* when one sees that same action being performed by someone else. Since then, we have learned that, as Gallagher says, mirror neurons "constitute an intermodal link between the visual perception of action or dynamic expression, and the first-person, *intra*subjective . . . sense of one's own capabilities."[22] A neonate is able to imitate a facial expression on the part of another person because it has the capacity to know, as it were, from the inside what it is that the other is doing.

It now seems as if the mirror neuron system is the foundation for the capacity of all fully functional human beings at any age to know the mind of another person.[23] When John sees Mary smile at him and reach in a certain way toward a flower, he knows that she is going to pick the flower to give it to him.[24] How does he know what she is doing? How does he know what she is feeling and intending to do? The Italian team of researchers responsible for the discovery of mirror neurons says:

A decade ago most neuroscientists and psychologists would have attributed an individual's understanding of someone else's actions and, especially, intentions to a rapid reasoning process not unlike that used to solve a logical problem: some sophisticated apparatus in John's brain elaborated on the information his senses took in and compared it with similar previously stored experiences, allowing John to arrive at a conclusion about what Mary was up to and why.[25]

The discovery of the mirror neuron system has made this sort of attempt at under-standing the human ability to mind-read look Ptolemaic. Trying to summarize their discovery, the Italian researchers say: "John grasps Mary's action because even as it is happening before his eyes, it is also happening, in effect, inside his head ... mirror neurons permit an observed act to be directly understood by experiencing it."[26]

This summary of theirs is not entirely perspicuous, since it is not clear what it is to experience an observed act. Nonetheless, the research of these neurobiologists, as well as that of many others, has shown convincingly that mirror neurons underlie the human capacity to know not only someone else's actions, but also her intentions and emotions. Describing their research on the role of mirror neurons in mediating the knowledge of intentions, another team of researchers says:

the ability to understand the intentions associated with the actions of others is a fundamental component of social behavior, and its deficit is typically associated with socially isolating mental diseases such as autism ... Experiments in monkeys [have] demonstrated that frontal and parietal mirror neurons code the "what" of the observed action ... The findings [of this study] ... strongly suggest that this mirror neuron area actively participates in understanding the intentions behind the observed actions ... The present data show that the intentions behind the actions of others can be recognized by the motor system using a mirror mechanism.[27]

Researchers in another study sum up their work on the mirror neurons in the inferior parietal lobule by saying: "these neurons not only code the observed motor act but also allow the observer to understand the agent's intentions."[28]

And they generalize the results of their research this way:

Understanding "other minds" constitutes a special domain of cognition ... Brain imaging studies suggest that several areas might be involved in this function ... Given the complexity of the problem, it would be naïve to claim that the mechanism described in the present study is the sole mechanism underlying mind reading, yet the present data show a neural mechanism [i.e., the mirror neuron system] through which a basic aspect of understanding intention may be solved.[29]

Other research has shown that the mirror neuron system is also involved when a fully functioning person knows the emotion of another. Exploring mirror neurons and emotion, Rizzolatti et al. make it clear that, in their view, the mirror neuron system mediates one particular kind of knowledge of emotion. So, for example, as regards disgust, they say: "populations of mirror neurons in the insula become active both when the test participants experience the emotion and when they see it expressed by others. In other words, the observer and the observed share a neural mechanism that enables a form of direct experiential understanding."[30]

Like many people working in the field, these researchers are concerned to distinguish a mind-reading kind of knowledge from knowledge *that*. And so they put the results of their research this way:

Observing another person experiencing emotion can trigger a cognitive elaboration of that sensory information, which ultimately results in a logical conclusion about what the other is feeling. It may also, however, result in the direct mapping of that sensory information onto the motor structures that would produce the experience of that emotion in the observer. These two means of recognizing emotions are profoundly different: with the first, the observer deduces the emotion but does not feel it; via the second, recognition is firsthand because the mirror mechanism elicits the same emotional state in the observer.[31]

It is not entirely clear what these researchers mean by saying that the mirror mechanism elicits the same emotional state in the observer. It is certainly not the case that every time a person observes the emotion of another, he comes to have that same emotion himself. But perhaps these researchers mean only that one can feel something of the emotion of another *as that other's emotion*. At any rate, that is how other researchers qualify the point.[32]

Still other researchers try to explain the cognition in question by claiming that the mirror neuron system allows us to simulate the mental states of others. So, for example, one prominent team of neurobiologists says:

One of the most striking features of our experience of others is its intuitive nature . . . in our brain, there are neural mechanisms (mirror mechanisms) that allow us to directly understand the meaning of the actions and emotions of others by internally replicating ('simulating') them . . .[33]

And in an effort to give their own philosophical explanation of what they take simulation to be, these neurobiologists say that the particular kind of cognition subserved by the mirror neuron system is achieved

without any explicit reflective mediation. Conceptual reasoning is not necessary for this understanding. As human beings, of course, we are able to reason about others and to use this capacity to understand other people's minds at the conceptual, declarative level . . . [but] the fundamental mechanism that allows us a direct experiential grasp of the mind of others is not conceptual reasoning but direct simulation of the observed events through the mirror mechanism.[34]

This is not completely clear and accurate either, of course. For example, it is not correct to describe the cognition subserved by the mirror neuron system as non-conceptual. When John knows the emotion Mary is feeling, he must know it by means of some concept, such as the concept of affection, say, or gratitude. In my view, for reasons that will emerge below, it is also not appropriate to try to understand the mirror neuron system in terms of simulation.[35]

Still other researchers highlight the intuitive character of the cognition mediated by the mirror neuron system. Raphael Bernier and Geraldine Dawson put the point this way:

The mirror neuron theory of autism simply proposes that dysfunction . . . [of the mirror neuron system] does not allow for the internal representation of others' observed behavior, expressions, movements, and emotions. This prevents the individual with autism from having an immediate, direct experience of the other through this internal representation. Social deficits . . . therefore cascade from this lack of immediate, experiential understanding of others in the social world.[36]

What all these researchers are struggling to describe is one person's knowledge of another and of that other's mental states when the knowledge in question shares features with the phenomenology of certain kinds of perception. Like the perception of color, for example, the knowledge of persons at issue here is direct, intuitive, and hard to translate without remainder into knowledge *that*, but very useful as a basis for knowledge *that* of one sort or another. John knows *that* Mary is going to give him a flower because he first knows Mary, her action, her emotion, and her intention—but these are things which he knows by, as it were, seeing them, and not by cognizing them in the knowledge *that* way.

And so these discoveries about the mirror neuron system help to explain the Wittgensteinian point Hobson made in the quotation above. We *see* emotion, as we *see* intention, because the mirror neuron system gives us some sort of direct apprehension of someone else's mental state. Or, as Hume put it, many years before the discovery of the mirror neuron system: "The minds of men are mirrors to one another, not only because they reflect each others' emotions, but also because those rays of passion, sentiments, and opinions may often be reverberated."[37] And that is why Hume says of himself: "A cheerful countenance infuses a sensible complacency and serenity in my mind, as an angry or sullen one throws a sudden damp upon me."[38]

This kind of social cognition or mind-reading, subserved by the mirror neuron system, is in effect the phenomenon of the Franciscan knowledge of persons.[39]

Mirror neurons and Franciscan knowledge

No doubt, further research will demonstrate that, besides the system of mirror neurons, there are also other neural systems that enable the human capacity for mind-reading.[40] Whatever these neural systems may turn out to be, however, it does seem to be the case that the mirror neuron system has a large role in the brain processes that underlie the Franciscan knowledge of persons. Of course, this is not to say that the mirror neuron system is necessary for all varieties of Franciscan knowledge. Franciscan knowledge, as I attempted to capture it in the preceding chapter, is not confined to knowledge of persons; and chances are excellent that parts of the central nervous system other than the mirror neuron networks will be found to underlie those other abilities.

So, for example, the noted Russian neurologist A. Luria reported the case of an early twentieth-century composer, Shebalin, who lost virtually all of his linguistic abilities as a result of a stroke; but while he was in this condition, he composed a symphony now highly regarded by musically literate listeners. Shebalin's cognition of music was preserved in the face of his stroke because it was not mediated by a natural language and did not constitute knowledge *that*. In general, the basics of language are processed in the left cerebral hemisphere, but many elements of music are processed in the right.[41] If at least some of the knowledge of music that allowed Shebalin to compose after his stroke counts as Franciscan, then this Franciscan knowledge is subserved at least in part by the particular right-hemisphere systems involved in music.[42]

Furthermore, there are also neural systems that process the musical elements in the production and comprehension of ordinary natural languages; these can be undermined or destroyed independently of other linguistic capacities. For example, the knowledge of whether an English-language question such as "Do you want coffee or tea?" admits of a yes-or-no answer depends on a direct intuitive understanding of the import of the intonation with which the question is uttered. The knowledge of the import of intonation seems to be a case of Franciscan knowledge too, and it is also processed in the right-hemisphere systems involved in music.[43]

Or consider the case of the fine arts. In his insightful study of the knowledge mediated by the visual arts, Dominic McIver Lopes says:

Even Plato should grant that some knowledge can be obtained from pictures. Looking at Rembrandt's painting *Belshazzar's Feast* in the National Gallery . . . you may learn that it is painted in oils, that there are paintings by Rembrandt in London, and that it depicts the divine hand. These are instances of 'knowledge about' a picture . . . We can know these facts about a picture just as we know similar facts about any object.[44]

Lopes calls this sort of knowledge 'knowledge about' pictures. Obviously, however, knowledge *about* a picture does not exhaust the knowledge mediated by pictures. Lopes calls the special kind of knowledge mediated by pictures 'knowledge in,' because it is knowledge that is garnered from seeing into a picture, as it were. Struggling to give an explanation of his notion of knowledge-in, Lopes says in frustration: "[knowledge-in] is not propositional knowledge amenable to analysis by the standard . . . account of knowledge. It is a different creature entirely. Nobody has managed a remotely clear description of the creature."[45] And Lopes goes on to ask: "How can pictures convey knowledge-in if the contents of knowledge are propositions? . . . A still life by Chardin depicts a collection of objects as appearing a certain way, and a grasp of the picture requires only that its viewer see the objects in it; but seeing-in is arguably non-propositional."[46]

Part of the problem here is that Lopes is trying to fit the knowledge gained through contemplation of pictures into the prevailing epistemological view which takes all knowledge (or virtually all knowledge) to be propositional knowledge or knowledge *that*,[47] and part of the solution to Lopes's puzzle is just to accept that knowledge-in is *not* propositional. In fact, Lopes's "knowledge-in" is analogous to the knowledge of persons, not only in the sense that it is not reducible to knowledge *that*, but also in the sense that it is immediate, intuitive, and difficult to articulate in language.

Lopes tries to answer his own question about the non-propositional knowledge mediated by pictures with the help of contemporary virtue epistemology. He says, "a picture may . . . have cognitive merit because it fosters or reinforces an intellectual virtue."[48]

This is a promising, if undeveloped, idea for an explanation of Franciscan knowledge of pictures, and it may be helpful for thinking about Franciscan knowledge in general. On this suggestion about the nature of Franciscan knowledge, Franciscan knowledge could be understood as the veridical delivery[49] of a cognitive faculty when that cognitive faculty is aimed at veridicality and is functioning properly in its typical environment,[50] where veridicality is a matter of an epistemic connection to things in the world that is correct and reliable[51] but that is nonetheless not propositional.[52] When the cognitive faculty in question is operating in this way at some particularly high or meritorious level, then its deliverances count as the manifestation of an epistemic virtue of some kind. But these are very controversial matters that cannot be adjudicated in passing in a chapter, and I raise them here only to leave them to one side.

Whatever the appropriately clear description is of the knowledge of pictures of concern to Lopes, or of Franciscan knowledge in general, no doubt this sort of knowledge is subserved by central nervous networks different from those involved in the knowledge of music and also different from the mirror neuron system underlying the Franciscan knowledge of persons. So the mirror neuron system is not the whole of the neural systems underlying Franciscan knowledge; as far as that goes, it is unlikely to be the whole even of the neural systems underlying the knowledge of persons.

For that matter, it seems unlikely that experiences of an immaterial deity, if there are any such experiences, would be mediated in part or in whole by the mirror neuron system either. Nonetheless, attempts by theologians and others to describe such experiences resemble descriptions of the ordinary experiences that are mediated by the mirror neuron system. So, for example, Martin Buber says:

The essential element in our relationship to God has been sought in a feeling that has been called a feeling of dependence . . . the one-sided emphasis on this factor leads to a misunderstanding of the character of the perfect relationship . . . feelings merely accompany the fact of the relationship which after all is established not in the soul but between an I and a You.[53]

The cognition human beings have in the so-called 'I–Thou relationship' is immediate, in Buber's view. He says: "It is not as if God could be inferred from anything . . . It is not as if something else were 'given' and this were then deduced from it. This is what confronts us immediately and first and always, and legitimately it can only be addressed, not asserted."[54]

No doubt, whatever cognitive capacities might underlie the sort of I–Thou experience of God Buber is concerned with here, it will have a substrate that is, at best, only analogous to the mirror neuron system.

A caveat: The fallibility of Franciscan knowledge

Even if the Franciscan knowledge of persons is not mediated solely by the mirror neuron system, thinking of it as having a source in the mirror neuron system is propaedeutically helpful in various ways. For example, it renders unworrisome, because familiar, the undeniable conclusion that Franciscan knowledge is fallible, however generally reliable it may be. Given the importance of Franciscan knowledge in the chapters that follow, it is prudent to say something more about this fallibility here.[55]

One team of Italian researchers introduce their overview of the mirror neuron system by saying: "Humans are an exquisitely social species. Our survival and success depends crucially on our ability to thrive in complex social situations."[56]

Like the sensory system subserving perception, the mirror neuron system is built to enhance survival in the particular social circumstances in which it works reasonably reliably; but, as in the case of more familiar human cognitive capacities, there are undoubtedly also circumstances and conditions in which it will yield erroneous results.

We can think of Franciscan knowledge of persons as roughly analogous to perception in the nature of its reliability. Perception, too, is generally reliable, and yet it can go wrong in more than one way. So, for example, there are perceptual illusions: I think that I see water on the road ahead of me; but the appearance of water is an optical illusion, and there is no water there. There is also perceptual ambiguity. I think that I see a bear, but in fact the thing that is the object of my visual experience is a bear statue. In this case, I do see something that is really there, something bear-shaped; but the visual information is insufficient to determine what exactly it is that is bear-shaped, and I form a false belief on the basis of that perceptual information when I think that I see a bear. So, the perceptual faculties can give information about the object of perception that is ambiguous, and judgment based on this information can consequently be incorrect.

Roughly the same sorts of things can be said about the brain systems and cognitive capacities that produce Franciscan knowledge of persons. Although for fully functioning people in typical circumstances, these systems and capacities are generally reliable,[57] they can go wrong. When they go badly wrong, they yield not so much *illusions* as something that might appropriately be called 'delusions.' There are perfectly ordinary cases of this sort of fallibility in the cognitive capacities underlying Franciscan knowledge of persons. For example, a battered wife looks at her husband, in the aftermath of a beating, and it seems to her that she sees love in his face; but she is deluded. There is no real love in the batterer.

In addition, there is obviously also ambiguous information that can yield incorrect judgments. A teacher confronting two students she believes to have cheated on an exam may get ambiguous information from her face-to-face encounter with them, and that ambiguous information may not be sufficient to enable her to perceive which of them is lying in protestations of innocence. For that knowledge, the information she gets from her interaction with the students may well be insufficient. If she feels she knows which of the students is the cheater, she deludes herself, we might say.[58]

On the other hand, there are also core cases of perception in which, in ordinary circumstances, we find it virtually impossible to doubt a particular perception. In ordinary circumstances, I cannot be shaken in my belief that *this* in front of my eyes is my hand. There are analogous cases for Franciscan knowledge, too. In ordinary circumstances, when my daughter is immediately before me, I cannot be shaken in my conviction that *this* before me is my daughter. In ordinary circumstances, a man coming home late and drunk to confront a furious wife has no doubts at all about the general tenor of her mental state.

It is noteworthy that some religious believers have supposed that certain religious experiences carry with them conviction of this kind. So, for example, Teresa of Avila gives as one mark of a genuine religious experience of God that the person who had the experience is unable to doubt that she was in the presence of God during it.[59] In the biblical stories examined in the chapters to follow, there are biblical characters who manifest such core cases of Franciscan knowledge in their interactions with God. Job's response to God's speeches, for example, strongly suggests that, in the narrative, for Job the experience of God that he had while God was talking to him gave him conviction of this sort of God's presence and love.

And so there are core cases of Franciscan knowledge, just as there are core cases of perception; and these somehow carry conviction of their veridicality with them. Furthermore, for the core cases of ordinary knowledge of persons, like the core cases of ordinary perception, it seems unreasonable not to accept the cognitive capacities in question as generally reliable. The fallibility of Franciscan cognition does not take away its general trustworthiness. In subsequent chapters, I will therefore leave to one side questions arising from concern over the reliability of Franciscan cognition.

Second-person experience

One group of neurobiologists try to explain the knowledge mediated by the mirror neuron system by relying on a familiar philosophical distinction. They say:

> The novelty of our approach consists in providing for the first time a neurophysiological account of the experiential dimension of both action and emotion understanding. What makes social interactions so different from our perception of the inanimate world is that we witness the actions and emotions of others, but we also carry out similar actions and we experience similar emotions. There is something shared between our first- and third-person experience of these phenomena: the observer and the observed are both individuals endowed with a similar brain–body system. A crucial element of social cognition is the brain's capacity to directly link the first- and third-person experiences of these phenomena . . .[60]

These neurobiologists are here availing themselves of the distinction by now familiar in contemporary philosophy between a first-person and a third-person experience or point of view. But, contrary to their claims, it does not seem right to take the experience of persons in which the mirror neuron system operates as a first-person experience of oneself, or a third-person experience of another, or some combination of both together.[61] Rather, it seems to be something entirely different. Under one or another description, some philosophers are now drawing our attention to the importance of what can be called 'a second-person point of view' or 'a second-person experience.'[62] In my view, this is more nearly the notion that the neurobiologists need to express what is of interest to them.[63]

For my purposes, I will understand a second-person experience in this way.[64] One person Paula has a second-person experience of another person Jerome[65] only if

(1) Paula is aware of Jerome as a person (call the relation Paula has to Jerome in this condition 'personal interaction'),

(2) Paula's personal interaction with Jerome is of a direct and immediate sort,

and

(3) Jerome is conscious.[66]

These conditions are necessary for second-person experience and sufficient for a minimal degree of it. (It is clear that there can be more to a second-person experience than this bare minimum. It is evident that knowledge of persons comes in degrees.[67])

Condition (1) implies that Paula does not have a second-person experience of Jerome if Paula is dumped unconscious on top of Jerome. Even if Paula is conscious, if she is not aware of Jerome—say, because Jerome is hiding and Paula does not know he is present —then Paula does not have a second-person experience of Jerome. Finally, if Paula has perception of Jerome but is not attending to him, so that she is not aware of him in spite of her perception of him,[68] then Paula does not have second-person experience of Jerome. On the other hand, condition (1) can be met even if Paula does not have perception of Jerome.[69] It is possible for one person to be aware of another as a person without seeing, hearing, smelling, touching, or tasting that other person. For example, if Paula and Jerome are engaged in an animated conversation with one another that they conduct by means of email, Paula is aware of Jerome as a person, even if she does not perceive Jerome.[70]

As for condition (2), I take Paula's personal interaction with Jerome to be mediated and indirect just in case Paula has personal interaction with Jerome only in virtue of having personal interaction with a third person, such as Paula's daughter Julia.[71] So condition (2) rules out cases of personal interaction which are mediated by one or more other people, but it does not rule out intermediaries which are machines or mechanical devices, such as glasses, telephones, and computers. If Paula's only contact with Jerome is by computer, but if the computer contact between them meets the other conditions for second-person experience, then Paula's computer contact with Jerome counts as a second-person experience.[72] On the other hand, Paula does not count as having a second-person experience of Jerome if her contact consists just in Julia's reporting to Paula something Jerome has said or done. In such a case, Jerome is conscious, and Paula is aware of Jerome as a person, in some sense; but this sort of awareness of Jerome is insufficient to count as a second-person experience of Jerome because it is mediated by a third person Julia.[73]

Finally, condition (3) requires that Jerome be conscious for Paula to have a second-person experience of him. It is not necessary, however, that Jerome be conscious of Paula. Paula has a second-person experience of Jerome even if Paula is hidden from Jerome behind a screen, watching Jerome interact with Julia.[74]

So this is how I will understand a second-person experience.[75] This characterization of a second-person experience makes it clear that a second-person experience is different from a first-person experience. In a first-person experience, I am directly and immediately aware of a person as a person, but that person is only myself. It is also clear that a second-person experience is different from a third-person experience. For a third-person experience, one person has knowledge of the states of another but not in virtue of being conscious of that other as a person.

A second-person experience is, therefore, different in character from a first-person or a third-person experience because it is necessary for a second-person experience, as it is not for a first- or third-person experience, that you interact consciously and directly with another person who is conscious and present to you as a person, in one way or another.[76]

We are not yet in a position to give a clear and complete account of knowledge which is not knowledge *that* or even just of the knowledge of persons directly subserved by the mirror neuron system. But, however we are to describe the knowledge of persons enabled by the mirror neuron system, in my view, it cannot be captured appropriately as knowledge of either a first-person or a third-person kind, contrary to the claims of the neurobiologists quoted above. It is more nearly accurate to describe it in terms of a second-person experience. Although the mirror neuron system no doubt also facilitates knowledge in ways which are at best variants of a second-person experience,[77] the paradigmatic sort of experience in which one gains the kind of knowledge of persons subserved by the mirror neuron system is a second-person experience. The mirror neuron system seems to be a brain system designed primarily to enable second-person experience and the knowledge of persons such experience generates.[78]

Second-person accounts

With so much clarification of the notion of a second-person experience, I want to consider the means by which the Franciscan knowledge communicated in a second-person experience is shareable with someone who was not part of the second-person experience in question. It will be helpful to have some short designation for this vehicle for sharing knowledge. So call it 'a second person account,' by analogy with the more customary notions of first-person or third-person accounts or reports.[79]

Why think that there is such a thing as a second-person account? What would differentiate it from either a first-person or a third-person account? In a first-person account, I give a report about some first-person experience of mine. In a third-person account, I give a report about some feature or condition of someone else. What is there left for a second-person account to do? Why would not a report of a second-person experience simply be one more first-person account—if I report the conscious states that I had while in the second-person experience[80]—or one more third-person account—if I report something about some other person that I observed during my second-person experience of her? Why could not a second-person experience be represented adequately in ordinary expository prose[81] of either the first-person or the third-person variety?

If everything knowable in a second-person experience could be expressed in terms of knowing *that*, with regard to either oneself or the others with whom one interacts, then no doubt a second-person experience could be captured by first-person and third-person accounts, and there would be no room for anything that could be considered a second-person account. But the cumulative weight of the evidence and arguments I have given about the knowledge of persons is sufficient to show its distinctive character. Second-person experiences cannot be reduced to first-person or third-person experiences without remainder, and so they cannot be captured by first-person or third-person accounts either. As I have been at pains to show, knowledge of persons accessible in second-person experiences is not reducible to knowledge *that*.

To some people, this conclusion might seem equivalent to the claim that a second-person account is impossible. If the Franciscan knowledge of persons is difficult or impossible to express in terms of knowing *that*, how can any account of it be given at all?

In one sense, the implied point of the question is right. There is no way to give an adequate account in expository prose (a Dominican account, that is) of the Franciscan knowledge given in a second-person experience. But it does not follow that no account of such knowledge is possible at all. While we cannot express the distinctive knowledge of such an experience as a matter of knowing *that*, we can do something to re-present the experience itself in such a way that we can share the second-person experience to some degree with others who were not part of it, so that at least some of the Franciscan knowledge garnered from the experience is also available to them.[82]

This is generally what we do when we tell a story.[83] A story takes a real or imagined set of second-person experiences of one sort or another and makes it available to a wider audience to share.[84] It does so by making it possible, to one degree or another,[85] for a person to experience some of what she would have experienced if she had been an onlooker in the second-person experience represented in the story. That is, a story gives a person some of what she would have had if she had had unmediated personal interaction with the characters in the story while they were conscious and interacting with each other, without actually making her part of the story itself.[86] The re-presenting of a second-person experience in a story thus constitutes a second-person account. It is a report of a set of second-person experiences that does not lose (at least does not lose entirely) the distinctively second-person character of the experiences.

We can put the point the other way around by noticing what we lose if we try to reduce a narrative to expository (that is, non-narrative) prose. Of course, a story typically does include within it many propositions expressing knowledge *that*, in the narrative line of the story and also in the statements the story puts into the thoughts and utterances of the story's characters.[87] But if we boil a story down just to non-narrative propositions, so that all the knowledge it conveys is knowledge *that*,[88] then we lose the knowledge that the story distinctively provides just because we cannot convey by means of expository prose alone even a simulacrum of a second-person experience.[89] A real story cannot be captured in a set of non-narrative propositions; Cliff Notes, even ideally excellent Cliff Notes, are no substitute for the literary work itself. Even a very good Cliff Notes-style summary of *The Brothers Karamazov*, for example, would lose what is best about the novel itself.

A storyteller, like an art photographer, directs attention to reveal elements (or to portray elements) in what is depicted that might otherwise have escaped the attention of onlookers. That is why the same events can give rise to highly variant stories even when all the stories are veridical.[90] How much of what can be known through a real or imagined second-person experience is made available to others to learn by means of a story depends in part on the artistry of the storyteller. Harlequin romances no doubt give us something; the world's great literature, drama, and film[91] give us much more. If, in her isolation, the Mary of the thought experiment described earlier[92] had had available to her not only science books but also, for example, the works of Eliot, Dickens, Tolstoy, Dostoyevsky, Angelou, and Achebe, or an array of the best movies and films of theater productions, it is indisputable that her first experience with her mother would have been less of a surprise.[93]

So far I have been considering the way in which the knowledge of persons in real or imagined sets of second-person experiences can be transmitted. But, for my purposes in this book, it is more important to consider how the knowledge of persons in fiction can be appropriated by the audience for that fiction. Philosophers have puzzled over audience reaction to fiction.[94] In my view, consideration of the mirror neuron system lets us think about audience appropriation of fiction in a helpful way.

We can begin by comparing the mirror neuron system with perceptual systems. Recent studies of the visual system, for example, have investigated what happens when a person sees a complex object and then watches that object rotating in space. Studies on visual imagery have shown that those parts of the visual system that are involved in the sight of the rotation of objects are also the parts of the system that are used when a person imagines the rotation of imagined objects.[95] It is now clear that the visual system can be used for the actual visual cognition and inspection of objects in physical reality, or the same neural system can be used to form images of objects and to inspect the imagined rotation of those objects.

Nothing keeps us from supposing that the mirror neuron system that subserves the knowledge of persons can also be used in this dual-purpose way, for the appropriation of second-person experience either in actuality or in thought only. If this is right, then it might be that, when we engage with fiction, we also employ the mirror neuron system, but in an alternate mode, just as the visual system is employed in an alternate mode when we imagine the rotation of an imagined object.[96] If the mirror neuron system is like the perceptual system in this regard, then the same system that explains our knowledge of persons in second-person experience could also explain our appropriation of the knowledge of persons through fiction.[97]

I am not claiming here that the mirror neuron system is used in the appropriation of fiction to give us actual second-person experience.[98] The appropriation of fiction does not give us real second-person experience, any more than the imagined rotation of imagined objects gives us real visual inspection of such objects. I mean only that when fiction functions as a second-person account and we gain some knowledge of persons from fiction, one possible explanation for why we do so is that the mirror neuron system can also be used in an alternative mode, for the engagement with fiction.[99]

On this hypothesis, then, the Franciscan knowledge garnered in real or imagined second-person experiences and preserved in narratives is communicable to those capable of exercising the cognitive capacities for Franciscan knowledge in engaging with the story. Excellence in interpretation, like excellence in narrative construction itself, will be, at least in part, a function of excellence in the exercise of the capacities for Franciscan knowledge of persons on the part of the interpreters of the narrative.

Caveat about literary form

Finally, it is worth pointing out here that, strictly speaking, not every narrative is a second-person account, as I have described second-person accounts. In general, narratives have interactions among people as their centerpiece, but there are stories in which the narrator relates experiences that include no persons except himself. Jack London's story "To Build a Fire" is a narrative of this sort. Even stories such as "To Build a Fire," however, have this much of the second-person about them: in re-presenting for us what is in the narrative only the experience of one person, such stories turn that experience into something at least approaching a second-person account, insofar as one's engagement with the single character of the story is analogous to a second-person experience. The author's presentation of the character, if it is well done, makes that character available to us in somewhat the same way the character would have been if he had in fact been directly and immediately present to us. The story thus contributes to our having and learning from something like a second-person experience, only it is our experience with the character of the story.

Conversely, it is also true that some forms of literature that, strictly speaking, do not count as stories can sometimes qualify as a second-person account. So, for example, some poems serve the same function as stories in portraying for us the interactions of persons;[100] and even some poems that have very few features of stories may still be successful in re-creating for us an image of one person's relations to others. So, for example, as I will discuss in Chapter 9, the poems that are God's speeches to Job present for the reader a picture of God's relations to his creatures, and the picture is vivid and lively enough to make it at least arguable that the poems are second-person accounts, too. But the clearest examples of second-person accounts are stories (in one medium or another) involving more than one person.

Conclusion

There is, then, a broad array of knowledge commonly had by human beings that cannot be formulated adequately or at all as knowledge *that*. Such knowledge is provided by some first-person experiences, especially those in which the qualia of the experience are among the salient parts of the knowledge. One important species of such knowledge is the Franciscan knowledge of persons.

In fully functioning human beings, such knowledge has a source in the mirror neuron system, which enables a person to know the actions, intentions, and emotions of another person in a direct, intuitive way analogous in some respects to perception. Such Franciscan knowledge of persons is gained paradigmatically through second-person experiences. And, although Franciscan knowledge of persons gained through second-person experiences is not reducible to knowledge *that*, it can be made available to others who lack the second-person experiences in question by means of a story that re-presents the experience. A story is, then, a second-person account.

Second-person experience and stories thus play a role with regard to the knowledge of persons analogous to the role played by postulates and arguments with regard to knowledge *that*. Experience and stories, on the one hand, and postulates and arguments, on the other, are devices for the acquisition and transfer of knowledge, although the kind of knowledge acquired or transferred and the sort of acquisition or transfer involved differ.

The Franciscan knowledge of persons which is not reducible to knowledge *that* but which is transmitted through stories is also philosophically useful. And this is why narratives have a role to play in philosophy, even philosophy of the analytic type.

With this, my explanation of the nature of my project and my defense of the methodology I mean to employ in it is complete. No doubt, a great deal more needs to be done to explain and defend the notion of Franciscan knowledge. But this is not a book on epistemology; it is a book on the problem of suffering. I have tried to show the appropriateness of using narratives in the examination of philosophical issues and to give some idea of the reasons for that appropriateness; more than that I have neither the space nor the desire to try to accomplish.

As I explained in Chapter 1, my plan in this book is to present a representative medieval worldview and theodicy—that of Thomas Aquinas—and let it, together with the stories I examine, count as a defense, a description of a possible world in which there is suffering and also an omnipotent, omniscient, perfectly good God. In the next part, I will begin the construction of this defense by presenting Aquinas's account of the features of the possible world in question that are most important for my purposes: the nature of love and the obstacles to love. When I have laid out this basic Thomistic worldview, which I will take to be true in the possible world of the defense, I will then turn to the biblical narratives I have chosen to consider, proceeding Franciscanly in their examination to the best of my (Dominican) ability. The examination of these narratives constitutes the third part of this book. In the fourth part I will examine Aquinas's theodicy, with the narratives as its context. The Franciscan knowledge mediated by these stories, understood in the framework of the possible world embodying Aquinas's philosophical and theological worldview, will be the basis for the defense I then construct.

PART 2

THE WORLD AT LARGE: LOVE
AND LONELINESS

Chapter 5

The Nature of Love

Then live, my strength, anchor of weary ships,
Safe shore and land at last, thou, for my wreck,
My honour, thou, and my abiding rest,
My city safe for a bewildered heart.
What though the plains and mountains and the sea
Between us are, that which no earth can hold
Still follows thee, and love's own singing follows,
Longing that all things may be well with thee.
Christ who first gave thee for a friend to me,
Christ keep thee well, where'er thou art, for me.
Earth's self shall go and the swift wheel of heaven
Perish and pass, before our love shall cease.
Do but remember me, as I do thee,
And God, who brought us on this earth together,
Bring us together to his house of heaven.[*]

Introduction

With so much said about the project of this book and its methodology, I want now to begin the description of the possible world of the defense that is my purpose by presenting those parts of the medieval worldview relevant to that defense. The most important of these has to do with the nature of love, as Aquinas understands it.

It is easiest to explain Aquinas's view of the nature of love by contrasting it with contemporary accounts of love. Two competing accounts of love have become familiar in recent philosophical treatments of the subject.

---

[*] Rabanus Maurus to Grimold, Abbot of St Gall, in *Mediaeval Latin Lyrics*, trans. Helen Waddell (London: Penguin Books, 1929; repr. 1962), 120.

On one account, love is a response of the lover to qualities he perceives and values in the beloved.[1] On this way of thinking about love, there are intrinsic characteristics of the beloved person that are especially attractive to the lover, whose love is engendered in him by these characteristics.[2] So there is a reason for the love the lover has for his beloved, and that is the set of characteristics that the lover finds so valuable in the beloved. Differing philosophers give different variations on this account of love;[3] but, for ease of reference, we can call the view common to all these variations 'the responsiveness account of love.'

There is something intuitively appealing about the responsiveness account, not least because we are accustomed to lovers who are filled with praise for the people they love. A mother who loves her young child, for example, can typically be counted on to regale her friends and acquaintances with the wonders of the child's many excellences. Nonetheless, the responsiveness account suffers from problems that have been amply expounded by its critics.

To begin with, any intrinsic feature possessed by a beloved person is one that other persons do have or could have. Consequently, it seems that, on this account of love, another person could be acceptably substituted for the beloved, provided only that the new person had the valued characteristics of the beloved. But the non-substitutability of the beloved is sometimes taken as a hallmark of love. Robert Kraut, for example, says: "The non-transferability . . . of love is a defining condition of its being directed toward a unique individual."[4] Centuries earlier, in Latin that needs no translation, Richard of St Victor described the four marks of great love as "insuperabilis, inseparabilis, singularis, insatiabilis."[5]

In addition, if love is a response to intrinsic features in the beloved, then it seems not only that the love would be generated by those intrinsic features in anyone else but also that the strength or intensity of the love would co-vary with the degree of the valued property. But this is manifestly not the case. As Harry Frankfurt aptly remarks: "It is quite clear to me that I do not love [my children] more than other children because I believe that they are better [than other children]."[6]

Furthermore, there is a problem as regards the constancy of love.

Love is, of course, not invariant. As Kraut says, "genuinely 'person-directed' loves [do not] endure through *all* changes of characteristics . . . Every love has its limits."[7] And Amelie Rorty gives a vivid description of the way in which a lover *should* change with changes in the beloved. As she puts it, "every change [in the beloved] generates new changes, in the lover and in [the lover's] interactions with [the beloved] . . . [Louis] would be cruel to love [Ella's] way of playing Scarlatti if her hands had been mangled in an accident."[8]

For all this, however, we still expect that real love will last even when the lover finds that his beloved no longer has the characteristics that originally entranced him in her. But the responsiveness account implies that, if the beloved loses the characteristics valued by the lover, then the lover's love must cease. On the responsiveness account, then, the well-known Shakespearean line is wrong: *pace* Shakespeare, love *must* alter when it alteration finds. This implication has the counter-intuitive result of making love very fragile, contrary to what we expect and find. As Frankfurt says of his children: "If [they] should turn out to be ferociously wicked . . . I might perhaps recognize that my love for them was regrettable. But I suspect that after coming finally to acknowledge this, I would continue to love them anyhow."[9]

Problems such as these that arise in connection with the responsiveness account have led some philosophers to an opposite theory of the relation between love and value in the beloved. We can call this theory 'the volitional account,' after Frankfurt's version of it, which highlights the role of the will in love. Frankfurt says: "The lover does invariably and necessarily perceive the beloved as valuable, but the value he sees [the beloved] to possess is a value that derives from and that depends on his love."[10] Speaking of his love for his children, Frankfurt says:

It is not because I have noticed their value, then, that I love my children as I do . . . It is really the other way around. The particular value that I attribute to my children is not inherent in them but depends upon my love for them. The reason they are so precious to me is simply that I love them so much.[11]

Frankfurt is willing to extend this point to all love. On his view: "This relationship between love and the value of the beloved—namely, that love is not necessarily grounded in the value of the beloved but does necessarily make the beloved valuable to the lover—holds not only for parental love but quite generally."[12]

Unlike the responsiveness account, which highlights the objective element of care in love, the volitional account focuses on the subjective element, which makes the value of a thing derivative from a person's care for it.[13] There is certainly something appealing about this position, too. It does seem right to think that the value a child has for its parents is a function of the parents' love for the child, and not the other way around. A mother whose love of her child was a response to the intrinsically valuable features she took herself to perceive in her child would be bizarre.

But the problem with the volitional account is that it assigns no reason for love, or at least no reason rooted in the beloved; and this is a counter-intuitive result. If there is no such reason, then it seems as if the lover could just as easily have loved some other person. Since there is nothing about the particular person he loves that is the reason for his love, there is also no reason why he should love her rather than anyone else. Contrary to the volitional account, then, and in accordance with the rival responsiveness account of love, it seems as if there ought to be *something* in the beloved that prompts the lover's reaction of love.

One way to think about the puzzle posed by these two opposing accounts of love is to see that each of them appears to give a wrong answer to the question a beloved person might well ask the lover: "Why do you love me?" On the responsiveness account, the answer is the unsatisfactory line: "Because I love in you characteristics X, Y, and Z, which I find intrinsically valuable"—with the unpleasant implications just canvassed. On the volitional account, the answer is the equally unsatisfactory: "Oh, there is no reason, at least no reason having anything to do with *you*."

Kolodny's account of love

In a recent article, Niko Kolodny sums up the state of the contemporary discussion of the nature of love by saying: "We will not get beyond this impasse so long as we assume that any reason for loving a person would have to be a nonrelational feature that she has."[14] Kolodny's own suggestion is that a lover does have a reason for loving her beloved, but that the reason is the lover's relationship with the beloved. We can call Kolodny's account 'the relational account of love.'

By 'relationship' in this context,[15] Kolodny has in mind a connection that persists over time and that has a history of interactions between the persons so connected.[16] So, for example, he says, "relationships are *historical*. Whether I stand in a relationship to someone at a given time depends on some fact about our pasts. Kevin is my friend only if there has been a historical pattern of attitudes and actions between us."[17] Although he excepts what he calls 'attitude-independent relationships', such as family relationships, from "any historical pattern of concern,"[18] he understands "attitude-dependent relationships" such as friendships or romantic relationships to be "just . . . an ongoing pattern of concern," characterized by "activities characteristic of the relationship," such as "spending leisure time together."[19]

On Kolodny's account of love, "one's reason for loving a person is one's relationship to her; the ongoing history that one shares with her,"[20] rather than any intrinsic characteristic of the beloved's.[21] On his view:

the reason one has for loving Jane, in any given case, is that she is one's daughter, sister, mother, friend, or wife. This proposal avoids the problems that plague the views that cite nonrelational features as reasons for love. For instance, the fact that Jane is one's daughter is a reason for loving her, but not a reason for loving a substitute with identical nonrelational features. And this proposal identifies the distinctive reasons for love that views such as Frankfurt's ignore at their peril.[22]

For Kolodny, then, "love consists (a) in seeing a relationship in which one is involved as a reason for valuing both one's relationship and the person with whom one has that relationship, and (b) in valuing that relationship and person accordingly."[23]

Kolodny thinks that understanding love as relational in this way enables his account to handle a case on which its competitors founder, which he describes as the case of the amnesic biographer. Kolodny imagines a scholar who writes and publishes an excellent biography of a woman named Mary and who subsequently meets Mary, falls in love with her, and marries her. Some time afterwards, the biographer develops amnesia of such a sort that he can remember the period of his life up to the publication of his biography but not after it. In this condition, he knows everything about Mary before the point of his meeting and marrying her, but he does not remember his own relationship to her. Kolodny says, in his amnesic state, we "would not expect him to love her, and it is hard to see how he could. To him, she is no longer the woman he fell in love with, but simply the attractive and admirable subject of his biography."[24]

Kolodny argues that the rival accounts of love give a wrong result with regard to this case. Since the amnesic biographer's perception of Mary's intrinsic qualities does not change with the amnesia, he should still love Mary in his amnesic state, on the responsiveness account of love. And on the volitional account of love, which assigns no reason for love, it seems that the amnesic biographer's love should not change just because he now lacks the memory of his relationship with Mary. But, Kolodny rightly claims, these are counter-intuitive results. By contrast, Kolodny claims that his own relational account gives the right result. Since the amnesic biographer no longer believes that there is a relationship between him and Mary that renders love appropriate, he no longer loves her.[25]

Despite the ability of the relational account to handle cases troublesome for its competitors, however, there are problems with it as well.[26]

Consider, for example, one of the Western world's most famous cases of romantic love, Dante's love for Beatrice, immortalized in his *Divine Comedy* as well as in his earlier writings. Dante, who was scarcely older than Beatrice, saw her once when she was 9 years old; and once, when she was a teenager, he was greeted by her in passing her on the street. But these events and some occasional sightings of her from a distance seem to have been the extent of Dante's connection to her. When Beatrice was barely out of her teens, she was married to someone else; and, at about the same time, Dante himself married Gemma Donati. Shortly after the time of these marriages, at the early age of 24, Beatrice died. When Dante was expressing his most fervent love for her in his great epic poem, Beatrice had been dead for many years. But even while Beatrice was living, there was no ongoing history of interactions between them.[27] For Dante and Beatrice, there was virtually no interaction at all, let alone a history of interactions, unless (*per improbabile*) one person's seeing another from a distance counts as an interaction between them. Consequently, there was also no relationship between them, in Kolodny's sense of 'relationship.' Nor did Dante suppose that there was. In his account of his love of Beatrice, in his *La vita nuova*, the way Dante himself describes his connection to Beatrice is just that he loves her, from a distance, with a love unrequited by her, for all he or anyone else knows.

There are various complaints that might be leveled against Dante's love of Beatrice as he describes it. The reformation Protestants thought that love such as Dante's is inimical to marriage, for example, and Dante himself supposed such love could be morally risky.[28] But, on Kolodny's account, we have to say not that there is something defective or deplorable about Dante's love for Beatrice, but just that he did not love her. Dante did not suppose that he had a relationship (in Kolodny's sense of 'relationship') with Beatrice, and so he also did not believe that there was such a relationship between him and Beatrice that rendered his love of her appropriate.

Kolodny seems willing to bite this bullet. He says: "Special concern for a person is not love at all when there is no belief that a relationship renders it appropriate."[29]

On Kolodny's account, then, we have to say that Dante did not love Beatrice. This, of course, is a highly counter-intuitive claim.[30] But then so is Kolodny's implication that self-consciously unrequited love is only concern. Unrequited love is famous for its painfulness, but there need not be anything painful about unilateral concern for another person. A Westerner who supports a particular third-world child through the medium of an international charitable organization might feel special unilateral concern for that child without experiencing pain in consequence.

Someone might suppose that Kolodny's account could be rescued from such implications if he just broadened his conception of relationship so that it could accommodate the example of Dante and Beatrice. But this is not the case. Consider, for example, Dante and his wife, Gemma Donati. Dante most certainly had and believed he had a relationship (even in Kolodny's sense of 'relationship') with Gemma. On the available evidence, it also seems true that Dante valued Gemma and his relationship to Gemma. She was the daughter of a politically powerful man in Dante's home city of Florence; she was the sister of one of his close friends; and she was Dante's wife and the mother of his children.[31] In all these ways, she and her relationship to Dante were important to him. But for almost twenty years of his life, although Dante remained married to her, he seems to have had no desire for *her*; he lived in a different city from her and made no effort to bring her to live with him.[32] In that period, Dante's attitude toward his wife meets Kolodny's conditions for love; but the claim that Dante then loved Gemma Donati is even more counter-intuitive than the denial that he loved Beatrice.[33]

Finally, consider again the beloved's question "why do you love me?" Unlike the volitional account, Kolodny's relational account can give an answer to this question; but, unlike the responsiveness account, the relational account's answer does not consist in pointing to valued intrinsic features of the beloved. For the relational account, the answer is "Well, it's because I value you and my relationship to you." Although this is less infelicitous than the answers of the competing theories, it is not satisfactory; and its unsatisfactory character can be seen by extending the imaginary conversation between the beloved and the lover just a little further. To the obvious next question on the part of the beloved: "but why do you value me and your relationship to me?," the relational account can give no answer, or at any rate, no answer having to do with the beloved herself.

Against the backdrop of these attempts to give a satisfactory account of the nature of love, I want to consider the theory of love given by Aquinas. I do not have space here for a detailed scholarly exposition of Aquinas's position or for a defense of my interpretation of it, which is not controversial in any case. Instead, I will simply sketch briefly the main line of Aquinas's account and then consider its implications, not only for the contemporary debate but also for the related issue of the nature of forgiveness, which is relevant to my purposes in this book, too.

Aquinas's basic conception of love

Aquinas uses four words for love; in Latin, they are *amor*, *dilectio*, *amicitia*, and *caritas*.[34] The first of these is love in its most generic sense, which is included in all the other kinds; for Aquinas, even a rock falling from a higher to a lower place can be said to have love for the place to which it falls, in this generic sense of 'love'.[35] The second, *dilectio*, emphasizes the element of voluntariness in the love of rational persons; and the third, *amicitia*, picks out the dispositions of love in friendship. But, for Aquinas, the fourth, *caritas*, is the word for love in its real or complete sense. Since Aquinas privileges *caritas* in this way, I will focus on *caritas* in explaining his account of love, although I will understand his views of *caritas* in light of what he says about the more generic *amor*.[36]

For Aquinas, the ultimate proper object of love is God;[37] but since, on the doctrine of simplicity, God is, in some very complicated way, the same as his goodness,[38] it is also true that the ultimate proper object of love is goodness.[39] On Aquinas's views, every human being is made in the image of God and is the child of God, so that the goodness of God is reflected in every human person. Consequently, the proper object of love also includes human beings. On Aquinas's views, then, love is primarily the love of persons;[40] and the *genus* of the love of persons, which encompasses all the various kinds of love between persons, is friendship. The love of other, non-personal things is somehow tied to the love of persons.[41] A person who loves wine, for example, is someone who desires wine as a good for himself; for such a person, his love of wine is part of his love of himself.[42]

The *end* of the love of persons—that is, the ultimate thing toward which love is directed—is union with God shared in the union with other human beings. Aquinas does not mean that anyone who loves is aiming at union with God. He means only that, if real love has its way and is not somehow driven off course, it will eventuate in shared union with God. On his view, the ultimate home of real love is in such shared union. But this view is compatible with supposing that a person who has real love for another has never entertained the idea of such an end for his love and would reject it if he did entertain it.

Some contemporary proponents of the volitional account argue that love consists primarily just in a desire for what is good for the beloved or in the interest of the beloved.[43] But this is not a position Aquinas would endorse.[44] On Aquinas's account of the nature of love, love requires two interconnected desires:[45]

(1) the desire for the good of the beloved,[46]

and

(2) the desire for union with the beloved.[47]

In the next chapter, I will examine the nature of union and the conditions necessary for bringing it about; and in Chapter 13, I will consider the standard of value by which Aquinas measures the good for human beings. In this chapter, my focus will be just on the nature of these two desires themselves and the nature of the love that emerges from their interaction. To ward off gratuitous confusion, however, it is worth pointing out here that, whatever exactly the union is which is desired in love on Aquinas's account, the desire for it is not equivalent to the desire to be in the company of the beloved.[48]

Other philosophers have remarked that one can love a person without desiring to be in that person's company,[49] and being in someone's company is obviously not equivalent to being united to her. It is manifestly possible to be in the company of someone when one is alienated from her, rather than united to her. So desiring union with a person might not include a desire to be in that person's company, at least not now, as that person currently is.

It should also be added here that, for Aquinas, the presence of a desire does not imply the absence of the thing desired. The fulfillment of a desire is compatible with the continuance of the desire. When both the desires of love are fulfilled, the lover finds joy in the beloved, but he does not cease desiring what he now has—namely, the good of the beloved and union with her.[50]

The strength of the desires of love can vary, and so love comes in different degrees of intensity; but, in the interest of brevity, I will leave to one side all the complications raised by consideration of the varying strength of the desires of love.[51] And this is only the beginning of the list of things I am omitting here. On Aquinas's philosophical psychology, there is no desire in the will without a preceding act of intellect, so that cognitive states also are part of love. There is a role for the passions as well, because the passions act on the intellect to influence its determinations of reasons for actions and desires.[52] But in the space of this one chapter I will not be able to discuss the role of beliefs and passions in love on Aquinas's views.[53] I will also not be able to explore what Aquinas has to say about the pleasures associated with love—or many other things also connected to his theory of love.[54] Space precludes a treatment of Aquinas's account that explains it in the whole context of his philosophical psychology and theology. But, for my purposes in this book, a brief presentation of the central elements of his account is sufficient.[55]

Preliminary points about desire and Aquinas's account of love

There are also myriad questions of contemporary philosophical psychology that are relevant to this discussion but that have to be left aside, too. It will be helpful, however, to call attention to one feature of the nature of desire. For my purposes, it is important to recognize that desires are not transparent.

Consider, for example, the desire for a hike in the Rockies on a summer day. A person may think that she has such a desire. It may be, that is, that she subjectively seems to discern in herself a desire and that she subjectively takes the object of that desire to be a hike in the Rockies on a summer day. Clearly, it is possible for her to be mistaken about both apparent apprehensions. For example, contrary to what she believes about herself, it may be that what a hike in the Rockies on a summer day really is is something that she herself does not want. That is, she may genuinely have a desire for something that she supposes is a hike in the Rockies; but she may be mistaken about what a hike in the Rockies is, so that, if she gets a hike in the Rockies on a summer day, she will be disappointed or even desire not to have what she is getting. Alternatively, she may understand the true nature of a hike in the Rockies on a summer day but be deceiving herself when she believes that a hike in the Rockies on a summer day really is an object of her desire. In either of these ways, it is possible for a desirer to be alienated from, rather than attracted to, what she herself believes is her desire or the object of her desire.

It is possible for a person to be mistaken about the object of her desire in other ways as well. For example, a person might indeed be attracted to, rather than alienated from, what she correctly believes to be the object of her desire; but she might nonetheless not recognize that object under one or another accurate description of it. For example, a person might really desire to hear a certain piece of music again, and that piece of music might in fact be Mozart's *Ave Verum*. But the desirer might be confused about the identity of the piece; she might think, for example, that it is a Mendelssohn motet. So, if she were asked whether she desired to hear Mozart's *Ave Verum* again, she would sincerely say 'no;' and if she were asked whether what she desired was to hear a Mendelssohn motet, she would sincerely say 'yes.' But, if she were presented with the Mendelssohn motet, she would be disappointed, because *that* was not what she wanted to hear again; and if she were presented with the Mozart *Ave Verum*, she would be glad, because *that* is what she wanted to hear.

So a person can be mistaken in more than one way in her beliefs about her own desires, and a person's desires need not be transparent to that person. I will presuppose these features of desire in the discussion of Aquinas's two desires of love.

It is also helpful to note that there is an implicit condition on each of the desires of love in Aquinas's account. It is not the 'for its own sake,' which we might have expected, although Aquinas certainly supposes that the beloved cannot have a solely instrumental value for the lover. Instead, the relevant implicit condition is 'for the sake of goodness.'[56] That is, if we ask the lover, "why do you want the good of the beloved?," or "why do you want union with the beloved?," on Aquinas's view the answer should not be "I just do; it's a final end for me." Rather, the answer should be, "because it's good"[57]—because it is good that the beloved should have what is good for him; because it is good that the lover should be united with the beloved.[58]

Goodness here is not to be identified with moral goodness only. It is goodness in the broader sense that encompasses beauty, elegance or efficiency, and metaphysical as well as moral goodness.[59] The good of the beloved is to be understood in this broader sense, too. Furthermore, because Aquinas holds that there is an objective standard of goodness, the measure of value for the goodness at issue in love is also objective.[60] Given Aquinas's ethical views, then, the good of the beloved has to be understood as that which truly is in the interest of the beloved and which truly does conduce to the beloved's flourishing. What exactly this is depends, of course, on the standard of value adopted. For Aquinas, as I will explain at length in Chapter 13, the ultimate good for any human person is union with God. But because of the strong connection Aquinas sees between God and goodness, anything that contributes to the objective good for a person also brings her closer to God. The beloved's closeness to God and her flourishing as the best person she can be will, therefore, be co-variant, for Aquinas. So to desire the good of the beloved, on the standard of goodness Aquinas accepts, is to desire for the beloved those things that in fact contribute to the beloved's flourishing, and these will also increase the beloved's closeness to God.[61]

On the other hand, although the lover must desire *as good for the beloved* what he wants for the beloved, nothing in Aquinas's account requires that the lover understand that good as something conducing to the beloved's flourishing or to the beloved's union with God. What the lover desires for the beloved must in fact do so; but the lover need not understand that it does so in order for the lover to desire these things as good for the beloved, since, as I explained above, a person may fail to recognize the object of his desire under one or another description of it. Nonetheless, because the standard for value is objective, the things that the lover desires as the good of the beloved have to be things that actually do, directly or indirectly, contribute to the beloved's flourishing and nearness to God. If what a person desires as good for another is not in fact the beloved's good by this objective measure, then, to one degree or another, the lover does not love him, whatever she may believe about herself. A parent who desires to beat her child because she supposes that beating is a good for the child is wrong in that supposition; and her desire to beat her child does not therefore count as a desire of love, whatever the parent may believe of herself.[62]

It is easy to become confused here, because there is an ambiguity in the notion of desiring something as someone's good.[63]

Consider, for example, a mother who gives her sick child a drug that has been prescribed by her pediatrician but that, contrary to the hope of the mother and the belief of the pediatrician, somehow damages the child rather than healing him. The drug is thus not a good for the child, but the mother does desire to give that drug to the child. Are we then to say that the mother is unloving? This would clearly be a counter-intuitive claim.

What, then, are we to say about the mother's desire as regards her child? Her desire is certainly not to damage the child. On the contrary, what she wants for her child is health, and she believes that the drug prescribed by the pediatrician is a means to her child's health. So she desires to give the drug to the child as a good for the child, but she desires the drug as a good only because she takes it to be a means to the good of health. The good of health for her child is the end of her desire for the drug; she would be just as glad to give the child any other drug, if that other drug were prescribed by the pediatrician as conducive to the child's health. In this case, then, the mother desires the drug not in its own right but only as a means to that thing which is in fact what she wants as the good for her child—namely, health. She has, therefore, only a derived and not an intrinsic desire for the drug.[64]

Contrast this case with the case of a sadistic schoolmaster who inflicts a humiliating punishment on a misbehaving student as a means of correcting him. It may be that the schoolmaster desires the punishment as a means to the correction of the student, but he also desires the punishment insofar as it gives him the pleasure of inflicting humiliation and pain. Unlike the mother who gives her child a harmful drug in the mistaken belief that the drug is a means to the child's health, the schoolmaster would not find any other means[65] to the same end of correction equally good. He desires that particular means in its own right. The mother's desire to give her child the drug would evaporate if she stopped believing in the connection between the drug and her child's health. The schoolmaster's desire to hurt and humiliate the student would not similarly disappear if he lost his belief in the connection between humiliation and correction for students. The schoolmaster has an intrinsic desire for the student's humiliation.

Given this difference between intrinsic and derived desires, we can say that, on Aquinas's account of love, the mother who gives her child the harmful drug under the misimpression that the drug will heal the child is nonetheless loving, as the schoolmaster who humiliates the student is not, in virtue of the fact that what is actually not good for the child is not something for which the mother has an intrinsic desire. For these reasons, it is possible, on Aquinas's account, for a lover to have the two desires of love with respect to a certain person and yet to do harm to that person, provided that what does harm to the beloved is not something for which the lover has an intrinsic desire.

In what follows, I will understand the desire for the good of the beloved in the ways qualified by these remarks.

It is worth noting that, on this understanding of the desire for the good of the beloved, it is possible for one person Jerome to think that he loves another person Paula when he does not, in virtue of the fact that he has an intrinsic desire for what is actually harmful for Paula. On Aquinas's views, then, a person can be mistaken in his beliefs about whom he loves.[66] One's love for another person, or its absence, is yet another thing that is not transparent.

The inter-connection of the two desires of love

It is important to see that, for Aquinas, the two desires of love are not independent of each other but rather interrelated. And when the two desires of love appear to conflict, Aquinas's claim that the ultimate good for human beings is union with God gives a method for harmonizing them. Union with God is shareable, and persons united with God are also united with each other. *Ultimately*, then, the same thing—namely, union with God—constitutes both the final good[67] for each of the persons in a loving relationship and also their deepest union with each other.[68] But God's nature is equivalent to goodness; and so it is also true, on Aquinas's views, that persons can be ultimately and deeply united with each other only if they are united in goodness.[69] Consequently, on Aquinas's account, shared union with God is the ultimate good for any human person. To this extent,[70] what is sought in the desire for the good of a person and what is sought in the desire for union with that person must *ultimately* converge.[71]

Consequently, if the desire for union is to be a desire of love, what is sought in this desire has to be compatible with the true good of the beloved. If a mother tries to prevent her son from ever leaving home, when leaving home is necessary for his flourishing, then she is not in fact desiring the good for her son. Her desire for what she takes to be union with him will, therefore, also not be a desire of love. Furthermore, because, ultimately, persons are united with each other only around the good, what the mother is desiring when she wants what is not good for her son is not in fact union with him, however much she supposes that it is. In this respect, too, her desire fails to be a desire of love.

To count as a desire of love, the mother's desire to be united with her son therefore has to allow for his being at some physical distance from her if that is, in fact, what is good for him. On Aquinas's account, a mother who wanted to keep her son with her when he was able and eager to join a resistance group working to overthrow the evil oppressors of his country (supposing that this is necessary for his flourishing) would not be loving him in trying to keep him with her.[72] And because by staying with her he would be abetting her failure to love him, a failure not conducive to her good as his mother, he would not be loving her if he gave in to her unloving desire.

On the other hand, if the desire for the good of the beloved is to be a desire of love, the good desired for the beloved has to include union with the lover, as also a good.[73] A lover's desire for the good of the beloved which failed to take note of the beloved's union with the lover as a good would not be a desire of love either. In order to count as loving, then, the son who left his mother to join the resistance would need not only to provide for her as best he could in his absence because he desired her good; he would also need to do what he could to further union between them at a distance, if by no other means than by longing for a time when peace was restored so that he could return to her.

The two desires of love are therefore interrelated in mutually governing ways.[74]

The character of the two desires of love

Although the two desires of love are interconnected, they are nonetheless very different in character.

To begin with, the desire for the good of the beloved does not depend on anything about the beloved. One can desire another person's good independently of any particular intrinsic features of that person and independently of any particular relational features as well.[75] A desire for the good of a person requires only a certain state of will in the desirer; it does not depend on anything in the person for whom the good is desired.[76]

For this reason, the desire for the good of the beloved need not be affected by variations in the beloved's intrinsic characteristics; the constancy of the desire requires only the willingness of the desirer to persist in that desire. Changes in the *desirer* might affect the constancy of the desire, but changes in the person for whom the good is desired need not do so.

By contrast, the desire for union with the beloved is very much dependent on the characteristics of the beloved, both the intrinsic and the relational characteristics. Aquinas thinks that it is possible to desire the good for humanity in general and also to desire some sort of union with all humanity—say, in the shared beatific vision of heaven.[77] And so, on Aquinas's account of love, a person can have an impartial love of all human beings. But Aquinas also supposes that some loves are and ought to be greater than others.[78] A person ought to love all human beings, but not equally. She should love some people more than others in virtue of having certain relationships with them, which ought to make her love for them greater than her love for humanity in general. On Aquinas's views, some relationships make possible a deeper and more intimate union between the people so related.

And so the desire for union with a beloved person *is* responsive to the beloved, as the desire for the good of the beloved is not.

Love as responsive to the intrinsic and relational characteristics of the beloved

The relational characteristics of the beloved determine the kind of union that is appropriate for the lover to seek. The same person may be a husband, a son, a colleague, a teacher, and a penitent, and all the people to whom he is related in these ways may love him. But the love they have for him should not and typically will not be of the same kind. That is because the kind of union with him appropriate for the people who are his wife, mother, colleague, student, and priest will be different, depending on the relationship in question.[79]

What determines the nature of a relationship is hard to capture succinctly, because many things are involved. In some cases, a relationship exists for reasons independent of the wills of the people in the relationship, and the obliteration of the relationship is not in the power of the people so related. The relationship of a parent to a child is of this sort. One can turn one's back on a hated father, for example, but one cannot bring it about that the hated person is not one's father. In other cases, the relationship is established just because the persons in the relationship want it, and the relationship will cease if one or the other of them repudiates it. Friendship is a clear case of this sort. And there are mixed cases. One can end one's marriage by divorcing one's wife, but one cannot thereby bring it about that she is not the mother of one's children. Temporal duration of the connection can be a factor in a relationship, and so can personal commitment to the relationship. People tend to cringe if a complete stranger who happens to have the adjacent seat on a plane wants to share intimate details of his life story. But circumstances are also a factor and can complicate the case. As we know, complete strangers can become familiar quickly in circumstances that appear to warrant it. If the plane were going down, for example, confidences otherwise inappropriate might be gratefully given and received. Because the subject is complicated in these and other ways, in what follows I will simply rely on our intuitive understanding of the nature of particular relationships.

A relationship of love is a particular kind of relationship between persons that shapes the sort of sharing and closeness suitable in that relationship and thus circumscribes the kind of union appropriate to desire in love.[80] A relationship is a relationship of mutual love only if each of the persons in the relationship has the two desires of love for the other.[81] For ease of exposition, I will refer to the differing kinds of relationships of love as 'the offices of love.'[82] However exactly we are to understand the different kinds of loving relationships, the nature of an office circumscribes the sort of union that is appropriate to the love of that office, and so it also delimits the sort of love appropriate within that office.

The locutions I have just used in describing the offices of love—circumscribing, delimiting—may make it seem as if offices keep love from having its full force. But this is a mistaken way of thinking about the matter. Although some offices are indisputably more important than others in a person's life, it is arguable that at least the loves of the most important offices are incommensurable. It is because of such incommensurability that it is possible for a person Paula to love her daughter neither more nor less than her mother or her husband. It is not that she loves each of these people equally either, however. What is more nearly right to say is that, because the loves of these offices are incommensurable, each of these beloved people can hold an unrivaled position in love within the office that each has in Paula's life. So the offices of love do not suppress love; they provide for it.

Offices are correlative, but they need not be symmetric. The office of mother is correlative with the office of daughter, but these are plainly not symmetrical offices. A mother holds the office of mother but not the office of daughter with regard to her daughter; and a daughter holds the office of daughter but not the office of mother with regard to her mother. Offices need not be reflexive either. A mother does not hold the office of mother to herself. And, finally, offices need not be transitive. If Paula holds the office of friend with regard to Jerome, and Jerome holds the office of friend with regard to Julia, it does not follow that Paula holds the office of friend with regard to Julia.

It is, of course, possible for two people to be connected through more than one office of love. A mother who is a professor might serve as a teacher for her own child, for example. On the other hand, some offices render others inappropriate; the widespread taboo against incest is the most obvious example. It is also possible for the relationship between two people to change, so that the office between them changes as well. A person might divorce her husband but remain friends with him, for example. Finally, it is possible to desire the good for a person and union with that person when one has no office, no current established relationship of any sort, with that person. And so it is possible for a lover to love someone who shares no office of love with him. But it is clear that union and the love of union will be possible only within an office of love of one or another sort. Consequently, although it is possible for a person to love someone with whom he has as yet no relationship, it is not possible for a person to be united to someone without having a relationship to her.[83] What is being desired in the desire for union thus in effect includes an office of love of some sort.

The two desires of love are also interconnected within the offices of love. If the lover desires to unite herself with the beloved in a way inappropriate to the office of love that currently holds between them, she violates the office;[84] and the violation of the office will be something that is not good for the beloved, insofar as it undermines or breaks the relationship of love currently obtaining between the beloved and the lover. To desire a kind of union with a person that is inappropriate for the current office with him is thus to fail to desire his good and therefore also to fail to love him.[85] So, for example, a priest who has sexual relations with a child entrusted to his care is not loving that child, however caring the priest may suppose himself to be, because, in pursuing a kind of union with the child that is outside the bounds of the office that he holds as priest in the life of that child, what the priest desires is in fact not the good of the child.

For these reasons having to do with the offices of love, on Aquinas's account, the second desire of love, for union with the beloved, has to be responsive to characteristics of the beloved, as the first desire does not, because the offices of love are dependent on *relational* characteristics of the beloved.

In addition, however, the *intrinsic* characteristics of the beloved also affect the second desire of love, not by determining an office for love but rather by affecting the character and extent of the union appropriate within an office.[86] I am postponing a detailed examination of the nature of union to the next chapter; but, whatever exactly union consists in, it is clear that, in order to unite with the beloved, the lover must share something of himself with her. What he can share and the degree to which he can share it, however, will be dependent on her as well as on him. A man who is a composer may want to share his labor and joy in composition with his much-loved sister; but if she is tone-deaf and musically illiterate, what he is able to share with her will be different from what he could share with her if she herself were a musician. The union appropriate for him to desire with her will thus be shaped by intrinsic characteristics of hers and by his perception of those characteristics. To this extent, his love of her will be responsive to her, or to what he sees of her.

It is important to recognize that, although the intrinsic characteristics of the beloved will affect the character and extent of the union possible within an office, they do not determine the *type* of the union appropriate; that is a function of the office itself. It is appropriate for a musician to share himself in his music in one type of union with his partner and in another type of union with his mother. On the other hand, if his mother is musical and his partner is not, then the musician will in fact share more of himself in his music in his office with his mother than in his office with his partner.

We can sum up this comparison of the two desires of love by noting that, although the first desire of love, for the good of the beloved, is not responsive to anything in the beloved, the second desire definitely is. The union possible and appropriate for the lover with the beloved is dependent on both the beloved's intrinsic and relational characteristics.

Finally, it is important to see that a person can be mistaken about both the intrinsic and the relational characteristics of the person beloved to him. We are all familiar with the case of the stalker who mistakenly believes that his victim is his girlfriend. The case of Oedipus and Jocasta shows that it is possible to be mistaken even about the most basic of human relationships. It is even more apparent that it is possible for a person to be mistaken about the intrinsic characteristics of his beloved. Such mistakes make a difference to the lover's ability to love his beloved. If a musician, for example, takes his sister to be musically imperceptive, when in fact she is sensitive to music but untrained, then his mistake will keep him from sharing music with her. To this extent, his mistake will also keep him from sharing himself with her and thus from loving her as he could. On Aquinas's account, therefore, there is truth in the saying that one cannot love what one cannot see.

The special cases

We can conclude this part of the presentation of Aquinas's account of love by considering the way in which it applies to the special cases of a human person's love of herself, a human person's love of God, and God's love of human persons.

Given Aquinas's account of the nature of love, to love oneself is to desire the good for oneself and to desire union with oneself.[87] But someone might object that the notion of desiring union with oneself makes no sense. Union, the putative objector might suppose, is the coming-together into some kind of unity of things distinct from one another; but no one is distinct from herself.

This objection, however, fails to take account of the fact that a person can be divided against herself. She can lack internal integration in her mind, and the result will be that she is, as we say, double-minded. She can also lack whole-heartedness or integration in the will. Aquinas describes a person who lacks internal integration in the will as someone who wills and does not will the same thing, in virtue of willing incompatible things, or in virtue of failing to will what she wills to will.[88] There is no union with herself for such a person. Furthermore, without internal integration, some goods important for a person's flourishing are ruled out.[89] Aquinas, for example, thinks that there is no peace for a person who is internally divided in herself, since, if she is divided against herself, she will have some unfulfilled desire no matter which part of her conflicting volitional states she acts on.[90] The good for a person thus requires internal integration.

So the desire for union, Aquinas's second desire of love, does have a role to play in self-love, if we understand it as a desire for internal integration. In fact, because of the importance of internal integration to human flourishing, in the love of oneself what is desired in the desire for union will converge with what is desired in the desire for one's own good.

In the case of a human person's love of God, the apparent difficulty arises not from the desire for union, which is understandable enough, but from the desire for the good of the beloved. It might seem to someone that desiring the good for God makes no sense, since there is no good that God lacks. But this objection is confused. Since God desires the good for all things, insofar as a human person desires the good for herself or for any other persons, on Aquinas's views she is in effect desiring what God desires. In that way, she desires the good that God desires to have; to that extent, she also desires the good for God.[91] And so it is possible to desire the good for God, in virtue of desiring what God desires as good.[92]

In the history of thought about love, some philosophers and theologians have supposed that the two kinds of love just canvassed, love of self and love of God, are in tension with one another or even incompatible with one another. In their view, a love of self is to one degree or another at odds with a perfect love of God. For such thinkers, the ultimate test of a person's love of God is whether or not she would be willing to desire her own everlasting misery if such misery were God's will.[93] On their view, a person who had perfect love of God would be willing to give up the desire for her own good if the loss of her good were God's will. For my purposes, it is important to see that this view of what the love of God requires is not one that Aquinas can endorse. On his view of love, love of oneself cannot be in competition with a love of any other person, even God.

To see that this is so, consider what happens, on Aquinas's account, if a person who wants to be in a loving relationship with anyone else does not love himself because he lacks for himself one or the other of the desires of love.

On Aquinas's views, for every person, internal integration is necessary for the real good for that person,[94] and the ultimate real good is union with God. So, if Jerome does not love himself because he lacks either of the desires of love for himself, then in one way or another he is not desiring what in fact is or contributes to the ultimate good for himself—namely, union with God. Now, if Jerome lacks the desire for what is or contributes to this ultimate good for himself, then either he will nonetheless desire this ultimate good for another person Paula, or he will not. If he does not, then he lacks one of the desires of love for Paula—namely, the desire for the good of the beloved. If he does, then he lacks the other desire of love, for union with the beloved. That is because, on Aquinas's views, ultimately, to be united with Paula requires being united with her in the union with God. If Jerome fails to desire the good for himself, however, or if he fails to desire the internal integration necessary for it, then he fails to desire for himself union with God. And for this reason, he also fails to desire what is or is necessary for ultimate real union with Paula. In such a case, although Jerome might believe of himself that he desires union with Paula, what he is desiring with respect to Paula is not in fact union with her, in virtue of the fact that Jerome does not desire for himself what is or what leads to union with God.

For these reasons, on Aquinas's account, a person who does not love himself cannot love another human person either. *Mutatis mutandis*, the same reasoning holds even if the other person in question is God. In failing to have the desires of love where another human person is concerned, even if that human person is himself, Jerome fails to desire what God desires, since God loves every human person. Jerome therefore lacks one of the desires of love for God, in virtue of not desiring the good for God—that is, the good that God desires to have. And in not desiring what is the true good for himself, Jerome lacks the other desire of love for God, insofar as he lacks the desire for what is or what contributes to his union with God.

So, on Aquinas's account, love of oneself is in fact necessary for any love of another, even God. A perfect love of God, therefore, cannot compete with love of oneself. A perfect love of God *requires* love of oneself.[95]

It is an implication of this conclusion that, just as it is possible for a person to desire as good what is in fact not good for the beloved, it is also possible to desire as uniting with the beloved what in fact does not unite the lover with the beloved. Consequently, it is possible for a person to be mistaken in more than one way about whether he loves another. Jerome can be mistaken in thinking that he loves Paula because he fails to understand and desire as good for her what is in fact the good for her or because he fails to understand and desire what will in fact unite him to her.

Finally, Aquinas's account applies also to God's love for human persons. God loves every human being, and so he desires the good of each human person and union with her, which is also her ultimate good and her ultimate flourishing.[96]

Problems and solutions

For Aquinas, then, love is, as it were, a systems-level feature, emerging from two interconnected, mutually governing desires, for the good of the beloved and for union with the beloved. Because love is complex in this way for Aquinas, his account can handle the problems troublesome for contemporary theories.

Consider, for example, the criticisms leveled against the responsiveness account of love. The responsiveness account has difficulty explaining the love of a parent for her children, because that love does not seem generated by the parent's perception of her children as particularly valuable or as more valuable than the children of others. Furthermore, a parent's love does not seem to co-vary with the parent's perception of valuable characteristics of the children. The parent's love does not typically decrease, for example, if she notes with sadness that her children are becoming deplorable. The constancy of love and the non-substitutability of the beloved are also problems for the responsiveness account.

Aquinas's account can explain what the responsiveness account cannot. The office of love between a parent and her children determines the kind of love between them, and the office is a function of the relational characteristics of the lover and the beloved. But the office is not a function of the intrinsic characteristics of the beloved, and so it does not co-vary with the beloved's intrinsic characteristics either. That is why the love of the office can remain through variations in those intrinsic characteristics of the beloved that are valued by the lover. And so Aquinas's account can explain not only these features of parental love but also the constancy expected of love. Furthermore, on Aquinas's account, love will not be readily transferable to any others whose valuable intrinsic characteristics are the same as those of the beloved, since the mere possession of the beloved's valuable characteristics on the part of some person other than the beloved is not enough for establishing that other person in an office of love with the lover.

Aquinas's account can handle equally readily the problems that are a stumbling block for the volitional account. Because, for Aquinas, the nature and degree of what can be shared in an office of love *is* a function of intrinsic features of the beloved, the lover must be responsive to things in the beloved herself. So, when the beloved asks, "Why do you love me?," on Aquinas's account, the lover does not have to answer by saying, "Well, there is no reason, or, at least, no reason having to do with *you*." Rather, on Aquinas's account, the lover can answer not only by calling attention to his relationship with the beloved, but also by praising the beloved herself.

For this same reason, since the lover's love is responsive in this way, the lover's love can vary with changes in the beloved. Although the office need not alter when it alteration finds, nonetheless, within the office, there may be alterations in the lover's love that respond to alterations in the beloved. So, what the lover praises in the beloved, or what the lover shares with the beloved, will change with changes in the beloved, as it in fact has to do if what the lover loves is *her*. In this way, Aquinas's account can validate the much-touted Shakespearean line without ruling out change, and growth, in a relationship of love. The office of love can remain the same through great changes in the intrinsic characteristics of the beloved, but the nature of the sharing in that office can and should vary with those changes.

Similarly, although Aquinas's account of love can explain the fact that parental love is not generated as a response to the perceived value of the children, it can also explain the compatibility of that fact with the observation that parents often dote on their children as specially wonderful. The office of love between parents and children is particularly important in human lives and makes possible a particularly powerful type of union in love, independent of the intrinsic characteristics parents suppose their children to have. And yet this fact is compatible with a parent's being responsive to her child's intrinsic characteristics, on Aquinas's account, because the character and extent of the uniting appropriate in an office are a function of the intrinsic characteristics of the beloved to which the lover responds.

Finally, since Aquinas's account gives an important place to the relational characteristics of the beloved, it can handle Kolodny's test case of the amnesic biographer who loses his love for his wife when he becomes amnesic about his relationship to her. But it can also accommodate the kind of case that is troublesome for the relational account, exemplified by Dante and Beatrice and Gemma Donati.[97] Because it is possible for a person to desire good for and union with a person with whom he does not have a relationship in Kolodny's sense of 'relationship,' on Aquinas's account (but not on Kolodny's) it is true to say that Dante loved Beatrice, even if his love was unrequited throughout Beatrice's life and Dante knew that it was. Furthermore, Aquinas's account explains the notorious painfulness of unrequited love. Because love includes a desire for union with the beloved, there is pain for the lover when it looks as if that desire is not and will not be fulfilled. Finally, it is possible to value a person and a relationship with her without desiring union with her. On Aquinas's account of love, love requires more than the valuing of a person and a relationship. If Dante had no desire for union with Gemma, then, no matter how much he valued her and his relationship to her, on Aquinas's account (but not on Kolodny's) it is not true to say that Dante loved Gemma.

Love and forgiveness

Finally, Aquinas's account of love has implications for the concept of forgiveness that are worth seeing. It is not part of my project here to try to define forgiveness;[98] but, whatever exactly is required for forgiveness, it must involve some species of love for the person in need of forgiveness. A person who refuses to forgive someone who has been unjust to her is not loving toward the offender, and a person who does forgive someone who has injured her also manifests love of one degree or another toward him. So, whatever else forgiveness is, it seems to include a kind of love of someone who has done one an injury or committed an injustice against one.

Since love emerges from the interaction of two desires, for the good of the beloved and for union with her, the absence of either desire is sufficient to undermine love.[99] To the extent to which love is implicated in forgiveness, the absence of either desire undermines forgiveness, too.

So, for example, a resentful desire for revenge is incompatible with love of the person against whom the desire for vengeance is directed. A resentful or vengeful person does not love his enemy in virtue of the fact that he desires the bad, rather than the good, for his opponent. For that same reason, such a person does not forgive his enemy either.

On Aquinas's account of love, however, this is not the only way to fail to forgive. To forgive a person who has perpetrated an injustice against one, it is not enough to have just one of the desires of love, the desire for the good of the perpetrator. It is also necessary to have a desire for union with him—if nothing else, then at least the generic desire for union that is an element of the general love for humanity. A person who desires the good of someone who has injured her but who refuses to have any contact with him whatsoever fails to love him, in virtue of having the opposite of a desire for union with him. For that reason, she also fails to forgive him.

So failure to forgive can find expression not only in resentment or vengefulness but also in a desire for withdrawal from the wrongdoer. On Aquinas's account of love, one person Paula forgives another person Jerome who has injured her only if she desires the good for Jerome and union with Jerome even in the face of his injustice against her.

This way of thinking about forgiveness illuminates the notion of forgiving oneself, too. Consider a person who believes she has committed some wrong and who fails to forgive herself for it. On the view of forgiveness at issue here, her failure to forgive herself will find expression in self-loathing or self-laceration, or both. That is, she will be alienated from herself, or she will want what in other circumstances she would reject as not good for herself, or both. In other words, she will resist one or the other or both of the desires of love for herself.

So to forgive a person, even if that person is oneself, requires maintaining toward that person both the desires of love.

On the other hand, what those two desires imply in any given case is a function of the condition of the person being forgiven.

To desire the good for Jerome is to forgo desiring the bad for Jerome, but what the good for Jerome actually is will depend on Jerome. The desire for Jerome's good need not include the willingness to waive punishment for him. Desiring Jerome's good requires forgoing punishment for him if that would be for his good—or insisting on punishment for him if *that* would be for his good. What is best for Jerome is whatever it takes to bring him to a more just condition in mind and will. Paula's calling the police or hiring a lawyer might be the best for Jerome in some circumstances. So for Paula to forgive Jerome, she must desire the objective good for Jerome—but *what* that good is will be determined by Jerome's character and the current state of his mind and will.

For this same reason, even if there was a previous relationship between Paula and Jerome, Paula's desire for union with Jerome need not include a desire to return to her former habits of companionship with Jerome. If Jerome is entirely unrepentant, or if his repentance is genuine but not trustworthy, because chances are excellent that he will soon abandon it, then Paula's desire for union with him need not and should not involve a willingness to return to her former companionship with him. At worst, by his actions, Jerome can destroy any significant office of love with Paula. In that worst case, Paula's desire for union with Jerome can appropriately come to no more than the sort of desire for union involved in the generic love of humanity provided for in Aquinas's account of love.

So, when Paula forms the two desires of love in forgiveness of Jerome, the nature of the appropriate fulfillment of those desires is a function of Jerome's state. Whether Paula can and should have any continued relationship with Jerome, and the character and extent of whatever company is warranted between them, depends on Jerome's state. On the other hand, if Jerome has not destroyed the relationship he had with Paula and if Jerome is genuinely and trustworthily repentant, then, if Paula persists in seeking what is bad for him or in withdrawing from him, she does not forgive him.[100]

The example of Paula and Jerome is a matter of injustice between people already in a relationship; but similar things can be said if the wrongdoer is a complete stranger to the person he injures.[101] In that case, there is no question of a return to former habits of companionship, of course, but there is still room for the sort of desire for union appropriate to the general love of humanity. Paula need not want any particular relationship with a stranger who has injured her, because none is warranted by their respective characters and conditions in life. But if, in virtue of the injury the stranger has done her, Paula is determined to ensure that there never is any human contact between the two of them, if she would be unhappy at any change in the stranger that *would* warrant a relationship between her and him, then she has not forgiven him.[102]

One way to test for forgiveness on Paula's part is thus to consider Paula's reaction to the possibility of complete, genuine moral reform on the part of the person who has injured her or been unjust to her. If the prospect of Jerome's reform is dismaying to Paula, if she is in effect hoping for the absence of such reform so that she can justifiably long for Jerome's punishment or stay at a distance from him, then she does not forgive him.

Furthermore, because to love and forgive Jerome is to desire the good for *Jerome* and union with *Jerome*, Paula must see Jerome as he is if she is to love and forgive him. But his actions against her and the cast of mind and will in him that are the source of those actions are part of him; and so Paula must see these things too if she is to see *him*. Misperception of the person loved undermines love; it does not enhance it. For this reason, forgiveness does not require forgetting what Jerome has done. Rather, it requires remembering it and nonetheless loving Jerome as he is.[103] If there is an obligation to remember great wrongs, as is sometimes claimed,[104] then, on Aquinas's views, forgiveness is compatible with that obligation.

Understanding forgiveness in terms of the two desires of love helps to resolve a familiar set of perplexities regarding forgiveness. Can forgiveness be granted unilaterally? Or does the granting of forgiveness require that the perpetrator repent his wrongdoing?[105] Can one forgive his enemy while he is still hostile? For that matter, can one forgive someone who is long since dead? Does forgiveness require reconciliation? Or is it possible to fail to be reconciled with someone and still forgive him?

These perplexities arise because we reflect on forgiveness from two different vantage points. Sometimes we consider forgiveness from the point of view of the person wronged, and in that case our intuitions are that a person can forgive unilaterally, in a way that does not require either repentance on the part of the wrongdoer or reconciliation with him. On the other hand, sometimes we consider forgiveness from the point of view of a wrongdoer who desires forgiveness because he is hoping for reconciliation. In that case, our intuitions are that, if the wronged person refuses reconciliation, she has not forgiven the wrongdoer. Aquinas's account of love helps explain the compatibility of these intuitions. A person who has been wronged can forgive the wrongdoer even if the wrongdoer is not repentant, because she can *desire* the good for him and union with him, no matter what his condition may be. But the fulfillment of those desires depends also on the will of the person being forgiven; his repentance and desire for reconciliation are also necessary if both the desires of love are to be fulfilled. So when we think about forgiveness from the point of view of the penitent wrongdoer, with the conditions requisite for full reconciliation presupposed, our intuitions are that forgiveness requires reconciliation.

On Aquinas's account of love, then, it is possible for Paula to forgive Jerome unilaterally, without repentance on Jerome's part, because it is up to Paula alone whether she desires the good for Jerome and union with him. For this reason, it is also possible for Paula to forgive an enemy of hers while he is still filled with hatred against her, and it is even possible for her to forgive the dead. But *the way* in which the desires of love are fulfilled, or whether they are fulfilled at all, will depend crucially on the condition of the wrongdoer being forgiven. Paula's *desire* for the good for Jerome cannot be fulfilled if, in self-destructive impulses, Jerome refuses the good offered him. And Paula's *desire* for union with Jerome cannot result in any kind of union with him as long as his state of character and current condition keep her from being close to him.

So a person can forgive unilaterally, as she can love unrequitedly. But the desires of love in forgiveness, like the desires of love generally, are inefficacious by themselves to bring about what they desire. A person who forgives, like a person who loves, has to be responsive to the person who is the object of her desires, and so she cannot have what she wants, in love or forgiveness, just by wanting it.

It is worth seeing that these conclusions apply also to God. God can forgive wrongdoers unilaterally, in the sense that he can desire the good for them and union with them. But these desires alone, even on the part of God, are unavailing to produce what is desired. For that, the wrongdoer has to have at least enough repentance to be willing to accept forgiveness. Even the love and forgiveness of God, then, have to be responsive to the beloved.

Chapter 6

Union, Presence, and Omnipresence

I venerate you with devotion, hidden truth,
who lie beneath these forms, truly hidden.
My whole heart gives itself to you
because it is wholly undone, contemplating you.

Sight, touch, taste are deceived in you;
hearing alone is safely believed.
I do believe whatever the Son of God has said;
nothing is more true than this Word of truth.

Only deity was hidden on the cross;
humanity lies hidden here as well.
And I, believing and confessing both,
seek from you what the thief sought, repenting.

As Thomas, I do not see your wounds,
and yet I confess you as my God.
Make me increase steadily in faith in you,
in hope in you, in love of you.

O memorial of the death of the Lord,
bread providing true life to us,
provide life for my mind, that I might always
know the sweet taste of you.

Pelican of pietas, Jesus Lord,
cleanse my unclean self in your blood;
one small drop of it could make
the whole world clean, purged from every evil.

Veiled Jesus, whom I now look upon,
when will what I so desire come to be?

When will I see your face, unveiled,
and in the vision of your glory blessed be?*

Introduction

In the previous chapter, I outlined the medieval view of the nature of love, as it is found in the thought of Aquinas; and I showed the way in which, on Aquinas's account, love for another person includes two desires: a desire for the good of the beloved and a desire for union with the beloved. In this chapter, I want to explore this account of love further by focusing on the notion of union. Aquinas himself makes considerable use of this notion, especially in his biblical commentaries; but he does not offer any extensive philosophical treatment of it. For my purposes in this book, however, it is helpful to have a more detailed understanding of the nature of union in love. In this chapter, therefore, I will develop a part of Aquinas's account of love that he himself relied on but left relatively unexamined.

For the sake of simplicity, I will focus on the sort of union of love appropriate within the office of friends; and I will understand this office narrowly, as distinct from the sort of friendship that can hold also between lovers or family members.[1] But at the end of the chapter I will say something briefly about the way in which the understanding of the union appropriate between friends, narrowly understood, can be expanded to all the offices of love.

It will be my contention that the sort of union of love appropriate to friendship among mentally fully functioning adult human beings[2] requires two things: personal presence and mutual closeness. In the end, I will also claim that, across all the offices of love, some variety of mutual closeness, which stems from and also makes possible occasions of personal presence, is necessary for the union desired in love. It may be that personal presence and mutual closeness are also sufficient for the union of love, but I will not claim that they are. For my purposes in this book, I need only to elaborate what is necessary to make possible the union of love on the medieval view I am explaining. I do not need to define union or find the necessary and sufficient conditions for it.

In addition, I will argue that presence and closeness of the sort needed for the union of love require internal integration of the psyche, and I will consider briefly one prominent account of such internal integration—namely, that given by Harry Frankfurt. By contrast with Frankfurt's position, the medieval account I am explicating, that of Aquinas, supposes that a self cannot be integrated around just anything; it has to be integrated around the good. I will conclude this chapter by adumbrating the implications of Aquinas's account for my project.

---

* Thomas Aquinas, "Adoro devote," in *The Oxford Book of Medieval Latin Verse*, ed. F. J. E. Raby (Oxford: Clarendon Press, 1959), 403–4. (The translation is my own.)

Closeness and presence

It is helpful to begin the consideration of the two relationships at issue here, closeness and presence, with an examination of presence.[3] What is it for one person to be present to or with another person? Can one person be present to or with another without being close to that person? Is being close to a person just one way of being present to or with that person? That is, is *being present* a genus within which *being close* is a species? Or is it the other way around? Is it the case that when there is a deep enough degree of mutual closeness between two people, it is then possible for each of them to be truly present to the other? Is *being close* a genus within which *being present* is a species?

The right answer to all these questions is 'yes,' in my view. The notion of one person's being present to or with another person is ambiguous. Sometimes *being present* is a genus within which *closeness* is a species, and sometimes it is a species which is within the genus of *closeness*. When *being present* is a genus such that *closeness* is one of its species, I will talk of the relation as 'minimal personal presence' or as 'minimal being present.' When *being present* is a species within the genus *closeness*, then for want of a better term I will call presence in this stronger sense 'significant personal presence' or 'significant being present.'

Minimal personal presence is at issue when we say things such as:

(i) "Some of those present were already asleep."
(ii) "Her family was present with her while she was comatose in the last hours of her life."
(iii) "The doctor himself was present and available to her only in the early morning."

Being present in these cases need not include much or any closeness among the persons involved. Instead, as presence is understood in these cases, it is just a generic connection between persons, which can vary from minimal to great, depending on what else is true of the connection.

Even within *minimal* personal presence, there are gradations; and we sometimes express these by differences in the prepositions indicating the relation. When the relation can be expressed without any preposition at all, as in (i) above, the kind of presence at issue is often only a matter of one person's being physically in a space picked out by reference to someone or something else. More is needed when the relation is expressed appropriately by adding the preposition 'with,' as in (ii). In that case, the person said to be present needs to be conscious, although the person he is present with does not need to be. These first two cases are the limiting cases for presence. The sort of personal presence at issue in those cases is *so* minimal that I will leave it largely to one side in the rest of the chapter. Finally, when the relation uses the preposition 'to' for its proper expression, as in (iii), all the persons standing in the relation need to be functioning as persons, as distinct from being comatose or otherwise unconscious, even if they are not conscious of each other. In what follows, I will take being present in this sense, as illustrated in case (iii), as the exemplar for minimal personal presence.

Significant personal presence, on the other hand, is a species within the genus *closeness*, and the preposition 'to' is usually required for formulations indicating this sort of presence. So, for example, we say such things as:

(iv) "She was distracted all through dinner and was never really present to me."

 (v) "He was more present to his children after he had lost his fortune than before."

(vi) "In mystical visions, Christ was present to Francis of Assisi."

Here we are thinking of presence in a different way from that in the preceding examples. In (iv), (v), and (vi), *being present* is a particularly significant or powerful way of being close to a person. On this sense of *being present*, being close to another person is necessary for being present to her (but not sufficient for it, as I will explain below).

So personal presence comes in two sorts, which have different connections to closeness. Minimal personal presence can occur without closeness between persons; but closeness is required for significant personal presence. When there is sufficient closeness between two or more persons,[4] that closeness enables them to be mutually present to each other in the stronger sense of *being present*.

This ambiguity in the notion of being present holds also when the presence of God is at issue. So Augustine, for example, talks in one place about God's being present to everyone everywhere always;[5] in another place, however, he describes the sadly ephemeral presence of God to him as he perceived it in a powerful religious experience.[6]

An insufficient account of presence

Recognizing that personal presence comes in these two kinds is helpful, but it still leaves open the nature of personal presence. What is required for one person to be present to another, in either the minimal or the significant sense?

In earlier work,[7] in an attempt to take account of the doctrine that God is omnipresent, present always to everyone everywhere, Norman Kretzmann and I tried to capture the relation of being present in terms of one person's having direct and unmediated causal contact with and cognitive access to another.[8] I now think, however, that the attempt to capture personal presence in terms of direct and unmediated cognitive and causal contact misses something even in the minimal sense of personal presence. Consider, for example, Homer's depiction of Zeus. Wherever in physical reality he is, Homer's Zeus has direct and unmediated causal connection with the Trojans and also direct and unmediated cognitive access to them. That is, Zeus knows directly and immediately what is happening to the Trojans in the fighting with the Greeks, say, and he can affect the way the fighting goes just by willing it. But Zeus can continue to have such cognitive and causal contact with the Trojans even when he is (as Homer sometimes says) having dinner with the Ethiopians. While Zeus is among the Ethiopians, however, he is absent from the scene of the Greek and Trojan War, not present to it.

Direct and unmediated causal and cognitive contact is even more inadequate for the stronger sense of presence. If Paula is blind and falls over Jerome when he is unconscious in her path, she may cause him to be moved by falling over him; and she may know by touch that it is a human person she has fallen over. Paula will thus have direct and unmediated causal and cognitive connection with Jerome; but she is not present to Jerome, in the stronger sense of personal presence, in virtue of falling over his unconscious body.

Second-person experience

What has to be added to the condition of direct and unmediated causal and cognitive contact, I now think, are two things—namely, second-person experience and shared attention. The first of these, second-person experience, is necessary for both kinds of presence and sufficient for minimal personal presence. For significant personal presence, shared attention is needed as well.

As I explained in Chapter 4, for purposes of this book, I will understand a second-person experience in this way.[9] One person Paula has a second-person experience of another person Jerome just in case

(1) Paula is aware of Jerome as a person,

(2) Paula's personal interaction with Jerome is of a direct and immediate sort,

and

(3) Jerome is conscious.

So described, a second-person experience is a matter of one person's attending to another person and being aware of him as a person when that other person is conscious and functioning, however minimally, as a person.

It is clear that Paula's having a second-person experience of Jerome is necessary for her being present with or present to Jerome, for all but the limiting cases of being present represented by (i) and (ii) above.[10] For example, if Paula were unconscious on the floor behind a screen in the room where Jerome was quarreling with Paula's daughter Julia, it would not be true that Paula was present with Jerome during the quarrel, except in the most minimal sense that her unconscious body was there. And the point remains the same if the roles were reversed, so that Jerome is the unconscious party in a room where Paula is quarreling with Julia. It would not be true that Paula was present with or to Jerome while she was quarreling with Julia, except in the most minimal sense that she had his unconscious body near her. With the limiting cases excepted, then, second-person experience is necessary for minimal personal presence.

Second-person experience is also sufficient for minimal personal presence. Suppose that Julia contrived to hide her mother behind a screen so that Paula could be an observer of Jerome's quarrel with Julia, and suppose that subsequently Jerome discovered that Paula had been there. Then, if Jerome challenged Julia, Julia would surely have to concede that her mother Paula had been present during the quarrel. Paula's second-person experience of Jerome in these circumstances is sufficient for her having minimal personal presence on this occasion.

Clearly, however, Paula's second-person experience of Jerome is not sufficient for her being present to him in the stronger sense of presence represented by (iv), (v), and (vi). Paula is not present to Jerome in this stronger sense just in virtue of being hidden behind a screen, secretly watching Jerome.

These points apply, *mutatis mutandis*, even to God.[11] It is one thing for God to be present always and everywhere with direct and unmediated causal and cognitive connection to everything but hidden from human view, and it is another thing entirely for God to be present to a human person in the stronger sense of presence represented by (iv)–(vi).

What, then, has to be added to second-person experience for significant personal presence? In my view, the answer to this question can be found in recent psychological and neurobiological literature on joint or shared attention in autistic and typically developing children. Joint or shared attention has been extensively investigated in infants, and I will present it first in that context. Then I will show the connection between it and significant personal presence.

Joint attention

As I explained in Chapter 4, the increase in the incidence of autism has prompted an outpouring of studies on the development of both autistic and typically developing children.[12] Two lines of research have proved particularly promising. One, discussed in Chapter 4, has to do with mirror neurons; the other, which I reserved for discussion in this chapter, has to do with joint or shared attention.

The form of joint attention that has been most extensively investigated is what researchers in the field call 'triadic attentional engagement' or just 'triadic shared [or 'joint'] attention.' This is "the (conscious) joining of two people's attention upon a 'third' element or target."[13] It is not easy to give an analysis of what is at issue in triadic joint attention. For example, one author says: "Joint attention . . . occurs when an individual (say, P1) is psychologically engaged with someone else's (P2's) psychological engagement with the world."[14] Another researcher says of two subjects engaged in joint attention directed toward some third object that "each subject is aware, in some sense, of the object *as* an object that is present to both subjects. There is, in this respect, a 'meeting of minds' between both subjects, such that the fact that both are attending to the same object is open or mutually manifest."[15] Yet another says:

for an instance of infant social engagement to count as joint attention, it is not enough that the infant attends to some object or event that just happens to be at the focus of someone else's attention. Critically, the infant needs to be aware of the object or event *as* the focus of the other person's attention—and in addition, for full 'jointness,' he or she should share awareness of the sharing of the focus, something that often entails sharing an attitude towards the thing or event in question.[16]

Whatever the difficulty of finding a correct formulation for describing the phenomenon, the phenomenon itself is easy to recognize. To take just one example, somewhere in the period between 9 and 12 months of age, most infants begin spontaneously to use a pointing gesture to call things to the attention of their care-givers and to share attention directed toward the object with the care-giver.[17] This pointing gesture "is intentionally addressed . . .This is shown by gaze alternation between referent and addressee . . ."[18]

Autistic children show significant deficits in the triadic form of joint attention. In one study, "not a single infant with autism . . . during the first 2 years . . . [showed] referential use of eye contact . . . and pointing at objects and following others' points."[19]

But impairment in triadic joint attention is not the most significant deficit autistic children show in this regard. There is a form of joint attention even more fundamental than triadic joint attention, and that is what researchers call 'dyadic shared attention.'

It is now apparent that triadic joint attention is a development of dyadic attention-sharing, which begins much earlier in infancy, in mutual gaze and in gaze-following. So, for example, one researcher says that gaze-following "is the earliest joint attention behaviour to appear in normal development, emerging some months before the onset of other joint attention behaviours . . . ,"[20] and it involves "a dyadic component."[21] Autistic children are impaired in this regard as well.

Dyadic attention-sharing can be a matter of the infant's and the care-giver's joint focus on the infant, or on some part or aspect of the infant. As one author explains,

Another set of phenomena involving others' attention . . . emerges before infants begin to direct others' attention to distal targets by pointing to them. Infants begin to detect others' attention to aspects of the self . . . These aspects may involve *temporary features* of the body, such as . . . a revealed tummy, or *acts* by the self, such as shaking the head . . . In two studies . . . it was found that from about 7 to 8 months, infants not only appear to be appreciative of attention to themselves, and seek to elicit attention to the self as a whole, but also seek to elicit attention to these specific aspects of the self.[22]

By as early as two months of age, infants already have some sophistication with regard to dyadic attention-sharing. They can, for example, "respond to attention from others with ambivalence. The onset of mutual gaze is sometimes accompanied by the aversion of gaze or head or both . . . [these reactions] are a response to mutual attention."[23]

In fact, there is "a fairly substantial body of evidence demonstrating the very young infant's capacity both to discriminate and express human features . . . Newborns are able to discriminate quite specific facial movements . . . and, moreover, are able to imitate these movements . . . and there is a close correspondence between the emotional expressions of mother and infant."[24]

It is hard to overemphasize the importance of dyadic attention-sharing to the appropriate development of normal human cognitive capacities. As one researcher says, "this is the most direct sharing of attention and the most powerful experience of others' attention that one can have."[25] Some researchers now propose that autism is most fundamentally an impairment in the capacity for dyadic joint attention:

Early research findings focusing on the joint attention impairment [of autistic children] initially emphasized a specific impairment in triadic interactions rather than dyadic interactions . . . Recently, however, the tide has begun to turn. Several studies show group differences in dyadic interaction between children with autism and those with other developmental delays . . . The research shows that certain measures of dyadic interaction predict diagnosis of autism several years later.[26]

Given the importance of vision in mediating dyadic shared attention, some researchers speculated that congenitally blind infants might suffer some of the impairments of autistic children; and this is, in fact, what they found. There is also an autistic-like syndrome that afflicts some of the congenitally blind.[27] On one account of this phenomenon,

there are specific forms of interpersonal communication and psychological co-orientation between a young child and others that provide a necessary psychological basis for understanding "minds" . . . and for comprehending and using context-sensitive language . . . most sighted autistic children are impaired in reacting to and identifying with the emotional attitudes of others; and . . . congenitally blind children . . . have a special problem with perceiving how attitudes are *directed* at objects and events in a shared world.[28]

One researcher sums up recent studies on the autistic-like characteristics of some congenitally blind children by pointing to the "functional overlap in the developmental psychopathology of congenitally blind and autistic children . . . [highlighting] the blind child's difficulties in apprehending and identifying with other people's attitudes as these are outwardly directed to a shared, visually specified world . . . "[29]

Manifestly, an autism-like disorder afflicts only some of the congenitally blind. Apparently, this is just because it is possible for the primary care-giver of a congenitally blind child to develop mechanisms for shared attention that do not rely on the visual system. As one researcher says, "there are alternative ways to help a constitutionally social child to coordinate her own attitudes towards the world with those of someone else."[30]

One puzzle with regard to autistic children and dyadic joint attention has to do with the root source of the autistic impairment. As one researcher asks, "why don't autistic children [engage in dyadic joint attention] . . . Our early research showed that it wasn't simply that they *can't* do it. In certain circumstances children with autism are actually very competent [at it] . . . "[31]

What, then, is the explanation for the failure of autistic children to engage in dyadic attention? Part of the answer has to do with the fact that there is voluntary control of attention:

Research studies of attentional orienting in typically developing infants suggest that there are two critical abilities that should be present as early as the first year of life: first, an ability to reflexively orient to sensory stimuli . . . second, an ability to control attention. . . . This capacity for voluntary control shows itself in the form of two corresponding developments. These are the capacity to disengage from one stimulus and shift to another and the ability to form an expectation from a cue . . . "[32]

"[Autistic children] have difficulties at the level of . . . voluntary control of attention . . . "[33]

These difficulties with the voluntary control of joint attention are not across the board, however.[34] They appear almost exclusively in response to social stimuli. As one researcher explains:

The initial problem for a child with autism, therefore, may be that they fail to benefit from face-to-face interaction . . . In ongoing work we are investigating the link between early dyadic gaze patterns and triadic communicative gestures and language . . . [our] findings all indicate that very basic dyadic difficulties affect later triadic joint attention.[35]

The same researcher sums up those findings by saying: "For individuals with autism, human stimuli may simply not be important early in development, and this may have serious implications for later development."[36]

These and many other studies make plain the importance of joint or shared attention, particularly dyadic joint attention. They do not give us a philosophical analysis of the concept of sharing attention, but they do give us some intuitive understanding of its nature and value for human life, even in infancy. In the discussion of joint attention that follows, although for ease of exposition I will omit the qualifier 'dyadic,' it is dyadic shared attention that will be at issue.

Joint attention and personal presence

Joint attention obviously also occurs among adults. For adults, as for infants, it is partly a matter of mutual knowledge, of the sort that prompts philosophical worry about the possibility of unstoppable infinite regress: Paula is aware of Jerome's being aware of Paula's being of Jerome's being aware, and so on.[37] In dyadic shared attention, the object of awareness for Paula is simultaneously Jerome and their mutual awareness—Jerome's awareness of her awareness of his awareness and so on—and the object of awareness for Jerome is simultaneously Paula and their mutual awareness.

Even this much insight into the nature of shared attention enables us to see that a second-person experience is just an ingredient of shared attention; and so it also helps us understand why a second-person experience is needed for minimal personal presence.

Paula's second-person experience of Jerome is just her being aware of Jerome and attentive to him when he is in a position to share attention with her, whether or not he actually does so. Without this much connection to Jerome on Paula's part, Paula is not personally present to Jerome in any except the limiting senses of personal presence.[38]

In my view, for mentally fully functional adult human beings, full-fledged dyadic joint attention is required for significant, as distinct from minimal, personal presence. If Jerome were to say of Paula, "She was distracted all through dinner and was never really present to me," one of the things he would be complaining about would be Paula's failure to share her attention with him. Conversely, if Paula was more present to her daughter Julia after she had given away her fortune than she was while she was wealthy, then Paula in her poor state would be more often or more deeply attentive to Julia, where the attentiveness in question requires shared attention of the dyadic sort. Finally, once we see that shared attention is required for personal presence, we can see why someone's having direct and unmediated cognitive and causal connection with another person is insufficient for her being present to him. In the case of Zeus and the Trojans, it is possible for Zeus to have such a causal and cognitive connection with the Trojans when he is not in a position to share attention with any of them because he is absent from the scene of the fighting.

Mutatis mutandis, this point about the connection between shared attention and significant personal presence applies also to God. God's having direct and unmediated cognitive and causal contact with everything in creation is still insufficient for God's being omnipresent. In order for God to be omnipresent, that is, in order for God to be always and everywhere *present*, it also needs to be the case that God is always and everywhere in a position to share attention with any creature able and willing to share attention with God.[39]

This way of understanding omnipresence has a notable implication. Given divine omnipresence, the only thing that makes a difference to the kind of personal presence, significant or minimal, that God has to a human person is the condition of the human person herself. If Paula wants Jerome to be significantly present to her, she alone will not be able to bring about what she wants, because the relationship she wants is up to Jerome as much as it is up to her, and, for one reason or another, Jerome may fail to meet the conditions requisite for significant personal presence. But, on the doctrine of omnipresence, things are different when it comes to God's being significantly present to a human person. If Paula wants God to be significantly present to her, what is needed to bring about what she wants depends only on her, on her being able and willing to share attention with God. Because God is omnipresent, then, if Paula is able and willing to share attention with God, the presence omnipresent God has to her will be significant personal presence. If she is not able and willing, then God will have only minimal personal presence with respect to her. (I will nuance the apparently over-optimistic character of this claim later in this chapter by showing that there can be obstacles *internal* to a human person that interfere with her having significant personal presence with anyone, including God, even if she is willing to have it, in some sense of 'willing'.)

Unlike infants, normally functioning adult human beings bring developed minds and wills to the sharing of attention; and they can employ more or less of their minds and wills in the process. For this reason, whatever the case may be for infants, for adults shared attention comes in degrees. There is a certain sort of shared attention when a husband ventures a quick glance at his angry wife as she is looking at him. There is a different, richer sort of shared attention in a romantic encounter of the sort John Donne describes in his poem "The Extasie":

> Our eye-beames twisted, and did thred
> Our eyes, upon one double string
>
> .   .   .   .   .
>
> Our soules, (which to advance their state
> Were gone out) hung twixt her, and me.

It is not surprising that Donne (and many others) point to interlocked gaze as the prime indicator and vehicle of shared attention in memorable romantic encounters. For adults as for infants, mutual gaze is a powerful mechanism for producing shared attention. Although vision is the most common or the ordinary mode of sharing attention, however, it is obviously not the only mode, since congenitally blind children can learn to share attention, too. Plainly, for mentally fully functioning adults, as well as for infants, shared attention can occur through modes of perception other than vision. In appropriate circumstances, any of the other senses can also be employed for the sharing of attention. In fact, as I explained in the discussion of second-person experience in Chapter 4, it is even possible that one person be presently aware of another and sharing attention with that other without having perception of him. As far as that goes, whatever means God uses to achieve shared attention with human beings, on theological views of God's presence to human beings, it presumably does not involve mutual gaze in any literal sense either. So shared attention does not require mutual gaze; but it does require mutual awareness among persons, whether or not it is awareness through a particular sensory modality.

For these reasons and others, it is clear that shared attention can be more or less deep and rich. In order for shared attention to be rich, there has to be a relation of mutual closeness between the persons sharing attention. A shared glance between relative strangers may be potent and exciting. But it is also possible for there to be sustained shared attention between two people, involving insightful mental seeing (as it were) of one another, and this can occur only between people who are close to each other.

So to understand shared attention fully, and the personal presence it makes possible, it is necessary to consider the nature of close relationships.

Interim conclusions

Before turning to the subject of closeness in relations, however, it may be helpful to review the nexus of relations sketched so far.

I claimed at the outset of this chapter that two things are required for union between persons, of the sort desired in the love of friendship: personal presence and mutual closeness. Personal presence needs to be distinguished into two sorts, minimal personal presence and significant personal presence. A second-person experience is necessary for minimal personal presence, and it includes (but is not exhausted by) direct and unmediated causal and cognitive contact between persons. Something more—namely, shared attention—is necessary for significant personal presence. Since shared attention comes in degrees, significant personal presence also comes in degrees. Rich shared attention is necessary for the most significant sort of personal presence. And mutual closeness is necessary for rich shared attention.

It is clear, then, that a complicated kind of personal engagement, based ultimately on knowledge of persons and shared attention between persons, is necessary for union. (It may also be sufficient, but I am not making this stronger claim here.) Given this nexus of connections, it is possible to refine the original claim about the union of love this way: the union of love requires mutual closeness and mutual personal presence of the most significant kind.

To ward off possible confusion here, it is important to add that, as regards union, the foundational role of cognitive states—the knowledge of persons and shared attention between them—should not obscure the role of the will. Especially with regard to knowledge of persons, what one knows is at least partly a function of what one wants to know. Volition also plays a part in attention, as we indicate when we talk of turning our attention to something or paying attention to someone. As far as that goes, even for infants, joint attention has a volitional component. In the view of some psychologists studying joint attention in infants, "selectively attending to something can be an intentional activity . . . 'the meeting of minds' characteristic of joint attention is primarily a 'meeting of wills'."[40]

As we will see, the role of the will in effecting union is even more evident when it comes to mutual closeness.

Closeness: The revelation of thoughts and feelings

With this short review, we can turn to an examination of the relation of mutual closeness by starting with the more basic relation of one person's being close to another.[41] When each person in a relationship is close to the other, then they are mutually close to each other.[42]

What is it for one person to be close to another? We can look for the answer to this question by acknowledging what is not sufficient for one person's being close to another. Propinquity alone is not sufficient for closeness, not even propinquity prolonged or often repeated. There is mere propinquity but not closeness between a person and the old man who regularly sits by her in the pew at church or the teenager who always gets on the subway when and where she does after work. Just adding conversation to propinquity will not produce closeness;[43] general benevolence plus conversation and propinquity is not enough either. The bright benevolence and lively conversation of a packed party is compatible with radical isolation on the part of those participating in it. As most people have experienced, it is possible to be more lonely and distant from others at a party than in the solitude of work in one's home or office.

What, then, can be said on the positive side?

This much seems relatively clear at the outset. The relation *being close to*, which holds only among persons as I am employing it here, is irreflexive (a person cannot be close to himself), asymmetric (a priest can be close to a family in crisis without its being the case that they are close to him), and intransitive (a mother can be close to her son and he can be close to his wife without its being the case that the mother-in-law is close to her daughter-in-law). So much seems relatively easy—at least, on first pass. (There is one complication even here, though, that I will consider later in this chapter.)

It is also easy to see that there are some necessary conditions involving openness of mind. For example, Paula is close to Jerome only if Jerome shares his thoughts and feelings with Paula. Furthermore, not just any thoughts and feelings will do here. For Paula to be close to Jerome, Jerome has to share with Paula those thoughts and feelings of his that he cares about and that are revelatory of him. Jerome would not be close to Paula if he shared with her a great many of his most trivial thoughts but nothing of what was important to him or revealing of him.[44]

It may seem as if I have things backwards here. That is, it may seem to some people that Paula is close to Jerome only if *Paula* reveals her mind to him, rather than the other way around. A little reflection, however, will show that my first formulation is correct. A priest is close to a family in his parish if one or more members of the family take him into their confidence. If the order of revelation were the other way around, if the priest shared his thoughts and feelings with one or more members of the family, we would say that the family was close to the priest. So Paula's closeness to Jerome requires self-revelation on the part of *Jerome*, not Paula.

Furthermore, Jerome's being actively engaged in self-revelation is requisite. If Paula is simply the sort of person who can see into others, so that she knows a great many things about Jerome without his telling them to her, she is not close to Jerome. Jerome's choosing to reveal his thoughts and feelings is necessary for Paula's closeness to him.[45] In addition, Paula has to receive Jerome's self-revelation, not only in the sense that she is willing to have him communicate his thoughts and feelings to her but also in the sense that she can understand what he is trying to reveal to her. If she is willing enough but uncomprehending, she will not be close to him.[46]

Closeness: Needs and desires

Plainly, there are also other necessary conditions involving desires and states of will, and these are even harder to spell out. If Jerome reveals very many of his thoughts and feelings to Paula but what Paula thinks or feels about what Jerome is telling her does not matter to Jerome, if her reactions to him are a matter of indifference to him, then, it seems evident, she is not close to him. If Jerome reveals a great deal of himself to a slave whose life is entirely in his power, but if the slave's reactions to Jerome do not matter to Jerome, then Jerome is only using the slave as a sort of sounding board. Most of us would consequently not see the slave as close to Jerome.

It is not clear how to frame this intuition as a positive claim.[47] I am inclined to think it has to be spelled out in terms of needs, but the notion of need in this context itself requires clarification. It helps to begin by thinking about the nature of a need on the part of some person. Jerome has a need for something S if S is, or is necessary for, something M that matters greatly to Jerome.[48] Consider:

(1) Jerome needs air.

(2) Jerome needs morphine.

(3) Jerome needs consolation.

(4) Jerome needs land.

(5) Jerome needs Paula (where Jerome and Paula are distinct persons).

In the first four cases, it is not so hard to know what the M in question is; roughly considered, it is:

(a) life,

(b) the warding-off of physical pain,

(c) the warding-off of psychological pain,

and

(d) the attainment of a goal to which Jerome is committed, respectively.

But what about (5)? What is the M in question for (5)? It *is* possible for one person to need another person in such a way that the M accompanying the need is any one of (a)–(d) in the list above, or something similar to these. Hitler, for example, needed his personal physician for (b), Eva Braun for (c), Goebbels for (d); when he was a child, he needed his mother for (a). There is at least one other sense, however, in which Jerome can need Paula; but it is not for any of the things in the list of (a)–(d), or for anything else that remedies something defective in Jerome or otherwise needed by Jerome for prudential purposes but missing.

When Augustine says to God, "You have made us for yourself, and our hearts are restless till they rest in you," he is evincing a need for the person of God; but the M in question is not readily reducible to anything that addresses or wards off something missing in or for Augustine. It is true, of course, that a creature needs its creator to live, and also for the rest of the things on the list (a)–(d). But the need Augustine is trying to call attention to in this line of his does not have to do with any inadequacy on Augustine's part. What sort of need is this?

Needs and desires are commonly associated, but they are nonetheless not correlative. It is possible to need something (for example, a reform in one's eating habits) without desiring it; but it is also possible to desire something without its being necessary for anything *other than the fulfillment of the desire itself*. If I have a great desire to hear Beethoven's *Christ on the Mount of Olives*, there may well be nothing for which my hearing that piece of music is necessary, other than the fulfillment of my desire to hear it. There is no lack or defect in me that is remedied by my hearing the music. I simply have a passion just then for hearing that particular piece of music. Would it be true in such a case to say that I need to hear that work? In one sense, the answer is manifestly 'no,' since there is no M in this case apart from the fulfillment of the desire for the music. But in another sense, if the desire is very powerful, then—looking for the CD and being unable to find it—I might say truly, with exasperation, "I *need* to hear it." In this sense of 'need,' then, if there is an M in question, it is only the fulfillment of the desire for the object of the need.

One person can need another in *this* sense, in my view. It is possible for a person to be the object of a need. As I argued in Chapter 3, there is a desire for persons that is like the knowledge of persons in being irreducible to propositional formulation. Just as it is possible to know a person, with a knowledge which is not reducible to knowledge *that*, so it is possible to desire a person with a desire which is not reducible to desire *that*. When Jerome desires Paula in this way, and when the desire is sufficiently great, then Jerome will need Paula in the sense of need at issue here. Jerome's needing Paula in this sense is, then, a matter of Jerome's having a great desire for Paula and Paula's being necessary for Jerome's fulfilling this desire for *Paula* (as distinct from anything else that is lacking to Jerome). Augustine's memorable line can be understood as expressing a need of this sort for God.

Need of this sort is requisite for closeness, in my view. Paula is close to Jerome only in case Jerome needs Paula in this sense. If Jerome had no need for Paula, he would not care whether or not he had Paula in his life; it would be a matter of indifference to him one way or another. In that case, it would be counter-intuitive to suppose that Paula is close to him. Furthermore, insofar as the fulfillment of Jerome's need for Paula is at least in part in Paula's control rather than Jerome's, Jerome's having a need for Paula makes Jerome vulnerable to Paula.[49] And so Jerome's being vulnerable to Paula is also requisite for Paula's being close to Jerome. *Mutatis mutandis*, the same point applies where relations of closeness between a human person and God are concerned. If God is to be close to Jerome, Jerome must have this sort of need and vulnerability where God is concerned.

It is clear that there also have to be correlative desires on Paula's part. Paula has to be willing to have Jerome need her and be vulnerable to her. If Jerome needed Paula but she took great care to avoid him, she would not be close to him.[50]

And this is not nearly the end. A great deal more could be said about what it is to have a need and desire for a person or what the satisfaction of such need and desire would consist in. Although I do not want to prolong the discussion of closeness any further by exploring these questions in detail, perhaps this much can be said briefly. Whatever exactly it is for Jerome to need and desire Paula, it must include at least Jerome's desiring in Paula those states of mind that are necessary for her being close to Jerome—namely, her understanding of his self-revelation to her and her willingness to have him need her and reveal his mind to her.

Paula's being close to Jerome thus not only involves certain states of mind and will in both Paula and Jerome, but also involves relational attitudes on Jerome's part. It involves Jerome's having desires about Paula's desires about Jerome and her understanding of him, and it requires his having a need and desire for her.

A worry: Closeness to God

Mutual closeness is necessary for the union desired in love, however; and so union between God and a human being Jerome requires not only that God be close to Jerome but also that Jerome be close to God. It will occur to someone to worry that the conditions for closeness I have been arguing for cannot be applied to God, especially given the classical theism Aquinas espouses. In my view, however, this worry is mistaken.

In the first place, insofar as God puts a revelation into history, as Aquinas supposes God does, God reveals his mind and will to human beings; and in this respect God meets one of the conditions for allowing human beings to be close to him.

Secondly, since the sort of desire at issue in one person's needing another is not correlated with any defect or lack on the part of that person, nothing about the classical divine attributes rules out such desire, and so also such need, on God's part. In this sense, even the God of classical theism can need his creatures. Aquinas can accept the view Job expresses when Job says to God, "You will call, and I will answer you. You will have a desire to the work of your hands" (Job 14: 15). In fact, on Aquinas's account of love, which takes a desire for union with the beloved as one of the constituent desires of love, God has to have a desire of this sort for his creatures if he is to love them.

But what about the condition having to do with vulnerability? On the Thomistic conception of God as sovereign and ultimately self-sufficient, it certainly looks as if nothing that matters to God is dependent on anything human beings do; a fortiori, it appears as if it is not possible for God to be vulnerable to human beings. But these appearances are mistaken, too. According to a biblical text that Aquinas accepts as literally true, God wants all human beings to be saved; but, on a Christian doctrine Aquinas also accepts, not all human beings are saved. That is because God created human beings with free will; and, on yet another Christian doctrine Aquinas accepts, some human beings misuse their free will in such a way as to reject God forever. Because God gave human beings such free will, God allowed certain things that matter to God—the salvation of all human beings—to depend on wills other than God's own. In this sense, God makes himself vulnerable to human beings.

In addition, of course, there is also the doctrine of the incarnation. On that doctrine, God makes himself radically vulnerable to human beings, in virtue of taking on human nature and becoming incarnate in Jesus.[51]

And so it is not the case that classical theism rules out a human person's being close to God, on the analysis of closeness I have been arguing for here.[52]

Closeness: Internal integration

Even if everything in the preceding account of closeness were spelled out accurately, however, we still would not have a complete account of what it is for one person to be close to another. At a minimum, we also have to say something about higher-order desires and acts of will. If Jerome wants to reveal his thoughts and feelings to Paula and if Jerome desires Paula in the sense just described, but if Jerome is alienated from his own desires as regards Paula—if he desires to have different desires from those he has regarding Paula because he thinks that his relationship to Paula is detrimental to his flourishing, for example—then Paula is not close to Jerome. Catullus's self-recriminating passion for his beloved Lesbia is a famous example of a relation that has such a conflict between higher- and lower-order desires. Speaking of Lesbia, Catullus says, "Odi et amo" (I love, and I hate).[53] He has this attitude toward the woman he loves because she is someone he himself wishes he did not love. She makes havoc of his psyche and his life, and he hates it that he loves her anyway. For Catullus, then, there is a mix of attraction to Lesbia and repulsion from her, mingled with self-loathing.[54] The relation that results from such an internal conflict on the lover's part undermines the lover's closeness to the beloved. For one person Paula to be close to another person Jerome, it is therefore necessary that Jerome have psychic integration of desires, or whole-heartedness.

These considerations also show that there needs to be some qualification of my original claim that the relation *being close to* is irreflexive.

As the case of Catullus shows, it is possible for a person to be internally divided in will from himself. Jerome might desire not to have the desires he has for Paula; his second-order desires might be in conflict with (at least some of) the first-order desires he has, and he might identify with his second-order desires. In that case, Jerome would be alienated from (some of) his own first-order desires.[55] It is also possible for there to be something analogous as regards the intellect. It is possible for a person to be unclear, uncomprehending, or even mistaken about his own beliefs. A self-deceived person, for example, is someone who has invested considerable psychic energy in hiding from himself some of the beliefs (or the beliefs and desires) he has. He has a stake in not recognizing some of his beliefs (or beliefs and desires) as his own, and he cares about seeing himself as other than he is. Such a person is divided within himself as regards his beliefs (or beliefs and desires). So, a person can be alienated from himself in mind as well as in will.

A person in such an internally divided condition is someone who is in some sense at war with himself. Typically, also, he is not a neutral bystander to this internal conflict. Generally, a person takes sides, as it were, in the battle within himself. There are some parts of himself, we might say, from which he stands at a considerable distance. In this sense, then, it is possible for a person to fail to be close to himself. And so, my earlier claim has to be modified: there is a way in which the relation *being close to* is reflexive. An internally divided person is someone who is, in some analogous or extended sense, not close to himself.

Or, if that is too much to say, this much at any rate seems to be right. A person alienated from himself cannot have someone else close to him. Jerome cannot reveal his mind to Paula if Jerome has hidden a good part of his mind from himself. And, if Jerome desires not to have the desires he has with regard to Paula, then to that extent he does not desire closeness with Paula either. For that matter, if Jerome is divided within himself as regards any of his desires, Paula will be distant from some part of Jerome, no matter which of his conflicting desires she allies herself with. So, for Paula to be close to Jerome, it is necessary that Jerome be integrated in himself.

Constraints on internal integration

I argued above that shared attention of a rich sort is necessary for the most significant sort of personal presence, and I claimed that mutual closeness is necessary for rich shared attention. I have tried to show some of the conditions necessary for one person to be close to another, and I have argued that internal psychological integration is one of them. Union in love requires mutual closeness and rich shared attention, and so it also requires that each of those united in love be internally integrated in this way. (If this is what Aquinas has in mind in claiming that love of another is predicated first on love of oneself, then he seems to me right.[56])

Harry Frankfurt has done more than anyone else in contemporary philosophy to call our attention to the importance of internal integration in the will. On his view, integration among hierarchically ordered desires and volitions—whole-heartedness, for short—is necessary for more than one of the features of personhood we value. On Frankfurt's view, caring about something can be understood as a matter of volitional integration. To care about something is to be committed to the desire for it; it is to have a higher-order desire in harmony with one's first-order desire for that thing.

It is notable that for Frankfurt a person's will can be hierarchically integrated around *any* sort of desires. For Frankfurt, structural harmony in the will is possible no matter what it is that is being desired. Although Frankfurt accepts objective standards of value, including moral value, he does not think that these standards constrain the ways in which agents can be identified with their own volitions. That is, it is possible, on Frankfurt's view, for an agent to be entirely identified with his higher-order volitions when those volitions are for a will which wills something that is objectively morally wrong. The will of such an agent would be hierarchically integrated around moral wrongdoing; he would be whole-hearted in evil.[57]

For Aquinas, such a case is impossible. So, for example, he says,

Even if bad people do not suffer temporal pains sometime in this life, they do suffer spiritual pains. That is why Augustine says in the first book of the *Confessions*, "It is the sentence you have given, Lord, and it is so, that a disordered mind is painful in itself." And [Aristotle] says about bad people, in the ninth book of the *Ethics*, "their soul is in strife; this part pulls this way, and that part pulls that way." And then he sums it up by saying, "If indeed it is in this way miserable to be bad, we should with intensity flee from evil."[58]

Aquinas, too, thinks that there is an objective moral standard, and he supposes that it can be known by the exercise of reason. In fact, he thinks that the objective moral standard, at least in its rudiments, is so accessible to ordinary reason that no human intellect is ever totally in ignorance of it. A human being Jerome who takes something objectively evil—say, beating his partner Paula—as a good morally acceptable for him to do will, therefore, always be double-minded.[59] With some part of his mind, Jerome will take beating Paula to be good; but with some other part of his mind, however far from full conscious awareness it may be and however vague and uncertain it may be, he will nonetheless understand that beating her is morally wrong. Because Aquinas supposes that desires and volitions are responsive to the willer's states of mind, Aquinas also thinks that double-mindedness of this sort in an evil agent generates a correspondingly conflicted set of desires and volitions. If Jerome is double-minded about the goodness of beating Paula, Jerome will have some first-order desires for beating her but also some first- and second-order desires opposed to doing so.

Unlike Frankfurt, then, Aquinas holds that no one can be whole-hearted in evil.[60] For Aquinas, it is not possible for a person's mind or will to be internally integrated in moral wrong. Rather, internal integration is possible only for a person single-mindedly understanding and whole-heartedly desiring the good. In the next chapter, I will return to this issue to discuss it in more detail. For my purposes here, however, what is most important to see is just that Aquinas, unlike Frankfurt, supposes the moral wrong a person does has the inevitable result of fragmenting him. To one extent or another, a person engaged in moral wrongdoing will be double-minded and also internally divided in will.

It is, therefore, a remarkable consequence of Aquinas's views that the ability of one person Paula to be close to another person Jerome is a function of *Jerome's* own integration in goodness. A person who is not integrated in goodness will hide one or another part of his mind from himself. To this extent, he will not be able or willing to reveal his mind to someone else. He will also have first-order desires that conflict with some of his other first-order desires or with his second-order desires or both. Consequently, he will be alienated from some of his own desires, whichever desires are operative in him.[61] Insofar as Jerome is in such a condition, Paula cannot be close to him, no matter what she does. Paula's becoming close to Jerome, or growing in closeness to Jerome, therefore requires that Jerome grow in single-mindedness and whole-heartedness. And, on Aquinas's views, this growth can occur only to the extent to which Jerome becomes integrated around the good. Without this sort of integration, closeness, personal presence, and therefore also union in love are all undermined or obviated.

All these points hold, *mutatis mutandis*, for God's being close to a human person, too. Aquinas assumes that God himself has the attitudes and desires needed for God's closeness to any human being. What is crucial, therefore, for God's being close to a person such as Jerome is Jerome's attitudes and desires with regard to God and Jerome's internal integration around the good.[62] I do not mean to say that anything about a human person could keep God from loving that person, since it is possible to love someone unilaterally. The internal fragmentation of a human person cannot keep God from exercising his providential care to work that person's good and to bring that person to union with God. Nor am I implying that there is anything about a human person which could keep God from being focused in attention on that person, more present to that person in second-person connectedness, than any human lover could be. The point here has to do only with that closeness that is an ingredient in union. As regards the closeness constituent of union, on the account of closeness I have argued for here, even God cannot be close to a person and united with a person who is not close to himself.

Summing up: Internal integration, closeness, presence, and the union of love

As I explained in Chapter 5, on Aquinas's views, love includes two desires, one for the good of the beloved and one for union with the beloved. In this chapter, I have tried to explicate the notion of union operative in this understanding of love.

I have claimed that two things are necessary for union among friends: the most significant personal presence and mutual closeness. As I have been at pains to show, personal presence and closeness are interconnected in complicated ways. Minimal personal presence, including second-person experience, is required for closeness; and mutual closeness is itself required for rich shared attention, which is in turn required for the most significant personal presence. My formulation of union as a matter of the most significant personal presence and mutual closeness is therefore pleonastic. As I have explained closeness and personal presence in this chapter, the most significant personal presence entails all the rest of the items on the list of things required for union, including mutual closeness. There is nonetheless some heuristic value in the pleonastic formulation. In human interactions, significant personal presence can be momentary or episodic, whereas mutual closeness is a matter of dispositions and considerable shared history as well. The pleonastic formulation keeps us from thinking of union itself as an ephemeral thing.[63]

I have also argued that a person's being internally integrated in himself is required for someone else's being close to him. This view has the implication that Paula does not have sole control over whether or not she is close to Jerome. If Jerome is not integrated within himself, then Paula's ability to be close to him is limited or inefficacious, no matter what she chooses to do. This point holds even if it is God's closeness to Jerome, rather than Paula's, that is at issue.

On Aquinas's optimistic view of human nature, which rules out the possibility of being whole-hearted in evil, a person can be integrated only around the good. Since union requires mutual closeness, on Aquinas's views, union is possible only among persons each of whom is integrated in goodness. The proverbial line that there is no honor among thieves becomes, for Aquinas, the contention that there is no union among thieves. To the extent to which a human person is not integrated in the good, then to that extent even God cannot be present to him in significant personal presence or be close to him with the closeness ingredient in union.

Finally, union comes in different sorts depending on the office of love at issue. In this chapter, my focus has been on the office of friend (where *friend* is narrowly understood, so that it excludes lovers and family members). But the account I have given of union can be extended to other offices of love as well, if it is relativized to the office in question, so that the degree of significant personal presence and the sort of closeness at issue are those that are appropriate for the office.

And so, while we may certainly fall into love, on Aquinas's views, the union desired in love is more nearly an accomplishment than an accident like falling. For Aquinas, this accomplishment is problematic for all post-Fall human beings, who are powerfully inclined to prefer their own power and pleasure over greater goods and who are thus not willing to be integrated around the good.

On Aquinas's worldview, therefore, the post-Fall human condition carries with it a kind of willed loneliness. In the next two chapters, I will consider the nature of this willed loneliness and Aquinas's understanding of the ways in which it can be overcome.

Chapter 7

Willed Loneliness

Aria de las lagrimas de Pedro

Lua descolorida
como cor de ouro palido
vesme i eu non quixera
me vises de tan alto.
O espaso que recorres
levame, caladina, nun teu raio.

Astro das almas orfas,
lua descolorida,
eu ben sei que n'alumas
tristeza cal a mina.
Vai contalo o teu dono,
e dille que me leve adonde habita.

Mais non lle contes nada,
descolorida lua,
pois non neste non noutros
mundos tereis fertuna.
Se sabe onde a morte
ten a morada escura,
dille que corpo e alma xuntamente
me leve adonde non recorden nunca,
nin no mundo en que estou nin nas alturas.

Aria of Peter's Tears

Colorless moon,
like the color of pale gold:
You see me here and I wouldn't like you
to see me from the heights above.

Take me, silently, in your ray
to the space of your journey.

Star of the orphan souls,
Colorless moon:
I know that you do not shed light on
sadness as sad as mine.
Go and tell it to your master
and tell him to take me to his place.

But don't tell him anything,
Moon, colorless,
because my fate won't change
here or in other worlds.
If you know where Death
has its dark mansion,
tell him to take my body and soul together
to a place where I won't be remembered
not in this world,
nor in the heights above.*

Introduction

In the preceding chapters, I showed that, on Aquinas's account, love emerges from the interaction of two mutually governing desires, for the good of the beloved and for union with the beloved; and I argued that union requires significant personal presence and mutual closeness. But, as I explained, mutual closeness and significant personal presence are undermined or obviated by a person's lack of internal psychic integration. To the extent to which a person is divided against himself, to that extent he cannot be at one with others either. The lack of internal integration is therefore inimical to the union desired in love.

For that matter, a person's alienation from himself is inimical to love itself. When a person lacks internal integration in will,[1] he wants and does not want the same thing, in one or another kind of conflict within the hierarchically structured will.[2] Consequently, what is needed for psychic integration depends on the will of the person who is divided against himself and not on anything external to him. If he wills whole-heartedly, he will *ipso facto* be integrated in will. A person who lacks internal integration in the will is, then, a person who does not will what he needs to will in order to be internally integrated. Consequently, the fact that others are kept from being close to him because of the lack of internal integration in his will is a result of the state of his own will. For this reason, there is a sense in which it is not true that he desires closeness with others. If he did, he would form those desires requisite for closeness; nothing prevents

---

* Galician poem by Rosalia de Castro; the poem is cited and translated by Osvaldo Golijov, in the notes to his *Passion according to Saint Mark* (Haenssler-Verlag, 2000); used by permission of the composer.

him from doing so except the desires of his own will. But, since it is the state of his own will that keeps others at a distance from him, there is a sense in which it is not true that he desires union with those others.[3] And so he is deficient, to one degree or another, in one of the desires of love where others are concerned. It is therefore arguable that internal integration in the will is necessary for love, as well as for union.[4]

These conclusions about union and love are stern claims that some people will be inclined to resist. To them, it will seem as if the condition requiring internal integration for union and even for love is strenuous. As far as that goes, some people will also object that internal integration is not needed for mutual closeness either. On this objection, even a person seriously alienated from himself can have other people close to him. How else, such putative objectors will argue, can we explain the way in which troubled people succeed in finding help from counselors or spiritual directors, for example? An internally conflicted person opens his mind and heart to the counselor who is helping him; and so his counselor becomes close to him. By this means, with the counselor's help, the troubled person begins to achieve a more harmonious inner state. How could psychic healing ever occur, the objectors will ask, if a person alienated from himself could not have other people close to him?[5]

This objection seems to apply in the case of union with God and closeness to God as well. Surely, the objectors will say, Aquinas supposes that God is providentially present to all human beings in this life, however subject to internal fragmentation they may be. It is central to classical Christian belief of a Thomistic sort that a perfectly good God loves all people and that an omnipresent God is always present to everyone. And so it cannot be, the objectors will argue, that a person's internal integration is necessary for God to be close to her or united with her, on Aquinas's sort of worldview.

According to these putative objectors, then, the account of love, closeness, and union that takes internal integration to be requisite for these good things must be mistaken. It is *too* strenuous.

A strenuous account of free will

The problem with trying to evaluate this objection is that it presupposes a certain identification of the true self of an internally divided person. It presupposes that a person is to be identified with the part of himself that seeks help from counselors, for example. If this identification were not presupposed, in what sense would it be true that a counselor is close to the troubled person who seeks his help? The locution 'the troubled person' suggests that there is just one true self in that person—namely, the self that is seeking help. But, when a person is divided against himself, it is hard to know what to count as his true self. In fact, there does not seem to be *one* self at all in such cases; rather, there seem to be at least *two*, and two that are at odds with each other. When we say of a person alienated from himself that *he* is close to his counselor, we are supposing that the part of his internally divided psyche that wants healing and help is to be identified with his true self. But why should we suppose that? Why should we think that the self that seeks closeness with the counselor is the true self? How is the true self to be identified?

This problem has received considerable attention in contemporary analytic philosophy, not least because of its discussion in connection with Harry Frankfurt's work on the hierarchical structure of the will; and it will be helpful to examine the problem in that connection here.

In various places, Frankfurt has claimed that the hierarchical structure of the will is central to personhood as well as to other things we value, including freedom of the will. According to Frankfurt, our ability to be reflexive in reason and in will also enables us to be divided against ourselves. We can accept some of our desires and volitions[6] and repudiate others. As Frankfurt maintains in various places, those desires and volitions that a person desires to have or wills to have or is content with or identifies with or accepts in some other way—*these* are really his own and really convey what he himself really wants. Those he does not desire, accept, and so on are in some sense external to himself and so *not* really his own. For Frankfurt, a human being's personhood requires that he have higher-order desires and volitions; and, for various reasons, Frankfurt thinks that a person's true self is to be identified with the higher-order states and acts of his will.

On Frankfurt's views, freedom of the will is a function of the hierarchical structure of the will. Freedom of the will can be understood on analogy with freedom of action. A person is acting freely when he does what he wants to do, so that freedom of action is harmony between what a person does and what he wants to do. By analogy, a person is willing freely when he wills what he wants to will, and freedom of the will is harmony between what a person wills and what he wants to will. A person's will is free, on Frankfurt's account, only if the "desire that governs him as he is acting is in agreement with a higher-order volition concerning what he wants to be his governing desire."[7]

Intuitively, then, the heart of freedom is being able to do what *you* want to do. But, on Frankfurt's views, an agent who is divided against herself will not be doing what *she* wants to do no matter what side of her divided self she acts on. That is because, when an internally divided agent acts in accordance with some desire of her divided will, the other part of her divided self will not want to do *that*. Consequently, in order to act with free will, she has to be whole-hearted in acting, and being whole-hearted requires her identifying with her higher-order volitions when she acts.

So, on Frankfurt's views, in order to count as having free will, an agent has to have hierarchically ordered desires and volitions and has to be internally integrated with respect to them. There has to be a harmonious mesh between an agent's second-order and first-order volitions. For this reason, according to Frankfurt, an agent who acts against her own second-order desires might be morally responsible for what she does, but she nonetheless does not act with free will. Contrary to a long-established tradition in philosophy, then, for Frankfurt there can be acts for which an agent is morally responsible but which are not done with free will.[8] On Frankfurt's account, more is needed for freedom of the will than simply being morally responsible for what one does of one's own will.

In the view of many people, however, Frankfurt's various attempts to explain a person's identification with his higher-order will do not succeed in settling the question of the true self. When an agent is divided against himself, which of the divided parts of himself is his *true* self and which parts give expression to what *he*—the true self—*really* wants? Why should we think, as Frankfurt does, that a person's true self is to be identified with his desires about desires? Why should not a person be identified with whichever of his conflicting desires he acts on or, for that matter, with the whole set of his conflicting desires? On the other hand, if a person's identifying with his desires or his accepting them in some way is what makes those desires authoritative for him, then what makes his desire for those desires authoritative for him? Does he also need to have and identify with third-order desires, and so on, ad infinitum? Alternatively, if his second-order desires can be constitutive of his true self and authoritative for him without his identifying with them, then why could not the same thing be said about his first-order desires? So, with what part of his divided self is a person really to be identified, and why?

Until these questions are answered, it is not clear that internal integration is needed for free will or that free will should be understood as a function of the hierarchical structure of the will. Even at this point, however, it is helpful to see that, if we do understand free will as Frankfurt does, then the condition for free will, like the condition I have proposed for union and for love to which the putative objectors take exception, is strenuous.

The true self

Elsewhere, in trying to answer questions raised in connection with Frankfurt's account of free will and true selfhood, I argued that two different kinds of identification are at issue in the notion of a true self, not just one, and that two different accounts of true selfhood are needed in consequence.[9] One account explains the metaphysics of personal identity, and the other explains what we might call 'the psychology of personal identity'—that is, the psychological identification of a person with certain higher-order states of hers.

On Aquinas's account of personal identity, a person is an individual substance of a rational[10] nature, where the rational nature is comprised of both intellect and will. There are, of course, other theories of the metaphysics of personal identity. But, whatever the details, virtually all reasonable metaphysical theories of personal identity count a mentally normally functioning adult human being as one person. For purposes of such theories, no matter what internal divisions there may be in such a person's psyche, as long as those divisions do not render that person psychotic or mentally non-functional in some other way,[11] he is still just one, metaphysically considered. He is one agent and one self.

In addition, however, a metaphysics of personal identity, such as Aquinas's, or any other that gives a privileged place to the rational faculties of mind and will, can serve as the basis for a particular psychology of personal identity. Aquinas thinks that a person's desires and volitions reflect the reasons she has for taking something to be good (where the good is to be understood broadly enough to include the beautiful, the efficient or elegant, the useful, and the metaphysical, as well as the moral). A person's first-order desires reflect her reasons relating to her actions; that is, her first-order desires are correlated with her reasons about the goodness of some particular action in some particular circumstances. But her second-order desires and volitions have to do with the kind of will she wants to have. Her second-order desires reflect her all-things-considered reasons about what would be good in general to do in circumstances generally of this sort, and these desires are correlated with her all-things-considered determination about the sort of volitional structure it is good for her to have.

For Aquinas, in the psychological sense of identity, a person is to be identified *with* her higher-order desires and volitions because they reflect the whole view of her intellect, in a way that her first-order desires and volitions do not. And the reason for this psychological identification is that, in the metaphysical sense of identity, a person is to be identified *as* an individual substance with a rational nature. Aquinas's metaphysics of identity, then, helps to explain and support a psychology of identity, according to which a person is to be identified with her higher-order desires and volitions.[12] Given Aquinas's view of identity in the metaphysical sense, when a person is divided against herself, her true self is to be identified with her higher-order desires and volitions because that part of her divided psyche reflects most the considered determinations of her own intellect or reasons-responsive capacities, and *she* is an individual substance of a rational nature.

And so, by using both the metaphysical and the psychological senses of the true self, we can give a principled answer to the questions about the identification of the true self. In the psychological sense, a human being's true self is to be identified with her higher-order desires, because they reflect the all-things-considered judgment of her rational faculties; and her rational faculties are constitutive of what is truly *her*, in the metaphysical sense.

For these same reasons, when a person's first-order desires conflict with her higher-order desires, she can unify her desires by bringing them into harmony with her higher-order desires, but not the other way around. As long as she has not lost her reason and as long as she does not change her mind about reasons for action in general, she could not harmonize her divided desires by bringing the higher-order desires into conformity with the lower-order ones. That is because, no matter how strong her lower-order desires are, she will also always have some desires not to have those desires, in virtue of the fact that her intellect repudiates them as not good. On Aquinas's views, therefore, an agent will be able to be integrated only in acting in accordance with her higher-order desires; in acting against them, she will invariably be fragmented.[13]

The strenuous and the ordinary: Freedom in will and action

In my view, the distinction between the metaphysical and the psychological senses of the true self allays the unease generated by the strenuous account of closeness, union, and love, as well as some of the concerns generated by Frankfurt's strenuous account of free will.

Consider, to begin with, Frankfurt's view of free will. If we think of the self in the two different ways just outlined, then we get two correspondingly different modes in which an agent can do what *she* wants to do.

Imagine an agent Paula who is internally divided against herself and who in this condition performs some act of her own will, without any external coercion.[14] When Paula does this act in these circumstances, she is acting on her own rational faculties of intellect and will. But these are constitutive of her as the person she is, in the metaphysical sense of the self. Consequently, when Paula acts in these circumstances, she is doing what *she*—the person constituted by these rational faculties—wants to do. As long as the intellect and will operative in her action are hers, then it is Paula who acts, even if she is internally divided in intellect and will when she does.

For this reason, it is true that in this case Paula acts freely, insofar as freedom of action is a matter of an agent's doing what *she* wants to do. As far as that goes, it is also true that Paula acts with free will, insofar as her freedom of will is a matter of her willing what she wants to will. The volition on which Paula acts is the volition *Paula herself* willed. It is the volition that Paula herself formed, even if when she formed it she also had higher-order desires that some other volition be her will.

Taking the true self in the metaphysical sense, therefore, gives us the ordinary view that Paula acts with free will in these circumstances even if she lacks internal integration when she acts, and it therefore also gives us the ordinary association between moral responsibility and free will. In the ordinary course of things, an agent who was morally responsible for an action that he did would be greeted with derision if he claimed that he lacked free will in acting because he was alienated from himself when he willed to act as he did. On the metaphysical sense of the true self, the things that make Paula morally responsible for what she does—that without coercion she acted on her own intellect and will—also make her action freely willed.

But this is only the ordinary mode of freedom in will and actions. Clearly, there is also a more strenuous mode.

Consider, for example, these sentences:

(1) "You'll never be free of pain as long as the shrapnel remains in your leg."
(2) "Paying your creditors is the only way to be free from them."
(3) "You will never be free of anxiety as long as you're a slave to your work."
(4) "Facing up to your past will free you from it."

In all of these sentences, freedom is connected to the removal of an obstacle that is hindering a person from having what she presumably wants: the absence of pain and financial stress in (1) and (2), the absence of psychic pain and psychological distress in (3) and (4). Unlike the cases in (1) and (2), however, in (3) and (4) the obstacle in question is not external to the psyche of the agent. In (3), the person who is being exhorted regarding his slavery to work is someone who wants to work as he does but who also feels distress at the diminished life left him by his endless work. He is someone whose desire to work is in conflict with his higher-order desires to be the sort of person who has "a real life," with all that is implied by that overused phrase. In (4), the person being exhorted to face up to his past presumably has something he wants to hide from himself and others, and yet he also has higher-order desires for a life of peace and companionship rather than guilt and secrecy. So, in (3) and (4), the obstacle to a person's having what he himself wants is something that is within that person's own will.

In cases such as those in (3) and (4), the freedom being recommended will come only when the exhorted person's conflicting desires are harmonized around her higher-order desires. When she acts or wills with such internal integration, she is doing or willing what *she* wants to do or will in a way which is stronger than in the ordinary mode. Consequently, if she does what she is being exhorted to do, she will also be free in a stronger sense of freedom. In the cases in (3) and (4), the freedom at issue is freedom in a strenuous sense, and it is a function of internal integration.

It is evident, then, that, when a person is free in the ordinary mode of freedom, his having freedom in the ordinary mode is compatible with serious failure on his part to do or will what he himself wants to do or will. If he acts with freedom in the ordinary mode but is alienated from himself in his acting, it will also be true that, in another way, he is not free. Because of his own internal psychic divisions, *he* is an obstacle to his doing what he himself wants to do or to his willing what he himself wants to will. Freedom in the ordinary mode can coexist with a significant lack of freedom. Complete, satisfactory, thoroughgoing freedom is therefore freedom of the strenuous kind.

The strenuous and the ordinary: Closeness, union, and love

It should be clear that something analogous can be said about closeness. If Jerome is a counselor for an internally divided person Julia, Jerome can be close to Julia if closeness is understood in an ordinary mode. That is, Julia can reveal things about her life and feelings to Jerome, and Julia can have higher-order desires about the sort of person she wants to be which lead Julia to want to reveal herself to Jerome. And so on. But, insofar as Julia is alienated from herself, she will also have conflicting desires, desires to hide things from herself as well as from her counselor. That is why expertise and training are needed on the counselor's part. In order to help Julia, Jerome will need to deal skillfully with Julia's resistance to what she also desires. The kind of closeness the counselor has to Julia is, therefore, compatible with his being closed out—*by Julia*—of a great deal of Julia's inner life. And so complete, satisfactory, thoroughgoing closeness to Julia is closeness of a more strenuous kind. That kind of closeness requires internal integration on Julia's part.

The same point holds as regards union. As I showed in the preceding chapter, union requires mutual closeness. If there is only mutual closeness in the ordinary mode between two people, it might be true that they are united in an ordinary mode of union, too. But that ordinary mode of union will be compatible with considerable distance and discord between them. Union in the ordinary mode is a far cry from the sort of union one hopes for when one longs to be united with a person one loves.

The same points apply also to love, *mutatis mutandis*; and it is important for my purposes to see that they do.

In her autobiographical record of her reunion long after the Second World War with her mother, who had been a camp guard at Auschwitz-Birkenau, Helga Schneider gives a vivid description of the difficulties of trying to have loving relations with a person severely fragmented in psyche.[15] When Helga finds her mother again, after a separation of many years, Mother Schneider is entirely unrepentant for her past morally monstrous actions but also severely alienated from herself because of them. She brazenly validates her past, even while she tries desperately to hide it or explain it away. She is deeply divided within herself; and, in consequence, all her human relations are damaged. Anyone who might be close to her is simultaneously welcomed in and shut out, whipsawed between the conflicting parts of her personality.

Helga's efforts to find some connection of filial love with her mother are marked by Helga's own care for her mother and her great desire for loving relations with her mother. But in the end Helga gives up. As Helga tells the story, Mother Schneider takes pleasure in the reconnection with her daughter and does what she can to try to fasten Helga to herself, so that there is no chance of losing her again. But her attempt to attach Helga to herself is marked by alternations between clinging to Helga, on the one hand, and complete coldness and rejection, on the other. The vectored result of these opposed forces, where Helga is concerned, is a kind of infantile narcissism on Mother Schneider's part that very effectively wards off any real closeness with Helga. When Helga finally abandons her efforts to establish loving relations with her mother, she sums up her recognition of the hopelessness of the attempt by saying about her mother: "I realize that if . . . [before having found her again] her absence was a presence that obsessed me, now her presence is an irrevocable absence."[16]

Helga's account makes clear that Mother Schneider loves her daughter in some ordinary mode of love, but that mode is compatible with Helga's feeling overwhelmed by the absence of any *real* love for her—any love in the strenuous mode—on her mother's part. The case of Mother Schneider is, of course, an extreme case; but its extreme character is propaideutically helpful. It presents starkly what can also be seen but with more difficulty in more common cases.[17] Love that stills the hunger for love is love of a strenuous kind; and, like closeness, union, and freedom in the strenuous mode, it requires internal integration on the part of the person whose love is at issue.

Like freedom, therefore, closeness, union, and love come in two modes, an ordinary and a strenuous mode. The ordinary mode may be acceptable to many people in many circumstances. But the ordinary mode of all these things is compatible with the absence of what we yearn to have, in love as well as in freedom. For what we hope to have for ourselves, the strenuous mode is necessary.

The general point holds also as far as God is concerned. On Aquinas's views, in this life, God is always present to every human person. Self-destructive or internally fragmented persons are no exception to this claim. Even those who believe in God but feel that God has deserted them, those who are painfully conscious only of God's absence, are enveloped in God's presence.[18] For Aquinas, God abandons no one;[19] on the contrary, God loves every person and is present to every person with providential care.[20] But this presence is nonetheless without the closeness ingredient in union. There is an ordinary mode, so to speak, and a strenuous mode as regards God's relations to human beings, too.[21] And, while God has the power to produce unilaterally some kind of personal presence, for significant personal presence even God's power is not sufficient. Significant personal presence of God to a human being requires mutual love and mutual closeness, and what is mutual cannot be produced unilaterally.

Internal integration and moral goodness

As I explained in the preceding chapter, although Frankfurt accepts objective standards of value, including moral value, he does not think that these standards constrain the ways in which agents can be identified with their own desires and volitions. It is possible, on his views, for an agent to be integrated around his second-order desires when those desires are for a will which wills something that is objectively morally wrong. Such an agent would be whole-hearted in evil.[22] By contrast, on Aquinas's views, an agent can be internally integrated only around the morally good. And so, for Aquinas, in order for a person to have freedom, closeness, and love in the strenuous modes of these things, that person must be not only whole-hearted but also whole-hearted in moral goodness. For Aquinas, a case of the sort Frankfurt envisages, in which a person is internally integrated wholly in moral evil, is impossible.

Aquinas's position has its roots in his optimistic view of human nature.[23] Like Frankfurt, Aquinas thinks that there is an objective moral order; and he holds that it can be known by the exercise of reason. In fact, he thinks that the objective moral standard, at least in its rudiments, is so accessible to ordinary reason that no normally functioning human intellect is ever totally in ignorance of it. No one ever gets so evil that there is nothing in his intellect or will that holds back from the evil he is immersed in, that disapproves of that evil and desires something better. Somewhere, however deeply buried in his psychic structure, there will be some part of the evildoer's intellect and will that dissents from the evil approved of by the rest of his intellect and desired by the rest of his will. Consequently, a human being who takes to be good something that is objectively evil will always be double-minded, in some complicated way that need not be accessible to the agent's own consciousness,[24] and the doubleness in his reason will be mirrored by a corresponding doubleness in his will. (Given the connection Aquinas maintains between mind and will, a double-minded person cannot be whole-hearted.[25]) For these reasons, on Aquinas's account, but not on Frankfurt's, there are limits to how evil a human being can become. For Aquinas, a human being can never become so evil that some part of his mind and will are not still on the side of the good. That is why, on Aquinas's views, moral wrongdoing inevitably fragments a person.

If Frankfurt's account were right, if a person could be internally integrated around just anything, then one would expect to find historical cases, in some time and place, of individuals or communities of people who were both wholly integrated around what is objectively evil and who also evinced love, closeness, union, and freedom in the strenuous modes. But this is not in fact what we find. On the contrary, groups comprised of individuals given over to moral evil are marked by self-seeking servility to those in command,[26] mutual strife and discord with their peers, and social isolation from others, including the members of their families. The high-ranking Nazis are our most thoroughly studied examples of people who would be the best candidates for persons integrated around evil if any persons ever were; and they are as remarkable for their self-regarding slavishness to power, internecine infighting, and loneliness as for their evil.

Take, for example, just the matter of internal fragmentation and loneliness. It is notable how often high-ranking Nazis were thought by others to be both divided within themselves and isolated from others. Even Himmler saw his closest subordinate Heydrich in this way. Heydrich was notoriously inaccessible to others, and Himmler explained him by saying that Heydrich was "an unhappy man, completely divided against himself."[27] In describing the state of his own psyche during the Nazi years, Adolf Eichmann said: "It would be better to call it a split state, a form of splitting, where one fled from one side to the other side and vice versa."[28] The social isolation and loneliness of the upper-echelon Nazis is in fact a feature regularly remarked on by their biographers. For example, one of Ribbentrop's biographers comments that by the mid-1930s Ribbentrop was characterized by "an insensitive remoteness" that left him "extremely difficult to like."[29] There were, of course, eminent Nazis who were regarded by some of their peers as cultured family men; but that appearance now seems to historians to have been only a thin covering for inward isolation. Even when it comes to the most gregarious and social of the Nazi elite, Goering, one of his biographers, says: "Few got close to him. Indeed for all his excessive sociability he remained an outsider, keeping people at a distance . . . his sociability was a mask."[30]

Although the Nazis as a group are the best-known among contemporary perpetrators of great evils, other studies of individuals widely regarded as moral monsters, such as Mao Tse-tung in his later years, give a similar picture.[31] So the historical record gives some evidence for thinking that Aquinas is right and Frankfurt is wrong. A human being cannot be internally integrated around evil. Great moral wrongdoing has the effect of fragmenting the wrongdoer's psyche, and those who are internally divided against themselves in moral evil are also isolated from others.

But, for my purposes, it is not necessary to adjudicate between Frankfurt and Aquinas on this score. Aquinas's claim that a person can be integrated only around the good is based on his view of the ability of human reason to discern objective value. He does, however, recognize that it is possible for a person to lose his reason and become insane. A person who has lost his reason is obviously not in a position to discern objective value by means of reason. So Aquinas could accept the possibility of a person of the sort imagined by Frankfurt—a person who is single-minded and whole-hearted in evil—as long as he could judge such a person insane, in virtue of that person's lacking the ability to discern by reason the objective value that is really there in the world. In such judgment, of course, Aquinas would not be dissenting from common opinion. The famous examples of people who might be proposed as exemplars of human beings who are internally integrated around evil—Hitler, for instance—are also people who are widely regarded as mad. Consequently, it would be possible to harmonize Aquinas's views with Frankfurt's on this score by claiming that internal integration, required for the strenuous modes of love, closeness, union, and freedom, can occur only around the good except in the case of those who have entirely lost the use of their reason.

If we harmonize the views of Frankfurt and Aquinas in this way, then Frankfurt's whole-hearted, single-minded totally evil person would fall outside the boundaries of my project, which is limited to considerations of mentally normally functioning adult human beings, as I explained at the outset. So those readers who are not inclined to accept Aquinas's views on this score can just bracket the totally wicked from the domain of cases under consideration in this book.

Therefore, either because Aquinas is right that a human being can be internally integrated only around the good, or because the totally wicked are exempted from the discussion here, in what follows I will include in the defense under construction the claim that the strenuous mode of love, closeness, and union, like the strenuous mode of freedom, is possible only for people internally integrated around the morally good.

The problem of shame

I have been at pains to show the connection between a person's alienation from himself and his moral wrongdoing, but it would be a mistake to suppose that moral wrongdoing is the only road to internal psychic fragmentation. Moral wrongdoing is sufficient for such fragmentation, but it is not necessary for it. Although internal integration around the good is necessary for union, closeness, and love, the absence of moral wrongdoing is not sufficient for these things. That is because shame also fragments a person, and guilt and shame are not the same.

In connection with the problem of evil, Marilyn Adams has emphasized the importance of what she calls 'the devaluation' of human beings. Contrasting her own approach to the problem of evil with that of other analytic philosophers, she says that they emphasize human free will and so focus on "what humans *do*," whereas her approach to the problem highlights "a metaphysical devaluation of humankind in relation to Divinity, and so in what both God and humans *are*."[32] She goes on to identify this devaluation as a kind of defilement, in ways which make clear that at least some kinds of shame are at issue for her. Summing up her own position, she says: "the honor code, with its calculus of honor and shame, is better equipped than morality to conceptualize the problems posed [to religious belief] by horrendous evil."[33]

While I do not share Adams's privileging of shame as regards the problem of suffering, I certainly concur with her view that there are special issues connected with shame and that these also need to be dealt with. A full philosophical exploration of the nature of shame is outside the bounds of my project; but, because shame does figure in the problem of suffering, something needs to be said here about the nature of shame.

In fact, the nature of shame is hard to capture; and the distinction between guilt and shame is also difficult to express clearly. The relations between guilt and shame, even when they are suitably distinguished, are complicated as well. For example, it is possible to feel shamed for being guilty of doing morally wrong acts. It is also possible to feel guilty for being a person who is shamed. (Imagine, for example, a person in Nazi Germany who rejects the Nazi worldview but feels shame by its standards anyway, contrary to his own determination to be defiant of those standards, and who consequently feels his susceptibility to the feeling of shame as a moral weakness in himself.)

There is also a complication stemming from the fact that, for shame as for guilt, there are three possibilities.

First:

(i) Just as a person can be guilty without feeling guilty, so a person can be shamed without feeling shame.

In such a case, we say with disapproval of the person who feels no shame that he is shameless—even if he is shamed by standards he himself does or should accept. Goering is a good example of this case. Although he *was* shamed at the Nuremberg trials, the accounts of others then present testify to the absence of any *feeling* of shame in him. (He also seems to have felt no guilt over the horrors he helped to perpetuate, but he was guilty of them nonetheless.)

Second:

(ii) Just as a person can feel guilt without in fact being guilty of any wrongdoing, so a person can feel shame without being shamed.

In such a case, we suppose that the person feeling shame is in need of comfort or counseling or something of this sort, but not that he needs any remedy for actual shame. Imagine, for example, a person who feels shame because she believes that she has failed an exam of great significance in her life, when in fact she has passed with distinction but has been sent, by accident, an erroneous report of her score. (Clearly, she might also feel guilty for not having done what was necessary to pass the test, but she would not in fact be guilty on this score.)

Finally:

(iii) Just as a person can feel guilty and also really be guilty, so a person can both be shamed and feel shamed.

Sophocles's Oedipus is an excellent example of this sort of case. He felt deeply the shame that he in fact incurred in the community in which he lived. (Analogously, Oedipus might have felt guilt for his act of killing an old man in a dispute over position on a roadway, and in that case he was also really guilty of this homicide.)

For ease of exposition, in what follows, unless explicitly specified otherwise, cases of either shame or guilt should be understood to be of this third sort, where the fact and the feeling coincide. But it is worth noticing that *each* of the three conditions of shame listed above is a source of internal psychic division. A person who feels shame, whether or not he is in fact shamed, is a person who is divided between the self that experiences shame and the self that has internalized the standards by whose measure he feels shamed. He stands at a distance from himself because he is divided between the shamed self that he feels he is and the evaluating self, which rejects as somehow unworthy or deficient the self that he feels himself to be. A person who *is* shamed but feels no shame has to suppress in himself a care for the standards and for the real or imagined community embracing the standards with respect to which he is shamed. And so he will be alienated from the part of himself that is connected to the world in which he lives. (*Mutatis mutandis*, the same points clearly apply also to guilt.)

There is a large literature on the distinction between shame and guilt. To take one classic source, Ruth Benedict is widely cited for her distinction between guilt cultures and shame cultures. Benedict claimed:

True shame cultures rely on external sanctions for good behavior, not, as true guilt cultures do, on an internalized conviction of sin. Shame is a reaction to other people's criticism . . . it requires an audience or at least a man's fantasy of an audience. Guilt does not . . . a man may suffer from guilt though no man knows of his misdeed.

But this way of distinguishing shame from guilt is now largely rejected. Both shame and guilt can come from internalized standards and sanctions, and a real or imagined audience is no more necessary for the one than for the other.[34]

Currently, it is common to take guilt as a person's negative reaction to what he does and shame as a person's negative reaction to what he is. So, for example, Martha Nussbaum says:

Guilt is a type of self-punishing anger, reacting to the perception that one has done a wrong or a harm. Thus, whereas shame focuses on defect or imperfection, and thus on some aspect of the very being of the person who feels it, guilt focuses on an action . . .[35]

By itself, however, the difference between what one is and what one does is not a good way of marking the difference between shame and guilt. Sophocles's

Oedipus expresses great shame over what he has done; and, at the outset of the work, the protagonist of Bunyan's *Pilgrim's Progress* feels guilt over the kind of person he is. In his excellent discussion of shame in ancient Greek culture, Douglas Cairns says:

It is very doubtful that such a fine-tuned distinction between focus on self *simpliciter* and focus on self as agent of specific acts can be maintained in practice . . . Shame . . . is not simply generalized dissatisfaction with the self, but rather involves a negative evaluation of the self in the light of some specific shortcoming; where a shortcoming is highlighted by a specific action contrary to one's moral standards, it is impossible that shame should not have a reference to the discrepancy between conduct and ideal self-image. Thus even a straightforward case of shame . . . might focus on both specific action and ideal self-image. Equally, the guilt that is caused by specific acts is caused by specific acts that set up a discrepancy between self-image and conduct, and thus guilt will always involve reference to both ideal self and conduct.[36]

And Cairns goes on to say: "any focus on oneself as a certain type of person must take into account the character of one's acts, and any rejection or repudiation of a specific act must encompass a conception of one's selfhood."[37]

As regards the distinction between guilt and shame, then, Claudia Card is nearer the mark when she focuses on the difference between what guilt and shame each seek or fear. She says: "In expiating guilt, we seek respect and reacceptance. In removing shame, we seek esteem or admiration . . . guilt can be relieved by forgiveness, whereas shame cannot."[38]

Moshe Halberthal's approach is also helpful; he focuses on the differing desires of guilt and shame. He says: "Guilt is expressed in the desire to clean a stain that sticks to a person, and expresses the need to reinstate the self that has been sullied. Shame, by contrast, colors the entire self. Shame does not stain, but defiles the entire surface. It arouses the desire to disappear and be effaced . . . "[39]

Nussbaum notes the difference in antidote as regards guilt and shame. Although forgiveness is an obvious antidote to guilt, "the shamed person," Nussbaum says, "feels a pervasive sense of inadequacy, and no clear steps suggest themselves to remove that inadequacy."[40]

Of course, if guilt is great enough or complicated enough, no clear steps may suggest themselves for removing guilt either. There may be cases in which forgiveness is virtually impossible, either psychologically or morally.[41] Nonetheless, it is helpful to think about the difference between shame and guilt in terms of the things desired and the penalties feared in each condition. The response on the part of real or imagined others that is anticipated with anxiety by a person feeling guilt is anger, and the penalty anticipated with anxiety is punishment of one sort or another. But shame is not like this. The response that is anticipated by a person feeling shame is more nearly rejection than anger, and the penalty dreaded is ostracism or abandonment. Cairns shows effectively that, for the Greeks at any rate, the connection between the shameful and the ugly is very close; and this is also helpful. A shamed person feels himself ugly, in one or another sense, and therefore *worthy* of being abandoned, just as a guilty person feels himself worthy of punishment. In extreme cases, guilt can give rise to self-hatred;[42] shame, by contrast, can give rise to self-loathing.

Shame, guilt, and the two desires of love

These reflections do not give us an analysis of the difference between shame and guilt, but they are suggestive nonetheless because they indicate a connection between shame and guilt, on the one hand, and the two desires of love, on the other. A shamed person and a guilty person each anticipates a repudiation, on the part of real or imagined others, of both the desires of love: (1) the desire for the good of the person in question, and (2) the desire for union with him. But the considerations above suggest that guilt is focused more on the first desire, and shame more on the second. A guilty person anticipating anger and punishment on the part of real or imagined others is anxious about things others may impose on him that are not for his good, at least not in his own view. By contrast, the shamed person anticipating rejection and abandonment on the part of real or imagined others is anxious about marginalization or isolation; his anxiety is directed towards a distance, an absence of union, forced on him by others with whom he himself desires some kind of closeness.[43] Of course, an absence of union can be taken as a kind of punishment, and a punishment can introduce distance between the punished person and others. Still, a man who feels guilty with respect to his wife and a man who feels shamed before his wife will have different anxieties. There is a psychological difference between the fear of anger and punishment, on the one hand, and the fear of rejection and abandonment, on the other.

In this connection, it is important to see that there is a discrepancy between the two desires of love. The first desire, for the good of the beloved, is easy to parse as a desire *that* something or other be the case. The lover desires that the beloved have health or that the beloved have meaningful work, or something of this sort. But the second desire is different. As I explained in Chapter 3, desire is like knowledge in coming in two basic varieties, one of which is reducible to propositional form—knowing *that*, desiring *that*— and the other of which is not.[44] Odysseus's desiring Kalypso is not equivalent to any desire *that*, and any desire *that*, where Kalypso is concerned, is a desire Odysseus could have without desiring Kalypso. But, as I argued in the discussion of the nature of union in Chapter 6, the desire of love for union is the desire for a person. Odysseus does not love Kalypso if he has no desire for Kalypso herself; his desire for Kalypso is integral to his desire for union with Kalypso and so also to his love of her. So, unlike the first desire of love, the second desire of love, for union with the beloved, is a desire which is not reducible to desire *that*.

For these reasons, when one person wants to be loved by others, he wants those others to have what in effect are two different sorts of desire as regards himself. What Jerome desires when he wants to be loved by Paula includes Paula's having a desire *that* Jerome have what is good for him. But it also includes Paula's having a desire *for him.*

If we see the second desire of love in this way, as a desire for a person rather than a desire *that* something or other be the case, then the connection between shame and the second desire of love is illuminating as regards the nature of shame. What is of most concern to a shamed person is the repudiation on the part of real or imagined others of the second desire of love. A person who feels guilty believes it would be appropriate for others to be angry at him and to punish him, where the punishment is something he does not want because he does not see it as good for himself, in some sense of *good*. And so a guilty person is concerned about a desire, on the part of others, that is opposed to his good, as he himself understands his good. But a person who feels shamed believes it would be appropriate for others to reject not his good but *him*.

It is not easy to find a clear formulation for a desire that is the opposite of the second desire of love. As in the case of guilt, what is at issue as regards shame is not simply the *absence* of one of the desires of love. Latin has a convenient pair of terms, missing in English but helpful here: *volo* ('I will'), *nolo* ('I nil,' as it were). The best we can do in English is to distinguish not willing, on the one hand, and willing not, on the other. To "nil" is to will not. A person who feels shame believes that others would be warranted if they were to "nil" him—that is, to repudiate a desire for him, rather than to desire union with him. That is surely at least part of the reason why a person suffering from shame wants not to be seen. He supposes that, if he were seen, others would be justified in rejecting him. That is why shame is characterized by a desire to avoid the gaze of others, to be invisible.[45]

Since for the shamed person the desire of love at risk is the desire on the part of others for *him*, it is easy to see why shame has been understood as a negative reaction to what a person is, rather than to what he does. The objection to this same understanding of shame is consequently also easy to grasp. On the view of shame I am arguing for here, it is not hard to understand why a person could feel shame over what he has done. Jerome may do some action such that Paula turns away from him and repudiates any desire for him. In that case, Jerome is shamed because of an action of his. And yet the shame is focused on his whole self, rather than on the action giving rise to Paula's rejection of him. That is because what Paula loses because of Jerome's action, and what Jerome wants her not to lose, is a desire for *him*. Consequently, there is something right both about the view linking shame and the whole person and about the objection to that view.

And so we can take the distinction between shame and guilt as a function of the difference between the two desires of love. A person who feels guilt has a conviction that his actions warrant others in desiring that he have what he takes to be opposed to his good. A person who feels shame has a conviction that something about himself—his own ugliness, on some standard of desirability—warrants others in repudiating a desire for him.[46]

This way of putting the point also helps us to see that there can be different varieties of shame, because there are different sorts of reasons for rejecting the second desire of love with regard to a person. A shamed person can be thought seriously deficient by others on the basis of highly varying scales of value, ranging from religious standards to standards of fashion current in a particular community. Just think of the difference between a drunken priest who scrambles in some terrible way the most sacred words of a significant religious ritual and a sick priest who loses control of his bowels while at the altar. Very different varieties of shame will afflict them.

The connection between shame and the second desire of love also helps explain the otherwise puzzling fact, noted above, that moral wrongdoing can give rise to shame as well as guilt, as careful studies such as that by Cairns have shown. This is so because a person might be as concerned about the alienation of others from him because of morally wrong actions on his part as he is worried about their desire to punish him for that action. What he has done may prompt in others a repudiation of him as well as a desire to punish him, and he may care more about the first possibility than the second. In fact, this understanding of shame also explains why a person who cares about some moral wrong he has done can be shamed just in his own eyes because of it. In consequence of what he has done, he himself can have the opposite of a desire for himself; he can find himself ugly and repulsive. In addition, this understanding of shame helps explain why a person who is unable to forgive himself for evil he has done can be characterized by self-loathing as well as self-laceration. Self-laceration is a person's attempt to punish himself; self-loathing, which is a response of shame, is a person's desire, as it were, to divorce himself. Finally, this way of thinking about the connection between shame and moral wrongdoing helps explain why so many people are inclined to believe that shame is nothing more than an auxiliary to guilt and that it should melt away with the forgiveness or absolution of guilt. Such people miss the fact that shame and self-loathing can be stimulated by many things other than care about one's own moral wrongdoing.

The antidotes for shame: Shame and ugliness, beauty and honor

Thinking of shame in terms of the second desire of love taken as a desire for a person also illuminates the connection between ugliness and shame. We are accustomed to think of what attracts us in another person as that person's beauty—the beauty of face and body or the beauty of the psyche. A physically ugly but much beloved person will be praised as having inner beauty. The admiring biography of John Nash, the mathematician who became schizophrenic and was dysfunctional for much of his life, is entitled 'A Beautiful Mind'.[47] When a person strikes us as admirable, as distinct from worthy of shame, we tend to find him, and not just some capacity of his, beautiful in some sense. To describe his own reaction to a group of young people who were working with the poor in an inner-city neighborhood, but who were rejected and marginalized by mainstream community groups, Jean Vanier says of them simply: "I found that group . . . quite beautiful."[48] Or, to put the point the other way around, a person who feels ugly by some standard or scale of value will also expect others who accept that standard to turn away from him.[49] Such turning-away is the opposite of a desire for union, however.

Even if we think of shame, as some people do, in terms of weakness or powerlessness rather than ugliness, the point remains fundamentally the same. We are attracted to power, and there is a kind of ugliness about those without it. We refer to those who lack power or are fallen from it as the devalued, degraded, debased, defiled, despoiled. They are diminished somehow in social standing or cultural stature, and they lack attractiveness for us in consequence.

This understanding of shame illuminates the antidote for shame, too. It is widely agreed that the antidote for guilt is forgiveness. On the account of love I gave in Chapter 5, Paula's forgiving Jerome is a matter of her willingness to maintain the desires of love for Jerome after he has hurt her or injured her in some way. Her forgiving Jerome consists in her desiring the good for Jerome and union with Jerome when he has perpetrated an injustice against her. And so forgiveness is a remedy for a person who is and feels guilty. But, as Nussbaum says, the remedy for a person who is and feels shamed is harder to see.

In his wonderful book about the loneliness engendered by shame, Vanier talks about the antidote to shame as a celebration of the life of the shamed person.[50] This allusive, obscure line seems to me on the right track entirely. A person whose life is celebrated is someone who has something lovely about him. The others celebrating his life with him have—and show him that they have—a desire for *him*. And so the natural remedy for shame is honor. A person who is honored has something attractive about him, and those who are attracted to him have some desire for him. One significant way to honor a shamed person is to be willing to receive nurture or care *from* him.[51] That is because, while people sometimes do not mind reaching down to the shamed to offer them help, the receiving of care from the shamed can seem to debase those who accept it. And so the antidote for shame can consist in enabling a shamed person to *give* to those who are not themselves shamed, or not shamed by the same standards.

Jean Vanier built an insight about this antidote to shame into his L'Arche communities for the severely disabled, when he stipulated that the disabled and those who are whole should live together in one community, so that they could be mutually care-giving. At the beginning of his description of L'Arche, Vanier says:

In August 1964, I founded l'Arche: a network of small homes and communities where we live together, men and women with intellectual disabilities and those who feel called to share their lives with them . . . Living in l'Arche, I have discovered a lot about loneliness, belonging, and the inner pain that springs from a sense of rejection. Community life with men and women who have intellectual disabilities has taught me a great deal about what it means to be human.[52]

Vanier has done as much as anyone to care for human beings with severe disabilities. And so it is notable that Vanier's opening remarks about L'Arche describe not what he has done for the disabled but rather what the disabled have done for him. His care for those with severe disabilities includes letting them care for him; and, no doubt, this is part of the healing he brings to those afflicted by the shame that can accompany serious disabilities.

Shame and willed loneliness

This much insight into the nature of shame is sufficient to show that shame is another route to internal fragmentation. A shamed person is divided into the self that is shamed and the self that has internalized the standards giving rise to a feeling of shame. A shamed person's repudiation of himself, as ugly or otherwise understandably rejected, is as effective as the inner dividedness generated by moral wrongdoing at preventing or undermining union, closeness, and love.

For my purposes in this project, the most salient difference between shame and guilt is that, on the face of it, the alienation from the self produced by shame does not have its source in the will of the shamed person. Unlike the loneliness stemming from the internal fragmentation of moral wrongdoing, the loneliness stemming from the internal division within the psyche of a shamed person is not primarily a function of the state of the will of the person shamed. Overcoming it is not within the power of the shamed person either. Rather, shame seems to stem from an involuntary suffering forced on a person by things that happen to him, outside his control.

Or so it seems on first view. But, in fact, this claim needs nuancing. For a person to be and to feel shamed, he needs not only to be deficient by some standards that are an objective measure for human attractiveness, at least as his community sees things; but he also needs to accept those standards as ultimate for him, as somehow binding on him and not overridden by other standards. For any particular debility of body or mind or any particular oppressive social status, however, a true story can be found about some actual person who has had that debility or status but who has nonetheless found some other, trumping standard of value by which to govern his life and by which he is not worthy of rejection. By the trumping standard, such a person is honorable and also in fact honored by others who know him intimately or who have come to know his story.

Joseph Merrick, the so-called Elephant Man, is as good an example of this point as any. When he was a child, Merrick suffered horribly not only from the disease that afflicted him but also from the depredations of those who prey shamelessly on the shamed. But as he grew to adulthood, the nobility with which he endured his suffering eventually caught the attention of his community. By the end of his life, even Queen Alexandra was among those who publicly honored him. Although Merrick always felt the dreadful ugliness of his physical condition and the shame concomitant on it, he did not accept the standards for attractive physical appearance as the ultimate standard for human loveliness; and he was lovely in this attitude. Frederick Treves, the doctor who rescued and befriended Merrick, plainly admired him. At his death, Treves said of Merrick:

As a specimen of humanity, Merrick was ignoble and repulsive; but the spirit of Merrick, if it could be seen in the form of the living, would assume the figure of an upstanding and heroic man, smooth-browed and clean of limb, and with eyes that flashed undaunted courage.[53]

Of course, there are also cases in which a person shamed for some reason simply lives out his life shamed by the standards operative in his culture, rather than lionized, as Merrick was. Yet even such cases are not a counter-example to the point at issue here. Consider, for example, Sophie Scholl, the student executed in Nazi Germany for her efforts at resistance.[54] She is an example of someone who was shamed by the standards of her culture and who died without honor in that culture. But she is now widely regarded as worthy of great honor, by standards the Nazis repudiated. One element among the many that make her so admirable is her refusal to accept the standards by whose measure she was shamed in her time in her culture.

And so it seems that, whether or not a shamed person accepts the standard by which he is shamed as the ultimate standards of judgment is, somehow, up to him.

I am *not* here claiming that those who are lonely in their shamed condition are to blame for either their shame or their loneliness. To accept such a claim would be monstrous, in my view. The relationship between loneliness and shame is very different from that between loneliness and moral wrongdoing, and it is inhuman to fail to see the difference. The point at issue here is only that there is a way in which even a shamed person is not totally helpless or at the mercy of others in his community. Seeing that this is so is not a monstrous blaming of the victim of shame. On the contrary, it is a validation of the fact that a person's human dignity cannot be totally taken from him by other people or external forces. Insofar as the standards by which a person is shamed are not the ultimate standards of human loveliness, it is open to a shamed person to refuse those standards and to align himself with a deeper measure of beauty, by which he himself is lovely and worthy of honor.

By the same token, however, it is also possible for a shamed person to cleave to the standard by which he is adjudged ugly, by his community or by some part of his psyche or both.[55] Embracing the standard shaming him allows a person to shut out other people in his community who are likely to reject him. That is, it allows him to reject them before they can reject him; it enables him to reject himself on their behalf before they have a chance to do it themselves. By this means, a shamed person keeps himself from the risk that attends all attempts at trust and that is specially dangerous and difficult for the shamed.

There is, then, a kind of willed loneliness even in shame.

Conclusion

Even without taking shame into consideration, it is the case that willed loneliness is a ubiquitous condition. Moral wrongdoing is sufficient for self-alienation, and it is hard to deny its universality. Some wit has said that the doctrine of original sin is the only theological doctrine overwhelmingly confirmed by empirical evidence, and it is hard not to accept the truth beneath the bitter joke. At any rate, it does seem amply demonstrated that human beings (or post-Fall human beings, as Aquinas would think) are powerfully inclined to prefer their own power and pleasure over greater goods. Consequently, even if shame could be erased from the picture, even if the only road to internal fragmentation were the lack of integration around the good, it would be the case that the condition of willed loneliness is all-pervasive, and the problem it poses is so also.

With this, then, my presentation of Aquinas's account of love is complete, or at least complete enough for my purposes. The love Aquinas describes, and the union desired in that love, with the closeness requisite for union, can have its full actualization only in case the person who loves is internally integrated. This is union, closeness, and love in the strenuous mode; and the lack of internal integration around the good undermines or destroys it. Shame is an obstacle to it as well.

It is important to see that the implications of these conclusions are not the same for love as for closeness and union. Paula's ability to love Jerome in the strenuous mode is entirely determined only by Paula. Whether or not she is internally integrated around the good is up to Paula, and whether or not she has for Jerome the two desires of love is also determined by her. But the situation is different with regard to closeness and union. No matter what Paula does, no matter how internally integrated she is, she will not be able to be close to Jerome or to be united with him, in the strenuous mode, if he is divided within himself. So, although it is entirely up to Paula whether or not she loves, it is not entirely up to Paula whether she has what she desires in love.

Mutatis mutandis, this same point holds also for God's love. Whether or not God loves a person is up to God alone. But even God cannot be close to a person or united with her, in the strenuous mode, if that person is alienated from herself.

Furthermore, as I was at pains to show in Chapter 5, if Jerome's moral alienation from himself creates a distance between himself and Paula, who desires to be close to him, Paula's forgiveness of Jerome is not sufficient to bridge that distance. Paula's forgiveness of Jerome is not enough to produce closeness or union between them as long as Jerome is divided against himself. And this conclusion remains the same even if we substitute God for Paula in the example. For God, too, forgiveness is unavailing for closeness to a person who is not internally integrated in the good. Even the love and forgiveness of God, then, have to be responsive to the beloved;[56] and, unless the beloved is internally integrated, even God is kept from closeness and union with the person he loves.

Whatever the case may be as regards shame, then, the human proclivity to moral wrongdoing is enough to guarantee that willed loneliness is common to human beings, affecting relations both among human persons and also between human persons and God.

In the next chapter, I will turn to Aquinas's explanation of the solution to this problem, the redemption of human beings from their willed loneliness. I will try to show the way in which that solution is, in effect, a remedy for shame as well as guilt.

Chapter 8

Other-Worldly Redemption

Purgatorio

the light being nearly faded,
. . . we met God's glad angel standing there

on the rocky ledge beyond the reach of the fire,
and caroling *"Beati mundo corde"*
in a voice to which no mortal could aspire.

Then: "Blessed ones, till by flame purified
no soul may pass this point. Enter the fire
and heed the singing on the other side."

. . . . .

I lean forward over my clasped hands and stare
into the fire, thinking of human bodies
I once saw burned, and once more see them there.

. . . . .

. . . and Virgil said: "Within that flame
there may be torment, but there is no death.

. . . . .

. . . turn here with whole assurance.
Put by your fears and enter to your peace."
And I stood fixed, at war with my own conscience.

And seeing me still stubborn, rooted fast,
he said, a little troubled: "Think, my son,
you shall see Beatrice when this wall is past."

. . . . .

. . . [my] paralysis melted from me,
and I turned to my Leader at that name
which wells forever in my memory

. . . . .

Once in the flame, I gladly would have cast
my body into boiling glass to cool it
against the measureless fury of the blast.

From the other side, to guide us, rose a paean,
and moving toward it, mindless of all else,
we emerged at last . . . .*

Introduction

In the previous chapter, I showed the way in which shame and moral wrongdoing leave a person alienated from herself; and I argued that such divisions in the self undermine or prevent closeness, union, and love, at least in the strenuous mode. On Aquinas's views, the internal integration necessary for closeness, union, and love is possible only in integration around the good. Although shame is internally alienating too, moral wrongdoing is therefore sufficient for inner fragmentation.

But, if this is right, as I have argued it is, then we are all in trouble. When we reflect on the many evils of the world—murder, rape, torture, racism, sexism, economic oppression, exploitative warfare, terrorism, and on and on—we often wonder how a good God could let such things happen. But another thing to wonder about is the moral evil of human beings, who in all cultures and all ages can be so vicious to one another. Considering the possibility that some human evils are unforgivable, one scholar expresses the human moral condition this way:

The examples in which the judgment of unforgivability gets the clearest justification are atrocities and brutal and relentless terror and oppression. When victims of these say 'never again' . . . they express the sense that particularly brutal or horrific wrongdoing should set permanent limits on the trust or hopefulness *in humanity* with which human beings may in conscience comfort themselves.[1]

Furthermore, people not only will what is morally wrong; they cling tenaciously to the moral wrong they will. They not only fail to will the good; they also fail to will to will it. They lack—or, what is more nearly true, they reject—a will for integration around the morally good. If Genghis Khan actually said what is commonly attributed to him—"The greatest joy a man can know is to conquer his enemies and . . . see the faces of those who were dear to them bedewed with tears, and to clasp their wives and daughters in his arms"[2]—he was giving expression to a monstrous cast of will that in its vastly more innocuous, little-league versions is known to everyone. That is why people laughed at the "Just Say 'No'!" campaign against illegal drugs. No one expects an exhortation to be availing against a human will that, for one reason or another, wills what it ought not to will.

---

* Dante, *Purgatorio*, xxvii, ll. 5–57, trans. John Ciardi (New York, Signet Classics, 1961).

Aquinas thought that the doctrine of original sin adds something to our understanding of the moral record of human history and psychology. What the doctrine contributes, on his view, is a story designed to explain why the moral condition of human beings is not God's fault. Those who are philosophically willing to do so can add the doctrine of original sin into the description of the possible world sketched in my exposition of Aquinas's views. But the doctrine of original sin is not essential to that description. It can be omitted, and those readers who want to do so should feel free to leave it out of the description of the possible world of the defense under construction. Readers who accept the existence of a perfectly good God but reject the doctrine of original sin and readers who reject the existence of God can substitute for the doctrine of original sin their own explanation of the human propensity to evil. Clearly, whatever explanation either of these groups gives for the human propensity to moral wrongdoing, it will not assign responsibility for this propensity to God.

Someone may object here that the human tendency to moral wrongdoing, however it is explained, is itself incompatible with the existence of a perfectly good, omnipotent, omniscient God.[3] On this objection, there is no possible world in which God exists and in which human beings are prone to moral wrongdoing; and the supposition that there is begs the question of the problem of evil.

But this objection is mistaken. To see that this is so, consider that, on the view of the putative objector, there is a sound argument that uses a description of the human propensity to moral wrongdoing as a premiss and that has as its conclusion the claim that God does not exist. How would such an argument go? Presumably, something like this:

(1) Human beings have a propensity to moral wrongdoing.

(2) A propensity to moral wrongdoing is itself an evil.

(3) If there is a perfectly good, omnipotent, omniscient God, he would prevent or eliminate any evil in the world unless he had a morally sufficient reason to allow it.

(4) There is no morally sufficient reason for God to allow the human propensity to moral wrongdoing.

(5) Therefore, there is no perfectly good, omnipotent, omniscient God.

But why think that the second and fourth premisses of this small argument are true?

Consider first the second premiss. Not only is it not obviously true, but some philosophers go so far as to maintain that a propensity to moral wrongdoing is a significant *good* in the world, because it is an essential prerequisite for moral goodness in human agency. So, for example, Richard Swinburne says:

Just as if reasons alone influence action, an agent inevitably does what he believes to be the best, so if desires alone influence action, an agent will inevitably follow his strongest desire. Free choice of action therefore arises only in two situations. One is where there is a choice between two actions which the agent regards as equal best which the agent desires to do equally; which . . . is the situation of very unserious free will. The other is where there is a choice between two actions, one of which the agent desires to do more and the other of which he believes it better to do . . . the more serious the free will and the stronger the contrary temptation, the better it is when the good action is done.[4]

Swinburne is here in a long philosophical tradition that includes Kant among others. The various historical formulations of this position are different in significant ways from Swinburne's;[5] but what those formulations and Swinburne's have in common is a rejection of premiss (2). On the view shared in this tradition of thought about the will, without a propensity to what is not morally good, human beings would lack significant free choice and, with it, the ability to do morally good actions. Consequently, on this position, not only is the human propensity for moral wrongdoing not an evil, but it is in fact actually an important good in the world because, without it, freely willed morally good actions are not possible.

As the rest of this chapter will show, this is not a Thomistic view, and I myself do not accept it. But it is an entrenched position, with a venerable ancestry; and a definitive, persuasive argument against it is not a simple or straightforward matter. Premiss (2) therefore is, at best, not easy to defend. It is certainly not *obviously* true.

Premiss (4) is even more difficult to support. Consider explanations of the human propensity to wrongdoing. There are secular explanations: evolutionary explanations, genetic explanations, sociological explanations, and, no doubt, many others as well. There are also theological explanations, including all the varieties of the doctrine of original sin. For premiss (4) to be true, all of these explanations would themselves have to be incompatible with the existence of God. That is, suppose that the right explanation for the human tendency to evil has to do with evolution. To argue that premiss (4) is true would, then, require showing that a perfectly good, omnipotent, omniscient God would never allow things to come into existence through a process such as that of evolution. For my part, I do not think that a good argument to this effect would be at all easy to construct.[6] But even if *per improbabile* we *could* build a good argument of this sort, it would not be remotely sufficient for an argument concluding to the truth of (4). That is because an argument for the truth of (4) would have to show that *all* the secular and theological explanations for the human propensity to evil are ruled out by the traditional divine attributes. An attempt to show this would be as contentious and unpersuasive as arguments get in philosophy, in my view.

So focusing on the mere propensity of human beings to moral wrongdoing is not itself a hopeful or promising way to construct an argument against the existence of God. But, without such an argument, nothing *forbids* the assumption that the existence of God and the existence of a propensity to wrongdoing in human beings are compatible. A fortiori, the objection that it is *question-begging* to suppose that they are compatible is clearly mistaken.

For my project, it does not matter which of the explanations we accept for the compatibility of God's existence and the human propensity to wrongdoing. In particular, as I explained above, nothing in my project requires that we accept the doctrine of original sin. On this score, I will assume only the two things on which secular and theological explanations of human wrongdoing can agree: that human beings have a propensity to moral evil and that this propensity is not attributable to a fault or defect on the part of an omnipotent, omniscient, perfectly good God. So although in this chapter, for ease of exposition, I will use Aquinas's terminology of original sin and the Fall, readers should feel free to take this terminology as shorthand for the explanations in their own preferred account of the human inclination to moral wrongdoing.

In subsequent sections of this chapter, I will examine Aquinas's understanding of the nature (as distinct from the origin) of the human propensity to moral evil, and I will explain the remedies Aquinas supposes to be necessary to alleviate it. The introduction of these remedies makes a divide in the discussion of this book. Up to this point, in laying out the methodology of this project and in presenting Aquinas's account of love, developed in the light of contemporary philosophical psychology and neurobiology, I have been arguing for a certain view of the world that is open to anyone to accept without a personal commitment to any particular religious belief. But the same cannot be said about Aquinas's account of the remedies for the human tendency to evil. And so it is important to make clear that, in expounding in this chapter the remedies for human evil as Aquinas understands them, for the purposes of my project I am describing *only* a possible world. It is no part of my purpose in this book to identify this possible world with the actual world, although nothing that I claim in this project rules out that identification either. As I explained in the first chapter, it is this character of my project that makes it a defense rather than a theodicy. Readers who do not share Aquinas's theological views can take them as theology fiction for the purposes of the defense at issue in this book. On the other hand, of course, readers who do share Aquinas's theological views can take what follows as a theodicy, as Aquinas himself supposed it to be.

The main aim of this chapter is the exposition of Aquinas's account of sanctification and justification, which he takes to be the remedies for the psychic sickness whose source is the human propensity to evil. Alleviating the psychic fragmentation stemming from this propensity is *necessary* for love and union in the strenuous mode, as the preceding chapters have argued. It emerges that the remedies Aquinas accepts for the problem caused by the human inclination to moral evil are an antidote not only to guilt[7] but also to shame. When shame and guilt are the sole obstacles to love and union in the strenuous mode—as they are where human relations with God are concerned—these remedies are also *sufficient* for such love and union. On Aquinas's worldview, without these remedies, even God cannot be close to a human person or united to him. With these remedies, however, on Aquinas's account, there is nothing to prevent the ever-present powerful love of God from finding its fruition in union with a human person.

Willed loneliness: A summary of the problem

Because the human propensity at issue is a disposition to moral wrongdoing, Aquinas understands it primarily as a defect in the will;[8] and he takes this defect to be part of the universal post-Fall human condition.[9] On Aquinas's view, all human beings have a sort of latent disease in the will. In the right circumstances, it blows up into moral monstrosity; in all circumstances, it sooner or later eventuates in moral wrongdoing of one sort or another.[10] The pure and innocent among human beings are no exception to this rule. When, for example, the biblical text says that Job was righteous, Aquinas takes the text to mean that Job was pure by relativized standards of human conduct in this world. By the objective, non-relativized standards of God, even Job was infected with the radical human tendency toward moral evil.[11] If we think of this tendency in the will as an analogue to the AIDS virus in the body, then the innocent are those in whom the virus has so far remained latent; they are not healthy so much as asymptomatic.

Given Aquinas's optimistic account of human nature and his view that inner integration is possible only around the good, it follows that all human beings in the post-Fall condition lack internal integration to some degree. They lack it not in the way in which a person lacks a limb, by some accident external to the will, but in the way in which a person lacks a reform in his destructive drug habits, by a resistance to it on the part of a person's own internally divided will. Consequently, it is an implication of Aquinas's views that, while human beings are wholly in the post-Fall human condition, they are not capable of love, closeness, or union in the strenuous mode.

Since a person's being in this human condition is a function of his will, the distance from others implied by this condition is also a function of his will. Its source, that is, is his own will. On Aquinas's views, therefore, there is a kind of willed loneliness, an isolation of one degree or another, which is part of the human condition. It is not that in being alienated from himself a person *ipso facto* wills to be at a distance from others. Rather, the divisions in his self carry distance from others as an inevitable concomitant. On the other hand, however, to the extent to which a person resists healing of his internal fragmentation, he also in effect resists closeness to others. This distance from others will not leave him until he is willing to let go of some part of his divided will.

Some people are lonely because age, illness, war, or other external circumstances have left them bereft of company. But, beneath ordinary, externally imposed loneliness, there is a deeper willed loneliness shared by all human beings, because the lack of internal integration in the human will excludes closeness, love, and union in their strenuous modes.

This willed loneliness shuts out even God. As I argued in earlier chapters, whether one person Paula is close to another person Jerome, whether she is united to him in love, is not within Paula's sole control. It requires also certain states of mind and will in Jerome, including most notably Jerome's being integrated in himself. *Mutatis mutandis*, claims such as these about Paula apply also to God. As I have been at pains to emphasize at various points in what has gone before, on Aquinas's views, nothing about human beings can separate them from the powerful, providential, ever-present love of God. But what is *desired* in love is union. And even omnipotent God cannot unilaterally fulfill this desire of love. Even God cannot be united to Jerome if Jerome is alienated from himself. Insofar as Jerome is resistant to internal integration, he is in effect also resistant to union with God.

Contrary to what someone might think, forgiveness is of no avail here.[12] God can forgive Jerome unilaterally, in the sense that God can desire the good for Jerome and union with Jerome, no matter what Jerome's internal condition. But even God's love has to be responsive to Jerome's own will.[13] To the extent to which Jerome is alienated from himself, the desires of love in forgiveness, even on God's part, will be unavailing. God can forgive Jerome unilaterally, but he cannot unilaterally have what he desires in forgiveness. In particular, even through forgiveness God unilaterally cannot bring it about that he is united to Jerome in love. A person's cleaving to his tendencies to moral wrongdoing closes a forgiving God out as well as forgiving human persons.

Something similar can be said about the willed loneliness stemming from shame. Unlike guilt, shame can be at least to some extent something inflicted on a person, as distinct from something whose source is solely a person's own acts, volitions, or dispositions. Any suggestion that shame shares with guilt the property of having human wrongdoing as its sole and invariable source is repulsive.[14] It would be inhuman to blame a person for being shamed when his shame is imposed upon him by things outside his control. And yet, insofar as a human person cleaves to the standards by which he is shamed, as if they were the ultimate standards of evaluation for him, there can be a willed loneliness induced by shame, too, even when it has its source in things external to the shamed person. It is possible for even the most shamed person, such as the Elephant Man, for example, to find a deeper standard of beauty by which he is lovely, rather than shamed.[15]

By the same token, however, it is also possible for a person to reject a deeper standard that affirms him for the sake of cleaving to the standard by which he is shamed. In the *Iliad*, when Agamemnon dishonors Achilles and Achilles in consequence withdraws from Agamemnon's army in rage, an embassy is sent to Achilles to try to make restitution for Agamemnon's dishonoring actions by honoring Achilles through the bestowal of great gifts and other blandishments. But the embassy's efforts are a total failure. Achilles explains to the embassy that he cares only about the honor which comes from Zeus, that he could hardly care less about the honor which comes from men.[16] Having laid out that useful distinction, self-serving in the circumstances, Achilles disdainfully rejects all efforts to allay his wrath over Agamemnon's shaming of him. In effect, Achilles cleaves to the standard of honor from men, and the shame which he has incurred by that standard, in order not to have to put aside his anger over having been shamed.

While a person's will is fixed on the standard by which he is shamed, and on the shame accruing to him by that standard, he remains alienated from himself, and from other people, too. In his shame and his wrath over having been dishonored by Agamemnon, Achilles remains isolated from the people who are his community; and he is divided within himself, too. It is notable that, when the embassy sent to Achilles first finds him—that very embassy to which Achilles praises honor from Zeus as the only honor worth having—Achilles is sitting alone, singing to himself songs about the honor given by men to men.[17] In his isolated and internally divided state brought about by his clinging to the standard that shames him, Achilles is an extreme exemplar of a kind of condition common to human beings.[18]

Apparent but unworkable solutions

On the face of it, the remedy for the willed loneliness springing from guilt or shame seems simple: nothing more is required than a person's willing in a certain way. Repairing a problem in one's will, unlike fixing a problem in one's leg or one's liver, requires only an act of will. What could be easier than a remedy that one has as soon as one wills to have it?

But, in fact, the truth is just the other way around. When the problem is in the will, the problem is, in one sense, insuperable. If a person has a bodily part that fails to function optimally, she can choose to do certain things about it. She can choose to take medicine or to have surgery, for example. Alternatively, if she is not able to make such choices, say because she is unconscious, then someone competent, a doctor, for example, can simply choose these things for her, on her behalf.

But when the problem is in the will, neither of these approaches will be successful.

If Paula could effectively choose of her own accord to be integrated in will, she would already be whole-hearted, or on her way to that state. Her lack of internal integration is just her unwillingness to unify herself in will. She is not internally integrated in will because she does not *want* to be. So, if the remedy consists in her willing whole-heartedly, the remedy is available to her only when the defect it is meant to remove is already gone.

Augustine has given us one of the classic descriptions of this difficulty. In an autobiographical passage in the *Confessions,* he says:

the mind commands the body, and is presently obeyed: the mind commands itself, and is resisted . . . it commands that itself would will a thing . . . [and it] never would give the command, unless it willed it; yet it does not [will] . . . [what it] has commanded . . . it commands . . . [because] it wills: and . . . the thing [is not] done which . . . [it] commanded . . . [because] it wills it not . . . But it does not command fully, therefore is not the thing done, which it commanded. For were the willing full, it never would command it to be, because it would already be.[19]

So the defect in the will is such that it could be fixed by the person who has it only if she did not have the defect.

On the other hand, no one else can fix Paula's will for her either, not even God. To the extent to which God fixes Paula's will, he wills for Paula a certain state of Paula's will. But, then, to that extent, what is in Paula is God's will, not Paula's. If the lack of internal integration in Paula's will is an obstacle to God's being close to Paula, God's determination of Paula's will is an even greater obstacle. Mutual closeness of the sort required for union depends on an agreement between two different wills. But, if God determines Paula's will, then the only will operative in Paula is God's will. In that case, there will not be two wills to bring into union with each other. There will be only one will, God's will, that is in Paula as well as in God. Union between Paula's will and God's will is not established by such means; it is obviated or destroyed.

How, then, is the problem in the will to be remedied? On the standard Christian answer to this question, which Aquinas inherits and develops,[20] the solution to the internal alienation resulting from the human propensity to moral wrongdoing consists in the paired processes of justification and sanctification.[21] Though the fact goes largely unnoticed, these same processes are also an antidote to shame. The healing of the will that mends the psychic fragmentation springing from moral wrongdoing also repairs the inner alienation stemming from shame. As I will argue below, when the processes of sanctification and justification are properly understood, it emerges that justification and sanctification are a solution for the internal divisions arising from shame, too.

With this much summary of the nature of the problem, we can now turn to Aquinas's understanding of the solution, the processes of justification and sanctification. It will be helpful to consider these processes in the reverse of the order in which the medieval tradition supposed them to occur.

Sanctification

In trying to explain the propensity of human persons to will their own pleasure and power over greater goods and the human culpability for this propensity, Augustine takes a surprising stand. According to Augustine, what human beings are culpable for is not the weakness of their wills when it comes to willing the good, but rather something very different—namely, the failure to seek help. Speaking to his audience about God, Augustine says:

There is everywhere present someone who in many ways, by means of creatures who serve him as lord, calls the man who is turned away [from him], teaches the man who believes, consoles the man who hopes, exhorts the man who loves, helps the man who strives, [and] hears the man who prays . . . And [so] it is not attributed to you as a fault that you fail to bind up the parts [of yourself] which are wounded but that you disdain him who is willing to heal them.[22]

Here Augustine is apparently thinking of God as always willing to aid the will of any person who wants God to strengthen him in his willing of the good. A person whose higher-order desires to will some particular good are too weak to produce a will for that good is nonetheless culpable for the evil he does, on Augustine's view, because that person could have asked God to help his will; and if he had done so, God would have given him the help he needed to do the good. Even if that person's will is not strong enough to bring his first-order volitions under the control of his good second-order desires, it is strong enough to enable him to form the first-order volition to ask God to strengthen his will; and, if he were to do so, God would give him the strength of will he wants and needs.

Aquinas is in the Augustinian tradition on this score. On Aquinas's view, one kind of grace that God bestows on a human will is the grace God gives to strengthen a human person's will for added power to will some particular good in response to that person's higher-order desires that God do so. In Aquinas's terminology, this is cooperative grace, because in giving it God is cooperating with a person's own higher-order desires. Suppose, for example, that Paula wants to become a vegetarian but finds it very difficult to give up meat. She finds eating meat morally objectionable and so she has a higher-order desire for a will that wills not to eat meat; she has corresponding first-order desires not to eat meat, too. But because she is habituated to eating meat, she also has first-order desires to eat meat; and those are the desires on which she often enough acts, to her own moral consternation. Like the Augustine of the *Confessions*, her will commands itself to will some good to which she is committed; but her will nonetheless does not will the thing it has commanded. On the theological view Augustine and Aquinas accept, if in this condition Paula asks God for help, then God will strengthen Paula's will so that Paula has the strength of will to will the good she herself wants to will—namely, not eating meat.

The process in which God cooperates with a human person's higher-order desires for a will that wills one or another particular good is the process of sanctification. If Paula petitions God for help in her struggle with her divided self,[23] then God can bring about changes in Paula's will so that Paula is enabled to bring her first-order desires into accord with her own second-order desires. By this means, Paula will make progress in integrating her will around the good. If it is only not interrupted but continued to its final conclusion, this process of moral improvement will eventually culminate in a state of complete moral goodness in Paula.[24]

If God were simply to produce a first-order volition[25] in Paula without Paula's having the corresponding second-order desire, God would be violating Paula's free will, since (as Aquinas thinks) if a person's volition is produced as a direct result of the exercise of efficient causality on the part of something external to that person's will, even on the part of God, the volition caused in this way is not free.[26] But, if God brings about a volition in Paula (either directly, by operating on her will, or indirectly in some way) when Paula has a second-order desire that God do so, then in helping Paula to integrate her first-order and second-order desires God does not undermine Paula's free will. Instead, he enhances or evokes it.[27] That is because Paula's own will brings it about that she has the first-order volition she does, not in the sense that it is the strength or even the agency of Paula's will that produces the desired first-order volition in her, but rather in the sense that, unless Paula had desired that God do so, God would not have acted on her will in this way. So, if Paula's second-order will had been different, her first-order volition would have been different also. God operates on Paula's will to enable Paula to have the will she herself wants to have.

Furthermore, if God simply altered Paula's will without Paula's desire that God do so, then the resulting will would be God's and not Paula's. God's acting on Paula's will in that way would replace her will with God's. On Aquinas's view, that is something which God, who does not undermine the nature of his creatures, would not do. But if God aids Paula's will because Paula herself wants God to help her have the state of will she herself wants to have, then the resulting will in Paula is the one she herself desires. For this reason, the ultimate source of the condition of Paula's will is not God, but Paula. In aiding Paula's will in this cooperative way in the process of sanctification, God is therefore not taking her will away from her. Rather, he is making her will more her own; he is providing its freedom, in the strenuous mode, in virtue of enabling Paula successfully to will what she herself wants to will.

Someone might suppose that, if this position were right, then, with one act of higher-order will, a human person could achieve, all at once, a full integration of her will around moral goodness, if she would only desire that God unify her will in this way. But this supposition fails to take account of the reality of human psychology. Sanctification is generally a lengthy process just because, typically, a human person's will is recurrently liable to internal division. Furthermore, even a particular higher-order desire for help in willing some one particular good can be wavering. Augustine is one of our most famous examples here, too. As he reports himself in the *Confessions*, in the period in which he was unsuccessful in his struggle to choose a celibate lifestyle, he prayed that God would give him chastity, *but not yet.*[28] Finally, even a higher-order desire for a good first-order will that is not wavering in this way can still subsequently fade or fall away. But, on pain of undermining a human person's will, God cannot make it stronger in its willing of the good than that person wants it to be.

Consequently, although sudden wholesale changes in the organizational structure of a person's will are in principle possible,[29] they are very rare and subject to back-sliding. And so, ordinarily, the path to full internal integration is slow. Typically, the higher-order volition for some particular good first-order volition on the part of some person Jerome, and his desire for God's aid in strengthening him in that willing, will result in some integration in Jerome's will. As Jerome's higher-order desires become effective in their command of Jerome's first-order desires, as Jerome's will becomes more unified, Jerome will be in a position to form further higher-order desires that further his will's integration around the good. In consequence, God can also give Jerome more aid to strengthen Jerome's will still more in willing what Jerome increasingly wants to will; and this strengthening of Jerome's will will enable Jerome to desire yet more cooperative giving of grace, and so on.

There may also be a kind of kindling effect. Being effective in her higher-order desire to become a vegetarian will change Paula's life as well as her will, and she will grow and develop in consequence. What began as a worry over the ethical treatment of animals may grow into a broader ethical ecological concern or may branch out into other concerns with social justice. Such development on Paula's part will typically be accompanied by new higher-order desires as well. Those people we admire greatly for their whole-heartedness and moral excellence grew into the characters for which they are admired. They were not born with them.[30]

Sanctification therefore generally takes time. On the theological doctrine that Aquinas accepts, the process of sanctification is not finished during a person's lifetime. If it is brought to completion at all, that completion occurs only in the afterlife.

For philosophical and theological reasons that will become clearer below, it is worth noticing the anti-Pelagian character of sanctification on Aquinas's account.[31] In the process of sanctification, Paula wants to will a particular good thing, and she does not despair of being successful in this higher-order desire of hers. But she does let go of her efforts to be successful on her own. She abandons the attempt to use her own strength of will to make her will be what she wants her will to be. Instead, she recognizes her own impairment in will and her need for help. Rather than struggling for what she wants to be, she in fact lets go of the struggle and seeks God's aid.

Sanctification and love

Even with so much clarification, the account of sanctification is still incomplete. To add what is missing, it is necessary to call to mind again Aquinas's account of love and the special cases of self-love and love of God.

The explanation of self-love in Chapter 5 has the implication that, in the higher-order desire of sanctification, a person is in effect loving herself. That is because in sanctification she is willing what integrates her around the good, and this is truly the good for herself. Consequently, what she is willing in the higher-order desire of sanctification is in fact a good for herself. But it is also the case that, in growing in integration in the good, she is being united with herself, to one degree or another. For this reason, in the higher-order desire of sanctification, what she wills is in fact union with herself. Both the desires of love are thus contained implicitly in the higher-order desire of sanctification. And so, in sanctification, a person is loving herself.

This is not to say that in sanctification she is self-consciously focused on herself. On the contrary, if she were, she would no doubt be desiring something other than a first-order will that wills some good. But because, in the process of sanctification, a person does have a second-order desire for a first-order desire for a particular good, the state of her will is what it needs to be in order for her to count as loving herself.

In addition, in sanctification a person is also loving God. By desiring a good will, she desires a good that God himself desires—that is, her internal integration and with it the possibility of her union with God. She thereby also desires what is good for God—namely, that God have the good that God desires. So, in the higher-order desire of sanctification, at least one of the desires of love for God is explicitly or implicitly present. Furthermore, as I will show below, sanctification presupposes justification; and justification includes the other desire of love for God, the desire for union with God. Since this is so, both the desires comprising love of God are contained at least implicitly in the higher-order desire of sanctification. Another way to think about sanctification, then, is to see it as a matter of increasing in love of God.

Justification

The process of sanctification not only involves a higher-order desire for a will that wills some particular good thing, but it also presupposes a more general higher-order desire as well. That is because a person in the process of sanctification must have a higher-order desire for a will that wills to will the good. Paula's second-order desire for a first-order desire not to eat meat, for example, is predicated not only on her desires as regards her own contribution to the ethical treatment of animals but also on her general higher-order desire to be an ethical person. She cares about the sort of person she is; she wants her will and character to be such that she herself can approve them as good. So, in the process of sanctification, all the more localized higher-order desires of the person being sanctified are predicated on a global second-order will for a will that wills the good.

But where does this global higher-order will come from?

The answer to this question is contained in the complicated doctrine of justification, which is the technical theological term for moral and spiritual[32] regeneration.[33]

We can begin unraveling the complications of this doctrine by considering briefly the nature of faith and its role in justification. For Aquinas, faith is the necessary and sufficient condition for the rescue of a person from her own propensity to moral wrong and from the isolation to which it gives rise. Or, to put the point in its more familiar terms, faith is the necessary and sufficient condition for salvation from sin and for the attainment of shared union with God in heaven. On Aquinas's views, a person's moral and spiritual regeneration requires only faith on her part; a person is justified by faith alone.[34]

Aquinas takes faith to include crucially a free act of will, in which a person hates his own moral wrong and longs for the goodness that is God's.[35] This act of will depends on a recognition of one's own moral wrong and a grasp of the goodness of God, and it consists in a higher-order desire for a will that does not will evil but wills the good instead.[36] In the desire for the goodness that is God's, it also includes a willingness to accept God's help, to one degree or another, in making that sort of goodness one's own. The will of faith is therefore a global second-order desire to have, through God's help, a will that wills the good. The formation of this act of will and the perseverance in it is necessary and sufficient for justification.

Because of Aquinas's commitment to a tight interconnection between the faculties of intellect and will, on his account the will of faith is necessarily accompanied by the beliefs of faith, which include most centrally the belief that God will give help if the help is not refused. In the act of faith, a person has the belief that God will instill into his will what is needed for goodness if only he does not resist God's doing so. But I mention the matter of the state of the intellect only to set it to one side. For my purposes in this project, the salient thing is the condition of the will in justification.

To ward off gratuitous confusion, however, it should be pointed out that, as regards the intellectual component of faith, for Aquinas, there is implicit as well as explicit faith. That is because Aquinas believes it is possible to be rightly related to the object of faith without knowing some of the theological truths about that object.[37] That is, he thinks it is possible to know God, with a knowledge of persons, without knowing all or even very many truths about God.[38] According to Aquinas, some of those who lived before the advent of Christ or who live in places where Christianity is not known might nonetheless count among those saved by faith because of their right relation to God, the object of faith, even if they do not explicitly hold the articles of faith. As far as that goes, even as regards knowledge about God, Aquinas's views validate implicit faith. So, for example, Aquinas thinks that pagans before the time of Christ might have implicit faith in virtue of believing in the providence of God.[39] For Aquinas, such faith is justifying, too.[40]

Finally, it is important to add here that the global second-order desire of the faith that justifies a person is compatible with any amount of first-order willing of particular evils, provided that that first-order willing does not destroy the second-order desire of faith. It is possible, in other words, for a person to have a second-order desire for a will that wills the good and also to reject a particular reform that he sees as morally needed but that he finds himself unable to accept at a particular time. This condition is, of course, one way of being divided against oneself.

Justification and love

A person's forming the justifying global second-order desire for a will that wills the good is the beginning of a process of moral and spiritual regeneration for that person. Sanctification is the continuation of that process, in which God works together with the will in a cooperative enterprise that gradually integrates the willer in goodness. Aquinas thinks that a person's justification is inevitably followed by her sanctification if only she perseveres in the global second-order desire of the act of faith. That is because Aquinas, like Augustine, believes that God loves all human persons; and so, on Aquinas's account of love, God desires the good for each human person and desires to draw every person to union with God. As long as a human person does not resist God's help or reject God's grace, God's desires for that person will be efficacious. For this reason, as long as a human person has a second-order desire for a will that wills the good, she will eventually have what she wants: a will entirely integrated in goodness. Aquinas's view of moral regeneration is thus a variation on an old proverb: *If wishes were horses, then beggars would ride.* For Aquinas, wishes *are* horses, and beggars *do* ride.

For justification as for sanctification, the higher-order desire of the will of a person in the process is a desire for a desire for what is good—and so it is also a desire for the good. To that extent, it is a desire for the good God desires to have and consequently a desire for the good for God. Like the higher-order will in sanctification, the second-order desire of justification is, therefore, one of the desires of love of God. In justification, however, the higher-order desire is not just a desire *that* there be something which is good—for God or for the desirer or both. On Aquinas's account of faith, it is also a desire for the goodness of God. As I have explained elsewhere,[41] because Aquinas sees goodness as God's nature under a certain description, on Aquinas's views a person who longs for God's goodness is a person who longs for God. The second desire of love is, therefore, especially ingredient in the act of will essential to faith. It is a desire for a person, where the person is God. Justification can therefore also be thought of as the beginning of love of God.

Sanctification and justification are thus two parts of one and the same process—namely, the process of growing in love for God. Since God is perfectly loving and always present, at least with minimal personal presence, to every human person, the only thing missing for mutual closeness between God and a human person is on the side of the human person. For this reason, justification and sanctification not only integrate a person around the good and thereby unite her with herself; they also unite her, in increasing degree, with God in love.

Grace and free will

Given this necessarily brief exposition of the theological doctrines of justification and sanctification, we can profitably return to the question I raised above: where does justification's higher-order desire for a will that wills the good come from? How does it originate?

We might suppose that it originates, like any other desire, in the will of the desirer. But, from Augustine's time onward, for philosophical and theological reasons, the tradition of thought Aquinas inherited rejected this answer. It is not possible to review that history in passing here, but the basic idea behind it is not hard to understand. If what needs to be explained is the ultimate origin of a moral and spiritual rebirth, then it is hard to see how it could be explained as a function of the will of the person whose moral and spiritual regeneration it is. Any will that wants to will the good is already in the process of such regeneration.

The impetus for the regeneration therefore has to come from without. But, for the same reason, there can be no question of *cooperative* grace in justification. God can cooperate with the will in the process of sanctification because God's grace can work together with the good higher-order desire that is already present in the will of the human person being sanctified. The very beginning of moral regeneration, however, is the point at which the will first forms the global higher-order desire for a will that wills the good. The formation of that higher-order desire in the will cannot be the result of cooperation between God and a higher-order desire in the human will, because the thing whose origin needs to be explained is precisely *that* higher-order desire in the human will.

It is Aquinas's position that a human person's global second-order desire for a will that wills the good is both free and also produced in her by God's action on her will. The grace that produces the will of faith is *operative*, on his views, not cooperative; and yet the will of faith is also a free act of will on the human willer's part.

There is probably more contention over how to understand this position of Aquinas's than over any other part of his work. Elsewhere I have tried to produce textual evidence to show that Aquinas cannot be classed as a theological compatibilist but has to be taken as a libertarian of a certain sort. And I have argued that Aquinas's philosophical psychology contains the resources for explaining the compatibility of his claims that the will of faith is produced in a human person by God and yet that it is a free act on the part of the human willer, in the libertarian sense of 'free.' Here I can only summarize that work briefly.

On Aquinas's account of the nature of the will, the will can assent to something or reject it, but it can also simply do nothing at all. It can just be turned off; it can be inactive or quiescent.[42] As regards volition, therefore, there are *three* positions available to the will, on Aquinas's views. Furthermore, in theory, the will can move directly from any one of these positions to any other.[43] That is, it can move from rejecting to quiescence, from quiescence to assenting, from assenting to rejecting, and so on. The will's motion is thus analogous to bodily motion. I can walk east, or I can walk west; but I can also simply cease walking east. My ceasing to walk east is not by itself an instance of my walking west. Furthermore, I can move from walking east to ceasing to walk east without having to walk west in order to do so. Finally, my ceasing to walk east is not a special kind of walking; it is simply the absence of walking, an inactivity or quiescence in those particular bodily parts that function to produce walking. The will's ability to be quiescent is like this, and the notion that the will can be quiescent in this way is an important part of Aquinas's account of justification, in my view.

As Aquinas sees it, before the beginning of the regeneration of justification, a person has a resistance to forming the second-order desire in which one repudiates one's own evil and wants the goodness that is God's; but the providence of God works in ways which, in effect, shepherd a person toward giving up that resistance. If in consequence a person's will gives up this resistance and becomes quiescent, then, at that point, God puts operative grace into the will of that person. In consequence of that divinely given grace, the human will forms the global higher-order desire that is the will of faith.

So, on Aquinas's views, before the beginning of a person's moral and spiritual regeneration, there are three possibilities for her will as regards the justifying act of will of faith.

(1) The will can detest its past wrongdoing and love God's goodness. (Call this 'an acceptance of grace.')

(2) The will can cleave to its past wrongdoing and reject God's goodness. (Call this 'a refusal of grace.')

(3) The will can simply be turned off as regards its past wrongdoing and God's goodness. (Call this 'the quiescence of the will as regards grace.')

On this third possibility, when the will is quiescent, it does not refuse grace, but it does not accept it either.

As Aquinas understands justification by faith, a mentally normally functioning adult human person Jerome who lacks faith has a will that refuses grace until at some moment, in surrender, that refusal gives way to a state of quiescence in the will as regards that person's volitional attitude toward his past moral wrongdoing and God's goodness. When and only when Jerome's will is quiescent in this way, God infuses grace into Jerome's will. With this infusion of grace into the will, Jerome forms the global higher-order desire that detests his own past wrongdoing and desires the goodness of God. In this condition, Jerome has a higher-order desire for a will that wills the good. On Aquinas's views, this higher-order desire is necessary and sufficient for justification; and, as long as it continues, it is inevitably followed by the process of sanctification, whose ultimate end is the human willer's complete internal integration in the good and his consequent union with God.

Aquinas does not discuss the subjective phenomenology of the psyche of a person who comes to a state of quiescence in the will with regard to something he had previously rejected. But it is not hard to find an example to illustrate the idea. Consider, for example, a person who is suffering a dangerous allergic reaction to a bee sting and who fears death, but who nonetheless vigorously refuses his doctor's attempt to inject him with the urgently needed antidote to the allergen because he has an almost ungovernable fear of needles. Such a person might not be able to bring himself to will that the doctor give him the much-needed injection. That is, if the doctor were to ask him whether he is willing to accept the injection, he might not be able to bring himself to say 'yes.' But he might nonetheless be able to stop actively refusing the injection, knowing that, if he ceases to refuse it, the doctor will press it on him. If he does this, then his will becomes quiescent with regard to the injection, neither accepting it nor refusing it, but simply turned off in relation to the injection.[44]

Although the psychology of a person in the condition represented in this example is complicated, it does seem to characterize people in the process of serious psychological change. To pick just one historical case, which makes it clear that quiescence in the will is not the same as peace or ease, consider again the case of Augustine. As Augustine recounts his struggle with himself to accept a celibate lifestyle, he seems for a short time to have been in a condition of this sort. After reading the texts that moved him strongly in the direction of accepting celibacy, he ran impetuously to a solitary place and wept bitterly. In the course of his weeping, he heard a child's voice prompting him to read a biblical text. It was only after reading that text that he finally brought himself to assent to the lifestyle change he had previously found it impossible to will. While he was still in the fit of weeping, then, he had not yet formed that assent. But it is also true that he was not any longer in the simple condition of rejecting celibacy that had marked him previously. Rather, in his anguished weeping in the garden, he was giving expression to the pain of his will's inability to accept celibacy and its simultaneous inability to reject celibacy any longer. The crisis begun in that weeping was a surrender of the will's resistance to grace, as Augustine understood it.[45] In the resolution of that crisis, Augustine brought an end to the divisions in his will by forming the second-order volition to adopt a celibate lifestyle.

A person whose will is quiescent with respect to grace and a global higher-order desire for a will that wills the good is in an analogous case, on Aquinas's account. When God gives the grace of justifying faith to such a person, he is infusing that grace into a human will that has ceased to reject it but that has not yet accepted it either. The will of such a person is in a state of privation with regard to the volition in question; in this regard, the will is just inactive. But the inactivity is a surrender, not a calm, because the person moving into that quiescence understands his quiescence as a letting-go of resistance to God and God's grace, just as the bee-sting victim understands his quiescence as a letting-go of resistance to the injection he fears.

On this interpretation of Aquinas's account of justification, the will of faith is brought about in a human willer by God; but the human willer is still ultimately in control of her will, because it is up to her either to refuse grace or to fail to refuse grace, and God's giving of grace depends on the state of her will. Because ultimate control over the state of her will is thus vested in the person being justified, Aquinas's account can give an answer to a question Augustine wrestled with unsuccessfully—namely, why God does not cause the justifying act of will in everyone. For Aquinas, whether or not God causes the justifying act of will in a person is dependent on whether or not that person's will has ceased to reject grace, and that is something for which she herself is ultimately responsible. Furthermore, since a human being not only is ultimately responsible for her state of will but also has alternative possibilities with regard to willing,[46] it does seem right to hold, as Aquinas does, that the justifying act of will is a free act, in a libertarian sense of 'free,' even though it is produced in the human willer by God.

Although the willer is in control of her will and responsible for it in this way, however, it is important to see that she manifests this control not by activity of one sort or another but rather by the abandonment of activity. Surrender of resistance and quiescence of the will are the start of the moral and spiritual regeneration required for internal integration, and for all the things for which internal integration is necessary, including especially love in its strenuous mode.

In this connection, it is important to see that surrender is not the same as submission. For Paula to submit to Jerome is for Paula to desire that something be done or that something be the case just because she believes that Jerome desires that she desire *this*, even when she herself would desire the opposite of *this* if it were not for her belief that Jerome desires that she desire it and her fear of what Jerome would do if she did not desire what he desires her to desire. It is certainly possible for Paula to submit to Jerome in this way while she helplessly hates Jerome. By contrast, in the sense of surrender at issue here, for Paula to surrender to Jerome is for Paula to come to desire *Jerome*. It is for her to desire him and union with him after a period of resistance to him.[47] On this way of thinking about the difference between submission and surrender, one can submit to someone without surrendering to him, and one can surrender to someone without submitting to him. Paula could desire Jerome and union with Jerome without thereby desiring *that* something-or-other be the case or be done just because she knows that Jerome desires that she desire this. Paula might in fact desire what Jerome desires, but only because she herself desires it as good, and not for the reason that Jerome desires that she desire this. On the other hand, Paula might desire Jerome but actually not desire what Jerome desires; she might instead desire that Jerome change *his* desires to bring them into harmony with what *she* desires.[48] So, surrender is not to be confused with submission.

In fact, Aquinas takes submission as I have understood it here as a kind of servility, and he sees servility as incompatible with love of any kind, including love of God. He says:

Servitude is the opposite of freedom. A free man acts of his own accord [*causa sui est*] . . . but a slave is a man who is moved by another in doing what he does, rather than acting of his own accord. But anyone who does something out of love for it acts of his own accord, as it were, because he is moved to act by an inclination which is his own. And so it is incompatible with the notion of servility that anyone acts out of love.[49]

Unlike submission, the surrender at issue in spiritual and moral regeneration is acting out of love; and, as I have explained it here, it is not only compatible with freedom, it in fact requires it.

Activity, personhood, and love

In various places, Harry Frankfurt has argued that the sure sign of the true self is activity, as distinct from passivity.[50] So, for example, Frankfurt says of the desires with which an agent has identified himself, "they are . . . wholly internal to a person's will rather than alien to him; that is, he is not passive with respect to them."[51] Elsewhere he says: "insofar as a person's will is affected by considerations that are external to it, the person is being acted upon. To that extent, he is passive. The person is active, on the other hand, insofar as his will determines itself."[52]

In other work, Frankfurt explicitly equates identification with caring: a person "*identifies* himself with what he cares about";[53] but to care about something, for Frankfurt, is to be active. So, for example, he says, "with respect to those things whose importance to . . . [a person] derives from the fact that he cares about them, the person is necessarily active."[54]

On Frankfurt's view, then, a person's true self is characterized by those things, especially those desires and volitions, that she cares about; and the things she cares about are the things with respect to which she is active. By contrast, for Frankfurt, those things with respect to which she is passive are not part of her true self.[55]

But here Frankfurt seems to have things wrong. Consider first the true self, where the self is understood in the metaphysical sense.[56] On the metaphysical sense of the self, a person's mind is constitutive of her; she is what she is because she is a thing with the cognitive capacities she has. These cognitive capacities include sensory perception. But to sense is to be passive; someone who senses something is receptive of sensory images and sensory information.[57] A creature that was only active and in no way passive would seem to be incapable of sensory perception. So, since being capable of cognition, including sense perception, is essential to being a human person, it seems as if a crucial element of being a human person includes being passive in certain ways.[58]

Or consider the psychological sense of the true self, and think about the human experiences we value as important for personhood. As Frankfurt points out, there are some experiences that are to be shunned as destructive of personhood and so pernicious to the true self of any human person. (One of his standard examples is prolonged boredom.[59]) By contrast, there are also experiences that people prize as greatly enhancing of personhood. The capacities that make these enriching experiences possible would seem to be part of personhood too. Such experiences include, for example, sublime aesthetic experiences and powerful religious experiences. But each of these sorts of experience has passivity as an inescapable essential element. So, for example, Edmund Burke says: "The passion caused by the great and sublime in *nature*, when those causes operate most powerfully, is astonishment; and astonishment is that state of the soul, in which all its motions are suspended . . . "[60]

Talking of her mystical experiences, Teresa of Avila says that, in the highest, richest sort of prayer, "all the faculties fail and they are so suspended that in no way . . . does one think they are working."[61] After such prayer, she goes on to say, the soul is so moved that it is almost consumed with joy.[62]

These are unusual experiences, of course, and so consider just love, which Frankfurt himself points to as particularly valuable for personhood and a significant part of a person's true self.[63] Frankfurt describes love in this way:

Loving of any variety implies conduct that is designed to be beneficial to the beloved object. In active love, the lover values this activity for its own sake instead of for the sake of advantages that he himself may ultimately derive from it. His primary goal is not to receive benefits but to provide them.[64]

Here Frankfurt's determination to anchor personhood in activity yields an unconvincing characterization of love: a selflessly active devotion to the interests of the person loved. On Frankfurt's description of love, a person could count as having active love of another and yet be indifferent as to whether or not he had any personal relationship with the person on whom he lavishes his selfless activity, as long as his activity serves the interests of that person. What is missing here is the other desire of love, the desire for union with the beloved.

To be united with another person, however, requires passivity as well as activity. Frankfurt is no doubt right in supposing that a lover wants to be active in the service of his beloved. But for a lover to be active on behalf of his beloved is only part of what his love for her consists in. The willingness to be the recipient of her loving activity is the other part. Insofar as a lover wants to be united with his beloved, he wants to receive from her as well as give to her.

Without an interweaving of reciprocal activity and passivity, then, love would be incomplete at best.[65] But, of course, even if Frankfurt were right about what love consists in, if the love in question were *mutual*, then *each* person in the mutually loving relationship would be active with respect to the other—with the ineluctable result that each would also be the recipient of the other's activity. So mutually loving relations require receptivity and passivity as well as activity, even on Frankfurt's position.

Pace Frankfurt, then, a person's true self is not just a matter of activity. Passivity of a certain sort is also important for it. In particular, love in the strenuous mode involves passivity as well as activity on the part of those who love. The union desired in love includes activity on the part of both of the persons in the relationship; and, for this very reason, it also includes passivity, since the activity of each of those who love must be accepted and received by the other. To the degree to which love is central to personhood, then, a certain kind of passivity is also among those things constitutive of personhood.

Conclusion

For Aquinas, the passivity of surrender is the necessary beginning of the regeneration on which love and union depend. Love in the strenuous mode requires that the lover be internally integrated around the good. For every human being, this internal integration is acquired with difficulty, against resistance to it—or, what is equivalent, from Aquinas's point of view, against resistance to God.[66] For Aquinas, justification and sanctification are not possible without the surrender to God that is the beginning of psychic regeneration.

In the surrender of sanctification, a person lets go of the effort to bring her will through her own activity into the state she wants it to have. Instead, she seeks God's aid for her will, to strengthen her will in the good she herself wants to will. In the process of justification, a person lets go in a more radical way. In justification, she surrenders to God by letting go of activity in the will entirely. She abandons her resistance to God by moving into quiescence in the will, so that God can regenerate her will without breaking it.

Both justification and sanctification are therefore essentially relational, and so is their goal. The point of justification and sanctification is not the growth of intrinsic, morally desirable properties in a human person Paula, even if such intrinsic increase in goodness is an outcome of these processes. The point of the processes is rather the establishment and deepening of a relationship of love between Paula and God that is undermined by the absence of psychic integration in Paula, and the ultimate end of these processes is a union between Paula and God. A second-person connection of love between God and a human person is thus what justification and sanctification aim at and effect.

Finally, for my purposes, it is important to see that justification and sanctification are also the remedy for shame, whatever its source. For shame, too, the antidote is a matter of second-personal connection to God. That is because, no matter what the standard is with respect to which a person is shamed, that standard is trumped by the standard constituted by loving relationship with God. If a person surrenders to God in the processes of justification and sanctification, he accepts that he is loved by God. To be loved by God, however, is not only to be someone for whom God desires the good. It is also to be someone for whom God has a desire.[67] In virtue of being desired by the most powerful and most good being possible, a human person is desirable by the ultimate of all standards. By *this* standard, then, all shame has to fall away. One traditional theological way of reading the erotic poetry of the Song of Songs is as a love song between God and each human person. That interpretation of the biblical text implies that every human person is, for God, "the fairest among women."[68] On the Thomistic account of love and union, justification and sanctification, the implication of this interpretation is right.

Since love requires that each of those in the loving relation be willing to accept loving activity on the part of the other, a person who receives God's love must also give to God, who must be willing to receive something from that person. The notion of an infinite God receiving something from a finite human creature may seem paradoxical, at best. But, clearly, at the very least, God can receive a human person's willingness to be in a loving relation with God. Furthermore, insofar as God does not unilaterally determine all the good things in the world that are in accordance with his will, a human being can help to bring those things about. And so God can receive the service of a human person, in that person's work for the good in the world.

It should also be said that on the Christian doctrine of the incarnation, which Aquinas certainly accepts, in becoming incarnate in Jesus, God makes it possible for human beings to give to God in a dramatic way—by feeding and sheltering him, as the mother of Jesus did, for example, or by washing his feet with her tears, as one of the women in his company is said to have done. It might seem that, even on Aquinas's theological views, that particular path for giving to God is restricted to those contemporaneous with the life of the incarnate deity. But, contrary to first appearances, Jesus in fact provides the possibility of similar service for those in times later than the earthly life of Jesus when he identifies himself with the poor: "inasmuch as you have done it to one of the least of my brethren, you have done it to me."[69] The later Middle Ages identified two kinds of lists of giving to Christ by giving to the poor. Feeding the hungry is at the top of one list; instructing the ignorant is on the top of the other. For Aquinas, then, in meeting the needs of others in the ways on either list, a human person is giving to Christ, and so also to God.

On Aquinas's way of thinking about the matter, therefore, God both gives and receives love in relationship with human persons. In this mutuality, there is a twofold remedy for shame. To be the beloved of God is to be ultimately desirable, and so there is here an antidote to shame as ugliness. To be someone who is able to give to God is to be ultimately honorable, and so there is *this* antidote to shame as well.

For these reasons, the surrender to God provided in the processes of justification and sanctification is the solution to the willed loneliness stemming from shame as well as the willed loneliness produced by the human propensity to moral wrongdoing. For Aquinas, willed loneliness is insuperable without this surrender to God, which is needed for moral and spiritual regeneration, which is requisite for internal integration, which is necessary for all love in the strenuous mode.

With this much understanding of love, its nature, the impediments to it, and the remedies for those impediments, we are now ready to turn to the biblical stories. The narratives explored in the chapters that follow are stories about a world in which God exists and is in relation with human beings, and in which there are nonetheless human persons who suffer dreadfully. In the next part, I will explore the biblical stories of

Job, Samson, Abraham and Isaac, and Mary of Bethany. When those stories have been expounded in detail, with the methodology I argued for in the first part of this book, I will then return to Aquinas's understanding of love, which plays a central role in his theodicy. I will argue that the stories and his theodicy, developed further along lines he would have found congenial, constitute an acceptable and powerful defense for the problem of suffering.

PART 3

THE WORLD OF THE STORIES: SUFFERING IN PARTICULAR

Chapter 9

The Story of Job: Suffering and the Second-Personal

It feels as though I make my way
Through massive rock
Like a vein of ore
Alone, encased.

I am so deep inside it
I can't see the path or any distance:
Everything is close
And everything closing in on me
Has turned to stone.

Since I still don't know enough about pain,
This terrible darkness makes me small.
If it's you, though—

Press down hard on me, break in
That I may know the weight of your hand,
And you, the fullness of my cry.*[1]

Introduction

In Part I of this book, I explained that my intention is to examine the problem of suffering through an exploration of biblical narratives, and I argued for the acceptability of that methodology. Now that, in Part II, I have also presented Aquinas's view of the nature of love, the obstacles to love, and the remedies for those obstacles, it is finally

---

* Rainer Maria Rilke, *The Book of Hours*, in *Rilke's Book of Hours*, trans. Anita Barrows and Joanna Macy (New York: Riverhead Books, 1996), 127.

time to turn to the stories. In this third part, I will illustrate the methodology I argued for and begin to use it for my announced purpose by examining biblical narratives, starting with the book of Job, the classical biblical book addressing the problem of suffering. In subsequent chapters, I will take up other biblical stories that, in my view, illustrate different elements of the problem of suffering. In the consideration of all these stories, I will presuppose the Thomistic account of love and union presented and defended in Part 2.

After the detailed examination of the stories, I will turn to the presentation of Aquinas's theodicy, which is the heart of the defense I am constructing. I will explain that theodicy, in which love plays an essential role, in the light of the stories considered in this part. (That is why the stories need to come before the presentation of Aquinas's theodicy and my use of that theodicy in the construction of a defense.) Aquinas's theodicy and my defense will constitute the fourth and last part of this book.

It will therefore *not* be my purpose in this chapter or any of the other chapters on the biblical stories to try to provide a theodicy or defense for the problem of suffering as the story raises it. Because I mean to use all the narratives I examine as the basis for reflection on the problem of suffering, it would defeat my purpose to formulate an attempted solution to the problem of suffering on the basis of one story alone. In this chapter, then, I want to use the methodology defended in the first part of this book to provide only a particular interpretation of the story of Job. Subsequently, after I have explored all the narratives I want to consider, I will use the interpretation of Job I offer here in the detailed presentation of Aquinas's theodicy. At that point, I will revisit the narrative and consider the hard questions it poses. In this chapter, however, I am leaving the questions of theodicy largely to one side, to be addressed later, in the light of all the narratives examined in this and the subsequent chapters.

In this chapter, then, and in the other chapters on the biblical stories, my purpose is limited. I will just focus on details of the story, and I will advocate for a particular interpretation of them. I say 'advocate,' rather than 'argue,' for the reasons that I set out in Part 1 of this book. Although it is not so difficult to rule out some interpretations of a story as false, it is much harder to make a case that one particular interpretation is the only right one. As I explained earlier, interpretations of texts can invite one to see the text in a certain light, but they cannot compel assent as philosophical arguments are meant to try to do.[2] In the chapters on the biblical narratives, I therefore do not take myself to be giving an argument that my interpretation is the only right one. Rather, my intention is to invite readers to see the text as I see it and to consider whether that view of the text makes sense to them, too. I am, of course, aware that the approach I am taking in doing so is not representative of current customs in academic biblical studies; but I have argued in Chapter 2 for the methodology I am employing on the biblical texts, and I will not repeat those arguments here.

On the other hand, it should also be said that I am hardly the first person to see the biblical stories as intricately crafted. To take just one contemporary example, Eric Auerbach's magisterial *Mimesis* made many people aware of the density characteristic of some biblical texts and the ability of those texts to convey an enormous amount with very few words.[3] Because my purpose in this chapter is not to contribute to professional biblical studies, but to give an interpretation of the biblical text useful for philosophical purposes, I have in general omitted discussion of the voluminous literature on the biblical stories under examination. Nonetheless, I have learned a great deal from other interpreters, including Auerbach, in both the contemporary and the historical periods. For the book of Job, these include not only historical biblical studies but also work by other contemporary and historical interpreters, most notably, the literary critic Robert Alter[4] and the medieval thinkers Saadya Gaon and Aquinas; but there are many others who could be mentioned as well.[5]

In this chapter, I will proceed to examine the story of Job in a way that does not track the order of the biblical book itself, for reasons having to do with the dialectic needed for a clear exposition of the interpretation I want to set out, as will become clearer in the course of the chapter.

I will focus first on the latter part of the book of Job, which contains God's conversation with Job. In order to highlight what is novel about the approach I am taking and its results, I will contrast the interpretation of that conversation produced by the methodology I am using with a very different contemporary account of the same part of the narrative given by a more familiar approach representative of current attitudes toward the book of Job.

With the illumination given by this examination of the latter part of the book of Job, I will then return to the beginning of the book in order to show something about the book as a whole. With this aim in mind, I will look in painstaking detail at the opening episodes describing God's interactions with Satan. Contemporary interpreters tend to gloss over this part of the book, partly because they take it to be extraneous to the philosophically and theologically interesting part of the book, and no doubt also partly because to contemporary sensibilities there is something vulgar and embarrassing about the whole notion of Satan. The idea of a conversation between Satan and the Deity is enough to make many people wince. Nonetheless, in the final form of the book of Job, the story of Job's life is framed by the story about Satan and Satan's conversations with God about Job. As I hope to show, there is incomparable intelligence and artistry in the form of the book taken as a whole when that framing story is understood as an integral part of it. In my view, if we abstract just the narrative of Job's life, separating it from the framing story about Satan, there is enough in that narrative by itself to show us something important about the problem of suffering. But if we see the narrative of Job's life within the broader context that includes God's conversations with Satan, the whole story that results illuminates a certain view of the operations of divine providence that considerably enriches the implications of the smaller-scale narrative of Job's life embedded within the whole.

So first I will look at the dramatic episode when God intervenes to talk to Job, which is the culmination of the dialogues among Job and the comforters. And then I will backtrack to the beginning of the book, to excavate with care the intricacies of the part of the book that involves Satan. I will have virtually nothing to say about the dialogues that make up the bulk of the book of Job, although I will presuppose some things drawn from the dialogues, such as Job's insistence on his own righteousness, as well as the nature of Job's sufferings. There are wonderful things in the dialogues, and they raise intriguing questions, the answers to which give insight into many things relevant to my purposes. For example, the speeches of Elihu contain many of the same sorts of claims about God as those that God makes on his own behalf in his conversation with Job; and consequently questions naturally arise about the relation of Elihu's claims to God's claims and to God's general condemnation of the speeches of the comforters.[6] But this is only a chapter in a book on the problem of suffering, and not a book on the story of Job; and it is not possible to do everything in one chapter. So, although I have let the dialogues inform this chapter, with regret I have left explicit consideration of them largely to one side.

The conclusion of the book of Job, which describes Job's return to prosperity and familial well-being, is regularly taken as the other part of the frame within which the real story of Job is contained; and it is also often dismissed as primitive and uninteresting. In my view, however, the conclusion of the book of Job is as important as anything else in the book for understanding the problem of suffering.

Although Job is important for my purposes because he is someone whose suffering stems from the loss of things central to earthly human flourishing, it is clear that his suffering also stems from the loss of his heart's desires. Both his wealth and his piety had given him a special position in his society as someone beloved of God. The fact of his suffering and the loss of his wealth are enough to cast doubt on that position in the eyes of Job's community, and so he loses his social standing as well as his wealth in his suffering. He also loses his children. As Job's complaints to the comforters make clear, all these losses deprive Job of the desires of his heart.

At the end of the story, however, these losses are made up in a certain respect. God's public conversation with Job has given him an even greater position in his society than he had before. After God's conversation with Job, everyone around Job makes a donation of some sort to him, with the result that Job comes to have twice as much wealth as he had before, at least insofar as wealth in his society is measured by the possession of animals. He also has ten children, just as he did before his sufferings started. So, in a certain sense, at the end of the story Job has restored to him in great abundance the things whose loss deprived him of his heart's desire. I have had to make this claim in a qualified way, of course, because at the end of the story the ten children of Job's who died in the catastrophes of Job's affliction are still dead. Although he has ten more children, these children do not restore to him the children he had lost.

So the end of the book of Job is in fact interesting for the light it sheds on suffering taken as the loss of the heart's desires. But what I want to say about this part of the book of Job cannot be adequately explained until after the discussion of the other narratives in subsequent chapters. I am therefore calling attention to its importance here only so that its reintroduction later will not come as a complete surprise or seem like an unexpected afterthought. In this chapter, I am intentionally omitting explicit consideration of this part of the book of Job, even though it will have a role to play in the final form of the defense I am constructing.

This chapter is thus limited in multiple ways. It leaves questions of theodicy or defense till later, and it looks at only some parts of the book of Job, postponing or leaving aside entirely consideration of other parts. My aim in this chapter is to examine just enough of the story of Job, as I read it, to illumine the relations between God and other persons in the story. Later in this book, I will return to those relations, to show their relevance for the problem of suffering.

Job's suffering

Because this chapter focuses on the narrative's concern with an explanation for Job's suffering, something should be said at the outset about the nature and intensity of that suffering.[7] In this connection, it is important to me to emphasize again a point made earlier in this book—namely, that nothing in any conceivable and reasonable explanation of suffering could undermine the fact or the force of that suffering. If it could, the explanation would not be an explanation of *suffering*. To explain suffering is not to explain it away. To find something that explains suffering or weaves it into some greater good in the sufferer's life is not to diminish in the least the torment of the suffering. For my part, I am awed by the suffering that, in the narrative, Job endured, and I honor the human spirit, which can stand under so much pain.

To understand the nature and extent of Job's suffering in the story, we can begin by noting that it comes to Job in two waves. The suffering in the first wave is itself complicated, but still much easier to describe than the suffering in the second wave.

In the first wave of suffering, Job loses in one day all his animals and servants, by a combination of natural disasters and human depredations; and all his children are killed by a freak accident in a sudden storm. Because of the nature of wealth in his society, the loss of the animals and servants swiftly reduces Job from great wealth to poverty, with all the wretchedness that such a precipitous change produces. The death of all his children at once plunges him into heart-cracking grief.

In these disasters of the first wave, and in their combination and suddenness, there are two different kinds of suffering for Job. I am not sure how best to define them, but it is easy to illustrate them. On the one hand, there is suffering such as physical pain or the psychological pain of sudden reversals of fortune. This sort of suffering can be shattering to the person compelled to endure it; but it is still somehow external, on the outside of personality, as it were. Job's loss of his wealth is a suffering of this kind. By contrast, the pain stemming from the death of a child is an agony of an inward sort.[8] Suffering of this inward sort is a rack on which the psyche is tormented without rest, struggling for breath. Each kind of suffering is dreadful, but the two kinds differ from each other at least in the phenomenological character of the anguish each produces. In the first wave, both kinds of suffering come to Job in the most intense way, not only because the disaster affects *all* his substance and *every one* of his children, but also because both kinds of losses happen at once.

In addition, however, the fact that they happen at once *and* the fact that some of the disasters are spawned by storm or other natural means produces a further suffering of the inward sort for Job. That is because when disasters have such suddenness and such genesis, they rattle the psyche, so that a person has trouble trusting things in the way he did before. The frightening vulnerability of human goods to forces beyond human control can be devastating to a mind forced to recognize it through catastrophic disasters. The mental distress a person endures in such circumstances can be at least as bad as physical pain, if not worse, as those who have suffered from it can attest. Psychic pain of this sort can result in nervous breakdown, when the afflicted psyche gives way under its burden.

All these kinds of suffering come to Job in the first wave.

In describing the suffering of the second wave, the text says explicitly only that Job had sore boils all over his body, so that the suffering of the second wave might seem to be just the external suffering of physical pain. But boils are disfiguring and repulsive, and therefore demeaning too. And so the affliction of boils does not consist only in the physical pain the boils cause. There is also the additional psychic distress of finding one's own body a disgusting, hostile stranger, instead of one's home, to which and in which one belongs.

Job's suffering in this second wave, however, is hardly limited to boils, even when we take into account the added psychic dimension of this physical disorder.

In the first place, there is also the ordeal of the social shunning that Job's suffering brings him by the time of his affliction with boils. As Job explains to the comforters, Job has become despised in his society because of all the bad things that have happened to him. He is publicly disdained and ridiculed even by people who are themselves outcasts in that community. Such extensive social shaming is a misery for the outcast.

But even this is not the worst of Job's troubles.

There is also the evident alienation Job endures from those who should be most supportive of him, most caring for him. The narrative highlights Job's interactions with the comforters, whose worthless, jarring efforts at comfort add to Job's suffering. But the problem is not confined to his experiences with them; it includes his relations with his wife, too. The distance his intimate companions introduce between themselves and him at the very time when he most needs their help and support is a betrayal of Job's trust in them. The endurance of the betrayal of deep-seated trust is also very painful.

But this is still not the worst.

In my view, the worst is the psychic trauma stemming from the nature and source of the accumulation of disasters that have overwhelmed Job. Job's experiences and his reactions to them leave him in a state of unending nightmare, as it were. In the narrative, Job gives a moving description of what it is like for him in this condition. In his daytime anguish, he says, he longs constantly for night and the relief of the unconsciousness of sleep; but at night, in waking and sleeping horrors, he cannot wait for day. And so neither by day nor by night does he find any rest from the torment of his mind. His suffering has plunged him into a state of mental disorder that Job himself describes as God's afflicting him with terror; this is a state closer to serious mental illness than it is to nervous breakdown. It is hard to explain the suffering of a seriously disturbed mind to those who have never experienced such a state; but the description given of it by the victims of the horrors of war, for example, has taught us to consider it with great respect. People who survive protracted bouts of this sort of suffering have endurance worth honoring, in my view. It is fearful.

This is the suffering of the second wave.

All of this, then, is what Job suffers, and it needs to be kept firmly in mind in the rest of this chapter. Explanations of Job's suffering are explanations for *this*, in all its consummate awfulness.

Second-person accounts and the book of Job

We can begin examination of the book of Job by noticing that it has a complicated form. As we now tend to read it, the heart of the book is a set of dialogues; but these dialogues are contained within a story about Job's relations to God. That story is in turn framed by a story about God's interactions with Satan, interactions that affect Job in crucial ways and cause him great suffering. The dialogues themselves consist in a heated debate between Job and the comforters about Job's suffering and God's role in it, so that the dialogues are a commentary on the story that contains them. But included within the set of dialogues is a conversation between God and Job. This conversation within the dialogues furthers the larger story within which the dialogues are contained because it consists in interaction between God and Job; the story of Job's relations to God, which is the subject in the dialogues, is ongoing in the conversation between God and Job. In addition, in his part of this conversation, God re-presents for Job God's relations with his creatures. God's speeches to Job, which are God's contribution to the conversation between God and Job and which are themselves a divine interaction with Job, consist in vivid descriptions of God's interactions with the non-human parts of his creation.

And so it is clear that, on the notion of second-person accounts I argued for in Chapter 4, there is an intricate set of nested second-person accounts in the book of Job. The description of God's personal relations with the non-human parts of his creation is contained within an account of God's conversation with Job, which is part of the dialogues commenting on God's relations with Job, which relations are themselves the subject of the story of God's relations with Job, which is in turn part of the framing story about God's exchanges with Satan. All of this taken together constitutes the book of Job.

And yet the book of Job is commonly treated as if it were little more than a philosophy treatise on the problem of suffering. The details and intricacies of the narrative and its second-person context are neglected as unimportant or dismissed as uninteresting additions to the philosophically important debate in the dialogues. Furthermore, the debate in the dialogues is treated as an unsatisfactory philosophical discussion because it is taken to break off without a decisive conclusion regarding the problem of suffering. The one thing Job wants, as he says over and over, is for God to explain to him why he suffers; and, on the common reading of Job, that is the one thing Job never gets from God.

The Anchor Bible commentary on Job is a good example of this sort of interpretation of Job, and I can show what I want to say about the book of Job more easily by taking the Anchor Bible commentary as my foil.[9] Contrary to the common interpretation exemplified by the Anchor Bible commentary, I think that Job does get what he wants in this story—namely, an explanation of why he suffers. Consequently, I also think that the book of Job is helpful for thinking about *solutions* to the problem of suffering—but only if the story is read with careful attention to its character as a series of second-person accounts.

The Anchor Bible interpretation of the book of Job

The Anchor Bible, which is typical in this respect of a common reading of the book of Job, supposes that the book gives us no help with the problem of suffering. The Anchor Bible commentator makes the point this way:

It has been generally assumed that the purpose of the book [of Job] is to give an answer to the issue with which it deals, the problem of divine justice or theodicy. This question is raised inevitably by any and every instance of seemingly unmerited or purposeless suffering, and especially the suffering of a righteous man. Job's case . . . poses the problem in the most striking possible way. A man of exemplary rectitude and piety is suddenly overwhelmed with disasters and loathsome disease. How can such a situation be reconciled with divine justice and benevolent providence? It must be admitted first and last that the Book of Job fails to give a clear and definitive answer to this question.[10]

The Anchor Bible quite rightly sees Job's reaction to his suffering as defiant. The commentator says: "Job bluntly calls into question divine justice and providence;"[11] his "bitter complaints and charges of injustice against God shock his pious friends who doggedly defend divine justice . . . "[12] Job, on the other hand,

vehemently denies that he has sinned, at least not seriously enough to merit such misery as has been inflicted on him. Justice, he argues, often appears abortive in the world and for this God must be held responsible. Hence Job infers that God has no concern for justice or for human feelings . . . [Job] wishes to argue his case with God, but he cannot find God nor force him to grant a fair hearing.[13]

On the Anchor Bible reading of the story, Job recognizes God's power;[14] but, in a series of protests against God, he calls into question God's goodness.

Here, at any rate, I think the Anchor Bible has it right. Job's passionate insistence on moral goodness in the governance of the world underlies his violent protests against

God and his demands that God be called to account. As the Anchor Bible commentator says, Job's friends are shocked at what they take to be his blasphemy. They repeatedly point out to Job the contrast between Job's limitedness, on the one hand, and God's power and knowledge, on the other.[15] "God's greatness is beyond man's comprehension . . . " the comforters say, and so, in their view, Job ought to appeal to God for mercy and forgiveness in order to be restored to God's favor.[16] But Job rejects the comforters' attitude with scorn. Job readily grants that God has power. As the Anchor Bible commentary maintains, what is at issue for Job is God's goodness. According to the Anchor Bible commentator: "[Job] charges God with vicious and unprovoked assaults . . . He cries out for vindication . . . God has afflicted him unjustly."[17] On *this* score, I agree entirely with the Anchor Bible: Job will not submit to a God who is not good, no matter how powerful he is.[18]

Because Job makes such a vehement indictment of God, the Anchor Bible commentator maintains that God's answer to Job, which comes in God's speeches near the end of the book, is

something of a surprise and . . . a disappointment. The issue, as Job had posed it, is completely ignored. No explanation or excuse is offered for Job's suffering . . . Job had already expressed his awe and wonder at God's power . . . He had questioned not divine omnipotence but [divine] justice and mercy. The complete evasion of the issue as Job had posed it must be the poet's oblique way of admitting that there is no satisfactory answer available to man . . . [19]

And, the Anchor Bible commentator adds: "The fundamental question [about suffering], If not for sin, why then?, is completely ignored . . . It is quite understandable that readers . . . are left with a feeling of chagrin at the seemingly magnificent irrelevance of much of the content of the divine speeches."[20]

What Job called into question with so much passion and rebellion was God's goodness. But, on the interpretation of the Anchor Bible, the only attribute of God's on display in God's conversation with Job is God's power.[21]

So the picture the Anchor Bible paints is this. God allows Job, an innocent person, to suffer terribly. In his suffering, Job acknowledges God's great power; but he complains bitterly about God's apparent lack of goodness. When God finally appears on the scene to answer Job's charge, however, all God talks to Job about is God's power. As the Anchor Bible reads the story, God simply fails to address Job's charge—and, if that is right, then this part of the story certainly is both surprising and disappointing, as the Anchor Bible commentator says.

A puzzle for the Anchor Bible interpretation

But I myself think that there is something even more puzzling about the story as the Anchor Bible interprets it, and it is something the Anchor Bible commentator fails to comment on. What does Job do in the face of the disappointingly high-handed description of God's power that he gets in God's conversation with him? On the view of the Anchor Bible, Job "answers with humble acknowledgment of God's omnipotence and his own ignorance;"[22] in the face of God's majestic declaration of his divine power, "Job repents and recants."[23] So, on the Anchor Bible interpretation, Job not only takes back his passionate protests, but he also submits to God with a good deal of humility.

But isn't this a surprising response to find on Job's part? It seems to me so surprising as to call into question the fundamental conclusions of the Anchor Bible interpretation. Is it really credible that, after all Job's fervent focus on goodness, after all his defiance of the power of God, he simply collapses into a heap of humility when the almighty ruler of the universe comes to talk to him and Job has impressed on him how really powerful God is? Are we to suppose that Job was something like a pompous windbag, willing to complain about the boss of the universe behind his back but utterly unable to stand up to him to his face? I do not see how one could read Job in this way. On this score, the Anchor Bible interpretation of the text seems to me very implausible.

Furthermore, the Anchor Bible interpretation cannot account for the intensity with which Job repudiates his earlier accusations against God. After God's first speech, Job says, "Behold, I am vile" (Job 40: 4);[24] and after God's second speech, Job says, "I recant and repent in dust and ashes" (Job 42: 6). If the divine speeches have as their only function reiterating the power of God, which Job has already acknowledged when he was indignant against God and insisting on an explanation of his suffering, why do God's speeches have this effect on Job? Why do they produce so powerful a repentance of his earlier attitude toward God? He could, after all, submit to God with suitable deference without going nearly so far.

The Anchor Bible interpretation thus gives us a serious incongruity in the character of Job. In the speeches to his friends, Job is heedless of everything except goodness, and he is willing to confront even the power of God to get it. But in his response to God's speeches, on the Anchor Bible interpretation Job in effect just cringes in front of power.

We can, of course, always chalk up an incongruity of this sort to the artistic incompetence of the author or editor of the narrative, though in this case it would be a fairly serious and dramatic incompetence. Even if the author or editor of the book wanted Job to be submissive to God at the end of the book, there are ways to write the story more plausibly than simply to have the rebel turn servile as soon as he hears God's assertion of his power. But impugning the competence of an author ought to be an interpretative strategy of last resort, to be employed when other attempts at explanation have failed. In this case, it would also be a particularly lame strategy, because of the magnificent artistry that is readily recognizable in the rest of the book.

An alternative interpretation of the divine speeches

The problem in the Anchor Bible interpretation arises, I think, because the Anchor Bible commentator is not attuned to the fact that, in the story, the two divine speeches are set in the context of a second-person experience, and they are also a second-person account, in their content.

Take, first of all, the content of God's speeches. The Anchor Bible summarizes the speeches this way:

Who is Job to speak out of ignorance? [God says, addressing Job]. What does he [Job] know of the founding of the earth, the subjugation of the violent sea, the dawn of day, the depths of the infernal regions, the expanse of the earth, the abodes of light and darkness, the treasure houses of the snow and ice, the ordering of the constellations and the rains . . . Can Job provide food for the lion and the raven? Does he know the birth season of the wild goats, the habits of the wild ass . . .Yahweh speaks to Job out of the storm and challenges him to show that he has divine powers.[25]

Without doubt, the Anchor Bible commentator is right in thinking that these speeches of God's describe God's power; God's great power and knowledge are certainly a central theme in the speeches. But the commentator misses an equally important feature of the content of the speeches, and it is crucial for an adequate interpretation of Job's response to them.

Consider, for example, the beginning of God's first speech, which the Anchor Bible characterizes as describing the power of God in the founding of the earth. That description is correct as far as it goes, but it is seriously incomplete. Here, in the Anchor Bible translation, is what God says to Job:[26] "Where were you when I founded the earth? Tell me, if you know so much. Who drafted its dimensions? Surely you know? Who stretched the line over it? On what are its sockets sunk, who laid its cornerstone, while the morning stars sang together, and all the sons of God rejoiced?" (Job 38: 4–7).[27]

As the Anchor Bible correctly maintains, these lines represent God as having the immense power to create the earth. But they also show God's role in a community that participates in God's creating by watching what he does and rejoicing in it. Furthermore, this community is not just passive in watching. It responds to what it sees God doing, and the response is communal, too: the morning stars sing together. When God creates the earth, then, he does not create alone. He shares his creating with a community of his creatures who rejoice together at his creating and sing. And part of the point of God's sharing with this community his creative acts is to bring such joy to them. God's communicating to Job this communal sharing of joy and song that surrounded God's creating of the earth is also part of the content of God's speech to Job. In addition, it is important not to miss the parental imagery in this part of God's speech. The group that rejoices is the group designated as the sons of God.[28] From the beginning of creation, then, and from the outset of God's conversation with Job, God is portrayed as a parent.

So what we see in this opening part of the first divine speech to Job is not just the metaphysical attributes of power and knowledge necessary for God's creation of the earth. We also see God as a person, in personal and parental relationships with his creatures, sharing what he has created with them and making them glad by doing so.

The Anchor Bible characterizes the next part of this divine speech as a description of God's subjugation of the sea. What God says in the part of the speech about the sea is this: "Who shut the sea within doors, when it came gushing from the womb, when I made the cloud its garment, dark mist its swaddling bands, when I put bounds upon it, set up bars and doors, saying, 'Thus far come, but no more. Here your wild waves halt'?" (Job 38: 8–11).

The imagery in these lines depicts God's dealings with the sea as maternal interactions between God and the sea. The sea is created by coming forth from a womb, and God deals with the sea as a mother deals with her child: he wraps it in swaddling bands; he clothes it with a garment. The description of God's relation to the sea is thus couched in the sort of language ordinarily used to portray a mother's care for her newborn baby.

Furthermore, the relations between God and the sea are characterized as personal relations.[29] The Anchor Bible takes these lines as a description of God's subjugating the sea; but it is noteworthy that in the story God controls the sea by *talking* to it. In fact, it is hard to see these lines as a description of a *subjugation*. God does not just bend the sea to his will. He does not simply wield his great power to decree what the nature and attributes of a sea must be. Presumably, God could do so with an act of will alone, without making any utterances. Or, if he wanted to determine what the sea did by means of an utterance, God could make an impersonal statement, addressed to no one in particular, of this sort: 'I decree that the sea will extend from here to there, but it will not extend any further.' Instead, what we get in God's speech is a description of a second-personal interaction between God and the sea. The speech portrays a second-person experience (as it were) between God and the sea, in which God says 'thou' to the sea.[30] As God describes his interactions with the sea in this part of the divine speech, God addresses the sea directly, in second-person forms of speech. In fact, God talks to the sea as if the sea were a rambunctious and exuberant child of his, but nonetheless a child who can hear him, understand him, and respond to him. And so, in God's description of himself in this part of his speech to Job, God brings the sea into conformity to his will by talking to the sea and explaining to the sea what it can and cannot do.

The remainder of God's speech describing the inanimate parts of God's creation continues in the same way. God portrays inanimate created things as if they were children of his with whom he has a personal relationship and for whom he has a parental concern. Furthermore, as the speech continues, God not only describes himself as talking to inanimate creatures, as he does in the section on the sea; he also describes these inanimate creatures as responding by talking to him in response. "Did you ever command a morning?," he asks Job (Job 38: 12), and a little later he says:

Where is the way to light's dwelling, darkness, where [is] its abode, that you may guide it to its bourne, [and] show it the way to go home . . . Who cleft a channel for the downpour, [or] a path for the thundershower, to bring rain on no-man's land, [on] the wilderness with no man in it, to sate the desolate desert, [and] make the thirsty land sprout verdure . . . Can you send lightning scurrying, to say to you, 'Here we are'?   (Job 38: 19–20, 25–7, 35)

Darkness and light have dwelling places, and God gets them to those places by personal interaction with them. He does not issue an impersonal decree stipulating where darkness and light must be. Rather, he himself guides them there. Darkness and light get to their proper places in the world because God shows them the way. Even the morning is disposed as it is because God talks directly to it and gives a command *to it*. And when God sends the lightning where it should go, the lightening responds by talking to God.

The explicitly parental terminology is also recurrent throughout the first speech. "Does the rain have a father?," God asks Job. "Who sired the dew drops? From whose womb comes the ice[?] The hoarfrost of heaven, who bore it . . . " (Job 38: 28–9).

As these lines indicate, then, the first divine speech constitutes a second-person account. It is not a story, strictly speaking, but it is story-like. It conveys, in the vivid sort of way a story would, a picture, an impression, of God's entering into second-personal relations with all of his creatures and dealing with them parentally.

That impression is only strengthened in the next part of the first speech that moves from describing God's interactions with inanimate things to sketching his relations with non-human animals. In that next part, what God tells Job shows not only God's power over the animals and his knowledge of their nature and ways, as the Anchor Bible maintains, but it also makes clear God's great care for the animals and his second-personal connections to them. God makes a home for the wild donkeys and gives the hawks the knowledge necessary for flight. Even in the case of the ostrich, who is portrayed as an inept and foolish mother, deprived of wisdom by God,[31] there is a loving note in the description of the beast. There is an implication that, if the ostrich's eggs and children survive, it is because God does the mother's job for the ostrich mother. She forgets, God says to Job, that the eggs she leaves in the sand are easily crushed and are vulnerable to animals that pass by. There is a tender note in the complaint that the ostrich mother *forgets*.[32] Who but God told her, or told her and reminded her, of what she was forgetting, and who but God preserved the eggs that the ostrich mother so forgetfully left vulnerable (Job 39: 14–15)?

Furthermore, the animals are portrayed as responding to God's attention to them by interacting with God in second-personal ways. For example, the raven's young do not just cry when they are hungry; they cry to God (Job 38: 41). Young and helpless animals are described as having a personal relationship with God—and so are powerful, fully grown animals:

"Will the buffalo deign to serve you?" God asks Job. "Will he stay beside your crib? Can you hold him in the furrow with rope? Will he harrow the valley after you? Can you rely on his great strength, can you leave your labor to him? Can you trust him to return and gather the grain of your threshing floor?"   (Job 39: 9–11)

The implication of these questions is that, even if a human being such as Job could not have the relationship with this fierce animal implied by the mention of all these activities characteristic of domesticated animals who live in close connection with human beings, God can and does.

The second of God's speeches to Job is different from the first in that it is focused narrowly on two great animals, behemoth and leviathan. Aquinas thought that the behemoth is an elephant; some modern interpreters take it to be a hippopotamus; and the Anchor Bible takes it to be a mythological beast. There is a similar spread of opinion about leviathan. For my purposes here, it is enough to take behemoth and leviathan as great and impressive beasts of some sort, real or mythological, which are difficult or even impossible for human beings to tame. I will refer to them just as behemoth and leviathan, with no attempt to take sides in the controversies about what exactly they are supposed to be in the book of Job.

Some of God's second speech is devoted to describing the strength of these beasts and the even more impressive power God has over them, including the power to capture or even to kill them. But there are also passages such as this: "Will [Leviathan] make long pleas to you, cajole you with tender words? Will he make a covenant with you, will you take him as [an] eternal slave? [Will you] [p]lay with him as with a bird,[33] leash him for your girls?" (Job 41: 3–5).

For Job, the obvious answer to all these questions is 'no.' For God, on the other hand, the answer is clearly different. God has a second-personal relationship even with these great beasts, who not only talk to him with tender words but cajole him, plead with him, play with him, and make covenants with him.

It is a mistake, then, to characterize God's speeches to Job as demonstrating nothing but God's power over creation. The speeches certainly do show God's power; but, equally importantly, they show God in second-personal connection to all his creatures. He relates to everything he has made in this second-personal way; and, in such second-personal interaction, God deals as a parent with his creatures, from the sea and rain to the raven and the donkey and even the monstrous behemoth and leviathan. He brings them out of the womb, swaddles, feeds, and guides them, and even plays with them. Most importantly, he talks to them; and somehow, in some sense or other, they talk to him in return. These speeches thus show God as more than powerful. They show him as engaged in second-person experience, as it were, with his whole creation, and they portray him as having a parental care toward all his creatures, even the inanimate ones.

Explanations for suffering

The divine speeches do not consist in non-narrative claims about God's relations to creation. If they did, they would be a third-person account laying out general theological claims about God's relations to creatures. Instead, each constitutes a second-person account that lets us participate, to some limited extent, in the perception of God's relation to inanimate things, plants, and animals. The speeches begin with an allusion to the morning stars singing together and the sons of God rejoicing as they watch God's creation. To some minimal degree, the speeches invite us to see what they saw. The implication is that, if we see it, we also will be inclined to rejoice. What Job wanted was an explanation of God's relations with him, and he does get it, but in the form of a second-person account. He had demanded goodness. What he gets is something of what caused the sons of God not just to find God good but to rejoice in him and in his relations to his creatures.

But what exactly is this? For the reasons I gave in earlier chapters, I do not think that this question can be answered, or at least not answered without remainder.[34] The question is a request that what is presented as a second-person account be translated into a third-person account, and I argued that this could not be done without losing what is most important about the second-person account. Nonetheless, I want to call attention to one thing that is suggested by the second-person account of the relations between creator and creatures constituted by the divine speeches.

The divine speeches suggest that God's relationship to all his creatures is personal, intimate, and parental. On one common moral intuition, a good parent will sometimes allow the children she loves to suffer—but only in case the suffering confers an outweighing benefit on the child who experiences the suffering,[35] and confers this benefit on him in some way that could not have been equally well achieved without the suffering. A good parent, that is, would not cause suffering to an innocent child of hers for the sole purpose of getting someone else to learn a lesson.[36] In the divine speeches, God is portrayed as giving the animals what they need just because they need it—food for the baby birds who cry to him, help in mothering for the foolish ostrich. Nothing in the speeches suggests that, when God considers what to do about the hunger of the baby birds, he thinks primarily about what might be a good thing for the cats in their neighborhood. God does not think about abandoning the baby birds in their need and weakness in order to benefit some other part of his creation; he does not consider whether letting them stay hungry would be justified by the good it produces elsewhere in the world. Rather, he considers what will be good for *them*, and so he feeds them when they cry to him.

In the divine speeches, then, there is not a claim but a suggestion, a picture, that leads us to think God operates on the principle I attributed to good parents. This principle applied to God is not equivalent to the justly ridiculed Leibnizian position that this is the best of all possible worlds in which everything that happens happens for the best. Rather, this is a principle just about one necessary condition for good parenting—namely, that, other things being equal, the outweighing benefit that justifies a parent in allowing some suffering to an innocent child of hers has to benefit the child primarily.[37]

Nothing in God's speeches to Job specifically describes God's relations with human beings, of course, but there is certainly a ready inference—both for Job and for the audience of the book—from the way God deals with the rest of his creation to the way in which he deals with human persons. If God deals as a good parent with even the inanimate parts of his creation, if he seeks to produce good even for infant ravens, then a fortiori in his dealings with a human person God will operate in the same way,[38] allowing that person's suffering only in case he can turn it to some outweighing good not otherwise available to the sufferer.[39] If an innocent person suffers, then, it will be only because a good and loving God, engaged in second-person interactions with his creatures, can produce out of the suffering an outweighing good for that person that is otherwise unavailable for him. The inference to this explanation about suffering is available to Job; but, in fact, Job does not need to draw it, since Job has accessible to him something epistemically and psychologically more powerful than inferential knowledge. This is cognition of the knowledge of persons sort, which is available to Job from the second-person account that God's speeches to Job are.

In addition to the second-person account of the speeches, however, Job has another, even stronger source of knowledge about God's reasons for allowing him to suffer. That is the second-person experience of God which Job has while God is talking to him. The Anchor Bible, which does not see or does not accord much weight to the second-personal interactions described in God's speeches, also does not recognize the importance of the context in which the divine speeches are set. While God has been talking to Job, what is the relation between Job and God supposed to be?

We do not have to speculate, because Job explains it in his last lines to God. "I had heard of you by the hearing of the ear,"[40] Job says to God, "but now my own eye has seen you" (Job 42: 5). While God has been talking to him, Job has been, somehow, seeing God. The communication between God and Job is thus, in some sense, face-to-face communication. I am *not* claiming here that Job's visual system, either functioning normally or in some non-normal way, is actually giving information about an embodied face. Rather, I mean that, in the course of the divine speeches, God has been somehow directly present to Job, where the presence at issue produces the kind of cognition that would require the literal sight of a human face if the cognition in question were of a human being. When Job says to God, "Now my own eye has seen *you*," he must be speaking metaphorically or analogously; the seeing in question clearly is meant to be a kind of seeing not mediated by the visual system. And yet, as the narrative portrays it, it is a kind of inner vision that is powerfully provocative of intimate acquaintance, as literal face-to-face interaction mediated by the visual system is. So, however exactly Job's seeing God is to be understood, in the narrative the second-person account of God's speeches to Job is set within the context of a second-person experience in which God is present to Job with significant personal presence.[41]

When Job raised his accusations against God's goodness, his charge was not a metaphysical complaint raised for philosophical reasons. It was a personal complaint. Before the start of the suffering described in the narrative, Job had a history of trust in God and obedience to God, as Job himself makes clear in his speeches to the comforters. Job's protest against God thus includes a charge of betrayal of trust. But for this charge, a face-to-face encounter can make all the difference. To answer a mistaken charge of betrayal, a person who loves you can try to explain, or she can just face you and let you see *her*. Barring the case of those who suffer from autism or similar disorders, a person who sees another can just *see* emotion in her;[42] and, presumably, a human person could also somehow see love in God, if the second-person experience of God were relevantly like a second-person experience between human beings.[43] Therefore, if in the narrative Job can somehow see God, who loves his creatures as a parent loves her children, he will also see, or know in some other way, that he is encompassed by that love as well.

So in the sight of God that Job has in his second-person experience of God in the course of God's conversation with him, Job has another powerful response on God's part to Job's demand for an explanation of his suffering. The sight of the face of a God whose parental love is directed even toward rain and ravens is also an explanation of Job's suffering. It explains Job's suffering to Job not by giving him knowledge *that*, but by giving him Franciscan knowledge of persons with respect to God and God's relations to Job. This is a second-personal explanation. Like knowledge of persons, it is non-propositional and so not the sort of thing to be true or false; but it can be a veridical explanation nonetheless.[44]

To say this, of course, is not yet to say that it is a *good* explanation. The question about whether it is a good and acceptable explanation, however, is one that I am postponing to the final section on theodicy and defense, after all the narratives have been considered.

One more puzzle

This way of understanding the divine speeches also makes sense of one other peculiar feature readily found in them.[45]

As many commentators have remarked, the divine speeches challenge Job. From their opening lines, with the exhortation to Job to gird up his loins, through their many prodding questions (where were *you* when I laid the foundations of the earth? does the hawk soar through your understanding?) to their final demands (who then is able to stand before me?), the divine speeches are aggressive toward Job. Instead of gentleness and consolation, the speeches have a distinct tone of indignant grandeur. It is as if God were saying to Job not "there, there, dear heart!" but rather "how dare you?!" And so the affect notable in the divine speeches implies that God is taking Job to task for complaining about God's apparent lack of goodness and love with regard to Job.

But there is a puzzle here, because, when God talks to the comforters about Job's complaints and the comforters' condemnation of Job for those complaints, God takes Job's part entirely. God says to the comforters, "My anger is hot against you because you have not said of me the thing that is right, as my servant Job has" (Job 42: 7). How are we to make sense of the narrative when it seems to be attributing to God both the view that the comforters were wrong to object to what Job said about God and also the view that Job was wrong in what he said about God?

If we simply take at face value the appearance in the divine speeches that God is somehow insulted by Job's complaints, then we will have an irresoluble incongruity in the narrative. As I said above, however, concluding that there is such an incongruity in a text ought to be a matter of last resort, especially when the incongruity is large and obvious and the text otherwise shows the marks of artistry. So before relegating this puzzle to a hopeless inartistic incongruity, it would be good to ask whether there is any way of reconciling these two elements in the narrative. One way to do so is to consider whether, in our own experience or in other narratives we know, there are ordinary occasions of the same sort. That is, are there familiar occasions on which one person

Julia accuses another person Paula of not loving her and not caring about her; and Paula responds with indignation that she is offended at the accusation, although she defends Julia to outsiders as entirely warranted in complaining as Julia does?

To put the question in this way is to suggest its answer. It is not uncommon for conflicts among people who love each other to have this feature. The same mother who is indignant with her teenage daughter for accusations that her mother lacks love will defend her daughter to outsiders for those very accusations. "When I was her age, I felt that way about my own mother," the mother may say to others who are inclined to censure the daughter's behavior; "if she were docile and obedient, I'd worry about her." And yet the mother might very well feel she had done the right thing in responding to her daughter with offended expostulation. In such a case, the mother is indignant with what her daughter has said but approving of her daughter's saying it.

Clearly, this is one among many sorts of circumstances in which it is good to give voice to an accusation that is believed to be true by the accuser but that is in fact false. But there are other circumstances as well. Sometimes an indignant response to an accusation has its source just in a healthy sense of the injustice of the accusation. But it can also stem instead from insightful care for the accuser. In these nutrition-conscious days, we have learned to ask about the bio-availability of nutrients in the things we ingest. We have learned, for example, that we do not absorb calcium from Tums, although Tums is full of calcium; we excrete the calcium we ingest in Tums, because that calcium is not bio-available to us.[46] As those who counsel the troubled know, there can also be a problem with the bio-availability (as it were) of love. Sometimes a troubled soul desperate to be fed with the love of another is surrounded by that love without being able to take it in, or even to understand that it is there for her. In her disturbed state, such a person is unwilling to believe that she is loved by or important to the person who matters to her. And, because she is in this troubled condition, she will sift expressions of love and concern on the part of the person who matters to her through the sieve of her bruised heart. She will interpret the other person's actions toward her in ways which only confirm her conviction that she does not matter to the person who matters to her. In this condition, even if the love of the person who matters to her is really there for her, it is not bio-available to her.

Sometimes the best way to convey love to a person in such a disturbed condition is precisely through indignation. The troubled person knows—we all know—that giving comfort to a person who is grieved because she believes she is unloved is perfectly compatible with not loving her. Well-bred, polite comforting is often enough accompanied by an underlying impatient uncaring. But being moved to indignation by an accusation of being unloving is not. A person who becomes indignant in the face of such an accusation is a person to whom the complainer manifestly does matter. Because this is so, and we feel it, a heartsore person can sometimes find love bio-available in an indignant rebuke when he cannot get it in any easier, softer way.[47]

And so it is possible to give a consistent interpretation of God's apparently inconsistent reactions to Job and to the comforters about Job. It is possible to interpret God as indignant with Job's accusations, either because God finds them so false or because God wants Job to understand that they are false or both. And yet it can also be the case that God approves of Job's uttering these accusations because something about giving voice to the accusations is good even if the accusations are not true.

Finally, it is worth remembering in this connection that the indignant person in this story is the Deity and the creator of Job. To appreciate the difference that this fact makes, imagine that a local political science professor at some state university has been complaining about the US president's policies. And then imagine that the president himself suddenly appears at the professor's house to remonstrate with him. The visit will astonish all those who know of it in the professor's community, and it will significantly elevate his status among them. The honor done him, the care given to him, the weight accorded his complaints will be evident to everyone, including the professor himself. Indignant remonstration on God's part in such circumstances has a connotation very different from that which such remonstration would have if it were impersonally delivered, without the visit. So, in this case too, it is important to be attentive to the second-personal context. The second-person experience between God and Job, which is the context for the divine speeches, alters greatly the import of what God says to Job.

This interpretation thus confirms the impression given by the second-personal elements in the content of God's speeches to Job. By multiple means, then, in second-person accounts embedded in second-person experiences, God is conveying to Job God's love for him. At any rate, it is worth keeping in mind that there are very few characters in any of the biblical texts to whom God speaks so much in such extended second-person experience; and there are also very few to whom God himself gives such public vindication as he provides for Job when he rebukes the comforters.[48]

Job's response to the divine speeches

The explanation of his suffering that Job gets in his face-to-face encounter with God is thus a second-personal kind of explanation. What exactly his suffering effects in him is not part of the explanation the divine speeches provide. But that they provide an explanation, and the right kind of explanation for Job, is shown by Job's response. I began by asking how we could explain Job's subsiding into humility and acquiescence after all his defiance of God and his insistence on goodness, if God's speeches to Job contain nothing but an assertion of God's power. What a closer look at the speeches makes clear is that this question rests on a false view of the content of the divine speeches and an obliviousness to their context.

If we see the speeches in the way I have argued for, a second-person account set in the context of a second-person experience, both of which show Job the love of God for him, then we can understand better why Job reacts to God's speeches as he does. Suppose you had been sure that the person who should love you the best had betrayed you, had abused your trust and used your vulnerability to her to cause you pain. Suppose that you had given vent to your anger and sense of betrayal in vehement speeches to her friends; suppose you had made these views known to her, too. And then two things happen. First, you are forcefully reminded, with a vivid second-person account, of the deeply loving character of your supposed betrayer and all the good she has done in the past. And, secondly, you see that powerful goodness and love directed toward you in her face. How would you feel? You might very well feel stricken, abashed, ashamed, and repentant—just the sort of emotions we find in Job. Job says, "Now my own eye has seen you," and he follows that line with this one: "So I recant and repent in dust and ashes" (Job 42: 6). Job wanted bare goodness, but his face-to-face experience with God goes past goodness to love.

Job does, then, have an explanation of his suffering; and, from his point of view in the narrative, it is sufficient to move him all the way from his preceding indignation against God through stricken repentance to reconciliation with God.

A broader lens

Having called into question the widely held view that in the narrative *Job* gets no explanation of his suffering, I now want also to consider the equally common belief that there is no explanation of Job's suffering *for readers or hearers of the story*. Obviously, if my interpretation is right and there is in the story an explanation available to Job, there is also *some* explanation for readers or hearers of the book, even if it is in the form of a second-person account about the second-personal explanation given Job. With entirely appropriate diffidence, however, I want to suggest that there is also available for the story's audience a further, supplemental explanation of Job's suffering, one that in the narrative is not accessible to Job. This explanation has to be teased out of the nested second-person accounts of the whole book of Job, including the parts that in the narrative are hidden from Job. Like the description of the explanation that is available to Job, this explanation for the audience of the book emerges only from careful attention to the second-person character of the narrative.

To see *this* explanation, we need to look at puzzling elements in the story apart from those in God's conversation with Job. Although at the end of this chapter I will say something briefly about some of these others, here I want to look in detail at only one of them—namely, the two episodes in the narrative having to do with Satan, which are part of the frame around the dialogues. (I will call these episodes 'the framing story involving Satan,' or just 'the framing story,' for short.) As I will show, careful reflection on the second-person experiences involving Satan and God in the framing story provides another philosophically and theologically sophisticated explanation for Job's suffering. Furthermore, as will become apparent, seeing the complexities of the second-person account in the framing story sheds light on the whole book of Job and its understanding of the nature of God's interactions with his creatures. In a sense, then, my interpretation of the narrative as a whole confirms the general medieval view that the book of Job is a story about God's providence and God's governance of creation.[49]

The framing story involving Satan that opens the book of Job suggests to many readers that, in the narrative, Job's suffering results from nothing more edifying or morally appropriate than a wager between God and Satan. Here, too, however, attentiveness to the second-person nature of the narrative and to the second-person experience between God and Satan described in it makes a significant difference to our understanding of the story. The second-person account involving God and Satan is centered on a pair of dialogues between God and *Satan*, each of which is focused on the second-person relations between God and *Job*. In these dialogues with Satan, God identifies Job as God-fearing, and Satan counters both with a prediction that in certain circumstances Job could be brought to hate God and with an exhortation urging God to bring about those circumstances. So the framing story is a complicated second-person account within which the nested second-person accounts comprising the story of Job's relations with God are embedded.

The dialogues between God and Satan are contained in two different episodes in the narrative. These two episodes resemble each other enough that they seem formulaic, in the way in which folklore and fairy tales often are, where repetition with variations on the theme is common enough to be a staple of the genre.[50] Large parts of the two episodes involving God and Satan are almost verbatim copies of each other, with a limited number of small variations. But careful attention shows that these few variations advance the story in significant ways. Furthermore, even the elements in the second episode that are verbatim or nearly verbatim copies of those in the first episode in effect have radically different import because of the different context in which they are set.

In what follows, I will examine the two episodes seriatim, in order to bring out the kind of explanation for Job's suffering implied in the framing story. At the conclusion of this examination, I will reflect on the reasons why the book contains two explanations for Job's suffering instead of just one. Why isn't Job simply given the explanation that, on my interpretation, is provided by the framing story of Satan? Alternatively, why embed the nested second-person accounts comprising the story of God's interaction with Job within the story of God's interactions with Satan? Why isn't the reader or listener simply presented with the explanation given Job? The answers to these questions show something more about the complicated structure of the book and about the workings of providence as the story portrays it.

The first episode of the framing story: Satan's coming among the sons of God

The first episode in the framing story of God's dialogues with Satan starts by noting that on a certain occasion the sons of God came to present themselves before God and that Satan also came among them. The text suggests that the gathering at issue is some sort of as-it-were family gathering—God and the sons of God—and that there is something odd about Satan's presence at it. On the one hand, Satan does come to the gathering, a fact that suggests he has a place in the as-it-were family. On the other hand, the text also makes it plain that there is something not right about simply including Satan as one more member of the group; his attendance has to be noted as a separate fact.

The ambiguous or troublesome nature of Satan's status in the group is emphasized by the way in which God greets him: where are you coming from? The question could indicate that there is something which God does not know—namely, Satan's previous location—and about which God desires information from Satan. But it could equally easily indicate God's desire to call something to Satan's attention—namely, that Satan is so far a stranger to this family group that his presence is a surprise and his previous location has been overlooked or left unremarked. Of these two possibilities, the latter is by far the more plausible. Certainly, if an adult child arriving for a celebration at his parents' house were greeted by his mother with the question "Where are you coming from?," he would know that he was being accorded outsider status and assigned responsibility for that status.

Sometimes such questions are put to adult children by a parent who is manipulative or lazily malicious. But questions of this sort need not arise from such unsavory motives. Sometimes a question of this kind is designed not to convey accusation and blame but rather to produce insight for the person being questioned; and the motive is not malice but care, or even love, for the person being questioned. There are famous examples of such questions in the ancient world, as, for example, when in the *Consolation of Philosophy* Lady Philosophy asks Boethius whether he knows he is a human being. But perhaps the most well-known examples of such questions uttered in a spirit of love and care are certain questions ascribed to God in the biblical texts. In Genesis, for example, when Adam hides himself after the Fall, God says to Adam, "Where are you?" (Gen. 3: 9). After Cain's sacrifice has been rejected, God asks him, "Why are you angry?" (Gen. 4: 6); and after Cain has murdered Abel, God returns to ask him, "Where is Abel, your brother?" (Gen. 4: 9). None of these questions is properly interpreted as a request for information God is lacking. All of them are intended to prompt introspective reflection in the person questioned, and the questions manifestly stem from care and love, not from contumely or any other kind of malice.

That God's question to Satan in the first episode of the framing story is designed to produce insight in Satan gets some confirmation from Satan's response to it, which is partly self-revelatory and partly evasive. He tells God that he has come "from roving in the earth and from walking back and forth in it." The ambiguity in Satan's status is brought out in this response. He is so close to God that he is able to join in a gathering of God's sons, and yet he nonetheless has to explain where he has come from; and when he explains it, the explanation names a process, not a location. Satan does not identify a place but rather describes the search for a place: he has been roving and walking back and forth. Satan comes to join the sons of God not from any settled spot but from a state of restlessness.

It is noteworthy, too, that Satan's restless roaming occurs on earth. The sons of God, who are described in God's speeches to Job as present with God at the creation of the earth, could be expected to find a place somewhere nearer to God than the earth. To the extent to which Satan is a member of the group of the sons of God, this point applies to him also. Why, then, does Satan have to describe himself as coming from a restless roving in the earth, apparently at some remove from God? Insofar as God's question elicits from Satan a response that clearly would prompt in Satan some reflection about himself if he pondered it, it seems reasonable to take the question as intended to elicit such reflection from Satan. Consequently, it is also reasonable to take God's question as caring, at least in a Socratic sort of way.

As far as that goes, Satan's restlessness and his ambiguous status among God's sons evince not only some degree of alienation from God on Satan's part but also some absence of peace in Satan in that condition. The alienation and the lack of peace constitute problems for Satan and also for anyone who cares for Satan. And it seems right that God should be among those who care for Satan, as God's opening question to Satan suggests he is, on my reading of it. Insofar as Satan still fits somehow into the group of the sons of God, to that degree God will have and ought to have for Satan the sort of attitude he has toward the group of his sons—that is, he will have at least some care and love for Satan.[51]

The first episode of the framing story: God's question about Job

In this context, it is helpful to think about the reasons why in the narrative Satan is in the ambiguous, unsettled condition he is. What makes a person restless? To rest is to stay somewhere without moving on. Moving on voluntarily, as Satan does in his restless roving, is prompted by a desire to be somewhere else; and that desire indicates that the place from which one wants to move somehow fails to meet one's needs or desires.[52]

The inability of a person to find a place that meets his needs and desires might stem from a fault in the world around him; all the places he has so far passed through might be seriously flawed, at least with regard to what the restless rover wants. But the inability might also stem from a flaw in the rover. A person who is not integrated in himself is someone who (in one way or another) wants and does not want the same thing. Catullus gives expression to this sort of psychic condition when he says about the woman who fascinates him, "odi et amo" (I hate, and I love).[53] He desired his beloved Lesbia and repudiated her at the same time. Consequently, whether he was with her or apart from her, he did not have what he wanted. A person in such a condition is certainly restless. And so restlessness can arise from an internally divided self, rather than from a flawed environment.

Since among the places open to Satan to go is God's presence, where (as the divine speeches describe) the sons of God find joy in shared attention with God, it is hard not to suppose that in Satan's case the flaw producing restlessness lies in him, rather than in the world around him. The turmoil in Satan shown in his subsequent exchanges with God only confirms this interpretation.

So the first episode suggests that Satan is an alienated and internally divided son of God, and it portrays God as exercising care for Satan through questioning intended to elicit insight on Satan's part about his condition.

Given this reading of the exchange between Satan and God in the dialogue of the first episode, one would expect that God's next part in that dialogue would be another question designed to push Satan further toward an understanding of Satan's internal state. At first glance, however, it seems as if that expectation is defeated. God does indeed ask Satan a second question; but, on the face of it, the question appears to be a change of subject, shifting attention from Satan to someone else entirely. God says to Satan, "Have you considered my servant Job, because there is no one like him in the earth, a perfect and righteous man, fearing God and turning away from evil?"

But this first-glance impression is deceiving. To see why, return to the previous example in which a mother asks her alienated son, newly arrived at a family gathering, where he has come from. Imagine that she then follows up that question by asking her son whether he has given any thought to his younger brother, who does everything right and always obeys her wishes. Only the unwary or oblivious would suppose that the second question is a change of subject. And so, although the introduction of Job might seem to be shifting the attention from Satan to Job, it would be naive to take it in that way.

How, then, should we understand God's question to Satan about Job?

One way of seeing the question as a continuation of God's earlier exchange with Satan is to understand it as exactly analogous to the mother's unpleasant question about the younger brother in the example I just gave. On this view, the question is simply a means of forcing on Satan a comparison that he is meant to feel is to his detriment. But, although this reading has the advantage that it understands the question to be still focused on Satan, however much it seems to be about Job, nonetheless it has disadvantages weighty enough to rule it out. Compelling a person to acknowledge someone else's superiority is contumelious, and malice is more evident in it than care. But, on the interpretation I am developing, God's first question stems from care for Satan. And so there would be a significant incongruity in the story if the motivations behind God's first and second questions were so opposed to each other.[54]

And that would not be the only aesthetic flaw. Read as malicious, God's question to Satan about Job would ignore all the interesting content of Satan's preceding remark, that he has come from roving in the earth. It would simply be a heavy-handed attempt to start a new attack on Satan. The content of that attack would itself be clumsy, too, because it would consist just in pointing out to Satan that there is somebody—somebody metaphysically littler than Satan—who is very good and who therefore constitutes a measure by which Satan can mark his own imperfections. Furthermore, if God's question to Satan about Job had no more in it than this, then its effect would only be to alienate Satan from God even more and to include Job in Satan's ire. On that view of it, God's question would, in effect, be an invitation to Satan to visit his disaffection on Job. The younger brother so unpleasantly brought to the attention of his estranged older brother by the spiteful question of the mother in my example can expect to feel his older brother's pain. And so not only is no care shown for Satan if God's question is interpreted in this way, but there is also no love lost on Job either. On the contrary, Job becomes just a pawn in the conflict between God and Satan.

I am aware, of course, that this is exactly how one very common reading understands the exchange between God and Satan. But, as I have been at pains to show, the rest of the story makes abundantly clear that God deals with Job in loving ways, and Job repents with vehemence after the divine speeches because he perceives the love God has for him. But if in the framing story God is simply using Job as a pawn to get at Satan, if God's question to Satan about Job were just an expression of malice toward Satan, then Job would be deceived about God when he sees God in the course of the divine speeches and finds God loving. Consequently, if we read God's question to Satan just as God's forcing an invidious comparison on Satan, the narrative as a whole would have a serious aesthetic incoherence. On this reading, the same narrative that makes God majestic as well as loving in the discourses with Job would have to be taken as making God petty and unloving in the conversation with Satan; and that would be a fairly dramatic aesthetic incoherence.[55]

The first episode of the framing story: Reprise and reconsideration

Is there, then, another way to understand God's question to Satan about Job that ties it more tightly to the preceding exchange between God and Satan but that also constitutes a further manifestation of divine care for Satan? And is there a way in which this question of God's can be read as integrally connected with Satan's immediately preceding answer that he has come from roving the earth restlessly? That is, is there any way of understanding God's question to Satan about Job as the appropriate next step in the conversation between God and Satan begun by God's first question to Satan and Satan's answer?

One clue to the complications of the conversation Satan and God are having is given by Satan's answer to God's question about Job. Satan's answer begins this way: "Does Job fear God for nothing? Haven't you made a hedge all around him and around his house and all that is his?" (Job 1: 9–10). One thing to ask about these lines of Satan's is how Satan knows that there is a hedge about Job, and about his house and all that he has. How is such a hedge perceptible to Satan? It is notable that neither Job nor the comforters seem to be aware of any such hedge. Job believes that God has made him prosperous; but that is not the same as believing that God has made him prosperous by making a hedge about him that wards off predators and disasters. Presumably, then, Satan knows about that hedge, as Job does not, because Satan has run into it and found he could not get past it. But Satan's knowledge would come through this route only if Satan had been trying to do some harm to Job—or to Job's house or to something that belonged to Job. If this interpretation is right, as I think it is, then it gives some insight into the nature of Satan's actions as he roves through the earth. He is trying to do harm to the inhabitants of the earth, and he is deliberately trying to thwart what God is doing with and for at least some of those inhabitants.

Furthermore, nothing in these lines of Satan's suggests that Satan supposes he is revealing himself to God by letting God see that Satan knows about God's hedge around Job. In fact, Satan is not in the least apologetic, or hesitant in any other way, about the implication that he has been trying to get past God's hedge. Presumably, Satan's attempts to harm a person God is determined to protect is old news to God, and Satan knows that God knows that Satan knows this. And so it is somewhat misleading to see Satan's coming among the sons of God as analogous to a wayward son's showing up unexpectedly at a family gathering. It is more nearly analogous to the sudden appearance at such a gathering of a son who has become a member of a group dedicated to overthrowing the things his parents love best.

On this way of understanding what is happening in the first episode of the framing story, we should take God's initial question to Satan—"Where are you coming from?—as a question not just intended to call Satan's restlessness to Satan's attention but also designed to bring out into the open the estrangement between God and Satan. Imagine that, in the turmoil of an election year, the son of a Democratic president who is up for re-election joined the campaign of the rival Republican candidate and worked hard to defeat his mother. If that son unexpectedly turned up at a family gathering and were asked by his President mother, "Where are you coming from?," we would understand clearly the complexity of the question. In answering, the son has to confront in his mother's presence his own alienation from his mother and his active efforts to undermine her. Reflection on the nuances of the dialogue between God and Satan suggests that Satan is in an analogous case. However candid it may appear, then, Satan's answer *(from roving in the earth and going back and forth in it)* has in fact got something evasive about it, as if her counter-culture son were to reply to the analogous question by explaining to his Democratic President mother that he had been steadily on the move for a while, covering and recovering a lot of territory—when he knows that she knows (and he knows that she knows that he knows that she knows) that he has been working against her.

This way of understanding God's first question and Satan's response to it illuminates the next part of the exchange between them, and it suggests one way of construing God's question to Satan about Job. On this interpretation, God's question about Job is not a change of subject from that of God's preceding question to Satan. Rather, it is as if the Democratic President were to respond to the evasive answer of her opponent-son by forcing out into the open a particularly sore spot in their relations—namely, the fact that her son has been trying to subvert (though entirely without success) the ultimate Democratic stronghold. It is as if the President mother were to say to her antagonist son, "Have you thought about my very strongest, most dedicated, most loyal supporters in Massachusetts?" If this question is asked when the President knows that her son knows that the President knows that the son has been laboring unsuccessfully to turn those very supporters against his mother, then the question makes perfect sense as a follow-up to the first question, "Where are you coming from?"

In fact, it is especially appropriate, given the evasive nature of the answer to that first question.

In just this way, God's question about Job overturns the evasion of Satan's earlier answer, brings the opposition between God and Satan out into the open where it can be examined, and also in effect puts Satan on notice that he is bound to lose in the course he has chosen. God's question about Job is, after all, not asked with any apparent anxiety.

This interpretation of God's second question to Satan, about Job, also helps to explain the unmistakable note of frustration that modulates the complaint in Satan's reply. When Satan says bitterly, "Does Job fear God for nothing?," it is as if the hostile son in my example were to respond to the President's indication of her diehard Democratic supporters in Massachusetts by expostulating, "Supporters?! *What* supporters! You *pay* them for their support!" Satan's response to God's question about Job remonstrates in the same sort of way. In response to God's asking whether Satan has considered God's specially devoted and God-fearing servant Job, Satan protests that God has made a hedge about Job and all that is his and has blessed the work of his hands and made him rich.

In this context, it is important to notice that there is something jaded or cynical in Satan's indignant response. Seeing that this is so sheds additional light on the character of God's question. God points to Job as the most righteous, the most pious, the most God-serving of men. Satan's rejoinder paints Job as hypocritical and self-seeking, as given to religion just for the sake of prosperity, as offering real allegiance only to wealth. The cynical tend to see everything through the projection of their own inability to integrate around goodness. The cynical person sees romantic love as only lust, political leadership as only power-seeking, disagreement as only personal enmity, compassion and benevolence as only manipulation. In short, the cynical person sees others through the lens of his own character; because his character is divided against itself, it tends to mix an evil, such as manipulation, with any good, such as compassion, that it sees. And so a cynical person, who sees others through his understanding of himself, has a seriously impaired vision.

In addition to the defect in vision it produces, cynicism has the additional drawback of impeding the very integration of character that the cynical person lacks and needs. All appeals, all examples, all loveliness that might call to him are disfigured and so undermined by the distorting lens of his cynical view. When God asks Satan to consider Job, he is therefore challenging Satan to come to terms with the fact that there is at least one thing in the world that is superlatively good. A cynical person who could be brought to admit that even one thing in the world was really good would have made a crucial concession, from which further internal integration could come.

And so we can understand God's question to Satan about Job as designed not only to bring Satan to honesty and insight about his relations with God but also to shepherd Satan toward some inner integration around the good. God's question about Job is therefore like God's initial question regarding Satan's whereabouts. It is born of care and expresses love.

A non-acerbic remark about patience

Before going further, I should acknowledge I am under no illusions that every reader will readily accept so complex an interpretation of these lines in the first episode of the framing story. For some people, this part of the book of Job has to be read as nothing more than a primitive bit of folklore, morally deplorable and devoid of artistic value. But I would say that, just as patience is needed for the intricacies of the left-brain pattern-processing characteristic of analytic philosophy, so a similar patience is needed for the kind of right-brained dissections of stories characteristic of those who are able interpreters of second-person experiences and second-person accounts.

Timothy Williamson says acerbically of those who are deaf to the detail of analytic philosophy: "Impatience with the long haul of technical reflection is a form of shallowness, often thinly disguised by histrionic advocacy of depth. Serious philosophy is always likely to bore those with short attention-spans."[56]

In my view, an analogous point holds for those impatient with the painstaking scrutiny of stories. Serious insight into second-person experiences and second-person accounts is always likely to strike those short-sighted in interpersonal relations as eisegesis.[57] So, if a tendency to eisegesis is the Scylla here, a tendency to autism (as it were) is the Charybdis. There is more than one kind of impatience to worry about in philosophy.

On the narrative's own showing, the story of Job is set within the context of the framing story of Satan, which grounds and explains it. In my view, seeing the love on God's part toward Satan is, therefore, important for understanding not only the framing story of Satan but the entire book of Job as well. It is my hope that those readers patient enough to make their way through this scrutiny of the framing story involving Satan will find that it gives an interpretation of the whole book of Job that has something intuitively compelling about it.

With this much *apologia* for my approach, we can return to the details of the framing story.

The first episode of the framing story: an objection

Someone might wonder why, in the narrative as I am reading it, Satan would bother to come to the gathering of the sons of God at all. In the analogous case of the President's son, we might well wonder why a hostile son would turn up at a family gathering when he is alienated from his President-mother and has been working to undermine her values and cherished projects. In the case of the President's son, the answer will be some complex mix of mutually undermining motives: a determination on the son's part to show that he has every right to attend family gatherings if he wants to do so; a desire to make trouble for his mother and show up what he takes to be her flaws and failures; an offensive glee at the thought of the discomfiture his family will have when they see him; and a real if unacknowledged yearning for the good he had when he was in harmony with his family. If we understand the son's motives as a mix of this sort and apply them in some analogous sense to Satan, then the nature of the complications of God's conversation with Satan—the need for such complications—becomes clear.

Here, however, our own impatience with people at enmity with us, together with a little folk theology smuggled in, might raise in someone a theological objection. If in the story Satan and God have the sort of relations I have been sketching, then why would God not just reject Satan? Why would God not, as it were, throw Satan out of the house, instead of letting him stay among the sons of God and asking him psychologically probing questions? What is the point of the complicated dance of conversation God initiates? After all, Satan is at enmity with God; and, on common theological doctrine about Satan, Satan's enmity is irrevocable. On this theological doctrine, for one reason or another, Satan's repentance and moral regeneration, his internal integration and return to harmony with God, are ruled out. Since this is so, why would God bother with him? Why would God talk to him? Why would God not just eject him and dismiss him?

But, even if it were true in the story (as distinct from theologically accepted) that moral regeneration were impossible for Satan, degeneration presumably is not. Surely, it is possible even for an irrevocably hostile Satan to become more internally divided and more alienated from God than he is. Therefore, even if the theological assumption in the objection were accepted in the narrative, there would still be some purpose in the care manifested by God's questions, which are designed to bring Satan to insight into himself and his actions. It is possible that God's care for Satan might keep Satan from getting worse, even if it were inefficacious to make Satan better.[58]

In addition, however, why suppose that real love, divine love, stops when it meets an irrevocably hostile response? There is love in a mother's trying to minimize the distance between herself and a hostile grown-up child, even if she knows that she will meet with nothing but enmity in response; and to the extent that her love is good, so is its expression in her relations with her antagonistic child. It is a sad thing in the world when an adult child is alienated from her mother, but it would not make the world a better place if the response of her mother were to become hostile toward her.[59]

So God's questions to Satan do not assert love, but they do express it by their delicate and ingenious probing of the internally divided part of Satan's mind. And there would be point and purpose in the loving care of God's dealing with Satan in that way even if it were true in the story that Satan's alienation from God is irrevocable and God knows it.[60]

The first episode of the framing story: Satan's answer to God's question about Job

Satan's response to God's question about Job is cynical, and it is important to see that its cynicism constitutes an accusation against God as well as against Job. Satan implies that

God is not playing fair in providing prosperity for Job and in protecting that prosperity against depredation. On Satan's view, God is buying Job's love and worship by trading prosperity for devotion. Furthermore, Satan also implies that God is colluding with hypocrisy and self-seeking on Job's part. On Satan's view, if prosperity and love of God were not on the same side but were rather separated, then Job would show what it was he really wanted. Job would make it plain that the main motivation for his behavior all along was only a desire for prosperity. Put out your hand against him, Satan says to God, and touch what belongs to him; he will curse you to your face then. With prosperity removed, on Satan's view of the situation, Job will not continue to love God but will rather rebel against God. For God to protect Job's prosperity is thus for God to enable Job's hypocrisy and to bribe him for his love. So Satan's answer to God's question about Job impugns not only Job's love of God but also God's goodness.

It is worth noticing in this connection that, when Satan describes the effect Job's loss of prosperity can be expected to have, what Satan imagines is that Job will make a violent break in relations with God. That is, Satan's prediction is not that Job will lose his faith, or that Job will find his way into the worship of some other god, or even that Job will despair and try to throw his life away. What excites Satan's interest and what he throws at God as a likely outcome is that Job will hate God and curse him to his face. In the story, although Satan is somehow still tied to God by a personal bond, he is also hostile to God and working actively and openly against him. Satan's assertions about Job imply that, if God were not improperly keeping Job attached to himself through bribery, Job would be like Satan in this respect.

Furthermore, Job's rebellion against God is not just an outcome that Satan is predicting; it is one that Satan has already been working hard to achieve. Since Satan believes that the loss of prosperity will turn Job against God and since he has discovered the hedge around Job as a result of trying to wreck Job's prosperity, then, manifestly, Job's rebellion against God has been Satan's aim all along. As far as that goes, in his response to God's question about Job, Satan is still working to achieve that same end. That is why Satan urges God to undertake a course of action that he predicts will have as its outcome Job's cursing God to his face.[61]

The first episode of the framing story: Trust in goodness

There are two further things about Satan's answer to God's question about Job that are helpful to see. In differing ways, each of these things has to do with trust in goodness.

In the first place, although Satan's view of Job is manifestly cynical, there is nonetheless still something disconcertingly on the mark in his claims about Job.

On the one hand, it is true that God praises Job to Satan as the best among human beings, either all the human beings of his time and place or maybe all human beings *simpliciter*. And surely the person singled out by God for being praised to Satan in this way had better really be an unusually good person. On the interpretation I have been developing, care for Satan in his internally divided state underlies God's question to

Satan about Job's notable goodness, but only a truly good person has any chance of getting past Satan's cynicism. Perhaps more importantly, for God to praise a person to Satan is to expose that person to a powerful enemy. Only a person manifestly meriting God's praise could be suitable for being made the object of Satan's attentions in this way. And so Job's being worthy of God's praise is important for this part of the story. We can take it, then, that in the world of the narrative Job is in fact outstanding in goodness.

On the other hand, however, the story tells us not only that Job was more righteous than everybody else but also that he was richer than everybody else (at least in his part of the world, at that time). And Satan's answer to God calls attention to this fact in a way designed to undermine trust in Job's goodness.[62] What should we think about religious devotion and compassion toward the poor evinced by a man who is enormously rich and living in great comfort? The piety and compassion of such a person are not bogus; a cynical attitude toward them is entirely out of order. But, as the later speeches of the comforters make clear, in the culture depicted in the narrative it is customary to suppose that affluence is the reward for piety and uprightness. In those circumstances, there has to be a certain inchoateness about the motivation for uprightness. When uprightness is joined to superabundant prosperity, the motivation for the uprightness is murky. At best, the source of the uprightness is uncertain; and, because it is untested, to that extent the commitment to righteousness is comparatively shallow. There is, therefore, something less than optimal about virtues developed and preserved in great affluence. So, until prosperity and goodness are pulled apart, it may not be a determinate matter whether Job loves the good for its own sake, or whether what he loves is mingled good and wealth.

This is not to say that Job's motivation is corrupt. If a woman's husband is never sick, it might be indeterminate whether her love for him is a love that would be strong in sickness as well as in health; but to say that it is an indeterminate matter is not to say that she does not really love him as things stand. Perhaps we could understand a psychic condition of this sort through an analogy with a person's physical condition. Physical condition is a matter of strength and of endurance, and these are not the same. No doubt, there is an analogous psychic distinction. A person with great but untested moral, spiritual, or psychological excellence has strength; but, without the exercise produced by testing, endurance is undeveloped or at least unclear. For this reason, it is uncertain what would happen if, for example, worldly ease and moral excellence were not conjoined. To the extent to which it is unclear, to that same extent the source of the moral excellence is also indeterminate.[63] Commenting on this very point, Thomas More says:

even when the wealthy are very good, their virtue in conforming their will to God's and in thanking God is still not like the virtue of those who do the same in tribulation. For as the philosophers of old said so well on that subject, virtue consists in things of hardness and difficulty. And . . . it is much less hard and less difficult, by a great deal, to be content and to conform our will to that of God and to give him thanks, too, when we are at ease than when we are in pain, or in wealth rather than woe . . . This the devil saw when he said to the Lord God, about Job, that it was no wonder Job had a reverent fear of God, since God had done so much for him and was keeping him in prosperity . . .[64]

If we think of Job's moral state in this way, concern about the source and power of his uprightness is compatible with the praise of him given by God and the narrator of the story. On the interpretation I have been developing, if Job had *not* been morally praiseworthy, God would not have risked him as he did when he praised him to Satan.[65] Just because Job is worthy of as much moral praise as God gives him, there is good reason for God (and also for us, the audience of the story) to think that Satan's prediction about Job will turn out to be false when Job has to choose for or against steadfastness in love of God.[66] On the other hand, the combination of untested moral excellence with great wealth does have something disquieting about it.

And so, as is often the case with those who are cynical, Satan's unwarranted attack on Job battens on something in Job that does warrant some attention, even if it in no way merits Satan's accusation. In this way, then, in the narrative what Satan says about Job calls into question trust in Job's goodness—on God's part, and on the part of the narrative's audience as well.

This is the first of the things implicit in Satan's claims about Job to which I want to call attention. The second emerges when we consider the way in which God grants Satan what he wants.

The narrative makes clear that God's trust in Job's goodness is in direct proportion to God's distrust of Satan's malice. In the story, God clearly expects that Satan will put out his hand against Job as soon as God removes his protecting hand from Job. God knows that Satan knows that God knows removing the hedge about Job is equivalent to delivering Job over to Satan's attack. And so, although in the first episode God does remove his hedge from around Job, he does not do so entirely. Satan had complained that that hedge was around Job, his house, and all that belonged to him. In this first episode, God is prepared to lift his protection only from Job's house and possessions. He does not remove the hedge from around Job himself. God thus takes no chances with Satan; he makes sure that Satan *cannot* lay a hand on Job himself.

More importantly, however, although God permits Satan to exercise his malice against Job in one way, God refuses to accede to Satan's malice in another way. What Satan wants is for *God himself* to attack Job's house and possessions, but in the story God does not in fact do so. Rather, he goes only so far: he removes his protection and thus leaves Job in Satan's hands. God does not reach out his own hand against Job.

It is as if Satan and God were both clear on the significance of the distinction between doing and permitting harm. God will allow Satan to harm Job, but he will not do so directly himself. That something important for each of them hangs on the distinction is confirmed by Satan's returning to the point later, when he comes back for another try at Job in the second episode in the framing story. At that point, too, what Satan wants and what God refuses to give him is that God himself turn his hand against Job.

Now why in the story does it matter to Satan (and to God) whether or not Job is afflicted at *God's* hands? It is worth noticing in this connection that God identifies Job in part by Job's relationship to God: Job is a servant of God's (as Satan clearly is not, at least not willingly) and God-fearing. Satan's own focus is also explicitly on Job's relationship to God. In each episode, what Satan predicts as the outcome of the action he is urging on God is that Job will curse God *to his face*. Finally, we should notice that Job's suffering and the test that it constitutes for Job remain the same whether that suffering is at Satan's hands or at God's. What is altered by having Job's suffering come at God's hands is only something in the relationship God has to Job. And so it seems as if what Satan seeks is precisely a disruption of that relationship between Job and God. What Satan anticipates and cares about is an alteration in Job's second-personal relation, his face-to-face relation, with God.

Satan's own story of alienation from God, marked by distrust on both sides, thus includes a struggle between Satan and God over an attempt on Satan's part to alienate Job and God from each other. Satan gains in that struggle if Job distrusts God and rebels against him. But Satan also gains something if God refuses to lift his hedge of protection from around Job. Job has a trust in God's goodness; but *God* also has a trust in *Job's* goodness, and this trust is challenged by Satan's charge against Job, as I explained above. If God were to insist on continuing to protect Job with a hedge around him, then we would quite rightly wonder whether God did not in fact share Satan's belief that Job's love of goodness and love of prosperity were inextricable. In that case, *God* would be distrusting *Job*. And then Satan would have succeeded, at least to that extent, in producing alienation between God and Job.

So Satan's accusation does not just call Job's goodness into question. By the charges that accusation raises, it creates a test for God as well as for Job. It puts to the test not only Job's trust in God's goodness but also God's trust in Job's goodness and Job's care for God.[67]

The end of the first episode of the framing story: Job's steadfastness

God's response to Satan is to trust Job's goodness. God wills to take the risk of removing his hedge from around Job's house and possessions. The foreseeable (and foreseen) malice moves swiftly: all Job's house and all Job has are removed from him by means of natural disaster and human predation, each of which somehow has Satan's hand in it.

It is important to see here that the events which bring about Job's suffering give the lie to Satan's presentation of his own attitude in his complaint about Job. In that complaint, there is a suggestion of offended rectitude in Satan's protest that God is inappropriately protecting Job and rewarding Job's righteousness and piety with prosperity. Satan's charge that Job would desert God if God and prosperity were separated implies that Satan objects to God's coupling wealth and piety. But Satan's charge would have been adequately tested if Job had been deprived only of his wealth. Manifestly, Satan goes much further. When God removes the hedge from around Job's house and possessions, Satan does not diminish or remove Job's *prosperity*; he strips Job of *everything*, and he kills all Job's children in addition.

Satan takes advantage, then, of the lifting of God's protection of Job to afflict Job as much as Satan is able to do, and much more than is necessary to try Job on Satan's charge. And so Satan tips his hand. His aim in afflicting Job is not to test the truth of his cynical charge that Job's only motivation for piety and uprightness is a desire for prosperity. What Satan cares about is Job's relationship with God. Satan's real aim is to use suffering as a means to drive Job into alienation from God.

And in *this* effort Satan fails. Although the disaster for Job is enormous, Job blesses God at the end of it; he does not curse God.

One obvious question to ask here is why God would let Satan go as far as he did.[68] Since the story makes clear that without God's withdrawal of his protection Satan can do nothing to Job, why does God withdraw as much of his protection as he does? Why not limit Satan's attack to the removal of Job's prosperity only and nothing more? This question should not be taken as equivalent to the question whether God is justified in allowing Job's suffering, which is the question of theodicy that I am postponing till after all the narratives have been considered. It is rather a question asking just for elucidation of God's motives in this story.

One way to answer this question is to consider what God's giving rein to Satan's malice brings about.[69] It is reasonable to suppose that the effects brought about by Satan's actions give us some insight into God's motivation for permitting those actions.

To begin with the obvious, then, Satan's attack effects changes in Job. There is Job's obvious and precipitous descent into grief and suffering. But, in addition, Job's suffering removes whatever indeterminateness there was previously in Job's motivations or dispositions as regards God and prosperity. In the aftermath of his suffering, Job takes his stand with God; and his love of God is only for God's own sake, not for the sake of wealth or its attendant community standing and other desirable effects. More importantly, Satan's attempt at introducing enmity between Job and God has not only failed, it has backfired. Job's manifold losses and his faithful response to God in the aftermath of those losses refine him by fire. In consequence of Satan's attack, because he is steadfast in his love of God under stress and in affliction, Job draws nearer to God instead of turning away from him.

In the narrative, these changes in Job are one important consequence of God's allowing Satan so much latitude in his depredations of Job, and I will return to reflect on it later in this chapter. But it is worth seeing that there is a further consequence which has to do with Satan himself. Job's steadfastness in suffering and his unambiguous adherence to God's goodness give Satan an example of moral excellence and love of God on which Satan's cynicism can no longer get any rational purchase. Consequently, Satan also gets what he himself needs and what the care evinced in God's questioning Satan was meant to give him. God's aim as regards Satan is thus also dramatically furthered as a result of Satan's attack on Job.

And so, one might have thought, the story should end at the point at which Job blesses God rather than cursing him, or maybe with Satan's response to Job's blessing God. God's permitting Satan's attack on Job has drawn Job closer to God; and it would have diminished the distance between God and Satan too if Satan would have let it do so. The story therefore seems over at this point.

But, of course, the story does not end here. It is only beginning here.

The second episode of the framing story: Satan's coming among the sons of God

The second episode in the framing story of Satan, and the next stage in the story of Job, is inaugurated by a repetition of the opening lines in the first episode: there is a gathering of the sons of God, and Satan also comes among them.[70] God asks Satan the same opening question as before and gets the same line as before by way of answer to it. As I explained at the outset, we could chalk these samenesses up to folkloric love of repetition; but the narrative does not support the theory that, like Homer, this biblical author or editor enjoys dilating his text with reiteration of details for no other reason than the pleasure that the reiteration gives him.[71] On the contrary, everything suggests that the biblical author or editor is a kind of miniaturist, who loves to make small details carry great weight. Furthermore, it is this second episode that inaugurates the entire rest of the book, including the dialogues about Job's suffering and Job's reconciliation with God in the end. In the story, therefore, the second episode of the framing story is pivotal. So it is worth considering whether there is a way to understand it other than as a folkloric repetition.

One thing to notice in this connection is that, although the opening lines are the same in both the first and the second episodes of the framing story, they must be taken with a different relish in the second episode precisely because they are set in the second episode, with the first episode as background. *This time*, when Satan comes among the sons of God, Satan comes from devastating Job, as God knows that Satan knows that God knows.

So God's line to Satan, "Where are you coming from?," has a different subtext from the earlier question expressed in the same words; and it invites a different response from the response God's first version of the question was seeking. There is something new and significant at issue between God and Satan now. It is evident now not only that Satan was wrong about Job but also that Satan has been unsuccessful in his attempt to introduce into the relations between Job and God that alienation which characterizes his own connection to God. So Satan ought now to retract his accusation against Job and his charge against God; he ought to concede that Job's goodness and God's trust in that goodness have been vindicated. More importantly, Satan ought now to acknowledge to himself and to God that his cynical view of things is wrong. As the first episode of the framing story makes evident, there is a need for some resolution of Satan's own alienation from God; and Satan's conceding that his cynical attitude has to founder on the case of Job would be a beginning of that resolution. To the extent to which Satan is willing to see and honor something that is really good, to that extent he and God will be on the same side.

Satan's answering God's question about his whereabouts with a retraction and concession would therefore be both warranted and beneficial for Satan. Given what has happened in response to Satan's attack on Job, given that Satan was entirely wrong about Job, the circumstances now demand an answer from Satan that is more, not less, yielding than before. But nothing of the sort is forthcoming from Satan. Instead, Satan simply gives God the same evasive answer as before, only with more intransigence than before in virtue of the context in which he says it. In the second episode, Satan gives his vague and insouciant answer in the face of the fact that he and God both know and care a great deal about where he has been and what he has been doing there.

The second episode of the framing story: God's question about Job

In the face of Satan's obdurate answer to God's question about Satan's whereabouts, God himself raises the subject of Job. God uses the same lines as in the first episode but with an addition to the earlier description of Job. In the first episode, God called Job to Satan's attention by praising him in the highest terms. Here in the second episode God repeats the praise but with an added assessment of what has just occurred. In addition to making explicit that Job has held steadfast in his love of God and love of goodness, God's assessment forces on Satan's attention an assignment of responsibility for Job's suffering.

The narrative makes plain enough that this has to be a complicated assignment. Human perpetrators are, of course, most immediately responsible for that part of Job's suffering not caused by the forces of nature. But Satan had urged God to reach out his hand against Job, and it is clear that Satan could not attack Job as long as God protected him. It seems, therefore, that God is the one ultimately responsible for Job's suffering. Furthermore, God went only so far as to leave Job in *Satan's* hands; Satan was the one who actually brought about Job's suffering. So, if we bracket the role played by human beings and the forces of nature, then we would expect that the assignment of responsibility for Job's suffering should go this way: Satan, not God, was directly and immediately responsible for that suffering, but God was ultimately responsible for it.

In what God says to Satan about Job in this second episode, however, God gives an assignment of responsibility that is the exact opposite of this. God says that Satan has incited God to move against Job. This explanation assigns *ultimate* responsibility for Job's suffering to Satan and *direct* responsibility to God. How are we to understand this? Why isn't God's line to Satan the claim we would have expected: God has permitted Satan to move against Job?

We can find the answer to these questions by seeing the problem with the explanation we would have expected, which assigns direct responsibility to Satan and ultimate responsibility to God. That explanation assigns to Satan too much control over Job and to God too little care for Satan.

It gives Satan too much control over Job, because it assumes that, in consequence of his conversation with Satan, God simply removes his hedge from around Job's house and possessions and then waits to find out what Satan wants to do to Job. If God had operated in that way, God would indeed have only ultimate responsibility, because his removing his protection would leave Job entirely vulnerable to Satan; and all direct responsibility would be Satan's, because Satan would be the determiner of the evil that befalls Job. What God actually says to Satan in his question about Job, however, implies that God and not Satan is directly responsible. And that would be the case if God did not lift his hedge *simpliciter* but rather just selectively, so that Satan is able to afflict Job only in those very ways determined by God to be acceptable. In that case, the design of Job's suffering is in God's hands, although the design is carried out by Satan. In this sense, then, it is true both that Job suffers at Satan's hands rather than God's and that God is directly responsible for Job's suffering.

Once we see the distinction at issue here, it is clear that God ought to operate in the way his speech to Satan implies that he does. The narrative makes it evident that Satan is too malicious for God to leave Job's house and possessions vulnerable to whatever it might occur to Satan to do to Job. Although the evils that befall Job are terrible and entirely worth fearing, it is also obvious (from the history of the twentieth century, if nothing else) that Satanic evil can be much, much worse than it is in the story of Job's losses. And so, however dreadful those losses are, there is some real point in God's not letting Satan have free rein.

In addition, the explanation we might have expected, with direct responsibility ascribed to Satan and ultimate responsibility ascribed to God, assigns to God too little care for Satan. That is because it implies a certain indifference to Satan on God's part. The explanation we might have expected makes God seem like a parent who has been pestered once too often by a troublesome, hostile child and who has finally said: "Oh, just do whatever you want to do! I don't care what you do as long as you don't kill anybody." But a parent who takes this sort of attitude has despaired of his child to some extent; to one degree or another, he has given up on nurturing him or being in harmony with him. That is, in the matter at issue, he has given up on wanting the good for his child or wanting to be united with his child; and, to that extent, he has given up on loving his child. On my reading of Satan's interactions with God, however, God has not given up loving Satan. On the contrary, God is doing things designed to bring Satan as close to God as Satan is willing to go, or at least to try to keep Satan from migrating even further away. So when God says that Satan incited him to move against Job, God is not only pointing out to Satan that he, rather than Satan, was in full control of the evil that befell Job, but he is also pushing Satan to acknowledge that God acted as he did for Satan's sake.[72]

There is some confirmation of this interpretation in the conclusion of God's question to Satan about Job, when God makes plain to Satan that the purpose of God's moving against Job did not have anything to do with what Job merited. It is worth noticing that

God calls this fact about Job to the attention of *Satan*, not Job or Job's comforters. In bringing this point home to Satan, God is preventing Satan from taking the point of Job's suffering to be the punishment of Job for any act on Job's part or any state of character in Job. Satan must not be allowed to see what God does as a matter of righting some injustice in the world.

It is clear that this point is of great importance to Job and Job's community. But why in the narrative is God concerned that *Satan* should know it? The answer, I think, is that a cynical person would prefer supposing that God acts for some impersonal good, such as the maintenance of justice in the universe, to the alternative of being forced into the acknowledgment that he himself is loved. That is because love that is given to an alienated person tempts, tugs, pushes that person to receive it. If that love were once received by Satan, then some peace and internal integration would also come for him; and if it did, the alienation between God and Satan would begin to break down, too. Because a cynical person has a stake in maintaining his cynicism, because he does not want to get sucked into believing in love and goodness, because he is afraid to find that what he thought was goodness is only a snare and a delusion, a cynical person also tends to ward off the love of others for him. In making sure Satan understands that Job did not merit his suffering, God is showing Satan implicitly, and delicately, that care for Satan is at issue here.

So God's giving Satan permission to afflict Job manifests not only trust in Job's goodness, but also love for Satan. It is in this sense that Satan is ultimately responsible for what happened to Job. And God's making sure that this point does not escape Satan is one more manifestation of God's care for him.

The second episode of the framing story: Satan's answer to God's question about Job

With this much insight into God's question to Satan about Job in this second episode of the framing story, we can turn to Satan's response to the question. Satan's response has a certain desperate tone to it. In the first episode of the framing story, Satan's answer to God's question about Job consisted of an accusation explicitly against Job, and implicitly against God; and it had the patina of an interest in morality, even if it was an interest motivated by a cynical attitude. There was some moral indignation in Satan's answer to God on that occasion. Satan's subsequent actions showed the false note in that indignation, because Satan destroyed not just Job's prosperity but everything Job had, including his children. Nonetheless, in the first episode there was at least a veneer of moral concern in Satan's response to God's question about Job. In this second episode, Satan has abandoned any attempt at self-justifying moral appearances. What Satan wants this time is just for God to hit Job so hard, and so unjustly, that Job will be driven past endurance into open conflict with God. Satan's response to his first failure with Job is not to recognize and admire goodness. Rather, it is to insist, urgently, on

Job's being struck again, worse than before, till suffering goads him into rebellion and hostility to God. It is surely not accidental that here, as before, Satan also pushes for Job's being afflicted at God's hands.

What is amazing is God's response. Although God does not accede to Satan's urging that Job's sufferings be at God's hands, God does nonetheless deliver Job into Satan's hands, with the sole proviso that Satan should not end Job's life. Why would God respond to Satan in this way? Why would God not rather scorn and repudiate Satan's overheated attempts to impel God himself to attack Job? There can be no question now of any moral concern about commingled prosperity and devotion to God. Job has come through Satan's previous attack with admirable steadfastness. And what Satan says about Job in this second speech can hardly be construed as any kind of accusation against Job. If God afflicted Job severely for no fault of Job's, Job would hardly be blameworthy if he responded with indignation. In fact, in the narrative, though the comforters think Job ought only to praise God and defer to him, Job *does* respond with passionate indignation, and God sides with *Job* rather than the comforters when he adjudicates between their differing attitudes. When God joins the dispute between Job and the comforters, as I pointed out above, what God tells the comforters is that they have not said of him the thing that is right, as his servant Job has.

Why, then, does God comply with Satan this time?

The second episode of the framing story: The effect of Job's suffering

In this case, as in the case of the analogous question raised in connection with the first episode of the framing story, one way to find the answer to the question is to consider what changes Satan's second attack effects.

When God complies with Satan, Satan moves swiftly to afflict Job with boils, with all the concomitant complicated suffering discussed at the outset of this chapter, including Job's pariah status in his community, his rejection by his closest companions, and the waking and sleeping nightmares that destroy Job's ability to find peace or rest. After Satan leaves the gathering of God's sons to attack Job the second time, Satan disappears from the narrative; and the narrative shape-shifts into a story about Job. Whatever other good Satan's attack may bring about, the narrative gives no sign that Satan's attack on Job or God's care for Satan produced any change for the better in Satan, either by furthering Satan's internal integration or by reducing his alienation from God. So, as far as the narrative is concerned, effective changes for the better in Satan are not among the changes produced by God's permission to Satan to afflict Job. But what about Job? What changes does Satan's attack ultimately effect in Job?

When the whole story starts, at the beginning of the first episode of the framing story, Job is a herder whose exemplary righteousness, piety, and prosperity mark him out from everyone else in his world. But, however noteworthy he was within that world, it is doubtful that he would have merited being remembered for long by it. Even superlatively righteous, rich, pious people are not, in the end, so very remarkable as they might seem to those within their own social milieu. Although, in their own immediate community, they are known as the good, devout, wealthy people they are, they are also rapidly and rightly forgotten. Who now remembers Paula of Bethlehem, Joanna of Naples, Glueckel of Hamlyn, or Abigail Williams?[73] Hardly anyone but the antiquarians who study the periods in which they lived—that is the answer. These people were noteworthy in the time in which they lived; but they were nonetheless not people of such distinction that they merited very much notice after their deaths.

By the end of the first episode of the framing story, because of the suffering he endured in consequence of the first episode, Job has become a more impressive and admirable person than the pious and wealthy herder he was in the beginning. He has become the sort of person whose story a culture strives to hand on, to help shape the ideals of the next generations. By the end of the first episode, Job is less like Paula of Bethlehem and more like a hero of a whole culture—like Olympias of Constantinople, in the Patristic period, or like Sojourner Truth and Harriet Tubman, in more recent times.[74] These were highly admirable people, who retained faith and remained steadfast under great suffering. Their communities wanted to preserve their memories from generation to generation; their societies honored them and hoped that succeeding generations would be formed by stories about them. Because of the way the suffering consequent on the first episode has shaped him, by the end of that episode Job has become the kind of person worthy of being a cultural hero of this sort. Under highly adverse circumstances, Job maintained uncorrupted moral uprightness and personal commitment to God, and there was power behind his goodness. Job found in himself the toughness to endure in conditions that would have crushed a lesser person. And so he became the sort of person who could inspire subsequent generations committed to the ideals the story of his life exemplifies.

But what about Job's state after the suffering stemming from Satan's second attack on him? There is a world of difference between Job at the end of the first episode's suffering and Job at the end of the second. Through the suffering of the first episode, Job became the sort of person worthy of being lionized by a whole culture; under affliction, he manifested in an exemplary way the values of his culture. Through the terrible suffering of the second episode, Job became a much greater person.

Olympias of Constantinople and Sojourner Truth were heroic women meriting the admiration accorded them in their culture, which kept their memories alive a long time. But, by way of contrast, consider Socrates. The story of Socrates is known to one degree or another by everyone educated in the West, and there is a reason for this fact. The greatness of Socrates transcends times and cultures. In consequence of his noble, steadfast pursuit of truth and goodness, in circumstances that led to his death at the hands of his own people, Socrates was a person worthy of admiration by everyone everywhere. For this reason, his life is a kind of cross-cultural icon. Or maybe even this way of praising Socrates is pale. Icons are static and mute, but Socrates's life has a kind of fire about it, a gloriousness, which inspires people, even (or especially) those with sharp minds and great hearts, through many centuries and cultural changes.

Something similar can be said about Job in consequence of the suffering inflicted on him by Satan's second attack. Through that suffering, Job attained a greatness of character like that of Socrates. Because of Satan's second attack and Job's endurance under it, in the story Job becomes the sort of person whose life captures the imagination of anyone who learns of it. Job stood up to the ruler of the universe, and in response God came to talk to him in one of the longest conversations between God and human beings in any of the biblical stories. Job's words and actions, described in the narrative in painstaking detail, now constitute a story that has contributed to molding all of Western civilization after it.[75]

Job would never have had this greatness if his suffering after the first episode between God and Satan had been the end of the story.

Job's endurance of the suffering that came to him after the first episode of the framing story built steadfastness and rooted commitment to God into him. That growth in steadfastness and commitment gives God in the narrative reason to think that Job could be stretched even further, into something luminously great. As it turns out in the story, God's high expectations of Job are not disappointed. Job's suffering in consequence of Satan's second attack on him does not eventuate in Job's cursing God to his face, as Satan had hoped it would. In the dialogues with the comforters after Satan's second attack, Job is vehemently indignant against God; but anger and indignation are one way to continue holding on to a relationship of love. A wife whose husband is furious at her is still very much in relationship with him. The distance indicated by cursing a person to his face requires something colder and harder than anger.

In fact, in a paradoxical way, Job's passionate accusations against God move Job closer to God. In his indictment of God, Job takes his stand fiercely on the side of goodness. Satan's first attack on Job has the unintended result of separating the love of prosperity from the love of goodness in Job. But Satan's second attack separates in Job two things that might be thought to be inextricably connected: the love of the office of the Deity, and the love of the goodness that is truly the essence of God. The comforters are shocked that Job refuses simply to take as good anything done by God. But Job is shocked by them and their willingness to abandon any objective standard of goodness in the interest of being on the side of the ruler of the universe. That is why Job issues his odd-sounding warning to the comforters. If you accept God's person, Job says in condemnation of their position, God will surely be angry at you.

In denouncing the comforters' willingness to kowtow to God, Job takes his stand with the goodness of God, rather than with the office of God as ruler of the universe. Without losing his personal commitment to the person of God, Job refuses to accept what God does just because it is God who does it. If, *per impossibile*, divine power and divine goodness were to be opposed, then in the way in which he reacts to his suffering Job is in effect choosing to be on the side of goodness rather than on the side of power, even if the side of power should be God's side.[76] In this choice, Job is as fervently on God's side as it is possible to be. Goodness separated from power still has something divine about it and is still worth committing oneself to; power separated from goodness is, one might say, just satanic.

Job's rebuke to the comforters implies that Job thinks God himself would approve of the attitude Job adopts, siding with goodness against power even in God's case, and the narrative implies that God takes Job to be honoring God by taking this stand. That this reading is right on both counts is made evident later in the story when God himself condemns the comforters' view.

And so by being angry at God and by insisting on goodness over power, even in God's case, Job in fact draws closer to God. At any rate, there is no other character in the biblical stories who is in a position to say what Job says at the end of the divine speeches: I had heard of you by the hearing of the ear, but now my own eye sees you. The devastating process that brings Job to that closeness with God makes him into an exemplar of the greatness possible for the human spirit in extreme and crushing circumstances.[77] The things Job suffers in consequence of the first episode between God and Satan move Job from being an outstandingly moral and pious prosperous herdsman to being a kind of cultural hero. The suffering consequent on the second episode moves him from there to a stature that manifests the greatness of the human spirit. There is something glorious about him in that condition.

It is important to see that, even if this conclusion is correct, by itself it does not give us a theodicy or a defense. At the outset of this chapter, I attempted to sketch in all their complicated variety the devastating losses and psychological trauma, shame included, that Job endures. The question of whether the changes in Job, as I have explained them here, constitute a morally sufficient reason for God to allow all this suffering is still an open question, and a hard one; and I am postponing it to the later chapter on theodicy. I am aware that for many people the very question is an offense. To them, it seems obvious that no effect on Job could justify what God allows Job to suffer. But this view is based on a scale of values for a human life that needs examination, and that examination also has to be deferred to the later chapter on theodicy. As I explained at the outset of this chapter, I am deferring considerations of theodicy and defense until all the narratives under consideration have been examined.

But this much can be said even at this point. The effects on Job, as I have described them, help explain why there are two episodes involving Satan, rather than just one. God could, after all, simply have lifted all his protection of Job (with or without the proviso that Satan had to spare Job's life) in response to Satan's first accusation against Job. But, by requiring two stages to the lifting of his protection, God brings it about that Job is tested and strengthened before undergoing the worst of the assault. It is as if Job needed to be tempered by the first attack in order to prepare him to sustain the second, much worse one. This is the way we would expect God to deal with Job if God's ultimate aim were to use Job's suffering to make him into a person who is exemplary of human glory.

And so the framing story of Satan does hold the key to the explanation of Job's suffering, as sophisticated repudiators of the story sometimes derisively claim that it does; but the explanation is not the primitive and morally offensive one they deride.

The explanation has to do with the effect of Job's suffering and the way in which it makes his life glorious. When we consider the framing story of Satan carefully, then, a third-person explanation of Job's suffering does emerge.

The nested stories: The fractal nature of the book of Job

On the narrative's own showing, the story of Job has to be understood as a small part of a much larger saga. As God explains in his conversation with Job, not only has God created the world, but he also governs everything in it, even the inanimate things. And, as the framing story of God and Satan implies, human history itself is subsumed within an overarching cosmic chronicle. So it is clear that in the narrative Job's interactions with God are a minuscule part of the things to which God's attention is turned. The book of Job is thus like an illustration in an art book that consists in a detail, greatly enlarged, taken from a much bigger painting that is outlined in a small box at the bottom of the page. The episode with Satan at the beginning of the narrative sketches in a few lines the general shape of a very big picture, and the divine speeches to Job provide small sketches of some other parts of that same big picture. The story of Job, which occupies the bulk of the book of Job, zooms in to enlarge a detail extracted from that whole enormous picture, which is drawn here only in part and in miniature.

In the whole picture within which the story of Job is a detail, God deals with Satan in a way which aims at Satan's good and which is designed to keep the distance between God and Satan as small as Satan will let it be.[78] Each episode involving God and Satan has the effect of making manifest to Satan, for Satan's sake, that Job is just as devoted to God and goodness as God tells Satan Job is when God singles Job out for praise. With regard to the story centered on relations between God and Satan, then, Satan is the primary beneficiary[79] of the lesson that can be learned from Job's reactions to his suffering, at least to the extent that the events involving Job make the lesson available for Satan if he is willing to accept it.[80]

But tucked within the overarching story of Satan's relations with God is the story that is focused on Job. With regard to *that* story, considered not as a detail in Satan's story (which it is) but as its own whole story—namely, the story of Job's life (which it also is)—*Job* is the primary beneficiary of the events involving his suffering. That is because the same acts on God's part designed to teach Satan that Satan's cynical view of the world is wrong make Job first a cultural ideal and then an exemplar of human greatness. So although, on the face of it, Job is simply an incidental part in the story of Satan's relations with God, nonetheless, in the story which is the narrative of Job's life God is concerned to deal with Job in a way that seeks Job's good primarily and aims to draw Job closer to God if Job stands steadfast. In fact, in the embedded story focused on Job God does not simply stand by to see whether or not Job will be steadfast. Rather, God intervenes to help Job by making himself present to Job and by talking to Job at impressive length. The protagonist of the embedded story of Job and the primary object of God's concern in that story is thus Job, not Satan.

In addition, contained inside the story of Job, in the content of the divine speeches to Job, there is the quasi-story of God's relations with the animals and the inanimate parts of God's creation. In each part of that quasi-story, the focus of the story is on the animal or thing in question. God finds food for the baby birds because they are hungry. God does not treat them just as incidentals in some other, bigger story. Nonetheless, the story of God's as-it-were personal relations with the beasts and the sea and all the rest of God's creatures is set within the story of God's personal relations with Job, which is itself set within the story of God's personal relations with Satan.

And so the book of Job consists in nested stories of God's personal relations with other persons and things. The nested stories resemble each other in several respects. The most important of these, in my view, is that within each of the nested stories the creature whose story it is is an end in himself, even if in some other story he is also a means to an end for some other creature. But there are other resemblances as well, pertinent for my purposes. For example, as the episodes involving Satan make clear, Satan's psychological state is troubled; he is restless and alienated from God, and his intense desire to alienate Job from God shows envy and hatred of Job because of Job's personal relationship with God. These are painful states; Satan suffers in them. Unlike Job's suffering, Satan's suffering is not externally caused, but internally generated by Satan's own psychic state. Nonetheless, in Satan's interactions with God, Satan has a second-person experience of God, which would reveal something to Satan about God's attitude of love toward him if he were willing to receive it. In this respect, Satan's story resembles Job's: Satan's face-to-face encounter with God makes possible for Satan some explanation and resolution of Satan's suffering. Like the explanation given Job, the explanation of his suffering available to Satan is not in the nature of a third-person account. Rather, Satan's second-person experience of God makes available for Satan a second-person explanation of his own condition, just as Job's experience of God does for him.[81]

And so the various stories contained within the book of Job are not only nested, but there are patterns of resemblance among them as well.

Here it is worth considering why the book of Job has this unusual feature. Why is it that the book tells the story of Job within the context of nested stories resembling each other? Why does the book present God's relations with Job as a detail in the larger picture of God's relations with Satan and God's relations with the rest of creation, too?

In my view, the book of Job is to second-person accounts what a fractal is to mathematics. A fractal is a set of points with this peculiar feature: when it is graphed, the shape of each part of the whole resembles the shape of the whole; and the shape of each of the parts of any one part also resembles that of the whole, indefinitely. That is, if a detail of the whole graph is enlarged, its graph looks like the graph of the whole; and if a detail of that enlarged detail is itself enlarged, its graph also resembles the graph of the part within which it is a detail, as well as that of the whole graph, within which the part is a detail. A graphed fractal is thus a picture within a picture within a picture, and so on, each picture of which is similar to the picture of the whole, only reduced in scale. For some fractals, such as the Mandelbrot set, when any detail of the whole graph of the fractal is enlarged, its graph closely resembles the graph of the whole but is not identical to it. Such fractals have infinite complexity. Insofar as the details of God's dealings with Job and also their outcome is very similar but not identical to the details and outcome of God's dealings with Satan or with the non-human animals and the other parts of creation, the book of Job seems to me the second-person analogue of a Mandelbrot set.

Extrapolations and suggestions

Understood as a kind of complex fractal, the book of Job is an illustration of the way in which God's relations with creatures is to be understood. God is able to use those creatures whom he treats as ends in themselves within their own stories *also* as means to ends for others of his creatures, who are ends in themselves within *their* stories.[82] This interpretation thus suggests a way of looking at all the other suffering, apart from Job's, mentioned or implied in the book of Job.

Consider, for example, Job's children. Some people suppose that in the narrative the death of Job's children is only instrumental to Job's story. If there is indeed a benefit for Job that comes to him in consequence of all his suffering, as I have argued there is, then it can seem as if, in a morally repulsive way, the suffering and death of Job's children are being used by God only as a means to an end involving Job. Their suffering apparently has Job, rather than the children themselves, as its primary beneficiary. But if we understand the book of Job as a kind of fractal, then it is clear that the fractal pattern can continue in indefinite extension. Just as Job is a means to an end in the story of Satan and yet is also the primary beneficiary of his suffering within his own story, so his children are a means to an end in Job's story; and yet—if we were to follow out the fractal pattern—we can suppose that there will be stories, contained within the story of Job, in which each of Job's children is the primary beneficiary of his or her suffering. The same point applies, of course, to the suffering of all the other characters in Job's story, including, for example, Job's wife, whose suffering is expressed in her despairing exhortation to Job to curse God and die.[83]

Furthermore, if the story of any one of those sufferers were told, it would contain mention of still other people—those grieved or harmed by the suffering and death of one of Job's children, for example—whose suffering would in turn have to be explained fully within the stories in which each of those people is the principal character. Within *those* stories each of the characters incidental in the stories of Job's children would be the chief beneficiary of whatever suffering occurs to them.

Although stories can be extended indefinitely in this fractal way, they obviously cannot be told in an indefinitely extended way in one narrative. And so the book of Job gives us Job's story. But, by explicitly giving us that story as an enlarged detail of a much larger story, it helps us understand the fractal nature of God's care for all of creation and the many stories we are *not* being given.

Not only does the book of Job give us this understanding of the basic principle of God's providence, but it also helps us understand how divine providence could possibly be exercised in this Mandelbrot way. Sometimes people reflecting on divine providence suppose that the good at which God aims is some form of prosperity or some version of desire satisfaction for every person. In the grip of this idea, mockers deride the whole idea of divine providence by asking how God could exercise care, for example, over a battle in which each of the opposed armies is trusting that it has God on its side.

But the story of Job suggests a very different goal for divine providence, and one that can be exercised at once even with respect to opposed warring parties. Both Job and Satan are the objects of God's providential care, and each is shepherded by that care toward the goal best for that person, even though Satan is Job's enemy. Providential care for each of the opposed parties is possible because the ultimate aim of God's providential care in the narrative is closeness to God and the greatness consequent on that closeness. But, as every part of the book of Job suggests, one important means by which God shepherds a person to that goal is God's second-personal interactions with that person. And, of course, nothing about God's second-personal interactions with one person keeps him from similar interactions with another. So the book of Job not only shows us something about the fractal nature of providence, but it also helps us see how such fractally exercised providence is possible.[84]

The doubling of explanation

In the narrative, as I have tried to show, there are two explanations for the suffering of Job, one set within the context of the other. In the narrative, one explanation is given to Job himself. That is a second-person explanation, which the audience of the narrative has at one remove, because the narrative gives the audience only a description of the explanation's being given to Job. The other explanation has to be teased out of the second-person account of the relations between God and Satan, but it is a third-person explanation; and it is available to the narrative's audience, but not to Job himself. With impressive ingenuity, then, the narrative not only explains Job's suffering to us within the context of two different but interwoven stories, that of Satan and that of Job, but it also invites us to see that we see what Job does not.

Why does the narrative contain two explanations of Job's suffering that differ in this way?

This question can be parsed into two subsidiary questions. (1) Why does Job not get the third-person explanation contained in the framing story of Satan? (2) Why is that third-person explanation given to the audience? That is, if the second-person explanation Job does get is sufficient for him, why should it not be sufficient for the narrative's audience as well?

It is not so hard to see why the explanation appropriate for Job is of the second-person sort. Such an explanation is short on what we might think of as engineering or medical details showing the precise nature of the connection between the suffering and the benefit that redeems it, but in certain sorts of cases a second-person explanation of suffering is a more potent explanation.

Consider, for example, a child with aggressive leukemia who is suffering the pains of a bone marrow transplant and who wants to know from his mother why she does not help him and stop his suffering when she so clearly could, just by taking him out of the hospital. His mother could respond to him by explaining about the benefits of the transplant—that is, by giving him a third-person, quasi-engineering medical account describing the reconstruction of healthy bone marrow. She might say to her son, "Well, see, you have a cancer that affects the blood, and the major blood products are produced by stem cells in the bone marrow. So what we are doing is removing some of your stem cells; the lab hunts through these till it finds some that aren't diseased, and then it clones them, for eventual reinfusion. Then we inject you with a series of cytotoxic drugs that destroy the diseased stem cells in your bone marrow. Those drugs work because they target fast-growing cells. The cancer cells in your bone marrow are fast-growing; but so are your hair cells and the cells in the mucus membranes that line your mouth, your esophagus, and your gut. The cytotoxic drugs kill those, too. That's why you have sores in your mouth; that's why you're throwing up, and why you're constipated." And so on and on.

This might be the right explanation for the son in the hospital, but then again it might not be. There are circumstances in which third-person explanations of this sort are inefficacious for comfort. The child undergoing a painful medical procedure may be at least as frightened and hurt by what he takes to be his mother's abandonment of him, her apparent indifference to his pain and need, as by anything that is happening to his bones and mucus membranes. In that case, the best response to his need for an explanation—perhaps the only response that makes love bio-available to him—is for the mother to give her son a second-person experience of her as loving of him. This may be the best means in the circumstances to show him that she would only let him suffer in order to bring about some outweighing good for him that she could not get for him in any easier way. In cases in which an apparent betrayal of trust is an important part of the suffering, second-person explanations have a special power to console. There is a particularly potent comfort for Job in the second-person explanation he gets in the narrative. Certainly, it is more intense for him than a third-person account could possibly be.

Furthermore, in the extended face-to-face experience Job has of God in God's conversation with him, not only does Job experience some sort of closeness with God, but also God honors Job in a signal way. The prolonged conversation with God and experience of God set Job apart from the others in his culture—as far as that goes, from all other human beings in any biblical narratives. At any rate, no other divine speeches recorded in biblical narratives are as extensive as those in God's conversation with Job. Insofar as honor from God is both comforting and restorative to a person who has been shamed by his friends and community as rejected by God, then in this respect also the second-person explanation given Job is appropriate for Job. So there is an antidote to psychic pain and to shame that stems from the second-personal character of God's explanation of Job's suffering, and this is also an important good for Job.

But why does not God *precede* Job's suffering with an explanation of the third-personal sort? Why not explain to Job before he suffers what is going to happen to him and why?

In my view, the answer to this question should be apparent. Neither one of Job's two experiences of suffering would have had the effect it does in the narrative if Job had had that suffering explained to him in advance. Consider just the first experience of suffering, in the course of which prosperity and moral goodness cease to be on the same side. An explanation of this suffering given to Job in advance would have made it clear to him that, although at least for a time, for Job, goodness and prosperity are not on the same side, nonetheless in fact goodness is ultimately allied with *cosmic* power. Job would then have had every reason to suppose that, if he only did not curse God, prosperity would at some point be returned to him (as it in fact is in the narrative). But in that case the entire episode of suffering would have lost much of its point.[85]

Similarly, calling Job's attention in advance to the way in which at the end of the story his suffering will have made him glorious by drawing him closer to God and deepening his commitment to God's goodness risks undermining those very things in him by showing him how prudentially beneficial it is for him to take his stand with goodness. Such an explanation given to Job would have opened Job's eyes to a coupling between commitment to God, on the one hand, and cosmic (rather than worldly) prosperity, on the other.

And so Job's flourishing through his suffering, in relationship to God, is incompatible with Job's having the explanation for his suffering given in advance in a third-personal explanation.

But what about the audience of the narrative? Why is Job's second-person explanation not sufficient also for the audience? Why does the narrative give the audience the third-person explanation that it denies Job?

It is helpful to see in this connection that the second-person explanation given to Job is not of the sort that people interested in theodicies often want, just because it is not a third-person account. A second-person experience in which one person conveys love to another can constitute a good response to a mistaken charge of betrayal for the mistaken accuser who has that experience. But it will be hard for a description of that experience to convince a third party, for the very reasons I gave when I explained why second-person accounts differ from third-person accounts. *How* Job knows what he knows—that his suffering is at the hands of a good and loving God—is hard to explain to someone who was not part of the same second-person experience. The best that can be done, as I argued earlier, is to turn that experience into a second-person account, of the sort we have in the story of the second-person experiences between God and Job.

Furthermore, there is a great variability in the reactions of people to a second-person account. When it comes to persuading its audience to share its perspective, a story is much more likely to be successful with those people who have themselves had some experience of the sort being described in the story. (That is why people reveal themselves when they explain what novels they find moving.) Second-person accounts involving God will be received differently by those who have their own religious experiences to draw on from the way in which they are received by those who do not, just as the second-person account contained in the divine speeches will strike Job differently from the way in which it will strike someone who receives it at one remove from the second-person experience in which it is embedded. (That is also why the problem of suffering presents itself differently to different people, depending on their own history of religious experience.)

So an explanation of Job's suffering that is in the form of a second-person account will be disappointing to some readers or hearers of the story, however satisfying it might be to Job, who has the second-person experience represented in the second-person account. *What* Job knows, that God loves him and did not betray his trust, may not be what someone looking for a third-person account wants. It may be enough for a sick child, who has a shared history of loving relations with his mother, to know that she allows him to suffer only because she loves him. But an outsider who does not know the mother, who has no relation to her, may well want to know exactly what the connection between the suffering and the child's well-being is, before he is willing to grant that the mother is justified in allowing the child to suffer.

And so, even if there is a point in the story for giving only one sort of explanation to Job, both sorts of explanation have a place in the narrative.

Conclusion

Whether the picture of providence portrayed in the book of Job is religiously or morally acceptable is a matter I am postponing for the last part of this book, as I have explained before. In this chapter, in this examination of the narrative, what I have been at pains to show is the picture we get of God's reasons for allowing Job's suffering, when we are attuned to the second-person character of the narrative, in all its complexity.

Focusing on the second-person account of the divine speeches and the second-person experience of God that Job has while God is speaking to him shows us that there is for Job a second-personal explanation of his suffering; and, through the second-person account of the narrative, it lets us share to some extent in the explanation Job gets by this means. Focusing on the second-person account of the framing story of Satan and reflecting on the second-person experiences between God and Satan which that account relates enables us to understand Job's suffering in another way, because we can tease a third-person account out of that framing story. It is not the primitive, morally repugnant folkloric story which the framing story is often enough thought to be—namely, that Job is a pawn heartlessly used in a wager between God and Satan. On the contrary, the nested stories of Satan and of Job show us God's providence operating in a fractal way, to deal with each of God's creatures as an end in himself, even while interweaving all the individual stories into one larger narrative. It is sometimes supposed that divine providence could not possibly operate in this way because it is not possible for there to be the sort of collocation of benefits necessary for each individual creature to be treated as an end in itself. But the story of Job shows that this attitude toward divine providence takes too limited a view of the nature of benefits and goods for human beings. There are also the goods of second-personal relations, and especially the potent goods of closeness between God and created persons. It is not impossible for God to provide goods of this sort to all his creatures.

Furthermore, the book of Job shows us God giving goods of this sort to created persons not by means of middle knowledge that lets him be the sole determiner of all the outcomes of his interactions with other persons.[86] On the contrary, in the case of Satan, Satan's own resolute hostility thwarts God's attempts to draw Satan closer to himself. Even here, however, divine providence is successful, in two respects. God uses Satan's malice toward Job to make Job magnificent in goodness, and by that means he thwarts Satan's efforts to turn Job into a rebel against God. And God succeeds in providing loving care for Satan, which would draw Satan closer to God if Satan were to accept it. In the narrative, then, divine providence succeeds in its aims not by determining what creatures do, but by being smarter than those creatures opposed to him. Maybe God does not play dice with the universe; but perhaps, like a consummate chess master, through the application of great intelligence, he is able to get to ends he wants through myriad possible disjunctive roads to it.

With this, my exploration of a narrative involving a sufferer who is a righteous, unwilling victim of the depredations of others and the forces of nature is complete. In the next chapter, I will turn to the story of Samson, which is the narrative of a person who suffers greatly, but as a perpetrator of great wrongs.

Chapter 10

The Story of Samson: Self-Destroying Evil

Batter my heart, three-personed God; for, you
As yet but knock, breathe, shine, and seek to mend;
That I may rise, and stand, o'erthrow me, and bend
Your force, to break, blow, burn, and make me new.
I, like an usurped town, to another due,
Labour to admit you, but oh, to no end.
Reason your viceroy in me, me should defend,
But is captived, and proves weak or untrue.
Yet dearly I love you, and would be loved fain,
But am betrothed unto your enemy.
Divorce me, untie, or break that knot again,
Take me to you, imprison me, for I
Except you enthrall me, never shall be free,
Nor ever chaste, except you ravish me.*

Introduction

In her book on the problem of suffering, Marilyn McCord Adams defines horrendous evils as "evils the participation in which (that is, the doing or suffering of which) constitutes prima facie reason to doubt whether the participant's life could (given their inclusion in it) be a great good" to the participant.[1] Although her definition specifically mentions the doing of evils as well as the suffering of them, her paradigm lists of horrendous evils typically include only examples of great suffering on the part of

---

* John Donne, "Holy Sonnet XIV," in *John Donne. Complete English Poems*, ed. C. A.Patrides and Robin Hamilton (London: J. M. Dent, Everyman Library, 1994).

unwilling innocent victims, such as the suffering of victims of rape, torture, and child abuse. A large part of her book is given over to considering whether there are benefits available to such an unwilling innocent victim that could possibly redeem his suffering and turn his life into a good for him. In this chapter, however, I want to focus on the other part of her definition of horrendous evil; I want to consider the problem of suffering as regards not the victims of horrifying evil but the perpetrators of it, whose own lives are wrecked in consequence of the evil they do.

Reflecting on horrifying suffering,[2] many thoughtful people feel strongly that there is nothing, there could be nothing, that defeats such suffering. In the view of such people, there is no outweighing benefit brought about by the suffering of horrifying evil that could not be gotten without the suffering, and the efforts of theodicy to find outweighing benefits strike such people as shallow at best and obscene at worst. On such a view, a person whose life includes horrifying suffering would have been better off if he had never been born. Job gives voice to this sort of attitude when he curses the day he was born and complains with bitter passion, "Why did I not die from the womb? Why did I not emerge from the womb and perish?" (Job 3: 11).

In the Greek world, the paradigm of a person whose life exemplifies horrifying evil is Oedipus. (It is a lamentable commentary on the course of the world from Sophocles's time to our own that, for us, the paradigms of persons whose lives are wrecked past fixing are heartbreakingly worse than the Greek paradigms. We do not need to remember the horrors of the Holocaust to see this point. The morning newspaper's most recent case of child abuse will demonstrate the fact.) Sophocles has Oedipus claim to be among the worst of the afflicted,[3] and it is not hard to see why Sophocles would put this claim in Oedipus's mouth. By the time Oedipus appears in *Oedipus at Colonus*, his unwitting parricide and incest (and his reactions to these things) have left him blind and disfigured, exiled and homeless, reduced to begging, bedeviled by fear, tormented by self-loathing, and shunned with horror by all who meet him. What is broken and ruined in Oedipus could not possibly be restored to wholeness. Surely this is horrifying suffering if anything is.

And yet Sophocles also has the ravaged Oedipus say of himself that he is a treasure superior to any lovely form.[4] In some sense, Sophocles thinks, the life of Oedipus, broken as he is, is a great good for Oedipus. How could this be? What could make the life of a person so broken nonetheless a good for that person?[5] What possible benefit for Oedipus could redeem his suffering?

The Greeks, who tended to value the life of the mind, thought that the benefit brought about by suffering is the intellectual virtue of wisdom.[6] An irrevocably damaged person can still be glorious in the excellence of wisdom. In fact, on the view of some of the Greek tragedians, the prize of wisdom comes only from suffering.[7] I understand that the mention of this view will only infuriate some people, who will point fiercely to cases that, in their view, cannot be seen in the manner of the Greek tragedians by any decent person. But I want to short-circuit the passionate production of such counter-examples. I am calling attention to this position here only to point out at the outset that believing in the redeemability of horrifying suffering is not, as some people seem to suppose, just a desperate expedient forced on those who are unwilling to give up their commitment to the existence of an omniscient, omnipotent, perfectly good deity. The Greeks could easily have explained horrifying suffering as a matter of conflict among the gods, not all of whom are perfectly good, on Greek views. So something other than theological scrambling for cover prompts the poignant trust of a tragedian such as Sophocles that even great suffering is redeemed by the benefit it brings to the sufferer.

Nonetheless, this view of Sophocles's is not one I will pursue in this book. That is because, although it has some significant similarities to the position I am going to defend, for all its loveliness its primary focus on an excellence of mind is misplaced, in my view.[8] From Augustine onwards, and certainly in Aquinas's work, Christian emphasis in reflections on human suffering has been primarily on the goods of relationship for the sufferer, not on the state of the sufferer's intellect.

For somewhat the same reason, it also seems to me important to have as an example of horrifying suffering the sort of case for the most part left in the background by Adams (although it is her work that is principally responsible for forcing it on our attention in recent times)—namely, the sort of case in which a human person's *doing* of evil wrecks his life (as well as that of others). Sophocles's Oedipus is pitiably anxious to make clear that his dreadful acts were in some important sense involuntary. "There is more of suffering than of violence in my deeds," he tells the Chorus.[9] And it is not hard to see why this claim matters to him. Job suffers unspeakably, but at least he suffers as a victim, not as a perpetrator. He is broken and his life is wrecked, but the responsibility for the horror does not lie with him; and so there remains this much beauty in him and in his life: he is innocent. But it is also possible to be broken and ruined and to know that one has brought the horror on oneself by the evil one has done.[10]

The story of Samson is like this. By what he did with the life he was given, Samson made a sort of abortion out of himself. He killed the good and lovely thing he might have been. The noble chronicle his life could have been was made by him instead into a moral horror story to inspire caution in others. His is a case in which it appears very doubtful that his life was a good to him. Only, it is Samson's fault that this is so. If the state of a person's will is important to his flourishing, then cases in which a person suffers terribly as a perpetrator of evil are among the worst cases of human suffering.[11]

Another version of the problem of suffering

There is therefore another version of the problem of suffering that also bears consideration—namely, that which focuses on the horrifying suffering of the lives of the perpetrators of evil, rather than the victims of it.

This version of the problem has largely been left to one side, I think, because we tend to react without pity to the perpetrators of great evil. If they themselves suffer dreadfully, we take them to get what they deserve. And yet imagine that Joseph Goebbels failed to kill himself, after his wife had killed their six children and herself at his instigation; imagine that he lived through the war into the new era and finally came to see himself just as we see him today. It is not hard to put Job's lines in Goebbels's mouth: it would have been so much better for Goebbels if God had let him die at birth. And if that line is true, as it seems at first glance to be, then the problem of suffering can surely also be raised about the perpetrators, as well as the victims, of great evil. Even if it were true that the suffering of the perpetrator were deserved, if both the evil and the deserved suffering could have been prevented, if the perpetrator would have been much better off dying young rather than living to perpetrate the evil he did, then why would not an omniscient, omnipotent, perfectly good God provide for the death of that perpetrator before he did that evil?[12]

This ought to be an especially troubling form of the problem of suffering for a worldview such as Aquinas's, for two reasons.

In the first place, as I explained in Chapter 8, the theological tradition Aquinas accepts takes moral evil to be something analogous to a cancer, but one that is in the will rather than the body. On Aquinas's views, the will of *every* human person is susceptible to this cancer. A moral monster is a person in whom time, circumstance, and choice have brought the disease fully to the fore. Of course, taken by itself, this attitude is not peculiar to worldviews such as Aquinas's. That many people hold an attitude of this sort is strongly suggested, for example, by the outrage that greeted a recent book attempting to pin the blame for the Holocaust on something specifically German—German history and German character.[13] To many people, me included, there is something almost childish about the book's attempt to defuse fear at the magnitude of the moral evil of the Holocaust by localizing its source in *Germans*. The adult view of the matter, many people are inclined to think, understands with sorrow that the potentiality for the Nazi sort of evil lies in all human beings. On this view of the human species, there is no one, not even asymptomatic Job, who is not subject to this moral disease.[14]

But if it is worse to suffer through one's own fault than as an innocent victim and if, on Aquinas's views, everyone is liable to suffer through his own fault to one degree or other, then this form of the problem of suffering has a special interest. There is, then, some reason for considering the problem of suffering in the form in which it has to do with the perpetrators of evil rather than with the victims of it.

Secondly, Aquinas's worldview itself has an odd feature built into it that makes this form of the problem of suffering appear particularly worrisome. As I explained in Chapter 8, on the traditional theological doctrines Aquinas accepts, the theological good news is that there is a cure for the moral disease of the will and that, furthermore, the cure can be had for the asking. One has only to want it.[15] What are we to say then about those who are not cured of it? The traditional answer, and one that Aquinas accepts, is that they do not want it, and so their failure to be cured is their own fault. Their own cleaving to their morally diseased state has kept them from availing themselves of the cure. It seems, therefore, that one symptom of the disease is that those who have it do not want the cure; and the worse the disease, the less likely the diseased person is to want the cure.

On these views, it appears especially hard to reconcile the existence of moral monsters with God's existence. If, in fact, there is a cure for the moral disease in people, as Aquinas holds, it seems that God could have used that cure on the perpetrators of horrifying evil to keep them from culpably refusing the cure; it seems as if God could have kept them from becoming moral monsters. On the other hand, if somehow their own evil keeps God from curing them, then it seems that it would have been better for God to have brought about the death of the perpetrators before their lurking moral cancer developed into full-blown moral monstrosity. Since everyone dies at some time, and since, presumably, an omnipotent, omniscient, perfectly good God can control the time of a person's death, it seems as if it would have been better *for the perpetrators* if God had brought about their death before they committed monstrous evils.[16]

The case of the perpetrators of great evil is, then, the hardest case for theodicy, at least in the sense to which Adams calls our attention, that a case of this sort is most likely to make us think the sufferer would have been better off not being born or dying before becoming a moral monster. If it can be shown that even a person whose own evil acts have broken him and left him in unspeakable suffering has available to him benefits that render his life a great good for him,[17] then there is an a fortiori argument to the possibility of such redemption of suffering in other less disturbing cases.

So, for all these reasons, I want to explore one case of horrifying evil in which the sufferer's own moral evil brings it about that his life is wrecked as it is. I want to look carefully at the story of Samson. I am going to focus not on all the moral wrong Samson does—either by our standards or by the standards operative in the narrative. Although many of the things Samson does are appalling, what is of concern to me in this chapter is just the wrong acts and attitudes by which Samson ruins himself. These are not in the same league as some of those on Adams's list of horrifying evils, but they are effective in breaking Samson.

Here, as in the preceding chapter, my aim is not to produce a theodicy or defense with regard to the suffering Samson undergoes. As I explained in the earlier chapter on Job, it would defeat my purpose in the book as a whole to try to build a defense before all the narratives have been examined.

Milton and Samson

I am not the first person to think that the case of Samson shows us the problem of suffering in a particularly disconcerting form but that it also gives us insights useful for theodicy. Milton thought so, too, and wrote a play incorporating his interpretation of the story of Samson and his reflections on it. Milton takes as his purpose in *Paradise Lost* to "assert Eternal Providence and justify the ways of God to men."[18] But, to my mind, Milton's best attempt at theodicy is in his powerful but less well-known tragedy *Samson Agonistes*.[19]

It is clear that Milton saw his own case as analogous to Samson's in many (but certainly not all) respects, and rightly so. When the Puritans fell from power, Milton, who had given so much of himself to their cause, was left blind, impoverished, and imperiled by his enemies. Because of the work he had done on behalf of the Puritans, after their fall Milton was a pariah even to those of his countrymen who were not actively seeking his death. And he was a failure at what he himself saw as his vocation to poetry. His great gifts for literature had been prodigally spent for two decades largely just on political pamphlets. The plan which Milton had announced in his youth, that he would produce a great English epic poem, looked at the time of the Puritan fall from power as if it had been mere bombast, inviting Horace's sort of scorn: "the mountains travailed to bring forth, and an absurd mouse was born."[20] By all accounts, Milton's political writings defending the Puritans cost him his eyesight; but the main effect of these writings, which constitute roughly four-fifths of Milton's entire corpus, was only to get Milton's name on the list of people excluded from pardon during the Restoration. The cause for which Milton had spent himself unstintingly had proved futile by that time; and everything about the succeeding Restoration period, from its lax morality to its anti-Puritan understanding of Christian doctrine and of the style of worship pleasing to God, was anathema to Milton. From Milton's point of view, the Philistines he had spent his life fighting had won, and their idolatry had triumphed. Milton's greatest poems—his magnificent epic *Paradise Lost*, but also *Paradise Regained* and *Samson Agonistes*—were all completed in the decade of his worst suffering, after the collapse of the Puritan revolution. *Samson Agonistes* is in fact Milton's last work; he died within three years of finishing it.

So Milton's interest in the story of Samson was not abstract, but personal and anguished. He thought about the unspeakable suffering of Samson's life out of the ruin of his own life. And the thought is very good. In Milton's case, at any rate, Sophocles had it right: suffering leads to wisdom. In considering the biblical story of Samson, then, I will take Milton's understanding of it as a guide but also as a foil, to highlight what is distinctive about the interpretation of the narrative I want to defend.

Samson in captivity

In introducing *Samson Agonistes*, the noted literary critic Douglas Bush picks out *Oedipus at Colonus* as one of the preceding works of literature Milton's play most resembles,[21] and it is not hard to see why Bush thinks so. Milton's view of Samson is in many respects similar to Sophocles's view of Oedipus. Like *Oedipus at Colonus*, *Samson Agonistes* begins by calling attention to the panoply of the protagonist's sufferings, and there is considerable similarity between the two characters on this score. To begin with, like Oedipus, Samson is blind. The lament over the loss of sight that blind Milton puts in blind Samson's mouth is heart-rending, and it reminds us not to gloss over blindness as a small suffering:[22]

> Light, the prime work of God, to me is extinct,
> And all her various objects of delight
> Annulled, which might in part my grief have eased,
> Inferior to the vilest now become

Of man or worm; the vilest here excel me,
They creep, yet see; I, dark . . .

. . . . .

. . . exiled from light,
As in the land of darkness, yet in light,

. . . . .

Myself my sepulchre, a moving grave,
Buried, yet not exempt
By privilege of death and burial
From worst of other evils, pains and wrongs . . .   (ll. 70–105)

For Samson, there are indeed many other evils. Oedipus is at least free to wander with his daughters. Unlike Oedipus, Samson is not only exiled, but also imprisoned and set to work at hard and demeaning labor, grinding grain like a beast for his enemies. Samson's blindness is also more destructive for Samson's life than Oedipus's blindness was for him. Samson was born to be a warrior for the liberation of his people, but hand-to-hand combat requires sight. In addition, like Oedipus, Samson is disgraced at home and a pariah to the community around him in his exile. But there is an extra measure of humiliation for Samson, because he is forced to use his strength, which was meant to be employed in the liberation of his people, to give food to their enemies; and his enemies exult over him in this condition.

For both Oedipus and Samson, the pain of their condition is made more bitter by the memory of the state from which they have fallen. Oedipus was the ruler of a city. Samson was something like a tribal Superman, an iron-age analogue to the man of steel, prodigious in his feats of strength, virtually invulnerable to the weapons of his enemies, and fearsome in his vengeance on wrongdoers. But for Samson the reversal in fortunes is considerably more complicated than it is for Oedipus, however tangled Oedipus's story is.

To begin with, that is because Samson was *called* to the state from which he fell. Rescuing his people from their oppressors was his vocation; it was, quite literally, what he was born for. The angel who announces Samson's birth to the hitherto barren woman who becomes Samson's mother tells her to avoid wine, strong spirits, and unclean food and to make sure that no razor ever comes on the child's head, because the child to be born will be a Nazirite from the womb.[23] This special son, the angel tells the woman, is destined to begin to deliver Israel from the Philistines.[24] Religion and patriotism are mingled together in this destiny; love of freedom, hatred of oppression, heroism in danger come into it also. Then, too, in that relatively small society, where Samson's exploits are widely known, the expectations and hopes of his family and his people are also part of the story; whether he means to or not, when Samson attacks the Philistines, he acts on behalf of his people.[25] Samson's fall is thus also the collapse of all these expectations and hopes. When Samson is captured, the enemies of Samson's people rejoice and give thanks to their god for defeating the champion of Israel and Israel's God. Samson's downfall is thus not just a personal catastrophe; his failure to fulfill his vocation is also the disgrace of his family and a national disaster.

Even more importantly, the disaster is Samson's fault. He is culpable for it, as Oedipus is not culpable for the acts that ruin him.

Samson's relationship to God

Milton sums up Samson's state succinctly by having Samson say:

> Now blind, disheartened, shamed, dishonored, quelled,
> To what can I be useful, wherein serve
> My nation, and the work from Heaven imposed . . .　　　　　(ll. 563–5)

Heaven is, of course, yet another problem for Samson. Not only is there the problem of intolerable guilt, which Milton unaccountably leaves off the list of Samson's troubles in these lines; there is also Samson's relationship to God.

That there was such a relationship, that it was direct and powerful, and that Samson trusted in it as a regular part of his life is shown by the episode of the battle at Lehi. There, the story says, Samson single-handedly slaughtered a thousand of the enemy, and the Philistines were soundly defeated in the battle. But afterwards Samson was very thirsty. And so, the text says: "Samson called to the Lord[26] and said, 'It was you who gave this great deliverance by the hand of your servant. And now I am dying of thirst, and I will fall into the hands of the uncircumcised' " (Judg. 15: 18). And, the story says, God provided water for Samson by breaking open a place in Lehi, from which water flowed.

It is notable that Samson not only thought to call on God when he needed a drink but that he called on God in such a familiar way. There is no worshipful address in his prayer. By way of contrast, compare, for example, the way in which Daniel begins his prayer to God: "Oh Lord, great and dread God, you who keep the covenant and give loving-kindness to those who love you and who keep your commandments" (Dan. 9: 4), or the invocation of Hezekiah's prayer: "Lord of hosts, God of Israel, you who dwell among the cherubim, it is you alone who are God of all the kingdoms of the earth, it is you who have made the heavens and the earth" (Isa. 37: 16). There is not only no reverent address in Samson's prayer; there is in fact no address at all. Samson simply turns to God to speak to him directly, as if invocation of the Deity, to get his attention and call him to listen, were unnecessary for Samson.

None of the other common elements of prayer are present in Samson's speech either. There is no plea for God's help, not even a single 'please.' In Daniel's prayer, by contrast, the opening plea to God, which intervenes between the prayer's invocation and its first petition, fills twelve verses. Even in Samson's own story, when Samson's father prays to God before Samson's birth, the father's very short prayer begins with an invocation and contains the elements missing in Samson's prayer, a "please" and a request for help. He says: "Oh my Lord God, let the man of God whom you sent [before] come to us again, I pray, and let him teach us what to do with the boy who will be born."[27]

As far as that goes, in his prayer Samson appears not to think it necessary even to make a petition. He asks nothing of God. He simply presents himself to God as thirsty and in want of water. The closest he comes to making a plea or a petition is to point to a danger to himself: unrelieved, the condition in which he is will lead to his being captured by his enemies. Samson points to this possible outcome as a sort of *reductio ad absurdum* of the idea that God could leave him thirsty.

As the prayer itself shows, Samson expects that his want of water and the unquestioned unacceptability (in Samson's mind) of Samson's falling to the Philistines will be enough for God to provide, immediately, on the spot, and without invocation or plea, what Samson needs. It is equally notable that in this story God seems to share Samson's attitude, at least to this extent: without comment, God provides the water.

Not only Samson's prayer but also the episodes recounting Samson's deeds and experiences suggest some intimate and strong connection between Samson and God. In the book of Judges, the story of Samson's exploits begins in this way: "the boy grew, and the Lord blessed him; and the spirit of the Lord began to move him in the camp of Dan . . . " (13: 24–5). Subsequently, when Samson engages in some feat of great strength, the story often (but not always) says that the spirit of the Lord came on him—or rushed into him, as the evocative Hebrew has it.[28] Samson is thus accustomed to tumultuous connection to God from his boyhood onwards.

On the other hand, in the catastrophe at the end of the story, the text explains, not only did the Lord's spirit not come on Samson, but in fact the Lord departed from Samson.[29]

What would it be like to find that the God who had only to see your need to satisfy it, who rushed into you and made you triumphant, was gone from you? Even Milton, I think, is not up to the challenge of depicting that misery for Samson.[30] The closest Milton comes to portraying the wretchedness that descends on Samson from his wrecked relationship to God is in a different poem, when Milton's Satan thinks about *his* lost relationship to God and addresses himself in soliloquy this way,

> cursed be thou, since against his thy will
> Chose freely what it now so justly rues.
> Me miserable! Which way shall I fly
> Infinite wrath, and infinite despair?[31]
>
> . . . I to hell am thrust,
> Where neither joy nor love, but fierce desire,
> Among our other torments not the least,
> Still unfulfilled with pain of longing pines . . .[32]

Among the things Samson must long for—light, freedom, home—the absent love of the God who rushed into him, with whose strength he was great, must prompt some of the most painful pining.

If horrifying sufferings can be ranked, if they are not simply incommensurable, then, taken all in all, Samson's sufferings are within the genus of the worst a person can endure with sanity.[33] At any rate, however great Oedipus's misery, it lacks the torment of being abandoned for cause by a deity once intimately, gloriously, with you.

Abandoned for cause

And it is indisputable that Samson was abandoned for cause; his fall is his fault. Oedipus's catastrophe is at every turn the work of his own hands, but it is easy to believe his anxious attempts to explain that he is not blameworthy for the acts that brought him down. No one would believe such a claim coming from Samson. Milton's Samson makes some feeble efforts to blame God—for giving the prodigious strength without which the catastrophe would not have occurred, for failing to give wisdom sufficient to match the strength—but in the end it is perfectly clear that the culpability rests with Samson. And so Milton has Samson say:

> Nothing of all these evils hath befall'n me
> But justly; I myself have brought them on,
> Sole author I, sole cause: if aught seem vile,
> As vile hath been my folly . . .
>
> (ll. 374–7)[34]

But what exactly is Samson culpable for?

Milton thinks that Samson's fault consists in having told Delilah his secret;[35] the confession Milton puts in Samson's mouth underlines the contemptibility (as Milton sees it) of Samson's act in disclosing the secret of his strength to Delilah:

> . . . my crime,
> Shameful garrulity. To have revealed
> Secrets of men, the secrets of a friend,
> How heinous had the fact been, how deserving
> Contempt, and scorn of all, to be excluded
> All friendship, and avoided as a blab,
> The mark of fool set on his front! But I
> God's counsel have not kept, his holy secret
> Presumptuously have published, impiously,
> Weakly at least, and shamefully . . .
>
> (ll. 490–9)

Here, however, I think Milton has to have it wrong. Although Milton is in general the most astute and insightful interpreter of this narrative that I know, for reasons perhaps best left to his biographers he is not perceptive here.

Samson and Delilah

To see that this is so, consider how we would have to read the story about Samson's capture if this interpretation of Milton's were right.

It is true in the narrative that Delilah wants Samson to tell her the secret of his strength.[36] But, by this point in the story, Samson has some experience of the suffering that comes from having his secrets betrayed by a woman he loves. Samson's earlier marriage to a Philistine woman at Timnath ended abruptly at the wedding when his bride treacherously revealed the secret she had wheedled out of him and Samson exploded in wrath, wreaking devastation on the Philistines before going home, without his bride. And so Samson, who is as capable of drawing inferences from bitter experience as other people, does not tell Delilah his secret when she tries to get it out of him. Rather he lies to her instead. He tells her *something* in order to stop her entreaties, but he does not tell her the truth.

The wisdom of his decision to lie is immediately apparent—to Samson as well as to the audience of the story—because Delilah loses no time in betraying him by passing his apparent revelation on to the Philistines, who use what Delilah tells them to try to capture Samson.

One might suppose that Samson would react to Delilah's betrayal in the same way that he reacted to the betrayal on the part of the woman of Timnath, by exploding into fury, leaving her, and killing Philistines. But, in fact, nothing of the sort happens: no fury, no leaving, no attacks on the Philistines. On the contrary, after Delilah's betrayal we simply get a repetition of the same scenario, with some shoddy additions: Delilah complains about Samson's lying and pushes him to tell her the truth. In the circumstances, Delilah's complaint is brazen, as she and Samson must both recognize. The *reason* Delilah knows that Samson has lied to her is that she betrayed his revelation to the Philistines and the Philistines were nonetheless unsuccessful in capturing him. The lack of Delilah's care for Samson is thus apparent, and she must know that he sees it, too. So, apparently, her attitude toward him matters little to either of them, provided that she is available for him.

But how are we to account for this? How are we to understand the fact that in the story hot-tempered Samson not only does not explode against Delilah and the Philistines in league with her when he finds that she has betrayed him, but instead tamely gives into Delilah's wheedling a second time and pretends again to tell her his secret? The explanation cannot consist just in the fact that he loves her, however we are to understand love in his case. He loved the Philistine woman of Timnath, too, and actually married her; Delilah, by contrast, is only a concubine of his. But his love for the woman of Timnath did not keep Samson from violent retaliation for her betrayal. Why is he so tame with regard to Delilah after he sees *her* betrayal?

The answer to this question is contained in effect in Samson's response to Delilah's initial request for his secret. Why is his response to her initial request a lie? Surely, because he does not trust her not to betray him to his enemies to be put to death. So here is what the narrative implies: Samson believes that the woman he loves, with whom he is sexually intimate, cannot be trusted not to want him dead. This is a fairly stunning failure to trust, on Samson's part.[37]

Samson's past relations with women give us some insight into his failure to trust Delilah. The first woman he loved, the woman of Timnath, betrayed him to his enemies during the wedding. When he was finally ready to forgive her and take her back, he found that she was sleeping with a man Samson had thought of as a friend, or at least an ally. Even we, who are used to finding life imitating soap operas, might be traumatized by two such betrayals in a row. Samson's next recorded intimacy with a woman is therefore, perhaps unsurprisingly, with a prostitute. But it turns out that a one-night stand with a prostitute is not much safer for Samson than accepting vulnerability by committing himself in marriage. While Samson was with the prostitute, the text says, his enemies were informed and gathered together to get him. It does not matter much whether his enemies were informed of his presence by the woman herself. Whether or not he was betrayed to the Philistines by her, it is clear that casual sex is no safer for Samson than giving himself in marriage to a woman he loves. And so we come to Delilah. The text tells us that Samson loves Delilah, and, in truth, Samson does stay with her; but he also keeps a considerable psychic distance from her, and he does not trust her not to betray him to his death.

So Delilah does not betray Samson's trust as his bride of Timnath did. On the contrary, Samson does not give her any trust to betray. He is prepared to take her and enjoy her; he is not prepared to give any of himself to her. And that is why Samson is not angry when he finds that Delilah is in league with his enemies. Because he has lied to her, she cannot do him any real harm; and because he has not invested himself in her, he does not much mind when she tries to do him in. She is like a cat one has carefully declawed; her attempts at attack may be occasions for amusement or annoyance, but they cannot cause any serious reaction. Delilah is right when she says to Samson in exasperation, after three futile attempts to learn his secret and betray him, that Samson has only mocked her and his heart is not with her.

Milton's interpretation of Samson's fault

Now, on Milton's view, how will we have to read the story of Delilah's fourth and final attempt to betray Samson? After three occasions on *each* of which it has to be obvious even to the most obtuse that Delilah has betrayed him to his enemies, on Milton's reading of the fourth occasion Samson is so wearied by the endless importunities of the woman he is besotted with that he tells her the truth about the way in which his enemies can do him in.

But, on Milton's reading of this episode, how are we supposed to understand Samson's beliefs and desires? It cannot be that Samson now believes Delilah is trustworthy,[38] and it is equally absurd to suppose that he tells Delilah his secret because he now desires to surrender to his enemies.

It is true that the story says Delilah vexed him practically to death, so that in the end he told her all his heart. And he does in fact this time, for the first time, tell Delilah something that is true: he has been a Nazirite from the womb, and he has never been shaven. But the question remains whether, in telling her this truth, Samson is telling her what he believes is the key to his capture by the Philistines. Does Samson believe, as

Milton supposes he does, that the rest of what he tells Delilah is also true: if he is shaven, his strength will leave him?[39]

If Samson did believe it, then, evidently, he would also have to think that Delilah would not use the information to do him in, or else it would have to be the case that he did not care very much if she did. If it is not sufficiently clear that neither of these states for Samson is psychologically credible, the rest of the episode shows decisively that postulating either of them is wrong.

If Samson had resolved to let Delilah in on the way in which the Philistines could capture him, then, when the Philistines did surround him, Samson would realize he was lost. Even if he had somehow supposed that, after three times of betraying him to his enemies for destruction, Delilah had somehow turned trustworthy, he would know how wrong he had been when he found the Philistines around him. If what he had told Delilah were in his own view the information needed to destroy him, then, when he saw himself surrounded, he would know that the Philistines finally had him in their power. Or, if he had anticipated such a result but did not care, then he would simply surrender tamely—or at least despairingly—when the Philistines attacked him.

But none of these things happens in the narrative. Instead, in the story, when Delilah wakes him with the cry that the Philistines are upon him, Samson responds by saying: "I will go out this time as before and shake myself free" (16: 20). To suppose that Samson has this reaction after having given the manifestly treacherous Delilah what he himself believes is the key to his destruction is to make psychological gibberish of the story.

So, although very many people read the narrative as Milton does here, Milton cannot be reading the story correctly at this crucial point.

And it is a good thing that Milton's reading is wrong, because otherwise we would have to suppose that Samson's fault is blabbing, as Milton says, and that in this story God punishes blabbing with blindness, exile, imprisonment, forced labor, and all the rest. On that way of seeing the story, Samson looks more pathetic than morally deplorable. Blabbing may be contemptible, as Milton says, but it is hardly a serious moral wrong. As far as that goes, it is not clear that it is a moral wrong at all in Samson's case. There is no indication in the story that Samson is under any obligation not to tell the source of his strength to anyone he chooses; in the story, neither God nor anyone else imposes secrecy on Samson as a moral obligation.[40]

But, then, how are we to understand this last episode with Delilah? If Milton is not right in the way he understands the cause of Samson's downfall, why did God depart from Samson, as the story says God does? What is it that Samson is culpable for?

Samson's exploits

Without doubt, the narrative of Samson's life and acts often makes Samson seem like a brute, and contemporary sensibilities can find plenty to censure in him.[41] We could engage in the much-indulged contemporary practice of trying to locate *every* outrage to our sensibilities in the narrative, everything from Samson's lamentable attitude toward women to his unspeakable treatment of foxes, to say nothing of his recurrent murderous mayhem; but we could also just take these things as deplored and skip the exercise. There are, however, some less obvious faults in Samson that are worth highlighting here; they have to do with Samson as the liberator of his people and with the mission for which Samson was born. Looking at these will put us in a better position to understand Samson's last episode with Delilah, and understanding that episode will in turn help us find an answer to the question about Samson's culpability for his own downfall and suffering. This may seem the long way round to that answer, but it is the quickest way I see.

Apart from the last and final episode that includes the events culminating in his death, there are six (or, depending on how one counts, seven) episodes in the narrative in which Samson demonstrates his great strength. They are these:

(1) the destruction of a lion (14: 5–6),

(2) the slaying of thirty Philistines (14: 19),

(3) the burning of the Philistine fields and the slaughter of the Philistines afterwards* (15: 4–8),

(4) the slaughter of the Philistines at Lehi (15: 14–15),

(5) the removal of the gates from a Philistine city* (16: 3),

(6) the first three escapes from the Philistines in the presence of Delilah* (16: 9–14).

The episodes asterisked in the list make no mention of the spirit of the Lord coming on Samson, and it is worth comparing those episodes with the others. It is helpful to begin by looking at those episodes in which the Lord's spirit does come on Samson.

Except for the first, all of the episodes involving Samson's demonstration of prodigious strength have to do with the Philistines; and even the first could be understood as involving the Philistines indirectly. Insofar as the work Samson was born to do requires him to live and the lion's attack threatens him, Samson's divinely appointed task of liberating his people from the Philistines requires him to ward off the lion. Perhaps that is why the spirit of the Lord came on him in that case. Or perhaps the episode was meant to be propaedeutic, teaching Samson what he could do, what he did not have to fear, to ready him for the warfare of liberation for his people that is his vocation.

In any event, the second episode is clearly connected to Samson's divinely appointed work. When Samson insists on marrying a Philistine woman over his parents' sensible objections, the text comments that Samson's parents did not know that God was seeking an occasion against the Philistines (14: 4). The occasion comes during the wedding when the Philistine guests succeed in getting Samson's bride to betray him in order to cheat Samson out of the prize set for solving a riddle Samson propounds. The ensuing violence, during which the Lord's spirit comes on Samson, could have served as the beginning of an Israelite revolt, led by Samson, against Philistine rule. At any rate, it is possible to read the text as providing *some* divine warrant for Samson's acts in this episode; and, to that extent, however attenuated the warrant is, those acts have some connection to Samson's mission.

The fourth episode can be construed in roughly the same way. The Philistines come in considerable numbers to take Samson, who is recognized by them as Israel's champion. There is, therefore, in this battle something connected to the public welfare, to the well-being of Samson's people. Not only Samson but also the Philistines and the Israelites can see the battle as having to do with Samson as the liberator of Israel. In this battle, too, the Lord's spirit comes on Samson.

In all these episodes, then, although, as the story makes clear, Samson's desire for survival or for his personal vengeance is his primary motivation for action, nonetheless Samson's victories are also understood by the Philistines and Israelites as victories for Samson's people. And, perhaps for this reason, in all these episodes, the text says that the Lord's spirit came on Samson.

The other episodes, those in which the text omits to say that the Lord's spirit comes on Samson, are considerably harder to construe in the same way. In those other exploits, Samson does not appear to be fighting as the champion of his people, even as a concomitant of his pursuing his own goals and desires. In these other episodes, he does not seem to be contributing in any serious way to the liberation of his people by his fighting with the Philistines. All of the episodes of this sort—the third, the fifth, and the sixth on the list above—are cases in which Samson's fighting seems prompted only by self-regarding vengefulness after self-indulgently imprudent liaisons with women.

For example, in the third episode on the list above, Samson is furious when he finds himself in effect divorced, without his consent, from the Philistine woman he had married and then deserted at the wedding ceremony. The father of this woman, Samson's Philistine father-in-law, assumed with some justification that Samson was never going to return to his daughter; and so he gave his daughter to another man, a friend of Samson's. When Samson discovered what his father-in-law had done, the havoc Samson wreaked on the fields of the Philistines in his wrath is understandably described by others in the story as a matter of Samson's vengeance for wrong done to himself in a private quarrel with his father-in-law: "The Philistines asked, 'Who did this?,' and they said, 'Samson, the son-in-law of the Timnite, because he took his wife and gave her to his companion' " (15: 6). The Philistines react to Samson's mayhem by killing Samson's bride and father-in-law, thereby prompting another round of violence from Samson, which Samson himself describes as his revenge for what his enemies did to him (15: 7). Whatever one may think of violence as a means of political liberation, neither Samson nor his enemies understand the violence in this episode as Samson's contribution to the liberation of his people from the Philistines. In this episode, Samson is using his great strength just for his own sake, in his private quarrel, seeking personal vengeance for the wrongs done to him in connection with his bride. In this case, the Lord's spirit does not come on Samson when he attacks the Philistines.

In the fifth episode, Samson seeks out a prostitute who is in Gaza, the Philistine territory to which Samson is taken at the end of the story when the Philistines finally succeed in capturing him. Clearly, there is a kind of complacency, if not arrogance, in Samson's taking the risk of visiting a prostitute in enemy territory; and, of course, in the story Samson's enemies do get wind of his presence, alone and unprotected, in their midst. They immediately form a plan for capturing him. That plan depends on the fact that the city's gates are barred at night. Because the gates are closed at night, the Philistines feel sure that they have Samson penned up in their city till the morning, when they plan to surround him and capture him, to put him to death.

But the story suggests that Samson also has a plan and that his plan involves the city's gates, too. The story says that Samson got up at midnight to leave through the barred gates. The story does not say that Samson knew his presence had been revealed to his enemies. As far as that goes, the story gives no suggestion that Samson is or needs to be worried about the Philistines, even if they were to surround him in the morning. He has, after all, single-handedly defeated a small army of Philistines in a battle not too long before. Nonetheless, Samson gets up in the night to leave the barred and gated town—and to make sure the Philistines know that the great Samson was in it.

Samson could leave the town in some simple way, by using his strength to get through the gates somehow. But getting away is not what Samson wants, or at least not all he wants. Samson removes the gates themselves, to flaunt his strength and to manifest his disdain of his enemies to them. Samson will have the whore he wants when he wants her, without hindrance from the contemptible Philistines, just because he is the mighty Samson. If there is any doubt about this reading, it ought to be dispelled by what Samson does with those gates. It would have been a sufficient thumbing of his nose at the Philistines for Samson to uproot the gates and throw them down outside the city wall. What Samson actually does is to put them on his shoulders and lug them all the way up to the top of a neighboring hillside, to deposit them there, in full view of the surrounding country. There is more than a little hubris in this. And the Lord's spirit does not come on Samson for this stunt.

The sixth episode: Samson's revelation to Delilah

In the third episode, involving his erstwhile father-in-law in Timnath, Samson used his strength to attack the Philistines for personal reasons, for his private revenge rather than for public reasons related to his mission as Israel's liberator. In the fifth episode, involving the prostitute in Gaza, there was an even worse misuse of the divine gift of strength in the arrogant willfulness of Samson's seeking sex in Philistine territory and in his manifesting an insolent disdain for his enemies by leaving their town in the manner he does. What shall we say, then, about the sixth episode, the episode involving Samson's affair with Delilah?

The first thing to notice is the time of the sixth episode; it is important to see the place of this episode in the trajectory of Samson's life. The sixth episode occurs shortly before Samson's death in the Philistine temple while the Philistines are celebrating Samson's capture. Now the narrative says that Samson judged Israel for twenty years;[42] and so, since the sixth episode occurs shortly before his death, at the time of Samson's affair with Delilah, Samson's career as liberator of his people has spanned almost two decades. And what does the story suggest? Certainly not that by that time Samson had succeeded in liberating his people from their oppressors, the Philistines. In fact, the Philistines are still at least a force to be reckoned with seriously, as their capture of Samson itself makes plain. But there is also no sign that, at the time the sixth episode takes place, Samson is planning any great public exploits designed for the liberation of his people. On the contrary, the only thing recorded of him at this stage of his career is that he is busy dallying with Delilah. His miraculous birth, his earlier victories over the enemies of his people, his intimacy with God have come to this: after twenty years, his people are not liberated from the Philistines, and his strength is going into preserving a liaison with a woman from whom he knows he has to keep a considerable, careful psychic distance.

Furthermore, consider the way in which his great strength comes into play in the episode with Delilah. With the Gaza prostitute, Samson used his power as a means of evading and scorning his enemies. With Delilah, he no longer cares to evade the Philistines, and he even seems bored with scorning them. He knows that they cannot beat him, and he no longer has much interest, apparently, in beating them. He is content just to let them surround him when they will and to brush them off like flies, as a nuisance not worth much notice, when they do. How glorious a flowering of his life and mission is this? The great gift of strength God gave him for the liberation of his people he is now using as a private resource to keep his dismal and inadequate love life going. The Lord's spirit does not come on him when he does.

But this small-mindedness and self-absorption are not the worst of the episode with Delilah.

On each of the first three times when Delilah presses Samson for his secret and he tells her a lie, the Philistines immediately afterwards do to Samson what Samson's lie leads them to expect will defeat Samson. At least after the first occasion, Samson cannot be surprised at what happens; he must expect it. So, at least after the first time, when Samson tells Delilah a lie about what will defeat him, he must expect that the Philistines will do to him whatever, with his lie, he puts into their heads to do. Furthermore, it is clear that, on each occasion, because he has lied about the thing that will (supposedly) render him weak, Samson expects to shake free of the Philistine devices, as he himself puts it in the story. This is also what he expects when, on the fourth time of being betrayed by Delilah, he finds himself surrounded by the Philistines and shaven. When he sees the Philistines around him after he has told Delilah about his Nazirite status, he supposes that he is going to experience nothing more than the fourth repeat of the same farce. On the fourth occasion, he tells himself that he will shake himself free this time as before.

It cannot be, then, that he himself really believed what he told Delilah on the fourth occasion—namely, that, if he were shaven, he would be weak like other men. And why would Samson believe a thing of that sort? It is so clearly false. Contemporary commentators themselves point out that in the previous episodes in the story the emphasis has been on the Lord as a source of Samson's strength; and so they think that this mention of Samson's hair as the source of his strength is a sign of different traditions in the Samson stories.[43] But, if we consider the story as a whole, in its final form, then both from the audience's point of view and from Samson's, there is just one correct explanation of the source of Samson's strength: it comes from the Lord.

Although the text makes plain that Samson's strength often comes to him with the tumultuous excitement of the Lord's spirit rushing into him, this is not, apparently, the way it always works. There is, for example, no mention of the Lord's spirit rushing into Samson when Samson brings down the pillars of the Philistine temple. In that case, however, the story also makes it evident that the regrowth of Samson's hair is not sufficient to restore Samson's strength.[44] His strength returns to him only after his prayer to God petitioning God to restore his strength. God's role in Samson's strength is therefore in fact implied by the story at that point. Furthermore, the narrative drives home the point that Samson's strength comes not from his hair but from God by its comment on Samson's mistaken belief that he can shake off the Philistines on the fourth occasion, as in the preceding three. The narrative explains Samson's mistake *not* by saying that Samson did not know he was shaven. Rather, the narrative says, Samson did not know that the Lord had departed from him. This text thus also confirms that the experience of the inrushing of the Lord's spirit is not necessary for Samson's being unusually strong. If it were, Samson could hardly have thought he was strong when he was not.

So the right way to understand Samson's fourth explanation to Delilah of the secret of his strength is as a mixture of truth and lies. Samson believes and says truly that he has never been shaven because he has been a Nazirite of God's from birth. But the next part of his speech is not true and he does not believe it: it is not the case that simply shaving him will destroy his strength. The lazy complacency that keeps him by Delilah lying and brushing off the Philistine attacks when they come leads to his revealing some deep and important truth to Delilah; but it does not give her the secret of his strength, and Samson does not expect that it will. When he tells Delilah that cutting his hair will make him weak, he is again lying to her, at least in the sense that he is telling her as true what he himself believes to be false.

Samson's culpability for his revelation to Delilah

It is important to see the implication of this last of Samson's explanations to Delilah. After the first three attacks by the Philistines, Samson has to know that his telling Delilah about his Nazirite status is tantamount to giving it up. If Delilah and the Philistines believe that Samson's strength is in his hair, then Delilah and the Philistines will shave him, and Samson must understand that they will.

In this light, consider the attitude that underlies Samson's telling Delilah about his Nazirite status. That status was given to him together with the mission to which his life was supposed to be dedicated. But Samson is not taking that mission seriously here.

In the episode with Delilah, Samson is fighting with the Philistines not for the sake of freeing his people but just as a way of continuing to sleep with Delilah. That in these circumstances Samson elects to tell Delilah about his Nazirite status is evidence that that status does not mean much to him. Samson does not suppose that his strength depends on his hair. Rather, Samson takes it to depend on God, and in the story he is right to do so; Samson's strength is God's gift to Samson. But, if strength is God's gift to Samson, Nazirite status is God's demand of Samson. To rely on having the gift and to be willing to dispense oneself from the demand is to treat God as if he were in Samson's service. Explaining his Nazirite status to Delilah as a means of placating his Philistine concubine and continuing to hang around in enemy territory enjoying her is a little like a Dominican's using his habit as a makeshift sheet for his mistress. The purpose for which the symbol is being used shows a disdain for the thing symbolized. It therefore also shows a disdain for God, to whom respect for the symbol and what it symbolizes is due.[45]

The worrisome element in Samson's attitude toward God after the battle at Lehi thus finds its full-blown awfulness here.[46] Here, with Delilah, Samson takes it for granted that, since he is the champion of his people, God will have to continue to bestow the gift of strength on him, but that it does not matter much what Samson himself does or how Samson treats God. As Samson sees it, dispensing himself from his Nazirite status as a means of mollifying his mistress carries no cost for him, the mighty Samson. With unreflective complacency, he simply assumes that God will keep him mighty when the Philistines surround him after shaving his hair.

And so, in an odd sort of way, by his attitude toward his Nazirite status and by lying about it, Samson makes true what was false before he lied about it: cutting his hair deprives him of his strength. Samson's strength departs from him when his hair is cut, not because his strength is in his hair but because the Lord departs from him when Samson does not care that his hair is cut. If Samson was insolent toward the Philistines in the episode with the Gaza prostitute, he is contumelious toward God in this episode with Delilah.

This, then, is what Samson is culpable for.

Love and closeness

At the start of the story of his exploits, Samson fills up with the spirit of the Lord; and when he does, the narrative makes clear, he is wild, invincible and triumphant. He has a certain sort of intimacy with God, or, at least, he is very familiar with God; and he is glorious in his victories for his people. At the end, by the time of the episode with Delilah, Samson seems just jaded as regards his mission and alienated from the people around him, with the kind of loneliness besetting a person who cannot trust even the woman with whom he is sexually intimate not to betray him to death. At this point in the story, he looks petty, isolated, and shabby. At the start of the story, Samson is so connected to God that he simply presents himself to God as thirsty, and almighty God provides the water. God is with him, as well as somehow in him through the inrushing of his spirit. At the end of the episode with Delilah, Samson is so disconnected from God that he does not even know God has left him, until he discovers it when the Philistines finally succeed in overpowering him. From start to finish of his career as God's warrior, until the ultimate episode in his life's narrative, Samson's trajectory is precipitously downward.

As I explained in Chapter 6, closeness to one person, Jerome, cannot be brought about unilaterally by someone else, Paula, who desires it; it is not up to Paula alone whether or not Jerome is close to her. *Jerome's* unwillingness to share his thoughts and feelings with Paula, for example, will be sufficient to isolate *her* from him. And, even if Jerome were willing to reveal his thoughts and feelings to Paula, Paula would still not be close to Jerome if he did not care about Paula's reactions to his revelations of himself to her. If the state of Paula's mind or will as regards Jerome would make little difference to Jerome, then Paula would not be close to Jerome. Paula is close to Jerome only if it is possible for Jerome to be hurt by Paula's reactions to him. And if he is willing to be vulnerable to Paula, then he is thereby also willing to let some of the things that matter to him be in Paula's control, not in his. So Paula's being close to Jerome also includes Jerome's being vulnerable to Paula. To this extent, Paula's being close to Jerome requires Jerome's being willing to be dependent on Paula for things he cares about, at least to some degree.

On this view of closeness between persons, it is evident that Delilah was never close to Samson. Where Delilah is concerned, it is obvious that Samson is largely self-protective; he hides his thoughts and feelings from her. It also does not seem to matter much to him whether or not Delilah betrays him. He takes great care not to let his welfare depend on her, and he tries to ensure that he is not vulnerable to her in any significant way. And so, although Samson sleeps with Delilah, and we have the text's word for it that he loves her, in some sense of 'love,' it is clear that, in manifold ways, Samson is not willing to let Delilah be close to him.

As I explained in earlier chapters, a person can have a kind of self-willed loneliness, in which other people are closed out from him because of his refusal to trust in them. Samson's relationship to Delilah has at its center a self-willed, self-protective loneliness of this kind. But it is important to see that, in the narrative, there is also an increasing distance, analogically considered, in Samson's relationship to God. By the time of his affair with Delilah, Samson has closed out God, too.

Nothing in the text supports the idea that it is possible for a human being to hide his mind or feelings from God; and so it might seem as if part of what is necessary for closeness between persons is always part of any relationship between God and a human person. But this would be a mistaken impression. If Paula were a specially intuitive person who succeeded in reading Jerome insightfully when he was trying but failing to hide his mind from her, she would not be close to him just in virtue of her insight into him.[47] In the same way, a human person can choose to bring his thoughts and feelings to God or refuse to do so. If he refuses, then not even the omniscience of God is sufficient to produce closeness between God and him.

Furthermore, a person can accept or reject his dependence on the deity, just as he can accept or reject his dependence on a human will other than his own. In Samson's case, the evidence in the story suggests that this condition for closeness between persons was somehow at risk or imperfectly present even at the outset of Samson's relationship with God, when God's spirit was rushing into Samson for his exploits of superhuman strength. At the outset, Samson wants God to provide him with what he needs—water, strength—but Samson gives no sign of accepting vulnerability to God in consequence. Even in the beginning of his exploits, Samson is not willing to let what he wants depend on what God wants; rather, he seems to expect that the nature of his own desires is sufficient to determine what God does for him. Early in the story, after the battle at Lehi, when Samson prays to God because he needs water, there is nothing conditional about his prayer. As I pointed out above, Samson does not say to God "if it be your will" or any other such formula—not even "please"—to indicate that the will of the deity being petitioned can or should have a role in determining the outcome of the petition. On the contrary, Samson's prayer for water seems to have as its unquestioned assumption only that *God* needs *him*—to be Israel's champion against the Philistines—and not that Samson's needs are in any way dependent on what God himself wants. To get God to give him water, Samson just points out to God that without water he will fall into the hands of the Philistines. He apparently supposes that that outcome would be intolerable to God, who can therefore be gotten to do whatever it takes to avoid it. (But there, of course, Samson would be mistaken, as the rest of the story makes painfully clear.)

It is true that in his prayer at Lehi Samson says to God, "it is you who have given this great victory into the hand of your servant." On the other hand, it is noteworthy that, when Samson rejoices over victory in the battle at Lehi, it is not gratitude for God's help, or even acknowledgment of it, which comes to his mind first. His initial thought is simply to exult in what he takes himself to have accomplished. What he says in the first flush of victory at the end of the battle is just this: "with the jawbone of an ass I have killed a thousand men!" By way of contrast, compare what Ehud says to his countrymen when he has single-handedly triumphed over the king of the Moabites: "The Lord has given Moab, your enemy, into your hands" (Judg. 3: 28). There is in Samson, then, at least some double-mindedness about whose strength it is that has gotten the victory over the Philistines at Lehi. That at bottom Samson takes pride in its being *his* strength and *his* victory, rather than God's, is strongly suggested by his triumphant line about himself at the end of the battle. If it is his own strength that brings him victory in battle, however, then he does not need to be susceptible to God's will or dependent on it for the victories and successes he desires.

So there is some isolating self-focus and self-will that closes others out even early in Samson's story. But things are much worse in the episode with Delilah. When Samson chooses to reveal his Nazirite status to Delilah, he thereby also wills to discard it for the sake of preserving his tawdry relations with her. At this stage of the story, then, he has wholly given up caring about what God wants from him. At this point, God's desires and constraints have lost any purchase on Samson. They do not matter to Samson, provided only that Samson can have what he wants; and he presumes that he can have what he wants from God without being vulnerable to God's demands on him. He is not close to God when he does so. In the final episode with Delilah, God is as closed out from Samson as Delilah is.

In Samson's case, neither erotic love nor the inrushing of the spirit of the Lord is sufficient for closeness between him and the persons (divine or human) who should be close to him. At any rate, it is clear that, where Samson is concerned, Delilah cannot get closeness by physical intimacy alone, and even God cannot bring it about simply by causing the impressive and uncommon spiritual connection of his spirit's rushing into Samson. God cannot break through Samson's self-willed loneliness to be close to Samson any more than Delilah can unless Samson is willing that he do so. As the narrative presents him at the time of his affair with Delilah, Samson has slipped very far, from the familiar connection to God Samson had at the beginning of his career and his gloriousness in military exploits to this pathetic condition at the end when the Philistines catch him with Delilah.

Here, at the end, then, there is a great distance between Samson and the other persons around him. Samson is willing to stay at a distance from Delilah, who is a woman he loves (as the narrative describes it); and there is also a serious distance between Samson and God. For closeness to Delilah or to God, Samson would have to be willing to be self-revealing and susceptible to each of them; and he would have to be willing to let what matters to him be dependent, at least to some degree, on what another (divine or human) person thinks and wants. But, in the course of his career, Samson is increasingly unwilling to do this, most manifestly in his shabby love affair with Delilah, but progressively also in his relations to God.

Early in his story, Samson takes God's gift of strength for granted, as if it were self-gotten, rather than being a gift of God's to him. At the end of his story, in the episode with Delilah, he shrugs off God's commands about his Nazirite status, as if in Samson's case obedience to divine commands was optional and up to him. Samson's distance from God in the episode with Delilah is the fruition of a distance from God that was there in Samson at least in embryo from the outset, even when the Lord's spirit came on him to make him triumphant and victorious. But, by the end of the story, the separation between Samson and those persons, divine and human, to whom he could have been close, leaves him in a lamentable condition. The intimate relationship he might have had with them could have been (and, in God's case, should have been) the basis for Samson's flourishing, as a man and as the liberator of his people. Instead, by the end of his life, neglecting his mission and his God, hanging around Delilah, he seems just a derelict version of what he might have been.

None of this is to deny that Samson in some sense loves either Delilah or God. The text explicitly says that Samson loves Delilah, and it seems to me Milton reads the story right in supposing that in some sense Samson loves God, too. Because human beings are complicated and can be severely internally divided, it is perfectly possible for a person to love double-mindedly (in an ordinary rather than strenuous sense of 'love'[48]) a person from whom he also keeps a self-absorbed distance. What should we say, for example, about a drug-abusing mother who tells her children that she really loves them as social services are taking them away? It does not seem right to think that people in such situations are invariably lying or self-deceived. And yet, clearly, they have not cared much about the deepest desires of the hearts of the people whom they claim to love. And so, in some double-minded (or double-hearted) way, love in the ordinary mode can coexist with the rejection of the care and closeness requisite for love. Love in the ordinary mode and lonely distance from the people one loves are compatible.[49]

On the one hand, then, it is true, as the narrative says, that Samson loves Delilah, in the ordinary sense of 'love;' no doubt, in this sense, Samson also loves God. But he does not let Delilah be close to him; and, *mutatis mutandis*, the same point applies to Samson's relationship to God. As far as his relationship with God goes, there is also a problem for Samson as regards the offices of love. It is clear that there can be an office of love between God and a human person, and that this office is variable, just as the offices of love between human persons are. But, whatever the variability, the office of love between God and a human person ought to fall within the genus of relations between creator and creature. In Samson's attitude toward God, as manifested in his prayer at Lehi or in his indifference to his Nazirite status, to one degree or another there is a violation of that office. In fact, by the time of his affair with Delilah, it seems evident that, whatever Samson may desire for himself from God, Samson no longer has a desire for God.[50] Finally, insofar as shame can consist in a failure to be desired in circumstances where such desire is appropriate,[51] Samson shames God in failing to have a desire for God. I do not mean that God either is or feels shamed in virtue of what Samson does. I mean only that in Samson's stance toward God in the episode with Delilah Samson's attitude toward God is a shaming attitude. That is, it is an attitude that would shame its recipient if the attitude stemmed from standards that were correct and appropriate. The alienation from God in this attitude is evident. And so, for all these reasons, it is also true that, on the strenuous account of love, Samson does not love God.

I have focused here on Samson's relation to God, because it is easier to miss the point in God's case; but, *mutatis mutandis*, the same things apply to Samson's attitude toward Delilah. When Delilah upbraids Samson for not caring about her, it is not hard to see the truth in her complaint. Since there are no characters in the story who are better candidates for persons close to Samson than Delilah and God, by the time of his connection to Delilah, Samson has become isolated within himself. Understanding Samson's self-willed loneliness in this way is helpful in considering the end of the story.

The end of the story

The part of the narrative that, in effect, constitutes the end of Samson's story begins with the text's comment that Samson did not know the Lord had departed from him (16: 20). Samson is culpable for the contumely that prompts God to depart from him;[52]

but God's departing from Samson is responsible for the catastrophe that follows, and it is worth noticing this fact. If God had stayed with (or in) Samson just a little longer, just until after the last Philistine attack when the Philistines shave him, then Samson would not have been captured by the Philistines. Samson is captured, blinded, imprisoned, subjected to hard labor, and paraded as a trophy to an alien god because God chooses to leave Samson just when he does.

As it turns out in this narrative, then, God does not have the sort of indirect responsibility for horrifying suffering at issue in the examples discussed at the outset of this chapter; in this narrative, God has direct responsibility for the suffering Samson undergoes at the hands of the Philistines. God could have waited till Samson was safe from Philistine attack before leaving him, and at that point he could have brought home to Samson that from that point onwards Samson would be bereft of the strength God had previously given him. God could have made sure Samson understood God had departed from him, so that Samson would know he needed to stay out of danger in consequence. In short, God could have let Samson off with a warning, as it were. Instead, in the story, without warning, God leaves Samson just when Samson must have his strength in order to avoid ruin.[53] So, although Samson brings the disaster on himself in the sense that his contumelious acts are responsible for God's leaving him, it is God's leaving Samson at that very time that lands Samson in the catastrophic condition he is in at the end.

Why does God do this?

This is not a question asking whether in the story God has a morally sufficient reason for his actions. It is only a question about the motivation that the story enables us to attribute to God for acting as he does. This question in effect returns us to that other question with which this chapter started—namely, whether the life of a person suffering horrifying evil because of his own evil actions can somehow be a good for that person. We will have an explanation of God's leaving Samson when he does if it emerges that, in the narrative, there is something brought about by the suffering resulting from God's leaving Samson that redeems the horrifying evil of Samson's life and makes Samson's whole life a good for Samson.

If there is anything of that sort in this narrative, it will have to come in the very last acts of Samson's life, when he is a captive among the Philistines. In his captivity among the Philistines, Samson is plunged into all the suffering described at the outset of this chapter. The mission for which he was born looks like a decisive failure, too. The victorious Philistines are having a celebration to thank their god for letting them capture Samson, and Samson is the main entertainment for the celebration. By the time of this celebration, Samson has been a Philistine prisoner long enough for his hair to have begun to grow back, and also long enough for some change to have taken place in his psyche, too.

The nature of the change can be seen in the prayer Samson makes to God in the Philistine temple. Blind Samson asks the unwary young man who is guiding him to let him feel the pillars on which the roof of the temple rests. As the subsequent events make clear, the plan Samson has in mind when he makes this request to his young guide is one which requires great strength; and that strength, as Samson has always recognized, depends on God—in this case, on God's coming back to Samson. That is why Samson prays to God for strength even though his hair is grown. The regrowth of Samson's hair is not the return of Samson's strength; the restoration of his strength requires the return of his God to him, and Samson knows it.

The prayer Samson makes on this occasion is significantly different from that other recorded prayer of his, after his victory at Lehi when he needed water. When he was in great need of water, Samson prayed to God in this way: "It was you who gave this great deliverance by the hand of your servant. And now I am dying of thirst, and I will fall into the hands of the uncircumcised." What Samson says now, standing between the pillars, is this: "Oh Lord God, remember me, please, and give me strength, please, just this once, O God; let me be avenged on the Philistines with revenge for my two eyes" (16: 28). The elements notably lacking in the earlier prayer are here now. There is not just one invocation of God in this prayer; there are two. And although the prayer is very short, just a sentence in effect, 'please' also occurs twice in it. There is a plea in it too, of the sort that was lacking in the earlier prayer. Someone who says "please, just this once" to another person thereby conveys the power of his own need or desire and his awareness of his dependence on the other person to give him what he wants.

These differences between the earlier and the later prayer may strike some readers as small or unimportant. But assessing the difference in that way is a serious mistake. In the first prayer Samson took for granted that God would give him what he wanted; in the second prayer he petitions God in the clear understanding that the granting of the petition is up to God, and God alone. In this understanding, there is also an acknowledgment of the importance to Samson of his relationship to God, for its own sake as well as for the strength that comes to Samson because of it. There is in it a desire for God as well as a desire for what God can give. It may help us to see the magnitude of this change by transposing it to a human case. In *Pride and Prejudice*, when the wealthy and aristocratic Darcy declares his love for Elizabeth and asks her to marry him, in the manifest conviction that a woman in her socio-economic position could not conceivably turn him down, she rejects him, with wrath barely constrained by civility, in these words: "You are mistaken, Mr. Darcy, if you suppose that the mode of your declaration affected me in any other way, than as it spared me the concern which I might have felt in refusing you, had you behaved in a more gentleman-like fashion." Months later, and much chastened, he renews his suit to her in these words: "You are too generous to trifle with me. If your feelings are still what they were last April, tell me so at once. *My* affections and wishes are unchanged, but one word from you will silence me on the subject forever." *This* time he really *asks* her if she will marry him. He may say that his affections and wishes are unchanged, but in fact they are in one sense radically altered. Now he desires her for what she is, a person in her own right, with a will and mind of her own, perfectly capable of refusing him if she chooses—and so she accepts him. He has learned to be open and even vulnerable to her, and she has learned to desire him because of it. She has grown close to him in consequence.[54]

The implicit repentance in Samson's later prayer of his earlier contumely toward God is by itself a huge change for the better in Samson. The things in the earlier prayer that showed that Samson was not willing to let God (or anyone else) be close to him are absent in this later prayer. In it, Samson's need, his vulnerability, his recognition that his own will is not enough to save him, are all manifest; and Samson is willing to let them be evident both to himself and to God. In this condition, he is no longer shielding himself in a loneliness that keeps even God at bay. For that reason, it is then possible for God to draw near to Samson. The value and the importance of the change in Samson are that it brings him to this condition. When the writer of the letter to the Hebrews includes Samson in the list of people who are paradigms of faith,[55] surely it is Samson's last prayer for strength which warrants that assessment.[56]

In the narrative, that God shares this view of Samson's prayer is made evident by the fact that God grants Samson's petition. God, who departed from Samson when he was distant from God and contumelious toward him, returns to Samson after this prayer. God fills Samson with enough strength to bring down the entire Philistine temple by pushing on its central pillars.

For my purposes, it is important to note that the turn to God represented by Samson's last prayer coexists with much of Samson's old spirit. Although Samson's suffering turns him, it does not tame him. However exactly the change in Samson is to be described, it would be a mistake to see Samson as quelled or made docile by his suffering. The prayer he makes to God in his Philistine captivity is not a prayer asking for forgiveness, of the sort that Daniel, for example, makes on behalf of his people in exile;[57] nor is it one asking for guidance in decision, of the sort that David, for example, regularly makes.[58] Samson asks neither for forgiveness nor for guidance. Samson forms a plan all by himself; he asks God only for strength to carry out the plan Samson himself has decided on.

In addition to the absence of any explicit request for forgiveness or for guidance, there is also the fact that in Samson's last plan he is still confusing his private concerns with his public role as the liberator of his people. In his prayer, he asks God for strength not in order to fulfill his mission, but in order to get personal revenge; he wants his strength back in order, as he says, to be avenged on the Philistines for his eyes. And then there is Samson's last recorded line: "Let my soul perish with the Philistines" (16: 30). This is a prayer, too, but one that is more nearly in the style of Samson's earlier prayer at Lehi. True, it is not a prayer based on a desire that God provide miraculously for him so that Samson might succeed in triumphing over his enemies. On the contrary, it is a prayer that God might not let him survive the general destruction of the temple's collapse. It is a complete giving-up on triumphing. In this sense, the line shows a change from the old Samson. But the style of this line of prayer is reminiscent of Samson's earlier prayer at Lehi; and the willfulness of it, the intransigent refusal to accept life on any terms other than his own, has a lot of the old Samson in it, too.

So God returns to Samson when Samson's turning to God is far from full and finished. God's return to Samson is thus not a reward for moral improvement in Samson or for complete and trustworthy repentance on Samson's part. The old character in Samson is evident enough to make such an interpretation of God's return implausible. Rather, God returns to Samson when there is just enough of Samson's turning to God to enable God to come close to Samson.

Reflection on Samson at the end of the story

The last part of the story of Samson's life and mission, and the final complication of Samson's turning-again to God, come in Samson's death in the collapse of the Philistine temple, which Samson brings down in virtue of God's returning to Samson and returning Samson's strength to him. It is not immediately clear how we should understand this conclusion of the story. Is Samson triumphant at the end of his life, when he dies in the destruction of the temple, or not?[59]

On the one hand, of course, the answer has to be 'no.' In the conclusion of the story, Samson dies, together with the Philistines whose deaths he has engineered through his bringing their temple down upon them; and he dies as a blinded Philistine captive among his enemies, a ruined wreck of what he himself had wanted to be. Where is the triumph in this? This is rather the culmination of the ruining of his life.

On the other hand, the text says that the Philistines who died in the temple's fall were many more than those Samson had killed in all his earlier battles taken together. It is also worth noticing that Samson's family came to get his body. If his family were able to retrieve his body from a Philistine temple in Philistine territory when Samson was responsible for the destruction of that temple and the death of the people in it, then we can reasonably assume that the collapse of the temple seriously undermined Philistine rule in that place at least for a time. In his death, therefore, Samson fulfilled his mission, finally, as he had not managed to do in his life. And he did so because in his suffering he turned to God, open to God as he was not before, so that God was able to be close to him. Surely, this is not defeat.

This odd and complicated mix, of conversion to God coupled to the old willful and self-destructive character, of defeat that nonetheless effects the fulfillment of a mission, of the most broken of lives that is somehow still glorious—this is what Milton also saw in Samson's story, and maybe in his own story as well. Milton sums it up this way:

> Samson hath quit himself
> Like Samson, and heroicly hath finished
> A life heroic . . .
>
> . . . . . .
>
> . . .To Israel
> Honor hath left, and freedom . . .
> To himself and his father's house eternal fame;
> And, which is best and happiest yet, all this
> With God not parted from him, as was feared,
> But favoring and assisting to the end.   (ll. 1709–20)

Milton's own appalling suffering entitles him to the next lines in the play. Lines that would be intolerable coming from those at ease are a kind of testimony from the world of horrifying suffering when they are written by Milton:

> Nothing is here for tears, nothing to wail
> Or knock the breast, no weakness, no contempt,
> Dispraise, or blame; nothing but well and fair,
> And what may quiet us in a death so noble.   (ll. 1721–4)

Gloriousness

Both the answer to the question about God's motivation for withdrawing from Samson and the answer to the chapter's initial question about redemption from horrifying suffering are implicit in Milton's interpretation of the narrative. On Milton's interpretation, in the end, there is, somehow, glorious flowering in the life of irremediably broken, defeated Samson.

This is, of course, not our ordinary notion of the flourishing of human beings. But the story of Samson prompts a more considered view of the nature of the good for human beings, and it will help us understand Milton's interpretation of Samson's story if we reflect on this view.

What is it for a human person to flower into glory?[60] On the standard of the good for human beings at issue for Milton, it is not winning your battles and building monuments to your victories. It is drawing near to God and letting him draw near to you. Of course, this may include much more than intimate communion with the deity, as it does in Samson's case. For Samson to draw near to God is also for him to fulfill the mission God has given him, and that mission has consequences for many people and more than one nation.[61] And yet surely there is also something glorious just in being close, to any degree, to the creator of everything, the ruler of the world.

It is worth recognizing that the general idea here is not confined to a worldview such as Milton's (or Aquinas's). Something roughly similar to it can be found in pagan Greece as well. It is what Achilles was thinking about, when he sat, grieved and angry, in his tent, refusing to join in the battles where Greek warriors got glory and died young. There are two sorts of honor, Achilles explains to the embassy that has come to try to persuade him to fight again. There is honor from men, and that is worthless. And then there is honor from Zeus, and that is everything—but *that* can also be had even by a person who dies without any battlefield glories.[62]

So, although Samson may look as if his life is a great good to him when he wins at Lehi or when he toys with Delilah and disdains his Nazirite status, it is not. A good life is not a matter of physical strength and health, or political power and honor (even with a mistress added in); and successful Samson's self-protective loneliness, at a distance from God as much as from Delilah, shows that Samson does not find it to be so either. Furthermore, what makes Samson triumphant at the end of the narrative of his life is not that God lets Samson win over his enemies as he dies. Consider how the scene in the Philistine temple would strike us if there were no prayer of Samson's and no renewed strength. Suppose instead that, in the story, the temple simply collapsed when Samson leaned on the pillars because of an architectural flaw that caused the pillars to give way just then. Samson would have trounced his enemies in that case, but he would not strike us as triumphant in consequence.

On Achilles's view of glory, on Milton's view, and on the view of Aquinas that I will go on to present and defend in Chapter 13, Samson is most magnificent not in his victory at Lehi or in the success of his Superman status at the time of his affair with Delilah. He is great at the end of the story but not because he kills many of his enemies; his renewed strength and victory over the Philistines are by themselves hardly anything admirable in him.[63] Rather, Samson's flowering comes in his worst suffering, in the period when his brokenness is providing his enemies with a celebration to an alien god. In his praying to God as he does then, and in the drawing-near to God that his prayer expresses, there is the culmination of the best in him. He is most glorious in the hopeful openness with which he makes his prayer and waits for God to flood him with strength.[64] In doing so, he is also enabled, finally, to act to fulfill the mission God gave him, to begin the liberation of his people and to honor the God who chose him for this mission. God is close to him when he does.

In a complicated way, then, at the end of the story, in his actions and in his relationship to God, Samson is what he was born for, what he himself wanted to be. The gift of strength Samson always wanted and accepted gladly was given by God for a purpose. By, in effect, finally accepting the giver with the gift in his last prayer in the Philistine temple, Samson opens himself to God and thus allows God to draw near to him. The real triumph for Samson consists in this closeness to God. This closeness, with the strength that God then restores to him, is what allows Samson to fulfill the mission God appointed him even before his birth.[65]

What is it that moves Samson from his corrupt and jaded state with Delilah, when his mission is forgotten and his divinely given gift of strength is serving only his liaison with his concubine, to his turning to God at the end of the story? Surely, it is his suffering. What else could have brought about the change in him? If we were going to rewrite the story of Samson, to take him from the episode with Delilah to the condition in which he makes his last petitioning prayer in which he turns to God, could we write scenes moving him from the first condition to the last without including serious suffering for Samson? Anything other than 'no' seems to me not a credible answer to this question.

And that is why in the narrative God leaves Samson when he does.

Conclusion

Nothing in the interpretation of Samson's story I have argued for diminishes one iota the horrifying suffering of Samson's life as the narrative portrays it. Nothing about the gloriousness diminishes the brokenness. The ability to see in retrospect the connection between Samson's brokenness and its redemption does not take away the misery and pain in Samson's life. The laments Milton writes for Samson in his *Samson Agonistes* are moving testimony to Milton's own raw sensibility not only to the appalling suffering of Samson in the story but also to the dreadful suffering of Milton's own life. And yet Milton bears witness, for himself and for the Samson of his play, that it is possible for even a life of horrifying suffering to be a great good to the sufferer. On Milton's way of reading the story of Samson, it is possible for there to be glorious flowering for the sufferer not in spite of the suffering but because of it. The suffering is not decreased by the flourishing; it is redeemed by it. And so it would not have been better if God had let Samson die before Samson fell into contumely against God. If Samson had died earlier, say because he had no water after the battle at Lehi, or because he had a heart attack in bed, Samson would have been the poorer for it.[66]

The view of Sophocles and other Greek tragedians with which I began this chapter therefore seems to me right but incomplete. There is an excellence of mind that can come from suffering, and, as in Samson's case, maybe only from suffering. There is more wisdom in Samson's final prayer than in his first; and it is only suffering, as Sophocles also believed, that has brought Samson to the wisdom underlying that final prayer. But, to my mind, there is an unacceptable sternness in supposing that an excellence of mind alone is sufficient to redeem suffering as great as Samson's, and the story of Samson is itself opposed to this view. The gloriousness of Oedipus at Colonus, as Sophocles portrays him, consists in his wisdom, in his ability to know things ordinary mortals do not know, including the precise time and place of his death. So for Sophocles, the suffering of a tragic figure such as Oedipus is redeemed by some extraordinary excellence of mind. But what redeems the suffering of Samson in the narrative is more nearly an excellence of heart and will than an excellence of mind.

And even this way of putting the point is too Greek. On the interpretation I have given here, and as Milton also thought, Samson's excellence consists not in intrinsic great-making characteristics of his, finally acquired at the end of his life, but rather in relationship, and especially in his relationship to God. In Samson's letting-go of his self-willed loneliness, in his willingness to be open to God, Samson allows God to draw near to him. And so Samson's suffering is redeemed in the closeness of his relationship with God. At the end of Samson's story, his irremediable brokenness has its culmination in his death among his enemies. But, in that death, he is also glorious.[67] He has opened to God, and in consequence both God and God's gift of strength have returned to Samson. The result is that, in his death, the mission of his life, to begin the liberation of his people, is fulfilled. And so, in the narrative, it is true both that Samson is irremediably broken and that his life is a great good for him.

It has to be said that, in this story, to some limited extent, Samson is repentant at the end of his life, but there are many perpetrators of great evil who, as far as human reason can see, die in the same monstrous condition in which they lived.[68] Nonetheless, Samson's turning to God at the end of his life does not by itself make the narrative of his life a fairytale. There do seem to be actual cases in which perpetrators of great evil rethink their lives and come to some moral or spiritual regeneration.[69] The story of Samson itself shows that we are in no position to know how many such cases there might be. The evidence for Samson's turning to God comes in his last prayer, which he might have uttered only in thought, immediately before his death. But, obviously, we are very rarely in a position to know the final thoughts of a dying person. In any event, Samson's story shows that there is a kind of redemption that is *possible* for a perpetrator of great evil. It says nothing about what *is* or *must be* actual for any and every perpetrator. That such redemption is possible at all is the salient point for my purposes.

To say this is not to claim to have a theodicy for the suffering brought on himself by a perpetrator of moral wrongs. That is because it is one thing to show something that can redeem suffering and another thing altogether to show morally sufficient reasons for God to allow that suffering for the sake of that redemption. Here, however, as in the case of the chapter on Job, considerations of theodicy are postponed until all the narratives have been explored.

Chapter 11

The Story of Abraham: The Desires of the Heart

By the rivers of Babylon, there we sat down, yea, we wept, when we remembered Zion.

We hanged our harps upon the willows in the midst thereof.

For there they that carried us away captive required of us a song, and they that wasted us required of us mirth, saying, Sing us one of the songs of Zion.

How shall we sing the Lord's song in a strange land?

If I forget thee, O Jerusalem, let my right hand forget her cunning.

If I do not remember thee, let my tongue cleave to the roof of my mouth, if I prefer not Jerusalem above my chief joy.*

Introduction

Both Job and Samson endure frightful suffering. Job is an innocent victim of catastrophic occurrences that overwhelm him and devastate his life. Samson ruins his own life, as well as that of others, through his reprehensible acts. But not all suffering is like the suffering of either Job or Samson. Even when suffering does not irrevocably wreck their whole lives, people who are somewhere on the continuum between perfectly innocent and morally monstrous endure heartbreak at the loss of things on which, for one reason or another, they have set their hearts.

Sometimes these are things we expect all people to care about, such as life and health, which are part of objective human well-being. But sometimes they are particular projects to which an individual is specially committed. In his diaries, Victor Klemperer

---

* Ps. 137: 1–6.

records his bitter grief at being prevented by Nazi depredations from writing the great book he had hoped would be the flower of his life's work.[1] One can set one's heart on particular persons, too. Even in an otherwise easy life, the loss of one much-prized person—in the ending of a marriage, for example, or in the death of a child—can produce terrible suffering. So a person can have his heart set on a particular person or project whose value for him stems at least in part from his own commitment to it. As I explained in the first chapter, appropriating an expression from the Psalms, I will refer to these sorts of commitments as the desires of the heart.[2]

In this chapter I want to explore a story in which suffering connected to the desires of the heart is central—namely, the story of Abraham's binding of Isaac.[3] That story elucidates the connection of the desires of the heart to the problem of suffering as well. Job and Samson are similar in that each of them emerges from his suffering as glorious in one respect or another. Their stories can therefore appear to confirm the strategy of those theodicies that try to justify divine permission of suffering by showing that suffering contributes (somehow, paradoxically) to the flourishing of the sufferer or of human beings generally. In the contemporary literature, such attempted theodicies include those which argue that suffering can be redeemed by contributing to the virtue of the sufferer or to the sufferer's usefulness to others.[4] The story of Abraham and Isaac, however, highlights the insufficiency of such a strategy for theodicy. It therefore also helps to confirm the view I argued for in Chapter 1—namely, that, in addition to the flourishing of a sufferer, the desires of a sufferer's heart need to be considered in any attempted theodicy or defense that is to have a hope of being satisfactory.[5]

The story of Abraham and Isaac is an especially good one for my purposes, not only for what it shows about the desires of the heart, but also for another reason connected to the problem of suffering, though in a different way. One traditional religious reaction to the problem of suffering has been to recommend that religious believers respond with faith to their own suffering as well as that of others. This recommendation has been made so often, in such varying circumstances, that it has become practically meaningless; and it is bound to strike many reflective people as deeply disappointing. Abraham, however, is traditionally considered the father of faith,[6] and on that view he becomes the father of faith because of his willingness to sacrifice his beloved son Isaac at God's command. So if faith is the recommended religious response to suffering, we can consider in some detail what that response is meant to be by looking carefully at Abraham's actions as he becomes the father of faith in the story of the binding of Isaac.

As I will show in this chapter, the response of faith is not an attempt to evade wrestling with the problem of suffering but, on the contrary, a challenge for those working to construct a defense or theodicy, because it sets a high standard for success at the endeavor. On my reading, the narrative makes the recommended response of faith not disappointing or vague but clear and demanding. I will argue that faith of the sort exemplified by Abraham consists not in detachment[7] from the desires of one's heart, as is often enough supposed, but rather in trust in the goodness of God to fulfill those desires.

In order to understand the nature of the faith being attributed to Abraham in the binding of Isaac and its relationship to the desires of the heart, however, we need to look carefully at the details of the whole narrative of Abraham's life, within which the story of the binding of Isaac is set. The narrative has neutron-star density, and it is not possible to do justice to all its artistry in one chapter. With regret, I will have to leave many details of the narrative unremarked in order to concentrate on just those features of it that are specially germane to my purposes. In what follows, I will examine the narrative of Abraham's life to bring out a view of the binding of Isaac that is different from some well-known and commonly accepted interpretations of that story. When I have made clear the interpretation I think is preferable, I will return to the problem of suffering, to consider what light the story of Abraham and Isaac sheds on faith as a response to suffering.

Kierkegaard's interpretation: Caveats

The story of the binding of Isaac has figured prominently in all three major monotheisms; in Judaism[8] and Christianity,[9] the story has been the source of endless discussion and commentary.[10] In the Christian tradition, which is the one I know best, there are insightful interpretations of it by Origen, Augustine, Jerome, Chrysostom, Aquinas, Nicholas of Lyra, Luther, Calvin, Kierkegaard, and hosts of others.[11] It is not hard to see why the story commands this attention. The story itself is poignant: Abraham obediently going to sacrifice at God's command the beloved, long-awaited child of his old age. And the story raises puzzling philosophical and theological questions. Why should God ask this sacrifice of Abraham? Why should he try Abraham as he does? And what is laudatory about Abraham's willingness to kill his own child? Why should Abraham's consent to destroy his son make him the father of faith?

Because Kierkegaard's reading of the story is as compelling as it is well known, I will begin with a rough summary of Kierkegaard's interpretation, as I see it. Although this is in fact my reading of Kierkegaard, I make no pretensions to Kierkegaard scholarship, which is as contentious as the scholarship on any major figure in the history of philosophy. I am not attempting to contribute to that scholarship here, and I do not mean to adjudicate among competing views regarding Kierkegaard's interpretation of this biblical narrative. But I can show more easily the interpretation of the story I want to offer if I take Kierkegaard's interpretation as a foil. Kierkegaard's interpretation is important for my purposes therefore, only insofar as it helps me bring out the salient features of the differing interpretation I mean to advocate. The reader who is primarily interested in the work of Kierkegaard himself and who dissents from the interpretation of Kierkegaard given in this chapter should feel free to take the section of this chapter on Kierkegaard's reading of the story as only a *Kierkegaard-like* interpretation.[12]

In general, as I understand him, Kierkegaard takes Abraham to be caught in a dilemma; but he thinks that that dilemma is resoluble, because he supposes that God's command produces a "teleological suspension of the ethical" for Abraham. The ethical prohibition against the killing of an innocent child is overridden by God's command to sacrifice Isaac. That Abraham understands and accepts this feature of his situation is part of what makes him a hero of faith for Kierkegaard. Interpreting the story as an instance of a moral or religious dilemma, whether resoluble or not, is a natural way of reading it. I am convinced, however, that this way of looking at the narrative is mistaken. To me, it seems blind to an important side of the story.

To show this side, it is important to place the episode of the binding of Isaac in the context of the whole narrative of Abraham's life, including especially the episodes involving Hagar and Keturah, Abraham's *other* wives or concubines,[13] and the children of these women. When the story of the binding of Isaac is read in this context, God's command to sacrifice Isaac cannot be understood as Kierkegaard does. God's command does not put Abraham in a dilemma where ordinary morality conflicts with obedience to God. Rather, it constitutes a test of Abraham's character that he passes precisely by committing himself to the belief that morality and obedience to God are on the same side.

When we see the story of the binding of Isaac in this way, we will be in a position to appreciate why in the narrative[14] a good God would test Abraham as he does. So understood, the narrative also gives us insight into Abraham's status as the father of faith, and, consequently, into one part of the nature of faith itself. Most importantly for my purposes, the narrative illumines the importance of the notion of the desires of the heart for the problem of suffering.

Kierkegaard's interpretation: Abraham's binding of Isaac

Kierkegaard calls Abraham a "knight of faith," and he explains this designation by comparing Abraham with a person whose life consists of "infinite resignation." Consider, says Kierkegaard, a young man who is hopelessly in love with a princess but who understands perfectly that there is no chance whatsoever of his winning her. He lets his love for the princess take over his life, but he gives up the princess. Such a man, Kierkegaard says, would no longer take "a finite interest in what the princess is doing,"[15] although he would preserve his love for her just as it was at the beginning. Like Dante in his love for Beatrice after her death, then, this lover would maintain his passion but without any practical or earthly interest in the human woman who prompted it. The life of such a lover is a life of infinite resignation, in Kierkegaard's view.

The knight of faith is different from such a lover, Kierkegaard explains, just because of the difference in his attitude toward the beloved. Someone who is a knight of faith and hopelessly in love with a princess also gives up the woman he loves and makes no effort to woo her. He, too, knows clearly that there is no chance of his winning her. So he "infinitely renounces claim to the love which is the content of his life, he is reconciled in pain."[16] But, says Kierkegaard, what makes him the knight of faith is that he simultaneously says sincerely to himself, "I believe nevertheless that I shall get her." This sincere belief is "absurd," although it is not strictly speaking crazy or incoherent, since "with God all things are possible."[17]

Kierkegaard's position is not entirely clear here. The knight of faith does sincerely renounce his beloved; like the person of infinite resignation who gives up the princess he loves because he knows he cannot win her, the knight of faith also makes an act of resignation. But, in a psychological movement that at first glance does seem to merit Kierkegaard's appellation 'absurd,' the knight of faith believes at the same time *also* that he will get the woman he loves. However we understand the simultaneous belief and disbelief at issue here, what makes the knight of faith such a prodigy, on Kierkegaard's view, is just that he manages to give up what he loves and at the same time to trust that he will have it.

Abraham is a knight of faith of this sort, in Kierkegaard's view. In an act of "infinite resignation," Abraham gives up his beloved son Isaac; but, because he is a knight of faith, he also expects to have Isaac, somehow. In this part of his interpretation, Kierkegaard is being true to a Christian tradition that is at least as old as the book of Hebrews. The author of Hebrews says that, when he was tested, Abraham offered Isaac in faith, with the belief that God could even raise the dead.[18] The implication of this text in Hebrews is, apparently, that Abraham believed he would not be losing Isaac even as he was going to sacrifice him.

What Kierkegaard's interpretation of the story adds to the tradition exemplified by the text in Hebrews is his explanation of the nature of Abraham's test when God commands him to sacrifice Isaac and his understanding of the conditions for Abraham's passing that test. According to Kierkegaard, when he was tested, Abraham was not a tragic hero as, for example, Agamemnon was. Rather, unlike Agamemnon, Abraham "overstepped the ethical entirely."[19] For Kierkegaard, a tragic hero such as Agamemnon "remains within the ethical."[20] When Agamemnon sacrificed his daughter Iphigenia to the gods at Aulis so that his fleet of ships could sail to Troy, Agamemnon was within the bounds of the ethical, because he resigned his own dearest desires in order to promote the well-being of the whole people for whom he was responsible. Agamemnon, then, is faced with a difficult moral dilemma, but it is difficult for him just because it pits his personal desires against his public duty. When Agamemnon picks his duty over his daughter, Kierkegaard thinks, Agamemnon has chosen the lesser of two moral evils. But, for Kierkegaard, Abraham is a different case. There is no ethical principle that overrides Abraham's duty to his son, Kierkegaard thinks. Instead, there is only the "teleological suspension of the ethical." Abraham was prepared to sacrifice Isaac "for God's sake, because God required this proof of his faith."[21] On Kierkegaard's views, what is higher than ethical principles is Abraham's obedience to God; and the demands of that obedience take precedence over morality. That is why, Kierkegaard thinks, there is a teleological suspension of the ethical in Abraham's case.

It looks, therefore, as if Kierkegaard understands the nature of Abraham's test and the conditions for passing the test like this. Morality imposes a requirement on Abraham—namely, that he not kill his son Isaac. But God's command also imposes a requirement. This is not a moral requirement; if it were, Abraham's case would be like Agamemnon's. Abraham would be subject to two conflicting moral requirements, of which one—namely, the one imposed by God's command—clearly took precedence over the other. But Abraham's case is significantly different from Agamemnon's in Kierkegaard's view, and the difference comes to this, that the requirement imposed on Abraham by God's command is not itself a moral requirement. So Abraham is faced with two requirements, one moral and the other religious. Since the requirement imposed by God's command cannot be overridden by anything and can itself override other obligations, what Abraham must do is sacrifice his son. For Kierkegaard, when Abraham assents to offering Isaac, Abraham's greatness is far beyond that of a tragic hero such as Agamemnon. It consists in his willingness to suspend the ethical for the sake of obedience to God's command.

Kierkegaard's interpretation of Abraham as in a dilemma where religion and morality conflict and religion overrides morality raises some perplexing questions. Why would a good God want to set his authority *against* morality, rather than with it? [22] Given the constant emphasis of the biblical texts on the sinfulness of human beings, surely we are not meant to suppose that Abraham needed no encouragement on the score of morality but could instead go on to something greater than moral goodness. And why is Abraham's act supposed to make him the father of faith? In his willingness to submit the concerns of ordinary morality to religious requirements Abraham is not unique; in fact, he is even superseded. Jephthah was not only willing to abrogate the prohibition against killing one's child; for the sake of his relationship to God, he actually did it[23]—unlike Abraham, who only got as far as raising the knife.[24] If the willingness to suspend the ethical in the interest of obedience to God is what makes a person the father of faith, why would that title not have been given to Jephthah rather than Abraham? Finally, what is the relation between Abraham's test, on this reading of it, and Abraham's conviction (as Kierkegaard sees it) that he will have the very thing he has resigned as lost to him? If willingness to subordinate morality to religious demands is success in passing the test, why suppose that the success would have been somehow lessened or undermined if Abraham had rejected the belief that he also would have the son he was resigning to God?

Abraham's offspring

With this much attention to Kierkegaard's reading of the story and the questions it raises, I want now to turn to the whole narrative of Abraham's life.

It will be helpful to begin by noticing the way in which that narrative is bounded by and focused on a concern with children. Among the first things we learn about Abraham is that he is married to a woman who cannot bear him children,[25] and among the last things we learn about him is that his children[26]—Isaac and Ishmael—have come together in order to bury him.[27] God's first recorded speech to Abraham occurs when Abraham is 75 years old,[28] and the last one takes place when Abraham is around 115.[29] In the forty-year interval, there are eight recorded occasions on which God visits Abraham to speak with him,[30] and every one of them has as its partial or total concern some issue involving Abraham's children or his descendants, the children of his children. In fact, every episode in which God visits Abraham includes at least one divine speech in which God makes promises to Abraham implying or stating explicitly that Abraham will have offspring.[31]

In the first of these eight visitations, God promises to make Abraham into a great nation and a source of blessing for all the families of the earth. In the second visitation, God's speech adds to the promise of the first visitation an additional promise to give to Abraham's seed the land in which Abraham finds himself—although this speech leaves open the way in which the notion of seed is to be construed. The divine speech in the third visitation repeats the divine promise made in the second visitation and elaborates on it by adding the promise that Abraham's seed will be very numerous. The fourth visitation is somewhat more complex. In it, God enters into a covenant with Abraham, and he makes prophecies about Abraham and Abraham's offspring. On this fourth visitation, God also reiterates the preceding promises but disambiguates them by adding the promise that Abraham will be the *biological* father of offspring. Finally, the remaining four divine visitations to Abraham, which are too complicated to summarize succinctly here, also each include promises about Abraham's children.

As the subsequent examination of the narrative confirms, God's promises in these visitations offer Abraham the reward of offspring because offspring is what Abraham wants most dearly. Being the father of children, the patriarch of a clan, the ancestor of a people is Abraham's heart's desire.

Promises

It will expedite the subsequent exposition of the narrative if we digress here briefly to reflect on the nature of a promise.[32] A promise is a performative utterance that expresses a speaker's commitment to a specific course of action in the future[33] (as, for example, "I promise I will return the axe to you tomorrow") or to a future state of affairs over which the speaker has some degree of control (as, for example, "I promise I will always love you"[34]) and that obligates her to perform that action or see to it that that state of affairs obtains.[35]

Correlative with a promise is an implicit future contingent proposition, a prediction in effect, which is, in general, true just to the extent to which the promise-maker is reliable as regards promise-keeping: Paula (the maker of the promise) will return the axe to Jerome (the recipient of the promise) tomorrow; Paula will always love Jerome.[36] I say 'in general,' because sometimes, although the promise-maker is completely reliable, circumstances external to the will of the promise-maker bring it about that the correlative prediction is false, contrary to the resolution of the promise-maker. Paula promised to return the axe to Jerome tomorrow, but the ice storm that descended without warning confined the whole community to their own homes and kept Paula from returning the axe to Jerome. Or Paula died suddenly of a heart attack today and so did not live to return the axe tomorrow. Or events occurred that made Paula's breaking her promise the lesser of two evils for Paula: she promised to return the axe to Jerome tomorrow;

but since Jerome is in a homicidal rage against his wife when he requests the axe, Paula breaks her promise and does not give it to him. Circumstances that render false the predictions correlative with the promises of reliable promise-makers are unpredictable, but also uncommon; and so, *in general*, the implicit prediction correlative with a promise is true if the promise-maker is reliable.

Since this is so and also generally understood to be so, the attitude of a promise-recipient toward the reliability of a promise-maker can (also *in general*) be ascertained on the basis of the recipient's tacit or occurrent belief in the truth of the prediction correlative with the promise. If Jerome responds to Paula's promise about returning the axe tomorrow by going to the store today to buy a new axe, we are within our rights to suppose that Jerome does not have much confidence in the reliability of Paula as a promise-keeper.[37] Furthermore, because keeping promises is morally obligatory, a lack of confidence on Jerome's part in Paula's reliability as a promise-keeper implies on Jerome's part a lack of belief, to one extent or another, in Paula's goodness. That is why Paula would feel insulted if, after hearing her promise to return the axe tomorrow, Jerome went to the store today to buy another axe.

In the narrative, it is evident that there is little or no likelihood that external circumstances will impede God's ability to fulfill his promises; and, in one place after another, the narrative makes clear that Abraham understands this fact about God. Abraham repeatedly shows that he believes in God's great power over nature and human affairs. He has no doubt, for example, that God can suddenly destroy Sodom and Gomorrah and everyone in those cities. Even when Abraham laughs at God's statement that Sarah will give birth to Abraham's child when he and Sarah are old, it is obvious that, although Abraham finds that statement funny, he does not think that what it foretells is impossible. And so we can take it that, where *God's* promises are concerned, Abraham understands that there is a strong connection between a promise and its correlative prediction. In the narrative, the likelihood that the prediction correlative with a divine promise is true depends entirely on the reliability of the promise-maker, not on that reliability together with the likelihood of external circumstances undermining the fulfillment of the divine promises; and Abraham recognizes that this is so.

For this reason, Abraham's attitude toward the predictions correlative with the divine promises is revelatory of Abraham's view of God's reliability as a promise-maker and consequently of Abraham's underlying attitude toward God's goodness as well. I am not suggesting that in the narrative Abraham deliberates about whether or not God is reliable as a promise-keeper or that Abraham consciously wonders about God's goodness or about how much trust to place in God's goodness. I mean only that, however unreflective Abraham may be about his attitudes toward God's goodness and God's promises and however tacit those attitudes might be, we can garner information about his attitudes toward God's goodness and reliability as a promise-keeper from Abraham's stance with regard to the predictions correlative with God's promises. To the extent to which Abraham does not believe those predictions, to that extent Abraham is also skeptical about God's goodness, even if his doubts are hidden from his own awareness and buried within his consciousness.

Because it is clumsy to talk about predictions correlative with promises, in what follows I will forgo this more careful locution and instead talk about the truth of a divine promise or Abraham's belief in the truth of a divine promise. But it should be clear that what is at issue in these locutions, strictly speaking, is just the prediction correlative with the promise.

In the narrative, what is striking is the double-mindedness of Abraham's attitudes toward God's promises.

The first divine promise

Consider, to begin with, God's first recorded speech to Abraham in the narrative in which God promises to make of Abraham[38] a great nation. Even with respect to this first promise, there is something odd about Abraham's response.

In this first speech to Abraham, God commands Abraham to leave his land, his family,[39] and his father's house. But this command comes to Abraham at a time when Abraham is already away from the land of his origins and from virtually all of his family. That is because by this time, after the death of Abraham's brother Haran, Abraham's father Terah has moved away from the family's homeland, taking with him Haran's son Lot and Abraham and Abraham's wife Sarah, and leaving the rest of whatever family he has behind. So when God tells Abraham to leave his country and his family and his father's house, there is less for Abraham to do to fulfill that command than there might otherwise have been. Abraham is already away from his home country; and, besides his wife Sarah, the only family of Abraham's (or the only family that the narrative mentions as with Abraham[40]) is his father Terah and his nephew Lot. To fulfill this command of God's, then, Abraham has only to leave his father and his nephew and their current dwelling place.

It is clear that on this occasion Abraham is ready to obey God's command, and it is equally evident that Abraham desires to have the promised divine reward. The narrative says that, in response to God's command, Abraham went out from his father's house and from the land where his father had settled. But the narrative *also* says that Abraham took Lot with him when he went.[41] Lot is part of Abraham's family and part of the house of Abraham's father Terah, since Terah took Lot in after the death of Lot's father. So, manifestly, Lot belongs to those whom God's command requires Abraham to leave behind.[42] Since Abraham takes action that is plainly intended to count as obeying God's command, why does Abraham take Lot with him when he leaves his father's house?

One obvious possibility worth considering here, and one which turns out to be amply confirmed by subsequent episodes in the narrative, is that Abraham is trying to help bring about the fulfillment of God's promise. He is trying to mitigate dependence on God for making the divine promise about his posterity true by arranging to make it true himself. In the narrative, at this period of his life, Abraham has been childless for a long time, long enough for him reasonably to suppose that he and Sarah will never have children of their own. And so, when Abraham sets out from his father's house in response to God's command, he takes his nephew Lot with him, contrary to God's command, as a kind of surety for the children Abraham does not have. If all else fails, Abraham seems to be thinking, God's promise to make of him a great nation could perhaps be made true through a foster son.

If this interpretation of Abraham's action is right,[43] as I think subsequent episodes in the narrative show that it is, how should we understand Abraham's attitude toward God as a promise-maker? On the one hand, it appears that Abraham believes in the truth of God's promise and trusts God as a reliable promise-maker. That is because Abraham does act on God's command, and with dispatch. On the other hand, however, Abraham's taking Lot with him in contravention of God's command indicates that Abraham thinks the divine promise will not come true unless, by bringing Lot into his household, he himself provides the offspring necessary to make the promise true. To this extent, Abraham does not believe God's promise that *God* will make him a great nation. And, to that extent, Abraham also does not trust God's goodness as a promise-maker.

Someone might suppose here that Abraham is simply trying to fulfill conditions on God's promise that are unstated but nonetheless implied. But why think so? There are indeed conditions conjoined to God's promise to make Abraham a great nation, but they are explicitly stated. They have to do with Abraham's leaving his family and land. Why suppose that there are further conditions that are unstated and that require Abraham to find somebody to serve as his heir? Furthermore, if it were up to Abraham to arrange descendants for himself, then, when Abraham did have descendants, in what sense would God be fulfilling his promise that *he*, *God*, would make of Abraham a great nation? So the supposition that, in taking Lot with him, Abraham is just trying to cooperate with God seems to me mistaken.[44]

Or consider the issue this way. On the one hand, if Abraham thought that God were good and could be trusted to keep his promises, Abraham would also believe that, as long as he fulfilled God's explicit commands,[45] the fulfillment of the promise God made him could safely be left to God. Abraham would not be trying to make that promise true himself by bringing his nephew into his household. On the other hand, of course, if Abraham thought God were not good and could not be trusted to keep his promises, then there would be no reason why he would leave his father to go wandering in foreign territory.

Consequently, when Abraham takes Lot with him, there is a certain double-mindedness in Abraham's attitude toward God.[46] Somehow, Abraham believes and also does not believe that God's promise is true. He therefore also believes and does not believe that God is a reliable promise-keeper. To this extent, therefore, Abraham is double-minded about God's goodness as well.

The fourth divine promise

By the time of God's fourth visitation to Abraham, in spite of the preceding three divine promises about his posterity, Abraham has remained childless. By this point in the story, the only thing that has changed as regards descendants for Abraham is that Abraham has adopted his steward Eliezer as his heir. That adoption seems to have occurred just because Abraham's nephew, Lot, who might have served as Abraham's foster son and heir, has ceased to be part of Abraham's household. Lot has left Abraham's household because of strife between the servants of Lot and those of Abraham. It is difficult to graze as many animals as Lot and Abraham have when the herds are being pastured together; and so their servants have quarreled. As a result, Lot and Abraham have agreed to put distance between them, so that the herds can be pastured without dissension. With Lot gone, Abraham has adopted as his heir his steward Eliezer.

Here we can ask a question analogous to the preceding question about Lot: why does Abraham adopt an heir? God's promises in all three of his earlier speeches to Abraham have specifically included promises about Abraham's seed. Even if the notion of seed could be construed broadly enough to include Lot, the notion of seed can hardly be extended far enough to include servants, as Abraham himself is aware. When God comes the fourth time to make promises about offspring to Abraham, Abraham complains that God has given him no seed, so that his heir has to be his steward Eliezer.[47]

If Abraham were to have seed, as God has promised he would, then Abraham would also have an heir. So if, in Abraham's eyes, God is good and his promises are trustworthy, why would Abraham adopt Eliezer as his heir instead of waiting for the promised seed? Adopting an heir in the face of God's promise about Abraham's seed argues a decided lack of confidence in the promise and consequently also in the goodness of God, the promise-maker. On the other hand, Abraham's willingness to complain to God is evidence of some trust on Abraham's part in God's goodness. Unless God is good and God's promises are trustworthy, what is the point of complaining to God that he has not yet made good on his promises? Why complain to God that God has not given Abraham seed unless God is good at least to the extent of caring about whether or not he keeps his promises? So, in Abraham's adopting Eliezer as his heir and then complaining to God, there is further evidence of Abraham's double-minded attitude toward God's promises and God's goodness.

In response to Abraham's complaint that God has given him no seed, God reiterates his promises and elaborates on them. Your descendants, he tells Abraham, will be as numerous as the stars. But this time God also disambiguates the preceding promises: biological offspring, not foster sons or adopted heirs, will be Abraham's promised seed. "He that will come from your own bowels," God tells Abraham, "will be your heir" (Gen. 15: 4). The narrative comments that Abraham believed this newly clarified promise of God's and that God counted Abraham's believing God as Abraham's righteousness.[48]

And yet, even if, at this moment in the development of Abraham's relations with God, Abraham did whole-heartedly believe in God's promises and thus also in the goodness of God as a promise-maker, this moment is followed almost immediately by the expression of a serious doubt on Abraham's part. When God goes on to repeat one of his promises, that he will give the land to Abraham, Abraham responds with a request for confirmation of the promise. How do I *know* that I will inherit the land?

he asks God. Here belief in God's reliability as a promise-maker is definitely not to the fore.[49]

Abraham's request for confirmation: A perplexity

Abraham's request for confirmation of God's promise to give him the land should remind us that Abraham has been hearing God's promises for a long time without seeing any sign of their fulfillment; and it is no doubt understandable that he would want reassurance about them. On the other hand, if one friend makes a promise to another and is rewarded with the question "How do I know this is true?," the promise-maker will be within his rights to be offended or to feel bad in some other way. If Paula asks to borrow some CDs from her friend Jerome and promises to return them, and Jerome responds by saying, "how do I know you will return them?," Paula will justifiably feel insulted. If Paula is still speaking to Jerome after that, she will say something like this: "because I promised I would, and my promise ought to be sufficient for you." And so one might be forgiven for supposing that the only right answer for God to give in reply to Abraham's "How do I know" question is an indignant "because I promised."

But in the narrative God does not respond with indignation. In fact, God's response is apparently to honor Abraham's request by giving Abraham the confirmation he wants that the divine promise is true.

I say 'apparently' because of the nature of that confirmation.

The confirmation has three parts. First, God comes to Abraham in a vision when Abraham is asleep. The vision seems to have something of the nature of a nightmare for Abraham, or at any rate to be accompanied by dread. In the vision, God predicts that at some future time Abraham's descendants will suffer dreadfully for 400 years, but that God will punish their oppressors and bring Abraham's descendants back to the land God is giving Abraham. Secondly, after this, there is a further vision, either when Abraham is asleep or after he wakes, in which Abraham sees smoke and fire passing between the halves of the bodies of animals that Abraham has divided and positioned in a ritual action of covenant-making. Finally, the confirmation finishes with God's explicitly making a covenant with Abraham to give him the land. So God's confirmation of the truth of his promises consists in divine predictions, delivered in visions, and more divine promises, this time made with the solemnity of a covenant.

It is obvious that this confirmation, including the ritual covenant, is worth only as much as the original promises. Someone who distrusted the original promise would not be helped much toward more trust by this kind of confirmation, would he? How could he possibly be? If Jerome says to Paula, "how do I know that you are trustworthy as regards your promises?," and Paula responds by saying warmly, "I promise you that I am!," Jerome would have to be benighted to suppose he had been given evidence warranting his trust in Paula's original promise or any real help with his doubt in that promise. Even if we suppose that Paula confirms her promise with a ritual act of impressive religious significance—swearing on a Bible, say—the ritual act will be worthless unless Paula is a trustworthy maker of promises and vows.

Analogously, the confirmation God gives to Abraham in the vision and covenant is only a more powerful variation on the original divine promise-making, and *it* is worth trusting only in case the original promises were, that is, only in case God is good and a reliable keeper of promises and covenants. At any rate, if this divine confirmation, in visions and covenant, of the original divine promises demonstrates anything not evident to Abraham earlier, it is only God's power—to produce visions, for example—and not anything about God's reliability as a keeper of promises and covenants or God's trustworthiness and goodness in general.

Why, then, does God respond in this way to Abraham's request for confirmation? Why should God offer what purports to be confirmation, rather than the rebuke that Abraham's request for confirmation appears to deserve? On the other hand, if confirmation rather than rebuke is the right divine response, why should God make the confirmation consist just in things that require the very same sort of trust as the promise for which Abraham wanted confirmation in the first place?

These questions should prompt us to ask the question that all the divine visitations and promises in the narrative so far cry out to have answered: why does God take such a circuitous route toward the end he promises Abraham? There are twenty-five years between God's first promise to Abraham and the birth of the promised heir Isaac. Why should God keep Abraham waiting such a long time, so that the much-desired son comes only in Abraham's old age? Why does not God simply remove Sarah's barrenness immediately after the first promise? In fact, why should God make any promises at all? If God wants Abraham to have a large posterity, why does not God simply ensure at the outset that Sarah is not barren?

Developing trust

The answer to these questions is implicit in the questions themselves, when we line them up in this way. That God is willing to respond to Abraham's request for confirmation by honoring it in any way, rather than rebuking it, is evidence of a surprising patience with Abraham on God's part. The point of that patience is hinted at by the nature of the confirmation God provides.

God's confirmation does indeed require the same kind of trust on Abraham's part as the original divine promise. But this response of God's to Abraham makes sense if God's aim in his dealings with Abraham—including his making promises to Abraham and then postponing the outcome Abraham so greatly desires—is not just the production of posterity for Abraham but also, and more importantly, the eliciting of a relationship of trust between himself and Abraham.

The story makes it clear that this kind of trust is hard for Abraham. That is why he takes Lot with him, adopts Eliezer as his heir, and asks for confirmation of God's promise—among many other things still to emerge in the story.

If God were to respond to Abraham's request for reassurance by giving Abraham real evidence (whatever real evidence might be in this context) that did actually constitute confirmation of the truth of the divine promises, God would be asking little of Abraham by way of belief in God's promises and even less by way of trust in God. As it is, the way in which God responds to Abraham's request for confirmation is reminiscent of the way a riding instructor will take a student who has pulled up short at a fence back around the riding ring again, faster and with more urging, for another try at that same fence. The vision and the ritual of covenant-making will confirm the divine promises for Abraham only if Abraham is willing to believe in God's trustworthiness and goodness.

The long process of God's repeatedly promising Abraham his heart's desire and then repeatedly delaying the fulfillment of those promises is thus not a peculiar way of producing offspring for Abraham but rather a taxing way of producing a relationship of trust between Abraham and God. It asks a considerable amount from God, as well as from Abraham, insofar as it requires divine ingenuity at the building of personal relations with human beings and divine patience with Abraham, to whom trust does not come easily. It is worth noticing that it also requires of God trust in Abraham[50]—trust that Abraham will not give up during the waiting period and turn irrevocably away from God in distrust and disbelief.

Midrashic commentators suppose that God will deal in this sort of way only with the spiritually strong, and so they see the ordeals God prepares for Abraham as evidence of Abraham's greatness.[51] However that may be, for Abraham, the process is not only challenging but also filled with pain. The pain that comes with waiting, interspersed with disappointment, and further externally imposed waiting, succeeded by reiterated disappointment, in apparently endless cycles, grinds the will down into misery. Pain of that sort wears away the heart. The anguish generated in Abraham by his assent to the sacrifice of Isaac captures the imagination of those who know the story, but we must not for that reason be oblivious to the suffering of Abraham's long wait for the children he so desires.

Seeing God's interactions with Abraham in this way—as a patient, trusting willingness on God's part to use his promises and Abraham's waiting to try to elicit a relationship of trust between himself and Abraham—helps to explain another, otherwise perplexing feature of God's promises.

In the first divine promise, God tells Abraham that Abraham will be the source of a great nation. In the second promise, God says that Abraham's seed will inherit the land. The second promise therefore disambiguates the first. Abraham will be the source of a great nation because he will have seed, and it is that seed that will become a nation and inherit the land. In the third promise, which comes after Lot has been separated from Abraham, so that Abraham has to understand God's promises will not be fulfilled through Lot, God implies that the seed in question is not some member of Abraham's extended family, but rather some more direct descendant of Abraham's. In the fourth promise, God makes this element of that third promise explicit by promising Abraham that he will be the biological father of the offspring who will count as Abraham's seed.

But in this fourth promise God still leaves notably vague the identity of the *mother* of the promised biological offspring. The fourth promise is disambiguated only in the fifth promise, when God makes clear that the promised seed will come to Abraham through Sarah.

Why is God's first promise characterized by an opaque vagueness, and why is that vagueness only slowly dispelled in the progression of promises? Clearly, God could have divulged to Abraham the full and complete promise, as it stands in its final unfolding, on the first occasion of his interaction with Abraham. On the first occasion of making a promise to Abraham, God could have explained to Abraham that Abraham would have a biological son by Sarah. For that matter, God could have specified the time at which this son would be born and all the other details of all his later elaborations on the original promise. That is, on the occasion of his first visitation to Abraham, God could have said to him: "Twenty-five years from now, you will have a son; the mother of this son will be Sarah; the son's name will be 'Isaac'; through him you will become the ancestor of a great people; these people will inherit the land"—and so on. God could have made his promise this way. Why did he not do so?

And here is the evident answer: because, if God had done so, then, for Abraham, there would not have been anything like the same process of growth in trust in God. The series of promises, with their increasing disambiguation, is clearly a kind of psychological or spiritual stretching for Abraham.

Abraham's reactions to the progression of promises show that, on the one hand, in some sense or to some degree, he does believe God's promises and does trust God to ensure their truth. And yet, on the other hand, in trying to make the promises true himself rather than waiting for God to fulfill them, he also shows that he does not entirely trust God as a promise-keeper. By starting with a vague promise that is gradually disambiguated and made more specific, God engages Abraham in a process that requires Abraham to grow in trust of God's promises and God's goodness. Each occasion on which Abraham tries himself to make the divine promises true is followed by God's reiterating and clarifying the promises. Each reiteration and clarification show Abraham both the futility of his own attempts to bring about the fulfillment of the promises and the rightness of waiting for God to fulfill them. And so through this demanding process Abraham is increasingly brought to trust in God. And there is also this: each time God returns to reiterate and elaborate the original promise, Abraham also sees that God does not give up on him or on his promises to him, even when Abraham has in effect been unwilling to wait in trust for God. For this reason, Abraham also gains a deeper insight into God's goodness and a greater appreciation of it. To this extent, as the relationship between God and Abraham deepens, the story shows that Abraham transfers to God some of the personal commitment that in the beginning Abraham seemed to reserve only for having offspring and being the progenitor of a people. The desires of Abraham's heart widen to include God as well as children and patriarchal status.

Abraham's first child: Ishmael

This way of interpreting God's interactions with Abraham and Abraham's reactions to God's promises is only confirmed by the fourth occasion on which God visits Abraham and makes promises to him.

This is the occasion on which God makes plain that Abraham will be the biological father of children—but leaves unspecified the identity of the mother of these children. In response to God's promise on this fourth occasion, Sarah proposes to Abraham that he take her maid Hagar to bed.[52] Since she herself cannot have children, she tells Abraham, perhaps he should try with Hagar. And Abraham agrees, thereby engaging in another attempt to contribute to making the divine promises true. It is notable that Abraham, who has the courage to ask God to confirm his promises and who (later in the story) is not afraid to cross-question God about the punishment for Sodom and Gomorrah, never thinks to ask God whether having sex with Hagar to try to produce offspring would be a good idea.

As could perhaps have been foreseen, this attempt of Abraham's to bring about the fulfillment of the divine promise initiates a new order of suffering—for Hagar most obviously, but also for Abraham and Sarah. Previously, the most evident pain for Abraham was the misery of the recurrent disappointment of reawakened hope that he might have his heart's desire. In having sex with Hagar, Abraham's double-minded response to God's promise sets in motion a train of events that eventuates in the distress of broken relationships, for Abraham and the rest of his small family too.

Sarah's stratagem for bringing about the fulfillment of the divine promise is successful, at least in the sense that Hagar quickly becomes pregnant. But Hagar's pregnancy almost immediately becomes the source of bitter discord between Hagar and Sarah. Given the wretchedness and injustice of a situation in which one woman offers another woman in her power to her husband for sex in order to make up for her own inability to produce an heir, *and* her husband accepts that abominable offer, it is not surprising that in this story there is discord between the two women when Hagar becomes pregnant.[53] According to the narrative, Hagar responds to her pregnancy by despising Sarah, who is her mistress and was her superior but who has now become her rival for Abraham's attentions; and Sarah is correspondingly furious. She complains vehemently to Abraham, and Abraham gives her permission to do whatever she likes to Hagar. Apparently, whatever she likes is bad enough to send Hagar out into the wilderness by herself, preferring the dangers of being alone in the desert to the perils of being left in Sarah's hands. It takes an angel of the Lord to send Hagar back.

As Hagar flees into the desert, an angel of the Lord appears to Hagar and tells her to return, to submit herself to Sarah, as Hagar will certainly have to do if she does return. But the angel also makes promises to Hagar, and it is worth noticing that these promises sound very much like God's promises to Abraham. Hagar will bear Abraham a son, the angel tells her, and he will be the progenitor of innumerable descendants. The angel's appearance obviously gives Hagar consolation. In fact, the name the angel assigns the coming child preserves this consolation in perpetuity. You will have a son, the angel says, and you are to call him Ishmael ("God heard"), because God has heard you in your time of affliction. It may be that Sarah and Abraham are willing to use Hagar just as a pawn in the pursuit of their own aims, but God is not. Although, as it turns out in the narrative, Hagar's child is not the promised heir, nonetheless God blesses her child too, to make this child as well the object of the very sort of promise that has captured Abraham's attention and desire. If Abraham is patriarch in consequence, then Hagar is the matriarch of the people that result from the birth of her son.[54]

Both the angel's appearance and the angel's promise give Hagar protection from Sarah. Although the text does not say so explicitly, it makes clear that Hagar told the story to Abraham, and by that means, at least, to Sarah, too.[55] At any rate, the narrative implies not only that Abraham was told Hagar's story but also that he believed what he was told. When Hagar's child is born, Abraham names him; and the name Abraham gives him is 'Ishmael.'[56] Plainly, once the story of the angel's appearance and the angel's promise, so like God's promise to Abraham, is known to Abraham and Sarah, it gives Hagar some status in that household. So far in the narrative, *only* Abraham has had divine visitations. But now Hagar—*not* Sarah, but *Hagar*—has been visited by an angel, who has spoken to her and made her promises. Furthermore, the content of the angelic promises will also add greatly to Hagar's standing in this family. Abraham will indeed be the father of many descendants, and the *mother* of these descendants will be Hagar. The increased stature given Hagar by the angel's appearance and promise thus protects Hagar, at least to some degree, from Sarah. Hagar is now not just Sarah's pregnant maid. She is the matriarch-to-be of the nation whose ancestor is *her* child and Abraham's.

With the comfort and protection provided by the angel's appearance and promise, Hagar does go back to Sarah and Abraham. The text records no further active discord between the two women, so that Hagar's new status seems to have been effectual in protecting her from further maltreatment at Sarah's hands. Apparently, at least for a while, this peculiar family group can now function with some semblance of peace. It is noteworthy, however, that the text also records no further offspring for Hagar by Abraham.

Hagar's pregnancy: A perplexity

At this point in the story, it could look as if the disambiguated divine promise of God's fourth visitation will be fulfilled through Hagar. The angel's promise to Hagar, that the son she will bear to Abraham will be the ancestor of a great nation, seems to recapitulate God's promise to Abraham, that he will be the biological father of seed that will become a great nation. And so it can look as if Abraham (and Sarah) had interpreted the fourth version of the divine promise correctly when Sarah offered Hagar to Abraham, to try to make the divine promise true.

But, of course, as the narrative makes clear and as we who know the story recognize, in this story Ishmael will not be the child of promise. Only the child born to Abraham by Sarah will have that status. And so it is worth wondering here why God would allow Hagar to become pregnant. Since God means his promises to be fulfilled only through offspring from Sarah, why does he allow Abraham to have a son by Hagar? If God can make a barren woman pregnant, surely he can also make a fertile woman barren, or at least prevent her from conceiving a child with Abraham.

Furthermore, in the narrative, it is clear that Hagar's bearing Abraham a child causes considerable suffering for all the people centrally involved in the story. The wretchedness of Hagar's forced surrogate motherhood has to be listed as the first of these sufferings, in a class by itself. But there is also noteworthy suffering for Sarah, as well as for Abraham, in the resulting tangle of relationships. And then there is the suffering of Ishmael, whose childhood takes place in Sarah's shadow, and who is subsequently expelled from home. Considering all the misery that arises from Abraham's having a son by Hagar, why does not God bring it about that Hagar is unable to conceive? Why does God let Sarah's misapprehension about the fourth version of the divine promises result in a living child born to Abraham by Hagar?

This question should not be interpreted as asking for a moral justification of God's action in allowing Hagar's conception. For the reasons I have given before, I am postponing questions pertinent to theodicy until all the narratives have been examined. The question I am asking here is looking not for theodicy as an answer but rather only for elucidation of God's motives in the story.

In considering the question so understood, it is hard not to think first of Hagar. Both Sarah and Abraham are willing to use Hagar in an inhuman way, as breeding stock. What redeems the situation for Hagar, if anything could, is precisely her pregnancy. It gives her status, which she evidently needs badly in that household; and it also gives her a son, who values her and loves her as his own, in a way that neither Sarah nor Abraham do.[57] And so thinking about Hagar sheds some light on the right answer to the question. If Abraham had accepted Sarah's offer of Hagar and Hagar had been barren, Hagar would have been used and then discarded, with no protective status and no love or family of her own afterwards. Insofar as in the story God has an interest in Hagar and a care for her, God's allowing her conception makes some sense as regards Hagar.[58]

But what about Abraham, whose story this is? Is there a reason relevant to Abraham for God's allowing Hagar to conceive?

It is worth noticing in this regard that God does not step in at any other point when, in a spirit of double-mindedness, Abraham tries to make the divine promises true. When Abraham takes Lot with him as he leaves his father's house or when Abraham adopts Eliezer as his heir, God does not do anything to stop Abraham from acting as he does or to prevent the natural consequences of his actions. God does not intervene to forbid what Abraham is doing, for example, or to coerce him into acting differently. God's pattern of action is to teach Abraham to trust in God's promises and God's goodness, but not to try to compel him into that state by any kind of threat or force.[59]

Seeing this pattern of divine action points us in the right direction for understanding why God's purposes as regards Abraham are also furthered by Hagar's becoming pregnant. The proper manifestation of the trust God is working to foster in Abraham would be Abraham's waiting in hope for the fulfillment of God's promises. There *is* trust of that sort in Abraham, but it competes in him with a strong desire to try to bring about the fulfillment of the divine promises by himself. God can thwart such moves on Abraham's part and compel him to wait for God to fulfill his promises. Alternatively, God can allow Abraham to try to take control of the fulfillment of the promises, and then let him discover that, after all, God will fulfill them himself. The first method is more likely to produce despair or fearful resignation than trust. The second method is the way in which one person Paula does often enough learn trust in another person Jerome—by being inadequately trusting in Jerome and then finding that Jerome is still there, still faithful to the relationship and to his commitment to Paula.

If God had kept Hagar from becoming pregnant, he would have been thwarting Abraham's attempt to bring about the fulfillment of the divine promises. And Hagar's consequent barrenness would have left Abraham with no options other than enforced waiting for God, with or without hope. In allowing Hagar to conceive, God first lets Abraham suppose Abraham has been successful in his stratagem for bringing about the fulfillment of the divine promise and then surprises Abraham with the news that, after all, the divine promises are still to be fulfilled, but by God and not by Abraham.[60] To me, it seems that real trust in God's goodness, as distinct from pained resignation or despair, is more likely to be generated in Abraham on *this* system.[61]

Hagar's return to Sarah: Another perplexity

There is one other perplexity regarding Hagar that is worth considering here. When Hagar flees from Sarah, an angel of the Lord sends her back into Abraham's household. But why? It is one thing to let Hagar conceive and bear a son. It is another thing to let her bear that son and nurture him in Abraham's household. In sixteen years (more or less), God will authorize Abraham to throw Hagar and Ishmael out. Then it will take a second angelic visitation to keep Hagar and her son from dying in the wilderness. Why, in the narrative, does not God simply let Hagar flee while she is pregnant, so that she can find a place and a community in which to stay, where she can raise her son in peace? Why send her back to Sarah and Abraham? Hagar's going back sets her up for the pain and the dangers of expulsion, and it inflicts that pain and those dangers on her child as well.

It is clear that there are some goods for Hagar and Ishmael that come to them from having their departure from Abraham's household occur when Ishmael is a teenager rather than when Hagar is pregnant with Ishmael. Wandering in the desert in the company of one's teenaged son is different from wandering as a single, pregnant woman. Giving birth alone in the wilderness or in a strange community and trying to care for a newborn in such circumstances is difficult, too. Furthermore, if Hagar had left

Abraham's household while she was pregnant, never to return, Ishmael would not have known his father. Whatever there is to be said about Ishmael's relations with Abraham, they are at least important enough and good enough *for Ishmael* that Ishmael is willing to join Isaac in burying Abraham after Abraham's death. But I want to leave considerations of Hagar and Ishmael to one side in order to focus the question on Abraham, as I did with the analogous question in the immediately preceding section. This is not the story of Hagar or Ishmael, but the story of Abraham; and the focus of this chapter is on Abraham, too. So, what difference does it make to Abraham that Hagar returns to his household when she is pregnant? What difference would it have made to Abraham if Hagar had fled and not returned instead of returning only to be expelled when Ishmael is adolescent?[62]

The answer is implicit in the question, I think. God's plan is to produce the promised seed from Abraham *and Sarah*, and in the process to elicit from Abraham trust in God's goodness. Forcing Abraham to lose the child he supposes to be the promised seed will grieve him, but it will teach him nothing about God's goodness. Abraham needs to learn that God can be trusted to fulfill the promises he makes. He needs to recognize that the seed of the divine promises is not the child resulting from his own stratagem for fulfilling God's promises but is instead a child given by God in a way and at a time Abraham did not choose. When Abraham comes to the point of being willing to let Ishmael go, he is acknowledging that the longed-for promised seed is the son God gave him, and not the son Hagar conceived because Abraham was trying to make the divine promises true himself. In that acknowledgment, made when Isaac is just weaned, in a culture that no doubt has a high infant mortality rate, Abraham is granting that a good God can be trusted to fulfill his promises.

And so in the narrative God allows Abraham to have and raise Ishmael, the son who results naturally enough from Abraham's attempts to make God's promises true. But, as the narrative goes on, God also brings Abraham to the point where he is willing to give Ishmael up, in recognition that God can be trusted to fulfill his promises himself.

The fifth divine promise: Abraham's second son

Ishmael is born when Abraham is 86 years old, eleven years after God's first promise to make of Abraham a great nation. When Abraham is 99 years old, and Ishmael is 13, almost a quarter of a century after that first promise, God returns to talk to Abraham, in the fifth divine visitation recorded in the narrative. On this fifth occasion, the divine speech does not begin with a promise, but with a command. "I am God Almighty," God says to Abraham, "walk before me and be perfect." And in the course of this divine visitation, God makes another covenant with Abraham, one instituted and signified by circumcision.[63] Abraham, Ishmael, and all the males in Abraham's household are bound by this covenant and thus obligated to undergo its identifying rite. All Abraham's promised posterity is included in this covenant and its ritual, too. It is on this occasion also that God changes the original names of the patriarch and his wife, from 'Abram' and 'Sarai' to 'Abraham' (which some interpreters take to mean 'Father of very many')[64] and 'Sarah'.

In the midst of this divine visitation, God repeats his earlier promises: Abraham will have innumerable descendants, and they will inherit the land in which Abraham has been living. But, for my purposes, what is especially noteworthy about this divine visitation is that God now makes the final clarification of his promises about Abraham's posterity: Abraham's posterity will be his biological offspring, *and* they will come from Sarah, not Hagar.

Abraham laughs[65] in response to God's promise that at his age he will have a child by Sarah, who is old too, as well as barren.[66] In response to this promise of God's, he makes a plea to God for Ishmael: may Ishmael live before you! From Abraham's point of view, whatever the truth of the divine promise about Sarah's having a child may be, in Ishmael he already has a seed (as the divine promises put it). Furthermore, the angelic speech to Hagar, when she was pregnant, contained a promise which seemed to be about that much-anticipated and hoped for seed: *Ishmael* will be the ancestor of a great posterity. What Abraham now asks for from God is in effect a confirmation of that angelic promise to Hagar; he wants God to bless *Ishmael*. And the blessing God does in fact give Ishmael in answer to Abraham's plea to God shows the desire behind that plea. God will multiply Ishmael exceedingly, he tells Abraham, so that through Ishmael Abraham will be the progenitor of a great nation.

Abraham's reaction to the fifth version of God's promise thus shows the same double-mindedness as Abraham's other responses to God's promises. Abraham's laughter at God's promise about Sarah's conceiving and Abraham's plea for Ishmael as the seed suitable for divine blessing stem from the same inner complexity as Abraham's earlier responses to God's promises. On the one hand, Abraham does believe God's promise that Sarah will conceive. Although Abraham laughs when he hears it, he does not dispute anything in God's promise that Sarah will have a son, nor does he ask for any confirmation of *this* promise. On the other hand, Abraham's petition for Ishmael also shows a certain unease about the divine promise regarding Sarah. If the coming child will be the child through whom Abraham has a notable posterity, why the special petition for *Ishmael* as the response to the promise about the son to come from Sarah?[67]

Although God blesses Ishmael as Abraham asks him to, God also answers Abraham by confirming and elaborating his promise about the child Sarah will bear. God tells Abraham that he will make his covenant with *Sarah's* son; the descendants of the divine promises to Abraham will trace their ancestry to Abraham *only* through Sarah's son.

The reason for God's taking this position is clear in the narrative. If God did not restrict the promises to Isaac and his descendants, then God would be supporting Abraham's attempts to fulfill the divine promises himself. By insisting that the only one who counts as the seed of the divine promises is Isaac—the heir produced by God's power and not by some stratagem of Abraham's designed to bypass Sarah's barrenness—God requires Abraham to see and accept that God can be trusted to keep his promises.

On the other hand, Ishmael is in fact now in existence and is also a beloved child of Abraham's; and God's protection has already been extended to him and his mother, beginning from the time when Ishmael was in the womb.[68] And so, in response to Abraham's plea for Ishmael, God reiterates and elaborates to Abraham the promise the angel had previously made to Hagar about Ishmael: "I have blessed [Ishmael] and will make him fruitful, and will multiply him greatly; he will beget twelve princes, and I will make him a great nation . . ."[69]

Abraham's double-mindedness and desire for descendants: The sons of Keturah

Because the next divine visitations are much more complicated than those examined so far and raise new issues, it is actually more efficient at this point to interrupt the natural progression of episodes in the narrative and jump ahead, for a moment, to the events involving Abraham and Keturah. People generally think only of Sarah's son when they think of a child of Abraham's, or perhaps they also remember Ishmael. But in fact the biblical narrative mentions *eight* sons of Abraham: Ishmael, Isaac, and *six* more sons by Keturah.

Sarah's reactions to Hagar, both when Hagar is pregnant and later, after Isaac's birth, are explosive and vindictive. And so it is not surprising that, in the sixteen years or so that Hagar lives with Abraham after Ishmael's birth, Hagar has no more children by Abraham. While Sarah lives, Abraham does not make the mistake of having more children by Hagar or of taking any other woman into his family. But once Sarah has died, Abraham does add another woman to his household; he takes a woman named Keturah as his wife or concubine. At that point in the story, Abraham is more than 137 years old,[70] but Keturah bears him one son after another.

Why does Abraham take another woman and start a new, large family?

There is a tradition in Rabbinic commentary that 'Keturah' is another name for Hagar.[71] On this tradition, the narrative is interpreted to mean that Abraham brought Hagar back into his household once Sarah was dead. The main evidence for this tradition seems to be only a sense of what Abraham *should* have done. By the time Sarah dies, however, it has been roughly thirty-five years (give or take a few) since Abraham expelled Hagar.[72] Even if at that point Abraham still remembered Hagar, still wanted her, and still knew where to find her, there is nonetheless some question whether after all those years Hagar would have wanted to return to the man who used his power over her to have sex with her and then threw her out to wander in the wilderness with the child he had fathered by her. If a sense of what ought to have happened can be the determiner of an interpretation of a story, as the tradition in this case appears to suppose, then in my view Hagar is *not* Keturah.[73] But, in any case, the text gives no indication that Keturah is not simply one more wife or concubine of Abraham's, and the list of the children Keturah bears Abraham does not include Ishmael. So it seems more reasonable to take the story at face value and assume that Keturah is not Hagar under another name, but just a new woman whom Abraham brings into his household when Sarah is dead.

Reasons of loyalty to Hagar can, therefore, not explain Abraham's taking Keturah into his household.

It might, of course, be the case that the narrative wants us to believe that Abraham was a virile old man who could not cope unless he had a woman living with him. But if that were the picture of Abraham the narrative was trying to present, then, we might reasonably enough suppose, the narrative would not have had *Sarah* laugh when she heard God tell Abraham that he would have a child when he was 100 years old.[74] If it was funny to Sarah to think that Abraham might father a child at *that* age, we could presumably expect that, in the world of the narrative, Abraham at almost 140 might have managed to live celibately without a struggle.

More importantly, by the time Abraham adds Keturah to his family, the divine promises have been fulfilled, at least in the sense that Abraham has the promised seed, Isaac, not to mention his *other* son, Ishmael, who is also destined to be the progenitor of a people. What, then, is the point of taking yet another wife or concubine and having so many more children by her?

It is helpful here to do the arithmetic of the story.

Abraham is 140 years old when Isaac marries Rebecca. (Isaac is 40 years old at this stage, and Sarah has been dead for three years.) Abraham is 175 years old when he dies. (He lives thirty-eight years after Sarah's death, and so thirty-five years after Isaac's marriage to Rebecca.) In the thirty-eight-year interval of time between Sarah's death and his own, Abraham has six sons by Keturah; and, in Abraham's lifetime, these sons grow old enough to be given gifts and sent away from home.

So when did Abraham add Keturah to his household? There is no evidence in the text beyond the facts in the preceding paragraph; and, on those facts, there is more than one option for the answer to the question.

Suppose that Keturah began to produce sons[75] in the first year of her life with Abraham. Presumably, there are at least seven years in age between the first of Keturah's sons and the sixth. In addition, it seems right to think that a son needs to be at least well into his teens in order to be sent away with gifts. And so we can reckon that there have to be *at least* twenty-five years between the time Keturah joins Abraham's household and the time the last of Keturah's sons leaves home (that is, seven years for the last son to be born, and another eighteen for that last son to be old enough to be sent away with gifts). There might be more, but it is hard to see how there could be much less.

So, if Keturah's sons started coming early and came in quick succession, and if Abraham sent them away in the last year of his life, then Abraham could have been as much as 150 years old when he began to have children by Keturah. (In that case, Abraham would have begun having children by Keturah when Isaac had been married to Rebecca for ten years.)

Alternatively, suppose that Keturah's sons came at three-year intervals, a common enough interval between children in cultures that breast-feed babies on demand. Then, on the supposition that the last of these sons was sent away at the end of Abraham's life and that he was teenaged when he went, Abraham could have been as young as 145 when he had his first son by Keturah. (In that case, Abraham would have begun having children by Keturah when Isaac had been married to Rebecca for five years.)

Finally, suppose that Abraham takes Keturah soon after Sarah dies and that Keturah becomes pregnant fairly quickly after joining Abraham's household. In that case, Abraham could have begun having children by Keturah when he was 140 years old. (In that case, Abraham would have had his children by Keturah throughout the first six or seven years of Isaac's marriage to Rebecca.)

Those are the basic options, if we do the arithmetic on the story. What does the arithmetic show us?

Abraham's longing to be a father and the ancestor of a people is plainly his heart's desire, and his whole relationship with God is shaped by it.[76] The first five encounters between God and Abraham are concentrated on Abraham's desire for descendants and God's promises to provide progeny for him. The double-mindedness of Abraham's belief in the divine promises and in God's goodness is equally evident, as I have been at pains to show. Abraham tries to bring about the fulfillment of the divine promises by devices of his own, all of which are predicated on an acceptance of Sarah's barrenness together with some stratagem for circumventing it. Abraham ceases trying to find some device that will make God's promises true in spite of Sarah's barrenness only when God makes clear that the seed of the promise will come from Sarah—and even then, in response to God's explanation that Abraham is about to have a child by *Sarah*, Abraham asks God to bless *Ishmael* and make *Ishmael* a great nation. The subsequent birth of Isaac does give Abraham what his heart had been set on—but *only* part of it, not the whole of it. That is because what Abraham has set his heart on is a posterity, not just a son. Abraham wants to be not merely a father but a patriarch. And so it is important in this connection to note that, in the narrative, when Isaac marries, Isaac's wife Rebecca is barren for the first *nineteen* years of her marriage. Isaac marries Rebecca when he is 40, but he does not become the father of Esau and Jacob until he is 60. At the point when Isaac's twin sons are born, Abraham is 160 years old. (The twins are 15 years old when Abraham dies.)

Given the arithmetic, on one set of suppositions or another, in the period when Abraham is having children by Keturah, Isaac and Rebecca are childless; in fact, it is possible that they have been childless for as much as a decade by the time the first of Keturah's sons is born. And so this is one plausible answer to the question regarding the time when Abraham adds Keturah to his household: Abraham is having children by Keturah at a time when it could look to a reasonable observer as if Isaac, the child through whom Abraham was going to become the progenitor of a great posterity, will not have children of his own.[77]

One explanation for Abraham's having children by Keturah is, therefore, that Abraham is continuing the pattern of his earlier responses to the divine promises.[78] When he takes Keturah, Ishmael is lost to him, wandering God-knows-where in the wilderness; and Isaac's wife seems to be barren.[79] In having children with Keturah in these circumstances, Abraham is making sure that there are children of his who *could* serve as the source of posterity for him in case his line through Isaac does not continue.

In fact, if Abraham takes Keturah as his concubine roughly a decade after Isaac marries Rebecca, which is also a decade before Rebecca has children of her own, and if there is a twenty-five-year interval between the time of Keturah's arrival and Abraham's sending away his sons by Keturah, then Abraham sends those sons off at a time when *Isaac's* twin children are in their teens—old enough for Abraham to feel reasonably sure that those twins will live into adulthood and be able to have children of their own. The narrative makes explicit that the point of Abraham's sending Keturah's sons away[80] is precisely to ensure that the offspring of the concubine do not inherit with the legitimate heir.[81] Perhaps the point at which Abraham decides he no longer wants the sons he produced with Keturah to be part of his legacy is the time when he is finally convinced that Isaac will have offspring of his own and that Isaac's offspring will survive to reproduce.[82]

Even by the end of his life, then, when he has Isaac and when Isaac himself is grown and married, the narrative suggests that Abraham is still double-minded about the fulfillment of God's promises, at least to the extent of providing a back-up plan for God, in case the original plan fails. Abraham's desire for progeny is great, and it never cohabits entirely easily in him with trust in God's promises and God's goodness. On the one hand, Abraham does indeed believe the divine promises and God's disambiguations of them, including the explanation that the only child of promise is Isaac, so that Abraham's status as patriarch of a divinely appointed people depends on Isaac alone. He does send Keturah's sons away just with gifts, rather than with a real share of his inheritance, which he saves altogether for Isaac.[83] And yet, on the other hand, Abraham's desire to be the father of a great posterity is so strong that he is still unwilling to risk it entirely on Isaac (or on Isaac and Ishmael). The sons of Keturah are there, too, just in case.[84]

And so the pattern of Abraham's being double-minded about God's promises to give him his heart's desire, which is evident in the narrative in the first five divine visitations to Abraham, is a pattern that characterizes all of Abraham's life. That pattern is interspersed with episodes in which Abraham's trust in God's goodness is whole-hearted, most notably in the binding of Isaac. But the overall pattern is only highlighted by the few notable exceptions to it.

The sixth divine speech: Sodom and Gomorrah

On the sixth occasion God comes to talk to Abraham, God's speech includes another reiteration, this time without elaboration, of his promises to Abraham about offspring. But after this part of the divine speech, the pattern of God's exchanges with Abraham established in the previous divine visitations alters. By the time of the sixth divine speech, the long crescendo in which God reveals increasingly more of his plan for making Abraham the patriarch of a great nation has finally come to an end; all the details are now known to Abraham, and to the audience of the narrative, too. Abraham will have numerous descendants, who will inherit the land of Canaan; these will be biological descendants; the line will go through Sarah, not Hagar; Sarah will begin the generation of that posterity by having a son in the coming year, and the son's name will be Isaac. From here on, God's exchanges with Abraham, including the rest of the interaction between God and Abraham on this occasion, are different from those in the preceding divine visitations. They are no longer concentrated on increasing specification of the divine promises of posterity for Abraham. Although they do still have to do with Abraham's children and also contain promises about Abraham's descendants, the focus of the remaining three divine visitations is more complicated than that of the first five. Their center of attention is elsewhere.

The sixth divine visitation comes hard on the heels of the fifth. On this sixth occasion, when God reiterates his promise that Abraham will have a son by Sarah, there is also some recorded interaction between God and Sarah. By overhearing the conversation between God and Abraham, Sarah now hears the divine promise for herself, as is appropriate since it involves her in an essential way. When she hears that promise, she laughs to herself not just at the thought that she will have a child at the age of 90 but also at the notion that she should "have pleasure," given Abraham's age. God reports her thought and her laughter to Abraham but diplomatically leaves out the part about Abraham; and when God confronts her for laughing, Sarah undiplomatically lies to God, denying that she laughed. God makes clear that he knows she has lied; but he does not scold her for lying to him. To Abraham, in Sarah's hearing, God responds to her laughter by saying "Is anything too difficult for God?,"[85] thereby commenting effectively on *all* the things prompting Sarah's wifely laughter. This incident in the story of the sixth encounter between God and Abraham is complicated and full of wonderful touches, which I pass over with regret, in order to concentrate solely on the part most directly of concern for my purposes.

That part of the sixth encounter is the conversation between God and Abraham about Sodom and Gomorrah.[86] It is the only recorded exchange between Abraham and God in the narrative that has as its entire ostensible object of interest something other than Abraham's desire for descendants—although, as we shall see, the tacit focus of this exchange may be nearer Abraham's customary concerns than first appears to be the case.

In this part of the sixth encounter, God begins by saying (or by reflecting to himself[87]) that it would be good for him to reveal to Abraham what he is about to do. Connected with this thought is a second divine assertion—namely, that Abraham needs to command his children (including the children Abraham does not yet have) to do justice and to keep God's ways, so that God can fulfill for them the covenant he has made with Abraham. This is the first explicit indication that there is anything conditional about God's covenant with Abraham, and it raises a great many questions, which cannot be dealt with in passing here. But it also reminds us that covenants are generally premised on the goodness of the covenant-makers. At any rate, those who are not good are also not trustworthy keepers of covenants. God's statement implies that the goodness of Abraham's descendants is a necessary prerequisite for God's electing to fulfill his part of the covenant. But, of course, it is also true that the covenant will be fulfilled only if there is goodness on God's side as well. That this is something Abraham must feel is made clear by the way this part of the story unrolls.

With so much clarification of his reasons for his revelation to Abraham, God goes on to tell Abraham that Sodom and Gomorrah are wicked cities and that he is about to visit them to determine the depth of their wickedness. Although nothing in this statement of God's asserts or even directly implies that God will somehow punish these cities, Abraham takes God's statement to mean that God intends to destroy both cities; and Abraham is greatly concerned at that implication. Would you really cut off the righteous with the wicked?, Abraham asks God. What if there were fifty righteous people in one of those cities? Would you not spare the whole city for their sake? Because, if you did not spare it, Abraham tells God, then the lot of the righteous would be the same as the lot of the wicked, and that would most certainly be unfair. "Far be it from you!" Abraham says; "Should not the judge of all the earth do righteously?!"[88] And Abraham goes on to work his way slowly from fifty innocents to ten. "If there were only ten righteous in the city," he finally asks God, "would you not spare the city for their sake?"

Abraham is assuming that in the destruction of a city all its citizens will also be destroyed; and he thinks that the injustice of God's killing ten innocent people would be terrible enough to warrant letting all the guilty of the city off their well-deserved punishment in order to protect the ten righteous. When God agrees that, if there are ten innocents, he will protect the city for their sake, even at the cost of forgoing the justly deserved punishment of all the many guilty, Abraham's concerns are finally allayed. When it turns out that God will not inflict on the innocent the punishment deserved by the guilty as long as the innocent number at least ten, then Abraham is satisfied that God has been bargained into justice.[89]

Although Abraham is usually praised for his concern with justice and for his courage in confronting God in this exchange,[90] the first thing to see here is in fact Abraham's double-mindedness about God's goodness. The double-mindedness that is evident in Abraham's reactions to God's promises about his descendants is even more pronounced and overt here. On the one hand, Abraham believes that God is the "judge of all the earth"; on the other hand, he feels that he needs to talk the judge of all the earth into acting justly.

The presumptuousness of Abraham's attempt to wrangle God, the judge of all the earth, into justice lies, of course, in Abraham's apparent presupposition that this wrangling is necessary in order to get God to act with justice. In fact, Abraham's bargaining with God is not only presumptuous but veers dangerously toward the comic. Abraham is supposing that the judge of all the earth would be willing to condemn the innocent with the guilty, and he is hoping to persuade that just judge God to act more justly than that—as long as there are a reasonable number of innocents affected.

The folly of Abraham's presupposition is pointed out in the very next episode of the narrative, in which God takes care to make sure that the *four* righteous people in Sodom are spared in the city's destruction. Abraham was willing to give up on the righteous if they were fewer in number than ten; but God, who (on Abraham's view) had to be bargained into protecting *ten* righteous people, actually spares the four righteous people living in Sodom. Without any arguing or bargaining by Abraham, God goes significantly further in the direction Abraham thought he needed to push God: God makes sure that *none* of the innocent is punished with the wicked.[91] And when Lot wants to escape Sodom and flee to Zoar, a little city that had been slated for destruction with Sodom and Gomorrah, God spares Zoar for the sake of Lot and the women (three, or two, depending on how one counts[92]) in his family.[93]

On the one hand, then, Abraham apparently believes that God is capable of unjustly causing the death of innocent people, so that God has to be bargained out of killing the righteous with the wicked. To this extent, Abraham plainly is not giving full assent to the belief that God is good. And yet, on the other hand, when God accedes to Abraham's pleas that he spare the guilty for the sake of the innocent, Abraham trusts that God will keep his word. Abraham asks for no confirmation or covenant to guarantee that God will do as he says. Abraham apparently thinks, then, that God's word alone is entirely trustworthy. To this extent, Abraham clearly relies on the goodness of God. And so, in his bargaining with God, Abraham is double-minded; he both believes and does not believe that God is good and worthy of trust.

The object of Abraham's concern in the exchange over Sodom and Gomorrah is also worth noticing. Contrary to common interpretations of this story, Abraham is not here manifesting some general concern with justice. To begin with, it is not at all obvious that there is more injustice in destroying ten righteous people in the process of punishing a city in which everyone else—*everyone else*—is worthy of death than there is in letting many people who are so evil go entirely unpunished for their crimes in order to protect ten righteous people.[94] As far as that goes, it is not at all clear why Abraham supposes the judge of all the earth could not manage to punish the wicked and preserve the innocent at the same time—as the narrative subsequently shows God can and does do. As the later episodes of the narrative make clear, it is not hard for God to do so; it does not even take a miracle. God simply tells innocent Lot and his family to leave the city, in order to avoid sharing in its punishment. So, if justice in general had been Abraham's concern, he might have tried to make sure that God would both spare the innocent and also punish the guilty. But this is not at all what Abraham does. It is evident, then, that the focus of Abraham's bargaining with God is not abstract justice.[95] Rather, the aim of Abraham's bargaining is only to ensure that God will not deprive righteous people of what they are in justice entitled to.

This concern of Abraham's reveals something else about Abraham's attitude toward God and about Abraham's anxieties where God's promises are concerned.

As I explained earlier, this divine visitation, in which God reveals his plans for Sodom and Gomorrah, begins with God's reiteration of his previous promise to Abraham about the descendants who will be the biological offspring of Abraham *and Sarah*. At this point in the narrative, childless Sarah is well past child-bearing age. This time, there is no stratagem of Abraham's that can make God's promise true; this time, only God can fulfill his promise. God's *power* to make it true—God's power to do whatever God says he will do—never seems in doubt for Abraham. At any rate, Abraham shows no surprise when he is told that God is able to destroy whole cities, or when he hears that nothing is too difficult for God. What Abraham is evidently not easy about, then, is the nature of the goodness which is yoked to that power.

The recipient of a promise is in justice entitled to the fulfillment of that promise. But, if God is willing to forget about what is owed in justice to the righteous for the sake of punishing others, then how safe is the hope and trust Abraham has put in God's promises? If God is not a perfectly trustworthy rewarder of the righteous, then what becomes of his promises to obedient, righteous Abraham?

So the double-minded conversation about Sodom and Gomorrah, in which Abraham tries to negotiate the judge of all the earth into justice, has behind it Abraham's own concerns about God's goodness and the trustworthiness of God's promises. In the initial divine speech or reflection that begins this episode, God implies that Abraham and his descendants need to be righteous in order for the covenant between God and Abraham to be effective. But, then, God needs to be a righteous rewarder of the righteous, too. Otherwise the covenant is worthless, even if Abraham and his children are righteous. A covenant can be rendered ineffectual by the failure of either party to it to be righteous.

The other noteworthy thing about this episode is God's great patience with Abraham's attempt to negotiate God into justice. Any human being who was addressed by someone close to him in the way Abraham addresses God would surely feel hurt and insulted. If the wife of an even ordinarily decent government official were to ask her husband whether he meant to kill innocent people in his next official action, or (worse yet!) if she showed that she was trying to talk him into a promise not to kill the innocent if there were at least ten of them, he would certainly be aggrieved and would let her know it. God's answers to Abraham's reiterated bargaining questions are eloquently brief, but nonetheless God does not rebuke Abraham for those questions. Why, in the narrative, is God patient in this way? As far as that goes, why does God explain to Abraham anything about God's intentions as regards Sodom and Gomorrah?

Here, as elsewhere in this chapter, it seems to me that the answer to the questions is evident, once the questions are plainly raised. There is love and care for Abraham in God's way of dealing with him. Given Abraham's uneasy attitude about God's goodness, his double-mindedness about God's trustworthiness with regard to God's promises to Abraham, there is wisdom in God's explaining to Abraham in advance divine punishment inflicted on others in Abraham's sight. And there is a parental patience and care in God's putting up with Abraham's questions to God about God's justice and the self-concerned anxiety underlying those questions.

The seventh divine promise: Hagar and Ishmael

God's goodness is also at issue, although in a different way, on the seventh occasion on which God comes to talk to Abraham. The conversation between God and Abraham then is no exception to the general rule: Abraham's children form the subject, or the partial subject, of the conversation, as they have on all the previous occasions on which

God has come to speak with Abraham. But this time the children in question are not the prophetically foreseen but not-yet-existent children of promise. This time they are real boys, Ishmael and Isaac. To understand the conversation between God and Abraham on this occasion, we have to be clear first about its context.

God's promise that Sarah would have a son has been fulfilled. When Abraham is 100 years old, Sarah gives birth to a boy, whom Abraham names Isaac.[96] Ishmael is 14 at the time of Isaac's birth. He has been Abraham's only child for all these years; now he has a brother.

The story skips over Isaac's infancy and focuses directly on his weaning. When Isaac is weaned, Abraham makes a great feast, the story says. It is not clear how old Isaac is at the time of weaning; at least 2 or 3 years old is not an unreasonable estimate. So Ishmael must then have been at least 16 or 17. During the feast Ishmael does *something*—the Hebrew can be translated variously[97] but has sometimes been understood to mean that Ishmael was mocking Isaac. Whatever it is Ishmael is doing, Sarah sees him and blows up. She has been violent toward her rival Hagar in the past. Given her history, the wonder is not so much that she blows up now as that with a son of her own she has tolerated Abraham's other son for so long.

What would be appropriate punishment for a teenage boy who mocked a younger brother, if in fact the reading that assigns this much culpability to Ishmael is right? Take his car privileges away for a week, we might say—but then we are a soft-hearted, child-centered culture. Nineteenth-century British educators, made of sterner stuff, might have prescribed a beating. What does Sarah want? She wants to have Ishmael, together with his mother, thrown out of the family, never to return. There is no suggestion whatsoever that Hagar has been in any way unkind to Isaac, but the punishment Sarah envisages for Ishmael encompasses Hagar, too. In the previous episode when God came to talk to Abraham, Abraham was concerned that the innocent not be included in the punishment of the wicked. Here Sarah is concerned that the punishment of the malefactor (if in fact Ishmael is a malefactor of any sort) not exclude his innocent mother.

If the punishment Sarah had in mind for Hagar and Ishmael were just banishment from the family, it would still be a terrible evil. Ishmael is Abraham's son, and Hagar, his mother, has been a part of this complicated family for almost two decades (or more). For years, before he heard God's promise about offspring by Sarah, Abraham no doubt thought *this* boy would be his only child. *Ishmael* was his son, his only son, the son of his old age, for fourteen years before Isaac came. The bonds of trust and love between Abraham and the boy must have been powerful. For Abraham to throw Ishmael out is a terrible betrayal of the boy's trust toward his father, and it can hardly be justified by whatever Sarah saw in Ishmael's relations with Isaac during the feast. There is no justification at all for the expulsion of Hagar.

But what Sarah wants is considerably worse than the mere expulsion of Hagar and Ishmael. In nineteenth-century Britain, sons thrown out by stern fathers were thrown into city life, where they might try to get their own living or sponge off friends or at nightmarish worst beg on street corners. But, if Hagar and Ishmael are thrown out, they will be expelled into the desert with all its perils. Being taken as slaves or chattel is the best that is likely to happen to them. If they are not found and preyed on by others, their chance of surviving alone in the wilderness is small. In fact, as the story develops, it takes divine intervention just to keep them from dying of thirst. Throwing a woman and her child out into the desert without protection is the analogue of exposing unwanted infants. Perhaps it is not identical to murder, but the difference does not seem to have much moral significance. If anything, what Sarah wants is worse than infanticide. At least, an infant has not built up trust in his father; a father's leaving his infant to die of exposure does not betray years of love and intimacy.

Clearly, Sarah is not interested simply in removing Hagar and Ishmael from the family. What Sarah wants is not just the absence of her rival's son but revenge on him, and on his mother, too. Her anger is murderous, and the depth of her passion is shown by that fact that she expresses it in a direct command to her husband: "cast out the bondwoman and her son." This is not the direction the order of command usually flows in this patriarchal society.

On the previous occasion when Sarah blew up over Hagar, Abraham acceded to her wishes; but then she just wanted to attack Hagar herself. Now, she wants the vengeance to be meted out by Abraham; she wants him to expel the son whom he loves and Hagar, the mother of that son, into the desert alone, in a way that puts their lives at risk. What Sarah wants is a heartbreaking wrong.[98]

That Abraham is willing to contemplate going along with Sarah at all is testimony to the implacability of her wrath; but, even so, he cannot bring himself to accede to her wishes. The narrative says: "The thing was very bad in Abraham's eyes on account of his son."[99] And so Abraham is caught between two options for action, neither of which he can find in himself the resources to do: on the one hand, to reject resolutely the command of his angry wife Sarah; on the other hand, to capitulate entirely to her demand for the expulsion of his son and the mother of his son. It should be clear that, although Abraham may be torn between these options, they do not constitute a moral dilemma for him. All morality is on one side. What the other side has to recommend it is just self-interested prudence and domestic peace.

This is the context for the seventh occasion on which God visits Abraham.

The seventh divine promise: God's concurring with Sarah

On this seventh occasion, God comes to talk to Abraham to guide the course of Abraham's action.[100]

Speaking of Abraham's reflection on Sarah's demanded expulsion of Hagar and Ishmael, the narrative says only that the thing was bad in Abraham's eyes because of his son. When God raises Sarah's demand with Abraham, God also takes note of Hagar and adds her to the list. God says to Abraham: "Let it not be bad in your eyes because of the lad and because of your bondwoman." And then God goes on to tell Abraham: "In all that Sarah says to you, listen to her voice."[101] So on this seventh occasion, God comes to talk to Abraham in order to break the deadlock in Abraham; and he breaks it, very surprisingly, by siding with murderously angry Sarah.

How can God tell Abraham to listen to his wife when what she wants is so evil? The answer to this question has two parts.

On the one hand, although Sarah's intentions are evil, the result she wants, that only Isaac should count as Abraham's heir, is the result God has foreordained all along. If, from the beginning, Abraham had been willing to trust whole-heartedly in the divine promises, Ishmael would not have come into being. If Ishmael were to remain in the household and be raised with Isaac, the two sons and their descendants would mingle and form one family. To that extent, Isaac and his descendants would not be singled out as the posterity of the promise that God originally made to Abraham and then reiterated for a quarter of a century. If God were now to allow Ishmael a status equal to that of Isaac's, so that Ishmael's offspring and Isaac's became one posterity of Abraham's, then God would be accepting and validating Abraham's previous failure of trust. And so, although with very different motivation, God sides with Sarah.

On the other hand, Ishmael *does* now exist, and he *is* a child of Abraham's, too. He, as well as Isaac, has a claim to be taken care of not only by his father Abraham, but also by God, whose complex dealings with Abraham have had a role in bringing about Ishmael's birth and his raising in Abraham's household.[102] And so God himself also undertakes to guarantee Ishmael's safety and his flourishing—only now away from Abraham's household.[103] In a reiteration of the promise the angel made to Hagar, God promises Abraham: "Of the son of the bondwoman I will make a nation."[104] If God promises to make Ishmael a nation in the wilderness, then God is promising that Ishmael will not die when he and his mother are expelled into the desert. On the contrary, God is promising that, in the wilderness, Ishmael, too, will live and have the status of progenitor of a people.

It is evident that God's message to Abraham makes all the difference to Abraham's decision about what to do. Without God's promise (or, more accurately, his confirmation of the angel's earlier promise), the action Sarah wants Abraham to engage in is manifestly immoral. For that matter, it goes directly contrary to the strong moral concerns Abraham evinced even for total strangers in Sodom and Gomorrah, where he worried about the injustice of condemning and punishing the righteous. Whatever can be said about Ishmael, Hagar is innocent; nothing in the text even hints that she is implicated in any activity worthy of banishment. God's promise to make of Ishmael a great nation enables Abraham to go along with Sarah without being guilty of injustice against Ishmael and his mother. It is as if the place where the stepmother wanted the father's son to be abandoned to his peril should turn out, unbeknownst to her, to be the boarding school from which the society's leaders and rulers come. God's promise to Abraham about Ishmael transforms Sarah's plan for abandoning Hagar and Ishmael and exposing them to the perils of the desert into a plan for Ishmael's flourishing—and Hagar's too, insofar as she is Ishmael's mother. To the extent to which Abraham wants what Sarah wants, but for a different motive, whose source is God's promise about Ishmael, not only

Abraham's action but also his intention in that action are saved from being morally reprehensible.[105]

God's promise also relieves Abraham, at least to a considerable extent,[106] of the evil of betraying his son's trust—because Abraham can tell Ishmael what God has said. He can explain that he is not acting in such a way as to bring about Ishmael's death (or even to wreck Ishmael's life), because God is guaranteeing Ishmael's flowering into a patriarch in his own right.[107] As far as that goes, because in the past Hagar has had her own experience of God's care for her and God's ability to protect her in the wilderness, Abraham's story will have a plausibility for her that it would not have for others without a similar experience. So Abraham's explaining to Hagar what God has promised will also save Abraham from betraying whatever trust in him Hagar might have.

As it stands, the narrative tells us nothing one way or another about what Abraham told Hagar and Ishmael, but it does give us one small clue about whether Abraham communicated to Ishmael this promise of God's about him. When Abraham dies, Ishmael comes to help his brother Isaac bury him. If all Ishmael knew is that, in response to Sarah's wrath, Abraham expelled him and his mother from the family to wander at risk of his life in the desert, is it believable that, after many years, Ishmael would return with filial piety to bury what would have to seem to him to be such a monstrous and unnatural father?

And so, because of God's promise, Abraham can acquiesce in Sarah's demands without thereby betraying either his moral convictions or his son and Hagar.

The expulsion of Hagar and Ishmael

In the narrative, on the strength of God's promise, Abraham sends Ishmael and Hagar off to walk into the desert. But it is instructive to contrast the way in which Abraham does so with Abraham's actions in other episodes where he is pursuing what he cares about.

When God made Abraham a promise that he would have biological offspring who would inherit the land, Abraham asked for some divine confirmation of the truth of God's promise. How shall I know this is true?, he asked. Here, where the life of his son (and his son's mother) is at stake, he asks for no sign.

When the issue was the lives of strangers in Sodom and Gomorrah, Abraham was willing to confront God and bargain with him. But here, where what is at issue is the expulsion of the child who has been a part of his life for sixteen years or more (and the expulsion of Hagar too), Abraham attempts no negotiations with God. He might have pleaded with God to let him keep Ishmael and Hagar with him. He might have tried to bargain God into letting him send Ishmael and Hagar back to his father's family at Haran, to be sheltered there; or he might have negotiated with God to be allowed to provide some other friendly community for Ishmael and Hagar. But he does not intercede for Hagar and Ishmael in any way. He just expels them into the wilderness alone, without any help of this sort.

And there are many other episodes relevant in this connection. When Lot was kidnapped by hostile warriors, in an episode of the narrative left to one side in this chapter, Abraham gathers an army and gets him back. Later in the narrative, when Abraham wants a wife for Isaac, Abraham puts together an enticing array of jewelry and other gifts, and he sends a servant and animals to his brother's household in Haran to bring back a woman for Isaac. When he sends Keturah's sons away, he sends them away with gifts. But Hagar and Ishmael get none of these things—no protective army, no servants, no gifts.

After all their years in Abraham's household, Hagar and Ishmael are sent away alone, with virtually nothing. The text says that Abraham rises up early in the morning, hands Hagar and Ishmael a bottle of water and a loaf of bread, and sends them off to walk into the desert—without any request for a confirmation of the truth of the promise, without any negotiations, without any gifts, without any entourage, without any supplies worth mentioning. Even given the reassurance of God's promise to Abraham about Ishmael, there is something distressing about the manner in which Abraham expels Hagar and Ishmael.

We could suppose that the distressing features of Abraham's action are Sarah's fault.[108] That is, we could chalk Abraham's action up to his acquiescing with Sarah, and we could see the treatment of Hagar and Ishmael as an expression of Sarah's anger against them. No doubt, Sarah's anger does contribute to some of the apparently punitive features of Abraham's action. But supposing that Sarah is solely responsible for the way in which Abraham turns Hagar and Ishmael out is an implausible explanation. Many things in the narrative suggest that Abraham dominates his household, and nothing indicates that he leaves major decisions to Sarah alone.

The other possible explanation is that there is more at stake for Abraham in the expulsion of Hagar and Ishmael than placating Sarah.

Throughout the narrative, God's promises to Abraham have reflected Abraham's heart's desire for patriarchal status. But, in the narrative, God does not promise Abraham just an end to his own childlessness, as if Abraham were pining for a baby. Rather, God promises Abraham *innumerable* descendants, as innumerable as the dust of the earth or the stars in the sky. And God promises that these descendants will hold a special place in the whole history of the world. But the fulfillment of these promises and the realization of Abraham's heart's desire will come to Abraham only through the child born by *God's* fulfilling the promises God has made—through Isaac, that is, not through Ishmael. Once Isaac has been born, Abraham finally understands this point and accepts it. To the extent to which he does, then, once Isaac is in existence, Ishmael is *de trop*, unnecessary for the thing Abraham wants so dearly.

Not only is Ishmael unnecessary, but in fact it is clear that Ishmael is in some sense even a threat to Abraham's having what he so desires. Ishmael is the first-born of Abraham's sons, in a society in which first-born status is of paramount importance (as the later story of Isaac and his sons Jacob and Esau highlights). Ishmael's status alone is, therefore, a threat to Isaac. In addition, there is a suggestion in the narrative's description of Ishmael's behavior at the feast celebrating Isaac's weaning that Ishmael feels a rivalry with Isaac. So Abraham might well feel that Ishmael could take action to undermine Isaac as Abraham's heir. To the extent to which Ishmael is separated from Isaac, Abraham might suppose, Isaac and his line are protected from Ishmael and his progeny.

And so Abraham's sending Ishmael away is, in a sense, Abraham's attempting to undo the past, the past in which, by getting Hagar pregnant, Abraham tried to bring about by himself the fulfillment of God's promise. For Abraham, the expulsion of Hagar and Ishmael is thus not just a matter of placating Sarah. Rather, their expulsion safeguards Abraham's self-interest in more than one way. By disinheriting Ishmael and his descendants, Abraham promotes Isaac and his descendants. He thereby protects his heart's desire, to be the patriarch of a great people—as God promised him he would be, only through Isaac. The story of Keturah's sons also confirms this interpretation of Abraham's motives. In that story, without any urging from Sarah, who is long since dead, Abraham sends the concubine's sons away at the end of his life so that they will not inherit with his son Isaac.

So when God tells Abraham to do what Sarah wants and expel Hagar and Ishmael, Abraham's self-interest is on the side of obedience to God. And the lack of care for Hagar and Ishmael evinced in the manner in which Abraham sends them away is troubling.[109]

The indiscernibility of mixed motives

Given the way they are expelled, things go for Hagar and Ishmael pretty much as one might have predicted: they wander aimlessly in the wilderness until the water in their water bottle is spent, without finding any shelter or protection, without finding any wells. After a while, Hagar is sure they will die of thirst; and she goes some distance from her son, weeping as she goes, in order not to be a witness to his death. At that point, God intervenes.[110] God sends an angel of the Lord to help Hagar find water, and the angel comforts her by repeating to her God's promise: "I will make [Ishmael] a great nation."[111] The narrative closes this episode by saying that God was with the boy in the wilderness as he grew. In other words, in the story God keeps his promise about Ishmael.

It is important to see here that God's promise to Abraham about Ishmael on the occasion of the expulsion of Hagar and Ishmael enables Abraham to send Hagar and Ishmael away without being guilty of a great moral wrong only if God's promises are trustworthy, and in two senses. In order for God's promise to Abraham about Ishmael in the desert to serve its morally beneficial functions, it must, first, be true that God does keep his promises. God must be good, unwilling to concur in the unjust punishment of the righteous, unwilling to accept or connive at the killing of an innocent child. As the story of Hagar and Ishmael in the wilderness makes plain, God's promise is trustworthy in this sense. But, secondly, it must also be the case that Abraham believes God is good in these ways. If God's promises were trustworthy in the first sense but Abraham did not believe that they were, then Abraham would be guilty of a great evil in agreeing to Sarah's plan, even if (contrary to what Abraham believed) God did in fact keep his promise to preserve Ishmael and make him flourish.

Furthermore, when Abraham was double-minded about God's goodness in connection with Sodom and Gomorrah, he was being presumptuous, but still fundamentally good-hearted. If Abraham is so much as double-minded about God's promise in this case, where the lives of Hagar and Ishmael are at stake, there will be nothing benevolent about Abraham. He will just be using God as an excuse to betray the trust of his son and to do a dreadful injustice to an innocent child and his mother. And that is not all. If Abraham is not whole-hearted in believing God's promise about Ishmael when he expels Hagar and Ishmael, he will be double-minded about God's goodness, too. To act on God's promise without wholly believing it would be to assume that God does not care much either about Abraham's trust in God as Abraham expels Ishmael or about Ishmael's safety in the desert. In effect, it would be to suppose that God would not much mind being used as an accessory to serious evil. A person who took this attitude toward God would be seriously alienated from God, as the focus on God's goodness and justice in the whole narrative makes plain.

So it makes a great deal of difference what we suppose Abraham's psychological state was when he expelled Hagar and Ishmael on the basis of God's promise about Ishmael. But what are we to say about Abraham's attitude toward God's promises in the expulsion of Hagar and Ishmael? Has Abraham's previous double-mindedness about the promises been resolved? Is Abraham now become whole-heartedly persuaded of God's goodness, convinced that the judge of all the earth would never do an injustice, would never destroy the innocent with the wicked, would always give the righteous their reward? Or is Abraham here simply grasping a face-saving excuse for getting rid of Hagar and Ishmael, without looking too closely at the nature of that excuse?

In difficult and complicated cases, where morality and self-interest are obviously on the same side, the problem is that there may not be a fact of the matter about the main motivator for the action.[112] When God tells Abraham to do what Sarah wants, what God decrees in effect enables Abraham to take an easy way out of the inner conflict in which Abraham was caught. When Abraham expels Hagar and Ishmael, is he doing what he does because he believes God is good and will keep his promises, or is he doing it because he wants to guard his heart's desire and his domestic well-being? Because in this case morality and self-interest converge, it seems likely that no clear and determinate answer can be given. To answer the question, we would have to know what Abraham *would* do if morality and self-interest were on opposite sides.[113]

God's command to sacrifice Isaac

The last recorded occasion on which God comes to talk to Abraham is the episode when, as the narrative says, God tests Abraham. This is the episode of the binding of Isaac.

On this occasion, God's speech to Abraham begins in a way dramatically different from that in the earlier divine visitations. In the narrative, on all the other occasions on which God comes to talk with Abraham, God begins straightway with the content of what he has to say. On this occasion, God begins just by uttering Abraham's name.

When God speaks Abraham's name, it is clear that Abraham recognizes God at once. Even with the long space of time since God's last speech to Abraham, Abraham (as it were) instantly knows the sound of God's voice, or is instantly cognizant of God in some other way in God's utterance of Abraham's name. In response to God's utterance of Abraham's name, Abraham responds: "Here I am."[114]

So God waits to convey his message to Abraham until Abraham has acknowledged that he recognizes God. First, God establishes Abraham's recognition of God and Abraham's shared attention with God. Only then does God communicate the content of his message. Once we grasp the content, it is not hard to understand the point of the deviation from past procedure on God's part. Given the content, it is crucial for Abraham that he have acknowledged, to God and to himself, that the speaker of that content is God. Without this preliminary step, it might have been possible for Abraham, once he heard the content of the message, to say to himself that he was not really sure about the identity of the speaker or about the veridicality of his apparent perception that he was being addressed by God. This initial step, in which God says Abraham's name and Abraham responds with immediate recognition and shared attention, makes subsequent doubt on Abraham's part much harder and less plausible.[115]

The content of God's message on this occasion is also dramatically at variance with that of all the preceding divine speeches. On all the earlier times of God's talking to Abraham, the content of the divine speeches has been or has at least included great promises about Abraham's offspring and their descendants. On this occasion, without explanation, God abruptly demands that Abraham sacrifice his son to him.

Abraham's silence

What shall we say about this demand of God's? For that matter, what should Abraham say to himself about it? Here is one possibility:

> *Everything in twenty-five years of building relationship between God and me is hereby over-turned. Everything I thought God was communicating to me is hereby shown to be a mistake or a delusion. Everything I believed would come to me because of my obedience to God is here-by destroyed. Everything I thought I knew about God is hereby shown to be illusory. Every preceding promise of God's to me is hereby falsified, and all the trust I placed in those promis-es is hereby shown to be betrayed. The judge of all the earth is a promise-breaker who desires the death of an innocent child in ritual sacrifice. And nothing is what it seemed to me to be.*

Is not this the import for Abraham of God's demand? How else would any ordinary human being, in Abraham's shoes, understand it? How else would any ordinary human being react?

Time stops in the trauma of such total disconnection between what was believed to be and what now has to be accepted as reality. Lesser souls have nervous breakdowns. If nothing is what it seemed to be, then, one asks oneself fearfully, is there anything at all that can be trusted? Greater souls are rebellious. Job attacks God himself and demands redress when he thinks the God whom he loved and served has unjustly overwhelmed him with catastrophe. Job demands God's reasons for his suffering; he calls God to account for the injustice of what has happened to him. In circumstances such as these, a great soul will be defiant, not fearful.

But what is Abraham's reaction? It is neither collapse nor revolt. As dramatic as God's command is in the narrative, there is equal drama in Abraham's reaction. He is simply silent. He says nothing to God, or to anyone else either. He simply prepares to obey.

How are we to understand this? Abraham's history shows that he is a man of energy and power, a warrior even; he and his servants pursue a marauding army and beat them in order to rescue his nephew Lot.[116] When he deals with kings, Abraham is authoritative; and when he has conflict with them, he wins.[117] Even more significantly, the exchange between God and Abraham over Sodom and Gomorrah shows decisively that Abraham is not afraid to stand up to God himself when it looks to Abraham as if God might be contemplating an injustice.[118] What is the bare possibility of injustice toward the complete strangers of Sodom and Gomorrah by comparison with this command of God's for the sacrifice of Abraham's son! And yet, in this case, Abraham opposes God in no way at all. He is silent in response to God's demand, and in silence he obeys God. Why does Abraham do this?[119]

And why does God issue this command? Why does he do this to Abraham?

In a sense, the answer to these questions lies in the whole narrative of Abraham's life, but it emerges especially from comparison of the details of the story of Isaac and the story of Ishmael.

Isaac and Ishmael

It is helpful to begin by noticing the timing of the episode in which God demands the sacrifice of Isaac; in fact, the episode begins by remarking on the time. It says, "it came to pass after these things" or "some time afterwards."[120] How much time afterwards? The only way to mark the time is by the description of Isaac. He is still young enough to be diffident and deferential toward his father. On the other hand, he is old enough to carry some distance up a mountain a load of wood big enough for him to lie down on. So it is not implausible to suppose that, when God commands Abraham to sacrifice Isaac, Isaac is somewhere in his adolescence, reasonably close, in other words, to the age Ishmael had been when his father turned him out into the desert.[121]

As virtually all commentators have noted, God's command begins with an elaborate identification of Isaac: "your son, your only son, Isaac, whom you love." But few commentators notice the striking character of the phrase 'your *only* son.' [122] If you had abandoned one of your two boys in the desert, would you be able to hear that phrase "only son" without wincing? If the phrase came from the person who told you to go ahead and abandon that son, wouldn't you wince all the more? And, if the person who guaranteed the safety of your abandoned son now uses the locution "only son" of the other boy, wouldn't you immediately think of that abandoned child and wonder in what sense Isaac is an only son?

So the trial of Abraham comes at a time when Isaac is about the age Ishmael was when Abraham turned him out, and it begins by calling Ishmael to the attention of Abraham (and the audience of the narrative) in virtue of referring to Isaac as Abraham's only son.

The content of God's message is enough to turn a father's heart to stone: take the only son you have—that is, the only son you have left—and offer him up to me as a burnt offering. But here we should again be brought to think of the expulsion of Ishmael.[123] Then God told Abraham to act in a way which, without divine intervention, seemed likely to bring about Ishmael's death. What made it morally permissible for Abraham to give in to Sarah and expel Ishmael was God's promise as regards Ishmael. To send Ishmael away without incurring serious moral culpability, Abraham had to rely on God's promise that God would make Ishmael a great nation. That promise entails not only that Ishmael survive but also that he flourish. So, if God's promise is trustworthy, Abraham can send Ishmael out into the wilderness without fear of harm coming to him, however reasonable it would otherwise be to believe that Ishmael would die in that place in consequence of being abandoned there. When Abraham expelled Ishmael, only a belief in God's goodness and in the trustworthiness of God's promises could keep that action on Abraham's part from constituting a terrible wrong against his own child.

Now God himself requires the death of Isaac. But, of course, as Abraham knows (and as the audience of the narrative knows), Abraham also has promises from God about Isaac. Isaac is the seed God has promised Abraham, the child with whom God will establish his covenant; through Isaac and Isaac's offspring Abraham will become the father of a great people. So the divine promises made about Isaac are equivalent to the divine promises made about Ishmael, at least in this respect: God has promised to make each of them a great nation. In that case, of course, each of them will have children before he dies. So, if God is good and does not break his promises, then Isaac (like Ishmael) will have children.[124] But when God tells Abraham to sacrifice Isaac, Isaac is still unmarried and without children of his own.

So here is where matters stand. If Abraham ends Isaac's life *now*, God's promises about Isaac will have been false, and God will not be trustworthy or good. Conversely, if God is good and his promises are trustworthy, then Isaac's life will not end now, however reasonable it seems from the human point of view to believe that sacrificing him will terminate his existence.

What should Abraham think?

The options for Abraham

The long process of the developing relationship of trust between God and Abraham comes to a head here, with no room left for ambiguity. Abraham now has to face up to all his previous double-mindedness about the truth of God's promises; he has to choose either trust in God's goodness or disbelief and rejection. And he has to confront in deadly earnest the fact that he was willing to expel his first-born son into the desert on the strength of God's promise to make of him a great nation. From a human point of view, abandoning a child in the desert is very likely to kill him. But if God is good and keeps his promises, then Ishmael will not only live but even prosper in the desert. How God can bring that about is not clear in advance; but, as God says to Abraham and as Abraham himself learns by experience in the conception and birth of Isaac, lots of things that look impossible turn out to be not too difficult for God. And so Abraham sent Ishmael out to wander in the wilderness, believing of himself that he was doing nothing wrong in the process. But that was then, when his self-interest was strongly on the side of supposing that God would keep his promises. Now things are different.

Doing what looks certain to bring about the death of Isaac is as strongly opposed to Abraham's self-interest as it could possibly be. Isaac, and the promise of posterity through Isaac, is Abraham's heart's desire. If Abraham now demurs, if he now finds that it is unreasonable to believe both that he could act in a way extremely likely to bring about a child's death and yet the child could live, or if he now conceives a great doubt whether he can trust the promises of God, what will we think, looking back, on the way he dealt with Ishmael? Will we not think that his apparent trust in God then was a mere excuse for doing a great moral wrong out of self-interest? Will we not suppose that Abraham in effect used God's promise to rationalize his own actions when it suited what he wanted and that Abraham is now doubting God and hanging back because his heart's desire is at stake and his self-regarding interests point the other way? If Abraham refuses to entrust Isaac to God's promises now, will we not be inclined to see his willingness to cast Ishmael out as a monstrous act toward his own son, rendered all the more sleazy by being cloaked in the hypocrisy of religion?[125]

In asking Abraham to sacrifice Isaac, God is asking Abraham what he would have done in the case of Ishmael if self-interest and trust in God had been on opposite sides, instead of converging. In effect, God's command to sacrifice Isaac asks Abraham to decide what he would have done on that earlier occasion if Isaac, not Ishmael, had been at risk, if morality and his heart's desire had come apart. Would Abraham have believed God's promises in *that* case, or did it make a difference that the child whose life was at risk was Ishmael? If Abraham really believed that God could be trusted to make Ishmael survive and flourish when Abraham sent Ishmael to walk into the desert with a bottle of water and a loaf of bread, does he not also have to trust God's promises with regard to Isaac? The moment of truth for the long process of Abraham's developing trust in God's goodness is here.

And perhaps because Abraham was so ready to obey God's command to give in to Sarah, perhaps because he expelled Hagar and Ishmael in the way he did, without any bargaining, without any attempt to help them in any way, the trial here is particularly difficult for Abraham. It is one thing to believe that God can make Ishmael (and Hagar) survive in the desert. It is another thing to believe that God can make Isaac the progenitor of a great people if he is sacrificed as a burnt offering before he has children of his own. The pain of this trial is also intense. In the case of Ishmael, Abraham exposed his son to the perils of the wilderness. In the case of Isaac, God is asking Abraham to do the sacrificing himself.

The testing of Abraham

If we look at Abraham's trial from Ishmael's point of view, with a certain interest in retribution, it might seem like punishment for Abraham. Looking at it from God's point of view makes it seem like a refining fire for Abraham. In the expulsion of Ishmael, Abraham's motives were mixed, so that there was perhaps no fact of the matter about whether Abraham acted out of trust in God's goodness or out of self-interest to protect his heart's desire. The command to sacrifice Isaac pulls apart self-interest and trust in God's goodness. Abraham must now place his hopes on God's goodness, or he must make clear that in the expulsion of Ishmael he was just using God as a means to a seriously wrong act, without supposing that God cared much or took much notice of that wrongness. So this trial refines Abraham. Whichever way he acts, he will act out of unmixed motives this time. He will act either out of self-interest with distrust of God, or out of belief in God's goodness but in a way that appears to jeopardize what he loves best.

And so this is indeed a test of Abraham, as the narrative says. God's command to sacrifice Isaac tries the measure of Abraham's commitment to the goodness of God. The way in which Abraham dealt with Ishmael makes the form of this test the right one for him, too. For Abraham to treat Isaac in the same way as he treated Ishmael is for Abraham to commit himself whole-heartedly to the belief that God is good. Furthermore, given Abraham's history with God, it is not unreasonable for God in the narrative, or for the audience of the narrative, to think that the previous episodes have made Abraham ready for this trial. It is not unreasonable to believe that Abraham can come through this test successfully.

Like some tests in quantum physics, this test also significantly affects what it measures. Whether or not Abraham passes the test by staking his son on God's goodness, the test is good for Abraham; and there is something right and loving about God's giving it to him. If the stories about Abraham had stopped with his turning Ishmael out, we would surely have been left with moral unease about him. The trial of the binding of Isaac requires Abraham to take an unambiguous stand, and so it also resolves what was ambiguous in the earlier expulsion of Ishmael. If Abraham passes this test, the test will constitute the refining of his character. On the other hand, if Abraham fails this test, the test will precipitate the morally troubling side of his dealings with Ishmael out of the murky mix of motives in which it was originally, and that clarification with its consequent self-knowledge will itself be a benefit to Abraham. This test alters Abraham's relationship with God, too. Either Abraham will now finally give whole-hearted commitment to God and the goodness of God, or he will have to take a stand at some distance from God and confront that alienation openly. It is worth noticing in this connection that God tells Abraham to sacrifice Isaac in a place three days' journey away from where Abraham is.[126] The long journey guarantees that Abraham will act only after ample reflection.

The poignancy of Abraham's predicament should also be clear. Even whole-hearted belief in God's goodness is not incompatible with great suffering regarding the outcome staked on God's goodness. (Think only of a parent's belief in the competence and truthfulness of the surgeon who tells her that her child will certainly come through the surgery beautifully and of her anxiety and misery while she waits for the end of the operation.) Even whole-hearted belief in God's goodness can coexist with anguish for Abraham, because it is Isaac's life that is at risk. Abraham's affliction is also compounded by the way God sets up the trial. If Abraham is wrong in trusting God's promises, then not only will Isaac be dead, but he will be dead by Abraham's hand.

Abraham's silence revisited

In these circumstances, Abraham's silence after God's demanding the sacrifice of Isaac is eloquent. To me, it seems to make clear that Abraham understood the nature of the test God was setting him and the reasons for that test. That is why Abraham does not ask for any explanation of God's command or any confirmation that God's earlier promises are true. That is why Abraham does not try to talk God out of his command or try to bargain with him for Isaac's life, as he bargained in the case of Sodom and Gomorrah. Furthermore, Abraham's silence also shows us how painful the ordeal is for Abraham. Not only does Abraham not object to God; he does not complain to anyone else either. His silence extends to the servants and even to Sarah. If Abraham were to complain to any of those around him, those others (and what should one say about Sarah here!) might well try to dissuade him. Or the very act of complaining might dissipate his own willingness to act. And so he is silent both as regards God and as regards the human persons around him, because he understands, and because he is holding his breath in the struggle with himself to trust Isaac to God.

Abraham's response to God's testing

In the circumstances, Abraham chooses to do what God has asked of him. Just as in the case of the expulsion of Ishmael, the narrative says that, in response to God's command, Abraham rises up early in the morning to do what he was commanded.[127]

But, of course, this information alone does not tell us whether Abraham passes the test God has set him.[128] Abraham might have been willing to sacrifice Isaac but in a spirit that would sour his relations with God ever after.[129] For example, Abraham might have found himself unable to trust God with Isaac but nonetheless have feared God's power; in that case, he would have obeyed God only to avoid God's wrath and punishment. And then he would not have passed the test.

To see whether Abraham passes the test, we need to be clear about what would constitute failing it. Abraham will fail this test if he does not treat Isaac in the same way in which he treated Ishmael. In the case of Ishmael, he was willing to act in ways that looked likely to kill his son, because he believed that God would keep his promises and God's promises entailed that Ishmael live and flourish. Abraham has similar promises about Isaac, and here, too, he is being asked to act in ways that seem sure to destroy the child. To treat the two cases in the same way, then, requires believing that, even if he sacrifices Isaac, Isaac will live and flourish. Is there anything too difficult for God?

So Abraham passes this test not in case he is willing to give up Isaac, as most commentators assume,[130] but just in case he believes that, if he obeys God's command to sacrifice Isaac, he will not be ending Isaac's life. He passes the test only if he believes that in obeying God he is *not* giving up Isaac.[131]

Not only that, but Abraham also has to believe that in sacrificing Isaac he will do Isaac no harm. Even if Abraham thought that sacrificing Isaac would not end Isaac's life—perhaps because God would resurrect Isaac or perhaps because God would somehow miraculously keep Isaac from death—Abraham might (reasonably enough, it seems) suppose that the process of sacrificing Isaac would cause psychological and physical suffering to Isaac. Such suffering on Isaac's part is obviously a significant harm to Isaac. If Abraham believed that in sacrificing Isaac he would not end Isaac's life but that he would nonetheless cause his son serious harm, then Abraham would also believe that God had commanded the harm of an innocent child. In that case, Abraham would not believe that God is good. It might be true that Abraham believed God could undo whatever physical damage God's command caused Abraham to inflict on Isaac, but the ability to undo evil caused is not at all the same thing as moral goodness.

It is, of course, hard to see how anyone could believe that sacrificing Isaac would not result in harm to Isaac. On the other hand, however, Abraham has already seen manifestations of God's great power, including the overthrow of Sodom and Gomorrah and the pregnancy of his barren 90-year-old wife. When God says to him, "Is there anything too difficult for God?,"[132] it is meant to be a rhetorical question. Furthermore, a little reflection shows that God *can* protect Isaac not only from death but even from harm in the process of sacrifice. That is, God can protect not only Isaac's life but also his psychological and physical well-being, even if Abraham were to plunge a knife into him. Contemporary surgeons can protect their patients in this way, first by explaining to them the point of the surgery and then by rendering them unconscious during the process. There seems no reason to suppose that God (and Abraham) could not do at least as well by Isaac.[133]

At any rate, what is clear is that Abraham cannot believe in the moral goodness of God and also believe that God is commanding him to harm an innocent child.[134]

So for Abraham to treat Isaac as he treated Ishmael earlier, Abraham needs to believe that, in this case, too, God is good and that following God's command will not result in the death of his son or in harm to him.

On this way of seeing the story, Abraham's line to the servants is not a polite fib. Abraham tells the servants: "You stay here with the donkey, and the lad and I will go over there, and we will worship, and we will come back to you."[135] On the interpretation I am arguing for here, in his line to the servants Abraham is not saying something he believes to be false in order to keep the servants from growing suspicious. Rather, he believes what he says. Similarly, when he tells Isaac, "God Himself will provide the lamb for a burnt-offering, my son,"[136] he is not engaging in tender deception or unconsciously cruel irony, as he would have to be doing if he thought he were about to kill Isaac. Abraham believes what he says to Isaac as well as what he says to the servants.

There is agony, though, if not irony, in these lines to the servants and to Isaac, because of what it takes to believe them. Think about a man mountain-climbing with his son, who finds that the only way to safety lies across a large crevasse. If he did not believe his son could make it, he would not ask him to leap. But he may be bathed in sweat, with years taken off his life, by the time the boy makes it over.

Abraham's lines to the servants and to Isaac are our main indication of whether or not Abraham passes the test, until God intervenes, dramatically halting the sacrifice at the point at which Abraham has raised the knife over Isaac. The angel of the Lord, speaking for God, says to Abraham: "Do not lay your hand on the boy or do anything to him, for now I know that you fear God, since you have not withheld your son, *your only son*, from me." And this line seems right. If Abraham had refused to trust Isaac to God after having been willing to expel Ishmael on God's promise, he would have been mocking rather than fearing God, acting as if God did not matter much or did not care much about the death of innocent children. But until Abraham had to choose whether to trust Isaac to God or not, perhaps no one, not even God, could have known whether Abraham feared God, because Abraham's motives in the case of Ishmael were mixed and confused. God knows now, because the trial over Isaac has refined Abraham.[137] Abraham has been willing to trust his son, his *only* son, to God. And so God says to Abraham at the end: "because you have done this thing and have not withheld your son, *your only son*, I will bless you and multiply your seed as the stars of heaven and as the sand on the sea shore; and your seed shall possess the gate of his enemies, and in your seed shall all the nations of the earth be blessed, because you have obeyed my voice."[138]

The impression given by Abraham's lines to the servants and to Isaac is thus confirmed when God comes to deliver his verdict: Abraham passes the test. The long process of God's patient attempt to develop a relationship of trust with Abraham and Abraham's double-minded finding his way into that trust has its flowering here, when Abraham is willing to sacrifice the son of the promise with faith in God and God's promise intact.

Abraham as the father of faith

If we read the story of the binding of Isaac in this way, in the context of the whole narrative about God's promises and Abraham's heart's desire for offspring, but especially in connection with the expulsion of Ishmael, we will be able to answer the questions that posed serious difficulties for Kierkegaard's view. The narrative makes it clear that there is a morally acceptable answer to the question why God should try Abraham and why the test should take the form it does. What is at issue is whether Abraham will believe in the goodness of God, in Isaac's case as well as in Ishmael's, and not whether Abraham will sacrifice absolutely anything to God if God commands him to do so.

Furthermore, what is praiseworthy about Abraham is not his readiness to kill his son in obedience to God. As I argued at the outset of this chapter, if that were what was supposed to make Abraham specially admirable, he would have to take second place to Jephthah, who not only raised the knife over his child but brought it down as well. Jephthah supposed that God and morality could be on opposite sides. But, in Abraham's case, it is precisely Abraham's willingness to believe in God's goodness, even against strong temptations to the contrary, that makes him the father of faith. When Abraham passes the test, he passes it just because he believes that God is good and will not betray his promises, so that sacrificing Isaac will not end Isaac's life. While Abraham goes to sacrifice his son, he believes that the God in whose goodness he has trusted will give him his heart's desire.

In one way, then, Kierkegaard's reading of the story of the binding of Isaac is right in its description of the knight of faith. Abraham does accept God's command to sacrifice his son, an acceptance that seems sure to result in Isaac's death; and, apparently absurdly, as Kierkegaard says, Abraham simultaneously believes that he will have his son. But Kierkegaard is mistaken in his understanding of God's test of Abraham and of Abraham's mental state as he endures it. On the interpretation of the story I have argued for, when God demands the sacrifice of Isaac, Abraham's options are to refuse to participate in what he believes will bring about the death of his son, because he does not after all trust God's promises to give him his heart's desire, or to be willing to obey God's command, believing that in so doing he will not be bringing about the death of his son because a trustworthy God has promised that Isaac will be the progenitor of a great nation. It is important to see that, contrary to Kierkegaard's view, on neither option is Abraham willing to kill his son,[139] although on the second option he is doing what, humanly speaking, *would* end the child's life save for the power and promise of God.

Furthermore, and also contrary to Kierkegaard's reading, there is no dilemma for Abraham here. No religious or moral obligation attends the first of Abraham's options. That is, there is no obligation for Abraham to believe that God breaks his promises or that God is not good; but, unless Abraham held such a belief, he would not think that, in sacrificing Isaac, he would be ending Isaac's life. On the contrary, Abraham has a moral obligation to reject that first option. Abraham ought to trust God with Isaac, not only because Abraham's long history of relationship with God makes it clear for Abraham that this is the right attitude to take toward God, but also because Abraham has already staked the life of one son on God's goodness. Consequently, Abraham is not caught in a moral or a religious dilemma between the two options open to him. The only option that is obligatory for him to take is the second one, to do as God has commanded him, and that option is both morally right and religiously good.[140]

If we read the episode of the binding of Isaac in the context of the whole narrative of Abraham's life, in which Abraham's double-mindedness about God's goodness is manifest, and especially if we see that episode against the backdrop of the expulsion of Ishmael, then it is clear that God is not pitting his authority against morality in asking Abraham to sacrifice Isaac, as Kierkegaard apparently supposed. The truly immoral response on Abraham's part would be to appear to trust God's promise to preserve Ishmael but then to act as if God could not be entrusted with Isaac. God's demand for Isaac and the requirements of morality are on the same side in this story, and the only obedience to God's command that will count as passing the test is the obedience which comes with a belief that by that obedience Abraham is not ending Isaac's life. There is, consequently, no teleological suspension of the ethical here.[141]

Reading the story of the binding of Isaac in this way also makes sense of the subsequent life of Isaac. As the biblical narratives go on to describe, Isaac retains the close relationship he had to his father after the episode of his binding, and his own commitment to God stays strong and deep. If what Isaac had seen and believed in consequence of his father's binding of him is just that God's commands abrogate morality, that God sometimes commands the killing of innocent children, and that in such cases his father is willing to obey, it is hard to know how Isaac could be anything but deeply angry at or deeply frightened of both God and his father. It is difficult to see how one could have a loving relationship with a father, human or heavenly, if one thought that father was willing to kill him.

So Isaac's own subsequent personal commitment to God and to Abraham supports the interpretation of Abraham's trial that I have been developing, and it also suggests that Isaac himself understood Abraham's test in the same way. Just as it seemed reasonable to believe that Abraham told Ishmael why he was turning him out into the desert, so it seems plausible to hold that at some point between the time they left the servants to go to the place of sacrifice and the time Abraham bound Isaac, Abraham gave Isaac Abraham's view of what Abraham was doing. At any rate, Isaac's subsequent history seems to require that he had some explanation that gave him a way of seeing his father holding the knife above him which let him believe that both God and Abraham loved him and would never do him any harm.[142]

Finally, it is also worth remembering here the story of Keturah. The narrative highlights Abraham's whole-hearted trust in God's promises in the binding of Isaac. But the story of Keturah makes evident, I think, that Abraham's double-mindedness recurs throughout his life. His status as the father of faith does not require, then, that he is always characterized by whole-heartedness. His having achieved it in his severe test is enough. In my view, there is a certain humanity about the narrative's ending not with the binding of Isaac but with the story of Keturah's sons.

Faith and the goodness of God

Interpreted in the way I have argued for in this chapter, the story of Abraham and Isaac gives us insight into the nature of faith, in the tradition that affirms Abraham as the father of all the faithful. Abraham's faith is not a faith in the existence of God, or in the power of the being who commands the sacrifice of Isaac, or in a duty to obey God's commands, no matter what. Plainly, Abraham has a belief in God's existence and power and in his own obligation to obey God, even before he decides what to do about God's command to sacrifice Isaac. But Abraham becomes the father of faith only with his willingness to sacrifice Isaac. No amount of evidence of the existence and power of God could have produced faith of this sort in Abraham. It required a particular state of will and character. Or, to put the point more accurately, it required Abraham to be willing to relate to God in a certain way. The faith that makes Abraham the father of faith has its root in Abraham's acceptance of the goodness of God, Abraham's belief that God will keep his promises, and Abraham's willingness to stake his heart's desire on that belief. In this state, Abraham is surrendering to God, letting go of his self-protective efforts to get what he wants for himself and committing himself in trust to God's goodness.

It is important to belabor this point a little, because the claim that God is good is often eviscerated of content, just as the notion of faith itself is. Sometimes when some suffering soul is told that God is good, the line seems to mean just that God is indeed hurting her but that, unlike Job, she must not complain about it. Not just any way of believing that God is good counts as Abraham's sort of faith, however. Job's comforters also insisted to Job that God is good, and they thought Job should take whatever happened to him as good and right because God did it. But it is noteworthy that, when God adjudicates the dispute between Job and the comforters, God comes down squarely on Job's side. It takes sacrifices and Job's prayers to keep the comforters from the wrath of God. How, then, does the position of the comforters differ from the position I am ascribing to Abraham as the basis for his status as the father of faith?

It is as if Job's comforters and Abraham came down on opposite sides of the Euthyphro dilemma.[143] "Do the gods will what they will because it is good," Socrates asks Euthyphro, "or is what the gods will good because they will it?" For Job's comforters, whatever God wills is good just because it is God who wills it. In deciding whether something that happens is good, on the comforters' view of it, we need only to consider the agency. If God is the agent of what happens, then that is sufficient for its being good; *any* other facts of the case are irrelevant to a moral evaluation of it. But, if Abraham took *this* attitude, he would be failing the test that the command to sacrifice Isaac sets him. He passes the test only in case he believes that God's promise regarding Isaac is trustworthy and that, contrary to all reasonable expectation, he will not end Isaac's life in obeying God's command to sacrifice him. For Abraham, then, there is an objective standard of goodness that includes the obligation to keep promises, and God does what he does because it is really, truly, objectively good.

So Abraham manages to believe that God is good and will keep his promises to Abraham, even while Abraham goes to sacrifice the son God promised at God's command, but to say this is not to say that Abraham is willing to call 'good' anything commanded by God. On the contrary, God promised Abraham that he would have descendants through Isaac; and, if what God wills is objectively good, God cannot be a promise-breaker. Abraham becomes the father of faith when he comes to believe that God is good in *this* sense and is willing to commit himself to God in consequence. Although Abraham clearly understands what it is to sacrifice a child, he nonetheless believes that, if he obeys God's command to sacrifice Isaac, Isaac will go on to live, to flourish, and to have descendants. And so he wills to stake his son on God's goodness. Abraham trusts that, if he consents to sacrifice at God's command his heart's desire—his son and through his son the office of patriarch of a people—he will still have his heart's desire, because God is good. The relationship Abraham comes to have to God is, therefore, what makes him the father of faith.

Abraham's attitude looks paradoxical or worse, of course; but it is important to see that, as the story itself shows, it is not contradictory. This paradoxical-looking attitude on Abraham's part turns out in the story to be entirely correct.

In fact, even this way of putting the outcome of the story is not quite right. With the begetting of Isaac but without the suffering of God's test, Abraham would have had the seed whose own progeny would eventually have made Abraham the patriarch of a tribe—an extensive tribe, but, still, just a tribe. In suffering and passing the test imposed by God's command to sacrifice Isaac, Abraham becomes the patriarch of the whole family of faith. So, in suffering the test and being willing to give up his heart's desire, Abraham receives it in a much more powerful form than he would otherwise have had.

Faith and the problem of suffering

At the outset of this chapter, I said that one traditional religious reaction to the problem of suffering has been to recommend that believers respond with faith, but that this reaction strikes many people as deeply disappointing. The story of Abraham's binding of Isaac gives us a second-person account of the nature of faith which makes that traditional reaction considerably less bland and not at all disappointing, in my view.

The unreflective inclination of many people, whether they are religious believers or not, is to understand the traditional recommendation of faith in this way. A sufferer who has faith is someone who is inclined to believe that God exists, that God is powerful, that God can arrange human lives as he likes, that God does not arrange them as the sufferer would like, but that the sufferer has to accept suffering at God's hand, because God is the all-powerful ruler of the universe. This may look like faith to many religious believers and non-believers, but it is not, as the story of Abraham makes clear. The faith of Abraham is a personal commitment to God, as someone who is really good and so keeps his promises, in a relationship of love.

To begin to see the point of the thrust of the story on this understanding of it, think of the promises of God, not just those directly attributed to God in the biblical texts but also those that the biblical texts make on behalf of God. Consider, for example, this one, important in my attempt to delineate the nature of suffering in the first chapter: "Delight yourself in the Lord, and he will give you the desires of your heart" (Ps. 37: 4). What difference would it make to a sufferer if, with Abraham-like faith, he managed in his suffering to believe that God could be trusted to keep this promise? It is important here not to empty the phrase 'the desires of your heart' of its meaning. It does not mean some great abstract good that a person ought to want but does not. It means what it says: "the desires of *your* heart"—and some general good a person does not want is not a desire of her heart.

If a sufferer managed in the midst of his suffering to hold the belief that God would give him the desires of his heart, it would not take away the pain of the suffering. How could it possibly? Nonetheless, the belief would radically alter his experience of that suffering. There is an appropriate analogy here to the suffering a woman goes through in childbirth. Although it does not take anything away from her pain, it makes all the difference in the world to a woman in the throes of the pain of childbirth to feel the presence of someone who loves her and to believe that her pain will eventuate in a baby who is the desire of her heart.

But, we might think, it is impossible even for an omnipotent God to give a heartbroken person the desires of her heart; for someone to be heartbroken is just for her to have lost the desires of her heart. I grant it looks this way—but then it must also have looked impossible for God to fulfill his promise to Abraham if Abraham sacrificed his son. And so it must also have been difficult for Abraham in his anguish as he was going to sacrifice Isaac to believe that God would give him the desires of his heart. Difficult to believe is not the same as irrational, however, as the narrative shows.

Abraham's willingness to trust God to keep Isaac safe even as he is going to sacrifice Isaac makes Abraham into something glorious. It moves him from being a prosperous nomad with powerful religious experiences to being the father of faith, and so it brings Abraham to the flowering of his life. But, paradoxically enough, that same trust and surrender to God also give Abraham the desire of his heart. In fact, somehow, it gives Abraham exactly what he wanted but in a form better than he would have known how to want it: both his son Isaac and the unique status of paterfamilias to the vast community of the faithful among all the nations of the earth.[144]

Conclusion

The story of the binding of Isaac thus illuminates the nature of faith as a response to the problem of suffering, and it sets a very high standard for acceptable solutions to the problem. I argued in Chapter 9 that Job's reaction to God after God's speeches is best understood as Job's having come to an assurance that God is good and loving, and that this attitude has implicit in it the conviction that God allows suffering only for the sake of an outweighing good that comes primarily to the sufferer. In the light of this chapter, we can add that, at the end of the book of Job, Job's attitude toward God in the face of his own suffering is faith of Abraham's sort.

But the narrative of the binding of Isaac adds an element not addressed in the earlier chapter's interpretation of the story of Job.[145] Abraham's belief in God's goodness is centered on a trust in the promises of God. Central among God's promises to Abraham, however, is the promise of Isaac and the posterity that comes to Abraham through Isaac; and precisely this is what Abraham has his heart set on. It is important to see that, in the story, the suffering of Abraham's trial is redeemed not only in his flourishing through the suffering of his trial, but also in his receiving the desires of his heart. It is hard to imagine a satisfactory conclusion to the narrative of Abraham's life that ends with Abraham being deprived of Isaac.

The story of Abraham's life illuminates, then, the claim I argued for in Chapter 1 —namely, that two things need to be considered when it comes to the benefits that could justify God in allowing suffering. One is the flourishing of the sufferer. But the other is what the sufferer himself has his heart fixed on, however that might relate to the sufferer's flourishing. There is something incomplete about any putative solution to the problem of suffering that neglects a consideration of the things the sufferer himself has set his heart on.[146]

This desideratum for solutions to the problem of suffering will, of course, strike most people as utopian, if not lunatic, because in our world the heartbrokenness caused by suffering is only slightly less obvious than suffering itself. In Chapter 14, I will return to this issue, not only to reflect further on the notion of the desires of the heart but also to examine in detail, in the light of all the narratives considered, the role of the desires of the heart in the problem of suffering.

Chapter 12

The Story of Mary of Bethany:
Heartbrokenness and Shame

Dear, all benevolence of fingering lips
That does not ask forgiveness is a noise
At drunken feasts where Sorrow strips
To serve some glittering generalities

.   .   .   .   .

Beloved, we are always in the wrong,
Handling so clumsily our stupid lives,
Suffering too little or too long,
Too careful even in our selfish loves:
The decorative manias we obey
Die in grimaces round us every day,
Yet through their tohu-bohu comes a voice
Which utters an absurd command—Rejoice.

Rejoice. What talent for the makeshift thought
A living corpus out of odds and ends?
What pedagogic patience taught
Pre-occupied and savage elements
To dance into a segregated charm?
Who showed the whirlwind how to be an arm,
And gardened from the wilderness of space
The sensual properties of one dear face?

Rejoice, dear love, in Love's peremptory word;
All chance, all love, all logic, you and I,
Exist by grace of the Absurd . . .*

* W. H. Auden, "In Sickness and in Health," in *W. H. Auden: Collected Poems*, ed. Edward Mendelson (New York: Random House, 1991), 317–20.

Introduction

In the preceding chapter, I noted the religious response of faith to suffering; and I argued that, as faith is portrayed in the story of Abraham's binding of Isaac, faith requires a personal commitment to God in trust and a belief in the objective moral goodness of God. The stories examined so far, the story of Job in particular but the others as well, bring home to us a common intuition shared by many—namely, that the benefit for the suffering God allows a person to endure has to be intended primarily for the sufferer if God is to count as objectively morally good. If in the story God allowed Job's children to be killed for the sake of some abstract general good to humanity or even for the sake of some benefit to Job, then the story would not portray God as good. In connection with the story of Abraham, I also called attention to the way in which a sufferer's desires of the heart have to be taken into account as regards suffering and its redemption.[1]

Abraham's suffering does not come to him because he is the victim of natural or human violence, as Job is, or because he destroys the promise of his own life by his own culpable actions, as Samson does. Abraham suffers just because he has his heart set on something that he does not have and that in his circumstances is difficult or even impossible for him to get (at least without God's promise and help). Even if Abraham had flourished in unbroken prosperity with no violence on the part of nature or other human beings, he would have been heartbroken if he had never had any children. I do not mean to suggest that there is no heartbreak for Job when his children die or for Samson when he is captured and blinded by his enemies. But Abraham's case is different from that of Job or Samson because it is true in Abraham's case, as it is not in the case of Job and Samson, that Abraham could have avoided his suffering if he had just picked a different thing to set his heart on having.[2] Abraham suffers because he has the heart's desire he does. He suffers during the miserable, wearying waiting for what he wants, and then he suffers the anguish of having to will to sacrifice his heart's desire once he has it.

Faith of Abraham's sort sets a high standard for a response to the problem of suffering, then, because it includes commitment to the belief that any suffering God allows is defeated by benefits for the sufferer of that evil, even if the suffering has its source in the desires of the heart.[3]

On the other hand, in the story of Abraham, on the interpretation I gave, it is also true that, after God's initial promise to Abraham, to one degree or another, Abraham always believes he will get his heart's desire. Abraham suffers because of his heart's desire, but it never seems to him that he has lost his heart's desire irretrievably. In the end, it turns out that this belief on Abraham's part is right. Abraham gets what he had set his heart on. The problem, of course, is that it so often seems that those who suffer do not get what they have their hearts set on; they are just broken-hearted in their suffering. Even for religious believers, in their suffering it can look as if God is betraying their trust rather than honoring it.

For this reason, many people think it is obvious that, if the standard for a successful defense or theodicy requires postulating the redemption of the suffering of broken-heartedness, that standard cannot be met. Such people will be inclined to pick any appalling instance of suffering in the morning newspapers and ask in perplexity how anyone could suppose there is or could be a benefit for *that* broken-hearted victim that would defeat her suffering. Consequently, although the story of Abraham exemplifies the suffering stemming from the desires of the heart, it does so in an anomalous way, one might say. Suffering stemming from the desires of the heart more often ends in heartbreak than in success and satisfaction, or so, at least, very many people believe.

Furthermore, heartbreak seems to afflict disproportionately those at the other end of the social spectrum from that exemplified by Abraham. When Abraham suffers, he suffers as a great man. The narrative makes it clear that Abraham is wealthy and that he has power of more than one sort in his society. At least at one point in the narrative, he has enough adherents and servants to give him military might;[4] at other points in the story, even rulers of the foreign territory he roams through treat him with respect.[5] But, in fact, poverty, powerlessness, and shame render people much more vulnerable to heartbreak. If even a little is taken away from him, a person who has very little will lose much more than a person rich in resources and status would. And, of course, without the protection offered by wealth, power, and status, of the sort Abraham had, it is very easy to lose very much.

Furthermore, shame itself can be a source of heartbreak. It is evident that broken-heartedness varies with the things we want. Some people are broken-hearted because of what has happened to them, because powers outside their control have deprived them of some person or project they set their hearts on. Abraham would have been broken-hearted in this way if he had remained childless all his life. Some people are broken-hearted over what they have done to themselves or to others. Samson is broken-hearted in this way when he is grinding corn in the prison of his enemies. But it is also possible to be broken-hearted just over what one is. This is the sort of broken-heartedness that is frequently accompanied by shame. It can derive from shame, too. One can be heart-broken *because* one is a shamed person.

In this chapter, I want to consider a story about heartbreak on the part of a person at the other end of the social spectrum from Abraham—namely, Mary of Bethany. She was without wealth or power; as I read her story, she was also a shamed person in her society. In highlighting shame in her story, I am not forgetting that the protagonists in the previous stories suffered from shame, too. Job reports as one of his afflictions his community's disdain of him. Samson is mocked and humiliated by his captors. And perhaps even Abraham felt some shame attached to childless status in his society. But shame, like heartbreak, comes in more than one variety.[6] It is one thing to be mocked or disdained by others, and it is another thing to be the sort of person from whose touch others shrink. Some kinds of poverty or powerlessness can leave a person degraded, so that those who are at ease shudder at the thought of contact with her. There is a special sort of shame about being a person whom others find defiling. On the reading of the story I will argue for in this chapter, Mary of Bethany suffers from this sort of shame.

In her story, Mary loses decisively what she had her heart set on, or so it appears to her for a certain time. She sets her heart on her brother's being cured of his illness, and there is a cure available for him; but he dies nonetheless. Furthermore, with his death she loses more than him. As I argued in an earlier chapter, a shamed person anticipates rejection on the part of others to whom she wants to matter; she expects that those others will find her ugly or worthy of dishonor and that they will turn away from her in consequence. For this reason, trust can come very hard to a shamed person. In the middle of her story, it looks to Mary of Bethany, and to the audience of the story, as if she is heartbroken at least in part because her hard-won trust is betrayed by the person to whom she had managed to give it without reserve. If closeness among persons can redeem suffering, as the story of Samson suggests, what can redeem suffering that stems from a betrayal of trust and the destruction of closeness?[7]

Suffering of the sort at issue in this chapter, in the story of Mary of Bethany, is not the kind that makes headlines in the newspapers; and so some readers may wonder why this story should be included in the list that begins with the sufferings of Job. But this is a mistaken way of thinking about suffering. Marilyn Adams says of horrendous suffering that it destroys the meaning of a life; on her view, such suffering is "defined in terms of the *prima facie* loss of the possibility of positive personal meaning."[8] And she adds: "This criterion is *objective but relative to individuals*."[9] She seems to me quite right in this remark. Suffering of the sort at issue here is a function of the desires of the heart had by a particular person. Depending on what a person sets her heart on, suffering that does not make headlines can be just as effective in destroying the meaning of her life as the more newsworthy sufferings are.

When his wife died, C. S. Lewis was a prosperous professor with a broad network of friends, a successful career, good health, meaningful work—in short, all the things that we think make for a good life. And this is what he said about himself:

there is spread over everything a vague sense of wrongness, of something amiss. Like in those dreams where nothing terrible occurs—nothing that would sound even remarkable if you told it at breakfast-time—but the atmosphere, the taste of the whole thing, is deadly . . . I hear a clock strike and some quality it always had before has gone out of the sound. What's wrong with the world to make it so flat, shabby, and worn-out looking? Then I remember.[10]

The death of one loved person can be a meaning-destroying event; and, unlike C. S. Lewis, some people never recover from the life-shattering grief such a death can leave. There are many things besides the death of a loved person, ordinary things, not in the same camp with the spectacular sufferings of Job, that are just as effective at devastating the life of the person who suffers them. Betrayal of trust, not morally monstrous but everyday and familiar, can be crushing in its effects in this way. People can take a very long time to recover from a divorce; some people never heal.

The broken-heartedness of such very ordinary suffering can leave a person in a state of apathetic unhappiness. In that state, Lewis says of himself: "I loathe the slightest effort. Not only writing but even reading a letter is too much. Even shaving. What does it matter now whether my cheek is rough or smooth . . . It's easy to see why the lonely become untidy; finally, dirty and disgusting."[11]

Similar things can be said about shame. Some people are shamed in spectacular ways, as Adolf Eichmann was, for example, at his trial in Jerusalem. But there is also shame that is, for those not suffering it, unremarkable and commonplace; and it can be life-destroying, too. A middle-aged, unaccomplished, dowdy wife, shocked to discover that her husband was leaving her for a younger, prettier, more successful woman, said of herself: "I am a worn-out shoe. What is there about me that anybody else could want?" Shame of this sort can rob life of its meaning, too, for the person who suffers it.

If there is a sociology of suffering, I do not know it; but it is hard not to suppose that the great mass of suffering in the world is of this ordinary sort, caused not by stunning evils but by ordinary heartbreak and shame. It would be a mistake to ignore it in a project of this kind, but nothing in the stories of Job, Samson, and Abraham captures it.[12] In this chapter, I will address it. I will look carefully at a story in which a woman without power or wealth, afflicted in consequence of everyday events, is broken-hearted in her suffering. The story of Mary of Bethany is the last narrative I will examine, and it is a good one with which to end. Her case is both poignant and challenging for theodicy.

A problem and an irenic solution

Unfortunately, although the unwary may find the preceding brief introduction reasonably straightforward, those sophisticated as regards biblical interpretation will not have read so far without alarm. The problem is that in these few preceding lines I have already crashed through more than one serious controversy. There is no consensus, neither among contemporary historically trained biblical scholars nor among major figures in the history of biblical commentary, about what texts are part of the narrative of Mary of Bethany or which women in the texts are to be identified as Mary of Bethany. But, of course, such controversies make a great difference to the enterprise of interpreting the narrative of Mary of Bethany or giving a summary characterization of her. Even in the little that I have said so far, I have implicitly taken sides in more than one of these controversies.

Part of the problem stems from the fact that, unlike the narratives examined in the earlier chapters, the story of Mary of Bethany is found in the Gospels; and there are *four* of them, each purporting to describe the life of Jesus, in roughly the same period and the same context, but with considerable variation in the episodes picked out for description and in the descriptions given of the episodes chosen for inclusion.

If one is willing to combine the four Gospels together, they will then form one much larger narrative, richer and more informative than any of the individual Gospels taken in isolation. I say "if one is willing," because another part of the problem has to do with which methodology one finds acceptable and appropriate for dealing with texts related to one another as the Gospels are. Patristic and medieval interpreters of the Gospels were agreed in supposing that all four Gospel texts could and should be combined into one larger narrative; and they supposed that that larger narrative is told only in part, and only from one point of view, by any one Gospel. The result of attempts such as theirs to provide a larger narrative and to defend its legitimacy on the basis of the texts in the individual Gospels is typically called a 'harmony' of the Gospels.

In the Patristic and medieval periods, considerable effort and ingenuity were expended on producing harmonies of the Gospels. Ingenuity is required, because there are places where the episodes in one Gospel are hard to fit into the space and time of one or more of the other Gospels and also because there are places in which details in one Gospel are in tension with those in another Gospel. So, for example, in one Gospel Jesus is said to be on a mountain top when he gives the Sermon on the Mount and the audience for his discourse is said to be his disciples;[13] in another Gospel, he is said to be on a plain when he gives this sermon, and the audience for it is a great mixed multitude of people.[14]

Contemporary historical biblical scholars sometimes speak of such passages as contradicting one another, not as being in tension with one another; but, in fact, these are tensions rather than contradictions, as philosophers understand contradictories. For example, in the case involving the Sermon on the Mount, the descriptions in the two Gospel narratives are not dated in any precise way; and so it is possible to understand the differing Gospel narratives as describing two different episodes that took place at two different times and in two different places. This is what Patristic and medieval harmonizers tended to do in this case in particular and in general in cases like this.[15] The basic hermeneutical principle of the Patristic and medieval harmonizers is relatively simple. They took everything in all the Gospels to be true; and then they tried to find a way in which to make the apparent discrepancies in the texts taken as true be consistent. And so harmonization of the Patristic and medieval sort tends to smooth out tensions in the Gospel texts by proliferating episodes. If one Gospel describes Jesus as giving a discourse on a mountain top and another one describes him as giving that discourse on a plain, then, the harmonizers conclude, he gave the same discourse twice, once on a mountain and once on a plain.[16]

The very different methodology of contemporary historical biblical criticism is itself a sort of harmonization, as I explained in Chapter 2. Like Patristic and medieval exegesis, contemporary historical biblical scholarship tries to remove the subjectively discerned tensions that it supposes are in a particular text or that it takes to emerge from a comparison of different texts claiming to describe the same events. Unlike the Patristic and medieval approach, however, contemporary historical scholarship tends to reconcile the tensions believed to be in the texts by sorting the apparently inconsistent bits into smaller stories or differing traditions, each of which is internally harmonious and self-consistent; and it then goes on to try to explain how these traditions or stories, at odds with one another, might have been woven together into the text as we now have it.

So, for example, one commentator writing on the passage in Luke in which the Sermon on the Mount is described as delivered on a plain says: "This Lucan detail differs from . . . the Matthean setting for the coming sermon . . ."; and the commentator explains the discrepancy in the two Gospels by saying that "Luke is at pains here to depict crowds coming to [Jesus] to *listen* [to him] . . . The emphasis in the Lucan form of the summary is on listening to him . . . "[17]

On this methodology, then, the two texts in Matthew and Luke are taken to be inconsistent descriptions of the same event, and the inconsistency is attributed to the ideological or theological predilections of the authors or editors who produced the texts.

As I argued in Part 1 of this book, the two methodologies—of Patristic and medieval interpreters, on the one hand, and historical biblical scholarship, on the other hand—can conveniently and appropriately be thought of as mirror images of each other. Each begins with a subjective perception of tensions within the texts under consideration. Beginning with such subjective (and no doubt often differing) perceptions of tensions, both methodological practices try to harmonize the perceived discrepancies. The methodology favored by Patristic and medieval interpreters is a harmonization by multiplication. It sorts the discrepant bits of the texts being interpreted into different episodes within one larger and more complex story. Sometimes contemporary historical scholars avail themselves of harmonization by multiplication, too;[18] but, on the whole, by contrast, the methodology practiced by contemporary historical scholars is a harmonization by division. It adjudicates the subjectively discerned discrepant bits into different stories, each of which is a self-consistent whole. And the discrepancies that the historical critic thinks he finds in the text he is examining are accounted for by assigning them to the person or community who combined the simpler stories together in an apparently inconsistent way.[19]

Although they disagree about many things, contemporary historical biblical scholars have been fairly united in their rejection of the Patristic and medieval style of harmonization. In the view of historical biblical scholars, Patristic and medieval harmonization does violence to the text.[20] This line, of course, presupposes that more violence is done to received texts by taking them to be true and combining them than by dismembering them and reconstituting the resulting bits into different wholes in accordance with the hypotheses of the interpreter. As far as that goes, the contemporary historical line also presupposes that we have some non-question-begging way of identifying 'the text.' For a successful charge that something does violence to *the text*, the objector needs to have a non-controversial view of what the text is. For interpreters such as Augustine and Chrysostom, however, all four Gospels together form *one* text, a Rashomon-like text of the life of Jesus. From the point of view of such Patristic and medieval exegetes, the charge of doing violence to the text is most appropriately leveled against historical biblical scholarship itself. On the Patristic and medieval understanding of *the text*, a methodology such as that of historical biblical criticism does violence to the text comprised of all four Gospels in virtue of refusing to recognize the unity of the text. Augustine speaks of such a methodology as shattering the text.[21]

But, leaving philosophical (and literary) questions of this sort to one side, it is clear that, on the contemporary historical biblical methodology of harmonization by division, the stories emerging from the application of that methodology will necessarily be fairly simple. Any tension discerned in a narrative will constitute an apparent inconsistency, which will be resolved by segregating the apparently conflicting parts of the narrative into different stories or traditions. And so it is hard to see how this methodology could ever leave us with a rich and complicated story. For my purposes, simple, tension-free stories do not offer much help. The large, rich, complicated sort of narrative that emerges from medieval-style harmonization is consequently of more interest to me than the stories that result from historical-style harmonization by division.

I recognize that some readers who care about history in virtue of their belief that the biblical texts are revealed may think that taking the biblical texts as revealed constitutes a compelling reason for reading the texts as historical biblical scholars do. It should be noted in this connection that Patristic and medieval commentators also took the biblical texts to be revealed, but they nonetheless supposed that access to divine revelation of historical events was afforded *only* by the larger narrative emerging from the use of their methodology. As the line from Augustine about shattering the text indicates, Patristic and medieval interpreters of the text thought that the best access to the history divinely revealed in the biblical texts is precisely through *their* methodology of harmonization by multiplication.

Clearly, the issues at stake here are too complicated to be examined briefly in passing.[22] For present purposes, then, I want just to point out that those readers who are antecedently convinced that the only route to accurate history is through the results of contemporary historical biblical scholarship can learn their history from that source and can simultaneously accept the larger narrative resulting from a different methodology when it is being used for philosophical reflection through narrative. Since the story, not the history, is what is salient for my purposes, this compromise position is open for those who are antecedently committed both to the view that the biblical texts are revealed and to the methodology of historical biblical scholarship.

Sad to say, however, even this leeway, which is afforded by my purposes, is not enough to determine what counts as *the* narrative of Mary of Bethany. So, for example, Augustine and Chrysostom are largely in agreement as far as methodology is concerned; they each accept the appropriateness of combining the Gospel texts into one larger narrative. But they are nonetheless miles apart as far as the identification of the texts comprising the narrative of Mary of Bethany goes. The root of the difference in their views is not a principle about the methodology of biblical interpretation but rather a serious disagreement about what can be acceptably attributed to Jesus as a moral exemplar. On anybody's view, all credible identifications of Mary of Bethany and the texts including mention of her present her as a friend of Jesus. But Chrysostom rejects with indignation the idea that Jesus would have been friends with any woman who was not herself exemplary in those virtues his culture thought of as womanly.[23] For this reason, he rejects a text that Augustine himself accepts as part of the story of Mary of Bethany, because he thinks that story portrays the woman in question as sinful.[24] So, because of their different understandings of what can be attributed to a moral exemplar such as Jesus, the expression 'the narrative of the life of Mary of Bethany' picks out different texts for Augustine and for Chrysostom.

In these circumstances, in order to avoid burdening this chapter with gratuitous controversy, I will adopt what I hope is an irenic procedure. I will begin with a careful look at just one story in just one Gospel, the Gospel of John. That story is uncontroversially a narrative about Mary of Bethany. The ending of that story, in which Mary of Bethany anoints the feet of Jesus, has echoes in other Gospels in stories of a woman who anoints Jesus;[25] but, in the initial examination of the story in the Gospel of John, I will leave the stories in those other Gospels largely to one side in order to avoid any controversies attendant on the combining of Gospel stories. After I have examined the narrative in the Gospel of John, I will consider another story in yet another Gospel, the Gospel of Luke, in which an unnamed woman anoints Jesus' feet. This story in the Gospel of Luke is accepted by some interpreters and rejected by others as a narrative about Mary of Bethany. I will not take sides in that controversy. Instead, I will proceed in this way. First, I will examine the story in Luke, considered in its own right, with the woman in the story left entirely unidentified. Once I have done so, I will then backtrack to the first story, which is uncontroversially about Mary of Bethany, in the Gospel of John; and I will ask what happens to our interpretation of that story in the Gospel of John if we take the story in the Gospel of Luke to be about Mary of Bethany, too. In asking this question, I am *not* committing myself to any identification of the woman in the story in Luke. Rather, I am interested only in a *conditional* interpretation. *If* the story in Luke is in fact about Mary of Bethany, *then* my initial interpretation of the story in John would need to be altered in ways that I will sketch out. This conditionally interpreted larger story will constitute the third narrative at issue in this chapter.

My description of Mary of Bethany in the introduction above is controversial, then, because I presented it without qualification. With this explanation of at least some of the controversies at issue in connection with the story of Mary of Bethany, I now officially qualify that initial description of her. It is an appropriate description of Mary of Bethany *if* the protagonist of the Lucan story is identified as Mary of Bethany. Without that qualification, not all of the description of Mary of Bethany in the introduction is appropriate, although, with the emphasis on shame moderated, the rest of the characterization remains apt.

The raising of Lazarus

With this explanation of my aims in this chapter and the complicated reasons for the ordering of the three stories examined in it, I need now also to yield to prevailing custom and confess that the well-known story of the raising of Lazarus in the Gospel of John is what I have been calling the uncontroversial narrative of Mary of Bethany. My unorthodox labeling of the story is a consequence of my interpretation of it, and so the reasons for that labeling have to be left to emerge in the course of this chapter. But, because I will read the narrative as focused on Mary, rather than on Lazarus, as is customary, I can show more easily what is of interest in the story from my point of view if I begin with a representative example of the more customary sort of interpretation. And so I will begin with the Anchor Bible commentary on the story. Against that background, it will be easier for me to present my reading of the narrative, which emphasizes its second-personal relations.[26]

Because the narrative in question is relatively brief, and because interpretation of it ineluctably focuses intensely on small details, in the case of this one narrative it will be helpful to have the text in front of us, at least in those parts that are most salient for the ensuing discussion. Since the Anchor Bible interpretation is the foil for my own reading of the story, I will quote the most relevant parts of the narrative in the Anchor Bible translation.[27] As the Anchor Bible translates it, the text reads this way:

XI. [1] Now there was a man named Lazarus who was sick; he was from Bethany, the village of Mary and her sister Martha. ([2] This Mary whose brother Lazarus was sick was the one who anointed the Lord with perfume and dried his feet with her hair.) [3] So the sisters sent to inform Jesus, "Lord, the one whom you love is sick." [4] But when Jesus heard it, he said, "This sickness is not to end in death; rather it is for God's glory, that the Son [of God] may be glorified through it." ([5] Yet Jesus really loved Martha and her sister and Lazarus.) [6] And so, even when he heard that Lazarus was sick, he stayed on where he was two days longer. [7] Then, at last, Jesus said to the disciples, "Let us go back to Judaea." . . . [11] He made this remark, and then, later, he told them, "Our beloved Lazarus has fallen asleep, but I am going there to wake him up." . . . [14] [F]inally Jesus told them plainly, "Lazarus is dead. [15] And I am happy for your sake that I was not there so that you may come to have faith. In any event, let us go to him." . . .

[17] When Jesus arrived, he found that Lazarus had [already] been four days in the tomb. [18] Now Bethany was not far from Jerusalem, just under two miles; [19] and many of the Jews had come out to offer sympathy to Martha and Mary because of their brother. [20] When Martha heard that Jesus was coming, she went to meet him, while Mary sat quietly at home. [21] Martha said to Jesus, "Lord, if you had been here, my brother would never have died. [22] Even now, I am sure that whatever you ask of God, God will give you." [23] "Your brother will rise again," Jesus assured her. [24] "I know he will rise again," Martha replied, "in the resurrection on the last day." [25] Jesus told her, "I am the resurrection [and the life]: he who believes in me, even if he dies, will come to life. [26] And everyone who is alive and believes in me shall never die at all.—Do you believe this?" [27] "Yes, Lord," she replied. "I have come to believe that you are the Messiah, the Son of God, he who is to come into this world."

[28] Now when she had said this, she went off and called her sister Mary. "The Teacher is here and calls for you," she whispered. [29] As soon as Mary heard this, she got up quickly and started out toward him. ([30] Actually Jesus had not yet come into the village but was [still] at the spot where Martha had met him.) [31] The Jews who were in the house with Mary, consoling her, saw her get up quickly and go out; and so they followed her, thinking that she was going to the tomb to weep there. [32] When Mary came to the place where Jesus was and saw him, she fell at his feet and said to him, "Lord, if you had been here, my brother would never have died." [33] Now when Jesus saw her weeping, and the Jews who had accompanied her also weeping, he shuddered, moved with the deepest emotions.

[34] "Where have you laid him?" he asked. "Lord, come and see," they told him. [35] Jesus began to cry, [36] and this caused the Jews to remark, "See how much he loved him!"

[37] But some of them said, "He opened the eyes of that blind man. Couldn't he also have done something to stop this man from dying?" [38] With this again arousing his emotions, Jesus came to the tomb. It was a cave with a stone laid across it. [39] "Take away the stone," Jesus ordered. Martha, the dead man's sister, said to him, "Lord, it is four days; by now there must be a stench." [40] Jesus replied, "Didn't I assure you that if you believed, you would see the glory of God?"

[41] So they took away the stone. Then Jesus looked upward and said, "Father, I thank you because you heard me. [42] Of course, I knew that you always hear me, but I say it because of the crowd standing around, that they may believe that you sent me." [43] Having said this, he shouted in a loud voice, "Lazarus, come out!" [44] The dead man came out, bound hand and foot with linen strips and his face wrapped in a cloth. "Untie him," Jesus told them, "and let him go."[28]

This, then, is the story of Lazarus's sickness, death, and resurrection. After Lazarus has emerged from the tomb, the narrative shifts its focus away from Lazarus and his two sisters. But all three of them come back into the story briefly in an episode in the next chapter, which I add here, also in the Anchor Bible translation:

XII [1] Six days before Passover Jesus came to Bethany, the village of Lazarus whom Jesus had raised from the dead. [2] There they gave him a dinner at which Martha served and Lazarus was one of those at table with him. [3] Mary brought in a pound of expensive perfume made from real nard and anointed Jesus' feet. Then she dried his feet with her hair, while the fragrance of the perfume filled the house. [4] Judas Iscariot, one of his disciples (the one who was going to hand him over), protested, [5] "Why wasn't this perfume sold? It was worth three hundred silver pieces, and the money might have been given to the poor." ([6] It was not because he was concerned for the poor that he said this, but because he was a thief. He held the money box and could help himself to what was put in.) [7] To this Jesus replied, "Leave her alone. The purpose was that she might keep it for the day of my embalming. [[8]] The poor you will always have with you, but you will not always have me.]"[29]

The Anchor Bible interpretation of the narrative

This, then, is what I have been calling 'the story of Mary of Bethany' in the Gospel of John. The Anchor Bible commentator Raymond Brown labels the text 'The Story of Lazarus,' and his comments on it are representative of a certain approach to the story. On his interpretation, Lazarus is the main character in the story (besides Jesus, of course), and the raising of Lazarus is the central focus of the story. Brown explains that focus this way:

the writer [of the Gospel of John] has chosen to take one miracle and to make this the primary representative of all the mighty miracles of which [the Gospel of] Luke speaks. With a superb sense of development he has chosen a miracle in which Jesus raises a dead man . . . the raising of Lazarus provides an ideal transition [between two parts of the Gospel of John], the last sign in the Book of Signs leading into the Book of Glory.[30]

On Brown's account, Lazarus is not only the main character of the story taken literally but he is also central when the story is understood symbolically:

[the Gospel of] John takes what may be a true reminiscence and uses it with theological purpose; for Lazarus, the one whom Jesus loves, is probably being held up as the representative of all those whom Jesus loves, namely the Christians . . . Just as Jesus gives life to his beloved Lazarus, so will he give life to his beloved Christians.[31]

As Brown himself recognizes, the narrative Brown takes to be 'the story of Lazarus' introduces Lazarus's sisters almost immediately. But, although the introduction of Mary and the identification of Mary as the woman who anointed Jesus is the second verse of the story, Brown discounts that verse because he thinks that it is just out of place at the head of the story. He supposes that this verse is meant only to call the audience's attention to the much later scene in Chapter 12 that describes an anointing of Jesus by Mary of Bethany. For these reasons, Brown takes the identification of Mary in this verse as an obvious editorial addition. He says: "This verse is clearly a parenthesis added by an editor: it refers to a scene in ch. xii which has not yet been narrated . . . "[32]

As is clear from this remark, Brown finds the placement of this verse in the story clumsy or literarily inappropriate in some other way. In addition, Brown takes other parts of the narrative involving either Martha or Mary to be deficient as well. In particular, he finds the narrative uninteresting in the lines that explain what happens after Lazarus's death when Jesus finally comes to Bethany to visit Martha and Mary. For example, Brown takes the description of Mary's meeting with Jesus to be monotonous, because, on his view, "[verses] 20–27 tell us how Martha came out from the house to greet Jesus, while [verses] 28–33 tell us how Mary came out from the house to greet Jesus. The two accounts are very similar, and both women utter the same greeting (21, 32)."[33]

In fact, Brown sees the descriptions of the meeting of each sister with Jesus after the death of Lazarus as just repetitions of each other. Speaking of the scene describing Mary's meeting with Jesus, he says: "As we have insisted, this scene really does not advance the action; vs. 34 could easily follow vs. 27, and no one would know the difference."[34]

That is, Brown thinks that, if the text omitted the entire description of Mary's meeting with Jesus, the omission would have lost nothing of any interest in the story; on the contrary, as it stands, the insertion of this description into the narrative is in Brown's view only a pointless duplication. As he sees it: "The only dissimilarity between Mary's greeting to Jesus and that of Martha is that Mary falls at Jesus' feet (32). Some would see in this the suggestion of a livelier faith on Mary's part, but it is noteworthy that Mary of Bethany is always pictured at Jesus' feet . . . "[35]

Here Brown is referring not only to the episode in this narrative in the Gospel of John in which Mary of Bethany anoints the feet of Jesus, but also to an episode in a story in a different Gospel, the Gospel of Luke.[36] In saying that Mary of Bethany is always pictured at Jesus' feet, Brown has in mind a Lucan story in which Martha complains to Jesus because Mary is sitting at his feet listening to him instead of helping Martha in her preparations of a meal for the assembled group. On that occasion, Jesus refuses to send Mary off to help with food preparation. Instead, he says to Martha: "Mary has chosen the best part; it shall not be taken away from her."[37] In this episode in the text of the Gospel of Luke, Mary of Bethany is portrayed not only as at Jesus' feet, as Brown's comment calls to our attention, but also as someone who is protected and encouraged by Jesus in her desire to learn from him.

As Brown's interpretation of the lines in John's Gospel portraying the sisters' meeting with Jesus continues, it is plain that Brown thinks the description of Mary's meeting with Jesus not only adds nothing to the story but in fact shows a lack of artistic skill on the part of the author or editor of the story. Brown says: "In comparing vss. 20–27 and 28–33 [the two episodes in which each sister encounters Jesus], we find that Mary's part is unimaginative and merely repeats what we heard in Martha's part . . . ."[38]

Brown accounts for what he takes to be an aesthetic deficiency in the narrative by means of a historical explanation. On his view, the elements of the story involving Lazarus are not only the focus of the story but are also the part of the story that is earliest and thus closer to historical events in the life of Jesus. So Brown claims, cautiously enough, that "From the contents of the Johannine account . . . there is no conclusive reason for assuming that the skeleton of the story [of the raising of Lazarus] does not stem from early tradition about Jesus . . . [T]he basic story behind the Lazarus account may stem from early tradition . . . "[39] On Brown's view, the parts of the story that involve the women, Mary and Martha, were added later.[40]

Brown argues that the first addition to the original story of Lazarus was the assignment of a role for Martha. As he reads the story, the elements involving Mary were a still later addition. Brown argues for that position this way:

granting that the role of one woman has now spread to the other, we are not so certain that the incident was first centered around Mary. Of the two, Mary is the better known; and we can see why, if Martha originally had a role, an editor might feel impelled not to slight Mary. However, if Mary had the original role, why would an editor feel impelled to give a longer role to the less important Martha?[41]

That is, on Brown's account, it is Martha who has the prominent place among the sisters in the Gospel narrative that constitutes the story of Lazarus as we now have it, and there is a historical explanation of this fact in the supposition that some lines about Martha were first added to what was originally a story about Lazarus. The role of Mary, like the initial identification of her as the anointer of Jesus, is a result of still later editing.

In fact, Brown thinks that the last episode in the story, in which Mary is said to anoint the feet of Jesus, originally had nothing to do with the story of the raising of Lazarus. On his view, these two separate stories were joined together only later. As he describes his position: "we suspect the mention of Lazarus and Martha [in Chapter 12] to be an editorial attempt to tie chs. xi and xii together. It is obvious that [Lazarus and Martha] have no important role in the scene of the anointing."[42]

Brown gives a similar historical explanation for what he takes to be the repetitive and unimaginative character of the episodes involving Mary in the earlier episodes of the story, in the description of the raising of Lazarus. Brown says: "this is what we would expect if a role for Mary was an afterthought. A study of vs. 2, which is clearly an editorial addition, suggests that later editing gave prominence to Mary."[43]

As for the story of Mary's anointing of Jesus, Brown sees this episode in the narrative as emerging from a confusion of two different incidents of anointing, both of which he takes to underlie the episode as it now stands in the narrative. In Brown's view, the confusion of these distinct incidents helps to explain some details in the narrative's version of the episode; Brown thinks that these details would fail to make sense if they were not understood as a result of the combining of two underlying incidents.[44] According to Brown, one of these underlying incidents is behind a different story in the Gospel of Luke, in which a shamed and sinful woman is said to let down her hair to wipe the feet of Jesus because her tears have fallen on his feet. The other is an incident in which Mary of Bethany uses an expensive perfume to anoint the feet of Jesus. On Brown's view, the Gospel of John has somehow conflated these two incidents, preserving elements of each.

So, for example, Brown thinks it makes no sense for the Gospel of John to attribute to "the virtuous Mary of Bethany" the letting-down of her hair, which Brown supposes would have been scandalous at that time, though on Brown's view a story (such as that in the Gospel of Luke) presenting a sinful woman as doing such a scandalous thing would make sense. Brown also thinks that it makes no sense for the Gospel of John to present Mary as anointing the *feet* of Jesus (as distinct from his head) and then wiping off the perfume she has just applied. But Brown thinks that these otherwise perplexing details can all be made sense of as a Johannine conflation driven by a Johannine desire to emphasize the burial of Jesus. He says:

> The theological import of the anointing in both John and Mark is directed toward the burial of Jesus . . . Mary's action constituted an anointing of Jesus' body for burial, and thus unconsciously she performed a prophetic action. And indeed this may explain why the rather implausible detail of the anointing of the *feet* was kept in the Johannine narrative—one does not anoint the feet of a living person, but one might anoint the feet of a corpse as part of the ritual of preparing the whole body for burial.[45]

So, on Brown's interpretation, if Mary has any importance in this narrative, it is just in consequence of what she does unwittingly, the significance of which she is not in a position to know. She is a minor figure in a major drama, and that drama is played out through her, rather than with her or because of her.

As for the role of Jesus in this story, here too Brown takes the main emphasis to be on Lazarus. He says:

> [the] setting of the stage [for the miracle of the raising of Lazarus] gives the author [of the Gospel of John] an opportunity to remind us of the themes that have run through the chapter so that we shall not miss the final significance of the miracle. Verse 36 recalls that Lazarus is the beloved (Christian?). Verse 37 calls forth the memory of the blind man, so that Jesus as the light and Jesus as the life will be juxtaposed. Verse 40 unites the theme of belief of which Jesus spoke to Martha in 25–26, and the theme of glory of which we heard in 4. It is fitting that glory be mentioned

here; for it not only gives an inclusion within the chapter, but also, as we have mentioned, forms an inclusion with the Cana miracle . . . thus bringing together the first and last of the signs. Moreover, the theme of glory serves as a transition to the Book of Glory, which is the second half of the Gospel.[46]

All Jesus' miracles are signs of what he is and what he has come to give man, but in none of them does the sign more closely approach the reality than in the gift of life. The physical life that Jesus gives to Lazarus is still not in the realm of the life from above, but it is so close to that realm that it may be said to conclude the ministry of signs and inaugurate the ministry of glory.[47]

Brown also turns his attention to some details in the story's descriptions of Jesus' attitudes and actions that have been the occasion of considerable commentary and debate, not only in the history of biblical interpretation but also on the part of contemporary historical biblical scholars. The narrative says that Jesus wept, that Jesus groaned, and that Jesus was troubled (or, as in Brown's translation, that Jesus shuddered and was moved with the deepest emotions). A lot of scholarship and a lot of speculation have been expended on trying to explain each of these three Johannine descriptions of Jesus, and the explanations have been highly various.

Of the three descriptions, the one for which an explanation *appears* ready to hand is the narrative claim that Jesus wept; and, in fact, Brown gives that apparently obvious explanation, though with a caveat. He says: "[Jesus'] weeping is caused by [Jesus'] thought of Lazarus in the tomb, but the verse [claiming that Jesus wept] is primarily intended to set the stage for vs. 36."[48]

Brown feels that he needs to explain why the author or editor of the story would portray Jesus' weeping as caused by the thought of Lazarus in the tomb, because the whole story is one in which Jesus' getting Lazarus *out* of the tomb is Jesus' original plan and is also the final outcome of Jesus' actions. In the story, Jesus does not expect Lazarus's death to be the end of Lazarus's life now; he expects Lazarus to be restored to health within minutes of the time when the narrative says that Jesus weeps. And so Brown feels the need to account for the narrative as he himself interprets it. He finds the point of the narrative's claim that Jesus wept to be in verse 36, where the people around Jesus take his weeping as a sign of his love for Lazarus.

The second of the three narrative claims, the description of Jesus as groaning or shuddering, is harder to explain. The Greek verb used here (*embrimasthai*) has some sort of indignation, anger, or annoyance as its root meaning. In the narrative, it is conjoined with another Greek verb (*tarassein*), whose basic sense is to trouble, disturb, or stir up. Brown supposes that, when the text says that Jesus groaned and troubled himself, it is attributing some sort of anger to Jesus. Unlike some other contemporary commentators, however, Brown does not suppose that the Gospel intends to imply that Jesus is angry at the sisters of Lazarus for their lack of faith. Instead, he interprets the passage in this way: "A better explanation of the anger of Jesus in [verse] 33 would be the reason offered for similar displays of anger in the Synoptic tradition . . . namely, that he was angry because he found himself face to face with the realm of Satan which, in this instance, was represented by death."[49]

As for the third claim, that Jesus was troubled, Brown says that, "used with the reflexive [the verb *tarassein*] means literally 'he troubled himself.' "[50] And he adds that the same verb is used to describe "the reaction of the disciples in face of the imminent *death* of Jesus . . . "[51] In this connection, Brown cites with approval Chrysostom's claim that in other Gospels the word *tarassein* is used of Jesus in the Garden of Gethsemane to indicate Jesus' "emotional distress prompted by the imminence of death and the struggle with Satan."[52]

In fact, on Brown's view, interest in the death of Jesus on the part of the author or editor of the Gospel of John is one of the main motivations for the inclusion of the story of the raising of Lazarus in the final form of the Gospel. Brown says: "[the Gospel of] John makes the Lazarus miracle the direct cause of the death of Jesus, for it provokes a session of the Sanhedrin . . . which reaches a decision to kill Jesus."[53]

The importance the Gospel places on the raising of Lazarus as a cause of the death of Jesus is, in Brown's view, "another instance of the pedagogical genius of the Fourth Gospel."[54] And Brown sums up his interpretation of the narrative by saying:

We suggest then that, while the basic story behind the Lazarus account may stem from early tradition, its causal relationship to the death of Jesus is more a question of Johannine pedagogical and theological purpose than of historical reminiscence . . . A miracle story that was once transmitted without fixed context or chronological sequence has been used in one of the later stages in Johannine editing as an ending to the public ministry of Jesus . . . Within the story itself, the miracle has been made to serve the purposes of Johannine theology . . . the raising of Lazarus in [chapter] xi is a dramatization of the theme of Jesus as the life . . . Jesus the incarnate Word gives light and life to men in his ministry as signs of the eternal life that he gives through enlightenment gained from his teaching . . .[55]

This, then, is Brown's interpretation of the story that he labels "The Raising of Lazarus" and its original theological concerns. It is a widely respected interpretation and representative of one kind of approach to the text.

The dramatis personae

With this presentation of Brown's interpretation as background, I want to approach the texts differently, focusing on the artistry of the story as we have it in its final form. This is the form of the narrative that is of interest for my purposes, which are not historical but philosophical, as I have explained.

With the concerns of historical biblical scholarship uppermost, Brown finds that, apart from Jesus, the most important person in the story is Lazarus. But, on the methodology I am employing, it seems to me that, besides Jesus, the main characters in the final form of the narrative are Martha and Mary and that (contrary to Brown's reading) Mary's role in the story is more prominent than Martha's.

It is helpful in this connection to see how the text introduces the characters who figure in the narrative. The narrative opens with the explanation that a certain man was sick, and it then proceeds to try to identify this sick man for its audience. It gives the sick man's name, 'Lazarus,' and the name of his town, 'Bethany.' But, apparently, from the story's point of view, this is insufficient identification of the sick man, because the story goes on to try to identify the town, too: the town is the town of Mary and Martha. So, from the point of view of the narrative, the town has to be identified by reference to the people whose town it is; and these people are Mary and Martha, not Lazarus. Furthermore, Martha herself apparently needs some identification, because she is presented as the sister of Mary. At the outset, then, the story identifies Martha by reference to Mary, not the other way around. Finally, the narrative wants to make sure that there is no ambiguity about the Mary in question. (This is a sensible concern, given the number of Marys involved in the life of Jesus; later in the Gospel of John, for example, there are *three* Marys mentioned as being near the cross of Jesus.[56]) And so the story ends this introductory section by identifying the Mary who is mentioned in order to identify Martha: It was that Mary who anointed the Lord with ointment and wiped his feet with her hair.[57]

The story begins, then, with the fact that a man was sick, and it proceeds through a complicated series of connections to identify the man: through his name, the name of his town, the identification of the town by reference to the people who can be expected to be known in connection with the town—Martha, who also needs identification, and then Mary, on whom all the other identifications rest. The story expects its audience to know this Mary and to know her as the person who wiped the feet of Jesus with her hair. Lazarus and even Martha are introduced and identified through their connection to her.

It is not uncommon for a man to be identified in Gospel narratives by his name and his place of origin—compare the story in John's Gospel of Pilate's writing 'Jesus of Nazareth' on the cross of Jesus[58]—and, of course, in this story Lazarus is identified at the outset by his town, Bethany. Furthermore, it is not uncommon for a woman to be identified by her name and her connection to her husband or her son—compare the identification in the Gospel of John of one of the women at the foot of the cross as "Mary, of Cleophas."[59] But it is less common to identify a man by reference to a woman, as in this case in which Lazarus is ultimately identified by his connection to Mary. Why would the story begin by identifying Lazarus in this way? The narrative itself suggests the answer: from the point of view of the story, Lazarus is much less well known than his sisters, and Mary is as well known as she is because of her anointing of Jesus.

Of course, we might wonder why the narrative would bother with the mention of Bethany if it wanted to identify Lazarus by his connection to his sister Mary and her connection to Jesus. Part of the answer seems to be that Bethany itself is known because of its connection to Jesus. In the other Gospels, Bethany figures as a place where Jesus goes when he needs a place to stay for the night (Matt. 21: 17, Mark 11: 11). Bethany is the place Jesus sends his disciples to get a donkey for his triumphal ride into Jerusalem (Mark 11: 1, Luke 19: 29). Bethany is named as the place from which Jesus ascended after his resurrection (Luke 24: 50). And three of the Gospels mention Bethany as a place where a woman anointed Jesus (Matt. 26: 6, Mark 14: 8, John 12: 1). So Bethany is a place that the Gospels portray as familiar to Jesus. It may be, then, that Mary is well known in connection with Jesus because she lives in a town that is well known in connection with Jesus. But, of course, it may also be that Bethany is a place well known for its connection to Jesus because, in consequence of the fact that Mary—and Martha and Lazarus—live there, it is a place Jesus frequents.

The identification of Mary as the anointer of Jesus comes at the outset of the story, in the second verse, which Brown finds obviously out of place because the audience has not yet been given the description of Mary's anointing Jesus. It is certainly true, as Brown notes, that there is an episode of anointing that comes into the story only at the story's end, after the raising of Lazarus. But it does not follow that the verse is out of place, as Brown claims. If the narrative's audience could be expected to know about Mary's anointing Jesus after the raising of Lazarus, then it is possible that the storyteller would use that episode to identify Mary, even in advance of telling the story of that episode. In the same way, one might, for example, begin telling the life of Augustine by saying, "That very influential Patristic Christian Augustine was born in Africa." But, as the narrator of that line would know and would expect his audience to know, Augustine was not from birth an influential Patristic Christian. In this case, the narrator would be identifying Augustine for his audience by some much later part of Augustine's history, which the narrator would expect his audience to know.

(There is still another possible explanation for this early identification of Mary as the anointer of Jesus, but it is one that I am leaving for later when I turn to the conditional interpretation of the narrative of Mary of Bethany. This is the possibility that, from the point of view of the storyteller, by the time at which the story of the raising of Lazarus begins, Mary of Bethany has *already* anointed the feet of Jesus, on some other occasion. In that case, on this hypothesis, the storyteller supposes that the previous occasion of anointing is so well known to his audience that the storyteller can identify the Mary in his story by reference to her anointing of Jesus on that earlier occasion. On this possibility, which I am leaving out of consideration until later, the narrative would in effect be presenting Mary as anointing Jesus *twice*, once much earlier in the events alluded to in the identification of her, and then again after the raising of Lazarus.)

Finally, it is worth noting that, in the introduction of them in the story, neither Martha nor Mary is identified by reference to a man who is her husband. The later parts of the story only highlight further the absence of any mention of husbands for either of them. In the later parts, there is no husband who helps in finding Jesus when Lazarus is sick, who mourns when Lazarus dies, who meets Jesus when he returns after Lazarus's death, who is present when Jesus raises Lazarus, or who has a place at table with Lazarus in the dinner that follows afterwards. As far as that goes, the narrative leaves the impression that neither sister was *ever* married. That is because there is also no mention of any children for either sister; in all the places in the story where a husband is absent, children are absent as well. Furthermore, the same things are true of Lazarus. At points in the story at which Lazarus's wife or children might have been expected to figure prominently if he had either, there is no mention of any such people. So the mode of introducing the figures of the story implies what the rest of the story confirms.

Lazarus, Martha, and Mary have neither spouses nor children. They live together, single and childless.

This is something of an odd living arrangement. There are, of course, explanations unflattering to the spinster for why a woman has never been married, but it is not so common to find that explanation applicable to each of two sisters. And, even if it were the case that, for whatever reason, neither sister had ever been able to attract a husband, one is still left to wonder why *Lazarus* has no wife or children. One can also wonder why the sisters are living with him. It might be sensible enough for two unmarried sisters to share a home, but why would they share it with Lazarus? If the answer is supposed to be that Lazarus is the breadwinner who provides the home for both his unmarried sisters, then the wonder at his having no family of his own is only enhanced. If he is able to provide for two women in this way, why would he not be able to support a family of his own? But, in fact, in none of the stories involving Mary and Martha is there a mention of Lazarus except here, where he figures in the story first as sick and then as dead. And so there is no suggestion that he is the head of this small household or the significant breadwinner for it. Jean Vanier gives one possible explanation for this living arrangement among the three siblings. He suggests interpreting the story on the supposition that Lazarus was not healthy enough to earn a living, but that his sisters took care of him and provided the income on which all three of them lived.[60] I myself find this interpretation plausible, but I will not insist on it here.

However we are to understand the living arrangements, then, this is the narrative's introduction of the characters of the story; and it is enough to make clear that Mary, Martha, and Lazarus are not among the great in their society.[61] Unlike Abraham, they are not possessed of wealth; they do not have an army of servants; and kings would have no interest in them at all. The narrative also makes it clear that they all have a special relationship to Jesus. Mary can be identified for the audience by mention of a close connection to Jesus, and Martha and Lazarus are related to Jesus through their family relationship to Mary, but also directly and in their own right, as the rest of the narrative plainly shows.

The plan of Jesus

The highlighting of Mary given in the introductory lines of the narrative set the stage for the rest of the story. In order to understand Mary's role in the story, it helps to think about the narrative from varying points of view. In fact, part of the drama of the narrative depends on the fact that the narrative enables its audience to be simultaneously aware of two differing perspectives. We can begin by considering the initial events in the story from the point of view of Jesus in the narrative. After that, we can return to a consideration of the same events from the perspective of the sisters of Lazarus.

Once the story has announced the sickness of Lazarus and has identified the people in the story, the events of the story unfold. The narrative says that Mary and Martha sent Jesus a message, to let him know that Lazarus was sick. By now, in the Gospel of

John, Jesus has healed many people of illnesses and infirmities, and that narrative fact seems common knowledge to the people in the story. (In fact, as we saw in connection with Brown's interpretation, after the death of Lazarus, the people around Mary and Martha wonder why Jesus, who was capable of curing even blindness, did not come to heal Lazarus.) The sisters are worried about their brother's sickness, but they are also hopeful that their friend Jesus will come and that he will heal Lazarus if he comes. That is why they send him their message.

When Jesus gets that message, he says: "This sickness is not to death, but for the glory of God, that the son of God might be glorified through it" (John 11: 4).[62]

And then, instead of going to Bethany to answer the sisters' appeal for help, to heal Lazarus or at least to check on him and comfort the sisters, Jesus simply stays where he is for some days. The narrative is sensitive to the unpleasant implications that could be drawn from this narrative fact. And so the narrative prefaces its recounting of Jesus' failure to go to Bethany in response to the sisters' message by saying baldly that Jesus loved Mary, Martha, and Lazarus.[63]

But, if Jesus loves them, why does he not simply head straight to Bethany, to console the sisters and to heal Lazarus? What are we to make of his response to the sisters' message? How are we to understand his words and his action—or inaction?

The most obvious thing to note about Jesus' reaction to learning of Lazarus's sickness is that it is unlike the reaction of Lazarus's sisters. Unlike them, Jesus apparently feels no anxiety or concern about Lazarus. One might suppose that, if Jesus were going to manifest any sorrow or anger over sickness and death, of the sort that Brown and other commentators attribute to Jesus in connection with Jesus' groaning, later in the story, then Jesus would do so here, where he is first confronted with news about the sickness of his friend. But, when Jesus gets the message that Lazarus is sick, he does not groan. He does not trouble himself, not about Lazarus, not about the lamentable state of the human condition. He does not weep. On the contrary, there seems to be *nothing* negative in Jesus' reaction to the news that Lazarus is sick, not even dismay or weariness at being called on yet again to heal the sick. If anything, Jesus' initial reaction seems almost positive, almost as if he had been waiting for something like this: *this* sickness, he says, will eventuate in *glory*.[64]

In light of the end of the story, which, of course, we know, there is something perverse about not just accepting the simple explanation of this reaction on Jesus' part. Either because he has had something like this in mind for some time or because the thought has come to him on the spot in response to the sisters' message, Jesus forms the plan to let Lazarus's sickness have its natural eventuating in death and then to raise Lazarus back to life.[65] Jesus is not sad or anxious about Lazarus, because his plan is the guarantee that in fact Lazarus will be just fine, no matter what happens to him now. And Jesus is apparently not worried about the sisters either; maybe he anticipates their joy at finding Lazarus restored to them by means of a notable miracle. Clearly, this notable miracle will make plain not only to others but also and especially to the sisters how very dear they are to him, how much they matter to him. Little-league analogues to the sort of attitude I am attributing to Jesus are familiar to us. The matriarch of the family thinks that her eightieth birthday has been forgotten by her family because no one has scheduled any celebrations for that day; and her family watch her being inwardly sad at the thought that she no longer matters very much to any of them. But they are waiting with anticipation for her joy and amazement when she discovers, on the day *after* her birthday, the huge surprise party they have planned for her, when all her old friends and all her family, from far and near, are gathering together to honor her. *Then* she will know how very much all of them love her.

To assume this explanation of Jesus' response to the sisters' message is certainly not to lay to rest questions over that response. It is just to set the stage for raising them. Why would Jesus form such a plan for Lazarus, Martha, and Mary? What is at issue in this case is not birthday parties but the life of one friend and the deep distress of the other two. Furthermore, what are we to make of Jesus' explanation of the purpose of Lazarus's sickness and death, if this is the plan he has in mind? How is God's glory or the glory of Jesus (or both) furthered by Lazarus's death? And, even if we can see the answer to this last question in the miraculous raising of Lazarus, why would Jesus let Lazarus die for the sake of this glory? In what sense is getting glory, for himself or for God, an acceptable reason for Jesus to let Lazarus die? The real difficulty in this part of the narrative lies not in comprehending *what* Jesus is doing in response to the sisters' message, but in understanding *why* he is doing it.

The first place to look for answers to these questions is in what Jesus says about glory. The glory of God is what he mentions first. In light of the end of the story, that Lazarus is raised from the dead, it is not hard to interpret this line. Raising someone from the dead requires a miracle; and miracles demonstrate the power that God has over nature, including the power that God confers on the person doing the miracle in God's name. Given that, in one sense or another,[66] Jesus is representative of God, it is not so hard to see why Jesus' raising someone from the dead redounds to the glory of God. And it is not hard either to see why it also redounds to the credit of Jesus, the person on whom God has conferred the power over nature enabling him to do the miracle. In virtue of having such power, Jesus can be supposed to be specially favored by God, in one way or another. So if (as Brown also does[67]) we interpret Jesus' use of 'the son' (or 'the son of God') as a way of referring to himself, we have a natural interpretation of Jesus' line that Lazarus's sickness will result in glorifying the son of God. The miracle of the raising of Lazarus adds to the glory of Jesus, as well as the glory of God.

On the face of it, then, it seems *per improbabile* as if the narrative is attributing a morally repellent attitude to Jesus. Imagine that a person Paula calls her friend Jerome to her aid because Paula's daughter Julia is sick and Jerome is a superb doctor who can heal her. And then imagine that, in response to this call for help, without a word of explanation to Paula, Jerome forms a plan first to wait and let Julia die and then to use the latest technology to restore her to life. And suppose that his motivation for this plan is the glory he will get from restoring Julia to life and health in this dramatic way. If this were Jerome's plan, then he would be morally reprehensible. He would be willing to let both Paula and Julia suffer for the sake of a good for himself; and the good for himself would be one he should not be seeking in any case—namely, his own self-aggrandizement. So there is a readily available interpretation of Jesus' motivation that is obviously worrisome, for the audience of the story, but also for the characters in the story who may hear this line of his or be privy to this explanation for his plan.

Clearly, then, this way of looking at Jesus' reasons for his reaction to the sisters' message only exacerbates the perplexity raised by his plan. In fact, however, taking Jesus' motivation as equivalent to that of Jerome in my example is confused in more than one way. To see why this is so, it is helpful to digress briefly to consider the nature of glory.

The nature of glory and the glory of God

It is apparent that glory can be understood in two different ways. On the one hand, glory can be taken as a matter of being widely admired, praised, or celebrated by others. Glory in this sense is akin to fame or honor. This is the sense of 'glory' at issue when we describe a person or his achievements as glorious and mean thereby that he has renown or is honored in his society or culture. So, for example, contemporary Romans thought that Octavius had achieved a glorious victory over Mark Antony at the battle of Actium and that Mark Antony had suffered a correspondingly inglorious defeat. On the other hand, glory can be taken as a matter of something's being exalted, of its having great intrinsic excellence or refulgent splendor, with no implications that it is widely known or honored.[68] A solitary hiker high in the mountains might quite correctly think the sunset that she (and only she) sees is glorious. A person can be glorious in this way, too. Now, many years after her death and because of contemporary media attention to her story, Sophie Scholl is glorious because of her courageous resistance to the Nazi government; but she would have been glorious in this way even if her story had been entirely forgotten.[69] Her gloriousness lies in what she did, not in the admiration and honor of other people for her.

So there are at least two senses of 'glory.' These two senses, of course, are not incompatible. Something or someone might be honored for some great excellence really possessed, as has come to be the case for Sophie Scholl. On the other hand, history is also full of anecdotes confirming the widespread feeling that honor and excellence are often unconnected. There is no shortage of rulers renowned in their day but now remembered for the antithesis of any kind of excellence.

When something is said to contribute to the glory of a human being, then, it could be glory in either or both of two senses. It might contribute to that person's excellence, whether or not anyone knows about it and honors it. Or it might contribute to that person's renown and honor, whether or not it did so because of some real excellence in the person achieving renown. Or it might contribute to both.

But what about the glory of God? Can God have glory in either sense of 'glory'? When something is done for the glory of God, what sense of glory is at issue? Can anything add to the glory of God? In what sense can the glory of God be increased?

Whatever can be said by way of a general answer to these questions, it is hard to suppose that anyone (in the world of the story or outside it) would seriously entertain the idea that a person's doing a miracle could increase the intrinsic splendor of God or add to the intrinsic excellence of God. So, if in the story the miracle of raising Lazarus contributes to God's glory, as Jesus predicts it will, then it seems reasonable to suppose that the miracle does so only in the other sense of 'glory'—that is, by adding to God's renown among human beings and increasing the praise given to God by human beings. So, if Lazarus's sickness is for the glory of God, as Jesus says it is when he receives the sisters' message to him, then one outcome of Lazarus's illness (or, more precisely, one outcome of the miracle of resurrecting Lazarus after he has died of his illness) will be glory for God in *this* sense, and only in this sense.

At this point, however, we need to think about the difference between glory understood as renown and honor for human beings and glory in this same sense for God. If Jerome gets renown for restoring Julia to health after she has been clinically dead, then the principal beneficiary of that renown is just Jerome. When the praise of Jerome for his quasi-miraculous healing of Julia is spread through his community, the primary person who reaps the tangible and intangible benefits of Jerome's enhanced renown is just Jerome. But it does not seem reasonable to suppose that things work in the same way where the glory of God is concerned. If it were God's gloriousness, rather than her doctor's, that was impressed on Paula, and if it were praise of God, not praise of Jerome, that Paula shared with her community, then the primary beneficiary of that increase in glory would not be God. It would be Paula. God's flourishing is not augmented when human beings praise him; *their* flourishing is. For a human being such as Paula to praise God and to have a better understanding of the things for which God is to be praised is for Paula herself to become greater. That is because in praising God she is recognizing the desirability of God and so desiring God. To this extent, she is also drawing nearer to God in love. And so she grows in greatness as well. Could there be a greater state for a human being than drawing near to God in love? So Paula's coming to praise of God will increase intrinsic excellence in Paula in virtue of increasing her second-personal connection to God.[70]

In an odd but understandable way, then, the increase in God's glory, where glory is taken as honor and renown, conduces to the increase of the glory understood as intrinsic excellence on the part of those persons who give God glory in the sense of renown. Insofar as, in the story, Jesus is God's special representative in one sense or another, the same point applies (*mutatis mutandis*) to the increase in the glory of Jesus resulting from the miracle of the raising of Lazarus.

Glory and the plan

It makes a difference, therefore, that the glory sought by Jesus' plan is the glory of God. Understanding that God's glory benefits those people who give God glory in this sense goes some way toward answering the questions I raised about Jesus' reactions to the sisters' message. But, as it stands, there is still something perplexing about Jesus' plan. That is because, on this explanation about God's glory, everyone who sees the miracle of the raising of Lazarus and is prompted to praise of God in consequence will gain by the miracle. But Mary, Martha, and Lazarus are not everybody. They suffer in ways particular to them when Jesus does not come to Bethany to heal Lazarus after the sisters' appeal to him. And so pointing to a general benefit made available to the whole community aware of the miracle does not by itself explain why Jesus would leave his friends unaided as he does.

Something of the original question still remains therefore: why did Jesus form the plan he did? It should be clear that this question is not asking whether Jesus is justified in doing what he does. What is at issue here is not theodicy. The question is asking only for a motive for Jesus' plan, a motive plausible in the story in which Jesus is portrayed as a good person and as loving Martha, Mary, and Lazarus.

The reflections on glory in the preceding section offer a helpful way to reformulate the question at issue here. Does the increase in God's praise and the renown accruing to Jesus from the raising of Lazarus somehow benefit Mary, Martha, and Lazarus in a way particular to them?

Put in this way, the question suggests one obvious answer. Plainly, Mary, Martha, and Lazarus are the primary beneficiaries of the miracle itself, because it restores Lazarus to them. But they are also obvious beneficiaries of the increase in the glory of God elicited by the miracle. Those who report the miracle and praise God for it will include Lazarus and his sisters in their telling of the story. The stories of the miracle will not only mention them but will also explain Jesus' performing this miracle on the basis of their special relationship to him. And so, in this case, what contributes to the glory of God, in the sense of honor and renown, also contributes to the honor and renown of the three of them. Apart from this story, nothing is known of Lazarus, and only slightly more is known of Martha; even as regards Mary, there is not a great deal more to report, and it seems doubtful that what else there is would have been preserved if it had not been for this story. Before the miracle, these three were undistinguished people of their period. After the miracle and because of it, their names and stories were passed on rapidly in the surrounding society. The story itself explains that, after the miracle, people came to Bethany for the purpose of seeing Lazarus, the person raised from the dead.[71] (As far as that goes, in consequence of the events involving the raising of Lazarus, the names of all three siblings have been passed on, commemorated, and celebrated for almost two millennia. Even among the twelve apostles chosen by Jesus, there are not many who can rival Mary, Martha, and Lazarus for their ability to capture the imagination of more than one culture in more than one age.) So, where glory is understood as honor and renown, Jesus' plan to increase the glory of God and his own glory by raising Lazarus has the clear effect of increasing the honor and renown of these friends of his, too. Insofar as this effect is easy for Jesus in the story to foresee, honoring them can be taken to be part of what he has in mind in forming his plan.

What is less easy but even more important to see is that, in this narrative, because of Jesus' plan, Mary, Martha, and Lazarus also gain in glory in the other sense of glory. In consequence of that plan, in a way particular to them as primary beneficiaries of the miracle, they grow in inner excellence as well as in honor.

Many people in the Gospel narratives ask Jesus for help with sicknesses or physical disabilities of some other sort, but ignoring their requests is not Jesus' usual response. The relative strangers who ask Jesus for help have enough trust in him to hope that he is both willing and able to help them. But they do not have the kind of second-personal connection to him that would enable such trust to survive in the face of no response at all on his part. In the story, the fact that Jesus picks Martha, Mary, and Lazarus as the ones whose request for help he will not answer immediately, at least not in the way they expect, is a sign of *his* trust in *them*. It suggests that he believes they can be counted on to maintain their trust in him, their willingness to be close to him, even in the face of a disappointment as severe as his not coming to heal Lazarus.

That belief on his part must be part of what underlies his plan to help them by resurrecting Lazarus rather than by healing Lazarus in response to the sisters' message. Clearly, Jesus' failure to come to Martha and Mary when they send their message to him will put pressure on them. It will confuse and perplex them; it will cause them pain. And no one in Jesus' position could fail to see that it will do so. Apparently, then, Jesus feels sure enough of their trust in him and their closeness to him to let them be subject to such pressure. Although they will be distressed and perplexed, or mad and miserable, when he fails to come, in the narrative Jesus apparently supposes that their second-personal connection to him will stay intact. And so he must expect that the pressure his inaction puts on them will eventuate ultimately only in deepened trust in him on their part and increased closeness. They will come to understand that he was not neglecting or disdaining them by failing to come to their aid. On the contrary, he was relying on them as his more advanced followers, as his closer friends. On his supposition, after the miracle, when Mary, Martha, and Lazarus come to understand his plan, they will gain a deeper insight into his love and care for them; and so their own love and care for him will deepen.

In addition, in the narrative Jesus is taken as God's representative in some special way. For example, Martha says to Jesus: "I believe that you are the Messiah, the Son of God, the one coming into the world."[72] (In this respect, Martha is the equivalent of Peter, who is generally assigned a place of honor in the Gospel narratives for his recognition of Jesus as the Son of God.) Because in the narrative Jesus is connected to God in a special way (whatever exactly that way is), to grow in understanding of the love and care of Jesus and to increase in love and care for Jesus are, in the narrative's own terms, also to grow in understanding of God's love and care and to increase in love and care for God. And so, when Martha, Mary, and Lazarus draw closer to Jesus, they will draw closer to God as well. As I said in connection with the discussion of God's glory, however, a person's drawing closer to God adds to the intrinsic excellence of that person.

By doing what he supposes will strengthen the second-personal connection Mary, Martha, and Lazarus have with respect to him, then, Jesus is also bringing it about that in the end they will grow in glory, in the sense of inner excellence and splendor.

In my example involving Jerome and Paula, what is offensive in Jerome's plan for the quasi-miraculous healing of Paula's daughter Julia is Jerome's willingness to use the suffering of Paula and Julia as a means to the enhancement of his own fame.

But the differences between Jesus' plan and a plan such as that of Jerome in my example should now be clear. As Jesus says, the miracle of the raising of Lazarus will contribute to the glory of God and to his own glory as well. But, for that very reason, because of their second-personal connection to him, it will also contribute to the glory of Mary, Martha, and Lazarus, in *both* senses of glory. By staying where he is until Lazarus is dead and then raising Lazarus in an astounding miracle, Jesus will increase both the honor and the excellence of his three friends to such an extent that this change in their stature and status will also be something to marvel at.

Insofar as this result is readily foreseeable, it is reasonable to suppose that it is part of Jesus' plan, or even at the heart of it.

Here someone may raise an objection. In the things Jesus says when he gets the sisters' message that Lazarus is sick, Jesus does not mention Mary, Martha, and Lazarus explicitly or imply that a benefit to any of them is part of his plan. Insofar as he mentions a benefit to human persons (other than himself), he seems to be thinking of his disciples. When Jesus is finally ready to go to Bethany, and his disciples wonder why he is going there then, he explains himself to them this way: "Lazarus is dead. And I am glad for your sakes that I was not there, so that you might have faith."[73]

In *these* words, Jesus is suggesting that one of his purposes in letting Lazarus die is a benefit for his disciples, not a benefit for Mary, Martha, and Lazarus. He says something similar as regards the surrounding crowd right before he does the miracle. At that point, he makes a prayer; and in that prayer he suggests that another purpose for his actions is that the people in that crowd might have faith.[74] An objector might suppose, then, that Jesus' main purpose in raising Lazarus was just the faith of his disciples and the onlookers.

On the view of this objection, Jesus chooses Mary and her family as the people for whom he will do this great miracle, because he thinks he can trust them to accept the suffering that his failure to heal Lazarus will cost them; but he intends the benefits of the miracle for very many people and not primarily for Mary, Martha, and Lazarus. And so, although Jesus loves Martha, and her sister, and Lazarus, he is willing to use them as means to his end of furthering God's glory and human faith. He is willing to let them suffer more than others for a benefit available equally to others who do not suffer as they do.

In my view, this objection is mistaken, and it rests on a reading of the story that is implausible for more than one reason. In the first place, it attributes to Jesus the willingness to let those he loves suffer great distress provided only that he can achieve his own ends of producing faith in his disciples and others in the community. But this view does not seem to me consistent with the text's portrayal of Jesus in the rest of the story. In addition, it is inconsistent with the narrative's picture of the reaction Martha and Mary have toward Jesus when he finally does come to Bethany. As their attitude toward him then makes clear, they expected that he would come to help them, and they were dismayed when he did not. They did not expect that he might be letting them suffer for some global purposes of his own. In the narrative, both before and after Jesus comes to Bethany, the sisters' expectation is that Jesus will care for their welfare as an end in its own right. By their reaction to Jesus after the miracle, they show that, in their ultimate view of the matter, that expectation was not disappointed. Finally, as I explained above, in the narrative, the raising of Lazarus *does* confer a great benefit on Mary, Martha, and Lazarus. If it was not part of Jesus' original plan that they should have this benefit, he would have had to be either unaccountably oblivious to that benefit for them or unaccountably uncaring that there be such a benefit for people whom the narrative says he loves; and these are both narratively implausible options.

So it makes more sense to suppose that providing the foreseeable benefits to Mary, Martha, and Lazarus is part of Jesus' original plan, even if there are also benefits to his disciples and to others in the surrounding community.

A puzzle

On this way of thinking about Jesus' plan, as Jesus conceives of it, the plan is motivated by Jesus' love for Mary, Martha, and Lazarus. Its purpose is to give all three of them a great gift—namely, glory, in both senses of 'glory.' And, of course, part of the cleverness of the plan is that at the end of the story Mary and Martha (and Lazarus) not only have a great gift they did not ask for (and presumably would not have imagined or known how to ask for). They also have the gift that Mary and Martha did ask for (and that Lazarus himself would have wanted): they have Lazarus restored to health and to life with them. In the end, then, Jesus grants them what they wanted and gives them far more than they asked.

But if this is Jesus' plan, then why does he not say as much to his disciples? As far as that goes, why does he not explain the plan to Martha and Mary (and Lazarus)? The answer to the second question contains implicit in it the answer to the first also.

It is a puzzling feature of the story that Jesus does not share with Martha and Mary what he is intending to do. The story makes it clear that Jesus sends no message to them in response to the message they send him; whatever messenger brought their message to Jesus apparently returns to Martha and Mary empty-handed. A flat-footed objection to the story might disapprove of this omission on Jesus' part. If Jesus wanted to do a notable miracle by raising Lazarus, this putative objector might think, Jesus ought at the outset to have presented his plan to Martha, Mary, and Lazarus. Then all three of them would have been reassured as they watched Lazarus's disease progressing. And Mary and Martha would not have wondered, with increasing anxiety and distress, why Jesus did not respond to their need—or even answer their message.

What makes this objection flat-footed is that it misses the effects that Jesus' communication of his plan would have had on Martha, Mary, and Lazarus. To share the plan with them is to ruin it.[75] If Jesus made sure Mary, Martha, and Lazarus understood what he intended to do, then the sisters would have sat by Lazarus as the disease progressed and Lazarus died, knowing all the while that Lazarus would be totally cured. They would know that his cure was just a matter of time and that this unusual way of curing him would render all three of them renowned, so that everyone would want to come to see Lazarus once he was raised.[76] No doubt, when their friends and neighbors worried about Lazarus and about them, the sisters would have explained Jesus' plan to them, too; and they would certainly have spread the news to still others, and so on—until the miracle of the raising of Lazarus becomes a kind of staged spectacle, to which an enterprising person might have sold tickets.

Nothing about *these* events would put much pressure on Mary, Martha, or Lazarus. Their trust in Jesus would not sustain much of a trial, and so it would not deepen either. It is certainly easier to sit by Lazarus's sickbed knowing that Jesus is going to restore Lazarus to life than wondering where he is and why he does not come. For these reasons, if Jesus were to share his plan with Mary, Martha, and Lazarus, they would not grow in stature in the way I argued above that they do grow in the story. Furthermore, if they did not grow in stature, the result of the miracle would also have much less by way of an impact on their honor and renown; it would not leave them the objects of lasting human admiration. On the version of the story where everybody knows in advance what Jesus is going to do, Mary, Martha, and Lazarus become just bit players in the events. It is still true that Jesus picks them for the miracle because they are his friends. But the focus of the story becomes almost exclusively on Jesus; Mary, Martha, and Lazarus become little more than part of the stage setting for the miracle he does. If the plan were shared with Mary, Martha, and Lazarus in advance, it is hard to see that anything would be lost if subsequent retellings of the story of the miracle made them anonymous. Nothing would be lost, that is, if the story of the events became just the sort of thing Brown thinks it originally was: a story that Jesus raised a person from the dead, where neither the name nor the history of that person matters very much to what is important in the story.

So, if Jesus had communicated his plan in advance to Mary, Martha, and Lazarus, as the objection supposes he should have done, then none of them would have gained in glory, in either sense of glory, in consequence of the miracle.[77] In that case, in planning to raise Lazarus, Jesus' concern would have been just for God's glory and his own; and Mary, Martha, and Lazarus would have been no more than means to that end. Jesus does not share his plan with Mary, Martha, and Lazarus therefore precisely because his plan is motivated by love and care for them. The great increase in their glory is part of the original plan.

Jesus' failure to reveal the plan ahead of time to his disciples is now also much easier to understand. How would he have revealed it to them? Would he have told them the plan and asked them not to tell Mary, Martha, and Lazarus? It is clear that the disciples have their own relationship at least to Lazarus. When Jesus is talking to the disciples about Lazarus, he refers to Lazarus as 'our beloved Lazarus.'[78] Would the disciples have been within their moral rights to keep such a secret from their beloved friend Lazarus or his sisters? It is one thing for Jesus not to divulge his plan, given the special status Martha takes him to have, as the son of God. It is another thing entirely for such a secret to be kept by the disciples, who are not in any way theologically significant superiors to Mary, Martha, and Lazarus. How would the disciples have felt about themselves if they had kept such a secret? How would Mary, Martha, and Lazarus have felt about the disciples if they had kept the secret? We do not have to work at answers to all these questions. That we can raise them is enough to show that it is much better if Jesus keeps his plan entirely to himself.

So this, then, is Jesus' plan. It will be helpful in what follows to have this understanding of the plan in mind.

Two worries, a response, and a workaround

Jesus' plan, born of love for Mary, Martha, and Lazarus, is a good plan; it is designed to bring a great gift to all three of them. And the plan might have worked exactly as he had intended it to do if Martha and Mary had been different people or had reacted differently to his failure to come. Imagine how differently the story would have gone if Martha and Mary had reacted to Jesus' failure to come to them by talking the situation over together and then sending Jesus a second message, one that began by telling him "We don't understand why you're not coming" and that concluded with a respectful request for an explanation. But Mary and Martha do not respond to Jesus in that sort of way; and, because they do not, Jesus' plan does not work as it was intended to do.[79]

To say this is in effect to suppose that the narrative attributes a mistake to Jesus—a non-culpable mistake, but still a mistake. Because my interpretation of the story does make this supposition, it is important to digress briefly to ward off possible worries.

First, someone might have a theological worry stemming from the doctrine of the incarnation, the theological position that assigns to Jesus a divine nature. If Jesus has a divine nature, this worry goes, then he also has the mind of God and knows everything; and so he cannot make a mistake. But this worry should be laid to rest. To attribute a mistake to Jesus does not saddle a story, or an interpretation of a story, with any noteworthy theological implications as regards the doctrine of the incarnation. Whatever else they may maintain, all mainstream theological explanations of the doctrine of the incarnation *also* assign to Jesus a fully human nature. If Jesus has a fully human nature, however, then he will be limited in knowledge in that human nature. And, if he is limited in knowledge in his human nature, then he is also capable of making a mistake when he is operating in that nature.

It is true that, on some understandings of the doctrine of the incarnation, Jesus also has to be taken as sinless or even incapable of sin in his human nature. But, manifestly, not all mistakes are morally culpable, let alone sinful. Even mistakes that cause serious distress or damage to other people can be completely non-culpable. Suppose that a father who has no idea that his little son has followed him out of the house, and whose ignorance is not itself culpable in any way, runs over his child as he drives out of the garage. The father acts on the mistaken supposition that his son is still in the house, and the result of the father's mistake is that the child dies. In that case, we pity the father; we do not blame him. So a person may be guiltless even for a mistake resulting in significant suffering or harm to others. The mistake my interpretation assigns to Jesus in the story is non-culpable; and so it has no implications for the theological position that takes Jesus to be sinless or impeccable.

On this same score, it is worth noticing that the Gospels themselves are not shy about attributing a mistake to Jesus, even a mistake that causes distress to others. So, for example, the Gospel of Luke tells the story that the mother of Jesus finally found her 12-year-old son after having had to search anxiously for him for a long time because he had failed to tell her where he would be.[80] When she remonstrated with him, his reply to her was an implicit admission of a mistake. "Why were you looking for me?," he asks her; "did you not know I would be *here*?" But, of course, on that occasion he was mistaken in thinking that she would know where he was; in fact, she did not know, and that is why she had had to search so long before she found him. (In this story, too, the mistake on Jesus' part is a matter of failing to take account of what another human person would understand about Jesus' own actions and purposes.)

So, interpreting the story as attributing a mistake to Jesus does not take sides in any theological controversies, any more than the Lucan story about the 12-year-old Jesus does. Those who reject the doctrines of the incarnation or the impeccability of the incarnate Jesus can accept my interpretation; but so can those at the other end of the ideological spectrum, who accept the whole Chalcedonian formula for the incarnation and take Jesus as the impeccable, omnipotent second-person of the Trinity made flesh.

Even with this worry laid to rest, there is a second worry that needs to be warded off in this connection. People who are not concerned about possible theological implications might still baulk at an interpretation attributing even a non-culpable mistake to Jesus, because they suppose such an attribution construes Jesus as inattentive or inept in some other way. There is something less than respectful, people having such a concern will think, about attributing a mistake to Jesus.

This concern would be appropriate if the mistake in Jesus' plan postulated by my interpretation was one that had to stem from some significant (even if non-culpable) defect or inadequacy on Jesus' part. But, as will become clear in what follows, the mistake my reading of the narrative attributes to Jesus is subtle, and his making it is perfectly compatible with both attentive sensitivity and attentive compassion. So there is no reason for concern about the attribution to Jesus of a mistake on this score either. On my view, as the unfolding events of the story show, Jesus' plan goes awry because he fails to predict correctly what the women will do, given the peculiarly double-minded mix of devotion and distance in their relation to himself. He expects them to stay committed to him and to retain their conviction that he loves them; and it is loving of him to have this expectation. It rests on a high assessment of them, and a high hope for them, too. In the event, he is mistaken on this score, but this is a mistake that any human person, however careful and astute, however admirable in every way, might make. Would Jesus be a more admirable character in the story if he tended to have a mildly cynical view of the people he loves, expecting the worst of them and doubting that they can be trusted to love him in times of trouble?

So I do not think that attributing to Jesus a mistaken belief about how the sisters will react makes Jesus seem in any way less than anyone might hope to see him.

But perhaps, for some people, even with all the benevolence-producing explanation I have just given, attributing a mistake of any sort to Jesus is unthinkable, and my attempts to ward off worries about such an attribution will not persuade them otherwise. And so, for such readers, I want to point out that it is possible to maintain most of the interpretation I give below even if this attribution is excised. That is, it is possible to suppose, contrary to my interpretation, that in the story Jesus makes no mistake of any kind and that in fact he predicts perfectly how the sisters will react to his not coming to their aid. On this supposition, what falls of my interpretation is only the explanation of Jesus' groaning, weeping, and being troubled. All the rest of the interpretation can be maintained, *mutatis mutandis*.[81] So readers who are immovably opposed to the attribution of any mistake to Jesus can simply omit that attribution, expunge my explanation for Jesus' emotive reactions, and then continue with the rest of the interpretation presented below. The result will be something less than the interpretation I offer and prefer, but I propose it as a workaround for such readers.

The sisters' message

With such worries attended to, we can now turn to the events of the story from the sisters' point of view. The first sign in the story that there will be trouble with Jesus' plan is evident even before Jesus' expression of that plan. It is there in the very message Martha and Mary send to Jesus. That message says just "Lord, look, the one whom you love is sick."

This message is not coy exactly, but it certainly is not frank and forthright either. A forthright message would have said: "Lord, would you please come and help us because Lazarus is sick, and we wish you would heal him." As it stands, the sisters' message does not give the name of the sick person, thereby leaving it to Jesus to know who is sick; and because the message does not identify the sick person, it also leaves it up to Jesus to understand why Martha and Mary care about the person who is sick. There is also a kind of uneasy delicacy in the identification of the sick person as "*the one* whom you love." Does Jesus love just that one? What about Mary and Martha? Does not he love them, too? And, if he does, why identify Lazarus as "the one" Jesus loves? Finally, it is notable that in this message there is no explicit request of any kind for help. Why not? If the sisters want Jesus to come to heal Lazarus, why do they not just say so?

To ask this last question is to suggest the answer to it and to the preceding questions as well. There are certainly familiar occasions on which one person Paula wants something from another person Jerome and yet fails to ask him for it when she could easily do so. Paula fails to ask because, if she has to ask, then, no matter what she gets in response to her request, she will not be getting what she wants, or at least not all she wants. What makes the complication in such cases is that, typically, Paula actually wants *two* things from Jerome: one is the particular object she is after (but does not ask for); the other is relational and second-personal. Paula's succeeding in having the *second* of these two things is dependent on Jerome's closeness and presence to Paula and on joint attention between the two of them with regard to the object Paula wants.[82] In order for Paula to have what she wants in this regard, Jerome needs to be attentive enough to Paula to know what Paula wants, and he needs to care about the fact that Paula wants Jerome to care about her having what she wants. We might say that Paula cares about Jerome's caring about Paula's caring about his care for her (and so on). Or maybe we could put the point this way: what Paula wants as regards her relationship to Jerome is that Jerome give her what she wants not only because he cares that she have it but also because he is attending to her and cares about her. It is hard to spell out the complications here, but the phenomenon is familiar and readily recognizable in its everyday occurrences.

In the story, Mary and Martha want healing for Lazarus, but they also care about Jesus and about their connection to Jesus. In their case, there is an extra complication as regards this latter concern because there is a significant inequality of status between Mary, Martha, and Lazarus, on the one hand, and Jesus, on the other. This inequality will drive desire and care of the sort characterizing Paula in my example into uncertainty and unease on the part of the sisters when Lazarus becomes sick and they are all three in need. Plainly, Jesus does care about all of them. The narrative explicitly says that he does; the sisters' message to Jesus explicitly says that he loves Lazarus. But the sisters are also bound to wonder why Jesus would love *them*. The most that can be said about the three of them is that they are very ordinary people. Jesus, by contrast, does miracles and is sought after by crowds; Martha takes him to be the son of God. Why would this extremely important person Jesus care about ordinary undistinguished people such as Mary, Martha, and Lazarus? And how hard would it be for Mary and Martha to have a whole-hearted belief that he does? What do they have to offer to attract the love and care of a man such as Jesus? How easy would it be for Mary and Martha to assume that, no matter how affectionate Jesus is toward them, in the end they are not in his inner circle; they are not people who really matter to him?

The nature of the sisters' message to Jesus suggests that, apart from their anxiety about Lazarus, they are also alive to what they feel is ambiguity in their relations with him. He matters greatly to them, and they believe that they matter to him. They believe that he loves Lazarus and them. But they do not believe these things whole-heartedly enough to bank on them, and so they do not ask him forthrightly to come to heal Lazarus. They assume that they are special to him; on the other hand, they are not sure that they are as important to him as he is to them. They believe that they are close to him; that is why they send their message. But they do not tell him openly what they want from him, so as not to presume on a closeness they might not have.

Any attempt of this sort to put into simple and direct words the double-minded attitudes on the sisters' part is bound to come out looking contrived, and so is any attempt to spell out straightforwardly the non-straightforward character of the sisters' message to Jesus. But that the message is not straightforward is clear, and the personal anxiety behind it is highlighted by the addition of the phrase "the one you love." They could, after all, have said just 'Lazarus.' Why do they feel they need to tell Jesus that he loves Lazarus? Can't he be trusted to remember or act on that fact himself?

In the narrative, then, the sisters' message sets the stage for trouble. It shows that the women have two powerful desires, one having to do with Lazarus's sickness, and the other having to do with Jesus' reaction to them as people who care about his caring about them.

Jesus and Martha

According to the narrative, after the sisters' message is delivered, Jesus waits for three days and then prepares to go to Bethany to put his plan into action. In a passage I did not quote above, the disciples with him are portrayed as concerned with their own issues. Is it safe to go back to a place so close to Jerusalem? Is it cowardly to worry about whether it is safe to go back?[83] As they head to Bethany, the disciples are focused on what they take to be—on what no doubt are—the larger issues of Jesus' ministry. Jesus himself is thinking about his great plan. What did the disciples expect to find, what did Jesus expect to find, when they arrived in Bethany?

Here is one possibility:

> Mary and Martha have been stricken by the death of their brother, and they have been unable to understand why Jesus did not come to heal him. But they know how much Jesus loves them. And so they are sure that there is an explanation for his absence that is consistent with his great love for them. Whatever it was that kept him from them, and that allowed Lazarus to die, it must somehow have been compatible with his love for them. Although they are grieved and confused, they have held fast to their trust in him; even with his failure to help them, they remain committed to their belief that they matter greatly to him. And so they are waiting for him with undiminished trust in him and with hopeful love of him to learn what happened to keep him from coming to them.

If this is what any of them were expecting, then the first meeting with Martha must have come as something of a shock.

We must not let the fact that we know the end of the story make us blind to what the women have been suffering in the time since they sent their message to Jesus. When they sent the message, they had a great hope: that Jesus would come because he loved them, and that, when he came, he would be able to help them in their pressing need. As their neighbors say, if Jesus could restore sight to the blind, then surely he could heal whatever ails Lazarus. The slow unraveling of a great hope, rooted in love for another person, is extremely painful. (Think about the anguish of even that paragon of self-control, Jane Bennett, in *Pride and Prejudice*, as she comes to understand that the man she loves has left and is not returning, or remember the growing desperation of pregnant Hetty, in *Adam Bede*, as she comes to see that her lover Arthur is not coming back for her.) There is the additional complication that for the sisters Jesus is a religiously significant figure; as Martha sees it and expresses it to Jesus, Jesus is the son of God. If the person by whom one feels betrayed is somehow specially representative of God, "the son of God," the pain of the apparent betrayal is greatly exacerbated.[84]

By the time Jesus arrives in Bethany, then, the sisters will have had ample time first for dismay, disappointment, and anxiety, then for pain and perplexity, and finally for the sodden misery that comes when the extinction of hope can no longer be denied. Furthermore, their misery will have a special suffering about it, because they loved Jesus and trusted in his love for them not only as the man he was but also as God's son, as Martha says. To understand what happens in the rest of the story, we need to be sensitive to the sisters' experience of Jesus' plan and the effects of that plan on them, when without explanation Jesus fails to come and Lazarus dies.

No doubt in differing ways, in virtue of having differing relations to Jesus, each sister has two desires of the heart, as the unfolding events of the story make manifest. One desire is that Lazarus might not die; the other, much harder to characterize, has to do with Jesus, with mattering to him and being loved by him. And so each sister has more than one reason for heartbreak when Lazarus dies because Jesus does not come. When Jesus goes to Bethany with his disciples, to raise Lazarus from the dead in a glorious miracle, what is waiting for him are two women who are heartbroken about Lazarus, but also about him.

As soon as Martha hears that Jesus is on the way to Bethany, she runs out of the house to meet him. Her sister Mary stays put in the house. Both these parts of the story give us useful information about the sisters, information that also comes to Jesus in the narrative. On his way to their house in Bethany, Jesus finds Martha—but not Mary—rushing out to meet him.

Martha's opening line, her greeting as she meets Jesus on the road, is "Lord, if you had been here, my brother would not have died." Some Patristic and medieval commentators take this line as evidence of Martha's faith in Jesus.[85] But there is something obtuse about that interpretation of her line in this part of the story. Martha's line is, of course, evidence of her faith in Jesus, particularly her faith in his ability to heal people of their diseases. But she is presenting her faith to Jesus in a way that conveys to him how much he has distressed her. Her line is an expression of hurt. It is the first thing she says to him, and it lets him know immediately how terribly he has let her down.

In the Gospel stories, Martha is portrayed as the practical, uncomplicated sister. In this narrative, although Jesus has caused her great grief, she is still speaking to him. Mary, on the other hand, is staying at home. Some commentators[86] have supposed that Mary did not know that Jesus was arriving. But the text says nothing to this effect, and the supposition is narratively implausible. As Martha's line to Jesus makes clear, Lazarus may be dead, but the sisters are still focused on Jesus' failure to come to them. Is it credible, in these circumstances, with both sisters in the same house and grief-stricken over Jesus as well as Lazarus, that Martha would learn of Jesus' imminent arrival and would fail to share this information with her sister? And, even if she did fail to tell Mary, is it credible that in those circumstances Martha could rush out of the house in excitement, and Mary would not quickly figure out where Martha was going and why? So it seems more plausible to suppose that, in the story, Mary and Martha had access to the same information about Jesus. But when they both knew that Jesus was finally coming, Martha ran to meet him, and Mary stayed exactly where she was.

Withdrawal and silence can also be an effective way of communicating to someone you love that he has hurt you. No doubt, for some temperaments, withdrawing into oneself is as natural a method of expressing pain as Martha's running out to confront Jesus directly is for her. In fact, it can be more self-protective for a person to withdraw, in rejection of a belief in the love of another, than to stay engaged with that other and maintain belief in the love of the other in the face of counter-evidence. Withdrawing in disbelief protects the person withdrawing against further hurt and against the vulnerability inherent in love. Mary's withdrawal is therefore a kind of willed loneliness. But the problem with her strategy for handling her hurt is that it shuts her out from what she herself wants, in an internally divided way, where Jesus is concerned.

For the person on the receiving end of it, withdrawal can be even more distressing than confrontation. When Martha confronts Jesus, she shows him in effect that she is still an active participant in their relationship; she is confronting Jesus because she still cares about him and is open to reconciliation with him. Or, if this is too strong to say, then at any rate since Martha has let Jesus know how she feels, he has a reasonably straightforward way in which to deal with her. Withdrawal can be more disturbing to the person left out or left behind than confrontation is just because it is not clear that the person withdrawing is in fact still open to reconciliation.[87]

And so, in the narrative, when Jesus is headed toward Bethany, it must be perturbing to him to find Martha coming to meet him to confront him, but it must be even more unsettling to find Mary not with her.

Practical Martha not only expresses her pain directly to Jesus, but she also offers him a way out of the trouble between them. She follows her opening words, "Lord, if you had been here, my brother would not have died," with this line: "But I know that even now whatever you ask of God, God will give you." In the circumstances, this is something of a broad hint, and it is not so hard to understand the attitude that underlies it. It is as if Martha were thinking to herself something like this: "You didn't come when we needed you, Jesus. Plainly, we don't have as important a role in your life as you have in ours. You are a busy man, with an important mission in life. And so you let us down. Well, never mind. Now you finally *are* here. Surely now you could get around to doing something for us, and that would be better than nothing." And so Martha says to him: "Even now, whatever you ask of God, God will give you." In this line, Martha is suggesting that, although in her view she and her brother and sister do not matter to Jesus as they believed or hoped they did, nonetheless she is willing to swallow her hurt and disappointment at this supposed fact as long as some practical good can come out of it all now.

Since Martha's hint at this possibility of a practical good is among the first things she says to Jesus, it seems clear that a hope for this good is one of the things motivating her to run out to meet him. Why does not Mary join Martha in a hope of this sort? Why does not Mary also run out to meet Jesus, to join her petitions to the petition implicit in Martha's hint? It is hard not to suppose that, in the story, Mary stays in the house when Martha runs out to meet Jesus because Mary minds so intensely about Jesus' treatment of her that she does not care what he does now. In the Lucan narrative about the sisters, Martha is the one who cares whether they all get lunch on time; Mary does not care whether they ever eat, as long as she can stay by Jesus listening to him.[88]

What about Martha's hint? It seems clear that the suggestion implicit in it puts Jesus in a bind. Jesus is, of course, coming to Bethany just for the purpose of raising Lazarus. But he cannot act on Martha's hint. If Jesus accepts and acts on the desire implicit in that hint, if he even appears to do so, he will have lost something he cares about and should care about.

Jesus' plan was to surprise the sisters by raising Lazarus; and the intended result of the plan was not just to restore Lazarus to life and to them, but to glorify all three of them with both kinds of glory. Their glory was to be his gift to them, born of his great love for them. But, from the sisters' point of view, the situation looks different. They trusted in his love for them; and, in a time of urgent need when they were counting on him, it seems to them that Jesus let them down. No matter what great gift he had in mind for them, is giving his friends good reason to think he has betrayed their trust an acceptable thing for him to do? An answer to this question will emerge in the course of the story; but I raise it here just in order to show how unacceptable Martha's suggestion is. If Jesus now accedes to what Martha is hinting at here, the result will be that Martha will have what she wants together with the belief that she does not rank very high in Jesus' list of priorities. She will settle into the conviction that he cannot be bothered to take any serious interest in ordinary, unimportant people in Bethany, certainly not while the rulers of Israel are next door in Jerusalem. To take Martha's suggestion, then, is to let Martha believe that Jesus has in fact betrayed her trust but that his doing so does not matter very much to him or in the world at large.

For this reason, whether or not Jesus' original plan was acceptable, acceding to Martha's hint is not. On the other hand, of course, it is not clear what Jesus *should* do now in the face of Martha's reaction to him. How could he carry out his original plan now without appearing to accede to Martha's hint?

Martha may put Jesus in a bind, but she is at least still talking to him. And so he talks to Martha in return, in a manner that seems on the face of it to be oblivious to the character of her remarks to him. "Martha," he says, "your brother will rise again." This line asserts a particular implication of what is in the story a general theological truth. In the circumstances, this line is also an unavailing broad hint to Martha on Jesus' part. He knows that Lazarus will rise again in a matter of minutes, as distinct from the general resurrection at some future time. But nothing in the content of Jesus' line *explicitly* recognizes Martha's feelings or addresses her distress, and the trouble between them is not brought out into the open either. Furthermore, in this line Jesus is also still not tipping his hand to Martha; his plan to raise Lazarus then, in a notable public miracle, is something he is still not telling Martha, at least not in any explicit way easy for her to appropriate. From Martha's point of view, then, all that Jesus tells her is a general theological point as it applies to her brother in particular.

So Martha takes Jesus' line, understandably enough, just as a pedestrian piece of preaching. Her response to his line is meant to let him know that she knows this already—though, in fact, she is fishing. Because she is not sure that she really does know what he means, she spells out what she takes him to be saying to see how he will respond. She says to him: "I know that my brother will rise again in the resurrection at the last day." So, in response to Jesus' oracular saying that Lazarus will rise again, Martha does not behave as his disciples sometimes do when they are faced with Delphic pronouncements from Jesus that they do not understand. Martha does not ask him to explain himself further or retire to ponder his meaning. Her overt response consists just in brushing his line aside. Although she is not completely sure that she has in fact understood him, nonetheless, in her view, if he means what she thinks he means by saying that Lazarus will rise again, then his line is not even relevant to the trouble between him and her. And it is certainly an uninteresting reply to her hint that even now God will give Jesus whatever he asks.

So, in the face of Martha's pain and disappointment in him and her hint that he might still do some good now, Jesus has tried to remedy things with a line that bypasses the personal trouble between the two of them and that moves a little way in the direction of the intended miracle: "Your brother will rise again." But Martha's answer to him—which is a version of "I know that already"—shows a disinclination to follow his lead. She will not let the conversation wander away from her opening rebuke to him and her hint. This response of Martha's must be worrying and exasperating to Jesus. From his point of view, his good plan is not working, and she is not playing her part in it, either in general or in this conversation. And so what Jesus says in response to Martha is a speech showing more vehemence and passion than he has so far shown in this story: "I am the resurrection and the life;[89] he who believes in me, even if he dies, shall live, and whoever lives and believes in me shall never die. Do you believe this?"

Martha seems to react to the vehemence of this speech of his, more than to the words themselves, which appear to convey an abstract theological lesson about the conditions for the general resurrection of all those human beings who believe in Jesus. In the context of their conversation, the content of Jesus' speech must be particularly baffling to Martha. Whoever lives and believes in Jesus shall never die—except, of course, that Lazarus believed in him and died, and that state of affairs is the source of the current problem for Martha. But Martha seems impressed with the evident passion of Jesus' speech. It tells her something relevant to her concerns, which are not abstract and theological but intensely personal: she is making an impact on him. The fervor of his words shows that her reaction matters to him. Although he has distressed her deeply, she can distress him, too. And, if she can, then, however he finally explains his apparent neglect of her when she needed him, she has it brought home to her here that he does care very much about her.

Responding to his tone rather than to the content of his words, Martha gives Jesus the appropriate variation on the natural human response to the passion in his speech. She lets him know that, after all, even so, her attachment to him is as strong, or stronger, than it was before: "I do believe in you," she says; "I believe you are the Messiah, the Son of God, the one we were waiting for."

Jesus and Mary

On the strength of this much reconciliation between them, still unexamined and as yet insufficiently understood, Martha has a heart for her sister, sitting at home, not coming to Jesus. The text says that Martha sent word to Mary secretly[90] and told her that Jesus was calling for her to come to him. Augustine supposes the text has just omitted to mention the fact that Jesus had called for Mary,[91] and Calvin thinks that Martha sent the message secretly because she was worried about Jesus' safety, given all the Jews in her house.[92] These interpretations are possible, but they are not at all plausible, in my view. In the circumstances, if Jesus had called for Mary, it would be an important part of the story, and we would expect it to be mentioned explicitly. Furthermore, it is hard to understand why Martha would send a message of that sort secretly. Calvin's conjecture, that she sent it secretly because she was afraid of the Jews in the house, is undermined by the context: the Jews who came in neighborly concern to comfort Lazarus's sisters, well known to be friends of Jesus, were hardly likely to be intent on harming Jesus. In any event, the text shows no evidence elsewhere that Martha had any concerns about Jesus' safety, either because of the people in her house or for any other reason.

In this connection, it is also worth noticing that, although Jesus set out with the purpose of going to Bethany to the house of Mary and Martha and Lazarus, nonetheless after his conversation with Martha he stops his journey and stays where he is. Why does he not continue to their house in Bethany? Why does he stay on the road where he was when Martha met him? If, as Augustine and Calvin thought, Jesus wanted to talk to Mary, why would he not simply continue his journey to Bethany to do so? Presumably, if Jesus continues on the road to Bethany, he will get to Mary much more quickly than if a message from Martha has to make its way back to Mary, and Mary then has to return that same distance, to reach Jesus on the road. And, in any event, why would Jesus want to meet Mary on the road, instead of in the obviously more appropriate and more comfortable place, her home? What purpose would Jesus have for staying put where he was on that road when Martha found him?

In fact, it is hard not to think that Jesus' staying put is an expression of perplexity on his part. Martha's broad hint that he could help them even now has made his raising Lazarus look like an afterthought to compensate for previous indifference. And Mary is simply absent, not coming to greet him, not speaking to him. Jesus has caused both the sisters great pain; it also looks as if he has hurt and alienated one of them very seriously. And so, it seems, Jesus miscalculated how the sisters would react to his failure to come to them. At this point, on the road, it is not clear what he should do, in the face of the sisters' reaction to him. If Jesus does not raise Lazarus now, it looks as if it will be true after the fact that he has betrayed the trust of all three of the siblings. On the other hand, in these circumstances, if he does raise Lazarus, chances are excellent that the sisters will conclude that he had betrayed their trust but was trying to compensate for it by doing this miracle afterwards. And, finally, if he tries to explain to the sisters that he had this great plan in mind for all three of them from the outset, would it be psychologically possible for them to believe him? Or would they always afterwards have a private and very skeptical doubt whether he thought of the miracle only when he saw their reaction to him and understood the depth of their distress? One explanation of Jesus' staying where he is on the road is that he now sees the problem with his plan and is stymied by it.

So, when it comes to Martha's sending Mary a secret message, I am inclined to read this part of the story differently from Calvin and Augustine. I think Martha fibbed. I think Martha understood and loved her sister and wanted to help her toward the comfort of a reconciliation with Jesus. And so, I think, Martha told Mary that Jesus was calling for her when in fact nothing of the sort had happened. Someone who responds to hurt by withdrawing from the person she thinks has hurt her may need the other person to make the first move toward reconciliation. She may need to know that her withdrawal matters to the person from whom she has withdrawn. But Martha apparently does not trust Jesus to understand Mary or to deal with her well in her withdrawal; and so, for love of her sister, she helps Jesus out. "The Master has come and is calling for you," she tells Mary; and she says it secretly because it is not true.

Martha's line has the sort of effect Martha hoped it would have, on my reading of this part of the story: it breaks the ice for Mary, the ice in Mary. The text says that, as soon as Mary heard Martha's message to her, she got up quickly to go to Jesus, with the sort of face that made the people around her think that she was going to the grave to weep. In response to Martha's telling Mary that Jesus is calling for her, Mary hurries to Jesus.

When Mary finds Jesus in the place on the road where he has stopped, she falls at his feet. Calvin sees this act on her part as a gesture indicating her reverence and devotion toward him.[93] But Calvin seems to me to miss the human drama in the scene. In this context, it seems incredible that Mary should be doing the equivalent of kowtowing to Jesus. Mary shares Martha's heartbreak over Jesus' failure to come to them; but, unlike Martha, Mary is not inclined to confront Jesus. When she falls at his feet, she demonstrates her pain in a way different from Martha's direct approach, but at least as expressively. She also avoids looking at Jesus. By that means, she does not abandon withdrawal altogether, which seems to be her mode of coping with pain in relationship.

As Brown remarks, Mary's first words to Jesus are exactly the same as Martha's, at least in their semantic content. "Lord," she says, "if you had been here, my brother would not have died." That is all she says. Unlike Martha, she offers no practical hints. She just weeps. But, although her line is the same as Martha's, her having stayed at home when Martha came to Jesus, her gesture of falling at Jesus' feet and failing to look at him, and her weeping all give her expression of these words to Jesus a very different resonance. Her *words* are the same as Martha's, but the information those words communicate in this context is very different from that conveyed by Martha's use of these words. Furthermore, if we think about Mary's expression of these words from the point of view of Jesus in the story, we can see not only that Mary's words tell Jesus something very different from Martha's words, but that Mary's words also put Jesus in a more difficult position. The expression of pain in Mary's line constitutes a rebuke to Jesus that must hit him harder for being the second time he has heard it from a person he loves. And this time the line comes not from a woman whose suffering has left her still robust enough to confront him. They come from a woman weeping and collapsed in front of him in consequence of what he has done to her.

The reaction of Jesus

Martha exasperates Jesus and inspires him to a passionate speech; but Martha is sensible and practical, and her distress is within bounds. Mary's distress is not; that is why she falls at Jesus' feet when she meets him. The text says that, when Jesus saw her weeping, and the company who had come with her weeping too, he groaned in spirit and was troubled.

As I explained in connection with Brown's interpretation of the story, the Greek verb often rendered 'groaned' here has some connotations of anger. In its noun form, it can indicate indignation. In its root meaning, it can signify the sound horses make when they snort in anger; Aeschylus uses the word this way in *Seven against Thebes*. But, of course, anger comes in various species, ranging all the way from, for example, self-loathing through vexation and annoyance to righteous wrath. What sort of state is being attributed to Jesus at this point in the narrative?

It helps in answering this question to think about Jesus' position here on the road. He is coming to Bethany, surrounded by his expectant and devoted disciples, intending to do a glorious miracle. He finds first Martha, greatly grieved but still practical—only in ways that run cross-grain to his own purposes—and then Mary, weeping, prostrate with pain, and surrounded by her sympathetic neighbors. In these circumstances, it must now be powerfully apparent to Jesus that, while he was waiting expectantly to put his plan for glory into effect, the women were distraught and uncomprehending over his failure to come to their aid. In one sense, Jesus' plan was a good one, full of love for the women and their brother. But at this stage his plan is not working; and it is not working precisely because the women loved and trusted him. At this point in the story, it seems to them, as it must seem to the people around them, that Jesus has betrayed their trust. Seeing Mary heartbroken at his feet, Jesus' disciples must also wonder whether the plan was a good one. Perhaps even Jesus now has a doubt about his plan. Perhaps that is why the story says that, seeing Mary weeping, Jesus was troubled.

If we understand the story in this way, a natural interpretation of the Greek word translated 'groaned' comes to mind. Jesus had a good plan that included bringing glory to these people he loves; but here in the story he is brought up short by the reactions of the women. He has to face the fact that, contrary to his intentions, it is precisely his plan that has left these women he loves heartbroken and alienated from him. Furthermore, his recognition of the problem for his plan comes not in private but in public, with a crowd of his disciples and other people around him, and with a woman at his feet, whose very weeping is a rebuke to him. What sort of reaction *would* a person in his position have in such circumstances?

Some commentators suppose that in groaning Jesus is expressing anger at the women's lack of faith,[94] but that interpretation is blind to the human interplay in this part of the story, which raises questions not about the women's conduct but about *his*. Other interpreters suppose that Jesus is expressing anger over the human condition or over death.[95] But this is to attribute to Jesus an academic leisure for intellectual pain about abstract problems—an utterly implausible attribution in this context, where he has weeping Mary, expectant Martha, distressed neighbors, and wondering disciples to deal with. On the other hand, the human equivalent of a horse's snort of anger is not hard to understand in these circumstances. That sound is the inarticulate vocal indication of a reaction to which ordinary people sometimes give expression with oaths or obscenities. It evinces a tangled mix of dismay, disbelief, disapprobation, and anger at oneself or the circumstances in which one finds oneself.

In any event, groaning and troubled, what Jesus decides to do, perhaps for lack of a better idea, is just to continue with the original plan, although that plan must now have a very different flavor for him. And it is hard to see what else he can do. To Martha who confronts him, he makes an impassioned speech. To Mary's weeping, he makes no answer of any sort.[96] He has nothing to say to her, at least nothing that she could hear and take as comfort now, in this condition. So, without saying anything to Mary, weeping on the ground in front of him, he just turns to the bystanders and asks the necessary question: "Where have you laid him?" They respond to him trustingly and respectfully. "Lord," they say, "come and see." And then Jesus weeps.

Why does he weep? The neighbors of Mary and Martha, who are not among the initiate in the story, think that Jesus is weeping because he loved Lazarus so much, and Lazarus is dead. But this seems to be the one explanation for Jesus' weeping that we can readily rule out. To see the point, consider that, if a man weeps because his friend is dead, that will be either because he is weeping for his friend or because he is weeping for himself (or for himself and others who loved his friend). He is weeping for his friend if he thinks it is very sad that his friend is not living anymore; he is weeping for himself (or for himself and others who loved his friend) if he thinks it is very sad that his friend will not be part of his life (or their lives) anymore. But neither of these reasons for weeping makes any sense in this case. Jesus cannot be weeping for himself or for others who would miss Lazarus, because he knows that in just a few moments Lazarus is going to be with them all again. And he can hardly be weeping for Lazarus. Death is not going to hold Lazarus, because Jesus is going to resurrect him now.

Some interpreters have supposed that Jesus is weeping over the awfulness of death itself; Calvin, for example, suggests that Jesus is weeping for the "common misery of the human race."[97] But this line, too, seems highly implausible. To weep for the common misery, the life of the person weeping needs to be cleared of messy, pressing problems, so that he has the psychological resources to spare for metaphysical sorrow. But Jesus in the narrative is not in that sort of situation; he has urgent problems of his own. Imagine, for example, a professor who is having to deal with one sister rebuking him and another weeping on the floor in front of him, with his undergraduates and graduate students all watching the scene, and one gets something of the right idea. In these circumstances, it is implausible to suppose that Jesus is meditating on the human condition and being brought to tears by his reflections.

Why is he weeping then? Perhaps because part of what goes with a state in which one is troubled and groans as Jesus does is a certain kind of discouragement.[98] (That the Gospel texts are willing to attribute discouragement to Jesus is plain from the story in which Jesus is said to grieve over Jerusalem because he wanted to gather its inhabitants in but they would not come.[99]) Jesus has more than a little reason for discouragement at this point in this story. If his good plan to draw his friends closer to him and make them glorious has resulted in their being alienated from him, how likely is he to be successful in dealing with those many people who are not his friends or are even his enemies? To suggest that he is discouraged in this way is not to attribute self-pity to him, or any variant on self-pity either. There can be discouragement over the failure of one's plans that has nothing of self-pity about it. Consider the kind of discouragement that rescue workers might feel if they could hear the moans and cries of the people buried under rubble, but their best plans to get those people out were failing. A person in such circumstances might well weep, without any suggestion of self-indulgence or any other culpable emotion.[100]

When the crowd around Jesus see him weeping, they respond to him in divergent ways. Some people remark that he must have loved Lazarus very much. Others give vent to a less emotional version of the sisters' line. They say: "Couldn't this man, who opened the eyes of the blind, have brought it about that Lazarus should not have died?" But both sets of remarks are confused or mistaken. Jesus is not weeping over the death of Lazarus, and he does not merit the rebuke that he should have healed Lazarus. For Jesus, who hears what the crowd says, these remarks must also exacerbate what is maddening for him about this situation. At any rate, at this point, the story says that Jesus groaned again.

The events at the tomb

In this state, Jesus comes to the tomb to carry out what is left of his original plan. The plan has not worked as he had trusted it would, but what else can he do now? For him, there is no help for it but to continue with the original plan as far as possible.

Martha, who had hinted at some sort of wonder-working action, has a failure of nerve when they get to the tomb. *I don't know*, she says uneasily to Jesus, in response to his command to take away the stone from the mouth of the tomb. *Do you realize he's been dead for four days? By this time, he stinks.* This is not like opening the eyes of the blind, Martha seems to be suggesting. The body of this dead man will have started to decompose. By now, as far as Martha can see, it would take a *big* miracle to restore Lazarus. And, while Martha believes that God will give Jesus anything he asks, that Jesus is the Messiah, the Son of God, the one they have been waiting for, she is nonetheless anxious about whether he can do anything for a body that has been dead for four days.

Jesus seems almost comforted by this fussy, double-minded anxiety on Martha's part. He has not yet uttered a word addressed to Mary, who seems to be by him but silent. Insofar as Jesus has made any response to Mary, it has been just to proceed, groaning, to do the miracle. But Martha's uneasiness prompts an answer from him: "Didn't I tell you," he says, "that if you would believe, you would see the glory of God?" The line calls Martha's attention to the thought she had been forcibly reminded of by the fervent speech Jesus made to her when she first encountered him on the road to Bethany. But maybe it is also the thought Jesus was hoping that Mary and Martha would rely on in the tough times when he did not come and Lazarus died.

After allowing himself this "didn't I tell you" speech and making a prayer that seems designed to instruct the surrounding crowd, Jesus finally does the miracle. He raises Lazarus. At this point the narrative shifts its focus and describes the subsequent action of the surrounding crowd that has gathered: many of them believed, but some of them went to conspire with the Pharisees against Jesus. The story tells us nothing further about Jesus' interactions with Mary and Martha on this occasion. And it is not an unreasonable speculation to suppose that the story does not say anything more on this score because it means us to understand that there is nothing more to be said. The narrative leads us to imagine that there was overwhelming excitement on everyone's part, but especially on the part of the sisters, to have Lazarus restored.

Besides the excitement, there is also the anxiety generated by the need to get Lazarus out of the grave clothes that bind him. In fact, Jesus calls attention to the grave clothes and the small but important task of removing them from Lazarus. That is, he directs attention away from himself and on to a practical job that is a need of the moment. There is some gentleness in his doing so. It would be churlish on his part, and a blot on the joy of getting Lazarus back, if he were at this moment to make another "didn't I tell you" speech. It is too much to expect Martha and Mary, but especially Mary, to absorb instantly what has happened, moving in no time all the way from heartbreak through relief and reconciliation to understanding and joy. So the story slips Jesus away from the scene, removing him from center stage, and turning that position over to Lazarus, who has a right to it in these circumstances. In doing so, Jesus gives the women time to reflect and meditate on what has happened.

The resolution of the drama

If the story stopped here, it would be frustratingly incomplete. There are so many things one still wants the story to show us. Once Lazarus is restored to his sisters and they reflect on Jesus' actions, how will they feel about Jesus' failure to come to them when they called for help? Were the sisters right to be so distressed by Jesus' failure to come? Was Mary right to be so hurt by Jesus and alienated from him? Was Jesus right in making the plan he did? And then there is the issue of reconciliation. When the sisters are reconciled to Jesus, what form will that reconciliation take? Will they, for example, chalk up their suffering to faults (small or large) on his part and forgive him for them?

The natural end of the story is not at the tomb when Lazarus is raised. It comes only in the next chapter. In that chapter, the immediate excitement generated by the miracle has subsided, and there is a dinner party. The story suggests that this party is not at the home of Lazarus and his sisters but in someone else's house. The narrative remarks that Lazarus was one of those who sat at the table with Jesus, but this would be a somewhat surprising thing to say if the dinner were in Lazarus's own home.[101] In fact, it is worth remarking that of the three of them, Mary, Martha, and Lazarus, *only* Lazarus seems to have a place at the dinner table. Martha is among those who serve the meal. And what about Mary? Mary has brought a large amount of an ointment so expensive that Judas judges it a sinful luxury.[102] With this sinful luxury of ointment, Mary anoints Jesus' feet. And then, as if that act of tenderness were insufficient to express what she feels, she wipes his anointed feet clean on her long hair.[103] Her action is one of love, even of adoration and self-abnegation. Why does Mary do this?

Before she understood his plan, Mary thought that Jesus had betrayed her trust and that therefore, to that extent, he did not love her. But with the raising of Lazarus she must come to see something of the original plan. She must see that Jesus had in mind both giving her the very thing she wanted, her brother Lazarus, and also giving her something beyond her imagination to desire, her own greatness and honor. To understand that plan is also to understand the deep love on his part for her that motivated it.

The recognition that Jesus does, after all, love her might move Mary to some act of devotion. But why the sense of self-abnegation shown by wiping his feet with her hair? Martha (and, for all the story suggests, Lazarus too) had a sense of having been let down by Jesus and then came to understand the plan Jesus had had in mind and the love behind the plan. But neither Martha nor Lazarus seem impelled to any acts of self-abnegation. Why does Mary feel driven to this course of action?

Of the sisters, it was Mary who would not come to meet Jesus until her sister called her; it was Mary who was alienated from him in heartbrokenness, in the belief that he had betrayed her trust. But when we see the whole story, it is not at all clear that Jesus' treatment of Mary constitutes a betrayal of her trust in him, however much it looked that way to Mary. Mary trusted Jesus to love her. In the circumstances, she thought she knew what he had to do if he did love her. Her brother was sick; Jesus was not far away; it would cost him little to get to her; and, if he got to her, he could heal her brother. In those circumstances, she thought that what she wanted more than anything else in the world was that her brother not die; and, if Jesus loved her, she thought, he could not do anything but come in response to her request for help. But he did not come; and so she thought that he did not love her.

But in the narrative it turns out that there are other things Mary herself wants and that she finds more worth having than the healing of Lazarus, although she did not know this fact about herself when Lazarus was sick. The restoring of Lazarus is more worth having, in her own eyes, than the healing she had thought she wanted more than anything else. It gives her Lazarus, as she wanted, in a glory-filled way that she would not have imagined, in a way that connects her more deeply to Jesus than she would have had courage or even imagination to hope for.

When Mary sees the raising of Lazarus in this light, what else will she see? She will see that Jesus formed this plan for her not only because she was dear to him but also because he supposed he could rely on her trust in him. Crucial to his original plan, in other words, was his trust in her, trust to be among those who were specially close to him, whose second-personal connection to him was especially powerful. He trusted her to believe in his love for her and to be committed to closeness with him enough to sustain her in the very bad days when he did not come and Lazarus was dying. But here, clearly, he was wrong about her. Her belief in him and her commitment to him were not strong enough to carry her through the suffering when he did not come.

When we look at the story only from Mary's point of view, we could be forgiven for wondering whether Jesus did not in fact betray her trust. But when we look at the story in its entirety, as Mary will have done after the raising of Lazarus, there is another way to see it. Seen in its entirety, the story shows that, contrary to first impressions, Jesus loved Mary as much as she wanted and more than she knew. She trusted him to love her, and he did not betray that trust. But there was a betrayal of trust—and it was on her part. In effect, Jesus trusted Mary to have toward him the sort of faith that Abraham had in God when he became the father of faith, the faith that in his love for her he would give her the desires of her heart. He trusted her to retain her commitment to him, to hold on to her willingness to be close to him, to believe in his goodness and his love for her, even in the face of Lazarus's death—and she did not. Seen in this way, the story shows Mary not as betrayed but as an unwitting and suffering betrayer.

If Mary comes to see herself in this way, it is easier to understand why she anoints the feet of Jesus and wipes them with her hair. Because she is not sensible, as her sister Martha is, her love is not sensible either. When Jesus did not come, Mary thought he had abandoned her; and she gave up on him, in a way Martha did not. Believing he did not love her, she was heartbroken. And he raised Lazarus after that.

And that is why Mary comes to anoint Jesus' feet and wipe them with her hair.

The end of this story of Mary of Bethany

In focusing on what he takes to be the history of "the Story of Lazarus," Brown sees Lazarus as the main character in the original form of the story, with the parts about Martha the result of later editing and the parts about Mary a still later addition. The main theological emphasis of the original story, as Brown reconstructs it, is on the glory of Jesus and the way in which power over nature manifests that glory. On my interpretation of the story in the form we now have it, however, the emphasis is not on Lazarus but on Martha and, even more so, on Mary. The predominant preoccupation of the narrative in the form we have it is still on glory, but it is the gloriousness of Mary that is at the center of the story's drama.

The sisters were heartbroken when Lazarus died. They must have felt sure that they knew what their heart's desires were, and they must also have felt sure that they had lost them forever. But what the story of Mary of Bethany shows is that a person can feel sure about these things and still be altogether mistaken.

Mary and Martha were not wrong about everything. They wanted to have their brother and to be loved by Jesus, and they were certainly right about the importance of these things to them. But they were mistaken about what the fulfillment of their heart's desires would look like. In that sense and to that degree, neither sister understood the desires of her own heart. Mary and Martha thought that they would have the desires of their hearts only if Jesus healed Lazarus and Lazarus did not die. Consequently, when Lazarus did die, they thought that they had lost what they wanted most. But, when Jesus raised Lazarus from the dead, Mary and Martha had their brother and the love of Jesus in ways more deeply fulfilling to them than those things would have been that they had supposed they wanted above everything. And so, contrary to what they thought they knew, Jesus did not fail them or betray their trust. He was in the process of giving them what they themselves wanted most even as they were firmly persuaded that they had lost it.

Paradoxically, it is the break in Mary's relationship to Jesus, occasioned by Mary's heartbroken suffering at his not coming to heal Lazarus, that is responsible for the power of the connection between Mary and Jesus at the end of the story. The story shows Mary at the feet of Jesus twice. The first time she was weeping despondently. The second time she was anointing his feet in an outpouring of love, overwhelmed by his love of her. There would not have been that second time if Jesus had simply come to heal Lazarus when the sisters sent their message to Jesus. But it is also hard to imagine how to write Mary's story in a way that would bring her to that second occasion at Jesus' feet without that first occasion when she was heartbroken.

We can see the last part of the narrative's artistry by recognizing that, in her action of self-abnegation and love, Mary does fulfill Jesus' original plan for her, although not in the way originally intended. In her act of anointing his feet and wiping them with her hair, she is glorious—in fact, more glorious than she would have been if things had gone as originally planned. Martha, who is sensible, did not separate herself so thoroughly from Jesus because of his failure to come to them, and therefore her turning back to him is sensible also. But Mary withdrew from him in her heartbreak; and her turning back to him after she understands him is equally passionate—unsensible, unrestrained, unstinting.[104] Even images of that fervent disciple Peter at his most generous are no match for this picture of Mary, with her hair down, heedless, anointing his feet in an outpouring of love. And so, the narrative suggests, although Jesus' original plan went wrong in one sense, in another, more complicated sense, it could not have been more successful.[105]

To say this is not to offer a theodicy for Mary's suffering; it is only to explicate the story. For theodicy, we want to know, in effect, whether the suffering was worth the prize it brought; and I am reserving that issue for the later chapters.

Another story of anointing

Martha's confronting Jesus expresses her sense that in not coming to help her in her need Jesus had behaved wrongly to her. When one person confronts another, she does so because she is seeking from him both some confession of his injustice against her and also some reparation for it. That is why confrontation is one path to reconciliation. Mary's sense of betrayal leaves her with a feeling that Jesus has not dealt with her as she wanted him to do, and her withdrawal from him is meant to prompt something on his part, too. Her withdrawal is also a means to reconciliation. But, unlike confrontation, withdrawal is not primarily seeking reparation for wrong done. Rather, it is looking for any sign on the part of the person from whom one has withdrawn that the withdrawal is causing him pain. If Paula confronts Jerome, she suggests in effect that he has been deficient in the first desire of love, for the good of the beloved. But, if Paula withdraws from Jerome, she evinces her feeling that he is in effect deficient in the second desire of love: he does not desire her as Paula wishes he would. When Mary withdraws from Jesus and weeps, she gives expression to her sorrowing sense that she does not matter to him, that he does not have a heart for her.

Of course, a person could engage in withdrawal from someone on purpose in order to try to manipulate the desires of that other person. But Mary's withdrawal is not manipulative. There is something simple about manipulation; Mary's condition is more complicated. On the one hand, as her actions make clear, she does not want to see Jesus. (Perhaps she is miserable enough that she even wants not to want to see him.) On the other hand, she has enough desire for Jesus that she wants him to desire to see her. That is why, when she thinks he is calling for her, she hurries to him. As Mary's alternation of withdrawal and hurrying to Jesus indicates, in withdrawing from him Mary is not giving up on him. On the contrary, she responds fast to the first sign that she has elicited in him some desire for her. But she comes to him only to fall at his feet weeping, not to look at him, not to be seen by him. And so she continues to withdraw from him even as she comes to him.

When Mary says to Jesus, "if you had been here, my brother would not have died," she, like Martha, rebukes him with that line. But her weeping and withdrawal show that, unlike Martha, she finds the explanation for his lack of love for her not in some deficiency in him but rather in herself. *She* has been insufficient to evoke from him the care she wished for from him. In an earlier chapter, I summarized the nature of shame by saying that a person who feels shamed believes it would be appropriate for others to reject not her good but *her*. She believes that those others would be warranted in repudiating a desire for her; that is part of the reason why a person suffering from shame wants not to be seen. As reflection on Mary's reaction to Jesus on the road shows, then, one source of Mary's suffering is the kind of shame a person feels when she believes she does not matter to someone who matters to her.

Shame is even more central in the story about a woman's anointing of Jesus that is found in the Gospel of Luke. Every Gospel has a story of a woman's anointing Jesus. It is widely agreed, however, that the anointing described in the story in the Gospel of Luke cannot be conflated with that described in the other three Gospels. The timing of the events in the Lucan story by itself is enough to make most interpreters, including the Patristic and medieval commentators, deny the possibility of such a conflation.[106] Summarizing a common view in the scholarship on the different anointing stories, Brown says that the stories of the anointing in Matthew and Mark and the story of the anointing by Mary of Bethany in John are in some sense intended to describe the same events,[107] but that these three stories have to be differentiated from the anointing story in Luke.

On the other hand, however, as Brown also points out, there are undeniable similarities between the anointing story in Luke and the anointing stories in the three other Gospels. As Brown explains: "No one really doubts that John and Mark are describing the same scene; yet, many of the details in John are like those of Luke's scene."[108]

As far as that goes, many of the details in the anointing story in Luke can *also* be found in the anointing stories in Mark and Matthew, too. For example, in both the story in the Gospel of Luke and that in the Gospel of Mark, a woman anoints Jesus while Jesus is at dinner in the house of someone named 'Simon;' and in each Gospel, the very expensive ointment is contained in a precious jar made of alabaster. So although, on the consensus view, the events described in the anointing story in Luke cannot be the same as the events described in the anointing stories in the other three Gospels, some details in the story in Luke can be found in the other stories as well.

Because the relations among the anointing stories in the four Gospels are thus complicated, and there is controversy about how to interpret the similarities and differences among them, I want to proceed by first considering the anointing story in Luke taken in isolation from all the other anointing stories.

It will be helpful in this case also to have the story before us. Here it is, in the translation of the Anchor Bible commentator on Luke:

7. [36] Then one of the Pharisees invited Jesus to dine with him; he went to the Pharisee's house and reclined at table. [37] Now there was a certain woman in the town known to be a sinner. When she learned that Jesus was at table in the Pharisee's house, she got an alabaster flask of perfume, [38] and went and stood crying at his feet. Her tears bathed his feet, and with the hair of her head she wiped them dry; she kissed them and anointed them with the perfume. [39] The Pharisee who had invited him watched all this and thought to himself, "If this man were really a prophet, he would know who this is and what sort of woman is touching him—seeing that she is a sinner." [40] But Jesus spoke up to him, "Simon, I have something to say to you." "Teacher," he says, "say it." [41] "A certain moneylender had two debtors. One owed him five hundred pieces of silver, the other fifty. [42] Since they could not pay it back, he graciously cancelled both debts. Now which of them should love him more?" [43] Simon replied, "I suppose, the one for whom he cancelled the greater debt." Jesus said to him, "You are right." [44] And turning to the woman, he said to Simon, "You see this woman? I came into your house, and you offered me no water for my feet; yet she has bathed my feet with her tears and wiped them dry with her hair. [45] You gave me no kiss of welcome; yet ever since I arrived, she has not stopped kissing my feet. [46] You did not freshen my face with oil, yet she has anointed my feet, and with perfume. [47] For this reason, I tell you, her sins, many though they are, have been forgiven, seeing that she has loved greatly. But the one to whom little is forgiven loves little." [48] Then Jesus said to her, "Your sins are forgiven." [49] And the guests who reclined at table with him began to say to themselves, "Who is this who even forgives sins?" [50] Again he said to the woman, "Your faith has brought you salvation; go in peace."[109]

The dinner party

This, then, is the anointing story in the Gospel of Luke. It is set in the house of a Pharisee named 'Simon,' who has the social and financial resources to invite a guest such as Jesus to dinner and have that guest accept. It is not clear who else is invited to this dinner, but it is clear who is not. The party is crashed by an unnamed woman, who simply makes her way into Simon's house and interrupts his dinner by attaching herself to the guest of honor. This is a bold, not to say brassy, thing for her to do. The narrative brings this point home by the way in which it identifies the woman: the narrative reveals her status, but not her name. Given that status, it is not surprising that the narrative omits the name. According to the narrative, the woman is an inhabitant of the same town as Simon; and, in that town—that is, the town in which she and other participants at the dinner live—she is known as a sinner. It will be less clumsy in what follows if this unnamed woman has a name by which we can refer to her; and so, for ease of reference, I will refer to her by the story's identification of her. I will call her 'Sinner.'

In the history of interpretation of this story, some interpreters have been swift to suppose that they knew exactly what kind of sinner Sinner was. They supposed she was a prostitute. There is certainly some evidence in the story to support this view. Simon looks askance at Jesus for allowing this woman to touch him. In fact, Simon thinks that the only reason Jesus would allow her to touch him is that Jesus, who is not an inhabitant of the town, does not know who this woman is. If Jesus knew, Simon supposes, Jesus would shrink from her touch. That is why Simon takes the willingness of Jesus to let Sinner touch him as evidence that Jesus is not a prophet. If Jesus had the knowledge of a prophet, Simon thinks, Jesus would make sure Sinner had no physical contact with him. So Simon takes the sort of sin Sinner is known for as the kind that defiles and degrades her. Her sin is such that socially respectable people who know about it fear contracting defilement just from being touched by her. As some recent feminist scholarship has highlighted, defilement that can be contracted by touch in this way is frequently taken to have a sexual connection.[110]

But, whatever the narrative means us to understand about the nature of her sin, the sort of sin for which Sinner is known in her community, on the narrative's own showing, is the kind that makes her a pariah in that community. The respectable people, the nice people, avoid touching her so as not to be defiled by her. So, Sinner lives in her community as a publicly shamed person. Furthermore, her shame is something for which her community blames her. In the story, it is her own doing, her sinning, that has made Sinner shunned by religiously respectable people such as Simon the Pharisee. Sinner's shame will therefore be complicated for her by guilt, at least felt guilt; and there will be a synergistic effect of the guilt and the shame.

If there is to be any healing of her shame for Sinner, it will be correspondingly complicated. It cannot consist just in forgiveness for guilt, even God's forgiveness, because Sinner's shame will remain even if her guilt is gone. Certainly, repentance on Sinner's part and reform of the source of the guilt in her life will not be enough for the people in her community to include her on their lists of guests for dinner. The sort of thing that healed the shame of the Elephant Man, for example—that the Queen herself wanted to be a guest in *his* home—will not help Sinner.[111] Since her shame stems from her past sinful activities, and since the past remains in the present at least through memory, Sinner will continue to suffer from shame even if she finds a remedy for guilt, because people in her community will remember what she was and will continue to shrink from her in consequence.[112] If there is a spectrum of religious status and social respectability, then Simon the Pharisee and Sinner are at opposite ends of it.

It must, therefore, be an act of almost desperate courage for a person shamed as Sinner is to break into Simon's dinner party for an honored guest. But, of course, this is only the beginning of what is courageous and remarkable about Sinner's actions. Sinner, who is in Simon's house as an uninvited, unwanted social pariah, goes on to make a public spectacle of herself at the dinner. If it is true that shamed people want to try to make themselves invisible to avoid the gaze of others, Sinner must be violating very strong desires of her own, as well as strong wishes of Simon's, in what she does at the dinner party.

Although Sinner's passionate reaction to Jesus argues that she knows something about who he is and what he teaches, there seems to have been no previous personal relationship between Sinner and Jesus; there seems to have been nothing that warrants Sinner's approaching Jesus in any personal way. Nonetheless, in Simon's house, Sinner treats Jesus in ways that would be worrisomely inappropriate if the two of them were in private. In public, they are simply scandalous. She weeps over the feet of Jesus. With a lotion that is outrageously expensive, brought in a container that is also outrageously expensive, she anoints his feet. And then she wipes his feet clean with her hair. Except for the sound of her weeping, she is silent. Maybe she does not know what to say; maybe she does not trust anyone to understand anything she could find to say. So she says nothing; she just weeps. She is at his feet, as the shamed woman that she is; but she anoints his feet and kisses them, in an act of adoration, close to him and intimate with him. Her actions are inappropriate, extravagant, wild. She is shamed and shameless at once.[113]

The giving and receiving of anointing

It must be evident to Sinner in advance that she will suffer for her actions at Simon's dinner party. How will respectable people describe her to one another after the fact? If she was shamed before, she will be shamed and notorious after this. So why does she do this? Why would she crash a Pharisee's dinner party and behave in this shameless way toward the guest of honor? Why would she *want* to do this?

We can begin trying to answer these questions by asking another. Why is Sinner weeping?

In explaining to Simon what he takes to be Sinner's motivation for her action, Jesus remarks just on the fact that Sinner's actions express very great love for Jesus. There is more than one way in which great love prompts weeping, however. As John's story of Mary of Bethany reminds us, sometimes a person weeps over someone she loves greatly because she is cut off from that person, by death or by betrayal (real or imagined). But a reason of this sort cannot be the explanation of Sinner's weeping. Sinner's anointing of Jesus is not the action of a woman who feels herself distant from the person she loves. On the contrary, her action is intimate and familiar—that is in fact part of what is scandalous about it. So why then is she weeping?

It helps in this connection to remember that people weep not only over bad news but also over good news. It is possible for people, especially those at the lower end of the social scale, to become accustomed to living in unending bad news. They learn to harden their hearts to the steady stream of suffering in their lives; they protect themselves against pain by becoming tough. When good comes unexpectedly to a person in this condition, it can crack her heart. If it does, it will make her feel the sorrows to which she had become dulled. It will also make her feel unexpected relief and gratitude, because against all hope there is this unlooked-for good and its tantalizing promise that there might be more good to come. All these things can bring tears with them. When a mother finds at her door, totally unexpected, a son she had long thought was dead, she will surely weep over him.

If we think of Sinner's tears along these lines, as the overflowing of a heart cracked by some unaccustomed good that she herself somehow associates with Jesus, then it is easier to understand both her tears and her actions. Her actions are certainly those of a person accustomed to being shamed. It is hard to imagine the respectable Simon drying anybody's feet with the hair of his beard. No doubt, he would find such an action inconceivable for him; the humiliation of it would be intolerable.[114] But Sinner is at home in her shame, and she uses her shame itself as a kind of gift to give to Jesus in return for what she feels she has found in him. The self-abnegation of her drying his feet on her hair is the means by which she expresses her honoring of him. The expense of the costly container of precious perfumed ointment, heedlessly spent on him, demonstrates the magnitude of her gratitude toward him, and her estimation of the greatness of the gift she takes herself to have received from him, for which she is returning what good she can.

Sinner treats Jesus as she does, then, because she loves him greatly, as Jesus explains to Simon. And she loves him because she has come to understand him as a person who will not reject her, who will not disdain her as the shamed person she is. She is entirely correct in this estimation of him, as the unfolding events of the story make clear. So Sinner loves Jesus because, somehow, in some sense, however inchoately, she understands that he loves her—not in the way Samson loved Delilah, which is quite compatible with causing her harm and shame, but in the strenuous sense of love, which seeks the real good of the one loved. The unexpected gift of this good is what causes her to weep. It should not be missed in this connection that her action of love and abnegation toward Jesus is fundamentally an act of cleansing him, as Jesus himself points out when he describes it to Simon. Defilement is at the heart of some kinds of shame, especially that kind that people feel can be caught by contact.

Defilement of this sort can feel to the shamed person as if it is impossible to wash away. Sinner washes Jesus' feet, with her expensive perfumed ointment and with her self. Maybe this action suggests itself to her because she feels, somehow, cleansed by him. This interpretation of Sinner's actions and motivations is strongly confirmed by Jesus' reaction to her.

In thinking about his reaction to her, the first thing to notice is that, while Sinner is anointing his feet, Jesus is doing nothing. The process of cleaning his feet with tears, ointment, and hair must take some time. During that time, Jesus is simply a passive recipient of action on Sinner's part. This is certainly not his normal manner. In the Gospel stories, he is portrayed as intensely active: teaching, exhorting, rebuking, commissioning, calling, doing miracles. Doing nothing is not his usual style. Furthermore, doing nothing in these circumstances at Simon's dinner party must take a considerable effort of will on Jesus' part. Sinner is, after all, making Jesus the centerpiece in a spectacle that causes the onlookers to cringe inwardly. Jesus could abort the whole messy and embarrassing process, which the onlookers think is degrading to him, by jumping up at the outset to preach to Sinner or about her.

It is easy to see, however, that Jesus protects Sinner precisely by being passive. By being willing to receive care from her, especially care of this socially unacceptable sort, Jesus honors her. As the narrative's report of Simon's thought to himself makes clear, Simon would never have allowed Sinner to touch him in those ways. Because Jesus, with his standing in this community, does allow Sinner to touch him as she chooses, in her extravagant and shameless way, he invalidates the judgment of her made by people like Simon.

Of course, Simon supposes that Jesus simply does not know who Sinner is. But Jesus' speech to Simon makes sure that everyone at the dinner table, and especially Simon, understands that Jesus certainly does know the nature of the woman who has been kissing his feet and anointing them. In fact, Jesus' speech to Simon is meant to teach that, as between Sinner and Simon, in Jesus' view Sinner outranks Simon by some ultimate measure of human excellence. Jesus grants that the sins of Sinner outweigh the sins of Simon (thereby implying that Simon, too, has sins). But the point of this concession on Jesus' part is to call attention to a measure of excellence deeper and more significant than the standard that weighs sins. Sins can be forgiven, and the love of the suffering sinner is what effects that forgiveness, which in its turn fans further love. A dynamic relationship of love between the sinner and the one competent to forgive sins is the ultimate measure of excellence.

That Jesus says such things about Sinner to Simon, in front of all those at the dinner, including Sinner herself, also honors Sinner. Jesus makes it clear to all his audience that he himself holds Sinner in higher esteem than he holds Simon, his host, who is able to have dinner parties and who is unwilling to touch Sinner. And we should not miss the way in which Jesus makes this relative ranking of Simon and Sinner. He begins his speech about Sinner by engaging in Socratic dialectic with Simon. The first ranking of excellence that privileges Sinner over Simon is actually uttered by Simon, who is sheepdogged into that utterance by Jesus' questions to him. If Simon grants the point to

Jesus in front of his guests and Sinner herself, it will be correspondingly much harder for Simon not to honor Sinner in future.[115]

Healing shame

We should not miss the fact that, up to the end of this part of his conversation with Simon, Jesus has as yet addressed no remark to Sinner. The first move toward any recognition on Jesus' part of Sinner, at his feet, anointing them and kissing them, occurs after Simon's response to Jesus, after Simon's implicit concession to Jesus regarding the relative ranking of himself and Sinner. At that point, although Jesus begins the next part of his conversation just with Simon, the narrative says that Jesus turned to the woman while he talked to Simon. Apparently, then, we are to imagine that, before this point in the narrative, in the earlier part of his conversation with Simon, Jesus has had his face turned away from Sinner. Only when Simon grants the point that in effect honors Sinner does Jesus first look at her. And even then Jesus does not talk to *her*. Here is the progression of events then. Jesus first talks to Simon (indirectly, in parables) about Sinner without looking at her. Then he looks at Sinner but talks (directly) about her just to Simon. (If at this point Sinner looks at Jesus in return, then there is shared attention between Sinner and Jesus while Jesus is talking to Simon about her.) Only after this does Jesus finally address Sinner directly.

If a shamed person has a hard time enduring the gaze of others, if Sinner has plunged into the dinner party and her actions at it, reckless of herself, then Jesus' abstaining first from looking at her and then from addressing her gives her a chance to catch her breath and regain her balance before Jesus speaks to her directly. Sinner's second-person encounter with Jesus comes by degrees, as it were, with Jesus' presence to her increasing as the events at the dinner unfold. Because of this slow progress toward mutual presence of each of them to the other, Sinner is given a chance to compose herself. When she has taken the opportunity offered her in this way to quiet herself, even if it is only a little, then Jesus not only looks at her but talks to her, and just to her. There is a kind of tender care for her in this indirection and incremental movement toward connection between them. It is the opposite of the callousness that the shamed so often experience.

The way in which Jesus treats Sinner in the progression of events before he begins to talk to her herself goes a long way toward healing her shame. But, as I explained above, one of Sinner's problems is that her shame is tangled with guilt; at least, her community attributes guilt to her, and the guilt is over things that defile her. The communal memory of her defiling guilt could easily rekindle shame for her in chronic ways, without ceasing, even after Jesus' public care for her at this dinner.

What Jesus says to Sinner when he addresses her directly, in front of all the other guests, is the help for this problem. When Jesus does finally speak to Sinner herself in this public setting, he says only two things to her. The first is, "Your sins are forgiven." The other guests at dinner wonder inwardly who he is to forgive sins. But, even if we take this as a skeptical thought on their part, it remains the case that Jesus, who has special religious status of a sort significant enough to be invited as guest of honor to Simon the Pharisee's dinner, this Jesus has told Sinner that her sins are forgiven. So, whether Jesus is engaged in a performative act in telling her that her sins are forgiven or whether he is simply describing what he believes to be the case, either way he puts his own honor behind the claim that the book on her sins is closed. Her sins are forgiven; and, as forgiven, they are over and done. Her slate is clean now.

The final part of his care for her is in the last thing he says to her: "Your faith has saved you. Go in peace."

With the first sentence of this small two-sentence speech, Jesus tells Sinner with authority that she is rescued. The past is over, and a new time is beginning for her, in which she has a new status. Whatever exactly it is to be saved, it is certainly meant to be something excellent and admirable, the antithesis of shame and guilt. In this regard, it is also worth noticing Jesus' assignment of responsibility for her rescue. His line asserts that she is saved by faith, presumably by her faith in him; and so he might have called attention to his own role in her salvation. But what he in fact says is *"Your faith* has saved you." And so he attributes to Sinner the credit for the new status she has. In this attribution, he honors her, too.

With his second sentence, Jesus gets Sinner out of the spot she is in. "Go in peace," he tells her—thereby helping her get herself out of Simon's house. By this point in the story, she must be as confused about how to make her exit from that dinner party as she is eager to do so. Jesus' words give her the opportunity she needs. His words are not only her exit line, but they are also her comfort. They are an imperative from him to her for her to be at peace. Surely, she will be grateful for this help to peace, given the excitement she herself has made at this dinner.

In his reactions to Sinner at the dinner party, then, Jesus gives Sinner's present shame over the past defilement produced in her by her sins the complicated remedy it needs. Jesus receives in public Sinner's socially unacceptable ministrations to him, her profligate and unconstrained care for him. In receiving it, he honors her; and in what he says about her to Simon, he honors her over Simon. Jesus sees to it that Simon participates in this honoring of her, too, and that the whole affair is a matter of public record. And then he separates for her the past from the present by putting 'forgiven' over the past sins so that they cannot serve to shame her now. In all these ways, he heals her shame and her suffering over it.

Jesus' last lines to her finish the story. They announce and illustrate her new status, and they praise her for it. And so they also comfort her for acting riotously in order to get this new status and the connection to Jesus, which is its source. By this means, they help her to quiet herself, and they get her out the door of somebody else's house so that she can finish quieting down in her own quarters. The tender care for her that characterizes all Jesus' dealings with her in this story finds its final expression here. We should not miss the fact that this tenderness on his part also honors her. She is the object of public care on the part of the guest of honor at the dinner, and so she is honored indeed.

Earlier, in describing Sinner's actions, crashing the party and making a public spectacle of herself where she is not wanted, I asked how the respectable people at the party would describe her to one another after the fact. It is worth asking that question again now. In the course of the events at the dinner, Sinner has not ceased to be herself; in this story, in this community, one might say, she is still 'Sinner.' But this designation, whose source is the narrative's sole identification of her, takes on different connotations as the events of the story unfold. By the end of the story, as all those at the dinner cannot help seeing, Sinner has been shown to be someone worthy of more regard than the dinner's host. She is held in more honor by Jesus, the guest of honor, than Simon is.

And so even the pejorative designation 'Sinner' in the end assumes a different connotation. In her courage, in her tears, in her reckless actions, in her loving Jesus, and in her being loved so gently by him in return, she looks beautiful. Her shame does not disappear exactly. But, by the events at the dinner, that shame becomes woven into a larger narrative of her life that makes her worthy of great admiration. The peace Jesus exhorts her to have as she leaves will come to her in consequence of this healing of shame for her. The internal fragmentation and self-loathing characteristic of shamed people will give way in the face of the memory of Jesus' treatment of her in front of all those guests at the dinner. Because Jesus honored her, and in that public way, Sinner will have been shown how to know herself, not by the local community measure that has shamed her, but by a deeper and more important measure that honors her. In the memory of the measure shown her by Jesus, she will learn the honor of herself, which is a necessary ingredient of her peace.

A stereoscopic view

There is undoubtedly a great deal more that could be said about this story in the Gospel of Luke. With regret, I have left unremarked more than one part of the story well worth commenting on; and I have said nothing at all about the way in which this story is read by other contemporary or historical interpreters. But this brief examination of the story is enough for my purposes. On the interpretation I have given here, the story is beautifully illustrative of the suffering shame can bring and also of the remedies for shame.[116] The story is therefore well worth considering in its own right in connection with the problem of suffering.

But I also want to ask what happens if we combine the two anointing stories, this one from Luke's Gospel and the one from the Gospel of John examined at length earlier. I share the view implicit in Brown's commentary on the story from the Gospel of John that it can be instructive to interpret the portrayal of Mary of Bethany in John's Gospel in the light of episodes in Luke's Gospel. What I want to ask now, however, is what happens if we add the Lucan story of anointing to the narrative of Mary of Bethany in John's Gospel. What does the narrative of Mary of Bethany look like if we take Sinner to be Mary of Bethany?

As I said at the outset, I explicitly *repudiate* the affirmation of the claim that Sinner is Mary of Bethany. By saying that I repudiate the affirmation of that claim, I do not wish to be understood as accepting its negation. On the contrary, my own strong inclination is to identify the women in the two stories. But I have neither the desire nor the space to argue the case for this inclination. And so in this chapter I will abstain from *any* judgment as regards the identification. In this chapter, I want to ask only this: *if* Sinner were the same person as Mary of Bethany, how would this identification alter the interpretation of the story of Mary's anointing of Jesus in the Gospel of John? Having examined each of the two anointing stories at issue here in isolation, I now want to explore how the interpretation of the story in the Gospel of John would be altered *if* it were to be the case that the woman anointing Jesus in that story were the same person as the woman anointing him in the story in the Gospel of Luke.

Because I am officially abstaining from judgment about the identification of the women in the two stories, the interpretation that will result from combining those stories is not one that I affirm as the correct interpretation of the narrative of Mary of Bethany.[117] I do offer it as an interpretation of the narrative of Mary of Bethany, but only conditionally: this interpretation *would* constitute the correct interpretation of the larger narrative of the life of Mary of Bethany *if* Sinner were in fact Mary of Bethany.

In the final part of this book, when I consider the problem of suffering in connection with shame, I will reflect on the two anointing stories in the Gospel of John and in the Gospel of Luke taken in isolation from each other. But I will also consider the larger narrative formed by combining them, understanding always that that larger narrative has to be taken conditionally, since the identification of the women in the stories is taken only conditionally.

So suppose that Sinner is Mary of Bethany.[118]

We can begin the interpretation based on this supposition with a consideration of the ordering of events. On interpretations of the Gospels as different as Augustine's and Raymond Brown's, the anointing of Jesus in the Gospel of Luke is much earlier than the episode of the anointing after the raising of Lazarus. The narrative of the anointing in the Gospel of Luke makes it clear that, before Mary of Bethany (Sinner, that is) crashes the dinner party, she has not been among the people close to Jesus. For these reasons among others, it seems right to read Mary's shameless actions in the story in Luke as marking the start of her personal relationship with Jesus. The supposition that Sinner is Mary of Bethany, then, yields a natural reading of the verse in John 11 that identifies Mary of Bethany as the woman who anointed Jesus. On this supposition, that verse is not a misplaced, forward-looking reference to Mary's anointing of Jesus after the resurrection of Lazarus; rather, it is a backward-looking reference to an earlier anointing of Jesus that was noteworthy enough that Mary of Bethany can be identified by mention of it.

If we compare that beginning of the relationship between Mary and Jesus to the relationship between them in the story in John, then it is clear that, after that riotous start described in Luke, the connection between Mary and Jesus developed progressively until Mary and her sister and brother became among the close friends of Jesus. In the only other incident recorded about Martha and Mary in the Gospels, Martha is busy preparing a meal for Jesus and his disciples, and Mary is determined to be among those listening to Jesus as he teaches. When Martha wants Jesus to send Mary out to the kitchen to help her, Jesus makes sure that nothing will separate Mary from him if she wants to be by him. On that occasion, too, Jesus protects her.[119]

Thinking of the relationship between Jesus and Mary as having this beginning and this past sheds a very different light on the shyness the sisters show in their message to Jesus about the sickness of Lazarus. It is one thing to be the friend of a great person if you yourself are only ordinary. It is another thing entirely for a person such as Mary of Bethany, who was Sinner, to believe that her needs will count as important in Jesus' world, given the difference between his status and position and her own. And this will be so for Mary even if Jesus often visits Mary and Martha or often honors them specially by coming to dinner at their house. In the fairy-tale story of Rapunzel, Rapunzel is greatly beloved of the Prince who comes to visit her frequently in her tower. He visits frequently, but somehow he never seems to think of bringing a ladder with him when he comes. No doubt, in the course of the Prince's visits to her tower, Rapunzel will come to believe that the prince loves her very much. But eventually, if she has any mind at all, she will also come to suspect that she is important to the Prince *only* in her tower, and not also in the castle where the Prince lives his official life. *That* is why he never brings a ladder. What would a strange thing like Rapunzel do in the court life at the castle? What would the Prince do with her if she showed up there? And so Rapunzel will come to believe both that she is very important to the Prince (as the person he is in her tower) and that she does not matter to him (as the prince he is in the castle).

Given Mary's background and the way in which her relationship with Jesus began, we can see that it must be easy for Mary to be double-minded in this sort of way. Mary's past shamed status will still be there in the background of her mind. However much she believes that Jesus loves her and her sister and brother, her past will greatly exacerbate in her own mind the difference between her position in her world and that of Jesus. It will, therefore, be easy for her to fall into a Rapunzel-like attitude toward Jesus. And so the double-mindedness and indirection of the message the sisters send Jesus have a special poignancy if that message is taken in the context of the story of the beginning of Mary's relationship with Jesus, on the supposition I am here exploring, that Sinner is Mary of Bethany.

Jesus' plan for the raising of Lazarus has a different flavor against this background, too. It is one thing for a shamed person to be honored in defiance of community standards by someone such as Jesus. It is another thing entirely to make such a person the recipient of a center-stage miracle, which manifests the kind of power over nature that can only have its source in the divine. After the way in which Jesus treats Mary at Simon's dinner, Mary will have acquired a new respectable status in her community, in consequence of being protected and honored by Jesus. But, after the miracle, Mary and her brother and sister become the kind of people whom strangers want to come to see, in wonder and awe.[120]

And so it may be that Jesus picks Mary, Martha, and Lazarus as recipients of this miracle just because Mary has the history of shame she does. Jesus' defiance of the community that disdains Mary, shown by his treatment of her during Simon's dinner party, might not have found its final outlet just in rebuking those who reject her. Maybe because of her suffering as shamed in her community, he has a special desire for glory for her, and for her brother and sister, too.

On the other hand, the misery of the sisters when Jesus does not come has a more poignant quality against the background of the story in Luke, too. There will be a wretchedness for Mary in particular as she waits for him in vain. Of all the people in her community (no doubt, aside from her brother and sister), he was the one she most trusted to care for her and love her. His apparent betrayal will therefore strike her very hard. It will seem to her as if her whole new world has evaporated; it will be hard for her not to suppose that, after all, she is still Sinner, even to him, even now. His failure to come to her in her need will, therefore, leave her shamed in a painful new way that also has something old and familiar about it. It will hit her on the raw.

That Mary is much more alienated from Jesus than Martha is when Jesus fails to come to them is now easier to understand. It is also easy to understand how Jesus could weep as he sees what has happened in the face of his plan. It is not hard to see why he would be troubled over Mary's heartbreak. Who would not wish that *this* woman might be spared this kind of pain? Who would not weep if he himself were the unwilling source of it?

But, for these same reasons, Mary will be overwhelmed when, with the raising of Lazarus, she sees how wrong she was about Jesus' love of her. When she understands his original plan and sees that it was designed to make her—her, the shamed wom-an—glorious, she will surely feel what she felt about him at the very beginning, at that dinner at Simon's house, only much more so, because she is now learning the lesson of his love for her in the context of her history with him and her experience of him. It makes sense, then, that Mary's reaction to the raising of Lazarus is so passionate and so much more intense than that of Martha (or Lazarus).

On this way of reading the story, Mary chooses anointing to express her response to Jesus after the raising of Lazarus because of the way her relationship with Jesus began. What her action of anointing Jesus after the raising of Lazarus is, then, is a function not only of what she actually does in anointing Jesus then but also of what she did on that earlier occasion at Simon's house. This second anointing is what it is partly because of all the resonance between it and the anointing that was the origin of the personal connection between Mary and Jesus. After the raising of Lazarus, in a public setting, at a dinner party, Mary anoints the feet of Jesus with a very expensive ointment and wipes his feet with her hair—reliving and recreating the beginning of her turning toward him in love and receiving love from him in return. (It is *not* part of my conditional interpretation to identify Simon as well as anointing women. But it is hard to leave unremarked the fact that in Matthew and Mark the name of the person in whose house Mary performs this second act of anointing is 'Simon.')

It is notable that on this occasion after the raising of Lazarus Jesus also just receives Mary's ministrations to him. He is not active with regard to her; rather, she is active in giving care to him. This time, however, Jesus is only silent. Her action speaks for itself this time. (In the corresponding stories in Matthew and Mark, when Jesus does speak, it is only to protect the woman anointing him, this time not against those who disdain her as shameful but against those who find her actions toward him excessive and profligate in the expenditure of funds for the ointment. He will not let her be put down or put away for the manner in which she chooses to express her love and gratitude to him.)

The wildness in Mary's actions on the first occasion of her anointing him, in Simon's house, is still there in this second anointing, after the raising of Lazarus; but it has a new form now. On this second occasion, Mary's actions are not scandalous. Rather, they express her understanding of Jesus' plan, her recognition of his love for her, and her love of him in return; and they are set in the context of her ongoing history of relationship with Jesus. Those who know her story, and that must be virtually all of those present on this second occasion of anointing, will understand her action as a re-enactment of her first anointing. Her repeating of her original anointing is, therefore, a recommitment to Jesus, and in a deeper way. Mary picks this way of expressing her reaction to his raising of Lazarus because the as-it-were liturgy of the repetition gives weight to her act. The unrestrained abandon she showed in her original anointing had its loveliness, but it had an out-of-control character about it as well. In the second anointing, because she is choosing in quiet to recreate her earlier action, there is not only control but also power behind the unrestrained character of what she does. It is hard to imagine her being double-minded or uncertain about his love of her after this. There is nothing disorderly in her psyche or her behavior in this second anointing. The surrender of love of her action has an authority about it, as we can recognize by considering how very different the reactions of the onlookers must be this time. The first time Mary anointed Jesus, the other guests must have been a bit afraid of her, wondering what else this crazy woman was likely to do. This time the onlookers will be a little in awe of her. The courage behind her action this time is not desperate; it has strength and discipline in it now. This time the story does *not* say that she wept when she anointed him.

In this anointing, then, Mary manifests the glory Jesus planned for her, in both senses of glory. Her standing in her community is here the mirror image of what it was when she anointed his feet the first time. And there is now something luminous and great about her. She is very different now from the frightened but fierce, shamed, and shameless person she was when she anointed Jesus the first time. Now she is both powerful and lovely.

So this is the narrative of Mary of Bethany[121]—if we identify the Mary in the story of the raising of Lazarus in the Gospel of John with the anonymous woman in the story of the anointing of Jesus in the Gospel of Luke.

Conclusion

These three stories, the two Gospel stories of the anointing of Jesus and the larger story consisting of the combination of these two, are narratives about a socially insignificant, suffering person who has a heart's desire of one kind or another.

Luke's Sinner is a shamed and broken person, but in her fierce desire for closeness to Jesus she is willing to brave even greater shame and scandal. Through her second-person experience of him—his reactions to her reactions to his reactions to her and so on—she finds an antidote to shame. She is honored by him in front of those who found her shameful, and the status he accords her outranks theirs, as all of them can see.

In the story in the Gospel of John, taken in isolation from the story in Luke, Mary loses what she thought she wanted more than anything, and she thinks that she has lost it irretrievably. Her brother is dead, and the person she had relied on to love her ignores her (as she supposes) in her greatest distress. She is heartbroken in consequence and shamed in her helplessness to ward off the evil that comes to her and the rejection of her that seems to be the root of that evil. That is why she falls at Jesus' feet weeping when she meets him on the road. She does not stand under her suffering; she falls in heartbreak.

But, as it turns out, what seemed to be irretrievable loss was not; and, however much it seemed to Mary that Jesus betrayed her trust, in fact in the story he did not. She was not wrong to be heartbroken, given her understanding of the circumstances and her understanding of her own heart's desires. Nonetheless, she was mistaken about what she thought she knew. When Lazarus is restored to her in a display of Jesus' love for her and for Martha and Lazarus too, what Mary is given is more what she really desires than she would have known how to want before the raising of Lazarus. What Mary could not have conceived of desiring is in fact somehow more what she herself wanted than that which she herself supposed she wanted. And that is why she reacts to Jesus as she does, once she understands what he has done for her. In her response to him, the glory that Jesus predicts as the outcome of the miracle clearly encompasses her, too. The greatness of her heart, the power of her love, make her lovely in ways very many generations of the story's audience have found worthy of admiration.

The conditional identification of Sinner with Mary of Bethany yields a larger narrative of great interest for considerations of shame, heartbrokenness, and suffering. As I explained in Chapter 7, a shamed person anticipates rejection and abandonment on the part of real or imagined others. She is anxious about marginalization or isolation. She expects that those with whom she herself would be glad of any kind of union will repudiate her. For this reason, heartbreak stemming from the loss of a loved person or from the apparent betrayal of a trusted person will hit a shamed person hard. In the larger narrative, Mary of Bethany's heartbreak at the death of her brother and at Jesus' failure to come is as anguished as it is because of her history of shame and her more recent history of Jesus' love and care for her.

The remedy for shame comes in stages, in the larger narrative. The second stage, which is the most powerful and effective at overturning the suffering of shame, comes paradoxically enough through the suffering of heartbreak in shame. Through that suffering, Mary of Bethany has what she thought she had lost forever during the time she was heartbroken, and she also has the final stage of her transformation from shamed to glorious. As the story shows, this transformation begins and ends in her second-personal connection of love with Jesus. When Mary anoints Jesus the second time, she does not need to avoid anyone's gaze. She is in a position to give care to Jesus as well as to receive care from him; and he honors her as she cares for him. The whole antidote to shame is here. In the power of her last wild gesture, there is a beauty about Mary that anyone might admire and honor.

As I have said in connection with each of the previous stories in the preceding chapters, to interpret the stories and sum them up in this way is not to give a theodicy for the suffering in the story. It is to explain why God (or Jesus, as representative of God in the stories of Sinner and Mary of Bethany) did not abrogate the suffering of the protagonist in the story. It does not yet touch the question of whether God (or Jesus) is justified in doing so.

With these stories interpreted in this way, however, we are ready for this question of theodicy (and defense). I will turn to it in the next and final part of this book.

PART 4

OTHER-WORLDLY THEODICY:
WHAT WE CARE ABOUT IN A
DEFENSE

Chapter 13

Theodicy in Another World

Have you not heard his silent steps?
He comes, comes, ever comes.
Every moment and every age, every day and every night,
he comes, comes, ever comes.

Many a song have I sung in many a mood of mind,
but all their notes have always proclaimed,
"He comes, comes, ever comes."

In the fragrant days of sunny April,
through the forest path,
he comes, comes, ever comes.

In the rainy gloom of July nights,
on the thundering chariot of clouds,
he comes, comes, ever comes.

In sorrow after sorrow,
it is his steps that press upon my heart,
and it is the golden touch of his feet
that makes my joy to shine.[*]

Transition

This is a chapter that is ineluctably burdened with preliminaries. Even before the introduction to it, some preliminary remarks are needed about the methodology of it.

The preceding chapters examined in detail four biblical narratives, the stories of Job, Samson, Abraham, and Mary of Bethany. How are these narratives now to be brought into the philosophical discussion of the problem of suffering? How are the narratives to

---

[*] Gitanjali, Poem XLV, in *Collected Poems and Plays of Rabindranath Tagore* (New York: Macmillan, 1966), 17.

be woven into the philosophical examination of the nature of love that was the subject of Part 2 of this book? How are the narratives to be used in this chapter, which is intended to present Aquinas's theodicy? How is the promise of the first, methodological section of this book to be fulfilled?

One possible answer to all these questions is that the narratives can be used as examples corresponding to philosophical points. There are important similarities and dissimilarities among the narratives, and it would be easy enough just to structure this chapter around the patterns among the stories. In this way, it would be possible simply to use the stories as illustrations of philosophical claims.

To take just one example, consider the end of the four stories. At the beginning of the stories, the sufferers are in different moral and spiritual conditions. Job suffers as an innocent victim and Samson as a perpetrator. Abraham is somewhere in between, and his mixed motives as regards Ishmael are tested in the trial over Isaac. Mary is an intimate friend of Jesus, and so, in the terms of the narrative, she is in a generally good moral and spiritual condition; but she loses heart and trust in Jesus in the course of her suffering.[1] Nonetheless, although in this way in the beginnings of their stories the protagonists are in varying conditions, at the end of the stories, in consequence of their suffering, they are alike in having come to some new greatness. Job has the most sustained face-to-face conversation between God and a human person recorded in the biblical narratives. Samson fulfills his mission and draws near to God when he does so. Abraham becomes the father of a whole people and also the father of faith. And Mary's act of adoration in anointing Jesus is so striking and great-hearted that she becomes emblematic in Christian thought for it. Suffering takes each of the protagonists from where that person is at the start of the story to something incomparably greater by the end of the story.

And so this chapter might well employ the patterns among the stories to provide examples illustrating one or more premises in an argument about suffering as a means to human flourishing. But, for the reasons laid out in Part 1 of this book, it seems to me that to use the stories in this way is to wreck them as stories. It is to use them only as a sort of picture-book illustration, gratuitous helps for those who like their philosophy with entertainment along the way.

There is something similarly inappropriate, in my view, about bringing the stories in simply as support for a particular premise in an argument about the problem of suffering. The stories can certainly serve such a purpose. So, for example, all of the stories taken together should motivate some diffidence in our assessment of individual cases of suffering. Because they are stories, each of the biblical narratives gives us considerable insight into the inner life of the protagonist in the stories, the place of the suffering in the trajectory of the protagonist's life, and the protagonist's relation to God. These are not things we generally know when we consider real-life cases of the suffering of others; sometimes, perhaps very often, even the sufferer does not know all of these things. And yet, as the stories make clear, seeing a possible justification for God's allowing suffering is a very different matter if we know the inside, as it were, of the suffering in question and its course.

The external description of a case of suffering, without insight into the inner life of the sufferer, can make the project of theodicy seem difficult or impossible. The external but superficial description of the suffering of Mary of Bethany, for example, is that her brother Lazarus was allowed to die when he could so easily have been healed by Jesus, who failed to come to his aid. Similarly, we can describe Samson's case in the same mode by saying that God allowed Samson to be captured and brutalized by his enemies when Samson could so easily have been allowed one more victory over them. Described in these ways, the suffering in question can look indefeasible, incapable of being redeemed. Is it not blankly unintelligible that God would have allowed Samson to suffer so dreadfully or that Jesus would have let Lazarus die? But, set in a context that includes the psychology and biography of the sufferer, the suffering acquires a very different look. In that context, the point of the suffering is not at all blankly unintelligible.

And so the stories could be used to support an agnosticism, a kind different from skeptical theism, as regards theodicy. Even if skeptical theism were wrong and there were no reason for doubting the human ability to understand God's actions and plans, the stories support the claim that it might still not be possible for us to see a morally sufficient reason for God's allowing suffering in any particular case because the inner life and the psychic trajectory of the sufferer in that case is opaque to us.

Nonetheless, although the stories can be used to support philosophical claims in this way, if this were the sole or main use of the stories, it would strike me as disappointing. That is because such use reduces the complicated richness of a story to some fairly simple moral, thereby undermining the whole point of introducing stories into philosophical reflection, as I explained it in Part 1 of this book.

But, if the narratives are not to be used as illustrations of premises in an argument about the problem of suffering, or as support for premises in such an argument, then how are they to be used appropriately?

In Part 1 of this book, I argued that a story, which is a second-person account, can give us something of what we would have had if we ourselves had been participants, even just as bystanders, in the second-person experiences that the story describes. In the same way, the biblical narratives examined in the preceding section constitute a way of sharing and passing on interpersonal experiences, including interpersonal experiences (whether real or imagined) with God, in all their messy richness. These narratively shared experiences can inform in subtle ways our intuitions and judgments, just as real-life experiences do.

As I was at pains to show in Part 1 of this book, I cannot explain exactly what way that is, but it is not necessary for me to do so. Even apart from the evidence and arguments in Part 1, we are all familiar with the phenomenon. What an American learns after numerous extended trips to China cannot be reduced to particular claims about the country, the culture, and the people; the experienced traveler will not be able to explain in numbered propositions what his previous trips have taught him. But, nonetheless, what virtually all of us believe is that, on his *next* trip to China, he will be readily distinguishable from his colleagues who are visiting China for the first time. He will be able to bridge the gap between American and Chinese cultures by myriad small or large insights hard to summarize or to express at all in any propositional way. Because of his previous experience with China, he will have an understanding of China and its culture and people that his colleagues on their first trip to China will lack; and he will not be able to convey to them in terms of knowledge *that* what he himself has learned. His inexperienced colleagues will have to learn it for themselves through experience on their own trips to China. Or, as I argued in Part 1, they might learn some of it in advance through stories, which lets them participate vicariously to some extent in the experiences their colleague, the experienced traveler to China, has had.

I think, therefore, that the best way to make use of the biblical narratives examined in Part 3 is to let the reflection on them presented in the chapters of that part serve as the equivalent of experience, not the experience of traveling through a country but rather something like the experience of immersion in a worldview. To experience this worldview is, of course, not the same thing as approving of it or being willing to adopt and accept as one's own the things peculiar to it. But, even if one rejects it, the as-it-were travel experience of it will broaden and enrich one's perceptions and judgments of things, altering them in subtle and not-so-subtle ways, much as travel to a very different culture will do even if one is alienated from that culture.

In what follows, then, I will treat the stories as one treats the experience of travel. I will not try to illustrate every philosophical point with an example from one of the stories or try to support every philosophical claim crucial to Aquinas's theodicy with evidence from the stories. Rather, I will let the memory of the preceding readings of the stories inform inchoately or tacitly the reflections in this and subsequent chapters, and I will call attention only to things specially worth remembering explicitly, and even then only where it seems particularly helpful to do so. In effect, I will count on the stories as a common store of experience shared by readers, in the way one might share with others the experience of having been to China, even if one disagrees with one's fellow travelers about the assessment of what one has seen, even if one disputes what the others take to be the facts with regard to the country and its people.

So, in this final part of the book, beginning with this chapter, I will outline and argue for a defense (as distinct from a theodicy); and, for the reasons given here and in Part 1 of this book, I will build that defense based on the stories examined in the previous part, but based on the stories in the loose sort of way in which very many of our views ultimately rest on our experiences.

This is as much as I am prepared to say philosophically on this score, and yet it does not seem to me to be the end of the matter. From my point of view, the stories have an almost inexhaustible richness, and only a fraction of it is extracted in any form in the chapters that follow. When questions arise, as they inevitably will, about the philosophical points made in this part of the book, it seems to me that one profitable way to deal with those questions will be to return to the stories.

With this preliminary consideration of methodology out of the way, the path is smoothed for this chapter and the real introduction to it. Readers should be warned, however, that the chapter that begins below has preliminaries of its own; given the complicated questions raised by theodicy, there is no professionally acceptable alternative. But readers uninterested in these details and impatient with preliminaries have my blessing to skip straight from the end of the introduction to the section headed "Aquinas's scale of values". The presentation of Aquinas's theodicy properly begins there.

Introduction

The suffering occasioned by the damaging forces of nature, the ravages resulting from the depredations of other human beings, the torment of pain and disfigurement, the anguish of psychic trauma and mental illness, the wretchedness of impoverishment, the misery of being unwanted, the affliction of pariah status, the brokenness of shame, the self-destruction of great moral evil, the ruin of a life and the blighting of its promise, the death of loved ones, the breaking of a heart in the loss of a heart's desire—have I overlooked any suffering of the characters in the stories canvassed in the previous chapters?[2] Surely no one needs to have it explained to him that all these variegated ills are only a beginning of a list of even the great evils that afflict human beings. For that matter, even a casual acquaintance with the primary sources from the Holocaust or the period of slavery in America is sufficient to show that there are far more cruel evils and agonizing sufferings than any of those described in the biblical stories surveyed in the preceding chapters.

And yet, together, Job, Samson, Abraham, and Mary give us an iconic representation of the panoply of human suffering. The physical pain and mental agony of an innocent victim are pictured in the story of Job. The self-destruction of human evil is evident in the story of Samson. The heartsickness whose source is the deprivation of a heart's desire is portrayed in the story of Abraham. And the misery of being unwanted, shamed, and heartbroken is shown in the story of Mary. Taken together, the sufferings of the characters in these stories constitute a kind of Aristotelian Categories of suffering. All the *modes* of suffering are here, even if many of its species are missing.

How could anything justify God's allowing such suffering? How could anyone believe that there is a world in which such suffering coexists with an omnipotent, omniscient, perfectly good God?

The great majority of philosophers and theologians of the major monotheisms did believe this, though; and Aquinas's position is representative of one strand of that thought. In essence, on Aquinas's theodicy, God is justified in allowing human beings to endure suffering such as that experienced by Job, Samson, Abraham, and Mary in the stories, because, through their suffering and only by its means, God gives to each of the protagonists something that these sufferers are willing to trade their suffering to receive, once they understand the nature of what they are being given.[3]

I suppose that few people will miss the stunning nature of this claim, but perhaps it is well to highlight it here nonetheless. Aquinas's theodicy commits him to the claim that, if a sufferer were single-mindedly rational in seeing what God was giving him through his suffering and were whole-hearted in responding to it, he would be willing to accept it on those terms. In such a single-minded, whole-hearted condition, Job would be willing to trade the loss of all his property, his health, his children, and all the rest, in order to receive it. Samson would be willing to trade his eyesight, his liberty, and even his moral decay to have it. Abraham and Mary would be willing to give up a heart's desire for it. Mary would be willing to have it even with the accompaniment of heart-breaking shame. The protagonists in the stories lost their wellbeing or their hearts' desires or both; for all of them, their sufferings were fearful. And yet, on Aquinas's theodicy, when these sufferers are single-minded and whole-hearted, they are willing to accept their suffering for the sake of having what God was offering them through the suffering.

But what is this? What would anyone care about more than his flourishing or his heart's desire? When Abraham, for example, whole-heartedly accepts the objective goodness of God, when he comes to faith and draws near to God, what does he understand about God and his relationship to God that moves him to this attitude? In this chapter, I will explicate Aquinas's theodicy and give his answers to these questions. In doing so, I will presuppose the whole complex discussion of love and union in Part 2 of this book and the exposition of the narratives in Part 3. With that discussion and exposition as the context, in this chapter I will sketch the general outlines of Aquinas's understanding of the solution to the problem of suffering.

Taken in the context of the biblical narratives and encompassed in Aquinas's whole worldview but especially his account of love, Aquinas's theodicy is the defense—or almost all of it—promised at the outset of this book. In my view, although Aquinas's theodicy constitutes a cogent defense as far as it goes, it omits reflection on one crucial element of the problem of suffering—namely, the suffering stemming from the loss of the desires of a person's heart. In Chapter 14, I will argue that this element needs to be taken into account in any theodicy or defense that has a hope of being acceptable. I think, however, that Aquinas's theodicy can be developed, along lines he himself would have approved of, to include this element. As I will try to show in Chapter 14, this development, Thomistic in character, can be woven into the theodicy that Aquinas himself held. The extended Thomistic account, Aquinas's theodicy and the emendation designed to take account of the desires of the heart, constitutes the defense that is the goal of this book.

In Chapter 15, I will turn to an evaluation of this defense; in that chapter, I will ask whether this account constitutes an acceptable response to the problem of suffering. I will argue that it does. In this chapter, however, my aim is not to evaluate Aquinas's theodicy. It is only to present it. Here I will lay out Aquinas's theodicy, taken in the context of the worldview in which it is embedded,[4] as if I were constructing a science-fiction story—a theology fiction story—about another world, which is still part of our universe of discourse, but which will strike many contemporaries as Martian. My hope in this chapter is to present this world clearly enough so that it constitutes a candidate for a depiction of a possible world in which God and human suffering coexist.

Obviating objections

Although, as I have explained earlier, I am not claiming that this possible world *is* the actual world since my project is defense and not theodicy, nonetheless some parts of Aquinas's theodicy will still prompt objections just because they seem to raise the problem of suffering over again in a different context. The issue here is not whether Aquinas's worldview is *true* but whether it is *consistent*. In particular, theological doctrines taken for granted in Aquinas's worldview include the doctrine of hell and the doctrine of original sin, but contemporary readers may wonder whether these doctrines are themselves compatible with belief in the existence of a loving God. What if, for example, in Samson's story, the narrative had ended in Samson's going to hell? That is, if in the narrative Samson had not turned again to God at the end of his life but had died in such a way that in an endless afterlife he was permanently alienated from God, would we suppose that, just in virtue of including hell, the story was narratively incoherent in trying to present God as loving?

On Aquinas's views, the doctrines of hell and original sin are certainly compatible with the doctrine that God is good and loving. In fact, Aquinas thinks that the doctrine of hell is an implication of the doctrine of divine love and the fact of the human misuse of free will.[5] But it is important to see that, if it could be demonstrated that Aquinas is wrong on this score, what would then be required is not a rejection of his theodicy as inconsistent but only a rearrangement of it.

For example, if the doctrine of original sin is rejected, some other explanation of the manifest phenomenon of the ubiquitous human disposition to moral evil will have to be found. And, unless one could make a successful argument for atheism out of such an explanation—something I do not think could be done[6]—that explanation itself will be compatible with belief in God and so can be substituted at the appropriate place in Aquinas's theodicy. The important contribution that the doctrine of original sin makes to the description of the possible world of the defense at issue in this book is just the claim that the human propensity to moral wrongdoing is not the fault of an omnipotent, omniscient, perfectly good God. Any other explanation of that propensity with this same implication and compatible with the existence of God is acceptable in the description of the possible world of the defense.[7]

Analogously, if the doctrine of hell is rejected in favor of, say, the position that God annihilates those unable to be saved, as some have argued it should be,[8] then annihilation will take the place of hell in Aquinas's theodicy. Or, if some version of Origen's universalism is one's preferred account,[9] then cycles of purgation will play the role that hell does in Aquinas's theory. And so on.[10] What the doctrine of hell contributes to the description of the possible world of the defense is an extrinsic lower bound to the scale of human flourishing. Any other extrinsic lower bound compatible with the existence of God is acceptable in its place in the description of the possible world of the defense.

So, for these reasons, examining the compatibility of Aquinas's theologically controversial positions with belief in the existence of God has considerably less bearing on my
project than it might initially seem. I will, therefore, not consider these issues further
here. I will incorporate the doctrines of hell and original sin in my description of the
possible world of the defense, and I will accept Aquinas's understanding of hell in the
theodicy I present in this chapter. But readers who find these doctrines unacceptable
should take mention of them as shorthand for their own preferred explanations of
the extrinsic lower bound of human flourishing and the human propensity to moral
wrongdoing.

The constraints and limits on Aquinas's theodicy

Before we turn to an examination of Aquinas's theodicy itself, something also needs to
be said about the constraints and limits on it.

Many of the constraints on theodicy that are insisted on by contemporary philosophers
also operate in Aquinas's theodicy. On Aquinas's views, if a good God allows suffering,
it has to be for the sake of a benefit that outweighs the suffering, and that benefit
has to be one that, in the circumstances,[11] cannot be gotten just as well without the
suffering; the benefit has to *defeat* the suffering.[12] If *per improbabile* something other than
suffering—conversations with God, for example—could have brought Samson to the
final redemption he has in his story, then, on Aquinas's views, in the story God would
not have been justified in allowing Samson's suffering. In addition, Aquinas accepts
a constraint that is controversial in the contemporary discussion[13]—namely, that the
benefit in question has to go primarily[14] to the sufferer,[15] whatever good might also be
done to other people.[16] If in the story it had been true that God let Job suffer only for
some good for Satan, or if God allowed the death of Job's children only for the sake of a
good for Job, then, on Aquinas's views, God would not have been justified in allowing
that suffering. The fractal character of providence, which is manifest in the story of Job,
has one source in this constraint. Since this constraint clearly makes the enterprise of
theodicy harder, I will simply note that Aquinas accepts it and leave to one side any
consideration of the controversy over it. In the discussion below of benefits correlated
with suffering, these constraints should be understood as applying.

As for the limits, as I explained in the first chapter, the suffering at issue in Aquinas's
theodicy as I am explicating it here is limited to the suffering of unwilling, innocent,
mentally fully functional adult human beings.[17] Aquinas himself pays little or no
attention to animal suffering[18] or to the suffering of human beings who are not mentally
fully functional adults; and, as I explained in Chapter 1, it is outside the scope of this
project to consider whether or not Aquinas's theodicy can be extended to apply to such
suffering.

I do not mean to say that in my view the defense I give in this book could *not*
be developed and extended in such a way as to apply to sentient sufferers other than
mentally fully functional adult human beings. On the contrary, I do not think it would

be easy to rule out the possibility that it could be so developed. In this regard, everything depends on the nature of the sentience of the creature suffering; and, for very many sentient creatures, we are only beginning to understand anything about their sentience.

So, for example, consider this passage from the book on bears by the experienced bear-keeper Else Poulsen:

Bears are born with the mental and physical flexibility required to negotiate the environment in which they are meant to live. This is true for spiders, humans, rats—all animals. Bears have personalities, individual differences, that set the template for how they address life . . . The twentieth-century dogma that we must not anthropomorphize, or attribute human character-istics like emotions to animals, has moved several generations of humans farther away from understanding the creatures we share the planet with. The self-aggrandizing and widespread assumption that we humans have the full complement of all of the emotions possible to all animals on Earth—basically, that all the marbles belong to us—is not only unscientific but also childish . . . Fortunately, human understanding is maturing, and we are learning that animals are emotional, thinking, and self-aware beings relative to the niche they were born to occupy . . . my everyday experiences with animals [have] left me wondering if the researchers who cling to the ideas that animals have no feelings, no problem-solving abilities, and no self-awareness [have] ever interacted with their family cat or dog.[19]

A bit later, describing her own process of coming to understand the nature of bears, Poulsen says about one particular bear, Louise: "I am indebted to Louise. She taught me early in my career that a zookeeper's most important tool is relationship."[20]

Whether the Thomistic defense at issue in this book can be modified and developed to apply to animals will depend on whether the animals in question have the cognitive and conative abilities that allow for relationship, as Poulsen supposes bears do. And so judging whether the Thomistic defense can be transformed to apply to particular cases of animal suffering would require a kind of detailed understanding of the sentience of animals that, for most species, is still largely lacking to us.[21]

On the other hand, of course, it might also be the case that the morally sufficient reason that on Aquinas's theodicy justifies God's allowing suffering of mentally fully functional adult human beings in fact just does not apply to the suffering of all sentient creatures. There is no guarantee that one and only one explanation of suffering applies to all the kinds of suffering that there are in the world.

For these and other reasons, as I explained in Chapter 1, I will leave out of account the suffering of sentient creatures other than mentally fully functional human adults. To reflect on such suffering, to explore whether a Thomistic approach could be developed with respect to it, and to consider what, if any, other approaches to it are possible would require a book in its own right. As I have noted with regret at other places in earlier chapters, it is not possible to do everything in one book.

Another limit on the Thomistic theodicy presented in this chapter has to do not with the nature of the sufferer but with the kind of suffering at issue for theodicy. It is neither suffering that is punishment for moral wrongdoing nor pain that is entirely voluntary.[22] The reason for this limit is just that the problem of suffering is not raised by either of these. It is clear enough why pain endured entirely voluntarily does not raise the problem of suffering. No one wonders about the problem of suffering in connection with such pain just because its endurance is entirely voluntary.[23] Things are somewhat more complicated in the case of suffering for moral wrongdoing, however. In this regard, it is important to distinguish two different ways in which human wrongdoing can result in suffering for the wrongdoer.

On the one hand, there is suffering that is just and appropriate punishment for wrongdoing.[24] It is hard to feel sorry for Samson when Delilah betrays him, because her betrayal seems to serve him right. He dallies with her for his own purposes; he is willing to enjoy her, but he does not give himself to her. And so she responds with a lack of commitment to him. She uses him for her purposes, too. If her doing so had caused him sorrow stemming from any care on his part about her relationship to him, it seems that he would have deserved that sorrow. If Samson had grieved over Delilah when he saw that Delilah had betrayed him to his enemies, his suffering would not make us wonder why a good God would permit it. Who minds when a man like Samson, accustomed to toying with a woman, gets a taste of his own medicine? We are not perplexed about what could justify God in permitting suffering of that sort. And so suffering that is thoroughly merited is outside the scope of this project.

By contrast, there is something horrifying about the wrecking of Samson's life. Even if we grant, with my reading of the story, that Samson is guilty of serious moral wrongdoing in his attitudes and actions toward God and in his use of God's gifts to him, the ruin of Samson's life seems out of all proportion to that wrongdoing. The irremediable wrecking of Samson's life, all the blighting of its initial promise, is in some sense the natural outgrowth of the moral evil Samson does. But something can be a natural consequence of moral faults without being appropriate punishment for those faults.[25]

As in the preceding case, the issue here has to do with what is voluntary or involuntary. Samson may have loved Delilah in some ordinary sense, but he did not mind the effects on her of his keeping her at a considerable distance from himself. In fact, it is hard to suppose that Samson gave much thought to the negative effects of any of his actions on Delilah, or that, if he had done so, he would have cared much about them. The same cannot be said about the catastrophe that Samson made of his life. Samson's deep alienation from God and the shambles of his God-given mission eventuate from the confluence of Samson's actions and the circumstances surrounding them. But, although the devastation of his relationship to God and his divinely appointed life-work was an outgrowth of Samson's attitudes and actions in those circumstances, that outcome was definitely against Samson's will.

In this one regard, Samson is like a negligent self-absorbed hunter who takes a careless shot after a quick glance at something moving in the woods and hits his hunting buddy instead of a deer. His grief over the outcome of his action is an indication of the fact that he would not willingly have brought about the state of affairs that is in fact the result of his morally culpable negligent action. In this respect, what the hunter does is against his will. Analogously, Samson would not willingly have made such a wreck of his life. The object of *his* involuntary manslaughter is himself. Of course, Samson is not entirely like the hunter. It is not ignorance of what he is doing that renders what Samson does involuntary in this way. It is rather that Samson is divided in will. Samson has a higher-order desire to be a person who is close to God and who champions the cause of his people. And so, when Samson desires to do, and does, those actions that take both these ends away from him, he is acting against his (higher-order) will, even if it is also true that Samson operates with his own will when he acts self-destructively. Samson's actions and the wreckage those actions make of Samson's life are contrary to Samson's desires about the sort of person he wants to be and the sort of life he wants to live. This is the sense in which what he does is against his will.

Because Samson is divided against himself in acting as he does, because he acts against his own higher-order desires regarding his life and his relationship to God, there is something tragic about his story, as there is about the story of a person guilty of involuntary manslaughter. For this reason, suffering such as Samson's, the wrecking of a whole life stemming from great moral wrongdoing, does fall within the purview of my project, as the suffering that is punishment for wrongdoing does not. With regard to suffering of the self-destructive, life-wrecking kind, we can understand Christ's line that it would have been good for a person who does such evil never to have been born.[26] That suffering of Samson's does prompt one to wonder how a good God could allow it.

The limits of this project therefore exclude the suffering that constitutes punishment for wrongdoing and yet include suffering such as Samson's. Given this distinction, it is true to say that the suffering at issue in this book is that of unwilling *innocents*. Samson, of course, is a perpetrator of great moral wrongs, not an innocent. And yet, to the extent to which there is something unmerited about the ruin of Samson's life, there is something undeserved about the suffering of that ruin. In this sense, and only in this sense, there is an innocence about Samson. That is why his destruction is horrifying to us, not satisfying, in the way deserved and appropriate punishment often is, in stories at least if not also in reality. In what follows, talk of the suffering of unwilling innocents should therefore be taken to include suffering such as that experienced by Samson in the ruin of his life.[27]

An additional clarification of the limits: Suffering unwillingly

I recognize that I have spent considerable space on preliminaries, but there is one more clarification of the limits of Aquinas's theodicy that will be helpful to have in what follows. Although suffering that is entirely voluntary is outside the bounds of this book, there are different ways of being an *unwilling* sufferer. There are those who are in every way unwilling to suffer—those unwilling *simpliciter*—and those who are unwilling only in a certain respect—those unwilling *secundum quid*. Aquinas does not discuss this distinction explicitly anywhere, as far as I know; but in effect he presupposes it and relies on it in many places. This distinction makes a difference in the theodicy Aquinas accepts and defends.

The suffering endured by a person in either group of sufferers is involuntary as regards any particular suffering a person experiences. What distinguishes the persons in one group from those in the other has to do with a particular kind of higher-order acceptance of suffering. It is possible for someone to endure a particular suffering involuntarily and yet to have given a kind of assent to the general endurance of suffering of that type. The possibility of division within the will and the hierarchical structure of the will allow for something to be against the will of the person suffering it, in one sense, while it is nonetheless in accordance with some acceptance of that type of suffering in the higher-order will of that same person.[28]

For example, when Samson goes to war against the Philistines, he suffers unwillingly anything the opposing Philistine warriors do to him when they attack him; certainly, any particular injury a particular Philistine fighter inflicts on Samson is an injury Samson endures unwillingly. On the other hand, however, in virtue of being willing to go to war, as war is practiced in his time, Samson is in effect accepting the endurance of battlefield injuries of one kind or another. To this extent, when Samson is injured, his suffering that injury is involuntary only in a certain respect. In wanting to be a warrior, Samson is willing to have a will that accepts enduring some battlefield injuries. Similarly, when Abraham obeys God's call to leave his home and wander among strangers, he suffers the depredations of some of those strangers involuntarily. He does not want the king of the country he is passing through to take away from him his wife Sarah, for example. But, insofar as Abraham has voluntarily left the safety and protection of his home, he has implicitly given a higher-order consent to the endurance of the kind of suffering inevitable in his period in the process of wandering as a stranger in foreign territory; and Abraham knows that he has. And so Abraham's suffering the particular depredations from strangers that he does is involuntary, but only in a certain respect. By contrast, when marauders take his cattle and kill his servants, Job's suffering is unconditionally involuntary. Job has not volunteered for it in any respect; it is not a suffering, or a type of suffering, to which Job has given any sort of consent with any part of his will.

The sufferings of the shamed should be classed with sufferings that are involuntary *simpliciter*, in my view, although the understanding of shame I argued for earlier might lead one to suppose otherwise. As I explained in Chapter 7, the suffering stemming from shame is different in important respects from unconditionally involuntary sufferings such as Job's. In order to feel shamed, a person has to assent to the standard by which others shame him (or by which his own psyche attempts to shame him), and he has to accept as appropriate the (real or imagined) marginalization or shunning of others. To this extent, and it is a very limited extent, there is a component of will in the suffering of the shamed; and we feel it. There is no similar component of will in the affliction that comes to Job in the loss of his children, his servants, and his property, or in the physical pain of his bodily ailments. If Job had willed otherwise, he would still have endured those losses and felt that pain. So, if someone supposed that the suffering of a shamed person such as Mary of Bethany had to be classified as involuntary only *secundum quid*, there would be some reason for it. Even so, however, I want to reject this classification of the suffering of the shamed. Mary's suffering in being shamed differs in relevant respects from Samson's sufferings in battle, for example.[29] Mary gives no kind of assent to what others do to her to shame her. To this extent, then, even if there is an element of will in the acceptance of the standard by which the shamed person is shamed, there is no similar acceptance of the suffering itself. The suffering of a shamed person such as Mary is, therefore, more like that of those whose suffering is involuntary *simpliciter* than it is like that of a warrior such as Samson, whose suffering in battle is involuntary only *secundum quid*.

Something similar should also be said about the suffering whose source is the desires of the heart. There is obviously a component of will in this suffering as well. If Abraham had been willing to give up the desires of his heart, he would not have suffered in not having these things.[30] And yet, in this case, too, Abraham's suffering is more like Job's suffering over the death of his children than like Samson's sufferings in battle. Of course, it is true of Job that he would not have suffered if, for example, he had stopped caring about his children, so that their deaths meant nothing to him.[31] But, although neither Abraham nor Job would have suffered as they did if they had not had the desires they did, it remains the case that the contribution of will to their suffering differs from that of Samson as regards the sufferings of battle.

The difference lies in the kind of change of will that would have warded off the suffering. If Samson had decided not to participate in battle but to retire to some island and live in isolation there, he would have evaded battlefield injuries.[32] He can escape the bad things that happen to him on the battlefield because he can escape the battlefield. In this respect, his battlefield sufferings lie within the control of his will. Job, on the other hand, can evade his suffering only by ceasing to care about what he in fact does care deeply about. He can do nothing to avoid the death of his children or the illness that brings him physical pain; *those* things are not in the control of his will. It is one thing to evade suffering by escaping injuries; it is another thing to evade suffering by ceasing to care about injuries.

To take suffering that could be evaded only by ceasing to care about something as a kind of voluntary suffering is a contentious and ultimately counter-intuitive interpretation of that suffering, in my view.[33] In any event, it elides the distinction I am concerned to try to draw here, between suffering that is involuntary *simpliciter* and suffering that is involuntary only *secundum quid*. Insofar as Abraham could not escape the things that threaten his heart's desires except by giving up his heart's desires, I will relegate his suffering to the camp of suffering that is involuntary *simpliciter*.

Aquinas thinks that it is possible for a person to have given a generalized assent (explicit or implicit) not just to one particular type of suffering but to suffering in general, understood as a means to inner healing and greater closeness with other persons, including God. On Aquinas's views, commitment to Christianity includes such an assent. That is because a generalized assent of this sort is part of the processes of justification and sanctification; it is at least tacitly included in the volitional component of faith, and it is explicitly part of sanctification.[34] For this reason, on Aquinas's views, a person who has faith, either explicit faith or what Aquinas calls 'implicit faith,'[35] suffers involuntarily only *secundum quid*.

The distinction between suffering that is involuntary *simpliciter* and suffering that is involuntary only *secundum quid* is significant in Aquinas's theodicy, as will be clear below.

What Aquinas's theodicy is not

Finally, to ward off gratuitous confusion, it is also necessary to say something briefly about what Aquinas's theodicy is not. Readers who have some acquaintance with the history of Christian thought in general and with Augustine in particular may expect Aquinas's theodicy to be some version of what is often understood, mistakenly, as Augustine's theodicy.[36]

Augustine struggled with the question of the metaphysical status of evil; and his ultimate conclusion, that evil is a privation of being, was shared by many later medieval philosophers, including Aquinas. 'Privation' here is a technical term of medieval logic and indicates one particular kind of opposition; its correlative is *possession*. A privation is the absence of some characteristic in a thing that naturally possesses that characteristic. Blindness is a privation of sight in Samson, but not in an inanimate object, because, unlike Samson, the inanimate object does not naturally possess sight. For these reasons, evil is *not* simply nothing on Augustine's views, as he is sometimes believed to have maintained. Rather, it is a lack or deficiency of some sort of being in something in which that sort of being is natural.

This position of Augustine's is an attempt to explain, as it were, the ontology of evil. Nothing about this position of Augustine's constitutes a solution to the problem of suffering, nor did Augustine or any later medieval philosophers suppose it did.[37] Aquinas himself would certainly not have supposed that anything about the metaphysical status of evil provided a reason for God's permitting suffering to occur.

Augustine is also known for his suggestion that the evil permitted by God contributes to the beauty and goodness of the whole universe, just as a dark patch may contribute to the lightness and beauty of a painting. Some people mistakenly interpret this suggestion on Augustine's part as an attempt at theodicy, too. But, to take this suggestion of Augustine's as an attempted theodicy is to suppose that, for Augustine, the answer to the question why God allows suffering is that suffering has an aesthetic value for God. It seems to me that the moral repulsiveness of such a position is obvious; it would most certainly have been obvious to Augustine and Aquinas.

Aquinas would reject both of these as-it-were theodicies sometimes mistakenly attributed to Augustine because neither of them is compatible with the claim that God would allow a human person to suffer only if through that suffering alone God can provide an outweighing benefit that goes primarily to the sufferer. This is a claim Aquinas himself explicitly asserts. So, for example, he says:

Whatever happens on earth, even if it is evil, turns out for the good of the whole world. Because as Augustine says in the *Enchiridion*, God is so good that he would never permit any evil if he were not also so powerful that from any evil he could draw out a good. But the evil does not always turn out for the good of the thing in connection with which the evil occurs, because although the corruption of one animal turns out for the good of the whole world—insofar as one animal is generated from the corruption of another—nonetheless it does not turn out for the good of the animal which is corrupted. The reason for this is that the good of the whole world is willed by God for its own sake, and all the parts of the world are ordered to this [end]. The same reasoning appears to apply with regard to the order of the noblest parts [of the world] with respect to the other parts, because the evil of the other parts is ordered to the good of the noblest parts. But whatever happens with regard to the noblest parts is ordered only to the good of those parts themselves, because care is taken of them for their own sake, and for their sake care is taken of other things . . . But among the best of all the parts of the world are God's saints . . . He takes care of them in such a way that he doesn't allow any evil for them which he doesn't turn into their good.[38]

In my view, those who interpret Augustine's aesthetic suggestion as a kind of theodicy have misidentified the question to which his suggestion was meant to be an answer.

For Augustine, and for Aquinas, God's original plan for the world was that the world have in it only good and not evil. On the view Augustine and Aquinas share, evil is first introduced into a good world created by a good God through the misuse of free will on the part of the creatures created good by God.[39] Without moral wrongdoing on the part of free creatures, there would never have been suffering in the world. So God permits the misuse of free will and all the suffering consequent on it; but the world as God permits it to be is not the world as God originally planned it. The world as it is now is therefore a result of God's "Plan B," not his "Plan A."

A more theologically respectable way to put this point is to distinguish God's antecedent will from God's consequent will.[40] God's antecedent will is what God would have willed if everything in the world had been up to him alone. God's consequent will is what God actually does will, given what God's creatures will. For Aquinas, the will with which God assents to suffering is only his consequent will, not his antecedent will. In the circumstances of post-Fall human life, with human misuse of free will, God's consequent will includes allowing human suffering in some cases. In the case of Samson, for example, even when God chooses to withdraw from Samson, so that Samson no longer has the special physical strength he needs to defeat his enemies, God's choice is nonetheless a matter of God's consequent will, not his antecedent will. God's antecedent will for Samson is that Samson have a life without suffering, in union with God.

The claim that all the suffering God allows is willed by God only in his consequent will, however, raises a question: why should we not suppose that there is a defeat for God, a sadness, a deficiency of *some* sort, in the fact that God's consequent will is different from his antecedent will, that God's "Plan A" for the world had to be replaced by God's "Plan B?"[41]

This, I think, is the question to which Augustine's aesthetic suggestion is the answer, and it makes sense as an answer to this question. The universe that results from God's

"Plan B" has suffering in it; but, as I think the stories in the preceding section illustrate, it has great compensatory beauty in it as well, a beauty that would not have been possible without the suffering. Plan B therefore is not a defeat. God is able to make a world with suffering in it even more beautiful than the world would have been had there been neither moral evil nor suffering. And so the point of Augustine's suggestion is that Plan B is a triumph for God, not a defeat.

To say this is not to imply that God did or must will the actual world as the best possible world, or that God did or must will the moral evil in the actual world because the actual world has more value than the world would have had without that evil and the suffering it produces. Moral evil is not like pain: it is not morally permissible to cause moral evil as a means to some good. In fact, God does not cause *any* moral evil. He only allows the moral evil introduced into the world by the free choices of creatures. And so, on Aquinas's views, God allows moral evil and its consequences in the sense that with his consequent will he permits it to occur; but God does not cause it or will its existence with his antecedent will. To claim that this world, even with its evil and suffering, is more beautiful than the world would have been without evil and suffering is therefore *not* to explain the morally sufficient reason for God to allow evil. It is one thing to ask why God's allowing moral wrongdoing and suffering does not constitute a defeat for God. It is another thing entirely to ask why God would allow moral wrongdoing and suffering in the first place. It is only the first question that is at issue in Augustine's suggestion about the aesthetics of the post-Fall world.

For these reasons, the two Augustinian positions sketched here will play no role in the Thomistic defense developed in this book.

Aquinas's scale of value

With all these various preliminary explanations behind us, we can begin the examination of what Aquinas's theodicy actually is by considering the standard of value he accepts for human flourishing. Any discussion of the problem of suffering presupposes some standard of value, in accordance with which the existence of suffering is judged at least prima facie inconsistent with the existence of a good God. And, insofar as the problem of suffering is an attack on the consistency of religious belief or the consistency of religious belief together with some uncontested empirical evidence, it is appropriate that the scale of value by which that consistency is judged be the scale of value embraced by the system of religious belief in question. It would make no difference to the argument over evil if it turned out, unsurprisingly enough, that the mix of religious beliefs with a scale of values antithetical to those beliefs was inconsistent.[42]

So suppose that we start with the extrinsic lower limit to human flourishing. What is the worst thing that can happen to a human being?[43] Serious illness? The loss of all one's children in a day? Capture and torture by enemies? These are indeed dreadful; but, like Job, a person can suffer the depredations of nature and other human beings as an innocent, and there is still a great good for Job in innocence. What then is the worst? Is it suffering the ruin of one's life and hopes because of one's own wrongdoing, as Samson did? Even this is not the worst, because, as Samson's story shows, it is possible for there to be re-formation and even flourishing in the wreckage of a life.

For Aquinas, the worst thing that can happen to a person is to become permanently psychically fragmented, permanently alienated from oneself, permanently separated from others, including God. Because a human will is free in a libertarian sense,[44] it is possible for a human being never to achieve or even to want real closeness or love with God or with any human persons either. And because, on Aquinas's views, human beings are everlasting and not transitory things, a human being is capable of being in such a condition forever.[45] *This* is the worst thing that can happen to a human being, on Aquinas's scale of value. To be in this condition is to be everlastingly at a distance from oneself, from all other persons, and from God.[46] It is to be endlessly isolated from God's redemptive goodness in self-willed loneliness, the full-blown horror only hinted at in Samson's sort of distance from Delilah. On Aquinas's worldview, then, not only does loneliness have something hellish in its ability to cause pain, but also hell, which is the worst thing made permanent, is unendingly lonely.[47]

What underlies Aquinas's adoption of this characterization of the worst thing for human beings is the conviction Aquinas shares with other thinkers in the Christian tradition that personal relationship is the genus within which the greatest goods for human beings fall.[48] The greatest good for human beings consists in personal relationships of a certain sort. For Aquinas, God is characterized by mind and will; and so, on Aquinas's views, God is a person, in our sense of the word 'person.'[49] A union of love with God is thus a personal relationship, too. On Aquinas's views, it is the greatest of personal relationships. The greatest good for human beings is to be in a union of love with God.

Furthermore, for Aquinas, this greatest good for a human being is also the best condition of a human being.[50] To be united with something is to be made one with it, in some sense. To be made one with God in any sense, however, is deification, at least in some analogous sense. And it is hard to see what could be a greater state for a human person than being made like God. So union with God in heaven is an intrinsic upper limit on human flourishing. For this reason, flourishing and greatness co-vary for human beings. For Aquinas, the good of union between a human person and God constitutes both the flourishing and the greatness of the human person in the union.

Finally, on Aquinas's views the hallmark of a great good is that it is shareable, that it is not diminished by being distributed. The union of love with God, which is the greatest of goods for human beings, is consequently also the most shareable. The love of one human being for another is a shareable good, and human loves can themselves be woven into the shareable love between God and a human person. Dante, who is a very good Thomist, tries to portray this idea of Aquinas's by picturing the community of human beings who are united with God and each other as joined through music into one great choral song of joy. On Aquinas's scale of value, the greatest good for a human being is, therefore, more precisely described as the shared union of love among human beings and God. For Aquinas, heaven is this greatest good made permanent and unending. *This* is the best thing for human beings.

Reasonably enough, then, the worst thing for human beings and the best thing for human beings are correlatives. The unending shared union of loving personal relationship with God is the best thing for human beings; the worst thing is its unending absence. Aquinas's views of the best thing and the worst thing for human beings thus mark out a scale of value on which human suffering and the benefits that might be thought to redeem it can be measured.

As is clear from this scale of value, it is also part of Aquinas's worldview that a human being's life is divided into two unequal portions, one very little portion before death and another, infinitely enduring portion, after death. For reasons having to do not with his theology but with his philosophical psychology,[51] Aquinas maintains that the state of a person at the end of the little portion of his life determines his state in the infinitely extended portion of his life after death. That is, on Aquinas's views, the state of a person after bodily death is *not* determined as a sum of merits or demerits in a life, contrary to what so many people imagine Christian doctrine mandates. It is determined more nearly in the way things go when one person proposes marriage to another: everything depends on the *current* condition, the *current* love, of the person to whom the proposal is made.[52]

For Aquinas, the openness to God's love that a person has at death becomes the enduring condition of that person thereafter; it is possible for her to grow in various ways thereafter but not to grow or diminish in her very openness to God's love.[53] With regard to the best thing for human beings, then, it is as if an Olympic gold-prize winner were to have won for herself not only that prize at that moment in the history of her life but also unending life in a physical condition at least as superlative as that which allowed her to win the Olympic prize. Presumably, that outcome for the athlete would be unending athletic excellence. For a person in heaven, it is a matter of unending excellence *tout court*, and the base-line degree of the excellence is set by her condition at the end of the first, little portion of her life.[54]

In what follows, I will presuppose this part of Aquinas's views as well as his scale of value.

Culture clashes and the logic of the argument

At this initial stage in the presentation of Aquinas's theodicy, some readers, who find mention of heaven and hell childish or worse, will be inclined to wonder whether these elements cannot be excluded from Aquinas's position. Other readers will be inclined to dismiss Aquinas's theodicy out of hand because of the inclusion of these elements.

In this connection, I want to call two things to attention.

First, although (as I explained above) it is possible to preserve the heart of Aquinas's theodicy with some substitution for the doctrine of hell, the same cannot be said about the doctrine of an afterlife for those united to God. It is not possible to excise the doctrine of heaven from Aquinas's theodicy; on the contrary, that doctrine is central to it in more than one way. So, while the extrinsic lower bound of Aquinas's scale of human flourishing can be understood variously without the destruction of Aquinas's theodicy, at least in outline, the intrinsic upper bound is not reformulable in the same way. It needs to be taken as everlasting shared union with God if Aquinas's theodicy is not to be lost.

Aquinas himself recognizes this point. He understands that to some people the notion of an afterlife will seem absurd, but he also thinks that accepting this notion is essential to his view of suffering. Without the worldview that holds that there is an afterlife and that true happiness consists in union with God in that afterlife, Aquinas thinks that the theodicy he adopts will appear entirely unacceptable. For example, he says:

If there is no resurrection of the dead, it follows that there is no good for human beings other than in this life. And if this is the case, then those people are more miserable who suffer many evils and tribulations in this life. Therefore, since the apostles and Christians [generally] suffer more tribulations, it follows that they, who enjoy less of the goods of this world, would be more miserable than other people.[55]

From his point of view, this last claim is a *reductio* of the rejection of the idea of an afterlife. And he continues his *reductio* in this way: "If there were no resurrection of the dead, people wouldn't think it was a power and a glory to abandon all that can give pleasure and to bear the pains of death and dishonor; instead they would think it was stupid."

So, on Aquinas's own view, in order to see suffering as he does in his theodicy, in order not to see the acceptance of suffering or the justification of God's allowing suffering as senseless, it is essential to include the doctrine that human beings are capable of everlasting union with God in the afterlife. For reasons that will emerge in the rest of this chapter and the next one as well, I concur with Aquinas's attitude on this score. Unlike the doctrine of hell, the doctrine of heaven is not an optional part of Aquinas's theodicy, and there is no substitute for it that will leave the basic character of the theodicy intact.

Secondly, for those whose reaction to this conclusion is "So much the worse for Aquinas's theodicy!," it is important to review briefly the logic of the argument from evil. That argument, which begins with facts about suffering in our world and tries to conclude to the non-existence of an omnipotent, omniscient, perfectly good God, is a challenge to the *consistency* of religious beliefs,[56] taken in the context of uncontested empirical evidence. A theodicy is an attempt to defend the consistency of religious beliefs (together with such uncontested empirical evidence) by giving the morally sufficient reasons that God in fact has for allowing such suffering. For this reason, the claims of a *theodicy* need to be true. But a *defense* is not a theodicy. A defense attempts only to tell a story about a possible world that contains both God and human suffering and that is enough like the actual world so that, for all anyone knows, this story *could* be true.[57] A defense, therefore, does not need to claim that the story it tells about this possible world *is* true.

Of course, if someone could demonstrate that the salient claims of the defense are *false*, *that* result would make a difference to the defense. Then it would not be the case that the story of the defense is true for all anyone knows. But, as far as I can see, for all the unpopularity in secular culture of the notion of an afterlife, no one has given even a remotely plausible argument, let alone a demonstration, to show the falsity of the claim that there is an afterlife in which some human beings are unendingly united to God.[58]

I recognize that some people who are committed to rejecting any variety of theism will think that no argument is needed to demonstrate the falsity of a claim that appears so totally counter-intuitive to them. But this is hardly a powerful attack on the Thomistic defense that includes this claim or a cogent support for the argument from evil. On the contrary, commitment to atheism is obviously incompatible with acceptance of the claim that human beings can be everlastingly united to God. The mere repudiation of this claim as counter-intuitive to atheists is therefore a question-begging basis for accepting the argument from evil or for rejecting the Thomistic defense against it. If the argument from evil rests on this question-begging basis, it does not constitute a serious challenge to religious belief.

There is consequently no philosophical reason for failing to include in the description of the possible world of the defense at issue in this book Aquinas's claim, essential to his theodicy, that human beings are capable of everlasting union with God.

Flourishing by degrees

Aquinas's scale of value for human life is thus bounded by upper and lower limits. The complete and permanent absence of loving personal relationships is an extrinsic limit on one end,[59] and this is hell. The shared and unending loving union with God is the intrinsic limit on the other end,[60] and this is heaven. Insofar as, ultimately, the only states for human persons are either being in heaven or being in hell, on Aquinas's views the best thing for human persons and the worst thing for human persons are not only mutually exclusive but also, ultimately, jointly exhaustive. Just to have warded off finally the worst thing is, therefore, to have achieved ultimately the best thing.[61]

It is important to recognize, however, that the best thing, the intrinsic upper limit of Aquinas's scale of value for human lives, itself comes in degrees. This claim may appear paradoxical, but a moment's thought will dissipate the appearance. As regards physical condition, the best state for human beings is to be in peak physical condition. But human beings differ greatly in what constitutes peak physical condition for them, depending on age, size, occupation, and other things as well. The peak physical condition for an 80-year old, for example, will be considerably less impressive as regards physical condition than the peak physical condition of a 20-year old; the peak physical condition for a person who is slightly built and small in stature will be different from that of someone who is big-boned and tall. Analogously, on Aquinas's views, human beings differ greatly in what constitutes for them the peak human condition of union with God.[62] That is because it is possible to have more or less of a loving relationship in union with any person. As I explained in Chapter 6, closeness can be more or less rich, and in consequence so can shared attention; since these are ingredients of union, union itself comes in degrees. So, for example, as the narrative presents things, there was some kind of union of love between each of the two sisters, Mary and Martha, on the one hand, and Jesus, on the other; but in the story it is clear that Mary is closer to Jesus than her sister Martha is.

So, on Aquinas's views, it is possible to have more or less of a loving relationship in union with God. The love and presence of omnipresent God are fully and equally available to all human beings. But there are differences in the willingness and the consequent capacity to receive God's love even on the part of those human beings who are in union with God. Even in heaven, then, the best thing for human beings comes in degrees. In consequence, on Aquinas's views, human greatness does so, too.

It is helpful to have some less clumsy way of referring to the great-making characteristics of human persons whose intrinsic maximum is found in one or another degree of union with God. For ease of reference, and in deference to a long tradition of religious thought, I will refer to the great-making characteristics of human persons stemming from their union with God as their 'glory.'[63] Glory, as I am using the term here, is thus *not* a matter of honor or fame. It is a matter of intrinsic and relational characteristics that render a human person objectively excellent as a person to some very great degree.[64] The peak human condition for a person, the intrinsic upper bound of that person's flourishing, is therefore also the glory of that person, as 'glory' is being used here.

Because union with God comes in degrees, human glory will also vary from person to person among those united to God in heaven. For these reasons, what constitutes the most excellent state for human beings is itself not an all-or-nothing condition; it comes in degrees. We are accustomed to such rankings of excellence, of course, but we are also accustomed to the misery that they bring to everyone except the prize-winners. How could there be human flourishing in heaven, someone might think, if even in heaven there are misery-inducing inequalities of excellence?

In my view, this question arises from a misunderstanding of the Thomistic idea of love. As I explained in Chapter 6, on Aquinas's views, it turns out that the degree of closeness between God and any particular human being is solely dependent on the will of the human being in question. This point applies even to those in union with God in heaven. For this reason, how close to God a human person is in heaven, and how much of glory there is for her, is a function only of how much of God's love she wants and is willing to receive.[65] Therefore, in the unending shared union with God in heaven, each person has all of the union with God and all of the greatness of human persons that she desires. On Aquinas's views, it is not possible for a person in heaven to want more union with God than she has. In the *Paradiso*, when Dante the traveler asks one of the redeemed in heaven whether she does not envy those among the redeemed who are closer to God, she cannot help it: she laughs at his question. *You don't understand how things work here,* she tells him kindly.[66] If she were to want more, she would thereby also have it.

I understand that some people will find this position difficult to grasp. They will suppose that any person will always want as much glory and greatness as it is possible to have; therefore, on their view, if a person's glory is a function only of her will for union with God, there could not be inequalities of glory in heaven. Rather, everyone in heaven would have the same maximal amount. But to think this is to confuse a will to win with a will to be open to love. Someone can want to be greater than others on some scale of value and nonetheless not want those things that are the necessary ingredients of that greatness. Even with regard to love, which one might assume every human being wants, the possibility of division in the human will allows for desire and resistance at the same time. Samson loves Delilah in some sense even while he lies to her and guards himself carefully against her. Problems generated by the double-minded mix of desire for love and resistance to it are a staple of love stories and a source of clients for counselors.

Two kinds of benefit for two kinds of sufferers

With this much description of Aquinas's scale of value for a human life, we can now turn to Aquinas's theodicy proper. As Aquinas sees it, what is the morally sufficient reason for God to allow the suffering of an unwilling, innocent, mentally fully functional adult human person?[67]

On Aquinas's theodicy, God is justified in allowing the suffering of such a person by one or the other or both[68] of two possible benefits, where Aquinas's scale of value is the measure of the benefits.[69] Which of the two possible benefits goes to a particular sufferer on any given occasion is a function of the nature of the involuntary suffering; it depends on whether the suffering is involuntary *simpliciter* or only involuntary *secundum quid*. For a person who does not have even implicit faith, whose suffering is involuntary *simpliciter*, suffering is defeated in virtue of its contributing to warding off a greater harm for her. On the other hand, for a person who is committed to a life of faith, whose suffering is involuntary only *secundum quid*, suffering is defeated in virtue of its contributing to providing a greater good for her.[70]

This result is as it should be, in my view. In ordinary cases of suffering permitted or brought about by one person for the good of another, if the suffering is involuntary *simpliciter*, then one person who allows (or causes) the suffering of another is not justified simply in virtue of the suffering's contributing to some greater good for the sufferer, even if the suffering is a necessary means to this greater good. So, for example, a person who is forced to endure semi-starvation and sensory deprivation during extensive confinement in a small space will emerge from that confinement to drink in with intense pleasure and gratitude experiences that other people take for granted. No doubt, the harsh imprisonment is necessary for that heightened pleasure in ordinary things. Even if we were to grant for the sake of argument both that the suffering in such a case is outweighed by the good that the suffering provides later and that this greater good could not be gotten without the suffering, no reasonable person would suppose that such a greater good justifies subjecting a person to such suffering involuntarily.[71] If a mother subjected a child of hers to such suffering for the sake of such a good, we would hope social services would remove that child from that mother.

It would not change our judgment if the mother incurred significant cost and risk to herself as a result of confining the child.[72] The connection of the involuntary suffering to the greater good of the child is not enough to justify the mother in bringing about such suffering for the child, regardless of what the mother herself might endure in the process.[73]

On the other hand, in a desperate effort to keep them hidden from the Nazis, certain people subjected Jewish children to just such suffering during the Second World War. And we now honor these people for doing so, because in those circumstances confinement of that sort, with its attendant suffering, was the best or only means available for keeping the children from a much worse fate at the hands of the Nazis. In these circumstances, the confinement with all its hard conditions warded off a greater harm for the children. What we find morally unacceptable when the benefit for the suffering is a greater good we find morally admirable when it involves warding off a greater harm.

On our ordinary moral intuitions, then, for suffering that is involuntary *simpliciter*, warding off a greater harm for a person is a morally acceptable reason for allowing suffering, if the suffering is the best or only means available in the circumstances to that end, but providing a greater good is not.[74]

Our intuitions are different, however, if a person's suffering is involuntary only *secundum quid* and not *simpliciter*. For example, *ceteris paribus*, we would not blame the coach of a team of cross-country runners who forced running up one more hill on his team against their vocal complaints. The greater good of the additional conditioning justifies the suffering inflicted on the team by the coach's demand for more training. In this case, because participation on the team is voluntary and presumably carries with it some assent to suffering in the interest of athletic excellence, our intuitions incline to the view that the involuntary suffering of the team members in their training is justified by the outweighing greater good of their resulting athletic excellence and competitive edge. On our ordinary moral intuitions, therefore, for suffering that is involuntary only *secundum quid*, providing a greater good for a sufferer is (*ceteris paribus*) a morally acceptable reason for allowing suffering if the suffering is the best or only means available in the circumstances for that end.

To hold, as Aquinas does, that warding off a greater harm for a person or providing a greater good for her justifies God in allowing suffering is not to say that God designed the world in such a way as to produce that suffering for that person. It is important to remember in this connection the distinction between God's antecedent and God's consequent will. Aquinas's theodicy rests on a claim about what justifies God in willing what he does in his consequent will. But that is not equivalent to a claim about God's antecedent will, about what God would have willed if human beings had themselves willed something other than they actually did. Aquinas does not think, for example, that God somehow determined tribal raiders to rob Job of his cattle or that the raiders were in accordance with God's antecedent will when they attacked Job. On the contrary, on Aquinas's views, the raiders acted on their own free will in attacking Job's herds. All that is claimed in Aquinas's theodicy is that, in his consequent will, God allows Job to suffer from the raiders as he does because God sees that this suffering can be turned into a benefit for Job. Because that benefit defeats Job's suffering, God is justified in allowing it. But nothing in this claim presupposes or implies that God wills this suffering for Job in his antecedent will.

Finally, it is helpful to note that, on Aquinas's view of the benefits justifying God in allowing suffering, the explanation for suffering has to do primarily with the state of the sufferer that comes *after* the time of his suffering. On the interpretation I gave of the story, what justifies God in allowing Job's suffering, for example, is not anything Job did before he suffered, contrary to what the mistaken Comforters suppose. Rather, the explanation for Job's suffering has primarily to do with what Job is enabled to become, in consequence of his suffering.[75] An analogy with medicine is helpful here. Doctors who put a cancer patient through painful surgery and strenuous chemotherapy cause the patient great suffering. The explanation of their justification for causing that suffering lies primarily in the future, rather than in the past. The medical treatments are justified by what they enable the patient to be—namely, a healthy or at least a living person. Two patients whose cancers are identical and identically advanced may get very different treatments from the same doctors, depending on the doctors' estimation of the effects of those treatments on the patients. The bone-marrow transplant that may cure the young woman of her multiple myeloma might kill the old man who has the same disease at the same state of development, because his system is no longer able to respond well to the treatments as hers is. And so the doctors will be justified in giving her the medical treatments they deny him based on their estimation of the future states of the patients. Although the doctors consider the current state of each patient, it is their estimate of the future state of each patient that justifies their decision to treat or not to treat the patient.

The nature of each benefit

On Aquinas's views, union with God features in each of the benefits justifying God in allowing suffering. The greater harm warded off is the permanent absence of union with God, and the greater good provided is the increased degree of everlasting shared union with God.

Since, on Aquinas's scale of value, permanent absence of union with God is the worst thing that can happen to a person, the negative value of the permanent absence of union with God outweighs the negative value of suffering of any other kind. Avoiding that outcome is, therefore, of more value for a person than avoiding any other kind of suffering. Analogously, since union with God is the intrinsic upper limit to human flourishing, attaining this union is of greater value for a person than avoiding suffering. On the face of it, then, the obvious question for Aquinas's theodicy is not whether the good of the benefit outweighs the suffering in any given case but rather whether the suffering is appropriately connected to one or the other of these benefits.[76] Even if we weigh the relative value of the benefits and the suffering as Aquinas does, why suppose that suffering is connected to these benefits as it needs to be for the purposes of theodicy?

I raise this question here only because it prompts us to take a closer look at the nature of the benefits that are supposed to defeat suffering. (I will raise the question again in a different way in the final chapter, when I turn to the evaluation of Aquinas's theodicy as a defense.) If we are going to understand Aquinas's claim that suffering can bring about these benefits for the sufferer, we need to be clear about the nature of the benefits. It is helpful in this connection to review briefly Aquinas's views of union with God as I explained them in earlier chapters.

For Aquinas, the primary obstacle to any person's flourishing in union with God comes from dispositions in that person's will that incline him to prefer his own short-term pleasure and power over greater goods. On Aquinas's understanding of the doctrine of original sin, all human beings have this disposition, which is a sort of cancer of the will,[77] a proneness to evil that eventuates in moral wrongdoing sooner or later and that can blow up into moral monstrosity.[78]

On Aquinas's views, a human person can be internally integrated only around the objective moral good. Not all internal fragmentation stems from moral wrongdoing; shame contributes to internal divisions in the psyche as well. The double-mindedness and internal conflict in Mary of Bethany, for example, have shame as at least one major source. Nonetheless, all moral wrongdoing contributes to psychic fragmentation, and so no human being who remains uncured of the disease of the will can be internally integrated.

This lack of internal integration undermines or obviates closeness between persons. Even God cannot be close to a human being who is internally fragmented and alienated from himself. Perfectly loving God desires the good for each human person and union with each person. And omnipresent God is present to each human person, in the sense that God is able and willing to be close to him and to share attention with him if he wants to share attention with God. But even God cannot be present to a person with significant personal presence unless that person is willing to be close to God, with all that that closeness entails.

On Aquinas's views, then, the obstacle to a person's having the best thing for human beings, shared union with God, is that person's internally divided state.[79] Since the best thing for human beings and the worst thing for human beings are jointly exhaustive, warding off the worst thing for any human person is also a matter of healing this internally divided condition. Aquinas takes justification and sanctification to be the means by which a person is healed of this disease of the will; by these means, a person becomes internally integrated around the good. Each of these processes involves a human person's giving up resistance to God.[80]

Justification occurs when a human person recognizes and rejects the moral evil in himself and yearns for God and the goodness of God. Aquinas takes this as the volitional component of faith. Faith includes an act of will that is a global second-order desire for a will that wills the good.[81] This volition is not a result of any kind of praiseworthy activity on the part of the willer. Rather, God forms this volition in a person once that person surrenders resistance to the love of God—that is, once he surrenders to God and lets the desire for God come to him. This kind of surrender can begin a first conversion to God, but it can also be the start of regeneration after the shipwreck of a life, as it is in Samson's case. Insufficiently reformed as they are at the end of the narrative, Samson's desires and his relationship with God at the end of his life are the result of a surrender to God that regenerates what is best in him and for him.

Aquinas takes faith to be the sole necessary and sufficient condition for warding off the worst thing for human beings. While the act of will of faith remains in a person, permanent willed loneliness is ruled out for him. Samson's surrender in faith to God's love is sufficient for saving him from that worst thing for human beings, even if a lot of the old Samson remains in him till his death. Warding off for a person the greater harm of permanent absence of union with God requires only bringing about and maintaining in him the volitional component of faith.

For Aquinas, the morally sufficient reason for God's allowing suffering that is involuntary *simpliciter* for a person is the role of such suffering in bringing that person to surrender to the love of God and, through that surrender, to the act of will in faith constitutive of justification.

The process begun by justification is continued by sanctification. It is possible for a person to have the second-order will of faith and also to have a first-order will that wills what it ought not to will, and so the act of will in faith is compatible with any amount of first-order willing of particular evils.[82] When a person's will is in this condition, he still fails to be integrated around the good to some degree. To this extent, however, he is also less able to be close to God, less united with God, than he might otherwise be. The desire for God in faith is the beginning of a relationship in love with God, and it culminates in union with God if a person perseveres in it. In the process of sanctification, however, God works together with the will of a human person in a cooperative enterprise that gradually integrates her more and more in goodness. Since internal psychic fragmentation is the sole obstacle to a person's union with God, sanctification thus brings a person into as deep a union with God as she is willing to have. Insofar as her greatness is correlative with the deepness of her union with God, sanctification glorifies her.

So sanctification presupposes justification, and justification includes a surrender to God in love. In justification, a human person is passive, rather than active; that is why, in justification, God's grace is only operative, not cooperative. On the other hand, unlike justification, sanctification is a matter of cooperation between God and a human person. A human person cannot be in the process of sanctification in an entirely involuntary way; just because sanctification is a matter of cooperation between God's grace and a human will, a human person in the process of sanctification actively wills to draw nearer to God. Insofar as suffering is a means to justification, therefore, the suffering involved is involuntary *simpliciter*; but the suffering resulting in sanctification is by contrast involuntary only *secundum quid*.

Consequently, the benefit for the suffering whose aim is the sufferer's surrender to God's love is the warding-off the worst thing for human beings. The benefit for the suffering whose aim is growth in internal integration in the cooperative process of sanctification is the increased closeness to God and the correlative increase in human flourishing and glory.

Finally, justification and sanctification are also the antidote to the internal alienation stemming from shame. The shame of Mary of Bethany is healed, partially and then wholly, in her relationship to Jesus, who is recognized in the story as the son of God (as Martha's confession to Jesus makes explicit). The love Jesus has for Mary and Mary's ability to accept and rejoice in that love are healing for those things in her psyche broken by shame. To be loved by God is to be desired by God, and so to be desirable by the greatest standard of all. To be in a relationship of mutual love with God is also to be able to give to God, as well as to receive from God; and there is ultimate honor in giving to the Deity. When Jesus protects Mary and allows her to anoint him, especially in the first anointing but also in the second, he honors her in a way that itself shames the standard by which her community originally shamed her. But neither of these healings of shame would have come to Mary if she had not been willing to be open to the love offered her, in the way Aquinas takes to be central to justification and sanctification. So the antidotes to shame—beauty and honor—are also effects of justification and sanctification.

On Aquinas's views, then, justification and sanctification include the healing of all the varieties of internal alienation,[83] and so they bring a person into as much union with God as she is willing to have. The resulting benefits defeat suffering for that person, on Aquinas's theodicy.

In discussing the book of Job, I argued that in that narrative there is a fractal character to God's providential care for sufferers. Any particular case of suffering is embedded in the story of that sufferer's life, and the sufferer is the chief protagonist of that story. But each such story will be thoroughly interwoven with the life stories of other people; and each of those other people is the protagonist in *his* story, even if he has only a small part in the life story of someone else. To talk about the suffering Job has in the loss of his children and the possible benefits that might defeat that suffering for Job is to say nothing at all about the suffering each of those children endures in consequence of dying in that way at that time, or about what benefits might defeat that suffering for that child. Each person's suffering is the proper topic for the narrative in which that person is the chief character.

If (contrary to Aquinas's view) the good for human beings were such things as winning a war, say, and if each side in a battle prayed to God to win that war, then it would be hard to understand how divine providence could find a way to deal providentially with all the parties in the war in such a way as to answer their prayers and defeat their battlefield sufferings. That is, of course, because, as long as both sides are actively engaged in war—that is, as long as the warring parties do not resolve their differences or puddle down into a truce—then *somebody* will have to lose that war. But, on Aquinas's scale of values, it is much less difficult to understand how providence can provide the good for every human person. Unlike the prize of winning a war, the relational good of union with God is infinitely shareable without diminution, and it is available to every human person no matter what that person's external circumstances might be.

Having that relational good is a matter of that person's psychic state, not his external circumstances.

And so the fractal nature of the providential guiding of human suffering and of the benefits able to defeat it are easier to see on Aquinas's theodicy and the scale of value it presupposes. In virtue of being a great good, the good that is the intrinsic upper limit of human flourishing, union with God, is a good that does not diminish when it is distributed, and so it is an infinitely shareable good. Of course, it is possible that a human person have her heart set on a *small* good—that is, a good that *does* diminish when it is distributed. But I mention this worry only to set it to one side; I will return to it in the next chapter, which is devoted to the desires of the heart.

The role of suffering in warding off the worst thing

Although Aquinas thinks that suffering plays an important role in the processes of both justification and sanctification, he gives few hints about the means by which, as he supposes, suffering has the effects it does in these processes. And so it seems to me better to leave out of the account of his theodicy any attempt at detailed explanation of the particular psychological mechanisms by which suffering influences the state of will sought in justification and sanctification. I will, therefore, highlight the role Aquinas attributes to suffering in justification and sanctification, but I will leave vague and unexplored the specific means by which Aquinas supposes suffering fills that role. (In the final chapter of this book, however, I will present and discuss studies in contemporary psychology that seem to confirm Aquinas's position on this score.)

Because Aquinas thinks of justification and sanctification as healing for a human psyche, he often speaks of suffering as God's medicine for the psychic disorder of post-Fall human beings. In this attitude, he is representative of a centuries-long medieval tradition. Augustine, for example, says:

The Physician to whom we have unreservedly entrusted ourselves and from whom we have the promise of the present life and of the life to come—that Physician sees these things [hunger, thirst, and other bodily sufferings] as helpful remedies . . . He governs and guides us so that we may be consoled and exercised in this life and so that in the life to come we may be established and confirmed in eternal rest.[84]

In his commentary on the Apostles' Creed, Aquinas himself says:

If all the pain a human being suffers is from God [as Aquinas thinks it is], then he ought to bear it patiently, both because it is from God and because it is ordered toward good; for pains purge sins, bring evildoers to humility, and stimulate good people to love of God.[85]

In his commentary on Thessalonians, Aquinas remarks on one part of the process he mentions in the quotation above. He says:

As water extinguishes a burning fire, so tribulations extinguish the force of concupiscent desires, so that human beings don't follow them at will . . . Therefore, [the Church] is not destroyed [by tribulations] but lifted up by them, and in the first place by the lifting up of the mind to God, as Gregory says: the evils that bear us down here drive us to go to God.[86]

Aquinas comments in great detail on the line in Hebrews: "whom the Lord loves he chastens."[87] He says, for example:

Since pains are a sort of medicine, we should apparently judge correction and medicine the same way. Now medicine in the taking of it is bitter and loathsome, but its end is desirable and intensely sweet. So discipline is also. It is hard to bear, but it blossoms into the best outcome.[88]

The same general point appears recurrently in Aquinas's commentary on Job. Arguing that temporal goods such as those Job lost are given and taken away according to God's will, Aquinas says:

someone's suffering adversity would not be pleasing to God except for the sake of some good coming from the adversity. And so although adversity is in itself bitter and gives rise to sadness, it should nonetheless be agreeable [to us] when we consider its usefulness, on account of which it is pleasing to God . . . For in his reason a person rejoices over the taking of bitter medicine because of the hope of health, even though in his senses he is troubled.[89]

In commenting on a line in the book of Job containing the complaint that God sometimes does not hear a needy person's prayers, Aquinas says:

Now it sometimes happens that God hearkens not to a person's pleas but rather to his advantage. A doctor does not hearken to the pleas of the sick person who requests that the bitter medicine be taken away (supposing that the doctor doesn't take it away because he knows that it contributes to health); instead he hearkens to [the patient's] advantage, because by doing so he produces health, which the sick person wants most of all. In the same way, God does not remove tribulations from the person stuck in them, even though he prays earnestly for God to do so, because God knows these tribulations help him forward to final salvation. And so although God truly does hearken, the person stuck in afflictions believes that God hasn't hearkened to him.[90]

For Aquinas, then, all suffering is medicinal for the parts of a person's psyche in need of healing. For those who are already internally integrated to one or another degree, the experience of suffering enables them to open in a deeper way to the love of God, as Aquinas says in the commentary on the Creed. But for those who are very divided within themselves, suffering is medicinal in the sense that, as Aquinas puts it, it helps the sufferer forward to salvation. Samson's distance from Delilah is symptomatic of a destructive internal division within Samson himself; it keeps not only Delilah but even God separated from him. There is something derisory about Samson in his jaded, self-protective condition when he is dallying with Delilah in enemy territory and using his great strength for nothing more admirable than fly swatting occasional Philistines. The subsequent wreckage of Samson's life is a natural outgrowth of his deplorable choices and acts. But the suffering that comes to Samson in consequence is also a means for healing Samson of the psychic ills that are deadly to what he himself cares about. On the interpretation of the narrative I argued for, God allows Samson's dreadful suffering in the spirit in which a loving mother allows her child to have a bone-marrow transplant: there is a chance that this suffering, however terrible, will save the loved person, who is otherwise in danger of something even worse.

On Aquinas's view, God is justified in allowing such suffering for a person in Samson's condition in virtue of the contribution suffering makes to warding off the worst thing that can happen to that person.

The role of suffering in providing the best thing

Given Aquinas's view of suffering as medicinal for the human psyche, one might be tempted to think that Aquinas would also take a person's suffering to be in direct proportion to her need for psychic healing. One might suppose, that is, that, since Aquinas thinks suffering is medicinal in integrating a person around goodness, then he would also think that a person who was more integrated in goodness would need and get less suffering. But, in fact, Aquinas's position is just the opposite. On Aquinas's theodicy, the more a person is integrated around goodness, the more likely it is that she will experience suffering. In explicating two metaphors in one of Job's speeches,[91] comparing human beings in this life to servants of a great lord and to soldiers on a military campaign, Aquinas makes the point in this way:

It is plain that the general of an army does not spare [his] more active soldiers dangers or exertions, but as the plan of battle requires, he sometimes lays them open to greater dangers and greater exertions. But after the attainment of victory, he bestows greater honor on the more active soldiers. So also the head of a household assigns greater exertions to his better servants, but when it is time to reward them, he lavishes greater gifts on them. And so neither is it characteristic of divine providence that it should exempt good people more from the adversities and exertions of the present life, but rather that it reward them more at the end.[92]

Aquinas's sense that the inner wholeness of a person renders her more, rather than less, likely to suffer can be understood in light of his taking suffering as medicinal. Strenuous medical regimens are saved for the strongest patients, in the hopes of bringing them to the most robust health and functioning. And so, on Aquinas's theodicy, for those people who are psychically more healthy, the benefit that justifies suffering is the connection between suffering and glory.

It is because of this understanding of suffering that, in the passage from Gregory the Great's *Moralia in Job* cited in Chapter 1, Gregory finds it so perplexing when good things happen to good people. If apparently good people really are good on the relativized human standard of goodness, that is, if they really are in the process of moral regeneration that integrates them around the good, then, Gregory thinks, God would bless them with the medicine of suffering to move them forward to even further sanctification. The absence of suffering in the lives of such people is, therefore, mysterious to Gregory. Chemotherapeutic regimens are withheld from people with cancer only in case they are so ill that the therapy cannot do them any good. That is why, when good things happen to good people, Gregory finds the ways of providence so hard to understand.

This is a common attitude in Christian thought and can be found much earlier than the work of either Aquinas or Gregory.[93] John Chrysostom, for example, puts the idea in terms of honor. He says: "What then? 'Is there nobody', someone asks, 'who enjoys comfort both here and hereafter?' This cannot be . . . it is impossible. It is not possible, not possible at all, for one who enjoys an easy life and freedom from want in this world . . . to enjoy honor in the other world."[94] And a little later Chrysostom adds: "The present life is an arena; in the arena and in athletic contests the man who expects to be crowned cannot enjoy relaxation. So if anyone wishes to win a crown, let him choose the hard and laborious life, in order that after he has striven a short time here he may enjoy lasting honor hereafter."[95]

Aquinas's position is similar. So, for example, he says: "All the saints who have pleased God have gone through many tribulations by which they were made the sons of God."[96] In his commentary on Thessalonians, Aquinas presupposes the same point in considering the ultimate tribulation, the sufferings in the eschaton: "Many who are alive [in the eschaton] will be tried in the persecution of Antichrist, and they will surpass in greatness the many who had previously died."[97] Elsewhere, in making the point more generally, Aquinas says simply: "from sufferings borne here a person attains to glory."[98]

These and many other passages make it clear that, for Aquinas, in virtue of the role suffering plays in the process of sanctification, there is a connection between suffering, on the one hand, and glory in shared union with God, on the other. It is not surprising, then, to find that Aquinas sees a person's enduring severe suffering as a sign of the spiritual greatness of the sufferer.

From Aquinas's point of view, then, the portrayal of the suffering of the protagonists in the preceding narratives makes sense. Abraham is called by God to endure the troubles of homelessness, the wearisome pains of a heart's desire recurrently disappointed, and the anguish of surrendering that heart's desire once he has it. At the end of his story, he has struggled his way to a deep trust in God that makes him a father of faith as well as a patriarch of many peoples. Mary is heartbroken when her beloved brother dies and she supposes she does not matter to Jesus, whom she loved, in whom she had reposed her greatest trust. But at the end of her story she has come closer to Jesus than even the apostle on whom Jesus founds his church. Peter assents to having his feet washed by Jesus, who thereby gives care to Peter. Mary washes the feet of Jesus, who is willing to receive care from Mary; and the way in which Mary washes his feet, heedless of herself and unstinting in love, becomes woven into the Gospel narrative itself. Job begins by losing all that apparently constitutes flourishing in his society. But at the end of his story God comes to talk to him face to face in the most extensive and powerful conversations between God and a human person recorded anywhere in the biblical narratives. After their suffering and because of it, these sufferers become icons of human greatness, whose stories are worth preserving through many centuries and cultures.

Something of the same sort is true even of Samson, as Milton's play about him illustrates. Given Samson's condition at the end of his life, his suffering is justified in virtue of its contribution to warding off for Samson the worst thing for human beings.

But, as things turn out, because Samson reacts passionately and positively in the process of his suffering, his suffering also contributes to making him glorious, in the way Samson himself wanted to be. For Samson, we might say, sanctification follows justification in swift succession.

In all the stories, then, in varying ways, each of the protagonists receives his own flourishing and greatness in exchange for what his suffering deprived him of in his earthly life. On Aquinas's theodicy, that benefit is everlasting, and the exchange is one that every person ought to be willing to make because he receives vastly more of what he cares about than he loses in his suffering.

Because Aquinas holds that the suffering for those able and willing to receive it as sanctifying contributes to the best thing for human beings, he also thinks that there is something to exult in as regards such suffering, however appalling it is in its own character as suffering. So, for example, he says:

It is a sign of the ardent hope which we have on account of Christ that we glory not only because of [our] hope of the glory to come, but we glory even regarding the evils which we suffer for it. And so [Paul] says that we not only glory (that is, in our hope of glory), but we glory even in tribulations, by which we attain to glory.[99]

If we saw only the pain and suffering of athletes training for major competitions and never saw any scenes of athletic glory and prize-winning, we would have a seriously wrong view of suffering in athletics. Analogously, from Aquinas's view, the involuntarily endured suffering of a person of faith has to be viewed in the context of that person's everlasting condition in the afterlife. The powerful admiration excited by the excellence of great athletes can inspire something close to envy about their ability to endure suffering in training. Analogously, although any reasonable person reading the stories in the preceding section would shrink from the suffering of the protagonists in those stories, most readers are also willing to accord those protagonists great admiration by the stories' end. From Aquinas's point of view, the greatness on the part of a person whose suffering has brought him to glory in shared union with God can make that person's endurance of suffering look worth having, too.

Many contemporaries will cringe at these lines, of course, but that is because they think there is no such thing as everlasting glory in heaven, not because they would be unwilling to accept suffering to win it if they thought it were there to be had.

A Molinist objection and a clarification

At this point, it will help elucidate Aquinas's position if we consider briefly a possible Molinist objection to it. Some people, the intellectual descendants of Molina, suppose that God has what is called 'middle knowledge.'[100] This includes knowledge of what a person *would* freely do in certain circumstances, as distinct from foreknowledge, which includes knowledge of what a person *will* freely do at a certain future time. If God has middle knowledge, as well as foreknowledge, then God knows what suffering would be efficacious in a person's life to bring that person to salvation and glory. In that case, Molinists will maintain, even on Aquinas's theodicy God would not allow any suffering that did not in fact bring inner healing to a person. There could not, therefore, be any suffering to which a person reacts by turning away from God.[101] But manifestly there is. And so, the Molinist objection runs, Aquinas's theodicy has a plainly false implication.

The contemporary debate over Molinism has prompted an extensive philosophical literature, and I cannot enter into that debate in passing here. As far as I can see, Aquinas does not accept Molinism. On his view of God's knowledge, it is not true, for example, that God knows what Job would have done if prosperity and commitment to God had never been connected either in Job's worldview or in Job's world, not because there is a defect in God's omniscience but because there is nothing there to be known. But it is not necessary to adjudicate the opposing positions in this case. That is because it is possible to sidestep the objection I am here attributing to the Molinists. This objection presupposes that, if God knew that a particular case of suffering would not have the effect of moving a person closer to God, God would not allow that suffering. But this supposition seems to me false, and its falsity does not depend on the truth or falsity of Molinism.

To see this point, consider that, in any given instance of the sort of inefficacious suffering at issue for the Molinist objector, it might be the case that without the suffering the sufferer would be moved even further away from God than he currently is or than he would be without the suffering.[102] Think of the example of Satan in the book of Job, for example. Or, for a case drawn from history, consider, for example, Albert Speer. Speer's suffering in consequence of the defeat of the Nazis did not in fact move him closer to God, at least not if his voluble expressions of repentance were self-deceived or hypocritical, as many people take them to be. But it also seems very plausible to suppose (even in the absence of middle knowledge) that without the suffering he experienced in Germany's defeat Speer would have become a much worse man than he actually was after the war. So, even if it does not produce increased closeness to God, suffering can be justified because it wards off even further distance from God.[103]

Furthermore, and more importantly for my purposes, there is something worthwhile about giving a person an opportunity for a good thing even if one were in a position to know he will not take that opportunity. This is the sort of case that would be exemplified in God's relations with Satan in the framing story in the book of Job if we were to read the story with the theological belief that Satan is incapable of repentance and reform. We can understand cases of this sort as a matter of giving power to a person, whether or not he is willing to use that power.

To see this point, consider an imaginary development of the narrative of the relationship between Abraham and his son Ishmael. Suppose that, when Abraham was an old man, he wanted to ask Ishmael's forgiveness for not having been a better father to him. But suppose also that at that time Abraham had moral certitude that his son Ishmael would never grant that forgiveness because he was so sunk in hatred of Abraham. It could still be good *for Ishmael* that Abraham ask Ishmael for his forgiveness.

The narrative of *Ishmael's* life would be better if Abraham asked his forgiveness; if the story of Ishmael's life lacked that petition on Abraham's part, it would be a worse story and a worse life for Ishmael. That is because, before Abraham asks forgiveness of Ishmael, it is not in Ishmael's power to be reconciled with Abraham.[104] After Abraham asks forgiveness, Ishmael does have this power. The acquisition of this power is a good for Ishmael even if he does not use it. So, even when one is in a position to know that a sufferer will not use the opportunity for healing acquired through suffering, it may nonetheless be good that the sufferer have it.

And, as I argued in connection with the portrayal of Satan in the story of Job, there is love in offering such power, such opportunity for good, to a person. Even if it were true in that story that God knew that Satan was irredeemable, there is still love in God's wrestling with Satan. God's engaging with Satan as he does contributes to a good for Satan and manifests a desire for as much closeness to Satan as Satan will allow; and so, on Aquinas's account of love, God's engaging with Satan in this way is an expression of love toward Satan. That love is a good thing to have in the world, even if Satan does not accept it.

On Aquinas's theodicy, then, suffering offers a power for movement toward God in the process of justification or sanctification. Even if this power is not used, even if God were to know in advance that it would not be used either for additional closeness to God or for less distance from God, there is still a good for the sufferer in having been offered that power. And there is God's love for the sufferer in offering it.[105]

For these reasons, the Molinist objection to Aquinas's theodicy is mistaken. Even if Molinism were true (contrary to what I take Aquinas's position to be), Aquinas's theodicy need not be committed to the implication that all suffering moves a sufferer closer to God, or to the implication that God is not justified in allowing suffering if it does not succeed in moving a sufferer closer to God.

The refolding phenomenon

As these remarks about the Molinist objection highlight, what effect any particular case of suffering has in the life of a particular person is a function of that person's freely willed reaction to that suffering. It is possible for a sufferer freely to reject the good of those benefits.[106] Because the benefit of justification or sanctification depends on being appropriated by the free will of the sufferer, suffering alone cannot cause these benefits. Aquinas's image of suffering as medicinal is therefore apt, because, on his views, suffering, like many life-saving medical treatments, is not guaranteed to be successful without the cooperation of the sufferer. Consequently, it would be more precise to say that, for Aquinas, the chance of keeping a person from the worst thing is the morally sufficient reason for God's allowing the suffering of those who are turned away from him; and the chance of transforming a person into something everlastingly glorious is the morally sufficient reason for God's permitting the suffering of those who are closer to him and morally and psychically stronger. If a person rejects the benefit of either justification or sanctification that might have been brought him by his suffering, that suffering will still provide at least this benefit for him—namely, the good of having been offered the opportunity to move closer to God in justification or sanctification or both.

Which of these roles suffering plays in regard to a particular person's suffering on a particular occasion—justification or sanctification—is a function of that person's response to that suffering on that occasion. In consequence of his response, any particular suffering can change its character. We are accustomed to the idea that a protein can be folded in different ways and that, at least in the case of proteins (if not everywhere), the Aristotelian idea that function follows form is right. The same protein can have radically different functions, depending on its folding.[107] Because of the role of free will in the appropriation of the benefits defeating suffering, suffering is also like this on Aquinas's theodicy. So, for example, a particular case of suffering that might have contributed to a sufferer's sanctification can, as it were, refold into a suffering contributing to the sufferer's justification if the sufferer reacts to the suffering by turning away from God and goodness. If Job had cursed God, as Satan hoped he would, then Job would not have emerged from his suffering glorious in the way that he does in the story. But then Job's dreadful suffering would have contributed to his justification, rather than his sanctification.

On the other hand, nothing keeps suffering whose main benefit would have been warding off the worst thing for the sufferer from being a benefit contributing to the glory of the sufferer because he responds to it in great-souled ways. In virtue of Samson's response to his suffering, for example, justification and sanctification are virtually simultaneously effected for him. Through his suffering, and his response to that suffering, Samson is not only restored to relationship with God but is brought to the fulfillment of his mission. He is made something that he himself wanted to be and that he himself would have found greatly admirable if he had seen it in others. As Samson's story shows, then, it is possible for a person to be simultaneously irremediably broken and also glorious. A person can be very far from physical or psychological well-being (or both), as Samson is in the story, and nonetheless have a life that exemplifies something of the best in human beings, in which the sufferer has his flourishing. Aquinas's scale of value, which ties human excellence and flourishing to relationship with God, supports such an evaluation.[108] But it is also an evaluation held by people who neither know nor care about Aquinas's views. A look at those among the poor who were broken in some way and yet are greatly admired by one or another subgroup within contemporary Western culture makes the point.[109]

Consequently, there is no one assessment of a person's condition on the basis of which all suffering in that person's life is distributed. Rather, the process of building a second-personal connection to God, in which suffering has a role, is like the analogous process between human persons, at least in this respect, that the nature of the connection is continually changing and shifting, depending on the choices of the persons involved, from one time to another.[110]

Suffering and consolation

Even with this much clarification, Aquinas's theodicy is still not presented in full. What is yet missing is his understanding of the role of divine consolation.

Because God is omnipresent[111] and perfectly loving, Aquinas thinks that all suffering is encompassed even in this life by the love of God. Some experience of the personal presence of God, significant personal presence with mutual closeness and shared attention, is possible for all people; it is not reserved just for mystics.[112] For those who are open to God's presence, the minimal omnipresence of God becomes significant presence in love; and this presence brings consolation with it.[113]

In fact, Aquinas thinks that, for sufferers who are open to God's presence, the consolation of that presence is felt with increased intensity in direct proportion to their sufferings. At the start of his commentary on 1 Thessalonians Aquinas quotes with approval the line in 2 Corinthians which says that, "as the sufferings of Christ abound in us, so our consolation also abounds by Christ" (2 Cor. 1: 5). This is not because God is willing to come closer to people who have fulfilled a certain quota of suffering. It is because through suffering a person can become more open to the love of God. Samson's distance from God, his willed loneliness even where human persons are concerned, begins to be overcome in consequence of his appalling suffering. When Samson is willing to be more open to God, God can come closer to Samson, with the consolation that such closeness brings.

It is clear that Aquinas's notion of consolation is not abstract or anemic; rather, it emphasizes the role of significant personal presence in relationship with God. So, for example, Aquinas says:

the ultimate perfection, by which a person is made perfect inwardly, is joy, which stems from the presence of what is loved. Whoever has the love of God, however, already has what he loves, as is said in 1 John 4: 16: 'whoever abides in the love of God abides in God, and God abides in him.' And joy wells up from this.[114]

Elsewhere, commenting on a text in the epistles of Paul, Aquinas puts the point this way: "When [Paul] says 'the Lord is near,' he points out the cause of joy, because a person rejoices at the nearness of his friend."[115]

Moreover, on Aquinas's views, the joy that comes from the experience of God's presence to a human person is essential to the religious life of a believer; and Aquinas expects that all persons of faith will have such joy.[116] As Aquinas puts it, without the joy of this relationship, no progress is possible for anyone in the life of faith.[117]

Someone might object that suffering interferes with the joy of loving relations, in all the different ways we could trouble to spell out, and that Aquinas simply fails to appreciate this point. I want to concede what seems to be a presupposition of this objection: loving relationship even with the deity does not prevent or take away suffering, as Aquinas himself recognizes.[118] On the other hand, however, Aquinas would reject the objection itself. Aquinas thinks that no sort of suffering, not even pain, can destroy the good of the loving personal relationship between God and a human being open to God's presence.[119]

I will have it pointed out to me also that there are well-known cases in which a sufferer complains bitterly of the absence of God. Sometimes the complaint that God is absent is simply a poignant way of calling attention to the suffering itself and to the fact that God did not prevent the suffering. So understood, the complaint is a passionate expression of the problem of suffering, but it has nothing to do with the availability of religious consolation. On the other hand, there are cases where the apparent lack of any sense of the presence of God is itself part of the suffering. Abraham endured long periods of deep disappointment without contact with God; Mary thought Jesus had neglected or forgotten her. Samson lost his connection to God and the strength it brought him in his hour of most need. And a central ingredient of Job's suffering was his experience of God as absent. Of course, Abraham and Mary do eventually receive such consolation. God returns to Samson, to empower him as God did on the earlier occasions when God's spirit rushed into Samson. And one of the longest speeches attributed to God in the Bible is the speech God makes to Job. When God's speech is finished, Job says: "I had heard of you before with the hearing of the ear, but now my eye sees you."[120] In the end, none of these sufferers could truly be said to suffer entirely without the consolation of God's presence.

Nonetheless, at least since the time of John of the Cross, the Christian tradition has recognized what John of the Cross called 'the dark night of the soul.' This phrase refers to a condition in which the consoling feeling typically brought about by experience of the presence and love of God is truly blocked for a person of faith.[121] The obstacle to such consolation is not some internal religious or moral dysfunction on the sufferer's part. Rather, as it is traditionally understood, the deprivation of this consolation is brought about by God for those who are already the most close to him, as a kind of intense training for those capable of the greatest union with him. Recently, this condition has been made the subject of considerable discussion because of the revelation that Mother Teresa suffered from it until her death.[122] Mother Teresa herself came to see the absence of spiritual consolation in her life as a special gift of God's to her, enabling her to grow powerfully in closeness to God. Why she would think so, however, or why the deprivation of consolation should be thought to have such an effect is a complicated story, which cannot be addressed in passing here; and so I note it only to leave it to one side.

For my purposes here, then, cases of the spiritually advanced who suffer the dark night of the soul have to be recognized as an exception to the claim that consolation increases with affliction. But, with the exception of such complicated cases, the consolation that accompanies suffering for those who are open to it, the shared attention with God and closeness to God, is available to all sufferers and is part of the benefit for those sufferers who are willing to receive it, on Aquinas's views.

Aquinas's theodicy and the mysteriousness of suffering

This, then, is the heart of Aquinas's theodicy. As I hope is clear, it is not to be confused with more pedestrian positions in its neighborhood. The goal of the redemptive processes of justification and sanctification is not growth in some non-relational inner state such as virtue, for example. The goal is the establishment and deepening of a relationship of love between two persons, one human and one divine. For Aquinas, redemption and glory, like consolation itself, are a function of relationship and can be had only in relationship.

In Chapter 1, I argued that, revelation on God's part aside, suffering is opaque; there is no transparency as regards flourishing or one's heart's desires. While Samson is engaged in his shabby affair with Delilah, he is not aware of the loss of that flourishing which he himself desires. In his odious condition, he thinks of himself as flourishing, as successful because of his physical strength. The same opacity attaches to the benefits that can defeat suffering. In the period when Mary was sure she had irretrievably lost her brother and the love of Jesus, which she wanted as much as she wanted her brother, Jesus in great love for her was preparing to restore her brother to her. So it is not the case that one has a benefit that defeats suffering if and only if one knows that one has it. A fortiori, others may also fail to see it. As I explained in that earlier chapter, on Aquinas's views so-called skeptical theism is false:[123] we *are* in a position to know what God's reasons are for allowing suffering—but only in general, in theory. For any *particular* case of suffering, because of the opacity of suffering and the opacity of the benefits defeating suffering, by means of unaided human reason a human person will typically not be in a position to know what justifies God in permitting *that* suffering.

The epistemic problem for Aquinas is not the inscrutability of God's mind (as some proponents of skeptical theism allege) but the inscrutability of the human heart and the complexity of a human life. In explaining why some things are not known to some people, for example, Aquinas says: "[one reason why something is not known is that] it is obscured by being inside something [else]. The things most obscured in this way are the things hidden in the [human] heart, which is exceedingly deep and unfathomable."[124]

What requires healing about a particular person, what suffering there is in the life of that person, what role suffering plays or might play in that person's redemption and glory—all these are things that no human being, including the sufferer, may be in a position to know. The role of any particular case of suffering in bringing about the things any particular person cares about can be evident only to a person in a position to see more than human persons typically can see. Furthermore, as the story of Samson makes clear, it is possible even for a person far from flourishing and internal integration around the good to turn toward it in inward ways at the very moment of death, in a manner not visible to external observers. Without the narrative's presentation of Samson's inner thoughts and words, to onlookers it could have seemed as if Samson had died just as alienated from himself and God as he had been during the latter part of his life.

And so, although Aquinas supposes that there is available to human beings a good and acceptable theodicy, it remains the case that, on his views, any particular instance of suffering is likely to remain a mystery to us. A theodicy, as Aquinas understands it, cannot by itself give a specific answer to the question why some particular person was hit by a car.[125] At least partly for this reason, the narratives canvassed in the preceding section have an advantage over real-life cases. The narratives give us details about the lives of the sufferers that we ordinarily would not have; and they also show us God in interaction with those sufferers, thereby giving us more insight into the relations between God and the sufferers than even religious believers would suppose is ordinarily possible in real-life cases, absent revelation from God.

It should also be said here that, in the same way and for analogous reasons, Aquinas's theodicy cannot give a specific answer to questions about the suffering of whole societies. If we want to know, for example, what reasons Aquinas's theodicy can give for God's allowing the suffering of the Western world during the First World War, what benefits in particular defeated the great communal suffering elicited by that social convulsion, then it is important to recognize that, on Aquinas's account, we are not in a position to give an answer to the question.

For Aquinas, such an answer would have to fall within the general outlines of his theodicy. That is, the benefits would have to go primarily to the sufferers, as measured by Aquinas's scale of value for human flourishing. Because the question asks about the communal suffering of many nations taken together, however, the benefit would have to be commensurate in scope and size. That is, the benefit would have to affect many societies, and it would also have to impact each society as a whole, influencing the entire community in such a way as to ward off the worst thing for the community or to contribute to the best thing for the community. Only someone in a position to be aware of the trajectory of whole societies could propose a morally sufficient reason for God's allowing suffering of this magnitude, but it is clear that human beings are very rarely in a position to grasp things of this sort. And so, although, on Aquinas's theodicy, there is no answer to the question about suffering affecting whole societies, we can see that we are rarely if ever able to see the things about such extensive organizations of people that we would have to see in order to apply Aquinas's theodicy to suffering on that scale.

All these conclusions apply only to unaided human reason, however. For those in union with God—to some very limited extent in this life and wholly in the afterlife—through their connection to the mind of God, the nature of their suffering and the benefits justifying it will be clear and comprehensible. It is no part of Aquinas's theodicy that suffering and its justifying benefits are opaque in every case or will *always* be opaque. On the contrary, one of the benefits of union with God is the resulting clarity about human lives, one's own, as well as that of others. The trajectory and flourishing of human communities is included in that vision as well.

A question and a brief answer

At this point, it may well occur to someone to wonder why, if Aquinas's theodicy is correct and if God can reveal the explanation for suffering to those united to him, at least in heaven if not also on earth, God does not make such a revelation in this life to everyone who suffers, in order to diminish their suffering.

Now in one sense this question is foolish. Aquinas develops his theodicy on the basis of passages from biblical texts, and he takes the Bible to be the revealed word of God. So Aquinas would undoubtedly suppose that God has in fact explained to human persons what God's purposes are in allowing human beings to suffer. But, in another sense, even with this response to the question, there remains something in the question worth thinking about. That is because, even if it were true that authoritative biblical texts provide a clear and definitive theodicy (something that many people who accept biblical texts as revealed would certainly deny), the theodicy in question is only general. It is theological, not personal, we might say. And so the question that looks foolish at first glance might be rephrased in this way: why does God not explain in detail and in advance to every sufferer why God allows that particular suffering for that particular person?

This is *not* a foolish question, but it has also been answered, in effect, in the course of the examination of the narratives in the preceding section. The very thing that justifies God in allowing the suffering of Job, or that justifies Jesus in allowing the suffering of Mary, would be lost if there were such advance notice and detailed explanation. In the case of Abraham, explanation in advance would undermine or destroy the process designed for the development of trust. In the case of Samson, if God had told Samson in advance that God was going to leave him, Samson would have avoided his capture by the Philistines; and then there would not have been any of the rest of the story that eventuates in Samson's final flourishing, in his being what he himself wanted to be.

The answer to the non-foolish question is, therefore, that, in different ways, for different reasons, God's explaining in advance to particular sufferers his reasons for allowing their particular suffering abrogates those very reasons. God cannot explain his reasons without losing them. And so the reasons that justify God's allowing human suffering are also the reasons that justify God's failing to explain those reasons to the sufferer. The benefits that, on Aquinas's theodicy, come to the sufferer are benefits defeating even the suffering of the hiddenness of God's reasons for allowing particular individuals to suffer as they do.

Aquinas's theodicy and the problem of callousness

For many people, the reaction to this Thomistic theodicy will be indignation. If it is taken not as piously platitudinous but as a serious expression of other-worldliness, some contemporaries are likely to find it so alien to their own sensitivities that they reject it out of hand as outrageous. One articulate formulation of this reaction is the charge that Aquinas's position is callous, because it finds a value in suffering and therefore seems somehow to make suffering acceptable. The most common expression of this charge consists in picking some horrendous case of suffering, typically drawn from newspapers or novels, and then asking with moral scorn if anything whatever could possibly justify suffering so terrible or so cruel.

But it is important to see that, on Aquinas's views, the typical presentation of cases of suffering in morally scornful objections to theodicy is incomplete. That is because, in such a presentation, the suffering at issue is typically reported from the outside, as it were; the mere facts of the bodily or psychological suffering constitute the whole description of the case. As the narratives in the preceding section make clear, however, in each such case there will also be a larger story, which the objector is in no position to describe, about the role of the suffering in the long-term psychic life of the sufferer. If we had only the newspaper version of the life of Samson, for example, no doubt his story would look very different to us.

In addition, even apart from the issue of incompleteness, the objector's description of the case, offered in moral outrage as a challenge to theodicy, would seem to Aquinas misleading at best and mistaken at worst. That is because typically such a description implies that the sufferer is isolated in his suffering, or at least is isolated from God. But Aquinas would not accept such an implication. As I explained above, on Aquinas's views, to one degree or another God is always present to every sufferer. No sufferer is isolated from the love of omnipresent God; and to the extent to which the sufferer is open to it, the presence of God to that sufferer comes with shared attention and closeness, for the consolation of the sufferer.[126] The stories in the preceding section are marked by a struggle for trust in God on the part of the protagonists of the stories, but they also include a depiction of the consolation for the sufferer in the presence of God, which at some point in the narrative is also part of the experience of the sufferer.

Someone might suppose that the consolation of second-personal connection to God is available only to sufferers who are religious believers, but this would be a hasty supposition. To see the point, consider the case of Cory Friedman, who suffered horribly with Tourette's syndrome from early childhood until early adulthood. At a certain moment in his life, in consequence of a set of traumatic events, Cory reached a point of no return, after which he began a heroic struggle to regain control of his life. As he describes himself and his family, none of them was a religious believer. And yet this is what Cory wrote on a yellow pad, on the night that marked the beginning of the struggle leading to a new life for him:

> I was born with the worst disease.
> My body wants me to suffer.
> My whole life, I've been gasping for air.
> The ground hasn't been there.
>   . . . . .

> I've lost the world. I've lost the world.
> I'm in myself and can't get out.
> The world's joy makes me feel like an outcast.
>
> . . . . .
>
> But I am alive. I am alive.
> I still have human feelings and needs.
> I have dreams.
> Don't desert me any longer, common goodness.
> How can you?
> You've already committed the biggest sin imaginable. Taking a good-hearted,
>   peaceful, intelligent person and making him come within a millimeter
>   of taking his own life . . .[127]

These words of this heartbroken, long-suffering atheistic young man are more than a little reminiscent of Job's complaints to God. When Cory cries to "common goodness" not to desert him, when he accuses common goodness of having hurt him enough, to whom is this cry and this charge addressed? Who is the referent of 'you?' Because Cory is atheistic, he himself will not take "God" to be the answer to these questions. And yet who does Cory think could be responsible for what Cory accuses common goodness of doing to him except the God Cory thinks he does not believe in? However we are to understand Cory's complicated psychic state at this point in his life, it is evident that Cory finds the bedrock on which to stand, to take the steps he does toward a regeneration of himself, in second-personal connection with what is from his point of view *je ne sais quoi*. It is therefore at least not clear that any kind of consolation of the presence of God is available only to those who believe it is available.

In a somewhat different vein but also connected to the issue of callousness, a complaint will arise that Aquinas's theodicy gives the wrong result as regards our attitude toward suffering. For example, someone will complain that on Aquinas's theodicy we ought to praise those who afflict other people because the moral wrongdoers are helping their victims to redemption or to glory. On this complaint against his theodicy, Aquinas is stuck with recognizing the Philistines as the heroes of Samson's story. But this complaint rests on a confusion. Someone who perpetrates an injustice against someone else does not do so in order to benefit that person. On the contrary, there is every reason to suppose that, if the Philistines knew that their actions would result in benefits for Samson, they would not have engaged in those actions. So, although a perpetrator of an injustice might without knowing it be bringing about some good for his victim, no praise accrues to the perpetrator from that fact. Rather, he is culpable for the injustice of his action and the malice with which it was done.

Along the same lines, someone might complain that on Aquinas's views we ought never to try to alleviate suffering since to alleviate suffering would also be to prevent the benefit brought about by the suffering.[128] On this complaint, Aquinas is stuck with censuring Martha for helping her sister Mary to the good of reconciliation with Jesus, since the suffering of Mary's alienation from Jesus is good for Mary. And, of course, if we interpret Aquinas's theodicy as holding, in general, that suffering is a good thing, then his view will be worthy not only of vituperation but of ridicule as well. It would then turn out, for example, that on his views anesthetics are to be eschewed[129] or, more generally, that any attempt to palliate or end anyone's pain is a bad thing. And it is certainly incontestable that other-worldliness *has* in the past been used in abominable ways as a basis for exploiting and oppressing the poor and defenseless. When the labor movement in the USA was trying to protect workers through unionization, part of its strategy was to cast opprobrium on hope in an afterlife. Instead of offering decent conditions and fair wages, union organizers said, the exploitative bosses held out to their workers the hope of "pie in the sky when we die."

But this complaint rests on a confusion analogous to that underlying the immediately preceding complaint. On Aquinas's views, *ceteris paribus,*[130] one person Paula's allowing some suffering on the part of another person Jerome that Paula could readily prevent or relieve is morally permissible only if Paula is justified in holding the true belief that that suffering is the best means in the circumstances for drawing Jerome closer to God in the processes of justification or sanctification. Unless it is true that this suffering of Jerome's serves this purpose, and Paula is justified in believing that it does, then *ceteris paribus* Paula's permitting this suffering of Jerome's is not morally permissible. But, as I have been at pains to show, neither suffering nor the benefits defeating suffering are transparent. It is not true that a person has them if and only if he knows that he does.[131] A fortiori, they are opaque to outside observers. In fact, unlike omniscient God, human beings are rarely in a position to see into the inner life of another person enough to know whether any particular suffering is likely to serve the purpose of justification or sanctification. And so it is also true that one human being Paula is rarely in a position to be morally justified in permitting the suffering of another human being Jerome when, *ceteris paribus,* Paula could readily prevent or relieve Jerome's suffering.

The putative objector might rejoin here that the possession of a Thomistic theodicy in effect provides what one might otherwise not have—namely, the basis for concluding that any particular suffering will in fact serve the purpose of justification and sanctification. The theodicy gives what unaided human reason cannot. And so, the putative objector will claim, a Thomistic theodicy provides what I have just claimed human beings rarely have: moral justification for permitting the suffering of others.

But this rejoinder is also confused. On Aquinas's theodicy, any particular suffering *allowed by God* will benefit the sufferer in the ways the theodicy explains. But when Paula considers whether she ought to try to prevent or relieve Jerome's suffering, she cannot know whether the future suffering of Jerome that she is considering is suffering that God will allow. That is because, if Paula does not do what she can to alleviate that future suffering of Jerome's, someone else might do so. In the biblical book of Esther, when Mordecai is trying to persuade Esther to speak to the King to try to prevent the genocide of the Jews officially proclaimed by the King, Mordecai says to Esther: "if you altogether hold your peace at this time [and do not speak to the King], then enlargement and deliverance will arise for the Jews from another place; but you and your father's house will be destroyed."[132] As this speech indicates, Mordecai is assuming that God has multiple routes to the end of preventing the suffering of the Jews. If Esther does not contribute to the prevention of that suffering, Mordecai supposes, someone else will. That suffering of the Jews therefore will not be among the sufferings allowed by God, even if Esther fails to try to prevent it; and Esther will be punished by God (Mordecai thinks) for her morally wrong action of not trying to prevent that suffering herself. Analogously, when Paula considers alleviating some future suffering for Jerome, she is not at that time in a position to know whether that suffering is suffering allowed by God. Furthermore, even if it were to be the case that God did allow Jerome's suffering, Paula would not thereby be retrospectively justified in having failed to try to prevent it. Since at the time she failed to try to prevent it, she did not know it would be allowed by God, her failure to try to prevent it is not justified for her.[133]

Therefore, although God is in an epistemic position to be justified if he allows suffering he could prevent, a human person very generally is not. From the fact that there is a morally sufficient reason for God to allow suffering, it does not follow that this reason also gives a human person moral license to allow suffering. Because God and human persons are not in the same epistemic condition as regards the permission or production of suffering, different moral judgments apply to God and human beings on this score. So the cynical use of other-worldly rhetoric receives no validation from Aquinas's position. Oppression of the poor by the rich is an injustice whose evil is in no way mitigated by any consideration of God's reasons for allowing suffering.

Finally, in a related vein, someone might object that, on Aquinas's theodicy, if a human person tries to alleviate suffering, he interferes with God's purposes as regards the role of suffering in the life of the sufferer. On this objection, Aquinas is stuck with disapproving of the attempt by Martha and Mary to get help for their brother when he was sick, because the suffering of his sickness was part of God's plan for good for Lazarus. But this objection is clearly mistaken. Mary and Martha do not defeat God's plan for Lazarus by seeking healing for Lazarus in his sickness. They are just unsuccessful in their efforts. An omnipotent God who has the power to prevent or allow suffering also has control over attempts to alleviate suffering. If God's purposes as regards the life of a sufferer would be thwarted by the alleviation of that person's suffering, then God could bring it about that attempts to alleviate the suffering were unsuccessful.

These objections, then, are confused about what Aquinas's theodicy implies. I want to say, however, that I affirm the affect underlying these objections, even if their content should not be conceded. A theodicy (or a defense) is an attempted explanation of God's allowing suffering. But nothing about such an explanation explains suffering away. Suffering remains suffering, and we need to retain our grief over it if we are not to lose our humanity.[134]

A brief word about two possible objections

At this point, it may occur to someone to object that the world as Aquinas understands it is not the best of all possible worlds. On this objection, there is a best of all possible worlds, and a perfectly good God has an obligation to create or produce it. But this is arguably not the best of all possible worlds. And so, on this objection, even if Aquinas's attempted theodicy is otherwise successful, the problem of suffering simply arises again in a different guise.

It is clear that there are a number of presuppositions underlying this objection, and each of them is controversial at best. There is a considerable philosophical literature discussing the issue of whether there is a best of all possible worlds. There is an equally substantial literature discussing the issue of whether an omnipotent God can unilaterally produce any world that is possible. And, finally, there is also a sizable literature discussing the issue of whether God is obligated to create a best possible world, even if there is one and God can unilaterally produce it. It is not possible to deal with all these issues in passing here. For the record, Aquinas thinks that 'the best of all possible worlds' is ambiguous as between a world that God governs in the best possible way and a world that is best *simpliciter*. Aquinas does think that there is a best possible world in the first sense; he believes that God governs this world in the best possible way. But he does not think that there is a best possible world in the second sense. From his point of view, an angel is a good immaterial creature; there is no limit on the number of angels God could make; and adding an angel to a world makes it better. So in principle for every world, there is a better world containing one more angel. On Aquinas's view, then, there is no best possible world *simpliciter*. For this reason, there is also no obligation for God to create one.[135]

But whether or not this position of Aquinas's is a successful rejoinder to the objection at issue here, the main problem with the objection, in my view, is that it disregards the dialectic of the discussion. The proponent of the argument from evil claims that it is not possible for there to be a world that is like the actual world as regards suffering (and other related empirical facts) and that nonetheless also contains an omniscient, omnipotent, perfectly good God. The challenge posed by the argument from evil is thus to show that there could be such a God in a world like ours. This challenge is met if one can find a morally sufficient reason for God's allowing suffering of the sort the actual world contains. In order to meet this challenge, it is not necessary to show that this is the best of all possible worlds *simpliciter*, even if, contrary to Aquinas's position, there is such a best of all possible worlds.

Something analogous should be said in response to the worry that the doctrines regarding the afterlife render Aquinas's theodicy more improbable than it would otherwise be. The issues involving probability and the problem of suffering are complicated, and I have neither the space nor the desire to engage them here. But this particular objection seems to me also to fail to engage the dialectic of the discussion. A theodicy does not seek to establish the existence of God or to argue for the truth of a particular set of religious beliefs. It seeks only to ward off an attack. The proponent of the argument from evil claims to be able to use the existence of the suffering in this world to show that God does not exist or that a particular set of religious beliefs is false. A theodicy such as Aquinas's is successful if it wards off this attack. To do so, it needs to provide a defensible morally sufficient explanation for God's allowing evil of the sort we find in this world. It is not meant to demonstrate the truth of religious claims, and it does not need to do so to succeed as a theodicy.

Conclusion

At the start of this chapter, I listed the sufferings of the protagonists in the biblical narratives examined in the preceding section, and I asked how anyone could justify God's allowing such suffering. The answer, on Aquinas's theodicy, is that this appalling suffering is the best or only means in the circumstances for the sufferer to have what he himself cares about.

In Samson's story, what Samson endures in the last, worst suffering of his life is unquestionably horrific. He is blind, defeated, captured by his enemies, exiled from home, and at a great distance from the God who once was so intimate with him. What is left to him of flourishing or heart's desire? And yet, if we think in terms of what Samson cares about, as the narrative shows it to us—Samson's relationship to God, his mission from God, his gift from God of great physical strength and the victory over the Philistines that strength wins him—it seems in the story that Samson has brought home to him both flourishing and heart's desire precisely by means of his suffering. Without Samson's suffering, by the time of his affair with Delilah what is left to Samson, what is left of Samson, is pathetic. On Aquinas's theodicy, through Samson's suffering, in the circumstances of Samson's life and choices, Samson has what he himself cares more about than the avoidance of that suffering. And that is why, on Aquinas's views, God is justified in letting Samson suffer these things. For Aquinas, *mutatis mutandis*, the same point would apply also to Mary of Bethany, Abraham, and Job. And it is not hard to see why Aquinas would think so. If we were in a position to ask these protagonists whether at the end of the stories, through suffering and because of it, they had what they themselves cared about enough to trade their suffering for it, Aquinas expects that the answer the protagonists would give would be 'yes.'

Aquinas thinks so because he is focused on human flourishing in relationship with God as the highest human good. And there is something intuitively right about interpretations of the stories that are seen through that lens. The sufferings of Mary of Bethany, for example, are appalling. And yet her endurance of that suffering makes her so much greater a soul than Simon the Pharisee, who disdains her at the start of the story. It is better to be Mary of Bethany, even with her suffering, than to be Simon, who suffers so much less than she does.

Nonetheless, there is also reason to worry about Aquinas's position. That is because it is possible for a person to care more about something that is his heart's desire than about his own flourishing. Aquinas's scale of value for human beings can measure suffering that stems from the loss of what we care about as regards flourishing, but, on the face of it, it gives little or no weight to suffering that has its source in the loss of the desires of the heart. The problem can be seen readily by considering Job's heartbreak over the loss of his children. We can suppose that Job might have been willing to accept his loss of prosperity, his physical suffering, his pariah status, and his psychological trauma in trade for his flourishing. That is, it might be the case in the story that Job cared more about his flourishing than about avoiding that dreadful suffering. There is also, however, the matter of Job's children. In the stories, in the end Abraham keeps Isaac, and Mary receives her brother again from the dead. But Job's children die; they are gone and do not return to him, at least not in his earthly life. It is entirely reasonable to suppose that, in the story, Job might have cared more about those children of his than about his flourishing.

I do not mean that Job might have wanted to suffer some harm to himself rather than allow harm to come to his children. This might be true, but it is not what I mean. I mean rather that, for Job, having his children with him in the course of his earthly life might be more worth having than his own flourishing. On this hypothetical version of the story of Job, not at all hard to imagine, when Job weighs his flourishing against his having his children with him, he cares more about the latter than the former: he would be willing to trade his flourishing to keep his children. But if this were so, then, it seems, Aquinas's theodicy would have nothing to offer the Job of this hypothetical story.

The relational character of Aquinas's scale of value gives his theodicy great strength, but it also focuses the theodicy on the objective side of what we care about, our own flourishing. As I showed in the first chapter, however, there is in addition a subjective side of what we care about. There are the heart's desires. In its concentration on the importance of union with God, Aquinas's theodicy in effect neglects suffering that needs to be addressed, the suffering generated by the loss of the desires of the heart.

In the next chapter, I will explain and defend this claim and consider how to develop Aquinas's theodicy to take account of it. In the final chapter, I will consider this developed theodicy and evaluate it. There I will argue that it can handle even the hypothetical case of Job and his children.

Chapter 14

What We Care about: The Desires of the Heart

If it is not my portion to meet thee in this my life then let me ever feel that I have missed thy sight—let me not forget for a moment, let me carry the pangs of this sorrow in my dreams and in my wakeful hours.

As my days pass in the crowded market of this world and my hands grow full with the daily profits, let me ever feel that I have gained nothing—let me not forget for a moment, let me carry the pangs of this sorrow in my dreams and in my wakeful hours.

When I sit by the roadside, tired and panting, when I spread my bed low in the dust, let me ever feel that the long journey is still before me—let me not forget for a moment, let me carry the pangs of this sorrow in my dreams and in my wakeful hours.

When my rooms have been decked out and the flutes sound and the laughter there is loud, let me ever feel that I have not invited thee to my house—let me not forget for a moment, let me carry the pangs of this sorrow in my dreams and in my wakeful hours.[*]

Introduction

Those theories of morality that make a connection between God and morality tend to take moral evil as something contrary to God's nature or to God's will or both. As I explained in Chapter 1, if the analogy is taken in a rough way, the evil human beings suffer can be understood analogously: suffering occurs when something goes

---

[*] Gitanjali, Poem 79, in *Collected Poems and Plays of Rabindranath Tagore* (New York: Macmillan, 1966), 29.

significantly contrary to the nature of the sufferer or to the will of the sufferer or both. On this way of thinking about suffering, suffering is a function of what we care about, our flourishing in our nature as human beings or our heart's desires in the central core of the web of desire in our wills.[1] To defeat suffering so understood, a benefit must also be something that we care about. It is hard to see how a benefit could defeat suffering for a person if that person did not care about that benefit. And so a benefit defeating suffering must also be a function of our flourishing or our heart's desires or both.

But, I asked in Chapter 1, if suffering is a matter of one's having one's flourishing undermined or of being kept from the desires of one's heart, how *could* there be a benefit that defeats suffering for the sufferer? If one did not care more about what one gained in the benefit than about what one lost in the suffering, the benefit could not defeat the suffering. But what could one care about more than one's flourishing or the desires of one's heart? There is a problem for any theodicy here, because it seems paradoxical or simply self-contradictory to suppose that one's flourishing or the desires of one's heart could be the benefit that defeats the suffering stemming from the loss of flourishing or the loss of the desires of one's heart.

Aquinas's understanding of the nature of the benefits defeating suffering shows us a road to a resolution of this paradox. On his theodicy, what we care about has to be considered relative to one or the other of two different contexts. The first is the small portion of a person's life before death; the second is the everlasting portion of it in the afterlife. Given Aquinas's worldview, it is possible that the loss of flourishing in this life and the loss of the desires of one's heart in this life be a means to flourishing in the afterlife. It is reasonable, however, to care more about flourishing in its everlasting form than in its limited form; there is more objective value in having flourishing forever than in having it for a finite time. Since this is so, then, at least with regard to flourishing, it is possible on Aquinas's views that both the sufferings that a person endures and the benefits that defeat that suffering be understood without paradox in terms of what one cares about.

It is worth reflecting a moment on this point. Aquinas's theodicy resolves the apparent paradox that threatens any attempt at theodicy—that there seems to be nothing a person cares about more than what he has lost when he is broken, or heartbroken, in suffering—because Aquinas's theodicy relativizes the things a person cares about to different portions of that person's life, the this-worldly portion and the other-worldly portion in the afterlife. Without this sort of relativization, it is hard to see how the paradox could be resolved. If there is only one realm within which to consider benefits for a person, then it does seem difficult, or even impossible, to find anything that a person would (or could) care about more than his flourishing or his heart's desires. For this reason, if we insist that there be some response to the challenge of the argument from evil that does not make mention of the afterlife, in my view we consign such a response to failure. I take it that this is another way of affirming the point Aquinas himself emphasized, that the notion of an afterlife is central to any attempt at theodicy (or defense) that is to have a hope of being successful. From Aquinas's point of view, trying to understand the pattern of suffering in this world without reference to an afterlife is just as Martian as trying to understand the pattern of suffering in a hospital without reference to life outside the hospital and after the hospital time.[2]

As I pointed out at the end of the last chapter, however, the strategy Aquinas's theodicy employs to resolve the paradox is based solely on what Aquinas takes to be the scale of objective value, on which human flourishing is measured. There remains the issue of the desires of the heart and the scale of subjective value for a person. As I explained in Chapter 1, sometimes a person's valuing of something is a response to the objective, intrinsic value that he thinks he sees in the thing he values. Value of this sort is measured by a scale for objective value. But sometimes a person's valuing of something gives that thing the value it has; its value *for him* is derivative from his care for it. The value a child has for its parents is typically of this sort. A child has the great value it does for its parents not because the parents suppose that their child is of more intrinsic value than other children but rather because the parents care so much for that child. Value of this sort is measured by the scale for the subjective value that things have for a particular person.

When someone is heartbroken because he has been deprived of the desires of his heart, how is that suffering to be redeemed for him? Abraham's suffering in his childlessness and in his binding of Isaac is defeated for him by his receiving Isaac as the child of God's promise and by his becoming the patriarch not only of a clan but even of the whole people of faith. But, if Abraham had never had the child on which he had set his heart or had never become the patriarch he wanted to be, would the role Aquinas supposes this suffering has in effecting Abraham's flourishing be for Abraham a benefit sufficient to defeat his suffering? It does not seem plausible to think so. And what happens if a sufferer cares more about the heart's desires he lost than he cares about his flourishing? If Job had cared more about keeping his children with him in this life than about his flourishing in any part of his life, this-worldly or other-worldly, then he would have repudiated what Aquinas's theodicy has to offer as a benefit redeeming his suffering.

So how is the suffering stemming from the loss of the desires of the heart to be woven into Aquinas's theodicy?[3]

The stern-minded attitude

One answer to this question is that people should focus their care only on their flourishing, their ultimate, spiritual flourishing. On the attitude underlying this answer to the question, the right way to harmonize the disparate things people care about, and the disparate scales of value by which the desires of the heart and human flourishing are measured, is just for people to give up the desires of the heart. In order to have some name by which to refer to it, I will call this stance 'the stern-minded attitude.' As the preceding chapters should have made clear, I myself reject the stern-minded attitude. But it has power and a venerable history. So, before considering what else can be said about the suffering stemming from the desires of the heart, some examination of the stern-minded attitude is necessary.

To appreciate the force of the stern-minded attitude, it is important to recognize that suffering which stems from a loss of the heart's desires is widely believed to be compatible with human flourishing.[4] For any particular historical person picked as an exemplar of a person having a flourishing human life, it is certainly arguable that, at some time in her life, that person will have lost permanently, or failed ever to get, something on which she had fixed her heart. Think, for example, of Sojourner Truth, who was sold away from her parents at the age of 9, or Harriet Tubman, who suffered permanent neurological damage from the beatings she sustained in adolescence. If any human lives manifest flourishing, the lives of these women certainly do. Most people would suppose that each of these women had a highly admirable, meaningful human life. And yet surely each of these women was irrevocably deprived of something on which, at some time, she had set her heart.

Thinkers in varying cultures, including some Stoics, Buddhists, and many in the Christian tradition, have been fiercely committed to the position that human flourishing is independent of the vicissitudes of fortune that cause heartbreak. On Aquinas's worldview, which takes flourishing to be a matter of union with God, most of the evils human beings suffer are compatible with flourishing. That is because a human person can be in a relationship of love with God and can also experience the consolation of that relationship, even when she is afflicted with serious suffering of body or mind. For all these thinkers, human flourishing is compatible even with such things as the depredations of other human beings, the torment of pain and disfigurement, the anguish of mental illness, the wretchedness of impoverishment, the misery of being unwanted, the affliction of pariah status, the brokenness of shame, and the death of loved ones, even though any of these things is sufficient to cause heartbreak to the person suffering it. In fact, this enumeration of sufferings is just a partial reproduction of the list I gave in the preceding chapter to summarize the afflictions of the protagonists in the biblical narratives examined earlier. On Aquinas's worldview, as well as on the views of those in the stern-minded tradition, the lives of people such as the protagonists in these stories exemplify flourishing even though they contain great suffering.

The belief that flourishing is compatible with great suffering and brokenness is also common among the reflective in our own culture. So, for example, in lines born of his long experience of living with the severely disabled, Jean Vanier says about the disabled and about himself, too:

we can only accept . . . [the] pain [in our lives] if we discover our true self beneath all the masks and realize that if we are broken, we are also more beautiful than we ever dared to suspect. When we realize our brokenness, we do not have to fall into depression . . . Seeing our own brokenness and beauty allows us to recognize, hidden under the brokenness and self-centeredness of others, their beauty, their value, and their sacredness. This discovery is . . . a blessed moment, a moment of grace, and a moment of enlightenment that comes in a meeting with the God of love, who reveals to us that we are beloved and so is everyone else . . . We can start to live the pain of loss and accept anguish because a new love and a new consciousness of self are being given to us.[5]

A particularly poignant example of this kind of view is given by John Hull in his memoir about his slow descent into blindness. Hull spends many pages documenting his strong aversion to going blind and the suffering caused him by the blindness that finally enveloped him. But then he recounts a religious experience he had while he was listening to music in a church. As he describes that experience, he summarizes his attitude toward his blindness in this passage:

the thought keeps coming back to me . . . Could there be a strange way in which blindness is a dark, paradoxical gift? Does it offer a way of life, a purification, an economy? Is it really like a kind of painful purging through a death? . . . If blindness is a gift, it is not one that I would wish on anybody . . . [But] as the whole place and my mind were filled with that wonderful music, I found myself saying, 'I accept the gift. I accept the gift.' I was filled with a profound sense of worship. I felt that I was in the very presence of God, that the giver of the gift had drawn near to me to inspect his handiwork . . . If I hardly dared approach him, he hardly dared approach me . . . He had, as it were, thrown his cloak of darkness around me from a distance, but had now drawn near to seek a kind of reassurance from me that everything was all right, that he had not misjudged the situation, that he did not have to stay. 'It's all right,' I was saying to him, 'There's no need to wait. Go on, you can go now; everything's fine.'[6]

Everything *is* fine, in some sense having to do with relationship to God, and so with flourishing also, on Aquinas's account of flourishing—and on mine, too. I wish only to affirm the attitude toward flourishing exemplified by the moving testimony of people such as Vanier and Hull.[7]

But because suffering is compatible with flourishing in this way, some stern-minded thinkers suppose that a person who is suffering because of the loss of the desires of his heart just needs to let those desires go.

Ordinarily, a parent's goodness is not impugned if the parent refuses to provide for the child anything whatever that the child sets his heart on. A child could set his heart on things very destructive to him, for example, or even on evil things. He could set his heart in random ways on continually changing things or on mutually incompossible things. And no doubt, this is not the end of the list of such very problematic instances of heart's desires. In such cases, even if it were possible to do so, a good parent would not give the child what the child desires just because the parent loves the child and wants what is best for the child; she is at cross-purposes with the child just because she cares as much as she does that the child flourish. An analogous point holds with regard to God and the suffering of adult human beings. In cases in which the desires of a person's heart are seriously inimical to his flourishing, reasonable people are unlikely to suppose that some explanation is needed for a good God's failure to give that person the desires of his heart. If we exclude such cases, however, there still remain many instances in which a person is heartbroken in consequence of having set his heart, in humanly understandable and appropriate ways, on something whose value for him is derivative of his love for it. Even with regard to this restricted class of cases, stern-minded thinkers suppose that, as long as flourishing is preserved, the desires of the heart should be abandoned if cleaving to them leads to suffering.

On the stern-minded attitude, there is no reason why a good God must provide whatever goods not necessary for her flourishing a human person has fixed her heart on. Stern-minded thinkers take human flourishing to be a very great good; for those who think of flourishing as a relationship to God, it can seem an infinite good or a good too great to be commensurable with other goods.[8] On the stern-minded attitude among religious believers, if God provides *this* good for a human person, then that is or ought to be enough for that person. On the view of the stern-minded, a person who does not find this greatest of all goods good enough is like a person who wins the lottery but who is nonetheless unhappy because she did not get exactly what she wanted for her birthday.

In effect, then, the stern-minded attitude is unwilling to assign a positive value to anything that is not equivalent to or essential to a person's flourishing. For stern-minded thinkers, the objective scale of value for human beings is the only *real* scale of value there is. Consequently, the stern-minded attitude is, at best, unwilling to accord any value to the desires of the heart and, at worst, eager to extirpate the desires themselves.

The stern-minded attitude in the history of Christian thought

A stern-minded attitude on the part of some (but not all) Christian thinkers is persistent in the history of Christian thought from the Patristic period onwards. In its Patristic form, it can be seen vividly in a story that Cassian tells about a monk named 'Patermutus.' It is worth quoting at length the heart-rendingly horrible story that Cassian recounts with so much oblivious admiration.[9]

Patermutus's constant perseverance [in his request to be admitted into the monastery finally] induced [the monks] to receive him along with his little son, who was about eight years old . . . To test [Patermutus] . . . and see if he would be more moved by family affection and the love of his own brood than by the obedience and mortification of Christ, which every monk should prefer to his love, [the monks] deliberately neglected the child, dressed him in rags . . . and even subjected [the child] to cuffs and slaps, which . . . the father saw some of them inflict on the innocent for no reason, so that [the father] never saw [his son] without [the son's] cheeks being marked by the signs of tears. Although he saw the child being treated like this day after day before his eyes, the father's feelings remained firm and unmoving, for the love of Christ . . . The superior of the monastery . . . decided to test [the father's] strength of mind still further: one day when he noticed the child weeping, he pretended to be enraged at [the child], and ordered the father to pick up [his son] and throw him in the Nile. The father, as if the command had been given him by our Lord, at once ran and snatched up his son and carried him in his own arms to the river bank to throw him in. The deed would have been done . . . had not some of the brethren been stationed in advance to watch the riverbank carefully; as the child was thrown they caught him . . . Thus they prevented the command, performed as it was by the father's obedience and devotion, from having any effect.[10]

What Cassian highlights in Patermutus is his determination to eradicate in himself one of the most powerful and natural heart's desires—a parent's love for his child—in the interest of focusing all his care solely on flourishing, spiritually understood. Plainly, Cassian prizes this determination; he admires Patermutus's actions and desires. But surely most people would find them chilling and reprehensible. For my part, I would say that one can only wonder why the monks bothered to catch the child, if the father's willingness to kill the child was so praiseworthy in their eyes. Can it be morally prohibited to do an act whose willing is morally praiseworthy?[11]

An attitude similar to Cassian's but less appalling can still be found more than a millennium later in some texts (but not others) of the work of Teresa of Avila, to take just one from among a host of thinkers who might have been selected as examples. Writing to her sister nuns, Teresa says:

Oh, how desirable is . . . [the] union with God's will! Happy the soul that has reached it. Such a soul will live tranquilly in this life, and in the next as well. Nothing in earthly events afflicts it unless it finds itself in some danger of losing God . . . neither sickness, nor poverty, nor death . . . For this soul sees well that the Lord knows what He is doing better than . . . [the soul] knows what it is desiring . . . But alas for us, how few there must be who reach [union with God's will!] . . . I tell you I am writing this with much pain upon seeing myself so far away [from such union]—and all through my own fault. . . . Don't think the matter lies in my being so conformed to the will of God that if my father or brother dies I don't feel it, or that if there are trials or sicknesses I suffer them happily.[12]

Not feeling it when one's father dies, not weeping with grief over his death, is, in Teresa's view, a good spiritual condition that she is not yet willing to attribute to herself. Teresa is here echoing a tradition that finds its prime medieval exemplar in Augustine's *Confessions*. Augustine says that, at the death of his mother, by a powerful command of his will, he kept himself from weeping at her funeral, only to disgrace himself in his own eyes later by weeping copiously in private.[13]

In the same text from which I just quoted, Teresa emphasizes the importance of love of neighbor; but in fact it does not seem possible for the love of neighbor to cohere with the stern-minded attitude manifested by Teresa and Augustine in the face of the death (real or imagined) of a beloved parent. As I argued in Chapter 5, it is the nature of love to desire the good of the beloved and union with him. But the desire for the good of the beloved is frustrated if the beloved gets sick or dies. Or, if the stern-minded attitude is unwilling to concede that point, then this much is incontrovertible even on the stern-minded attitude: the desire for union with the beloved is frustrated when the beloved dies and so is absent. One way or another, then, the desires of love are frustrated when the beloved dies. Consequently, there is something bad and lamentable, something worth tears, something whose loss brings affliction with it, about the death of any person whom one loves—one's father, or even one's neighbor, whom one is bound to love too, as Teresa acknowledges. Tranquility at the death of another person is incompatible with love of that person. To the extent to which one loves another person, one cannot be unmoved at his death. And so, contrary to what the stern-minded might suppose, love of neighbor is in fact incompatible with the stern-minded attitude.

Teresa's attitude toward her father's death, as she imagines her attitude would be if it were what she takes to be ideal, can be usefully contrasted with Bernard of Clairvaux's attitude toward the death of his brother. Commenting on his grief at that death, Bernard says to his religious community: "You, my sons, know how deep my sorrow is, how galling a wound it leaves."[14] And, addressing himself, he says: "Flow on, flow on, my tears . . . Let my tears gush forth like fountains."[15]

Reflecting on his own unwillingness to repudiate his great sorrow over his brother's death—his failure, that is, to follow Augustine's model—Bernard says

It is but human and necessary that we respond to our friends with feeling, that we be happy in their company, disappointed in their absence. Social intercourse, especially between friends, cannot be purposeless: the reluctance to part and the yearning for each other when separated indicate how meaningful their mutual love must be when they are together.[16]

And Bernard is hardly the only figure in the Christian tradition who fails to accept and affirm Cassian's attitude. Aquinas is another.

There are isolated texts which might suggest to some readers that Aquinas himself is an adherent of Cassian's attitude. So, for example, in his commentary on Christ's line that he who loves his life will lose it, Aquinas reveals that he recognizes the concept of the desires of the heart; but, in this same passage, he also seems to suggest that such desires should be stamped out. He says:

Everyone loves his own soul, but some love it *simpliciter* and some *secundum quid*. To love someone is to will the good for him; and so he who loves his soul wills the good for it. A person who wills for his soul the good *simpliciter* also loves his soul *simpliciter*. But a person who wills some particular good for his soul loves his soul *secundum quid*. The goods for the soul *simpliciter* are those things by which the soul is good, namely, the highest good, which is God. And so he who wills for his soul the divine good, a spiritual good, loves his soul *simpliciter*. But he who wills for his soul earthly goods such as riches and honors, pleasures, and things of that sort, he loves his soul [only] *secundum quid* . . . He who loves his soul *secundum quid*, namely with regard to temporal goods, will lose it.[17]

The implication seems to be that, for Aquinas, the person who does not want to lose his soul should extirpate from himself all desires for any good other than the highest good, which is, as he says, God.

But it is important to see that what is at issue for Aquinas in this passage is the desire for worldly things—that is for those goods, such as money or fame, which diminish when they are distributed. On Aquinas's scale of values, any good that diminishes when it is distributed is only a small good. Whatever we are to say about Aquinas's attitude toward goods of that sort, when it comes to the desires of the heart for things that are earthly goods but great goods, such as the love of a particular person, it is clear that Aquinas's attitude differs sharply from Cassian's. So, for example, in explaining why Christ told his disciples that he was going to God the Father in order to comfort the disciples when they were sad at the prospect of being separated from Christ, Aquinas says: "It is common among friends to be less sad over the absence of a friend when the friend is going to something which exalts him. That is why the Lord gives them this reason [for his leaving] in order to console them."[18]

Unlike Teresa, who repudiates grief at the prospect of losing her father, in his general reflection here (as in many other places) Aquinas is accepting the appropriateness of a person's grief at the loss of a loved person and validating the need for consolation for such grief. So Aquinas is not to be ranked among the members of the stern-minded group, any more than Bernard is; and, of course, in other moods, when she is not self-consciously evaluating her own spiritual progress, Teresa herself sounds more like Bernard and Aquinas than like Cassian.

On this subject, then, the Christian tradition is of two minds. Not all its influential figures stand with Cassian; and, even among those who do, many are double-minded about it. Speaking to a nun of his acquaintance, Anselm says: "This world is nothing to you, nothing but dung, if you wish to be a nun and spouse of God . . . Do not visit your relatives, they do not need your advice, nor you theirs . . . Let all your desire be for God."[19]

But writing to two relatives of his own who were coming to visit him, he says: "In coming . . . you have lit a spark; you have blown it into flame; and in this flame you have fused my soul with yours. If you now leave me, our joint soul will be torn apart, it can never again become two . . . If you stay with [my soul], we will be more than blood-relations; we will be spiritual partners."[20]

And in his last will and testament, he says to the men in his community: "even if I can no longer be present with you in body, I will never cease to remain with you in the love of my heart."[21]

A possible confusion

But, someone will surely object, is it not a part of Christian doctrine (and therefore also part of Aquinas's worldview) that God allows the death of any person who dies? Does anyone die when God wills that that person live? So when a person dies, on Christian (and Thomistic) theology, is it not the will of God that that person die? In what sense, then, could Teresa be united with God in will if she grieved over her father's death? How could she be united with God, as she explains she wants to be, if her will is frustrated in what God's will accepts or commands?

In my view, the position presupposed by the questions of this putative objector rests on too simple an understanding of God's will and of union with God.

To see why, assume that at death Teresa's father is united with God in heaven. Then the death of Teresa's father has opposite effects for Teresa and for God: it unites Teresa's father permanently with God, but it keeps Teresa from union with her father, at least for the remainder of Teresa's earthly life. For this reason, on the Christian doctrine Teresa accepts, as the quotations from Bernard also imply, love's desire for union with the beloved cannot be fulfilled in the same way for a human person as for God. If Teresa's will is united with God's will in desiring union with her father, then Teresa's will must also be frustrated at the very event, her father's dying, which fulfils God's will with respect to this desire.

Something analogous can be said about the other desire of love, for the good of the beloved. If Teresa desires the good of her father, she can only desire what her own mind sees as that good; but, unlike God's mind, her mind's ability to see the good is obviously limited. To the extent to which Teresa's will is united with God's will in desiring the good of the beloved, then Teresa will also desire for the beloved person things different from those desired by God, in virtue of Teresa's differing ability to see the good for the beloved person.[22]

It is easy to become confused here because the phrase 'the good' can be used either attributively or referentially.[23] That is, either 'the good of the beloved' can be used to refer to particular things that are conducive to the beloved's well-being; or it can be used opaquely, in an attribution of anything whatever under the description *the good of the beloved*. A mother who is baffled by the quarrels among her adult children and clueless about how to bring about a just peace for them may say, despairingly, "I just want the good for everybody." She is then using 'the good' attributively, with no idea of how to use it referentially.

If Teresa were tranquil over any affliction that happened to her father, it would be because she thought that by this tranquility her will would be united to God's will in willing the good for her father. In this thought of hers, 'the good' would be used attributively, to designate *whatever* God thinks is good. But this cannot be the way 'the good' is used in any thought of God's, without relativizing the good entirely to God's will. If we eschew such relativism,[24] then it is not the case that anything God desires is good just because God desires it. And so it is also not true that God desires as the good of a beloved person *whatever* it is that God desires for him. When God desires the good for someone, then, he must desire it by desiring particular things as good for that person. Consequently, to say that God desires the good for a person is to use 'the good' referentially.

For this reason, when, in an effort to will what God wills, Teresa desires *whatever* happens to her father as the good for her father,[25] she thereby actually *fails* to will what God wills. To be united with God in willing the good requires willing for the beloved particular things that are in fact the good for the beloved, and doing so requires recognizing those things that constitute that good.

At the death of Mao Tse-tung, one of the groups competing for power was called 'the Whatever Faction,' because the members of that group were committed to maintaining as true anything Mao said, whatever it was, and to maintaining as good anything Mao had commanded, whatever it was.[26] In trying to desire whatever happens as good because God wills it, a person is as it were trying to be part of a Whatever Faction for God. She is trying to maintain as good anything that happens, whatever it is, on the grounds that it is what God wills.

By contrast, in his great lament over the death of his brother, Bernard of Clairvaux is willing to affirm both his passionate grief over the loss of his brother and his acceptance of God's allowing that death. Bernard says: "Shall I find fault with [God's] judgment because I wince from the pain?;"[27] "I have no wish to repudiate the decrees of God, nor do I question that judgment by which each of us has received his due . . . "[28] Bernard grieves over this particular death as a bad thing, even while he accepts that God's allowing this bad thing is a good thing.

Understanding the subtle but important difference in attitude between Teresa and Bernard on this score helps to elucidate the otherwise peculiar part of the book of Job in which God rebukes Job's comforters because they did not say of God the thing that is right, unlike God's servant Job, who did. What the comforters had said was that God is justified in allowing Job's suffering. Job, on the other hand, had complained bitterly that his suffering was unjust and that God should not have allowed it to happen. How is it that, in the story, God affirms Job's position and repudiates that of the comforters? In my view, the answer lies in seeing that the comforters took Job's suffering to be good just because, in their view, Job's suffering was willed by God. In effect, then, the comforters were (and wanted to be) part of the Whatever Faction of God. Job, by contrast, was intransigent in his refusal to be partisan in this way. And so, on the apparently paradoxical view of the book of Job, in opposing God, Job is more allied with God's will than the comforters are. That is why, when in the story God adjudicates the dispute between Job and the comforters, he sides with Job, who had opposed him, and not with the comforters, who were trying to be his partisans.

The apparent paradox here can be resolved by the Thomistic distinction between God's antecedent and consequent will.[29] On this distinction, whatever happens in the world happens only because it is in accordance with God's will, but that will is God's *consequent* will. God's consequent will, however, is to be distinguished from his antecedent will; and many of the things that happen in the world are not in accordance with God's *antecedent* will. To try to be in accord with God's will by taking as acceptable, as unworthy of sorrow, everything that happens is to confuse the consequent will of God with the antecedent will. It is to accept as intrinsically good even those things that God wills as good only *secundum quid*—that is, as the best available in the circumstances. But God does not will as intrinsically good everything he wills; what he wills in his consequent will, what is the best available in the circumstances, might be only the lesser of evils, not the intrinsically good. On Aquinas's theodicy, as I explained in the previous chapter, God allows suffering that is redeemed by its contribution to the good of the sufferer. But for God to allow it is to will it with his consequent will. It is not for God to determine it to occur or to will it with his antecedent will.

And so to accept as good whatever happens on the grounds that it is God's will is the wrong way to try to be united with God. One can desire as intrinsically good what one's own mind takes to be intrinsically good in the circumstances, or one can desire[30] as intrinsically good whatever happens, on the grounds that it is God's will. But only the desire for what one's own mind takes to be intrinsically good can be in accordance with God's will. For the same reasons, only a desire of this sort is conducive to union with God. Although it appears paradoxical, then, the closest a human person may be able to come, in this life, to uniting her will with God's will may include her willing things (say, that a beloved person not die) that are opposed to God's (consequent) will.

It is also important to see in this connection that, on Aquinas's position, in principle, there cannot be any competition between the love of God and the love of other persons.[31] On the contrary, if one does not love one's neighbor, then one does not love God either. That is because to love God is to desire union with him; and union with

God requires being united in will with him. But a person who does not love another, his father or brother, for example, cannot be united in will with a God who does love these people. When a loved person dies, however, at least one of the desires of love for him, the desire for union with him, is frustrated. To be tranquil in the face of the death of another is therefore to be deficient with respect to one of the desires of love for him. And so, in being unmoved in the face of the death of a loved person, one is not more united with God, or more in harmony with God's will, but less.

Denying oneself

Something also needs to be said in this connection about the Christian doctrine (which Aquinas accepts) mandating denial of the self. This much understanding of the two different ways in which one can try to will what God wills shows that there are also two correspondingly different interpretations of that doctrine.

Cassian and others who hold the stern-minded attitude manifest one such under-standing. A person who shares Cassian's attitude will attempt to deny his self by, in effect, refusing to let his own mind and his own will exercise their characteristic functions. That is because a person who attempts to see as good whatever happens, on the grounds that whatever happens is willed by God, is trying to suppress, or trying to fail to acquire, his own understanding of the good. And a person who attempts to will as good whatever happens, on the same grounds, is trying to suppress the desires his own will forms, or trying not to acquire the desires his will would have formed if he were not in the grip of the stern-minded attitude. To attempt to deny the self in the stern-minded way is thus to try not to have a self at all. A woman who says sincerely to her father, "I want only what you want," and "whatever you think is good is good in my view, too," is a woman who is trying to be at one with her father by having no self of her own.

On the other hand, it is possible to let one's own faculties of intellect and will have their normal functioning and still deny oneself. Consider, for example, Abraham as he goes to sacrifice Isaac at God's command. The story says that God's command tests Abraham, and it is clear that the test pits Abraham's desires about his son against God's command to sacrifice him. In the story, then, it is evident that Abraham desires not to sacrifice Isaac. He does not see the sacrifice of his son as a desirable thing, and he does not want it. Abraham's intellect and will are thus opposed to the sacrifice of Isaac. On the other hand, however, Abraham does indeed go to the place God designates for the purpose in order to sacrifice his son. So Abraham sees doing what God wants as desirable, in fact as more desirable than doing what he himself wants. Abraham's intellect and will are thus committed to the desirability of letting God's desires take precedence over Abraham's own. In this rank-ordering of desires, Abraham does not give up his desire not to sacrifice Isaac. He still has that desire; he just acts counter to it because he desires to desire something contrary to his desire not to sacrifice Isaac. To act as Abraham does is to deny the self by first having a self to deny. Unlike the no-self position, this position is compatible with sorrow, and tears, for the things lost in the desires denied.

In fact, a little reflection shows that, contrary to first appearances, the no-self position is actually incompatible with the Christian injunction of self-denial. That is because one cannot crucify a self one does not have. To crucify one's self is to have desires and to be willing to act counter to them. C. S. Lewis, who is arguing for a similar position, puts the point this way: "it would not be possible to live from moment to moment willing nothing but submission to God as such. What would be the material for the submission? It would seem self-contradictory to say 'What I will is to subject what I will to God's will,' for the second *what* has no content."[32]

An adherent to the Whatever Faction of God cannot deny his self because he has constructed his desires in such a way that, *whatever* he wills, he does not will counter to his own desires. That is because a person who is a partisan of the Whatever Faction of God has a second-order desire for whatever it may be that is God's will, and he attempts to stamp out of himself any first-order desires which are in conflict with that second-order desire. He does not want to let God's desires take precedence over his own; he wants to have no desires in conflict with God's desires, whatever they may be. That is why (unlike the real Teresa, who was full of very human emotions) such a person would not weep if her father died. In theory, at any rate, *whatever* happens is in accordance with her first-order desires and is therefore not a source of sorrow to her. In virtue of the fact that she has tried to extirpate from herself all desires except the one desire for whatever it may be that is God's will, such a person has no desires that are frustrated by whatever happens, as long as she herself remains committed to willing whatever God wills.[33]

By contrast, a self-crucifying denier of the self, such as Abraham, has first-order desires for things his own intellect finds good, so that he is vulnerable to grief in the frustration of those desires. But he prefers his grief and frustration to willing what is opposed to God's will. In this sense, he wills that God's will be done. His second-order desire is that God's desires take precedence over his own. When Christ says, "not my will but yours be done," he is not expressing the no-self position, because he is in effect admitting that he has desires in conflict with God's desires.[34] On the other hand, in virtue of preferring his suffering to the violation of God's will, he is also willing that God's desires take precedence over his. This is the sense in which he is willing that God's will be done. C. S. Lewis says: "In order to submit the will to God, we must have a will and that will must have objects. Christian renunciation does not mean Stoic 'Apathy,' but a readiness to prefer God to inferior ends which are in themselves lawful."[35]

To deny oneself is therefore a matter of being willing both to have first-order desires and to go contrary to them. Or, put another way, it is a matter of being willing to suffer the contravening of one's will. Insofar as the stern-minded attitude seeks to eradicate desires other than the desire for flourishing, it in effect refuses to have a self to deny. And so it is more aptly characterized as an extreme attempt to avoid suffering than as self-denial.

The repudiation of the stern-minded attitude

So, for all these reasons, the stern-minded attitude is to be repudiated. Whatever its antiquity and ancestry, like many others in the Christian tradition Aquinas does not accept it. In my view, he does well to reject it. It is an unpalatable position, even from the point of view of an ascetically minded Christianity. It underlies the repellent and lamentable mindset exemplified in Cassian's story. It is also incompatible with the love of one's neighbor and consequently with love of God as well. Contrary to the stern-minded attitude, there are things worth desiring other than the intrinsically valuable things necessary for human flourishing, and the desires for these things should not be suppressed or stamped out. In fact, as Cassian's story of Patermutus makes plain, the attempt to extirpate the desires of the heart leads not to human excellence, as Cassian thought it did, but to a kind of inhumanity, exemplified by a willingness to murder one's own child in the service of a confused and reprehensible attempt at self-denial.

It has to be noted, however, that there is an apparent paradox in this repudiation of the stern-minded attitude. As I introduced the phrase, the desires of the heart are desires which are central to a person's web of desires but whose objects derive their value for that person from his love of them; they need not themselves be intrinsically valuable things or essential to his flourishing. As I have been at pains to make clear, for a person to lose the objects of such desires or to give up those desires themselves is therefore compatible with his flourishing. But the rejection of the stern-minded attitude seems to imply that a person's flourishing requires that he have desires of the heart and that he strive to have what he desires. Consequently, it also seems to imply that it is essential to a person's flourishing that he have desires of the heart. And, if the desires of the heart are required for his flourishing, then it seems that the objects of those desires are as well. So it seems to follow, paradoxically, that it is essential to human flourishing that a person desire and seek to have things at least some of which are not essential to his flourishing.

In recent work, Harry Frankfurt has argued that it is useful for a person to have final ends.[36] The core of his argument is the claim that a person with no final ends at all will have a life that lacks flourishing. And so, in an apparent paradox, final ends turn out to be useful for human flourishing. The apparently paradoxical claim about the desires of the heart can be understood analogously. Human beings are constructed in such a way that they naturally set their hearts on things in addition to and different from their own flourishing. That is why confining a person's desires just to his own flourishing has something inhuman about it. A person's flourishing therefore also requires that he care about and seek to have things besides those that are intrinsically valuable components of or means to human flourishing.[37] On Frankfurt's view, having something that is not a means to anything else, a final end, is a means to a person's flourishing. On the view I have argued for here, having a desire for things that are not necessary for flourishing is necessary as a means to flourishing. And so, although no particular thing valued as a desire of the heart is essential to a person's flourishing, human flourishing is not possible in the absence of the desires of the heart.

At the outset of this chapter, I suggested that Job might care more about the loss of his children than about his flourishing. For the stern-minded, if Job's suffering is really connected to his flourishing in the way I described in the preceding chapter, nothing more is needed for an acceptable theodicy: the good of flourishing given to Job through his suffering defeats all his suffering. To hold this view, however, is to accord no value to the desires of Job's heart. It is, in effect, to say with regard to Job a much sterner version of what (in the example of Chapter 1) the loving but exasperated father said to his little daughter when she was crying: it is not reasonable to weep about these things. But disregarding or downplaying the desires of the heart is itself unreasonable. Suffering is a function of what we care about, and we care not only about our own human flourishing; we care also about the things on which we have set our hearts, and it would be inhuman of us not to do so.

For all these reasons, we can safely leave the stern-minded attitude to one side.

Two problems for Aquinas's theodicy

The question therefore remains: how is the suffering stemming from the loss of the desires of the heart to be woven into Aquinas's theodicy? On Aquinas's theodicy, the benefit outweighing the suffering for Job outweighs it only on Aquinas's scale for objective value, which measures the intrinsic worth of things essential to human flourishing. The benefit does not automatically outweigh the suffering of any particular person on the scale that measures the value things have for him just because he has set his heart on them.

In fact, the problem is not just that Aquinas's theodicy is incomplete in this way. If the stern-minded attitude is repudiated, then Aquinas's theodicy looks self-defeating.

To see why, consider that, on Aquinas's views, a person's suffering is a means to his flourishing; but one source of suffering for a person is heartbreak, the loss of the desires of his heart. Because this is so, it seems that, for Aquinas, there is actually an opposition between the desires of a person's heart and that person's flourishing. The loss of the former can be a means to the latter. In effect, then, on Aquinas's theodicy, any desire of a person's heart, however innocuous its objects may be, apparently turns out to be inimical to his flourishing. Because this is so, and because a person cares about both his flourishing and his heart's desires, it seems that on Aquinas's theodicy there is ineluctably an incompatibility in the set of things a person cares about.

If this result is right, however, and if it does not lead straight back to the stern-minded attitude, then it seems pernicious for Aquinas's theodicy. On Aquinas's views, suffering is medicinal for internal integration, and internal integration is necessary for flourishing. But the side effects of the medicine now seem to be internal fragmentation, a division in the will, which undermines flourishing, as I was at pains to show in earlier chapters. By pitting one part of what a person cares about against another, Aquinas's theodicy seems to imply that the suffering medicinal for flourishing has as an unintended side effect the destruction of the flourishing it is meant to effect.

And so it appears as if Aquinas's theodicy is self-defeating—unless, of course, compatibly with Aquinas's theodicy, there is a way to overcome the apparent opposition among the things we care about.

It may help to see these problems for Aquinas's theodicy in the concrete. So consider the story of Mary of Bethany.

In that story, Mary has a heart's desire that her brother not die and that Jesus heal Lazarus out of love for her as well as love for Lazarus. As the story turns out, Jesus does not heal Lazarus and Lazarus does die. But, in the narrative that is Mary's story and not Lazarus's,[38] both these narrative facts contribute greatly to Mary's flourishing. Now suppose that the story is rewritten in such a way that—somehow—all these narrative facts remain the same but that Lazarus is not resurrected. To the extent to which Mary has the heart's desires she does, it seems that, in this rewritten story, Mary will remain heartbroken even if she cares very much about her own flourishing and even if she grasps the contribution of Lazarus's death to her flourishing. If the stern-minded attitude is repudiated, then the value Mary's flourishing has on the scale for objective value does not automatically override for her the value that Lazarus has for her, on the scale for subjective value particular to Mary.

How would Mary be internally integrated in psyche, as she needs to be for flourishing, if she were torn between her care for her flourishing and her love of Lazarus? That is the first problem for Aquinas's theodicy. And what would defeat the suffering of Mary's heartbreak over Lazarus, if her flourishing alone does not do so? That is the second problem.

Furthermore, it can appear that the second problem is intractable. As regards flourishing, Aquinas resolves the paradox that seems to damn all theodicies by relativizing flourishing to different portions of a person's life, this worldly and other-worldly. On his theodicy, flourishing of a very great sort in the everlasting portion of a person's life is the benefit redeeming the suffering of the loss of lesser flourishing in the short part of that person's life. So the introduction of an other-worldly element into Aquinas's theodicy renders non-paradoxical the claim that the loss of a person's flourishing is defeated for him by the gain of his flourishing. On the scale for objective value, great and everlasting flourishing is more valuable than lesser, limited flourishing; and losing the smaller short-term flourishing for the sake of acquiring the greater lasting flourishing is a trade worth making. But it is not easy to see how this Thomistic strategy can be applied to the scale for subjective value for a particular person. What relativization is possible as regards the desires of a person's heart? Given the repudiation of the stern-minded attitude, what could one gain that would make it worth losing the desires of one's heart other than the desires of one's heart? But how could a person gain the desires of her heart by losing them?

And if this second problem is intractable, then so is the first. On Aquinas's theodicy, it seems that the desires of the heart are inimical to a person's flourishing, so that, if a person cares both about his flourishing and also about the desires of his heart, he cannot be internally integrated. But, if there is nothing at all that can redeem the suffering stemming from the loss of the desires of the heart, then a fortiori there is nothing that can redeem that suffering as a means to flourishing. And so it seems that a person who cares about both his heart's desires and his flourishing cannot be internally integrated, as he needs to be for flourishing.

The stern-minded attitude solves both these problems by rejecting the desires of the heart. With the stern-minded attitude itself rejected, Aquinas's theodicy is in need of some other solution to these problems.

The end of the stories

In my view, the solutions to both problems for Aquinas's theodicy are evident in the endings of all the narratives examined in the preceding section. Franciscanly seeing this side of those stories is one thing, however; teasing it out and explaining it Dominicanly is another entirely. It is nonetheless a help to begin with the stories.

In the preceding paragraphs, I called attention to the heart's desires Mary of Bethany evinces; but, manifestly, each of the protagonists in the other narratives has heart's desires, too. Abraham wants a son, and children from that son, because he wants to be the patriarch of a people. Samson wants to be a great warrior, notable for his strength, successful as a liberator of his people, beloved of the Lord who gives him strength. And Job wants to be a prosperous paterfamilias known for his piety among his people.[39]

At a certain point in the stories, however, it seems to the protagonists of the stories, and to the audience of the stories also, as if the protagonists have lost their heart's desires. Jesus does not come when Mary of Bethany calls to him for help, and Lazarus dies. Abraham takes his son—"his *only* son," since Ishmael has been sent away—to offer him in sacrifice to God. Samson is captured by the enemies of his people, blinded, forced into manual labor for those he hoped to conquer, and made a spectacle for the enemies of his people, exhibiting the apparent power of their god over his. Job loses his wealth, his children, and his religious standing in his community. Whatever may need to be said about the suffering of each of these protagonists, whatever the case may be for each of them as regards flourishing, it is undeniable that, at some point in the stories, each of them is heartbroken over something unconnected to human flourishing, even flourishing understood as Aquinas does, as union with God.

But what else is notable about the stories is that, in the end, each of the protagonists in fact receives his heart's desire, although in a form he did not expect, and also by a means he did not expect: it comes in consequence of the suffering of heartbreak. The evidence for this claim is in the painstaking unfolding of the stories in Part 3, and that cannot be repeated here. Here just gesturing at the ending of the stories has to be enough.

At the end of the story of Mary of Bethany, the great love Jesus has for her is made powerfully evident to her, and Lazarus is restored to her in a more meaningful way than she could have imagined beforehand, through Jesus' miracle of the resurrection of Lazarus. Abraham has his son Isaac, and he becomes the patriarch of innumerable people through that son. In fact, Abraham becomes the father of all the faithful; as the story explains, all those who bless themselves will be blessed in Abraham's seed. Samson achieves a decisive victory over the enemies of his people, not by emerging glorious from hand-to-hand combat with them, but by bringing down the temple on them and him; in the process, he draws closer to God than he had ever been before in the story. And in all three of these cases, as I showed in the examination of the stories, the suffering of the protagonists is necessary, in the circumstances of the narrative, for them to have what is in fact their hearts' desires, even if those desires are in the altered form in which the protagonists have them at the end of the stories.

The case of Job is different from that of the other three in signal ways; but nonetheless something analogous can be said: at the end of his story, Job has a religious standing in his community much greater than he could have imagined earlier; and that standing has its source in his suffering. In addition, however, in a way that distinguishes Job's story from that of the other three, the story claims that Job has "double" of all the things he valued and lost at the outset of the story. He is twice the prosperous paterfamilias he was and wanted to be at the beginning of the story. What differentiates the end of Job's story from that of the others canvassed is the apparently adventitious addition of children and wealth in Job's return to prosperity. There is no essential connection between Job's suffering and his receiving double those things he lost in the suffering. It is also worth noting that although at the end of the story Job has double the number of camels and other beasts as he had before his suffering began, the number of the children he gains then is identical to the number of the children he lost, not double it.[40]

Later I will return to these features of the ending of Job's story that do not match features of the other three; but, for now, I want to call attention only to those things shared by the endings of all four narratives. In the stories, the protagonists suffer heartbreak in the loss of their heart's desires. But what they gain at the end of the stories is, somehow, their heart's desire, only, as it were, more so. And, somehow, with the one exception noted in the case of Job, what is gained by the protagonists is gotten through the suffering occasioned by the heartbreak. In all these stories, then, it is true that the sufferers gain the desires of their hearts by losing them.

To gesture toward this feature of all the stories, however, is not to explain it. Consider again the story of Mary of Bethany. If Jesus had come when the sisters called him and had healed Lazarus then, Mary of Bethany would have had her heart's desire in the form in which she had originally framed it. At the end of her story, however, she is plainly grateful for what she gained by means of the loss of that form of her heart's desire. Why would she be grateful in this way? What is the relation between what she received at the end of the story and what she wanted at the beginning of it? And how are we to understand comparisons of things on the scale for subjective value? Why would Mary prefer what she receives at the end of the story with all its suffering to what she would have had if she had gotten without the suffering what she originally wanted? How are we to understand the defeat of the suffering that comes to Mary of Bethany when she is heartbroken? In the story, it plainly *is* defeated, but how is that defeat to be explained? Here we are up against one of the problems for Aquinas's theodicy.

In addition, in her story the same outcome of events both conduces to her great flourishing and gives to her her heart's desires. Somehow there is a harmonization between the two disparate scales for value for her. What Mary of Bethany cares about as regards her flourishing and what she cares about as regards her heart's desires are not incompatible, at the end of her story; in fact, they converge. How is this harmonization of the scales of value to be explained? Here we are up against the other problem for Aquinas's theodicy.

The scale for subjective value

For the protagonists in the stories canvassed, it is apparent that what they receive at the end of the stories is somehow more their hearts' desires than what they thought their hearts' desires were at the beginning of the stories. In Chapter 1, I explained that what a person cares about need not be transparent to him, even when it comes to heart's desires. My example in that chapter was Victor Klemperer. Klemperer was heartbroken because he supposed that he would never write the great book he had it in him to write when he wanted to write a study of eighteenth-century French literature; but he recorded this heartbreak in his diaries, which have been hailed as one of the greatest works of confessional literature ever to come out of Germany. Presumably, if Klemperer had been offered the choice of writing a book that added to the existing secondary literature on a limited period in French literary history or writing a book that is one of the greatest German works of any kind, he would have wanted the latter much more than the former; and he would have recognized the desire for the latter as a version of the desire for the former. In thinking about the two problems of Aquinas's theodicy and the way in which both problems seem solved by the same set of events in the biblical narratives, it will be helpful to try to understand the relation between two forms of the same heart's desire, between what the protagonists of the biblical stories thought they wanted—and did want—at the beginning of their stories and the heart's desires they got at the end.

For this purpose, it is important to think more about the scale for subjective value.

To illuminate the characteristic features of the scale for subjective value, consider first the *other* scale, the scale for objective value, by which flourishing is measured. Intuitively, the scale for objective value runs from higher to lower, where what is best is highest and what is worst is lowest. In addition, the objective value some things have is derivative from their connection to things higher up on the scale. The objective value of exercise, for example, stems at least in part from the connection of exercise to health and the objective value health has.[41] In response to the question why exercise is valued, one right answer is that it contributes to health, which has a higher objective value. In fact, for Aquinas, until we come to that objective good which is highest on the scale, God and shared union with God,[42] it always makes sense to ask why something is valued. On Aquinas's views, if with regard to something good on the *objective* scale of value a person is asked why he values it, the answer "I just do" is never acceptable. From Aquinas's point of view, the answer needs to be "because it is good." As I explained in Chapter 5, Aquinas takes goodness to be a function of God's nature.[43] And so, for Aquinas, to value something because it is good is—ultimately—to value it for its connection to what is at the upper limit of the scale for objective value—namely, God and shared union with God.[44]

Against this brief review of the scale for objective value, we can begin to delineate the scale for subjective value, the scale by which heart's desires are measured, because analogous things can be said about that scale. Like the scale for objective value, the scale of subjective value for any particular person comes in degrees, and it is bounded as well. Intuitively, however, the scale for subjective value for a person runs from what is deeper to what is more superficial, rather than from what is higher to what is lower, as the scale for objective value does. For the scale for subjective value for a person, depth, rather than height, is a measure of greatest value. What a person values most as a heart's desire is not at the intrinsic highest bound of the scale but at the intrinsic deepest, so to speak.

In addition, just as on the scale of objective value, so on the scale of subjective value, for a person some things are valued derivatively from other things. The things that have deeper subjective value for a person can be the source of value for other things that have subjective value for him. Abraham values Hagar as he does at least in part because she is the mother of his son Ishmael; her value for him is at least in part derivative from the value Ishmael has for Abraham, who cares so deeply about having offspring. In the Lucan narrative of the anointing of Jesus, Sinner's heart's desire is set on Jesus; and so, for Sinner, the subjective value of the connection to Jesus makes her scandalous actions at Simon's party worth doing. The value of her actions at the party is measured for her by their connection to Jesus, on whom she has her heart fixed. That is why she is willing to endure the reactions Simon and the others take to her when she crashes the party and anoints Jesus as she does.

So the scale of subjective value for a person ranges from superficial to deep. The greatest value is had by those things that are deepest; and deeper things can be a source of value for other things valued by that person on this scale.[45] In all these respects, the scale for subjective value is analogous to the scale for objective value.

On the other hand, there is this apparent disanalogy between the two scales. If a person is asked why he values something, when the value is measured by the scale for subjective value, even something valued as the deepest heart's desire, it seems that the answer "I just do" has to be not only an acceptable answer but in fact the only answer conceivable. Because a thing measured by this scale has its value for a particular person derivatively from the fact that he cares about it, and not the other way around, it seems that the answer to the question "Why do you value this?" has to point only to the care for it had by the person doing the valuing, not to something intrinsic in the thing valued. For this reason, it seems that the care a person has for a thing is the sole appropriate explanation for the value things have as heart's desires for him. I will refer to this view as 'the quodlibet view'—'the whatever view'—since the view maintains that a person's caring about anything whatever is the sole source of subjective value for him; and I will call this view into question below.[46]

The deepest desires of the heart

On Aquinas's views, for all human beings there is one and the same intrinsic upper limit to the scale of objective value—namely, God and shared union with God. But what can be said about the intrinsic deepest limit to the scale of *subjective* value? It seems that the deepest limit must vary from person to person. In fact, on the quodlibet view, it seems that the deepest limit could be just anything at all.[47] In her endearing chronicle of the almost twenty years of her life devoted to the barn owl she rescued, Stacey O'Brien makes clear how deeply she cared for this bird.[48] She says about this owl: "He was my teacher, my companion, my child, my playmate . . . We were happy together . . . I loved him completely."[49] So, could there be a person for whom the deepest desire of the heart is an owl? On the quodlibet view, it certainly seems so. But matters are complicated here.

An objective scale of value for human beings is the same for everyone; that is why it is an objective scale of value. For this reason, the things valued on the scale can be characterized in terms of universals, one thing shared entirely by many: health, freedom, love, shared union with God. The nature of the things on the subjective scale is not like this, however. These things are particulars. No one sets his heart on health or on freedom; he sets his heart on his son's health or his people's freedom. For Aquinas (as for many contemporary thinkers, of course), human beings are embodied, made of matter;[50] and this fact makes us particular not only in what we are but also in what we love. There is the particular place in which a person is born, the particular time in which he grew up, the particular culture in which he lived, the particular nation, ethnicity, or people to whom he belongs; most importantly, there are the particular persons who are dear to him (or hated by him). Human beings are not like God in being capable of sharing intimately with endless numbers of people. Human beings are built for shared union in love with particular people—in fact, those few people on whom they have set their hearts. That is why someone who is everyone's friend is no one's friend. All friendship is particular friendship between one particular person and another, and a person who has no particular friends will simply have no friends.[51]

So, although on Aquinas's scale for objective value there is one objective, intrinsically valuable thing—namely, God and shared union with God, which is for every human being the greatest good—nonetheless this one common good has to be appropriated in particular ways by particular people with particular others. For this reason, the shared union with God that is at the intrinsic upper limit of the scale for objective value, on Aquinas's views, is after all not *exactly* the same for everyone, in virtue of the fact that, for every person, that union is not shared equally with everyone. For every human person, there are only particular human persons with whom he is most deeply united in love.[52]

Earlier I argued for the claim that it is essential to a person's flourishing that he set his heart on things not essential to his flourishing. The point at issue here is a variation on that claim: the greatest good that is common to every human being, God and shared union with God, has a particular character that makes it vary from person to person. There is, therefore, after all something ineluctably individual and particular, not abstract and common, about the highest good that has the greatest intrinsic value for everyone as measured by the scale for objective value. It is thus of universal objective value for every human being that he set his heart on particular things not the same for everyone.

Conversely, however, contrary to the quodlibet view, there is also a universal element, common to everyone, about the scale for subjective value. Since shared union in love with particular people is the greatest good for a human person, it is of universal objective value that the deepest things a person sets his heart on are persons. That is, for every human person, there is something right, something conducing to human flourishing, about having particular persons as the deepest desires of the heart. No one is surprised to find a survivor of some natural disaster saying on the evening news, "We lost everything in this fire, but we are all alive. We have each other; we have the things we care the most about." It is hard to imagine even that artist notorious for privileging art over family, Gauguin, saying in similar circumstances, "I have lost my whole family in this fire, but my pictures came through OK. I have my pictures, and so I have the things I care the most about." But, if some artist did say something to this effect, virtually all of us would be alienated from him. There is something inhuman about an attitude of that sort.

That this is so helps make clear that some things are not suitable as deepest heart's desires. The problem with owls as the deepest desire of a person's heart is that the communication between an owl and a human person is severely constrained, and in consequence so is the possibility for closeness between them. Very much of what constitutes union of minds and hearts for human persons is not possible between a human person and an owl. And so, if an owl alone is the deepest desire of some person's heart, then there will be a great deal of that person's psyche that is neither matched nor shared. Much of the shared union that is the greatest flourishing for human beings, on the scale of objective value for human beings, will be absent from the life of a person for whom the deepest desire of the heart, on the scale of subjective value for her, is an owl alone.

Consequently, just as there is a subjective element to the scale of objective value, because for each person only some people—*these* particular people—*can* be most intimately part of the shared union of love that is the greatest flourishing for all human beings, so there is also an objective element to the scale of subjective value for a person. It is not a matter of what *has* to be in this case, but a matter of what *ought* to be.[53] Anything *can* be the deepest desire of a person's heart, in the sense that a person can take it as the center of his web of desire. But only persons *ought* to be the deepest desire of a person's heart. In this respect, then, the quodlibet view is wrong. The care a person has for a thing, any thing, is an appropriate explanation of the value that thing has for him when it is a desire of his heart, but it is not the only explanation possible of the value of heart's desires. There is also the suitability of the things desired. Given the nature, history, inclinations, and circumstances of any particular person, some things are more suitable than others for him to set his heart on. For *these* things, it makes sense that he set his heart on them. For everyone, the most suitable of all are particular persons.[54]

God as the deepest desire of the heart

From Aquinas's point of view, however, even this much repudiation of the quodlibet view is not strong enough. Augustine's famous line addressed to God is pertinent here: you have made us for yourself, and our hearts are restless until they rest in you.[55] For Augustine, and for Aquinas, too, not only are human beings constructed in such a way that they hunger for the love of other persons, but in fact their deepest, inbuilt hunger is for God. On the Augustinian view shared by Aquinas, unless a person takes God as her deepest heart's desire, her heart will always have at its deepest core a yearning that is both inchoate and unsatisfied.

As his line indicates, Augustine thinks that this claim is true for all human beings, even those convinced that there is no God. Psychic hunger is no more translucent than suffering is. It is possible to hunger for something in particular without knowing what that particular is; for that matter, it is possible to hunger without knowing that one hungers.[56] The realization that one was hungry, in fact hungry for *this*, whatever this is, can sometimes come first when the hunger is satisfied. Then the relief, the gratitude, the joy, the determination not to lose *this*, reveals the hunger that was there before. People who find in unforeseen, unanticipated ways—in a drug, a relationship, a lifestyle—freedom from something that had previously afflicted them frequently have a reaction of this sort. They come to feel that *this* is what they had been hungering for all along, without realizing it. On Augustine's views and on Aquinas's too, every person for whom relationship with God comes belatedly and unexpectedly will have a reaction of this sort toward God and relationship with God.

In effect, the medieval tradition Aquinas accepts supposes that, just as some cognition appears to be innate,[57] so some desires also are hardwired into a human being. Certain biological desires, such as the desire for food, seem to be like this. For the medievals, the desire for God is like this, too. On their view, a desire for God is innate, whether or not a person is fully conscious of the desire or its nature.[58]

It is important to recognize that the claim that this desire is innate does not imply that a person has no control over it. The desire for food is innate, too, but a person can react to that desire in different ways. Depending on his own higher-order desires as regards his innate desire for food, a person can shape this innate first-order desire in different ways. For example, he can hate his desire for food or be alienated from it in some other way; in consequence, he can become anorexic or ascetic. Alternatively, he can care greatly about his desire for food and try to enhance it or train it; he can become a glutton or a gourmand. One way or another, in consequence of the higher-order desires he adopts toward it, a person can have considerable voluntary control over his desire for food. In the same way, although for Aquinas as for Augustine a deepest heart's desire for God and for shared union in love with God is innate, a person has considerable voluntary control over this desire. It is open to him to commit himself to it; alternatively, even if he cannot stamp out the desire entirely, he can fail to recognize or affirm it, and he can even repudiate it. Depending on his explicit or tacit and unacknowledged higher-order desires as regards it, he can shape this desire too in different ways. And so, although Aquinas supposes that the desire for God is innate in human persons, it does not follow that human persons lack all control over it.

In introducing the notion of the desires of the heart, I said that a heart's desire is something that matters greatly to a person but that need not be essential to her flourishing; for her, human flourishing could be possible without it. Unlike the value of things measured by the scale for objective value, on the scale for subjective value the value that the desired thing has for a person is derivative from the fact that she cares for it. On the medieval position I am sketching here, however, the deepest limit of the scale for subjective value is a special case. For Aquinas, what ought to be at the deepest intrinsic limit of the scale for subjective value for a person is not only essential to that person's flourishing but in fact equivalent to it. For Aquinas as for Augustine, it is possible for a human person to take as her deepest heart's desire the very thing that is also her greatest flourishing—namely, God and shared union with God. And so the intrinsic highest limit of one scale and the intrinsic deepest limit of the other can converge. On this view, unlike more superficial heart's desires, the intrinsic deepest limit to the scale for subjective value ought to be the same for everyone, at least to the extent to which the scale for objective value is the same for everyone.

It is important to see in this connection that shared union with God, which is a universal good for everyone, is also a union with something that is a particular, an individual with a mind and a will. For this reason, the question "Why do you value this?" asked of a person with regard to a deepest heart's desire for God and shared union with God can be given either the sort of answer appropriate for things valued on the scale for objective value or the sort of answer appropriate for things valued on the scale for subjective value. "Because God is good" is one appropriate answer; "because I love God" is another.

And so, although the two scales for value can converge on God and shared union with God, their convergence does not reduce the scale for subjective value, even at its deepest limit, to the scale for objective value. Although God and shared union with God is the greatest good for a person on the scale for objective value, if a person takes it as her deepest heart's desire as well, then the value it has for her will *also* be derivative from the fact that she has set her heart on it. It will have value for her not only because she is responding to the objective value in it; its value for her will also be derivative from the fact that she has set her heart on it.

Consequently, as regards the deepest desire of the heart, there is a sense in which the quodlibet view is entirely wrong. As Aquinas sees it, the deepest heart's desire is an inbuilt desire for God; even if a person ignores or repudiates it, it nonetheless remains in him. And so, although a person can take anything at all as his deepest heart's desire, unless a person commits himself to the inbuilt desire for God, it will be the case that in vague, ill-understood, or dimly grasped ways he will always be missing something on which his heart is set. On Aquinas's views, the deepest heartbreak will come to any person if he loses that thing which it is in fact his greatest good to have.

The interweaving of heart's desires

On the Augustinian view Aquinas shares, there is a connection between other desires of the heart and the innate deepest heart's desire for God and shared union with God. That is because, on this view, any created good loved for the real goodness in it will lead eventually to an awareness of the creator of that good and to a love for God, if only the love for the good in that created thing is allowed to deepen.[59] A noteworthy illustration of what Augustine and Aquinas have in mind can be found in O'Brien's chronicle of her life with Wesley, the owl she loved so deeply. As she describes herself in the period when she first began caring for this owl, she was an ordinary, secular, scientifically inclined young woman, working in a university lab. But her years of caring for the owl change her. Here is her own explanation of that change:

I gazed into the universe of Wesley's eyes almost every day for nineteen years . . . When I would look into his relaxed, at-peace-with-himself eyes, I felt like I was looking into something inscrutable, unobtainable, deeper than we can possibly imagine, an old soul that reflected something bigger, ineffable, eternal.

Even though I had been trained to exclude thoughts about spirits and unquantifiable, immeasurable feelings that could taint scientific conclusions, Wesley's presence in my life influenced my thinking. Now I see that to exclude a certain kind of idea is itself creating a bias. What if . . . we miss [the truth] because we have not allowed ourselves to listen to the channel it's on—or we've tuned it out? Wesley helped me feel God—to "get" the idea of God . . . in a way that I had not before and couldn't get from a theological sermon. I've decided not to discount those feelings and the wonder and gratitude that comes with them.[60]

At a certain point in her life, when O'Brien was debilitated by a serious, painful illness, she considered killing herself and also her owl, so that it would not suffer because she was no longer there to care for it. But she found that she could not do it. When she got close to doing so, she felt, as she says, that "it would have been an obscene act."[61] She explains her rejection of that double death in this way: "It's the Way of the Owl. You commit for life, you finish what you start, you give your unconditional love, and that is enough. I looked into the eyes of the owl, found the way of God there, and decided to live."[62]

And so what O'Brien began by thinking of as the way of the owl became for her one part of what she came to see as the way of God. Somehow, then, because of her love for this one particular owl, O'Brien came to set her heart on God and union with God; and the two loves, for God and for the owl, came into harmony for her. When they did, her heart's desire for her owl altered by being woven into an even deeper desire for God and union with God.

The refolding of heart's desires

Just as a protein can refold into a different configuration without any loss of its identity but with a great change in its functioning when it refolds, so the heart's desires of a person can also be reshaped by being woven into the deepest desire of that person's heart. The refolding of a heart's desires in this way makes a great difference to the character of suffering stemming from heartbreak and also to the possibility for its defeat.

When Abraham goes to sacrifice Isaac at God's command, he suffers because Isaac is his heart's desire; but he goes nonetheless, because his deepest heart's desire is God. At that point in his life, his desire for Isaac is encompassed within his desire for God. When Lazarus is resurrected, Mary of Bethany finds that what she could not have imagined in advance is in fact more her heart's desire than what she had originally thought she wanted. And then there is the case of Klemperer. It is hard not to believe that Klemperer would have greatly preferred being the author of the Klemperer diaries than of the critical work on French literature he thought it was his heart's desire to write. In the cases of all the protagonists in the biblical narratives, in Klemperer's case, and even in the case of O'Brien and her owl, intuitively it seems that there are two configurations of one single heart's desire, just as there can be two configurations of one and the same protein; and one of these configurations is deeper, closer to the center of the web of desire, than the other.

What is the relation between the two configurations of a heart's desire? And what does this relation have to do with a deepest heart's desire for God?

It is easiest to see the answers to these questions when the heart's desire has to do with a particular person. Lazarus is a heart's desire for Mary of Bethany. But when Lazarus is restored to her through resurrection, she has Lazarus as given to her by Jesus in love for her. After the resurrection of Lazarus, Mary loves Jesus in loving Lazarus, and she loves Lazarus in loving Jesus. What is new is not her love for Lazarus or for Jesus, but somehow the interconnection for her of these two loves. The interconnection of these loves is missing for her in the terrible time when Jesus does not come to heal Lazarus. In that time, Mary loses her belief that Jesus cares about her love of Lazarus. In effect, she thinks that the desires of her heart do not matter to Jesus, and so she believes that she has lost irrevocably the desires of her heart, for Lazarus and for Jesus. That is why she sinks into heartbrokenness. When Lazarus is restored to her through the miracle Jesus does, Mary's love for Jesus becomes part of her love for Lazarus. Her heart is still set on Lazarus then, but it is set on Lazarus as gift, as something given to her by a person on whom her heart is set in an even deeper way.

On the view I am trying to sketch here, what the poet Michael Dennis Browne says about the experience of two lovers when they are in romantic love's elated condition needs to be said about all the heart's desires of a person whose deepest heart's desire is for God: "everything is grace, is given."[63] In approving the poet's line that everything is a gift of the beloved and applying it to everything for a person who takes God as his deepest desire, I am not falling back into one species of the stern-minded attitude, trying to deprive everything of value except the love of God. Rather, it is the other way around. On the view I am trying to describe here, the deepest desire of the heart for God gives an added value to every other heart's desire, because it turns into gifts other things on which a person has set his heart.[64]

To see the point here, it is helpful to return to Aquinas's account of the nature of love. For Jerome to love Paula, Jerome must want the good for Paula. But it is part of the good for every human being to set her heart on things not connected to her generically human flourishing. Paradoxically but intelligibly, as I have been at pains to show, the generically human flourishing of any human being requires her to care for particular things not connected to her flourishing. In his writings about the raising of children, John Locke, who had no children, suggested that a child's asking for something is a prima facie reason not to give that thing to that child.[65] But this seems dead wrong. Because of the connection between heart's desires and flourishing, on the one hand, and the connection between desiring the flourishing of a person and loving her, on the other, no one who loves a human person can love her without also having some care for what she cares about, some desire that she have the desires of her heart. When Mary of Bethany thinks that Jesus does not care about what she cares about, in effect she is willing to accept a view of Jesus as unloving of her.

These points apply to God, too. For God to love Paula, God must care that Paula have what she cares about. Because this is so, a person who takes God as her deepest heart's desire ought also to accept that God cares about what she cares about. The alternative is to suppose that God is unloving. In taking this position, I am not forgetting the complications stemming from the human propensity for willed loneliness. When Catullus says of the woman on whom he has set his heart, "Odi et amo"—"I love her and I hate her"—he makes clear that it will be difficult to give him what he cares about. He is double-minded about this woman who is so important to him. He has some commitment to being united with her and also some commitment to rejecting her, and he cannot have both at once. The shortest route to giving Catullus what he cares about may be the long process of getting him to be integrated in psyche in his attitudes toward her. But the difficulty of doing so does not alter the fact that loving Catullus requires caring that Catullus have what he cares about.

It makes a difference therefore if the deepest desire of a person's heart is a perfectly good, perfectly loving God. If, like Catullus, someone takes something other than a perfectly good and loving God as his deepest heart's desire, the thing that is his deepest heart's desire will lack either the power or the will (or both) to give him what he cares about, at least as regards the deepest limit of the things on which his heart is set, but possibly as regards other heart's desires as well. The woman Catullus both loved and hated was destructive to him as well as enticing for him; when he hated her, he did so because she had very little care for what he cared about. But, on the Augustinian view Aquinas accepts, she would have been powerless to give him everything he wanted at his heart's core, even if she had cared to try. On this view, however beautiful or good they may be, all creatures are too limited to do so. A person whose deepest heart's desire is an owl alone, or even a human person alone, will find that she has some heart's desires unsatisfied, even if it is only the inchoate innate desire for God. On the other hand, if a person takes a loving God as her deepest heart's desire, then, as is also possible for her to understand, the perfectly loving person who is at the center of her web of desire cares about what she cares about and, as God, has the power to provide it for her, as gift, in love.

Plainly, this point holds even when the desires of a person's heart include a project. A heart's desire for a particular project is a desire for self-actualization in a certain mode, by being a victorious tribal warrior or by writing an excellent study of French literature. I have no idea how to individuate heart's desires; but, intuitively, it seems clear that it is possible for a heart's desire even for a project to be radically reconfigured and still remain the heart's desire it was.[66] When Samson has what he wants at the end of the story, it is very different from what he wanted at the outset; but it is still not the writing of a study of French literature. It is still recognizable as the desire to be a successful tribal warrior. And, as the detailed exposition of the story shows, when Samson dies as a blinded captive among his enemies, somehow that original heart's desire is satisfied.

If a person takes God as her deepest heart's desire, all her other heart's desires, including desires for a project, can refold, can reshape without losing their identity, by being woven into that deepest desire. If that happens, then the other things she had her heart set on become gifts, gifts had or hoped for, or even gifts lost or not given. A gift, however, is different from other transfers of goods; it differs, for example, from charitable donations. Unlike a charitable donation, a gift is second-personal in character; it is part of a story of second-personal relations and experience.[67] There is a giving-back in every receiving-as-a-gift of something given-as-a-gift. At the very least, there is on the part of the gift's recipient the recognition that there is a giver with the recognition that the thing given is a gift. There is, we might say, a kind of shared attention between giver and receiver around the gift because of the giving and receiving of the thing as gift.[68]

When *everything* is gift, as the poet Michael Dennis Browne wrote, then there is also a sense in which everything is meant to be given back. This is not the claim that every gift is to be received only long enough to be given back to the giver—and so to be refused as a gift. There is something of the stern-minded attitude about such a claim, if in fact it is not just stupid. The point is rather that, when the deepest desire of one's heart is for God and shared union of love with God, one gives oneself, together with all the other desires of one's heart, to the person from whom the other heart's desires are hoped for as gifts. *This* is the sense in which everything is meant to be given back. In my view, this is also the point of the processes of justification and sanctification central to Aquinas's worldview.[69] In drawing close to God or wanting to do so, as in more ordinary analogues of union in love, one surrenders oneself. But surrender in union of love with God is not submission;[70] and part of the difference between the two is that in such surrender but not in submission, because of the loving nature of the person to whom one surrenders,[71] it is right to trust that in surrendering one is not giving up the desires of one's heart.

Defiant, intransigent Samson surrenders to God at the end of his life, but with a prayer—an insistent prayer—to have what he has set his heart on. The result is that, when he gets it, he gets it as gift, as part of the second-personal connection, shared attention and personal presence, of union in love with God. What he had originally wanted is represented by his victory in the battle at Lehi. The refolded heart's desire is represented by his final triumph, with all its losses for him. As the story shows, the difference between the two lies in Samson's altered relationship to God. The final form of his heart's desire is interwoven into his deepest heart's desire for God, in a way that its earlier form was not. And Abraham is the father of faith just because, in extreme circumstances, he continues to hold on to both his heart's desires, for God and for Isaac, and to harmonize them. As he goes to sacrifice Isaac, he believes that God is good and will give him the desire of his heart—namely, Isaac. The deepest desire of his heart is for God, and the second-personal character of that commitment is part of his care for Isaac. By the time of the binding of Isaac, Abraham's heart is set on Isaac *as gift*, as given to him by God.

And so a heart's desire can change its configuration in virtue of its being interwoven into something deeper among the desires of the heart. When the deepest heart's desire of a person is for God and shared union with God, then the other things on which he has set his heart can be desired as gifts in the ongoing, dynamic second-personal connection between him and God. In being refolded in this way, those other heart's desires do not cease to be what they were or cease to be desires of his heart; but they are altered, and so is the suffering generated in case they are lost or not had. If God is the deepest desire of a person's heart, then in relation with God that person will have what he most deeply wants. But, like Abraham, he will also trust that the God who loves him will give him the other desires of his heart, as God can, compatibly with his flourishing. The suffering stemming from the loss of what he desires as gift in relation of love with God is still suffering, but it does not destroy either the center of the web of desire for him or his hope to have the other desires of his heart.

Refolded heart's desires and gifts

So, it is possible that a heart's desire broken in suffering be transformed and also fulfilled if it is woven into a deepest heart's desire for God. In particular, what was simply desired can through this process come to be desired as gift. This process does not diminish the suffering of the person grieving the loss of his heart's desire in its original form or the sorrow of others at his suffering; and it should not. There is inhumanity in shutting oneself off from suffering, whether through stern-mindedness or in more pedestrian ways. But refolding the heart's desires by interweaving them with a deepest desire for God alters the character of the suffering over the loss of them in their original form. When one of those in union is a perfectly loving God, the human person in that union can wait in trust even while he is grief-stricken over the loss or absence of something he had his heart set on. In such circumstances, both the waiting and the trust become a kind of giving back, which is part of the mutuality of love. Even the thing wanted as gift becomes wanted as something to be given back—not in the sense of being rejected, as the stern-minded attitude might suppose, but in the sense of being interwoven into the flowering of a life made into a gift for the person who is one's deepest heart's desire.

Moved and honored by the love Jesus reveals to her when he resurrects Lazarus, Mary of Bethany's desire is to shower love and honor on him in return; and she is glorious when she does so. But, in the story, this exchange between Mary and Jesus takes place at a dinner where Lazarus is one of the guests of honor. He is not lost sight of in the giving and receiving of love between Mary and Jesus; he is integral to it. At the start of the story, Lazarus is Mary's heart's desire. And he still is, at the end of the story. What changes is that her love for Lazarus becomes part of her love for God, as represented to her in Jesus. As part of that deeper love, Lazarus is loved as gift, in the ongoing, dynamic, giving and returning second-personal connection that is union in love.

These reflections also help to make sense of the odd feature of the book of Job to which I called attention at the outset of this chapter—namely, the adventitious character of Job's return to prosperity in his community. The protagonists in the other stories have their heart's desires, too, by the end of their stories, but there is a natural connection between their suffering and the mode in which those heart's desires are fulfilled. Their suffering is integral not only to their flourishing as they do at the end of their stories, but also to their having their heart's desires in the form that they do. Job's return to the status of prosperous paterfamilias is not like this, however. Prosperity in the form of herds of animals can readily be had, by Job or anybody else, without a story involving suffering.

Because of the adventitious character of Job's return to tribal wealth, it is not uncommon for readers to take the ending of the book of Job as an excursus stuck on to the real story, fairy-tale-like at best, at worst vulgar and whitewashing. But to read the ending of the story in this way is to join the stern-minded attitude in assigning no value to the desires of the heart or to join Locke in supposing that love has no pressing need to provide the desires of the beloved's heart. If we repudiate the stern-minded attitude and reject Locke's presupposition, then the apparently jejune ending of the book of Job is in fact a sophisticated comment on the problem of suffering and integral to the rest of the story. The iconic picture that the book of Job gives of the relation between God and a human person who loves him is incomplete without that ending. If the heart's desire of a human person is not naturally fulfilled through the suffering that brings him to flourishing, it is nonetheless not adventitious to his story that he have his heart's desires, in one form or another; and there will be a desire on the part of a loving God to give him his heart's desire, as God can, compatibly with making him glorious. Job's terrible suffering transforms him. It makes him exemplary of what is most admirable in the human spirit, and it bonds him to God, as his deepest heart's desire. If this condition is, as it seems to be in the story, compatible with a heart's desire on Job's part to be a prosperous paterfamilias, then there is nothing surprising about his having it at the end of a story focused on his second-personal connection to a good and loving God.

Seen in this way, what is surprising in the book of Job is not that Job gets tribal prosperity at the end of the story, but that he still wants it, after his face-to-face encounter with God. But, however it is to be understood, this ending to the story is a hedge against the stern-minded attitude. For the stern-minded, Job's momentous encounter with God ought to be enough good for him; every desire of his heart should be satisfied in this tremendous drawing near to God. Who would want camels if he has God with him? But the right answer to this question is that a human being can want camels or owls or the writing of books *anyway*, even so. The particular focus of a particular heart's desire on something accidental to flourishing, even flourishing in union with God, is natural to human beings and so also essential to their flourishing. When a heart's desire of this sort can be satisfied compatibly with flourishing, what would be loving about denying it?

Conclusion

At the outset of this chapter, I said that there are two problems for Aquinas's account.

The first is that it seems self-defeating. Internal integration in the psyche is needed for the closeness ingredient in union in love, and harmonization among the things one cares about is needed for internal integration. But, on Aquinas's theodicy, it seems as if the suffering Aquinas takes to be medicinal for such internal integration pits the desires of the heart against flourishing, so that a person who cares about both will be internally fragmented. The side effect of medicinal suffering therefore seems to be an enhancement of the disorder the medicine was intended to cure.

The second problem appears to afflict Aquinas's theodicy at the point where it initially seems strong. Anything that defeats a person's suffering has to be something he cares about more than he cares about the things whose loss occasions his suffering. But, since suffering stems from a loss of something affecting flourishing or heart's desires, it is hard to see what a person would care about more than these. Aquinas's strategy for handling the problem depends on dividing a person's life into two portions and relativizing suffering to one of these, the short, earthly portion. What defeats the suffering of the loss of flourishing in the earthly portion of the sufferer's life is the gain of flourishing in the everlasting portion. This is a powerful strategy, but it seems ineffective for the problem of suffering having to do with the heart's desires, because a person may not care more about his flourishing than about the loss of his heart's desires. And if he does not, then what could defeat the suffering stemming from heartbreak? If the strategy of relativizing flourishing will not work in such a case, what would?

The solution to the first problem lies in seeing that, on Aquinas's views, it is possible for the two scales of value to converge for a person. It is possible for her to take as her deepest desire what is also her greatest flourishing. To say this is not to adopt the stern-minded attitude. To harmonize the heart's desires with flourishing is not to stamp out the heart's desires. The subjective character, the particularity, of the heart's desires, is preserved. At the end of the story, Abraham still has his heart fixed on Isaac; Mary of Bethany still has her heart set on Lazarus. Convergence of this sort is possible even when other particular things taken as heart's desires are on the face of it unsuitable to be a person's heart's desire. O'Brien's care for God comes to underlie her care for her owl, not to eradicate it; the addition of the care for God changes her care for her owl, but it does not destroy it.[72] In cases where a person takes a project as his heart's desire, as Samson does, the project is a matter of that person's self-actualization in that particular mode. Transformed by being woven into a deepest heart's desire for God, a desire for flowering in a particular mode becomes a desire to flower in that mode *for the beloved*, to use what one has—one's gifts, as we say—to their fullest as gifts given for gifts received.

Consequently, it is false that, on Aquinas's theodicy, the heart's desire of a person must be inimical to her flourishing. It *can* be, but it is false that it must be. When a person takes God as her deepest heart's desire, what is highest on the scale of objective value and what is deepest on the scale of subjective value for her become the same for her. For this reason, it is also possible for her to weave together all the things she cares about, her care for her flourishing and all her heart's desires, into a unity governed by that deepest desire. A person in this condition does desire those things on which she has set her heart; but she desires them *as gifts* of God, the person who is her deepest heart's desire, to be given back as gifts to the beloved.

The solution to the second problem lies in seeing that there is a relativization possible also for desires of the heart. The relativization is not to two different portions of a person's life, with two different degrees of objective value. Rather, it is to two different layers of depth in the heart's desires themselves. Something can be taken as a heart's desire just in itself, or it can be a heart's desire as interwoven with a deepest heart's desire. When the deepest heart's desire is for God, then other desires of the heart become desired as gifts in the second-personal connection to God.

If a person desires as a gift what he has his heart fixed on, then something analogous to Aquinas's strategy for dealing with suffering and flourishing becomes possible. A thing can be desired in its own right alone, or it can be desired as gift, given and given back, interwoven into the deepest heart's desire for God. Just as, on Aquinas's theodicy, flourishing can be lost or undermined in one way and gained in a far more valuable way, so too for the desires of a person's heart. They can be lost in one way and gained in another way, much more deeply desired by that particular person. What defeats the loss of the desires of the heart for a person is his gaining of the desires of his heart in another mode.

On this view, if a person loses or fails to receive a heart's desires in the process of deepening her closeness to God, she will grieve, because she has lost something that she had set her heart on. But, even so, what is at the center of the web of desire for her is *not* lost. Things do not fall apart for her; the center holds. And, because what is at that center is a perfectly loving God, even in grief she need not, should not, abandon her desire for the heart's desires she lost or failed to have. If she does, she will be joining the stern-minded. What is open to her to do instead, what is good for her to do, is to adopt the attitude that characterized Abraham when he became the father of faith: because the person who is her deepest heart's desire is also perfectly good and loving, she can trust him to give her the desires of her heart, in one form or another, but recognizable still in their particularity.

And so all the things a person cares about, his heart's desires and his flourishing, are compatible, even on Aquinas's theodicy, which takes the suffering of the loss of the heart's desires as medicinal for flourishing. The suffering that stems from the loss of the heart's desire is defeated not just by flourishing but also by the gain of the heart's desires, even if in a refolded mode.

It is possible therefore to develop Aquinas's theodicy in a way compatible with his own worldview and his strategy for theodicy in a way that handles the problem of the desires of the heart. To say this is to finish presenting the theodicy as it forms the Thomistic defense of this book. What remains that needs to be said and can be said in the defense of this Thomistic defense is the job of the next and final chapter.

Chapter 15

The Defense of the Defense: Suffering, Flourishing, and the Desires of the Heart

Whither shall I go from thy Spirit? or whither shall I flee from thy presence?
If I ascend up into heaven, thou art there; if I make my bed in hell, behold, thou art there.
If I take the wings of the morning, and dwell in the uttermost parts of the sea;
Even there shall thy hand lead me, and thy right hand shall hold me.
If I say, Surely the darkness shall cover me, even the night shall be light about me.
Yea, the darkness hideth not from thee, but the night shineth as the day; the darkness and
the light are both alike to thee.*

Introduction

As the preceding chapters show, Aquinas's views give a rich explanation for human suffering. For those who share his worldview, his position yields a powerful theodicy. For those who do not, it can nonetheless constitute a defense, a description of a possible world in which God and human suffering coexist. As I explained at the outset, my purpose in this book is just with his worldview and theodicy considered as a defense.

In the preceding chapters, I presented and defended Aquinas's account of love and the obstacles to the union desired in love, and I explained his view of the way in which such obstacles can be overcome. With this as background and with the stories as help, in Chapter 13 I laid out Aquinas's theodicy and the scale of values it presupposes. The stories examined in Part 3 embody that theodicy, in my view, and give us insight into its central claims. In Chapter 14, with the help of the stories, I argued that Aquinas's theodicy is incomplete considered as either a theodicy or a defense, because it leaves out

---

* Ps. 139: 7–12 (KJV).

the redemption of suffering stemming from deprivation of the desires of the heart. But in that chapter, with the help of the stories, I also showed the way in which Aquinas's theodicy can be developed to incorporate suffering of that sort. In my view, the stories embody this developed Thomistic theodicy as well.

The developed Thomistic theodicy transformed into a defense is the Thomistic defense of this book. How are we to evaluate it? What does it take to evaluate a defense? What would an objector have to show to argue successfully that a defense is unacceptable?

The first thing to remember in this connection is that, since it is being proposed only as a defense, there is no need for a defender of the defense to argue that the Thomistic defense or the worldview in which it is embedded is true. Because it is a defense and not a theodicy, it needs only to be internally consistent and not incompatible with uncontested empirical evidence.

Consequently, one way an objector might try to show that the Thomistic defense is unacceptable is to argue that it is inconsistent. And one way in which it might be inconsistent is if something in the Thomistic defense is inconsistent with one of the standard divine attributes. In my view, however, possible objections along this line have been adequately dealt with in the preceding chapters. Throughout the preceding parts of this book, I have called attention to cases in which something in Aquinas's theodicy might seem to be in conflict with a standard divine attribute, and I have tried to show why there is in fact no conflict in each case. For example, in earlier chapters, I gave reasons for supposing that even an omnipotent God could not bring about flourishing for a person just by willing it; even God needs to be responsive to a human person's condition. That is because union with God cannot be gotten by God unilaterally, either through love or through forgiveness. Or, to take another example, for reasons given in earlier chapters, it is apparent that, if suffering is a means to human flourishing, then God's allowing suffering is compatible with God's character as loving. For God, the two desires of love, for union with the beloved and for the good of the beloved, are both aimed at bringing a human person into union with God. Because union with God is the best thing for human beings and its absence is the worst thing, it is worth suffering, however bad the suffering. If suffering has the role assigned to it in the Thomistic defense, then, allowing suffering for the sake of human flourishing in union with God is part of God's love, not contrary to it.

Another way in which the Thomistic defense might be inconsistent is if one element in it undercuts another. In my view, the most important objection along these lines is the one I raised in the preceding chapter. There I showed that the suffering medicinal for the psychic integration requisite for flourishing can look as if in fact it is actually destructive of the psychic integration it seeks. That is because it can seem as if Aquinas's theodicy pits the desires of the heart against flourishing, so that a person who cares about both will ineluctably be internally divided—and thereby kept from flourishing. But, as I also argued in that chapter with the help of the stories, this apparent inconsistency can be resolved. It is possible to harmonize the care a person has for the desires of her heart with the care she has for her flourishing without invoking the stern-minded attitude. What is the greatest good for a person on the scale for objective value can converge with what is the deepest heart's desire for a person on the scale for subjective value for her; and, when it does, all the things a person cares about can be interwoven into a unity with the deepest desire of her heart and with her care for her flourishing, too.

So, although questions can no doubt still be raised about the internal consistency of the Thomistic defense, in my view issues of consistency have already been addressed as much as is reasonable to require of one book.

Still another way to undermine a defense or theodicy, less discussed but much felt in the debate over the problem of evil, has to do with the palatability of a defense. Some attempts at theodicy or defense strike many people as unpalatable for reasons they find hard to articulate and so also difficult to discuss. Seeing benefits in terms of what we care about helps to explain this reaction. Sometimes a benefit proposed in an attempted theodicy or defense is in effect only one component of human flourishing—the acquisition of virtue, for example. Sometimes, the proposed benefit does not even go primarily to the sufferer but is rather a benefit just for the human species as a whole—the significant use of free will, for example. But, typically, none of these is anything we care about more than we care about the things suffering undermines or deprives us of, our flourishing or our heart's desires.[1] Attempted theodicies or defenses based on benefits that are only partial components of human flourishing or that go just to humankind as a whole seem insipid to us because we have no taste for the trade they offer. In exchange for what we most centrally care about, they offer us what very few of us care about very much.

Taking suffering and the benefits defeating it as a function of what we care about is therefore one of the strengths of the Thomistic defense. At the very heart of the Thomistic defense is an attempt to show that what is gained through suffering is what is more worth caring about, not just on the scale for objective value but even on scales for subjective value, than what is lost in the suffering. One of the advantages of bringing stories into the discussion is that the stories let us explore in depth, in a narrative analogue to a thought experiment, this claim on the part of the Thomistic defense. If in fact the Thomistic defense were insipid or unpalatable in what it offers as a benefit defeating suffering, we would feel it when we saw it in operation in the life of a sufferer with whom the story has brought us into sympathy.

So in this respect, too, the Thomistic defense has in effect already been amply defended in the preceding chapters.

At this stage, then, what evaluation does the Thomistic defense still need? Has it not been sufficiently defended as a defense in the course of its exposition and examination? Has it not been sufficiently exemplified, embodied, confirmed in action, and supported in the stories?

In my view, what still remains for the evaluation of the Thomistic defense is the question whether that defense contravenes uncontested empirical evidence. A defense is distinguished from a theodicy because a defense does not claim that the possible world it describes is the actual world. (It does not claim that it is not. It just does not claim that it is.) The point of a defense is, in effect, to undermine confidence in the crucial third premiss of the argument from evil:

(3) There is no morally sufficient reason for an omniscient, omnipotent, perfectly good God to allow suffering in the world.

For a defense to undermine confidence in this premiss, it has to be the case that, for all we know (as distinct from all that we are committed to believing), the claims of the defense could be true. It would therefore invalidate a defense if something about what we currently know demonstrates that the possible world of the defense is not the actual world.

It is important to see in this connection that the issue is not whether the Thomistic defense includes views rejected by many contemporary thinkers. Obviously, it does. Many contemporary philosophers reject the theory of libertarian free will included in Aquinas's worldview, for example, and secular thinkers reject Aquinas's account of the afterlife. For that matter, secular thinkers deny the existence of God, which is of course central to the Thomistic defense. As I have noted in other places above, however, it is important to remember the dialectic of the argument. An acceptable defense is certainly not an attempt to prove the existence of God, and it does not attempt to offer a proof of any other religious beliefs either. Rather, to be successful, a defense needs only to rebut an attack on the truth of a set of religious beliefs. This attack, the argument from evil, seeks to impugn the consistency of religious belief taken in itself or together with uncontested empirical evidence. But, given its purpose, the argument from evil cannot itself contain views incompatible with the religious beliefs under attack. It would not be surprising to discover that religious beliefs comprise an inconsistent set when they are combined with secular beliefs antithetical to them. And philosophical theories are not uncontested empirical evidence. As far as that goes, if there were a good argument from evil that relied on compatibilism, for example, it would show not that religious belief is inconsistent, but only that religious belief would be wise to reject compatibilism. If the argument from evil so formulated were successful, then those who are committed to compatibilism would have a reason for rejecting religious belief, but that reason would have to do with compatibilism, and not with the presence of suffering in the world.

So the question whether the Thomistic defense contravenes uncontested empirical evidence is not a question of whether secular thinkers will find it plausible.

In my view, an objection that the Thomistic defense contravenes uncontested empirical evidence will most profitably focus on the role the defense assigns to suffering. That is because many people suppose that one of the most manifest facts about very much suffering in the actual world is its pointlessness. This supposition is not the claim that

> for most human suffering, human beings are not in a position to see a point to those particular cases of suffering.

That claim is not an objection to the Thomistic defense; on the contrary, in Chapter 1, I argued *for* this claim, as an important element of the Thomistic defense, limiting the scope of applicability of the defense. A theodicy cannot, and is not meant to, explain in particular why God would allow the particular suffering of a particular sufferer at a particular time in a particular set of circumstances; the role of suffering in the life of any particular human being may not be evident even to the sufferer herself. What is at issue here is instead the claim that

for most human suffering, there is no point to that suffering.

This claim does constitute an objection to the Thomistic defense.

Consideration of this objection is the last thing needed for an evaluation of the Thomistic defense, in my view, and it is the work of this chapter. If, as I will argue, this objection cannot be shown to be true on the basis of uncontested empirical evidence, then, in my view, the Thomistic defense is successful. At any rate, it is as solidly defended as anything can hope to be in philosophy.

The central question

The question posed to religious belief by the problem of suffering is whether there is a morally sufficient reason for God to allow suffering. Call this 'the central question.' In light of the reflections regarding suffering in Chapter 1, the central question can be given a more specific formulation. I argued in that chapter that a person suffers when something undermines her flourishing or her having the desires of her heart or both. A morally sufficient reason for God's allowing suffering must therefore be something that somehow defeats the badness of suffering so understood. Given the constraints on theodicy explained in Chapter 13, a person's suffering is defeated by a benefit that goes primarily to her, that outweighs her suffering, and that could not be gotten just as well without the suffering.

On the Thomistic defense, the benefit defeating a person's suffering has to do either with enabling a person to have the best thing for human beings or with enabling him to ward off the worst thing for human beings; and, in the process, it also offers the sufferer the desires of his heart, compatibly with his flourishing. The benefit is, therefore, a matter of offering the sufferer what that sufferer cares about, either as regards flourishing, or as regards the desires of the heart when those desires are interwoven with the flourishing of the sufferer, or both. Plainly, then, the benefit outweighs the suffering. So what remains to be considered with regard to the central question has to do with the connection between a person's suffering and the benefits said to defeat it. In the context of the Thomistic defense, the central question can therefore be formulated this way:

(C) Does God's allowing the evil a human being suffers enable[2] her to flourish, or enable her to have the desires of her heart; and is her suffering the best available means, in the circumstances,[3] to achieve those ends?

I recognize that this formulation of the question will provoke incredulity or indignation in some people, who will take the very form of the question to be an insult to human suffering. Just raising the question in this way will seem to them to be offensive, because they take it as so obvious that most human suffering is entirely pointless. Here, as elsewhere in this book, I want to side with the affect underlying this attitude, even if I reject the claim that goes with it. Human suffering is appalling, and the horror of the whole of it has to be faced. But there is more than one way of facing suffering; and consigning those who suffer to the scrapheap of human history is not the only way to respect their suffering. And so I want to look carefully at the central question, but in the full acknowledgment that the fearfulness of human suffering has to be honored.

As I have formulated it, the central question plainly consists in two pairs of subsidiary questions. These two questions are the first pair:

(C a1) Does God's allowing a person's suffering enable her to flourish?

and

(C a2) Is a person's suffering the best available means, in the circumstances, for her to flourish?

And these two questions are the second pair:

(C B1) Does God's allowing a person's suffering enable her to have the desires of her heart?

and

(C B2) Is a person's suffering the best available means, in the circumstances, for her to be able to have the desires of her heart?[4]

In fact, we can refine the formulation of the first pair of subsidiary questions still further in light of Aquinas's scale of value. The problem of suffering presupposes a standard of value, and the logic of the argument requires that that standard be the standard of the religious system challenged by the argument from evil. For the purposes of the defense at issue in this book, the relevant standard of value is Aquinas's. On Aquinas's scale of value, the intrinsic upper limit of the scale for objective value for human beings is God and shared union with God. Given this scale of value and the requisite conditions for union with God, the first subsidiary pair of questions should be reformulated in this way:

(C A1) Does God's allowing a person's suffering enable her to be willing to let God be close to her?

and

(C A2) Is a person's suffering the best available means, in the circumstances, to enable her to be willing to let God be close to her?

This pair of subsidiary questions (C A1 and A2) and the other pair (C B1 and B2) together constitute the central question. These are the questions that need to be answered affirmatively if Aquinas's theodicy and worldview are to constitute a successful defense. Is there reason to think that an affirmative answer to these questions is incompatible with uncontested empirical evidence?

Here it is worth reflecting what such reason would be. Since what is at issue is the role of suffering in conferring a kind of power or capacity on the sufferer, it would not disprove the Thomistic defense if there were cases in which suffering did not result in the flourishing or the fulfillment of the heart's desires of the sufferer. To have a power is one thing; to exercise it successfully is another. Because the Thomistic defense includes a commitment to libertarian free will, it provides for the possibility that a sufferer might choose not to exercise the power mediated by suffering. Nonetheless, if all or even most suffering did not have any point for the sufferer, that would be some evidence against the Thomistic defense, since one would suppose that an omnipotent, omniscient, perfectly good God would not use a strategy that was a complete failure, or a nearly complete failure. So, if it turned out that most suffering really is pointless, as many people suppose, that would be evidence against the Thomistic defense.

In what follows, I will begin with the first pair of subsidiary questions (C A1 and A2), and then go on to consider what can be said with regard to the second (C B1 and B2).

The first pair of subsidiary questions: the first question

On Aquinas's view, suffering is a means to human flourishing either because it is medicinal for those things disturbed in the psyche of a human person that keep him from being willing to let God be close to him, or because it is healing and instrumental in bringing a human person to a greater closeness with God, or both. On Aquinas's view, the role of suffering in the process that leads to shared union with God is thus the answer to the first pair of subsidiary questions. Is there in fact, as many people suppose, uncontested empirical evidence showing that, for most cases, suffering does not have the role assigned to it in the Thomistic defense?

Here it is helpful to see that, for present purposes, (C A1) can be answered by considering an empirical issue regarding human psychology. For Aquinas the main obstacle to a person's being united with God, in greater or lesser ways, is that person's lack of psychic integration. Since this is so, we can evaluate an affirmative answer to (C A1) by asking whether a person's suffering enables her to grow in psychic integration. This is a question that can be answered either by reflection on our own experience and that of others, or else by empirical studies.

To my mind, reflection on our own experiences and those of others only supports Aquinas's position about the relation of suffering to internal integration. The view of some ancient Greek tragedians that the gods have put suffering before wisdom is also a witness on this side.[5] The plausibility of the stories in Part 3 is testimony too. We would not find the stories plausible as we do if our own experience did not move us to accept this connection between suffering, on the one hand, and psychic healing and spiritual growth, on the other. But it is not necessary to spend time on this anecdotal approach to the appraisal of the question, because, *mirabile dictu*, there are scientific investigations of the topic. The study of the role of great suffering—'trauma,' as the psychologists call it—in spiritual and moral regeneration is a recognized subdiscipline in psychology.

As one group of psychologists says:

researchers have become interested in how traumatic events can sometimes provide a springboard for people into greater personal growth . . . The phenomenon of positive change following trauma has been variously labeled as posttraumatic growth, stress-related growth, thriving, perceived benefits . . . and positive adjustment . . . The evidence base for the concept of posttraumatic growth is sound.[6]

Another group of researchers explains the introduction of the term 'posttraumatic growth' as a consequence of a surprising finding involving patients with cancer. They say:

Most people diagnosed with cancer report that they experience positive changes in their lives as a result of their disease, and may say their experience with cancer was more positive than negative . . . In the 1990s, Tedeschi and Calhoun (1996) coined the term posttraumatic growth (PTG) to describe reports of lasting positive change following an unusually stressful event. PTG has been a subject of considerable research interest since that time.[7]

Still another group of researchers refer to the phenomenon as 'adversarial growth,' and they review the growing literature in this area this way:

Positive changes following adversity have long been recognized in philosophy, literature, and religion . . . They have been reported empirically [by psychologists and other researchers] following chronic illness, heart attacks, breast cancer, bone marrow transplants, HIV and AIDS, rape and sexual assault, military combat, maritime disasters, plane crashes, tornadoes, shootings, bereavement, injury, recovery from substance addiction, and in the parents of children with disabilities . . . Studies of adversarial growth are an important area of research . . . [And from] an applied perspective, clinicians should be aware of the potential for positive change in their clients following trauma and adversity . . . the facilitation of adversarial growth may be considered a legitimate therapeutic aim.[8]

Another review article begins this way:

Research on perceived growth following stressful or traumatic life events has recently burgeoned . . . Of course, the notion that individuals can grow through struggle and strife is not new; in fact, over the millennia, many religious and philosophical systems have promoted this view . . . and even within psychology, these ideas have a long history . . . However, only recently have behavioral scientists begun to develop rich conceptual models and apply rigorous methodologies to this promising phenomenon.[9]

Other researchers introduce the idea this way:

only in recent years have positive changes following trauma and adversity been studied systematically . . . These positive changes have been labeled *posttraumatic growth* (PTG), referring to a positive psychological change arising from the struggle with a major life crisis. PTG refers to changes that include an identification of new possibilities, more meaningful interpersonal relationships, increased appreciation of life, changed priorities, an increased sense of personal strength, and growth in the domain of spiritual and existential matters . . . [10]

One pair of researchers, who call what they study 'quantum change,' transformative experiences associated with great suffering, say about such change:

One way of explaining quantum change experiences is that they represent . . . a turning point in the life journey where major change simply must occur because the person is unable or unwilling to continue in his or her present course. It is a point of desperation, a breaking point where "something has to give"—and it does. The result is a new, dramatically reorganized identity . . . Strained and separate aspects of identity are reordered . . . [11]

To the extent to which the positive changes after trauma documented in such studies are integrative for the person undergoing the change, then to that extent, on Aquinas's account, they also have a role in enabling her to be willing to let God be close to her. In fact, some researchers have become interested precisely in the relation between posttraumatic growth and religious attitudes, and there are studies supporting the kind of correlation between suffering and closeness to God at issue for the Thomistic defense. Reviewing a series of such studies, Shaw, Joseph, and Lanley say:

what the evidence shows is that religious and spiritual beliefs and behaviours can develop through the experience of traumatic events, that religious and spiritual beliefs can be helpful to people in their psychological recovery, and in their personal development and growth following trauma . . . Evidence suggests that religion and/or spirituality may lead to posttraumatic growth, but also that posttraumatic growth leads to a transformation in religion and/or spirituality. [12]

These studies and many others like them support the connection between suffering and psychic integration at issue for the Thomistic defense. [13]

Someone will protest at this point that suffering is associated with psychological disintegration, too; a person's suffering can also turn him away from flourishing and union with God. This is a point recognized also in the psychological literature on posttraumatic growth. The researcher studying quantum change, for example, says that trauma can function "as a catalyst for . . . [the] reconceptualization of the self,"[14] but that "such reorganization [of the self] can also occur in negative as well as positive ways."[15] So the putative protester's point is right; but it is nonetheless not a cogent objection to the Thomistic defense. Aquinas holds that human beings have libertarian free will; and he argues at length that, even in the giving of grace, God does not act on a human will with efficient causation.[16] Since this is so, a sufferer can react to his suffering negatively rather than in ways that contribute to "posttraumatic growth." Suffering can contribute to spiritual regeneration and growth; but it cannot guarantee them. And so the mere occurrence of negative reactions to suffering is not by itself evidence against this part of the Thomistic defense.

It is also not an objection to the Thomistic defense that sufferers often have no sense of spiritual growth in virtue of their suffering, or that others around the sufferers are similarly unaware of such regeneration in the sufferer. Neither suffering nor benefits justifying God in allowing suffering are translucent. They are more nearly like health than like pain: one can be mistaken in one's belief about whether or not one has them. It might take trained expertise, such as that had by psychologists or pastors and priests, to detect spiritual regeneration in consequence of suffering, just as it can take trained expertise to determine the presence or absence of health in a person.

Finally, someone might suppose that, if this is so, then the Thomistic defense suffers from being an unfalsifiable position, since the absence of posttraumatic growth after suffering does not falsify the claim that suffering contributes to psychic integration. But this would be a mistaken supposition. If all psychological research showed no posttraumatic growth, or virtually none, that would count as evidence against the Thomistic defense. For that matter, if our own experience or the experience of others were always only of psychic disintegration in consequence of suffering, that would count against the defense. It would also count against it if any stories illustrating posttraumatic growth struck most readers as implausible or unrealistic. Consequently, it is not the case that, with the inclusion of a role for freely willed negative reactions to suffering, the Thomistic defense becomes unfalsifiable.

To sum up, then, there is at least some empirical evidence confirming the role that the Thomistic defense assigns to suffering in psychic integration. And the existence of some cases in which suffering does not lead to psychic integration is not inconsistent with that defense. Finally, the emphasis of the Thomistic defense on the relational character of the benefit redeeming suffering highlights the point that a benefit redeeming suffering may be hard to see; it might take trained experts to see it, or it might not be evident to anyone lacking a God's-eye view of the whole life of the sufferer. For all these reasons, the connection between suffering and closeness to God integral to the Thomistic defense does not contravene uncontested empirical evidence. The evidence does not warrant the claim that most suffering is pointless, at least as regards flourishing, in the sense at issue in (C A1).

The first pair of subsidiary questions: The second question

Even if there is not uncontested empirical evidence contradicting an affirmative answer to (C A1), however, that is not enough to ward off the attack on the Thomistic defense as regards the connection between suffering and flourishing. Even if suffering can contribute to flourishing for the sufferer, and even if that flourishing outweighs the suffering, there is still the issue of whether the flourishing could have been gotten at least as well without the suffering. So what about question (C A2)? An affirmative answer to (C A1) is of no use to the Thomistic defense unless there is also an affirmative answer to (C A2). Is there uncontested empirical evidence to show that suffering is not the best means, in the circumstances of any particular sufferer, to the psychic integration needed for closeness to God?

Clearly, neither reflection nor psychological studies can demonstrate that in the particular circumstances of a particular person's life suffering is the best means for bringing about this result. That is because neither reflection nor psychological studies are sufficient to show what a particular person would have done in circumstances different from those that actually obtained. Unlike (C A1), (C A2) is not in fact a question whose answer can be evaluated through reflection on empirical research. On the contrary, answering it requires knowing what a person would freely do in circumstances other than those that actually obtained, in order to evaluate the efficacy of suffering in leading a person to spiritual or psychological regeneration. Knowing this, however, requires middle knowledge. There is serious dispute over whether even God can have middle knowledge. As far as I am aware, no one has yet suggested that psychologists or other human beings might have middle knowledge. But, unless we can know what a person would have done in non-actual circumstances in which he did not suffer, we are not in a position to compare suffering with other things that might have served as a means to the same end in order to evaluate which means would have been better.

It is, however, worth considering the stories of Part 3 in this connection. Could we rewrite those stories in such a way that the protagonist reaches the same level of closeness to God at the end but without the suffering the protagonist endures in the story as we have it?

Someone might suppose that we certainly could. For example, God might have spoken to Job for a long time and let Job see him without all that Job suffered. God might have restored Samson's strength so that he could fulfill his divine mission to liberate his people without Samson's being blinded and captured by his enemies. God might have taught Abraham to trust God and to form a firm belief in God's goodness without God's requiring of Abraham the agonizing trial of going to sacrifice his child. And Jesus might have been close to Mary in loving relationship without her having to endure the anguish of supposing that she had been betrayed by him in the death of her brother. So, someone might suppose, in every case it seems as if the suffering of the protagonist in the story is gratuitous, unnecessary for the closeness with God (or Jesus) manifested by the protagonist at the end of the narrative.

But the examination of the notion of closeness and union in the preceding chapters should show how facile and unreflective this supposition is. While it is true, for example, that God could have made long speeches to Job and shown himself to Job without Job's suffering, it is clearly a mistake to suppose that God's talking to Job and giving Job some sight of God is sufficient for God to be close to Job. For God to be close to Job it is not enough for God to be in the conditions requisite for closeness; Job also has to have certain states of mind and of will. As I have argued, these include not only relational attitudes on Job's part, but also internal integration around the good.

The human condition, however, carries with it a kind of willed loneliness. A double-minded person will hide one or another part of his mind from himself, and to this extent he will not be able or willing to reveal his mind to someone else. And a person whose desires are at odds with each other will have conflicting first-order desires or first-order desires that conflict with second-order desires. To this extent, such a person will be alienated from his own desires, whichever desires are operative in him. He will want and not want to reveal himself to another person. He will want and not want that person, so that his need for her and his vulnerability to her both are and are not acceptable to him.

On this understanding of the nature of closeness and the obstacles to achieving it, it is much easier to see the role that suffering has in bringing the protagonists in the stories to the kind of psychic growth needed for closeness with anyone, including God. Consider Samson, for example. At his worst with Delilah, he is a typological example of willed loneliness, with a mistakenly proud view of himself and a contumelious attitude toward God. He is not willing to need anybody or to recognize the things in himself that should prompt him to admit need of God. His terrible suffering at the hands of the Philistines changes him in mind and will, as the differences between his earlier and his later prayer make clear. Given the circumstances, the character he had formed for himself and the proud loneliness he had wrapped himself up in, it is hard to believe that anything other than suffering would have brought him to the state of closeness to God represented by his last prayer.

In the case of Abraham, the trial of the binding of Isaac refines him, in the sense that it integrates his mind and will around an acceptance of the goodness of God and the reliability of God's promises, in a way in which he was not integrated when he expelled Ishmael from his home. The trial integrates him in this way by pitting his commitment to God's goodness against his perceived (but not his real) self-interest. In the circumstances of the history with Ishmael, it is hard to see what would integrate him in this way other than separating trust in God from what Abraham feels (at least double-mindedly) is his self-interest. But, of course, that very separation is also what produces the suffering for Abraham.

The story of Job can be understood analogously. By insisting on goodness even to the extent of challenging the divine ruler of the world, Job in effect allies himself most effectively with God, who is good, although Job does not know it while he is so angry at God. Job sees it finally when he turns away from his anger and turns toward God to say, "*Now* I see you!" And in this turning, in the closeness to God it constitutes, Job is glorious, in a way he was not when he was simply a prominent member of a religiously oriented animal-herding community. But how would we write the story of this development on Job's part if suffering had to be left out of our narrative? How would we effectively sketch the change in him from being a relatively quiet, prosperous, pious paterfamilias to being a man angry enough to call God to account and passionate enough to abandon that anger in turning toward God when he sees him? Suffering effects this change in Job in the narrative as we have it. It is hard to see what else would.

The story of Mary of Bethany is the most complicated of the four in this regard. As the detailed examination of the narrative in Chapter 12 shows, however, it is, paradoxically, precisely the break in Mary's relationship to Jesus, occasioned by Mary's suffering at his not coming to heal Lazarus, which is responsible for the intimacy between them at the end of the story.[17] In the story's final scene, Mary is glorious in her love of Jesus and in the closeness between them, in a way she would never have been if Jesus had simply come to heal Lazarus in a timely way. But it is very hard to imagine how to write her story in a way that would bring her to that same final scene without the preceding suffering on her part.

And so, for all the protagonists in the narratives, sensitivity to the details of the story shows that, contrary to what one might unreflectively suppose, suffering is integral to the process producing the closeness with God (or Jesus) that constitutes the flourishing of the protagonist at the end of the story; and it is hard to imagine that it could have been gotten in some easier way, without suffering. For the protagonists in these narratives, then, the answer to the question

(C A2) Is a person's suffering the best available means, in the circumstances, to enable her to be willing to let God be close to her?

is not the easy 'no' it might have originally seemed to be, but a clear 'yes' instead.

No doubt, there is more that could be said about the first pair of subsidiary questions; but I do not want to pursue consideration of them further, because, in my view, the greater problem for the Thomistic defense is posed by the second set of subsidiary questions.

The second pair of subsidiary questions

Suffering stems from deprivation as regards the sufferer's flourishing or the desires of his heart; but, on the Thomistic defense, such deprivation can itself be a means to flourishing. The apparently paradoxical nature of this claim is resolved by recognizing that, on the Thomistic defense, flourishing can be relativized either to this-worldly elements of this-worldly flourishing, or to other-worldly elements of ultimate human flourishing that consists in closeness to God. For Aquinas himself, the loss both of this-worldly flourishing and of the desires of the heart are redeemed by the role of suffering in enabling the flourishing of human beings, either by enabling the sufferer to ward off the permanent loss of this flourishing or by enabling the sufferer to increase it through greater closeness to God. But, for the Thomistic defense at issue in this book, something more needs to be said, because the suffering stemming from the desires of the heart also needs to be defeated, and its serving as a means to flourishing is not sufficient for this purpose. Even if we give the Thomistic defense everything it needs as regards the relation between suffering and flourishing, there still remains the problem of suffering stemming from the loss of the desires of one's heart. Unless we adopt the stern-minded attitude, then, paradoxically, this suffering has to be defeated by the gain of the desires of the heart.

So consider again the second pair of subsidiary questions:

(C B1) Does God's allowing a person's suffering enable her to have the desires of her heart?

and

(C B2) Is a person's suffering the best available means, in the circumstances, for her to be able to have the desires of her heart?

What shall we say about these questions?

Contrary to the case as regards (C A1) and (C A2), it looks as if the answer to (C B1) and (C B2) is plainly 'no.' Just think again of the stories. The protagonists in the stories have desires of the heart. And they suffer as they do precisely because they lose, or risk losing, those desires. Their suffering does not enable them to have the desires of their heart; rather, they suffer because something takes those desires away from them or at least seriously imperils them. So, in the stories, the answer to (C B1) is 'no.' The answer to (C B2) is thus clearly 'no' as well.

But, on the Thomistic defense, the heart's desires of a person, taken on their own, can be inimical to his flourishing, however innocent or good those desires might otherwise be. That is because suffering has a role in flourishing and because the deprivation of heart's desires has a role in suffering. It is part of love to care that the beloved have what the beloved cares about, but there is no love in giving a person what he cares about at the price of his ultimate flourishing. So, the initial negative answer to the second subsidiary pair of questions are right, but that negative answer does not constitute an objection against the Thomistic defense, because the heart's desires at issue in that pair of questions are the heart's desires taken just on their own, in the form in which they can be incompatible with the desirer's ultimate flourishing.

It is, however, possible to relativize the desires of a person's heart, too. They can be taken on their own; or they can be taken as interwoven with a deepest heart's desire, when the deepest heart's desire and the greatest good for human beings converge on love of God. Insofar as suffering enables a human person to draw closer to God, it shepherds a person toward that ultimate flourishing. For that reason, it also steers him toward the integration of his heart's desires with his love of God, as his deepest heart's desire. When this happens, his other heart's desires are no longer inimical to his flourishing. In that case, on the Thomistic defense, a loving God will also fulfill them, in their altered condition, in which they are compatible with flourishing.

It is possible for a person to lose the desires of his heart when they are inimical to his ultimate flourishing, but to gain them again in their refolded form when they are interwoven with a deepest desire for God. On the Thomistic defense, the suffering endured by the loss of the heart's desires enables increased closeness to God. Flourishing of that sort enables an increase in desire for God and shared union with God as the deepest heart's desire. And this in turn enables the integration of other heart's desires into this deepest desire. In this process, the other heart's desires refold; and, in their refolded form, these desires can be fulfilled compatibly with the flourishing of the desirer. So, on the Thomistic defense, it is possible for a person to gain the desires of his heart by losing them.

In my view, the most challenging issue for the Thomistic defense is, therefore, the answer to the second pair of subsidiary questions if we take the heart's desires at issue as interwoven with a deepest heart's desire for God. That is, the second subsidiary set of questions crucial for the evaluation of the Thomistic defense needs to be formulated this way:

(C B1*)   Does God's allowing a person's suffering enable her to have the desires of her heart when they are interwoven with a deepest heart's desire for God and compatible with her flourishing?

and

(C B2*)   Is a person's suffering the best available means, in the circumstances, for her to be able to have the desires of her heart in this condition?

To these questions, the Thomistic defense has to give an affirmative answer. What are we to make of this answer?

The answer and the evidence

In my view, the major problem lies with the affirmative answer that the Thomistic defense gives to the first of these two questions, not the second. That is because, if in fact there were a person who got his heart's desire in some refolded fashion compatible with his ultimate flourishing, it does not seem hard to suppose that suffering would have gotten him to that point as nothing else could. The preceding reflections on the role of suffering in flourishing support an affirmative answer to the second question, even if there were not other reasons in its favor. What will strike many people as much harder to swallow is the affirmative answer the Thomistic defense gives to the first question. Are there not innumerable cases, such people will think, in which even a person whose heart's desires can be supposed to be integrated with a love of God nonetheless apparently loses irrevocably what he had his heart set on? Is there not incontestable evidence that there are innumerable such cases? Does not the Thomistic defense founder at this very point?

The stories themselves can appear to support the attitude behind these rhetorical questions. In the end, Samson won a great victory for his people. Abraham had and kept his beloved Isaac with him. And even Lazarus was resurrected. But what about cases like Job's? Unlike Lazarus, Job's children were not resurrected. And this is clearly only the beginning. Samson's eyesight was not restored, and he died in exile from his people, as a captive among his enemies. Hagar was sent away from Abraham's household, never to return. Maybe Hagar longed to live out her life in Abraham's home; maybe she had as her heart's desire being Abraham's wife, not his rejected concubine. Maybe Sinner longed for a life in which she had never been shamed. In the stories, none of these people had a resurrection of the lost and longed-for things.

I do not want to take away one iota of the grievousness of heartbreak for any human being. No matter what can be said by way of theodicy or defense, suffering remains suffering, execrable and lamentable, worth strenuous efforts on our part to avoid or to remedy. But, compatibly with this attitude, it also seems to me the case that the change made by encompassing all the desires of a person's heart within a deeper desire for God and shared union with God works a transformation not only as regards the character of the heartbreak over the loss of other heart's desires but also as regards the very nature of the loss and the possibilities for the redemption of it.

To see this point, consider first that, on the worldview of the Thomistic defense, many things that would otherwise seem irrevocably lost turn out to be lost only temporarily.[18] That is why, on Aquinas's views, the story of Job is not wrong to claim that at the end Job had twice as much as he had lost during his affliction, even though at the end of the story Job has gotten not double the number of offspring he had before but the same number—namely, ten. For Aquinas, in gaining another ten children, Job came to have *twenty* offspring. The first ten adult children who perished are not annihilated; though they are separated from Job for the duration of his earthly life, they are not lost to him forever. They will be among the particular people Job loves in shared union with God in the everlasting portion of his life; and, even now, they themselves continue to be his beloved children in the everlasting portion of their lives.

In fact, on Aquinas's theodicy, there is a connection between Job's loss of his adult children in the earthly portion of his life and his union with them in the everlasting portion. On the fractal character of providence, there is a narrative of the life of each of Job's adult offspring; and in that narrative each of those persons is the protagonist of the story. On the Thomistic defense, the suffering of each of those persons is redeemed by its contribution to that person's good, either in warding off the worst thing for that person or in providing the best thing for that person. And so the terrible event that separates Job from those offspring of his who perished and causes his heartbreak over his loss of them also contributes to his union with them everlastingly. If Job holds this view of shared union with God and takes God and shared union with God as his deepest heart's desire, he will not cease to grieve over the death of his children. Unless he is in the grip of the stern-minded attitude, how could he possibly not grieve? But his grief will have a different character to it than it would have had if having his offspring with him in this life had been his sole or deepest heart's desire.

Death itself looks different on Aquinas's worldview. With suffering understood as medicinal or otherwise healing, earthly life has the character of a hospital; and death has something of the nature of a discharge from the hospital. Assessment of life span alters accordingly. Those who die younger than others are not the more afflicted; they are those whose release has come earlier than that of others. Physical debility, shame, and other terrible losses of similar kinds also have a different nature if the deepest desire of one's heart is God, with whom shared union in love is everlasting. On this view, Samson's losses of freedom,[19] home, and eyesight become temporary, not irrevocable. And even the nature of the loss that is an irrevocable history is altered. As the story of Sinner shows, for example, the dreadful history of having been a shamed person in one's own community can alter its nature through being interwoven later into shared union with God. By the end of her story, what was Sinner's opprobrium has become a kind of badge of honor for her.

For these reasons, the character of the loss of a heart's desire is altered when the desire itself is altered by being interwoven into a deepest desire for God and shared union with God. In its altered condition, the heart's desire can also be fulfilled compatibly with the flourishing enabled by suffering. In the stories, at the end, the protagonist has what he himself cares about, not only as regards flourishing but as regards his heart's desires as well; and what he has been given is more what he cares about than what he lost. Even the short story of the prologue follows this pattern. In that story, Mary Magdalene was so heartbroken when she could not find the dead body of Jesus that she brushed off angels attempting to comfort her. In finding Jesus, as she finally does, she has more of what she herself had her heart set on than she would have had if she had gotten what at first in the story she thought she wanted most.

Two non-narrative exemplars

But these are stories, someone who is heartily sick of stories will think. What about real-life cases? Are not most real-life cases of suffering radically different from the suffering in these stories? In real-life cases, does not most suffering just end in pointless heartbreak? In real life, who gets the desires of his heart through suffering?

These are rhetorical questions, of course. To the person who raises them, it seems obvious that the vast extent of unbearable suffering in the actual world leaves uncountably many human beings irremediably heartbroken, with no fulfillment of their heart's desires. From the objector's point of view, it is callous, monstrous, to suggest otherwise.

In my view, however, it should be noted that it is not as evident as one might at first suppose where callousness lies in this dispute. If, contrary to the Thomistic defense, suffering leads only to the destruction of what people care about, then people in contemporary industrialized countries, or just the middle and upper classes in those countries, will have a vastly greater share of what human beings care about than everyone else. The bulk of the world's population will be ruled out of that good state. Aquinas's other-worldliness, alien to secular sensibilities, at least has the implication that the human good we care about is not another monopoly of the upper classes in the industrialized nations. On the Thomistic defense, there is an inalienable egalitarianism about opportunities for a fulfilled and flourishing human life, as there is not where wealth and the things wealth brings are concerned. To reject the Thomistic defense in favor of the view that most actual human suffering is pointless is therefore to privilege as models of human well-being the lives of the comparatively wealthy in the West and to relegate the majority of human lives in the West and elsewhere to the pitiable or the deplorable. So there can also be a kind of callousness in failing to find value in suffering.

On the other hand, if we are to take the objector's rhetorical questions seriously, and not just as an expression of indignation, then it would take sociological studies done in conjunction with psychological research to answer them; and even then the answer might not be reliable. As the story of Abraham shows, it can take a lifetime for the fulfillment of a heart's desire, of the sort at issue in the Thomistic defense, to emerge.

In the circumstances in which a real canvassing of the empirical data is not available to us, I want to approach a serious consideration of these rhetorical questions by considering two non-narrative exemplar cases. Each of them taken individually shows, in my view, two things. The first is the subtle and complicated way in which a heart's desire, altered in suffering and made compatible with flourishing, can be fulfilled. And the second is the opacity of that fulfillment. Without careful reflection and some testimony on the part of the sufferer, we would certainly suppose that, in each case, the sufferer endured only heartbreak. Because the two cases are so different, when they are taken together, they seem to me to undercut seriously the confident conviction of some people that most actual suffering is pointless.

As a first exemplar of real-life suffering, consider the well-researched life of the great English poet John Milton, already discussed earlier in connection with the story of Samson. Milton wanted to be a politically important promoter of Puritan causes; he had his heart set on the political success of the Puritans and his own contribution to that success. It is as clear as anything ever gets in philosophy that Milton could have had his heart's desire as regards the Puritan cause at least as well without his suffering as with it. In fact, to the extent to which his suffering included heartbreak over the failure of the Puritan cause, his suffering was inimical to his heart's desire. When the Puritans fell from power, Milton lost what he had given so much of his life to trying to achieve. He suffered because he lost the desires of his heart.

In Milton's case, it is certainly arguable that his heart's desire was inimical to his flourishing as a poet. Milton wanted to support the Puritan cause in some powerful way; and the particular way in which that heart's desire took form in him led him to give himself unstintingly to Puritan politics. The resulting administrative and political labor kept him from the leisure and the creativity needed for poetry. But, also arguably, Milton's ultimate flourishing included using the great gifts for poetry he himself took to be God-given, giving back to God the expression of his own deep commitment to God in poetry of epic proportions.

The problem for a person whose heart's desire is directly or indirectly inimical to his flourishing is that he will suffer no matter what happens. Someone in Milton's case will be blocked from having what he cares about, no matter what he gets, because what he cares about, his heart's desires and his flourishing, is in effect internally inconsistent. Since a person's flourishing is an objective matter, the internal conflict in such a case can be overcome only by his bringing his heart's desires somehow into harmony with his flourishing. But this harmonization cannot be at the cost of his simply giving up his heart's desires, if it is to be a harmonization rather than simply an abandonment of those heart's desires.

In Milton's case, the precipitous Puritan fall from power left Milton in great poverty and peril; his enemies in the new restoration society confiscated all his property and then searched for him to put him to death. In that impoverished and imperiled condition, Milton wrote virtually all of his greatest poetry, including the larger part of *Paradise Lost*, *Paradise Regained*, and also *Samson Agonistes*, which is his own story as much as it is Samson's. In his greatest suffering, he also somehow had his greatest flourishing, both in his own spiritual growth and also in its expression in his poetry, as Milton's reflections on suffering and closeness to God in his magnificent *Samson Agonistes* confirm.

But what about Milton's heart's desire to promote the Puritan cause? He was heartbroken when the Puritan regime collapsed, and with it the Puritan hopes for a new Jerusalem on earth. With the fall of the Puritans, we might suppose, it is evident, obvious, that Milton lost irrevocably what he had set his heart on.

And yet consider the outcome. Do the seventeenth-century British Puritans have any partisan as powerful or appealing as Milton? If there is anyone who can give pause to people who find those Puritans objectionable, is it not Milton? Can the Puritans point to anything more admirable or more moving as a fruit of the Puritan spirit than Milton's poetry? In the end, after the downfall of the Puritans, Milton became one of the most powerful promoters of the Puritan cause. In fact, then, Milton did get his heart's desire, only not in the way he himself originally sought to have it, by participating as a functionary in the Puritan administration. Rather, he achieved it by the glory of the poetry that he, a committed Puritan, wrote. As it has turned out, Milton has promoted the Puritan cause, not only in Britain in his own period, as he had wanted to do, but throughout the world from his time until now.

Chances are excellent, however, that Milton would not have written that poetry if he had not suffered as he did in the period after the collapse of Puritan rule. The way in which Milton sought his heart's desire made that desire inimical to Milton's own flourishing as a poet, to his using for God the gift for poetry he thought God had given him. But, as the outcome shows, it was possible for that desire to be fulfilled in a way different from the way Milton sought to do; and, in that alternative way, the desire was harmonious with Milton's flourishing, not opposed to it. While the Puritans were in the political ascendency, Milton put his poetry on hold, as relatively unimportant by comparison with politics. When the Puritans fell from power, Milton returned to poetry and found the true and rightful use of his gifts there. His last great work, *Samson Agonistes*, is a particularly personal reflection on the nature of relations between God and a person to whom God has given great gifts, but the problem of human suffering and closeness to God is at the center of all his great poems written in this period. When Milton writes so movingly of Samson's drawing closer to God through suffering, it is easy to understand that he is speaking out of his own experience.

And so, although in the collapse of Puritan rule Milton suffered the loss of his heart's desire, nonetheless, paradoxically, because of that suffering Milton came to a flourishing he would never have had without the suffering, and he also received his heart's desire, though in a way very different from—and much better than—the way he had hoped for.

Some people may suppose that taking Milton's life as a real-life exemplar case is unrepresentative because Milton is both an extraordinary human being and also a believing Christian. So I want to take as my second real-life exemplar the suffering of a contemporary, non-believing, highly admirable but not extraordinary mother of an autistic child. At the start of her book about that child, Jessy, Clara Claiborne Park describes her life before Jessy, her fourth and last child, was born and grew into autism. She says of herself:

I, who tell this story, was when . . . [Jessy, the fourth child] was born a typical college-bred housewife . . . I was like my friends in putting my full resources of intelligence and intuition into the task of bringing up my children . . . I had used to exhaustion the full abilities of a grown-up woman in overseeing the first years of these small humans, and I was terribly proud of what I had done. Anyone would have said—many people did say—that I had three lovely children . . . I was terribly proud to have produced three such lovely children . . . So much of pride had I invested in my bright and beautiful children and my great good luck.[20]

The desires of Claiborne Park's heart were her bright and beautiful children; when her fourth child was born, Claiborne Park yearned for that child to be one more of the same sort. This child, too, she thought, "would grow and take her place in a family lovelier than anybody else's."[21] But the fourth child was eventually diagnosed with autism.

After years of struggle with the ravages of autism on a child and a family, Claiborne Park summed up her reflections on her suffering in this way:

our lives change and change us beyond anticipation. I do not forget the pain—it aches in a particular way when I look at Jessy's friends, some of them just her age, and allow myself for a moment to think of all she cannot be. But we cannot sift experience and take only the part that does not hurt us. Let me say simply and straight out that simple knowledge the whole world knows. I breathe like everyone else my century's thin, faithless air, and I do not want to be sentimental. But the blackest sentimentality of all is that *trahison des clercs* which will not recognize the good it has been given to understand because it is too simple. So, then: this experience we did not choose, which we would have given anything to avoid, has made us different, has made us better. Through it we have learned the lesson that no one studies willingly, the hard, slow lesson of Sophocles and Shakespeare—that one grows by suffering. And that too is Jessy's gift. I write now what fifteen years past I would still not have thought possible to write: that if today I were given the choice, to accept the experience, with everything that it entails, or to refuse the bitter largesse, I would have to stretch out my hands—because out of it has come, for all of us, an unimagined life. And I will not change the last word of the story. It is still love.[22]

Claiborne Park's moving and insightful book shows that her flourishing included raising her family well, but it was not exhausted by that project. She also had it in her to write a superb book that has influenced many people by sharing with them her experiences and her successes in child-raising, including the child-raising of an autistic child. As the passage above and many other passages in her book make clear, her suffering brought her spiritual growth; it integrated her around goodness and love. In that condition, her gifts came to fruition. And so she came to see even the suffering of her life as a gift. It is a gift that is a largesse, in her view, even if it is a bitter largesse, as she says; and, on her own testimony, it is a gift she would not be willing to forgo if she had been given a choice.

She herself recognizes that, if something is a gift, there must be a giver of it; and, because she is worried about being sentimental, or religious, she assigns the role of giver of the gift to her daughter. But it is clear that her daughter is closer to being the gift than the giver. And so I would say that, in finding her life a gift, Claiborne Park is drawing nearer to a God whose existence she is not yet willing to grant. Cory Friedman, the Tourette's syndrome sufferer, found strength in second-personal confrontation with something that he took to be responsible for afflicting him even while he did not acknowledge its existence.[23] Analogously, Claiborne Park accepts her suffering as a gift from a giver whose existence she is not ready to recognize.

Aquinas accepts the idea of implicit faith. On his views, it is possible to be related to the person who is God, and to draw nearer to that person, without accepting theological truths about God. It is not the case, on his views, that a human person can draw near to God only after having explicitly accepted the truth of the claim that God exists. That is because, for Aquinas, it is possible to know God without knowing all or even very many truths about God. In my view, to know *that* one's life, even in its suffering, is a gift and to know *that* it is a gift of love is already to know (with the Franciscan knowledge of persons) the giver, even if in an unacknowledged way and to a very limited extent.

And so, as Claiborne Park herself testifies in the book that constitutes part of her flourishing, in the alteration affected in her by suffering, by her heartbreak over her daughter's autism, she somehow found her heart's desire anyway, only in a way much different from that in which she had originally sought it. As she herself testifies, in the bitter largesse of that gift—from her daughter, from a giver unacknowledged by a breather of thin, faithless air—she found something she cared to have more than she cared to have what she lost in the suffering.

Milton was heartbroken when the Puritans fell from power. Claiborne Park was heartbroken when her daughter was diagnosed with autism. Without careful examination of the details, and without the sensitive and intelligent autobiographical record left in different ways by each of the sufferers in these two real-life cases, surely we would have supposed just that they had lost irrevocably the desires of their hearts. But, as the preceding reflections and the autobiographical texts of these two people show, we would have been wrong in that supposition. If we could be wrong in these cases, which seem at the outset so obvious, then why would we suppose we are in a position to know, for cases in which we have so much less evidence, that the suffering in those cases is pointless?

More cases: Heart's desires and projects

An objector might suppose that the sort of argument for the Thomistic defense I have been giving runs aground when the heart's desire is for a particular project. It is possible for a person to suffer heartbreak because external circumstances prevent him from ever succeeding at a project on which he had set his heart. In cases of that sort, it is not difficult to discern whether or not that person was ever enabled to carry out that project. Surely, someone might suppose, many people set their hearts on projects and die without any fulfillment of their desires. At least for cases of this sort, the objector will suppose, we can just see that the suffering is pointless.

But if the heart's desire—say, for writing a book—is encompassed within an even deeper desire for God, the desire for the project becomes part of the second-personal connection with God that is itself the deepest heart's desire. The desire for the project refolds from what was a desire for a particular kind of (first-personal) self-actualization into a desire for some kind of (second-personal) gift-giving, the giving-back as a gift of something received as a gift. But this transformed desire can be fulfilled even in circumstances in which the original, untransformed desire cannot be. Anything one can do in one's circumstances, however constrained they are, can be a way of giving everything back as gift and flourishing in doing so.

Klemperer's case illustrates the point. He was fired from his job as a professor, denied access to libraries, barred from borrowing books from friends, stripped of his own book collection, and compelled to do strenuous manual labor many hours a day. In such circumstances, no one can write a study of eighteenth-century French literature. But, in his own love of the good, Klemperer determined to do what he could to resist the terrible evil overtaking him. He wrote a diary, a few pages at a time, in order to bear witness to the times. In doing so, his gifts and talents flowered and became influential in a way incomparably greater than they would have been otherwise. In my view, the spiritual growth in him during that time of diary-writing is one of the things made clear by the diaries; the cosmopolitan atheism characteristic of him at the beginning of the diaries loosens its grip on him, too. There must be everlasting life, he says to himself in some of the worst of the times, because real love is not something that can die.[24]

But what would we say if Klemperer had written nothing at all, not his study of eighteenth-century French literature and not his diaries either, because his circumstances kept him from the use of his talents? Surely, for every story that begins like Klemperer's, with heartbreak over talents rendered useless, there are innumerably many that do not finish as his did, with those talents marvelously brought to fruition. Or what about those people natively talented but deprived by poverty or other adversity of the opportunity to develop their talents? Consider someone such as the story's Mary of Bethany. What if she had had a project of some sort as her heart's desire? Who knows what she might have been in a more humane world, a more just society? Who knows what she might have written if the injustice of her society's treatment of women and its oppressive usage of the poor had not kept her from what she might have been? But, nonetheless, here is what can be said about her, even so. She did what she could in her circumstances: she loved greatly. And so what she produced is her life itself. The story of her life as she wrote it in living, like the story of others whose lives were stunted or cut short by things outside their control, is her project, her flowering. This is also what can be said about Klemperer: if Klemperer had written nothing, his flowering could still have come in the story of his life.

For those who reject these lines as mindless piety illustrated in fiction and thought experiments, think of the history of Sophie Scholl. She was executed by the Nazis for her participation in the abortive attempt of a tiny group to lodge a small student protest against the Nazi government.[25] She wrote no books; in fact, she did virtually nothing in her very short life. But her limited life was luminous in its courage, and the story of her life has captured the imagination of very many people in our own day. Even if no one had recorded the story of her life, it would still have been luminous.[26] On the Thomistic defense, her life was her giving back to God what she had to give in return for God's love given to her. The gift given, received, and given back was the exchange of love that was the fruition of her life. There are no external circumstances that can take away a flowering of her sort.[27]

And so, in the very worst of circumstances, a heart's desire for first-personal self-actualization in a certain way, through a certain project, can transform into a desire for second-personal closeness, for receiving one's life as a gift from God and giving it again as gift to God. That giving as gift what was received as gift, in second-personal connection to a beloved giver of gifts, can seem, even to the person suffering, more worth having than the flowering of the life she had originally hoped for. By her refusal to try to save her life by placating her persecutors, Sophie Scholl herself showed that she preferred being what she became, even with its suffering, to what she might have been without it. And, after the fact, who would not be glad to have been a person like her, even if her suffering seems fearsome?

To say this is not to adopt any of the hateful positions in the neighborhood. It is not to approve the actions of her persecutors or the evils of her society. It is not to suppose that God in his antecedent will choose this particular ghastly suffering for her. The good reasons for rejecting positions so worthy of repudiation have been discussed in Chapter 13, and they cannot be rehearsed in detail here; but it is important to see that nothing being said here invalidates the pertinent points in the earlier chapter. What is at issue here is only what happens when a person weaves her heart's desires into a deepest desire for God. In that case, it is possible for those desires to be transformed in one way or another so that even the worst external circumstances are not sufficient to prevent their being satisfied somehow in the union of love with God. Transformed in this way, the heart's desires are capable of fulfillment, compatibly with the flourishing of the sufferer, even in circumstances that seem to be utterly destructive not just of talents but of the whole person. The story of Samson illustrates this point, and so does the story of Sophie Scholl. In more complicated ways, Klemperer's story does, too. What was in him a desire just for his own flourishing becomes interwoven in him with a burning desire for justice and goodness, so that at great risk and with great effort he bears witness to his times in his diaries. Because of the connection he makes between goodness and God's nature, for Aquinas, any hunger for real justice and goodness is a nascent love of God.

The hardest cases

I think it has to be acknowledged, however, that none of the cases canvassed so far, not even the case of Sophie Scholl, is the worst or the hardest for the Thomistic defense. In my view, the hardest cases for the Thomistic defense are those in which love is permanently rejected. Suppose, for example, that Hagar had had Abraham as her heart's desire. If Hagar were heartbroken when Abraham sent her away never to return, what is there to be said about her suffering? Is not her suffering entirely pointless? What could redeem her heartbreak over Abraham's permanent rejection of her?

By his choices and actions, it is possible for one person to destroy entirely any office of love he had or might have had with another. The entire system of creation, as Aquinas sees it, is predicated on this sort of possibility, even for God. There cannot be a union of love between two persons, even if one of them is divine, unless there are *two* persons. Something whose will is completely determined by another cannot be united with that other; there is only one will in such a case, not the two needed for union. For God, as for Hagar, to be willing to take another person, with an independent will, as the desire of the heart is to accept the possibility of being rejected instead of being loved.

In my view, the interactions between God and Satan in the framing story of Job call this possibility to our attention and also suggest a way in which to deal with it. In the framing story, on the interpretation I gave of it, Satan is one of the sons of God, however this group is to be understood; but he is an alienated member of the group. In the story, it is not possible for God to be united with Satan at that time because at that time Satan is at odds with himself. In Aquinas's worldview, the alienation of Satan is irremediable. To the extent to which God loves Satan and wants to be united with him, then, in the story there is something that God, at least in his antecedent will, cannot have—for that period of time, as the story portrays it, or ever, as Aquinas understands it. Nonetheless, on Aquinas's account of love, it is possible, even so, for God to continue to love Satan—as Satan is, for what Satan is: cynical, double-minded, alienated from himself and others. As I have interpreted the framing story, that love on God's part, with its tenderness and compassion, brings God as much closeness to Satan as is possible for God or anyone else to have with Satan, given Satan's internal fragmentation.

But, in the story, when God cares for Satan in this way, God is not heartbroken by Satan's rejection of him. God's care for Satan, God's love for Satan, arise from within God's participation in shared union with all those other persons who are united to God in love, the morning stars who sing for joy at the creation, for example. The loneliness Satan has willed for himself cannot take away the joy of that shared union, not for God or for anyone else involved in it. On the contrary, the effect of Satan's rejection of love is to make Satan less able to attract the desires of love than he otherwise would have been. When Satan rejects love, he changes himself; and what he makes of himself, through his double-minded cynical hardness, is less worth having than what he might have been. For those like God who can see him as he is, the inner fragmentation in Satan that wards off the love of others will also diminish whatever loveliness Satan would otherwise have had in their eyes. When one sees him in this way, Satan shape-shifts from someone who excludes others to someone who excludes himself from joy. Seen within the context of God's shared union with others, Satan is more worthy of compassion than of desire. And so what might have been an active desire on God's part for real union with Satan becomes in the story an encompassing compassion, content to offer as much care as possible to a person who has walled himself off from love.

In my view, God's interaction with Satan in the framing story of Job models the way in which a heart's desire for a person can refold when that person rejects love. And it is suggestive for all the hardest cases in which one person suffers because another person has rejected him.

In Hagar's story, through the process that includes the suffering inflicted on her by Abraham, Hagar, who was an ill-treated servant, becomes the matriarch of a great people. God himself honors her. To protect Hagar from Sarah and from Abraham, God cares for Hagar in her affliction in ways that set her apart from all the other women in the narrative. Of the women in Abraham's life, it is not Sarah to whom God comes to talk. It is Hagar. Furthermore, although the narrative of Abraham's life highlights God's promises to Abraham, Abraham is not the only person in the story to receive God's promises. Hagar does too.

And so Hagar has her own story, only hinted at in the narrative of Abraham's life, of gift-giving and gift-receiving with a God to whom she is close. Singled out by God for honor, from within the care of closeness with God, Hagar has resources for reshaping her response to Abraham and her desire for him. What might have been a desire to be Abraham's wife can transform, in the face of Abraham's treatment of her, into a desire for whatever office of love is possible for her with Abraham. In the end, her response to Abraham might come to no more than an understandable desire to keep Abraham at a distance, only sharing with God whatever care or compassion for Abraham is appropriate for her to have, even so, in the circumstances of Abraham's treatment of her. For Hagar with Abraham, as for God with Satan in the framing story of Job, someone else's rejection cannot take away the goodness of an ongoing second-personal giving and receiving in shared union of love with God.

Even in these hardest cases, then, a heart's desire can refold. If Paula rejects love, or rejects the love Jerome has for her, it is still open to Jerome to love Paula as he can from within the joy of union with God. On the Thomistic defense, there is power for spiritual growth for Jerome in his suffering over Paula. If he takes the power offered him in suffering, it will bring him closer to God; and it will cause his heart's desires to converge on shared union of love with God. In that condition, even his grief over Paula can be encompassed in the fulfillment of his heart's desire to love and be loved. In the face of Paula's rejection, Jerome's heart's desire for Paula, like God's own desire for each of his creatures, has to refold from a desire for union to a desire for giving compassion and care. But, refolded in this way, it is also capable of fulfillment from within the joy of the shared union of love with God.

Even in this hardest of cases, then, on the Thomistic defense there is a point to the suffering; there is both flourishing and fulfillment of heart's desires. It is certainly not true that it is obvious that most suffering of this sort lacks this point.

A question of resistance

But, an objector to the Thomistic defense might ask, what if someone rejects the refolding of his heart's desires? As I explained it, a heart's desire is something that has the value it does for a person because he has set his heart on it. What if someone resists the refolding of his heart's desire? What if he just wants what he wants, without any refolding? What if Mary did not want Lazarus to be resurrected, but only just healed? What if Job wants his children with him in this life and is not willing to let that heart's desire be reshaped?

In all such cases, because of a person's resistance to the refolding of his heart's desires, it *is* true that his heart's desires are inimical to his flourishing, for the reasons I explained in Chapter 14. To say this is to point out both the problem and the solution. A person in this condition is internally divided in the things he cares about, and for this reason he cannot flourish either. To will for him both his good and union with him, that is, to love him, therefore requires first desiring his internal integration. Giving him the desires of his heart at the expense of his flourishing is giving up on the good for him and therefore also on union with him. There is no love in doing so. In cases of this sort, then, the point of the suffering of the deprivation of the heart's desires is in fact flourishing, at least enough flourishing so that the sufferer is in a condition to have all the things he cares about, his heart's desires as well as his flourishing.

Where things are

For all these reasons, then, the objection that the Thomistic defense contravenes uncontested empirical evidence is false. Since objections to the internal consistency of the defense and its palatability have already been adequately addressed, with this last objection laid to rest the Thomistic defense is successful. At any rate, it is as successfully defended as it is reasonable to hope any philosophical position to be.

As I have presented it in this book, the Thomistic defense is a limited one. It applies only to the suffering of mentally fully functional adult human beings; it does not apply to human beings who are not adult or not fully functional mentally, and it does not apply to non-human animals.

In my view, a limited defense is sufficient. There is no a priori reason for thinking that a solution to the problem of suffering has to be based on only one benefit, or only one kind of benefit, for defeating the whole panoply of the suffering of all sentient creatures; and it is enough work for one book to explain and defend a defense for one sort of suffering. On the other hand, it is not clear that the defense I have argued for cannot be adapted to cases other than those of mentally fully functional adult human beings. A great deal depends on the subjective states of the sentient creature that suffers, and its ability in that state to enter into any kind of personal relationship. In saying this, I am not claiming that the defense I have presented in this book could be transformed and extended to all other cases of suffering. I am pointing out only that it would be hasty to suppose that it could not be.

At any rate, the examination of the biblical narratives should give us increased imagination for the sorts of benefits that need to be considered in reflecting on suffering. It should also give us an increased awareness of the importance of the details of the stories of the sufferers in any assessment of the suffering. Our assessment of the suffering in the biblical stories would be skewed and wrong-headed without the insight the stories provide about the psychological states, the relationships, and the life trajectory of the sufferer. Part of the problem in thinking about suffering in the case of animals, very young children, and those whose mental capacities are seriously impaired is that so much of their inner life is opaque to us. Their stories are largely hidden from us.

For these same reasons, the Thomistic defense is limited in another way as well. It offers a theory about suffering, but it does not offer a system for applying that theory in any given case. In this respect, it is like other theories. Cardiology, for example, also offers a theory, a good theory, about what causes heart disease. But there are still people who lack any of the risk factors specified in the theory and who nonetheless have coronary artery disease. The theory is not flawed because this is so. It is just that cardiologists are not in a position in any given case to know all the things about a patient needed to understand why this patient got coronary artery disease of this sort at this time. Analogously, the Thomistic defense provides a powerful explanation of God's morally sufficient reasons for allowing suffering. But it still cannot explain why this particular human person suffered as she did at this time in these circumstances. It is not in the nature of a defense to provide this sort of explanation. For that, we need not universally applicable philosophical and theological theories, but a particular person's biography, her particular history and psychology; and this no theodicy should be expected to provide. A fortiori, *mutatis mutandis*, the same point applies to the suffering of communities, peoples, and nations.

On the Thomistic defense, even the worst and most apparently hopeless suffering has a point. On the other hand, nothing in the defense either explains suffering away or justifies indifference of any kind in the face of suffering. On the contrary, the Thomistic defense illuminates what is bad about suffering, the deprivation of flourishing or heart's desires or both; and it has the resources for explaining why God's having a justification for allowing suffering is not enough for any human being to be justified in allowing it.

The flourishing that suffering deprives a person of is this-worldly, and the heart's desires broken in suffering are those not yet compatible with flourishing. To say this is not to say that the suffering stemming from the deprivation of these things is not worth lamenting or striving to remedy. It is. But this is not the end of the story. On the Thomistic defense, it is possible to gain one's flourishing by losing it; it is possible to find the fulfillment of one's heart's desires through heartbreak. It is possible to gain what one cares about by losing it.

The apparent paradox in these lines is resolved by the relativatization the Thomistic defense makes. It relativizes flourishing either to goods of this world or to relational goods that are central to shared union with God. And it relativizes heart's desires either to those taken just on their own or to those interwoven with a deepest heart's desire for God. Because of this twinned relativization, on the Thomistic defense it is possible for a person to lack worldly goods or to lose his heart's desires, and yet to have a life of fulfillment and flourishing in closeness with a loving God.

Finding this closeness requires surrender, of the sort central to justification and ingredient also in sanctification. It requires a willingness to open to love, to God's love, but also to the love of human beings. The relationship to God does not take away suffering; but, in the second-personal presence between a human person and God brought about by surrender to love, there is consolation even in the face of suffering. The suffering itself is redeemed in flourishing and fulfillment in the shared union of love. What one cares about and loses becomes the best means available in the circumstances for finding and having what is infinitely more worth caring about than what is lost.

In the stories, what the suffering of the protagonist does is to make it possible for him to flourish and to have the desires of his heart simultaneously. In each case, although the suffering was unnecessary for the protagonist to have his heart's desire, through the suffering he in fact receives the fulfillment of his heart's desire in a way that is better, in his own eyes, than the good he had hoped for and fixed his heart on. The suffering that was the best available means to bring him to flourishing also in the end yields for him his heart's desire.

It is part of all love, including God's love, to want to give the beloved the desires of his heart. When a human person comes into relationship with God, through the surrender of justification and sanctification, and his heart's desires become interwoven with a deepest heart's desire for God, then God can give him the desires of his heart, in their refolded form, compatibly with flourishing. Because flourishing and the fulfillment of heart's desires compatibly with flourishing are a function of second-personal relationship to God, God's care for all human persons can be exercised in the fractal way illumined by the book of Job. There is no competition between human persons for union in love with God.

The promise of the Psalmist is nuanced in the right way then: delight yourself in the Lord, and he will give you the desires of the heart. The delight in the Lord and the desires of the heart, made compatible with flourishing and transfigured as gifts, are conjoined.

What adds bite to the thought here and strips it of the saccharine is the phrase "compatible with flourishing." If love wants to give the beloved the desires of his heart, it is because love wants the good of the beloved. But, when the greatest good is union of love, it is also very difficult to get for human beings, who can have a death grip on willed loneliness. Jean Vanier, who has lived most of his life with the severely disabled, is willing to accept anguish as a means to openness in love, with God and with other human persons, too. John Hull, whose heart's desire was to avoid the irremediable blindness that enveloped him, was moved to see his blindness as itself a gift, a satisfaction of his heart's desire in a radically transformed way.[28] Claiborne Park came to understand her sorrow-filled life with her much-loved autistic daughter as a gift. And so, on the testimony of people such as these, whose experience of suffering gives them a license to say it, brokenness in suffering can be a gift too, for those strong enough and open enough to love to receive it.

To take suffering as a gift is not to take it away. There are goods that, once lost, cannot be replaced, or, if they can be restored, it is only in an afterlife, not before. At the end of his story, Job fathers many more children; but the children he had lost are not thereby replaced. Children are not like camels; one cannot make up their loss simply by getting more of them. And maybe even camels are not like that. Maybe among the things Job lost irretrievably—camels or even inanimate material objects—there were things that were of inestimable value to him, irreplaceable for him, because of the love he had for them. Samson's blindness is irremediable, and so is the disfigurement which the Philistine method of blinding must have produced. And, if he had not died in the destruction of the temple, Samson would have ended his days not as the feared warrior he gloried in being, but as the wretched recipient of care from others. Abraham became the father of a great nation, and the father of faith, but Ishmael, his son, was permanently lost to him; and so was Hagar, the woman who bore Abraham that son.

So, although the stories support the Psalmist's lines about the desires of the heart by showing the way in which the suffering that breaks the heart yields for the sufferer the desires of her heart, they also illustrate the fact that there are good things, on which a human being can set her heart, that can be irrevocably lost in this life. Nothing about the claims of the Thomistic defense or the promise of the Psalmist alters this fact, or is meant to do so. The hope of the stories and the Thomistic defense is the redemption of suffering, not its elimination.

Conclusion

"Any form of theodicy," Susan Neiman says, " ... involves some form of bad faith."[29] It must follow on such a view that a human person whose life includes serious suffering—and surely, by the time of death, that will be every human person—is someone whose life is not a good for him. Every person whose life includes serious suffering would have been better off if he had died at birth or had never been born, because there is no point to his suffering; and there is no good in his life that has its source in his suffering and outweighs it.[30] This view seems to me false. As I have said repeatedly throughout this book, I too think that human suffering must not be glossed over; it must not be trivialized in the interest of ideology. But there can be ideology in the promotion of despair as well as in the raising of hope. And moral scorn is a delicate matter, easily mishandled. The avuncular Martian in my first chapter has moral scorn for doctors, but he does not understand hospitals. In seeking the moral high ground, moral scorn can fall short of a sufficient regard for truth.

On the Thomistic defense, the Franciscan type of good faith is Abraham. Abraham manages simultaneously to hold on to his desire for God and his desire for his son. In going to sacrifice his son, he is willing to sacrifice the desire of his heart for the sake of the closeness to God he would lose if he were not willing. But, as he goes, he does not give up the desire of his heart; he trusts God to give it to him. Faith is not a matter of having no self, contrary to one strand of thought, even in the Christian tradition in which the Thomistic defense is embedded. Rather, it is a matter of being willing to crucify the self one has. Having desires of the heart makes heartbreak possible. Retaining those desires in the face of heartbreak and being willing to draw close to God through suffering is Abraham's faith.

The faith of Abraham requires a kind of willingness to be open to pain that neither Job nor Mary had until the end of their stories. Job protected himself against it by hanging on to his heart's desire but rejecting God as not good. Mary protected herself against it, not by anger of Job's sort but by letting go of her heart's desires and putting distance between herself and Jesus. Neither of these attitudes is compatible with Abraham's faith. Each is a kind of rebellion (a rebellion commended by God, in the case of Job, and wept over with compassion by Jesus, in the case of Mary). But, of the two, Job's kind of rebellion is better. In angrily calling God to account, Job was less willing to give up on what he wanted, either his heart's desire or his relationship to God, than Mary was when she withdrew. And so, in the period of his suffering, Job stayed closer to God than Mary did during hers.

Mary reacts to her suffering as she does because at the heart of it is her heartbreak over what she takes to be a broken personal relationship with Jesus, the Son of God in her view.[31] And that may also be why her return to that relationship is so powerful. Both Job and Mary exemplify the faith of Abraham at the end of their stories. But, at the end of their stories, Mary is closer to God (in the person of Jesus) than Job was at the end of his story. Job's saying to God "Now I see you, and I repent in dust and ashes" is totally eclipsed by Mary's outpouring of love and devotion.

It is true that sometimes the suffering a person endures breaks that person past healing. There are things that can crush a person's mind or shatter his body past mending. Sometimes what is ravaged are hopes. There are things that can wreck a person's life irremediably, so it can never again be made whole; its initial promise can no longer be fulfilled. What was broken and ruined in Samson could not possibly have been restored to wholeness. And yet, as the story shows, as Milton thought, as I think, on the Thomistic defense, Samson's life was a great good for him, in spite of all its pain and its unalterable brokenness.

Samson's strength, and God's spirit with the strength, were God's gift to Samson. Using that strength to win victory for his people, with God's spirit rushing into him, was Samson's heart's desire. In the end, through his suffering and because of it, Samson drew near to God; and when he did, he found his heart's desire as well. He used his gift for the purpose for which it was given, only in a way very different from that which he had originally desired. In receiving his strength as a gift from God, he was enabled to give to God not only the use of God's gift but himself with it. His flourishing and his heart's desire come to him at the end of his life, despite the irrevocable ruin of all that had seemed most desirable in him; and he is glorious, even as the broken ruin of what he had hoped to be.

For my part, I would be willing to say more: there is something enviable about blind, imprisoned, disgraced Samson, sunk in many of the same vices as before, and yet also filled with the spirit of God and untamed. There is something glorious about him and about his life that dwarfs those who live at ease. And so I would say also about the other protagonists in these stories. Mary of Bethany was shamed and heartbroken; but she loved unstintingly, and she was so loved in return. There is a greatness about her life that overshadows that of a person who has every worldly good given him and gives very little back in love to anyone.[32]

And so, in the end, I think that these lines of Aeschylus, rich and deep, have truth in them, but not the whole truth, which is richer still:

Zeus, who puts mortals on the road to understanding, who ordains that suffering leads to learning, decrees that, in place of sleep, pain of remembered suffering drips against the heart, and wisdom comes to unwilling mortals. Grace comes violently somehow from the gods who guide the ship.[33]

If the part missed by Aeschylus could be summed up in a line, then, for me, this line addressed to God in a medieval Latin hymn would pick it out:

> Flendo et canendo
> Te . . . quaesumus.[34]
>
> In weeping, and in singing,
> You . . . are what we have sought.

There is grace, then, and wonder on the way, but they are hard to see, hard to embrace, for those compelled to wander in darkness.

DESINIT

Rise up, my love, my fair one, and come away. For, look, the winter is past, the rain is over and gone; the flowers appear on the earth. The time of the singing of birds is come, and the voice of the dove is heard in our land. The fig tree puts forth her green figs, and the vines with the tender grape give a good smell. Arise, my love, my fair one, and come away.

(Song of Songs 2: 10–13. KJV modified)

NOTES

Preface

1. The story of Jerome's relationship with Paula can be found in J. N. D. Kelly, *Jerome: His Life, Writings, and Controversies* (London: Duckworth, 1975; repr. 1998); for the quotation, see p. 278.

2. The image is *The Hands of Time*, © Laurin Rinder | Dreamstime.com. Dan Schutte is a member of the highly acclaimed St Louis Jesuits, and he is in his own right a sought-after musician and composer of liturgical music. Mike Gale's beautifully done book documenting the thirty-year history of the St Louis Jesuits made me think that if anyone could find an image that would capture the heart of my own book, Mike Gale could. (See Mike Gale, *The St Louis Jesuits: Thirty Years* (Portland, OR: Oregon Catholic Press, 2006).) In the event, he and Dan found the image together, and Dan worked with it to edit it for this book.

Prologue

1. See Matt. 27: 56, Mark 15: 40, John 19: 25.

2. Cf. Augustine, *Harmony of the Gospels*, in *Nicene and Post-Nicene Fathers*, ed. Philip Schaff, vi (Grand Rapids, MI: Eerdmans, 1996), cc. LXXVIII–LXXIX.

3. For Chrysostom's relations with his friend Olympias, see J. N. D. Kelly, *Golden Mouth: The Story of John Chrysostom, Ascetic, Preacher, Bishop* (Ithaca, NY: Cornell University Press, 1995).

4. Cf. John Chrysostom, *Commentary on Saint John the Apostle and Evangelist* (Homilies 48–88), trans. Sister Thomas Aquinas Goggin (Washington: Catholic University Press, 1959; repr. 1977), homily 62.

5. Cf. Augustine, *Harmony of the Gospels*, c. XXIV.

6. Jonathan Hull, *Touching the Rock: An Experience of Blindness* (New York: Vintage Books, 1991), 205–6.

Chapter 1

1. Cf. Matt. 24: 26.

2. Here I am appealing to intuition to support this claim; but Part 2 of this book provides arguments in support of it in the connections made there among love, internal integration, and moral goodness.

3. I do not have a precise definition of what it is for an adult human being to be mentally fully functional. For purposes of this project, I will assume only a rough rule of thumb: if an adult human being is appropriately held morally responsible for his actions and is appropriately the subject of the reactive attitudes, then he is within the bounds of the mentally fully functional.

4. An indicator of the complexity of the issue even for human adults who are not mentally fully functional is the recent study showing neurological processing of semantic information on command by a patient who had been relegated to persistent vegetative status by external indicators. See Adrian M. Owen et al., "Detecting Awareness in the Vegetative State," *Science*, 313 (Sept. 8, 2006), 1402.

5. Because the heart of the theodicy at issue in this book has to do with interpersonal relationships, the development of this theodicy to sentient creatures other than mentally fully functional adult human beings depends on the extent to which these other creatures can participate in interpersonal relationships. For a suggestive essay on this subject, see Barbara Smuts, "Encounters with Animal Minds," in Evan Thompson (ed.), *Between Ourselves: Second-Person Issues in the Study of Consciousness* (Charlottesville, VA: Imprint Academic, 2001), 292–309.

6. There are other limits on this project as well. In Chapter 13, I discuss these limits at length.

7. For an exception to this rule, see, e.g., Bruce Langtry, *God, the Best, and Evil* (Oxford: Oxford University Press, 2008), 42–7. His discussion focuses on evil rather than suffering; and although there are similarities between his account and that which is argued for here, the two accounts differ in significant ways.

8. For a helpful discussion of the difference between pain and suffering, see Laurence J. Kirmayer's essay "On the Cultural Mediation of Pain," in the section "When Is Pain Not Suffering and Suffering Not Pain" in Sarah Coakley and Kay Kaufman Shelemay (eds.), *Pain and its Transformations: The Interface of Biology and Culture* (Cambridge, MA: Harvard University Press, 2007), 363–401. The book as a whole is a helpful introduction to the complexities of pain and suffering.

9. Anton's Syndrome is a particularly bizarre version of a class of syndromes known collectively as 'anosognnoias,' in which a patient is unable to understand that she has a debility, however devastating that debility is. For a popular discussion of anosognosia and Anton's Syndrome, see Antonio Damasio, *The Feeling of What Happens* (New York: Harcourt, 1999), 209–13, 269.

10. I recognize, of course, that there are cases in which a human being's valuing pain positively counts, in the eyes of many people, against the mental health of that person. Pain sought for the sake of sexual pleasure is an example, and so are the ascetic excesses of such Patristics as Simeon Stylites.

11. After I had written this chapter, I discovered that a similar idea expressed in connection with the same sort of example had occurred to Richard Kraut (*What is Good and Why*, (Cambridge, MA.: Harvard University Press, 2007), 153).

12. Shelly Girard, "Why Have Natural Childbirth?" (http://pregnancyandbaby.com/pregnancy/baby/Why-have-natural-childbirth-606.htm).

13. I am emphasizing here the voluntary nature of this suffering in childbirth, because there are also cases in which women have no access to anesthetics in childbirth or have access to them but are denied them by others. In such cases, where the suffering in childbirth is involuntary, the problem of evil does arise in my view.

14. There are obviously connections among these three pairs: (1) pleasure and pain, (2) desire and aversion, and (3) volition and nolition (that is, willing against). The connections are complicated, however. The first member of each pair is not always accompanied by the first member of each of the other pairs; and the same point holds as regards the second member of each pair. It is possible, for example, to will against something and be averse to it even when it gives one pleasure; the pleasure of scratching a rash when one is determined to follow the doctor's instructions that the rash must not be scratched is an example. It is also possible for someone to desire something which he wills against or for someone to will something to which he is averse. A recovering alcoholic can desire alcohol but reject drinking it; a person can will to travel by plane even if he has a phobia as regards flying. As far as that goes, it is possible to have a volition just for something for which one has no desire. In a spirit of perversity, for example, one can form a volition to do that very thing among one's options for which one has no desire. And so on. (For excellent discussion of some of these issues, see Timothy Schroeder, *The Three Faces of Desire* (Oxford: Oxford University Press, 2004).) Breaking a person's will cannot, therefore, simply be handled as a special case of a person's enduring pain. A person might feel pain at having her will broken, but she need not. The means used to break a person's will might not involve pain at all; lobotomies and hypnosis are means of this sort. But, even in the cases in which a person feels pain at having her will broken, the badness of what she suffers is not limited to the pain. If the pain were alleviated—say, by some technological means involving drugs or surgery—her suffering would not thereby be ended. (Schroeder says, correctly in my view: "Pains are just one of many ways in which one may suffer" (p. 72).)

15. Ps. 37: 4–5.

16. The expression 'the desires of the heart' is ambiguous. It can mean either a particular kind of desire or else the thing which is desired with that particular kind of desire. When we say, "the desire of his heart was to be a great musician," the expression refers to a desire; when we say, "In losing her, he lost the desire of his heart," the expression refers to the thing desired. I will not try to sort out this ambiguity in my use of the expression in this book; in all cases, I will simply trust to the context to disambiguate the expression.

17. See Elinor Burkett, "God Created Me to Be a Slave," *New York Times Magazine*, Oct. 12, 1997, pp. 56–60. To say that this person consents to what is in fact non-consensual sex is to say that, because she feels her will rendered non-efficacious by her enslaved condition and also feels willed resistance to be useless, she ceases to resist or to will against things which she would will against if her will were allowed to affect what happens to her. And to say that she would will against it is to say that she now has dispositions and inclinations, including higher-order states of will, which are opposed to what she accepts with her first-order volitions.

18. There is a large literature on the notions of flourishing, well-being, happiness, and related concepts. Although in a later chapter I will briefly sketch the measure of human flourishing adopted by Aquinas, detailed discussion of the concept of flourishing has to remain outside the bounds of this book, if the book is to have any bounds at all. For an excellent discussion of human flourishing and the sort of ethics in which the notion of human flourishing is at home, see Kraut, *What is Good and Why*. Kraut ties flourishing to health, broadly understood. He says: "If you say of a human being that he is flourishing, your statement is thrown into doubt if he is correctly described as either *psychologically* or as *physically* unhealthy, weak, damaged, and stunted. Certainly, if he suffers from both kinds of disabilities, the claim that he is flourishing, or that he is doing well, is impossible to sustain" (p. 133). Although I find Kraut's views of flourishing insightful and helpful, I think the tight connection between flourishing and psychological or physical health is too restrictive. There is a kind of flourishing which a human person can have in circumstances in which both his physical and his psychological health are impaired. Consider, for example, people greatly admired for their behavior in terribly adverse circumstances. Think, for instance, of those people for whom a tree is planted at Yad Vashem for their willingness to risk their lives to rescue Jews during the Nazi period. Or think of those slaves in the American South who escaped their masters and went on to help others do so also. Under great stress, in terrible times, a person's psychological and physical health may both be severely impaired. And yet the acts of courage and altruism on the part of such people give their lives a flowering to be envied by those who live at ease and in health. Insofar as 'flourishing' and 'flowering' are cognate (as Kraut also points out (p. 131)), then it is possible to have a life which flowers in an excellent way even when one is both physically and psychologically impaired. (After I had written this note, I attended a dinner at which one of the other guests was Chaim Elata, professor emeritus and former president of Ben-Gurion University in Israel. He told me that when the Nazis invaded Holland, they took his father and stepmother away and somehow left him; at age 13, he was left alone, in dangerous circumstances, in an empty household. The psychological scars generated by those times, he said, will never go away; and it was clear that there were also lasting physical effects on him from that period of deprivation. And yet, by anyone's account, Chaim Elata has had a

flourishing life, and it is evident that he is held in great honor by his community. I report this conversation and these biographical details with his express permission.)

19. By the phrase 'what he ought to be' and variants on it I do not mean to pick out only a person's morally good qualities; rather I use the phrase in the sense glossed here—namely, to pick out those qualities which constitute the flourishing of that person.

20. Harry Frankfurt has written insightfully about this notion. See, e.g., *The Importance of What We Care About* (Cambridge: Cambridge University Press, 1988); and *Taking Ourselves Seriously and Getting It Right* (Stanford, CA: Stanford University Press, 2006). Frankfurt rejects the idea, important to me in this project, that there is an objective side to what a person cares about.

21. There has to be a *ceteris paribus* clause here, of course. If the magic genie's gifts had a cost to them, such as, for example, that the runner's mother died of a heart attack in the excitement of watching him win, or that he had to practice running so many hours a day that good things in life other than running were denied him, then the claim I am making here would be false.

22. In *Horrendous Evils and the Goodness of God* (Ithaca, NY: Cornell University Press, 1999), Marilyn McCord Adams makes a distinction that is at least related to the distinction I am after here. She says: "the value of a person's life may be assessed from the inside (in relation to that person's own goals, ideals, and choices) and from the outside (in relation to the aims, tastes, values, and preferences of others) . . . My notion is that for a person's life to be a great good to him/her on the whole, the external point of view (even if it is God's) is not sufficient" (p. 145).

23. It is worth asking about the modality in this claim, and I return to the issue in Chapter 14.

24. In saying this, I am not affirming a subjective theory of happiness that makes happiness a function of desire satisfaction. The desires of the heart are a particular subset of a person's set of desires—namely, those to which she is committed as foundational or central to her network of desires.

25. For further discussion of these issues, see my *Aquinas* (London and New York: Routledge, 2003), ch. 2, on God and goodness.

26. For further discussion of this issue, see Chapter 14.

27. There is a complication in need of further discussion in this claim, because there is a sense in which there is something involuntary even about the voluntarily chosen pains of natural childbirth. For discussion of two different ways in which something can be involuntary, see Chapter 13.

28. In the last part of this book, I will consider and argue against reasons for thinking that this claim is false.

29. On the other hand, it would be odd if a person *never*, throughout the entire course of his life, had insight into these things. For further discussion of this issue, see Chapter 13.

30. Peter Gay says: "Together, [volumes I and II of the diaries] make Klemperer into one of the greatest diarists—perhaps the greatest—in the German language" ("Inside the Third Reich," *New York Times Book Review*, Nov. 22, 1998).

31. Victor Klemperer, *I Will Bear Witness: A Diary of the Nazi Years. 1942–1945*, trans. Martin Chalmers (New York: The Modern Library, 2001). There are many places in the diaries where Klemperer gives voice to this sentiment. Cf., e.g., "The time in the factory does not pass so agonizingly slowly; but I am brought down by the mindlessness, the irretrievably wasted final span of my life, by having become mindless" (p. 286), and "The work of more than ten years is in vain: the 18ieme [the projected scholarly book on eighteenth-century French literature], the Curriculum, the LTI [other projected books]—nothing will be finished, nothing will be published. Vanitatum vanitas, but very bitter nevertheless. Perhaps none of it is any good anyway ..." (p. 313). In *The Third Reich at War* (New York: Penguin Press, 2009), Richard J. Evans reports that after the war Klemperer did also write and publish his study of eighteenth-century French literature (p. 757). I am unaware of reviews of that work.

32. See Timothy Williamson, *Knowledge and its Limits* (Oxford: Oxford University Press, 2000), 24–5, for an argument against the transparency of pain. For an intriguing study of the complexity of pain and for pain dissociation syndromes, see Nikola Grahek, *Feeling Pain and Being in Pain* (Cambridge, MA.: MIT Press, 2007).

33. The notion of defeat is not easy to spell out precisely. Roughly considered, a benefit defeats suffering when the suffering is somehow integral to the benefit and the benefit is such that it is rational to prefer having the suffering to not having it, given the benefit which the suffering brings. For discussion of complications stemming from the relationship between the suffering and the benefit that justifies God's allowing the suffering, see Chapter 13.

34. See, e.g., the papers by William Rowe in Daniel Howard-Snyder (ed.), *The Evidential Argument from Evil* (Bloomington, IN: Indiana University Press, 1996).

35. As pointed out by William Rowe, in his classic formulation of the argument from evil, it is also possible to rebut the argument from evil effectively without a theodicy by employing on it what Rowe calls 'the G. E. Moore shift' (William Rowe, "The Problem of Evil and Some Varieties of Atheism", *American Philosophical Quarterly*, 16 (1979), 335–41; repr. in Howard-Snyder (ed.), *The Evidential Argument from Evil*, 1–11.) As Rowe explains it, the G. E. Moore shift consists in taking as a premiss the negation of the conclusion of an opponent's argument and deriving as a conclusion the negation of one of the premisses in the opponent's argument. In the case of the argument from evil, the G. E. Moore shift is a matter of taking as a premiss the existence of God and concluding that there is a morally sufficient reason for God to allow evil. This response to the argument from evil depends on some support

for the premiss that God exists, support which is not effectively undercut by the problem of evil itself. The G. E. Moore shift has not received much attention by contemporary philosophers because they suppose that support for the premiss that God exists would have to come from arguments for the existence of God, and few people now have much confidence that such arguments can be adequately defended. So, for example, Peter van Inwagen says that a response of this sort to the argument from evil is

unappealing, at least if 'reasons' [for preferring the claim that God exists to the rival claim of atheism] is taken to mean 'arguments for the existence of God' in the traditional or philosophy-of-religion-text sense. Whatever the individual merits or defects of those arguments, none of them but the 'moral argument' (and perhaps the ontological argument) purports to prove the existence of a morally perfect being. And neither the moral argument nor the ontological argument has many defenders these days. (Peter van Inwagen, "The Problem of Evil, the Problem of Air, and the Problem of Silence," in Howard-Snyder (ed.), *The Evidential Argument from Evil*, 154.)

Even if none of the arguments for the existence of God is successful, however, it might still be the case that, for any particular individual, belief in God is rooted in religious experience or is in some other way a properly basic belief. In that case, the G. E. Moore shift would be an adequate response to the argument from evil for such a person. On the other hand, even if it were successful, the G. E. Moore shift would not obviate the usefulness of a theodicy, because a theodicy contributes an explanation of evil, as the G. E. Moore shift does not.

36. Skeptical theism comes in different varieties, some considerably different from or more complicated than the short description in the text here indicates. For a good introduction to the varieties of skeptical theism and objections to them, see Paul Draper, "The Skeptical Theist," in Howard-Snyder (ed.), *The Evidential Argument from Evil*, 175–92.

37. See, e.g., William Alston, "The Inductive Argument from Evil and the Human Cognitive Condition," Stephen Wykstra, "Rowe's Noseeum Arguments from Evil," Peter van Inwagen, "The Problem of Evil, the Problem of Air, and the Problem of Silence," Paul Draper, "The Skeptical Theist," and Peter van Inwagen, "Reflections on the Chapters by Draper, Russell, and Gale," in Howard-Snyder (ed.), *The Evidential Argument from Evil*, 97–125, 126–50, 151–74,175–92, 219–43, respectively.

38. An analogue to skeptical theism is the agnosticism of those who emphasize the doctrine of divine simplicity and derive from it the belief that human beings are unable to know God in any way. Some readers committed to a radical agnosticism of this sort would presumably also reject the possibility of theodicy, since, if it is not possible for human beings to know God, it is also not possible for them to know why God does what he does. (For a sophisticated presentation of a position rejecting theodicy based on the doctrine of simplicity, see Brian Davies, *The Reality of God and the Problem of Evil* (London and New York: Continuum, 2006).) *Pace*

those who hold such a position, it seems to me that nothing in the doctrine of simplicity rules out God's communicating his purposes to human beings in revelation. And so, contrary to what some might suppose, agnosticism of this sort is also compatible with theodicy, if the theodicy is grounded in revelation. I am grateful to Adam Green for calling to my attention the need to make this point clear.

39. Peter van Inwagen, who has contributed significantly to the support of skeptical theism, defends his own combination of skeptical and non-skeptical claims about God's values and aims this way:

for almost every theological proposition that I claim to know is possibly true and which I could not know was possibly true by means of my ordinary human powers of 'modalization,' I would claim the following: this statement is *in fact* true and I know it to be true and this knowledge essentially involves testimony, testimony that derives ultimately from divine revelation. (Van Inwagen, "Reflections," 238)

40. I do, however, return briefly to this issue in Chapter 13, where I discuss it in connection with Aquinas's scale of value for human beings and his theodicy, which is based on that scale of value.

41. I have explored this theodicy in detail in *Aquinas*, 455–78.

42. There is a nineteenth-century translation of the whole work: *Morals on the Book of Job by Gregory the Great, the First Pope of that Name* (Oxford, 1844). Although I have preferred to use my own translations, I give the reference both to the Latin and to this translation: Gregory the Great, *Moralia in Job*, bk. 5, intro.; *Morals*, 241–2. (A contemporary translation by James O'Donnell of part of the work is also available online.) The line taken by Gregory has the result that, if we come across saintly people who do not suffer much, we should be inclined to wonder whether they really are as saintly as they seem.

43. See Mal. 1: 2 and Rom. 9: 13.

44. Even so, of course, the notion of God's hating anyone is troubling, to the medievals as well as to us. For a discussion of hatred and a distinction of it into that which is compatible with love and that which is not, see Chapter 5.

45. For my attempt to understand the part of the Jewish tradition from which I have learned the most, see my "Saadya Gaon and the Problem of Evil," *Faith and Philosophy*, 14 (1997), 523–49.

46. Terrence Tilley, *The Evils of Theodicy* (Washington: Georgetown University Press, 1991).

47. See, e.g., Kenneth Surin, *Theology and the Problem of Evil* (Oxford: Blackwell, 1986). For critical discussion of Surin's arguments, see Langtry, *God, the Best, and Evil.* 4–6.

48. Simon Blackburn, "An Unbeautiful Mind," *New Republic*, 5 and 12 (Aug. 2002), 29–33. Both Hume and Blackburn acknowledge exceptions to the rule, and Blackburn allows for the possibility that Polkinghorne is one of those exceptions.

49. Blackburn, "An Unbeautiful Mind," 33.

50. Someone might suppose that I am being unfair to Blackburn in virtue of taking what he intended to be only a scientific description of the world as if it were Blackburn's description of the world *simpliciter*. But the characterization of Blackburn's picture as blind in certain respects remains apt even if we understand it to be limited to science. There are other sciences besides physics, cosmology, and the theory of evolution. As Chapters 4 and 6 show, recent developments in neurobiology and developmental psychology are also important for understanding the world we live in, and they give a picture of our world significantly less bleak than Blackburn's.

51. Blackburn, "An Unbeautiful Mind," 29.

52. The distinction has gained currency since Plantinga's introduction of it, and others have come to use the terms in varying ways. See, e.g., Van Inwagen, "The Problem of Evil, the Problem of Air, and the Problem of Silence," 156. On the other hand, Paul Draper says: "defenses are a proper subclass of theodicies. They are theodicies that are true for all anyone knows" (Draper, "The Skeptical Theist," 180). The difference between a defense and a theodicy is considerably less sharp on Draper's way of thinking of a defense. For my purposes in this book, I will be construing 'defense' roughly in Plantinga's and Van Inwagen's way.

53. James Tomberlin and Peter van Inwagen (eds.), *Alvin Plantinga* (Dordrecht: Reidel, 1985), 35.

54. Van Inwagen, "The Problem of Evil, the Problem of Air, and the Problem of Silence," 156.

55. Van Inwagen, "The Problem of Evil, the Problem of Air, and the Problem of Silence," 156.

56. E. J. Lowe, *Personal Agency: The Metaphysics of Mind and Action* (Oxford: Oxford University Press, 2008), 75.

57. Lowe, *Personal Agency*, 77.

58. Of course, nothing prevents someone who finds Aquinas's worldview veridical from accepting the defense as a theodicy.

59. This line does not have to be understood as a pious platitude. On Aquinas's analysis of beauty, beauty is goodness perceptible to the senses, so that beauty is a quasi-transcendental; that is, beauty is God's nature apprehended in a certain way. For some discussion of the medieval view of beauty as a transcendental or quasi-transcendental, see Umberto Eco, *Art and Beauty in the Middle Ages* (New Haven: Yale University Press, 1986). For a helpful discussion of the relation between beauty and religious sensibilities, see Frank Burch Brown, *Good Taste, Bad Taste and Christian Taste: Aesthetics in Religious Life* (Oxford: Oxford University Press, 2000). For my own attempt to explicate in detail the notion of beauty as a road to God, see my "Saint Louis Jesuits and Sacred Music: Beauty as a Road to God," *Sacred Music*, 134/4 (Fall 2007). In my view, awareness of beauty counts as a kind of Franciscan knowledge, of the sort explained in Chapter 3.

Chapter 2

1. Larry Benowitz et al., "The Role of the Right Cerebral Hemisphere in Evaluating Configurations," in Colywyn Trevarthen (ed.), *Brain Circuits and Functions of the Mind: Essays in Honor of Roger W. Sperry* (Cambridge: Cambridge University Press, 1990), 320–33. For some interesting recent work on the differences between the two halves of the cerebrum, see, e.g., Norman Geschwind and Albert M. Galaburda, *Cerebral Lateralization* (Cambridge, MA.: MIT Press, 1989). I am using the distinction between left-brain and right-brain skills here primarily as a heuristic device. Nothing in the claims I want to defend would be undermined even if it turned out (*per improbabile*) that all our cognitive capacities were processed on the left; and all the claims I make using the distinction between left-brain and right-brain skills can be rephrased without it.

2. Bas van Fraassen, *The Empirical Stance* (New Haven: Yale University Press, 2002), 3.

3. Bernard Williams, *Shame and Necessity* (Berkeley and Los Angeles: University of California Press, 1993), 13.

4. To attribute a weakness to a field is not the same as attributing a weakness to every thinker or every piece of research in the field. There are plenty of examples of analytic philosophy which show all the strengths of the discipline without what I have characterized here as its weakness. Such work exemplifies the care for detail and accuracy distinctive of analytic philosophy while ranging broadly, with depth and insight. For my part, I think that some of the work of the analytic metaphysicians targeted by Van Fraassen, especially that of Al Plantinga and Peter van Inwagen, for example, is admirable and exemplary in this regard.

5. And, of course, if the major Western monotheisms are right, then reality itself is personal as well as patterned. On the view the Western monotheisms have of the nature of reality, the Grand Unified Theory of Everything will have at its ultimate and irreducible foundation both persons and patterns.

6. I am here in effect claiming that what narrative has to contribute to philosophy is not just some affective influence on its readers, which stems from engaging the emotions and imaginations of readers as well as their intellects, but rather some cognitive content, which is explicable less well or not at all by non-narrative philosophical prose.

7. Particular uses of narratives have been common in some areas of Anglo-American philosophy at certain periods. For a discussion of the use of literary examples in twentieth-century Wittgensteinian ethics, see Onora O'Neill, "The Power of Example," *Philosophy*, 61 (1986), 5–29. As O'Neill explains the use of narrative in this sort of ethics, it consists largely just of prompting ethical reflection on particular ethical cases.

8. Quoted in Leslie Paul Thiele, *The Heart of Judgment: Practical Wisdom, Neuroscience, and Narrative* (Cambridge: Cambridge University Press, 2006), 263.

9. A good introduction to the literature can be found in Eileen John and Dominic McIver Lopes, *Philosophy of Literature* (Oxford: Blackwell, 2004). See also the collection of papers in Matthew Kieran and Dominic McIver Lopes (eds.), *Imagination, Philosophy, and the Arts* (London: Routledge, 2003), and Jose Luis Bermudez and Sebastian Gardner (eds.), *Art and Morality* (London: Routledge, 2003).

10. For an example of such criticism, see Jenny Teichman, "Henry James among the Philosophers (A Review of *Love's Knowledge: Essays on Philosophy and Literature* by Martha Nussbaum)," *New York Times Book Review*, Feb. 10, 1991, p. 24. I doubt whether anyone can give necessary and sufficient conditions for something's counting as philosophy, but surely *the search for truth, by means which give a prominent role to arguments, about matters of importance* is roughly the genus within which philosophy will be found. If that is right, and I think it is, then clearly Nussbaum's work counts as philosophy.

11. See Martha Nussbaum, *The Fragility of Goodness: Luck and Ethics in Greek Tragedy and Philosophy* (Cambridge, Cambridge University Press, 1986), 33–9.

12. Nussbaum, for example, tends to talk in terms of knowing through emotion and imagination, and she argues that there are some kinds of knowledge which cannot be grasped by the intellect. (See, e.g., Nussbaum, *The Fragility of Goodness*, 45–7.)

13. Van Fraassen, *The Empirical Stance*, 18.

14. Johnson is famous for having said: "A woman's preaching is like a dog's walking on his hinder legs. It is not done well; but you are surprised to find it done at all."

15. Williams, *Shame and Necessity*, 14.

16. For a recent treatment of Plato's dialogues, which takes the opposite tack and uses their literary character as a key to the interpretative analysis of the dialogues' philosophical content, see James Alexander Arieti, *Interpreting Plato: The Dialogues as Drama* (Savage, MD: Rowman and Littlefield, 1991).

17. It is my hope to turn to those narratives at some later time.

18. Much of the material on biblical narratives in this book was originally presented in Aberdeen as the Gifford lectures. Some people may wonder whether there is not something about Lord Gifford's will that rules out the consideration of biblical texts in the Gifford lectures. The terms of the bequest stipulate that "the lecturers are to treat their subject as a strictly natural science . . . without reference to or reliance upon any supposedly special exceptional or so-called miraculous revelation." But, of course, this stipulation rules out only the use of biblical texts *as revealed*; it does not exclude consideration of them as narratives. In fact, when Lord Gifford gives examples of the things he *does* want to have discussed in the lectures, he mentions not only such standard fare of natural theology as the nature and attributes of God, but also, as he puts it, "the knowledge of the relations which men . . . bear to [God]." Insofar as narrative has something to contribute to our knowledge of interpersonal relations, something which philosophy without such help would

pass by obliviously, examination of narratives in which God figures have a helpful role to play in reflection on relations, real or imagined, between human beings and the deity. My use of the biblical stories to illuminate philosophical reflection on the problem of evil is therefore well within the terms Lord Gifford set for the lectures.

19. These other sorts of biblical criticism include some which attempt to deal with the texts as a whole or in their final form, such as some varieties of literary criticism and canonical criticism.

20. With the conceivable exception of theological exegesis. Cf. W. Neil, in S. L. Greenslade (ed.), *The Cambridge History of the Bible* (Cambridge: Cambridge University Press, 1963; repr. 1988), iii. 238–93.

21. For one example of an attempt to canvass the new approaches, see Gale Yee (ed.), *Judges and Method: New Approaches in Biblical Studies* (Minneapolis: Fortress Press, 1995).

22. So, for example, J. P. Fokkelman, *Narrative Art in Genesis* (Assen: Van Gorcum, 1975), says:

If to the creators of the prose of the so-called historical books of the Old Testament it was of fundamental importance to express themselves in narrative art . . . then for the interpretation of the texts it is equally fundamental to understand these texts as literary creations and to recognize their mode of existence as linguistic works of art.   (p. 5)

An excellent and interesting instance of the use of feminist theory to examine biblical texts—to take just one example out of very many that could be given—is Margarita Stocker, "Biblical Story and the Heroine," in Martin Warner (ed.), *The Bible as Rhetoric: Studies in Biblical Persuasion and Credibility* (New York: Routledge, 1990), 81–102.

23. See, e.g., his volumes *The Art of Biblical Narrative* (New York: Basic Books, 1981), *The Art of Biblical Poetry* (New York: Basic Books, 1985), and *The World of Biblical Literature* (New York: Basic Books, 1992).

24. See Alter, *The Art of Biblical Narrative*, 13–14.

25. Alter, *The Art of Biblical Narrative*, 14.

26. Robert Polzin, *Samuel and the Deuteronomist* (New York: Harper and Row, 1989), 1–2.

27. Jon Levenson, "The Eighth Principle of Judaism and the Literary Simultaneity of Scripture," *Journal of Religion*, 68 (1988), 221.

28. Levenson, "The Eighth Principle of Judaism," 223.

29. For an example of this sort of complaint, see Marc Zvi Brettler, *The Book of Judges* (London and New York: Routledge, 2002). Brettler says that calling the Bible literature is "anachronistic, and often suggests inappropriately that the Bible is 'Literature.' . . . I am deeply sympathetic to a point made by Robert P. Carroll, that reading the Bible as literature is a 'misreading of the text' " (p. 9).

30. See, e.g., Marvin Pope (ed. and trans.), *Job* (The Anchor Bible; 3rd edn.; New York: Doubleday, 1973), pp. xl–xli. Pope acknowledges that the book of Job has a "single personality" among the sources of its composition; but he also thinks that "virtually all biblical books are composite in some degree."

31. See my "Visits to the Sepulcher and Biblical Exegesis," *Faith and Philosophy*, 6 (1989), 353–77.

32. James Alexander Arieti has pointed out to me that analogous problems arise with regard to such works as the *Iliad* and the *Odyssey*. Although many scholars believe that these works stem from multiple authors operating at different times, nonetheless classics scholars treat each work as a unified whole for purposes of literary interpretation.

33. So, for example, Raymond Brown objects to what he calls harmonistic approaches because in his view they "do too much violence" to the text; see his *The Gospel According to John* (The Anchor Bible; 2 vols.; New York: Doubleday and Company, 1970), i. 972. A similar complaint is made by historical scholars about literary criticism of the biblical texts. Brettler, for instance, says: "The comments made by Polzin and other literary scholars concerning the meaning . . . [of the texts of Samuel] are accomplished on the basis of a certain amount of violence to the text . . . ." (Brettler, *The Book of Judges*, 15).

34. An analogous point is made by Jon Levenson about Christian historical criticism which attempts to see the Hebrew Bible and the New Testament as part of the same book: "historical studies play for their Christian authors much the same role that midrash played for the classical rabbis: like the midrashim . . . this kind of historical inquiry serves to harmonize discordant texts" (*The Hebrew Bible, the Old Testament, and Historical Criticism: Jews and Christians in Biblical Studies* (Louisville, KY: Westminster/John Knox, 1993), 28).

35. The tensions and discrepancies are sometimes subjectively discerned in the details of the story, but sometimes the tensions in question have to do with other evaluations as well, including (but not limited to) the tension between the theology of the story and the period which the story purports to describe or the quality of the language in the narrative and the currently accepted understanding of the quality of the language in the time and place the narrative represents.

36. It has been objected to me that historical biblical scholarship relies much more on objective criteria and much less on subjective evaluation than the traditional harmonizing approaches do and that therefore there is something prejudicial in seeing the two approaches as analogous in their attempts to resolve tensions in the texts. But I am not persuaded by this objection. Its description of historical biblical scholarship is belied by the state of the discipline, which is as contentious as any humanistic field, if not more so. If historical biblical scholarship relied on objective criteria and eschewed subjective evaluations, we would expect to find much more convergence of views in the discipline than we do. For more argument in support

of this sort of response to the objection, see Peter van Inwagen, "Critical Studies of the New Testament and the User of the New Testament," in Eleonore Stump and Thomas Flint (eds.), *Hermes and Athena: Biblical Exegesis and Philosophical Theology* (Notre Dame, IN: University of Notre Dame Press, 1993), 159–90.

37. Alter, *The Art of Biblical Narrative*, 21. See also Polzin, *Samuel and the Deuteronomist*, 10–11, and 2–3:

   [The historical biblical scholar Martin] Noth's picture of how the [Deuteronomic] history came to be written . . . mostly fails to account for its artful construction because . . . it unduly concentrates on superficial aspects of the composition . . . and therefore completely neglects the many artful features of the text;

   [historical biblical scholars] are working hard to portray a supposed earlier stage [of the texts] as more coherent or clear before those inept redactors got their damned hands on it . . . [For example, the view of Miller and Roberts in their recent study of 1 Samuel] that the final hand at work on 1 Samuel 1–7 is a 'redactor' makes it impossible for [the] authors to recognize the many signs of the highly artistic composition that they worked on so assiduously as they reconstructed the prebiblical narrative . . . that is the subject of their monograph.

38. Alter, *The Art of Biblical Narrative*, 20.

39. See my "Revelation and Biblical Exegesis: Augustine, Aquinas, and Swinburne," in Alan G. Padgett (ed.), *Reason and the Christian Religion: Essays in Honor of Richard Swinburne* (Oxford: Clarendon Press, 1994), 161–97.

40. I am grateful to J. W. Case for calling my attention to the need to address this issue here. My own view of these complicated matters is closest to that of the medievals in the paper cited in n. 39.

41. Compare the analogous complaint about literary structure made by Brettler: "Too often scholars are creating, rather than seeing a structure" (*The Book of Judges*, 12).

42. There are, of course, also specious sorts of interpretations produced by forcing onto the text some tendentious psychological theory. The problem with such interpretations is not that they attempt to probe the thoughts and motives of the characters in a narrative but that they do so inadequately because they are in the grip of an ideology. I do not mean to be defending such ideological interpretations of narratives.

43. See Chapter 12 for detailed discussion of the text describing the weeping of Jesus. See also Chapter 9 for further discussion of the charge of eisegesis in this regard.

44. Chinua Achebe, *Hopes and Impediments* (New York: Anchor Books, Doubleday, 1989), 143–4.

45. Achebe, *Hopes and Impediments*, 144.

46. In subsequent chapters I argue that literature conveys cognitive content otherwise available to us only with difficulty or not at all. As will become clear, I also think that such cognitive content covers a broader range of things than Achebe's emphasis might suggest.

47. Van Fraassen, *The Empirical Stance*, 4.

48. Van Fraassen, *The Empirical Stance*, 37.

Chapter 3

1. I do not mean to say that there has been no interest on the part of analytic philosophers or others in attempts to capture the general distinction at issue for me in this chapter. Cf., for example, Bas van Fraassen's discussion of the difference between objectifying and non-objectifying discourse, in *The Empirical Stance* (New Haven: Yale University Press, 2002), ch. 5 "What is Science?"

2. The current interest on the part of some analytic epistemologists in the notion of vagueness shows that analytic philosophers are themselves concerned with the problems generated by an unvarying insistence on precision (see, e.g., Timothy Williamson, *Vagueness* (London: Routledge, 1994) and *Knowledge and its Limits* (Oxford: Oxford University Press, 2000)). For a detailed discussion of the problem with reference to analytic metaphysics, see Van Fraassen, *The Empirical Stance*, ch. 1.

3. Regis Armstrong et al. (eds.), *Francis of Assisi: The Early Documents*, i. *The Saint* (New York: New City Press, 1999), 72. In the face of the attitude expressed in the quoted text, one could be forgiven for wondering whether the solution of Origen is not preferable as an aid to celibacy.

4. Simon Tugwell (ed.), *Early Dominicans* (New York: Paulist Press, 1982), 10.

5. See Jean de Mailly, "Life of St Dominic," in Tugwell (ed.), *Early Dominicans*, for these stories about Dominic.

6. Tugwell (ed.), *Early Dominicans*, 66.

7. Tugwell (ed.), *Early Dominicans*, 92.

8. Regis Armstrong et al. (eds.), *Francis of Assisi: The Early Documents*, i. *The Founder* (New York: New City Press, 2000), 249.

9. Armstrong et al. (eds.), *Francis of Assisi*, i. 251.

10. Armstrong et al. (eds.), *Francis of Assisi*, i. 217.

11. Armstrong et al. (eds.), *Francis of Assisi*, i. 141.

12. Although I am not inserting this qualification at every point at which I hope it will be understood, it should be clear that I am in no way trying to characterize actual Dominicans and actual Franciscans, either in the past or in the present. Typology is not meant to be a characterization of reality, historical or present.

13. Regis Armstrong and Ignatius Brady (eds.), *Francis and Clare* (New York: Paulist Press, 1982), 44–5.

14. Philosophers sometimes distinguish ethics from morality, where ethics is a matter of any normativity with regard to human conduct and human character, and

morality is confined to that realm of ethics which has to do with the morally good
(whatever moral good is thought to be).

15. For helpful discussion of biblical interpretation among African-American slaves
in this period, see Cain Hope Felder, *Troubling Biblical Waters* (Maryknoll, NY:
Orbis Books, 1993), and *Stony the Road We Trod* (Minneapolis: Fortress Press, 1991);
Eugene Genovese, *The World the Slaves Made* (New York: Vintage Books, 1976);
and Dwight Hopkins and George Cummings, *Cut Loose Your Stammering Tongue*
(Maryknoll, NY: Orbis Books, 1991).

16. I am tempted to put the point in the terms Aquinas uses to describe our knowledge
of the nature of God: I do not know what this alternative kind of knowledge is,
only what it is not.

17. Peter Klein, "Epistemology," in *Routledge Encyclopedia of Philosophy* (London:
Routledge, 1999).

18. See, e.g., Peter Klein, "Knowledge, Concept of," in *Routledge Encyclopedia of
Philosophy*. For a powerful dissenting view that nonetheless remains within the
tradition that all knowledge is knowledge *that*, see Williamson, *Knowledge and its
Limits*; see especially pp. 27–33.

19. The main reason for the qualification has to do with what Bertrand Russell called
'knowledge by acquaintance,' which I will discuss below and in the next chapter.

20. See, e.g., Jason Stanley and Timothy Williamson, "Knowing How," *Journal of
Philosophy*, 98 (2001), 411–44. For a good survey of the recent neurobiological
literature showing that knowing how and knowing *that* are discrete capacities
served by different neurobiological systems, including different forms of memory,
see Eric J. Kandel et al., *Principles of Neural Science* (4th edn.; New York: McGraw
Hill, 2000), 1229–30.

21. Graham Oppy, "Propositional Attitudes," in *Routledge Encyclopedia of Philosophy*.

22. Some versions of virtue epistemology might be considered exceptions to the general
claim that contemporary views of knowledge take knowledge to be a branch of the
pattern-processing arts insofar as some proponents of virtue epistemology include
a motivational component in the analysis of knowledge. But even the versions of
virtue epistemology which mean to model epistemology as closely as possible on
virtue ethics take knowledge to be a matter of knowing *that*.

23. Timothy Schroeder, *The Three Faces of Desire* (Oxford: Oxford University Press,
2004), 11.

24. For the initial state of the discussion about knowledge by acquaintance, see, e.g.,
DeWitt Parker, "Knowledge by Acquaintance," *Philosophical Review*, 54 (1945),
1–18. For a specially helpful recent exploration of the topic, see Thomas Baldwin,
"From Knowledge by Acquaintance to Knowledge by Causation," in Nicholas
Griffin (ed.), *The Cambridge Companion to Bertrand Russell* (Cambridge: Cambridge
University Press, 2003), 420–48. Baldwin argues that in the years after 1914
Russell "was in fact developing a new conception of epistemology, linked to a

new philosophy of mind, which was so far ahead of his time that it passed by largely unappreciated" (p. 420). According to Baldwin, during this period Russell distinguished between knowledge of things and knowledge of truths, and he distinguished each of these further into two different kinds. Knowledge of things is divided into knowledge by acquaintance and knowledge by description, and knowledge of truths is divided into intuitive and derivative knowledge. The four resulting species of knowledge are interconnected on Russell's views. So, for example, intuitive knowledge of truths depends on knowledge by acquaintance of the things at issue in those truths. As Baldwin describes Russell's position at that time, knowledge by description of things depends on derivative knowledge of truths, which in turn depends on intuitive knowledge of truths, which, finally, depends on knowledge by acquaintance of things. Now, in some respects, Russell's knowledge by acquaintance of things looks like one kind of Franciscan knowledge. And so, if Baldwin's interpretation of Russell's epistemology is correct, for the Russell of this period, Franciscan knowledge is foundational for all knowledge *that*. So understood, Russell's position during this period is remarkably like the epistemology of Thomas Aquinas. See my *Aquinas* (London and New York: Routledge, 2003), ch. 8, on the mechanisms of cognition. See also Ch. 4, n. 39, below.

25. The most notable exceptions are the eliminative materialists who think that knowing the neurophysiology of color perception just is or else is equivalent to knowing what it is like to see color.

26. The thought experiment in question was introduced by Frank Jackson ("Epiphenomenal Qualia", *Philosophical Quarterly*, 32 (1982), 127–36) to argue that qualia, the states one is in when one is conscious, cannot be reduced to brain states.

27. For a good survey of current philosophical discussion of this thought experiment, see Peter Ludlow et al. (eds.), *There is Something about Mary: Essays on Phenomenal Consciousness and Frank Jackson's Knowledge Argument* (Cambridge, MA: MIT Press, 2004).

28. For a dissenting view and a discussion of other dissenting views, see Stanley and Williamson, "Knowing How," 442. For a different dissenting view, also based on considerations of knowing how, see Laurence Nemirow, "Physicalism and the Cognitive Role of Acquaintance," in William Lycan (ed.), *Mind and Cognition* (Oxford: Blackwell, 1990), 490–9.

29. It is perhaps worth pointing out that some philosophers and theologians have attributed to God a kind of non-propositional knowledge. See, e.g., William Alston, "Does God Have Beliefs," in William Alston (ed.), *Divine Nature and Human Language: Essays in Philosophical Theology* (Ithaca, NY: Cornell University Press, 1989), 178–96.

30. More than one person has suggested to me that what I am referring to as an alternative sort of knowledge really is not knowledge at all but that 'knowledge' is used equivocally in English because English lacks the terms enabling one to

make the distinction Germans, for example, make with the terms *kennen* and *wissen* (where *kennen* is supposed to pick out what I am referring to as Franciscan knowledge and *wissen* is supposed to pick out knowledge of the sort at issue in analytic epistemology). Bertrand Russell apparently attempted to distinguish knowledge by acquaintance from knowledge of truths by analogy with this supposed distinction in German and a similar one in French. (See Baldwin, "From Knowledge by Acquaintance to Knowledge by Causation," 422.) I am skeptical, however, that *kennen* and *wissen* in fact divide in the way this objection supposes. Consider, for example, 'Kennen Sie den neuen Beweis for diese logische Formel?' and 'Ich weis wie Rot aussieht.' More importantly, in Franciscan knowledge or knowledge by acquaintance, information about the world—about colors or faces, for example—is conveyed to a person in some generally reliable way by means of cognitive faculties functioning normally and that information is consciously available to the person to whom it is conveyed so that it can be used and reflected on. These features seem to me to make it reasonable to suppose that 'knowledge' is not being used equivocally when it is applied to cases of this sort.

31. For an analogous discussion of literature, examining the question of whether some of the knowledge mediated by literature is irreducible to knowledge *that*, see Catharine Wilson, "Literature and Knowledge," and Peter Lamarque and Stein Haugom Olsen, "Literature, Truth, and Philosophy," in Eileen John and Dominic McIver Lopes (eds.), *Philosophy of Literature: Contemporary and Classic Readings* (Oxford: Blackwell, 2004), 324–8 and 341–54 respectively. For a different analysis of the role of narrative in philosophy, see J. David Velleman, "Narrative Explanation," *Philosophical Review*, 112 (2003), 1–25.

32. Someone might suppose that in such cases the claim to know the music is equivalent to a claim that one has heard this music before in the past. But this supposition is mistaken. Suppose that a listener who has heard John Adams's opera *Doctor Atomica* is now hearing for the first time the symphony which Adams wrote based on the music from his opera. Then the listener might truly claim to know the music, in virtue of knowing the music from which the symphony is a transformed derivative, without its being true that the listener has heard this music before. Similarly, someone might suppose that the claim to know the music is equivalent to the claim to know that the music is familiar to one. But this equivalence will not hold either. An amnesic patient who cannot remember anything about his past might be told by his doctor, who is a reliable authority for him, that certain music is familiar to the patient; and the patient might come to know this claim in consequence of accepting it on the authority of his doctor. But, in virtue of the patient's amnesia for his past life, it would not be true in such a case that the patient knew the music. I am grateful to Ksenija Puskaric for calling to my attention the need to address this point.

33. Someone might suppose that knowing the music is also just a matter of pattern recognition, but this supposition is mistaken, in my view. Some people, such as

professional musicians, do recognize the patterns in music when they know music; but it is possible to know a piece of music without being musically literate enough to be aware of the patterns in it. In the rest of this chapter, I leave examples such as that involving music largely to one side in order to concentrate on knowledge of persons. But I think it would be worth reflecting further on cases, such as that of music, where the object of Franciscan knowledge does not have to do with persons. Other examples include the knowledge of fine wines ('he knew the wine right away' is not equivalent to 'he knew right away that the wine was ——', where the blank is to be filled in by the name of the wine) and perhaps even some instances of knowledge of numbers. (I owe the example of knowledge of wines to Kathleen Brennan.) Some mathematicians and scientists discuss their knowledge of their discipline in terms that suggest they at least sometimes rely on knowledge which is not reducible to knowledge *that* in their work. See, for example, Feynman's distinction between knowing arithmetic and knowing numbers: Richard Feynman, *"Surely You're Joking, Mr. Feynman!"* (New York: Bantam Books, 1985), 197–8. In yet another sort of case, the Nobel laureate biologist Barbara McClintock explained her success in her work with her plants this way: "I start with the seedling, and I don't want to leave it. I don't feel I really know the story if I don't watch the plant all the way along. So I know every plant in the field. I know them intimately, and I find it a great pleasure to know them" (quoted in Evelyn Fox Keller, *Reflections on Gender and Science* (New Haven and London: Yale University Press, 1985), 164). Some artists also suggest that inanimate objects need to be known in the same sort of non-propositional way if artistic creativity is to be exercised on them. So, for example, Rainer Maria Rilke says to an aspiring young poet, "draw near to Nature. Then try . . . to say what you see and experience and love and lose . . . seek [themes] which your own everyday life offers you . . . describe all these with loving, quiet, humble sincerity, and use, to express yourself, the things in your environment . . . . If your daily life seems poor, do not blame it; blame yourself, tell yourself that you are not poet enough to call forth its riches . . . (*Letters to a Young Poet*, trans. M. D. Herter (Norton, New York: Norton, 1993),19; I owe this reference to John Foley).

34. This example, and many others, make it clear that Franciscan knowledge admits of degrees. If knowledge by acquaintance does *not* admit of degrees, as Russell seems to have maintained, then that is one reason for supposing that Franciscan knowledge is not the same as knowledge by acquaintance. (It is not the only reason, of course; there are also others. For example, Russell's version of knowledge by acquaintance excludes physical things as its objects and is restricted to a small, peculiar set of objects; for discussion of these issues, see Baldwin, "From Knowledge by Acquaintance to Knowledge by Causation," 422–4.) On the other hand, of course, Russell might have been wrong in his view that knowledge by acquaintance does not come in degrees. Russell thought that knowledge by acquaintance does not admit of degrees because it is a simple act–object relationship. But, assuming

we understand what such a relationship is supposed to be, even if Russell were right that knowledge by acquaintance consists in such a relationship, it is still the case that the object known in the simple act–object relationship might be a composite object. And if it is, then one might have direct awareness of some part or property of that object, in a simple act–object relationship, without having such awareness of all the parts or properties of the whole composite. As more parts or properties of the composite become the object of awareness, the knowledge by acquaintance of that object will be deepened. That is why an amateur musician can know Mozart's *Ave Verum*, for example, but not know it as well, or as richly and deeply, as a professional musician who has performed the piece would know it. The amateur will know the music in some of its parts but not as many as the professional. Just as ordinary sensory perception can be trained, so that an experienced horseman can *see* (as a novice cannot) what lead a horse is on, so the cognitive capacities involved in Franciscan knowledge can also be trained. The professional will hear in the music what the amateur misses, and so the professional will know the music to a degree unavailable for the amateur.

35. See Laurence Bonjour and Ernest Sosa, *Epistemic Justification: Internalism vs. Externalism. Foundations vs. Virtues* (Oxford: Blackwell, 2003), 100.

36. More than one person has suggested to me that, if Mary had been kept from all second-person experiences, she could not have learned a language, and she would be unable to read. But this objection seems to me insufficiently imaginative. We can suppose that Mary has been raised in a sophisticated environment in which carefully programmed computers taught her to speak and to read.

37. Nicholas Wolterstorff has suggested to me in correspondence that, if Mary had had the requisite sort of experience of personal interaction before her period of isolation, then it would have been possible to communicate to her in the expository prose of a third-person account what personal interaction with her mother would be like. On this view, the difficulty in communicating to Mary by a third-person account the nature of a second-person experience with her mother is just a function of Mary's innocence of second-person experiences. But I am inclined to think this diagnosis of Mary's difficulty is not correct. In ordinary circumstances involving persons socialized in the usual way, it remains true that, when we meet a person for the first time, we learn something important which we did not know before we met that person, even if before the meeting we were given an excellent and detailed third-person account of that person.

38. Although insofar as some of what is at issue for Mary in the relevant first-person experiences has to do with qualia, it may be that what she knows in that first-person experience is *also* not expressible in terms of knowing *that*.

39. In correspondence, Al Plantinga has suggested to me that I am here in fact explaining in expository prose what it is that Mary learns—namely, what it is like to be loved by her mother, and so on. But that some sort of expository description

of what Mary learns is possible does not mean that we can explain what Mary learns adequately with an expository account. Consider, for example, that, while it is possible to describe the experience of seeing red to a person who has been blind from birth by saying that when a sighted person sees a red object, she knows what it is like to see red, this description is not an adequate explanation in expository prose of what the sighted person knows in knowing what it is like to see red.

40. The importance of this point should not be overlooked. Stories could not have a role in mediating Franciscan knowledge, as I am claiming in this book that they do, if Franciscan knowledge required the knower to have special causal contact with the object of Franciscan knowledge. For further discussion of the relation between Franciscan knowledge of persons gained through second-person experience and Franciscan knowledge of persons gained through stories, see Chapter 4.

41. What sort of combination is at issue here is not clear. Manifestly, it is not completely conscious and is not a matter of deliberation. Further analysis of it is beyond the scope of my project here.

42. Knowledge is said to be deep or capable of deepening in some figurative or extended sense which is hard to cash out, especially on any conception of knowledge as limited to knowledge *that*. Deepened knowledge is not a matter of additional items of knowledge *that* or a matter of holding the original items of knowledge *that* with more conviction. On the Franciscan approach to knowledge, deepened knowledge of something seems analogous to a stronger connection to a person to whom one already has ties. It consists at least partly in more insight and clarity of understanding, but neither is readily expressible in expository propositional form.

43. Sophocles, *The Oedipus Cycle*, trans. Robert Fitzgerald (New York: Harcourt Brace Jovanovich, 1977), scene I, p. 87: "slave as I am," Oedipus says, "to such unending pain as no man had before."

44. Sophocles, *The Oedipus Cycle*, trans. Fitzgerald, scene II, p. 96.

45. Sophocles, *The Oedipus Cycle*, trans. Fitzgerald, scene III, p. 112.

46. I am not claiming that all Franciscan knowledge is knowledge of persons, only that knowledge of persons of the sort at issue in the examples above is one species of Franciscan knowledge. For other species, not involving persons, see the remarks on music above and on the arts in general in the next chapter.

47. It should perhaps be said here that there are cases in which a prosopagnosic patient is able to pick out a person by face on the basis of certain features of the face which distinguish that face from others in a line-up. For example, if Paula is asked to pick out Jerome's face from a series of pictures that she knows includes Jerome's face among others, then it may be that Paula can correctly pick out Jerome's face by inference from one feature of it, say, because she knows that Jerome has a mustache and only one of the faces in the series of pictures has a mustache. But, clearly, this is not the same as the normal state of knowing Jerome by face.

48. In her wonderful book *Adam's Task: Calling Animals by Name* (New York: Knopf, 1986; Skyhorse Publishing, 2007), Vicki Hearne raises a similar issue about animals. Speaking of her dog Salty, she says: "I must be careful not to ask anyone who is a 'natural bitee' to approach and touch her. Natural bitees are people whose approaches to dogs (and perhaps to people as well) are contaminated by epistemology. They attempt to *infer* whether or not the dog will bite, jump up on them or whatever . . . They are—sometimes only momentarily—incapable of beholding a dog. It is not that the required information will follow too slowly on their observations, but that they *never* come to have any knowledge *of* the dog, though they may come to have knowledge *that* . . . " (pp. 59–60).

49. For a detailed discussion of the intellectual excellence of wisdom, see ch. 11 on wisdom in my *Aquinas*.

50. How the brain combines these two kinds of knowledge is not clear; but this is an empirical issue, not to be solved by philosophical speculation.

51. For further discussion of this conclusion about desire, see Chapter 5 on love and Chapter 7 on willed loneliness.

52. Richard Kraut, *What is Good and Why* (Cambridge, MA.: Harvard University Press, 2007), 70.

53. For this well-documented case of a feral child, see Roger Shattuck, *The Forbidden Experiment: The Story of the Wild Boy of Aveyron* (Tokyo: Kodansha International, 1994), and Harlan Lane, *The Wild Boy of Aveyron* (Cambridge, MA.: Harvard University Press, 1976).

54. For some discussion of this sort of case, see the suggestive article by Kendall Walton, "On the (So-Called) Puzzle of Imaginative Resistance," in Shaun Nichols (ed.), *The Architecture of the Imagination: New Essays on Pretence, Possibility, and Fiction* (Oxford: Clarendon Press, 2006), esp. p. 144.

55. On this score, see Jenefer Robinson, *Deeper than Reason: Emotion and its Role in Literature, Music, and Art* (Oxford: Clarendon Press, 2007), esp. ch. 1.

56. We think (and, for that matter, Aquinas thinks) that human mental faculties are connected and that all of them have some tie, direct or indirect, to the intellect. (For Aquinas's position, see my *Aquinas*, ch. 8, on the mechanisms of cognition, and ch. 9, on intellect and will.) We remember what intellect has apprehended; we desire what intellect apprehends as desirable; we fear what intellect apprehends as fearful. If this is right, then desires, memories, emotions and the rest have a certain derivative character, dependent on the apprehensions of the intellect. For this reason, we can take those desires, memories, and emotions which are not reducible to propositional form to have that character in virtue of being tied to an apprehension of intellect which also has that character. On this way of thinking about the general issue, the non-propositional character of certain deliverances of the intellect can transmit that character to the deliverances of other higher human

mental faculties. I am grateful to John Greco for prompting me to think about the larger issues here.

57. In "Francis and Dominic: Persons, Patterns, and Trinity," *American Catholic Philosophical Quarterly* (Proceedings of the American Catholic Philosophical Association), 74 (2000), 1–25, I argued that, if persons are irreducible to anything non-personal, then Franciscan knowledge will be a source of philosophical insight for us in all areas of philosophy that deal with persons, from epistemology and metaphysics to ethics. But there are two reasons for being unsatisfied with this answer. These reasons suggest that, even if it were true that a person is irreducible to the non-personal, that irreducibility would be neither necessary nor sufficient for the importance of Franciscan knowledge to philosophy.

In the first place, even if persons *are* reducible to something non-personal, it may be that there is a kind of knowledge of persons—Franciscan knowledge—which is irreducible to the kind of Dominican knowledge that can be had of the impersonal components of persons. Secondly, and on the other hand, some knowledge of persons is obviously knowledge *that*. It is, therefore, open to us to think that, even if persons were irreducible to the non-personal, Franciscan knowledge might not matter to philosophy. So for these reasons, the importance of Franciscan knowledge to philosophy does not depend on the irreducibility of persons to the non-personal.

58. There is an argument from authority available here, for what that might be worth. Consider, for example, the thought of Levinas. Levinas appears to think that ethics in particular, and insightful philosophical thought in general, are possible only for a person who has vividly in front of him the face of the other. Levinas's whole philosophy is marked by the emphasis on the importance of direct and immediate awareness of another person's face. Insofar as I understand Levinas's basic idea, it includes the point I have been at pains to defend here—namely, that there is something to know in experiences of persons which cannot be known in other ways. What Levinas adds to this idea is precisely the insistence that what is known in this way is foundational for philosophy. (It is also worth pointing out in this connection that, although Levinas is notable for obscurity in his philosophical writings, which are attempts to give third-person philosophical accounts of the importance of the encounter with the face of the other, he is much clearer and more compelling in his Talmudic commentaries, where what is at issue is often a narrative.)

But not everyone will find this sort of appeal to authority much help, especially since the philosophy of the authority I have selected, Levinas, strikes many people as controversial or at least as less than clear. (I am grateful to Jonathan Malino, David Hartman, and the Hartman Institute for compelling my attention to Levinas's work, and especially his superb Talmudic commentaries.)

59. For helpful discussion of the nature of thought experiments, their virtues and their limitations, see, e.g., Tamar Gendler, "Thought Experiment," in *Encyclopedia of Cognitive Science* (New York: Nature Publishing Group, 2002).

60. Van Fraassen, *The Empirical Stance.*

61. Van Fraassen, *The Empirical Stance*, 37–8.

62. See *Ystoria sancti Thome de Aquino de Guillaume de Tocco* (1323), ed. Claire le Brun-Gouanvic (Toronto: Pontifical Institute of Mediaeval Studies, 1996), ch. 47. I myself am inclined to think that Aquinas's works could seem like straw only to a person who had had the sort of overwhelming religious experience he seems to have had.

63. Armstrong et al. (eds.), *Francis of Assisi*, i. 227–8.

64. Cf. John Moorman, *A History of the Franciscan Order from its Origins to the Year 1517* (Oxford: Clarendon Press, 1968), 311.

Chapter 4

1. Vilayanur S. Ramachandran and Lindsay M. Oberman, "Broken Mirrors: A Theory of Autism," *Scientific American* (Nov. 2006), 64.

2. Peter Hobson, *The Cradle of Thought: Exploring the Origins of Thinking* (Oxford: Oxford University Press, 2004), 183.

3. Hobson, *The Cradle of Thought*, 183.

4. Clara Claiborne Park, *The Siege: A Family's Journey into the World of an Autistic Child* (rev. edn.; New York: Little, Brown and Company, 1995), 5–6.

5. Among philosophers, there is not one universally accepted understanding of the notion of mind-reading. It seems to me to be taken ambiguously, in a way analogous to the ambiguity in the notion of perception. The notion of perception can be taken as (i) perception, (ii) perception as, and (iii) perceptual belief. To say that Max has a perception of a cup can be understood to mean

   (i) the cup is an object of perception for Max,

   (ii) Max perceives the cup as a cup,

   (iii) Max perceives that that is a cup.

   The notion of mind-reading seems to me ambiguous in the same way. Paula can be an object of Jerome's cognitive capacity for mind-reading, or Jerome can use that capacity to mind-read Paula or her mental states as —— , or in virtue of using his cognitive capacity for mind-reading Jerome can believe that —— (where the blanks are to be filled in appropriately for the mind-reading capacity). The reason for the ambiguity is that, in ordinary cases in which the cognitive capacity is operating normally, it operates as part of a whole system to give information available to consciousness, connected with other information stored in the system, and formulable in beliefs. For reasons I have given elsewhere, it seems to me better to take perception in sense (ii) than in sense (i) or sense (iii). (See my *Aquinas* (London and New York: Routledge, 2003), ch. 8, on the mechanisms of cognition, the section on perception.) In this book, I will understand mind-reading analogously, in sense (ii), rather than sense (i) or sense (iii). In this respect, I dissent from Alvin Goldman's use of the term 'mind-reading'. His use of the term is a variant on (iii). He says: "By 'mindreading' I mean the attribution of a mental state to self or other. In other words, to mindread is to form a judgment, belief, or representation that a designate person occupies or undergoes (in the past, present, or future) a specified mental state or experience" (Alvin Goldman, "Mirroring, Mindreading, and Simulation," in Jamie Pineda (ed.), *Mirror Neuron Systems: The Role of Mirroring Processes in Social Cognition* (New York: Springer, 2009), 312). On Goldman's usage, it would not be true to say that autistic children are impaired with respect to mind-reading, since it is possible for them to form judgments about the mental states of others. But in order to explain what is impaired in autism, we need a term like 'mind-reading' in sense (ii). Since 'mind-reading' is the term already employed for this purpose by many philosophers and researchers on autism, it seems to me better to continue to use the term in that way rather than in Goldman's way. Goldman's goal is to interpret mind-reading in such a way as to make the new results in neurobiology compatible with his own attempts to understand mind-reading in terms of simulation theory. For arguments against Goldman's position, see Shaun Gallagher's article in the same volume, "Neural Simulation and Social Cognition," pp. 355–71.

6. See, e.g., the collection of papers in Naomi Eilan et al. (eds.), *Joint Attention: Communication and Other Minds* (Oxford: Clarendon Press, 2005).

7. For a philosophical attempt to explain the nature of mind-reading, see Shaun Nichols and Stephen Stich, *Mindreading: An Integrated Account of Pretence, Self-Awareness, and Understanding Other Minds* (Oxford: Clarendon Press, 2003).

8. Hobson, *The Cradle of Thought*, 59.

9. See Derek Moore et al., "Components of Person Perception: An Investigation with Autistic, Non-Autistic Retarded and Typically Developing Children and Adolescents," *British Journal of Developmental Psychology*, 15 (1997), 401–23.

10. For an article arguing to a similar conclusion with an extensive review of the scientific and philosophical literature, see Shaun Gallagher, "The Practice of Mind," in Evan Thompson (ed.), *Between Ourselves: Second-Person Issues in the Study of Consciousness* (Charlottesville, VA: Imprint Academic, 2001), 83–108.

11. Hobson, *The Cradle of Thought*, 143.

12. Ramachandran and Oberman, "Broken Mirrors," 64.

13. Hobson, *The Cradle of Thought*, 243.

14. Jana Iverson and Susan Goldin-Meadow, "What's Communication Got to Do with It? Gesture in Children Blind from Birth," *Developmental Psychology*, 33 (1997), 453.

15. Iverson and Goldin-Meadow, "What's Communication Got to Do with It?" 453–67.

16. See, e.g., Joseph B. Hellige, *Hemispheric Asymmetry: What's Right and What's Left* (Cambridge, MA: Harvard University Press, 1993), 38–40, 50–4. See also Eric R. Kandell et al., *Principles of Neural Science* (4th edn.; New York: McGraw Hill, 2000), 14–15, 1182.

17. See the discussion of second-person experience and joint attention in Chapter 6.

18. For a recent helpful review of the literature on autism and the mirror neuron system, see Raphael Bernier and Geraldine Dawson, "The Role of Mirror Neuron Dysfunction in Autism," in Pineda (ed.), *Mirror Neuron Systems*, 261–86. For a helpful reflection on the nature of mirror neurons and recent neurobiological research on them, see Lindsay M. Oberman and V. S. Ramachandran, "Reflections on the Mirror Neuron System: Their Evolutionary Functions beyond Motor Representation," in Pineda (ed.), *Mirror Neuron Systems*, 39–59.

19. Shaun Gallagher, *How the Body Shapes the Mind* (Oxford: Clarendon Press, 2005), 70–2.

20. An interesting discussion of the capacities of infants along these lines can be found in Ellen Dissanayake, "Antecedents of the Temporal Arts in Early Mother–Infant Interaction," in Nils Wallin et al. (eds.), *The Origins of Music* (Cambridge, MA: MIT Press, 2000), 389–410.

21. Gallagher, *How the Body Shapes the Mind*, 73.

22. Gallagher, *How the Body Shapes the Mind*, 220.

23. For a recent attempt to summarize research on mirror neurons and its importance for philosophy of mind, see Vittorio Gallese, "The 'Shared Manifold' Hypothesis: From Mirror Neurons to Empathy," in Evan Thompson (ed.), *Between Ourselves: Second-Person Issues in the Study of Consciousness* (Charlottesville, VA: Imprint Academic, 2001), 33–50. See also Gallese, " 'Being Like Me': Self–Other Identity, Mirror Neurons, and Empathy," in Susan Hurley and Nick Chater (eds.), *Perspectives on Imitation: From Neuroscience to Social Science* (Cambridge, MA: MIT Press, 2005), i. 101–18. Many other papers in this volume are also helpful for the issues of this chapter.

24. The mirror neuron system is predicated on recognition of a person as a person, but by itself it does not seem to facilitate that recognition, as we currently understand the workings of the mirror neuron system. So the knowledge of persons cannot be explained by the mirror neuron system alone, as far as we now know. For recent work on the neurobiology of social cognition, see, e.g., Chris Frith and Daniel Wolpert (eds.), *The Neuroscience of Social Interaction: Decoding, Imitating, and Influencing the Actions of Others* (Oxford: Oxford University Press, 2004).

25. Giacomo Rizzolatti et al., "Mirrors in the Mind," *Scientific American*, 295/5 (Nov. 2006), 54.

26. Rizzolatti et al., "Mirrors in the Mind," 56, 58.

27. Marco Iacoboni et al., "Grasping the Intentions of Others with One's Own Mirror Neuron System," *PloS Biology*, 3 (2005), 1, 4, 5.

28. Leonardo Fogassi et al., "Parietal Lobe: From Action Organization to Intention Understanding," *Science*, 308 (Apr. 29, 2005), 662.

29. Fogassi et al., "Parietal Lobe," 666.

30. Rizzolatti et al., "Mirrors in the Mind," 60.

31. Rizzolatti et al., "Mirrors in the Mind," 60.

32. In connection with a different discussion, Raphael Bernier and Geraldine Dawson say: "Empathy, the ability to experience the affective experience of others (while still recognizing this is the other's affective experience), is another important aspect of social cognition" ("The Role of Mirror Neuron Dysfunction in Autism," 267).

33. Vittorio Gallese et al., "A Unifying View of the Basis of Social Cognition," *Trends in Cognitive Science*, 8 (2004), 396.

34. Gallese et al., "A Unifying View of the Basis of Social Cognition," 396.

35. For some of the papers influential in the early discussion of simulation, see Martin Davies and Tony Stone (eds.), *Mental Simulation* (Oxford: Blackwell, 1995). In my view, the problem with trying to understand the cognition mediated by the mirror neuron system in terms of simulation is that it tries to turn into a first-person experience what is in its nature a second-person experience. For the notion of second-person experience, see the later sections of this chapter and the relevant sections of Chapter 6. For other arguments against the simulation account, see, e.g., Gallagher, *How the Body Shapes the Mind*.

36. Bernier and Dawson, "The Role of Mirror Neuron Dysfunction in Autism," 277.

37. Hume, *Treatise on Human Nature*, bk. 2, pt. 2, sect. 5. I am indebted to Annette Baier for this reference. As she herself makes clear, Hume's philosophy emphasizes the importance of what he calls 'sympathy' for all of ethics.

38. Hume, *Treatise of Human Nature*, bk. 2, pt. 1, sect. 11. I am grateful to Annette Baier for this reference.

39. These results from psychology and neuroscience should prompt us to reflect more broadly about knowledge which is not knowledge *that*. Like the things proposed as objects of knowledge by acquaintance, the objects of Franciscan knowledge can be even inanimate things. So, for example, an infant knows a ball as a ball before the infant is in a position to know that *this* is a ball. As far as that goes, even for fully functioning adult human beings, there is a difference between knowing something as a thing of a kind and knowing *that* this is a thing of that kind. A person who has a visual agnosia might not be able to know a glove as a glove, but he might still be able to know *that* this is a glove, say, because his physician has told him so. (See Oliver Sacks, *The Man who Mistook his Wife for a Hat* (New York: Summit Books, 1985).) For a helpful recent neurobiological study of agnosias, see Martha J. Farah, *Visual Agnosia* (Cambridge, MA: MIT Press, 1990).

In fact, it seems as if knowledge which is not knowledge *that* must be primary. Without *any* knowledge of a thing as a thing, it is hard to see how anyone could have knowledge *that* this something-or-other has certain properties or stands in certain relations to something else. Aquinas makes this point by saying that the primary act of the intellect is the knowledge of the quiddity of a thing—that is, the knowledge of a thing as a thing; on his view, this sort of cognition is prior to the intellect's having knowledge expressible in propositional form. (See also my *Aquinas*, ch. 8, on the mechanisms of cognition.) For a discussion of an analogous issue as regards reference, see John Campbell, *Reference and Consciousness* (Oxford: Oxford University Press, 2002). This broader claim about Franciscan knowledge is, of course, even more contentious than the claims about the knowledge of persons, and it cannot be adequately expounded or supported in passing here.

40. As far as that goes, it might turn out that future research somehow undercuts or invalidates the current work connecting mirror neurons and mind-reading. The importance of the recent research on mirror neurons lies *only* in its showing a means by which mind-reading could be subserved by neural mechanisms in the brain. What is important for my purposes is not the mirror neuron system itself. If some system other than the mirror neuron system should turn out to be the neural mechanism for mind-reading, my conclusions would still hold, *mutatis mutandis*.

41. There are complications here, however. In the case of professional musicians, some elements of music are *also* processed in the left hemisphere. Some of the relevant issues are canvassed in Nils Wallin et al., *The Origins of Music* (Cambridge, MA: MIT Press, 2000).

42. It should be said that mirror neurons have also been implicated in the knowledge of music. For a study of the neurobiology of the knowledge of music, see Daniel Levitin, *This is Your Brain on Music* (New York: Dutton, 2006); for the mention of mirror neurons, see p. 260.

43. For an interesting recent discussion of the brain systems involved in the processing of music and other significant sounds, see Steven Mithen, *The Singing Neanderthals: The Origin of Music, Language, Mind and Body* (London: Phoenix Books, 2006), esp. chs. 3 and 4. Luria's report of the case of Shebalin is discussed on pp. 33–4.

44. Dominic McIver Lopes, *Sight and Sensibility: Evaluating Pictures* (Oxford: Clarendon Press, 2005), 133.

45. Lopes, *Sight and Sensibility*, 144.

46. Lopes, *Sight and Sensibility*, 137.

47. For a brief discussion of prevailing epistemological views in analytic philosophy, see Chapter 3.

48. Lopes, *Sight and Sensibility*, 148.

49. In this respect, the object of Franciscan knowledge is more like a map or a scientific model than like a proposition. On this understanding of Franciscan knowledge,

knowledge of this sort does not imply the truth of what is known but the veridicality of it.

50. Here, of course, I am adapting for my own purposes a rough outline of Al Plantinga's account of knowledge. See his *Warrant and Proper Function* (Oxford: Oxford University Press, 1993).

51. One might well wonder on what basis the mirror neuron system, or whatever the accurately described neural system might be, is judged reliable. If this question is pushed far enough, it will lead to skepticism, since the reliability of any human cognitive system cannot be demonstrated in a non-circular fashion. (For an argument to this effect with respect to perception, see, e.g., William Alston, *The Reliability of Sense Perception* (Ithaca, NY: Cornell University Press, 1993).) If we put skeptical worries to one side, then the success of human beings in living and acting in concert in society is evidence of the general reliability of the neural systems in question. Of course, to say that the system is generally reliable is not to say that it works equally excellently in every case. Clearly, there is a great range of ability with regard to social cognition just as there is with regard to other human cognitive abilities. Among those within the normal range, the world's great novelists are at one end of the spectrum, and those who are very clumsy and uncomprehending in social situations are nearer the other end. I am grateful to Charity Anderson for calling my attention to the need to make this point clear.

52. I take it that perception is a more common case involving the veridicality of cognitive capacities. To see a cup which is in front of one, even to see it as a cup, is to have a correct but non-propositional connection to things in the world. A visual agnosic might not be able to perceive a cup, because his central nervous system defect renders some part of the relevant cognitive faculty dysfunctional. And yet the agnosic can know about some object in front of him that this is a cup—say, because he has perceived the cup through touch rather than vision or because the neurologist treating him has just told him so. What the agnosic lacks, even with the knowledge that this is a cup, is the knowledge of the cup, which his defective visual system no longer gives him.

53. Martin Buber, *I and Thou*, trans. Walter Kaufman (New York: Touchstone Books, 1970), 129.

54. Buber, *I and Thou*, 129.

55. I am indebted to Robert Pasnau for excellent questions that called my attention to the need to address this issue.

56. Gallese et al., "A Unifying View of the Basis of Social Cognition," 396.

57. The caveat here is necessary since, clearly, there are recognized cognitive debilities in which these faculties do not function properly. Autism is undoubtedly the most well known of these debilities.

58. Not only is knowledge of persons fallible, but neurological research has uncovered numerous syndromes in which the cognitive capacities correlated with Franciscan

knowledge of persons are so defective that the delusions they yield are intractable. In Fregoli's syndrome, a patient has the intractable delusion that he knows familiar people when he looks at the faces of strangers. In Capgras syndrome, a patient has the intractable delusion that he does not know the people he is looking at when he looks at the faces of persons who are in fact familiar to him. (For discussion of such syndromes, see, e.g., Sandra Blakeslee and Vilayandur Ramachandran, *Phantoms in the Brain* (London: Harper Perennial, 2005), ch. 8.) Both Fregoli's syndrome and Capgras syndrome are a kind of loss, after neurological damage, of the capacity to know something *as* the thing it is. Although these syndromes have been described largely as they affect the knowledge of persons, there are also reported cases in which the lost capacity extends to the knowledge of familiar things other than persons. So, for example, some researchers describe "a patient who claimed his actual home was not his 'real' home, although he recognized that the facsimile home has the same ornaments and bedside items as the original" (Todd Feinberg et al., "Right-Hemisphere Pathology and the Self: Delusional Misidentification and Reduplication", in Todd Feinberg and Julian Paul Keenan (eds.), *The Lost Self: Pathologies of the Brain and Identity* (Oxford: Oxford University Press, 2005), 103; see also pp. 105–6, 114–25). There are also cases where, as a result of neurological pathology, a patient fails to know a part of his own body as his own, in a way which is intractable to correction and delusional. (See, e.g., Feinberg et al., "Right-Hemisphere Pathology and the Self," 103–4.) One or another kind of right hemisphere damage seems to underlie the loss of the normal cognitive capacity in these cases. Feinberg et al. say: "right frontal hemisphere damage creates a disturbance in ego functions that mediate the relationship between the self and the world . . . ." ("Right-Hemisphere Pathology and the Self," 123). It may be that such syndromes do not result from a malfunction of the mirror neuron system in particular. But these odd conditions illustrate one way in which neurological damage to a brain system underlying an intuitive faculty for the knowledge of persons can malfunction to yield delusions in place of the Franciscan knowledge ordinarily provided by the fully functioning neural system.

59. Teresa of Avila, *The Interior Castle*, trans. Kieran Kavanaugh and Otilio Rodriguez (The Classics of Western Spirituality; Mahwah, NJ: Paulist Press, 1979), 89.

60. Gallese et al., "A Unifying View of the Basis of Social Cognition," 396.

61. Cf. also in this connection Gallagher, *How the Body Shapes the Mind*. Gallagher is concerned to show that so-called theory theory and simulation theory are inadequate to understand the phenomenon subserved by the mirror neuron system. Simulation theory tries to understand it in first-person terms; theory theory tries to understand it in third-person terms. Gallagher argues for a different approach, which tries to capture the second-person character of the mental phenomenon. Others attempting to explain that same character sometimes speak of it as 'intersubjective,' rather than second-personal. In this connection, see,

e.g., Evan Thompson, "Empathy and Consciousness," in Evan Thompson (ed.), *Between Ourselves: Second-Person Issues in the Study of Consciousness* (Charlottesville, VA: Imprint Academic, 2001), 1–32.

62. For use of the idea in ethics, see, e.g., Stephen Darwall, "Fichte and the Second-Person Standpoint", *Internationales Jahrbuch des deutschen Idealismus*, 3 (2005), 91–113; and *The Second-Person Standpoint: Morality, Respect, and Accountability* (Cambridge, MA: Harvard University Press, 2006).

63. In this chapter, I distinguish not only among first-person, second-person, and third-person experiences, but also among the corresponding points of view and accounts. I have no neat and precise definitions for any of these, but, put roughly, what I have in mind is this. A first-person experience is an experience I have with some degree or other of conscious awareness and which I could have by myself. A first-person point of view is my reflection on or observation of my (real or imagined) first-person experience considered as a first-person experience (as distinct, for example, from considering that experience as a neurologist or some other third person might consider it). And a first-person account is my account to someone else of my reflection on or observation of my (real or imagined) first-person experience qua first-person experience. So, my wanting a cup of coffee when I am in a normal cognitive and conative condition is a first-person experience; I want the coffee, and the desire is a conscious desire in me. My conscious, introspective reflection on or observation of that conscious desire is a first-person point of view. (I can have a conscious state without a conscious reflection on it or observation of it, as I do when I drive to work, conscious of the state of the road but focused intently on the news on the radio, so that I do not attend to the conscious visual states which guide my driving.) And my explaining my desire considered as a first-person experience to someone else is a first-person account. Something roughly similar distinguishes experience, point of view, and account for the second- and third-person analogues.

64. There are, of course, other ways of trying to capture the nature of second-person experience. Cf., e.g., Daniel Hutto, *Folk Psychological Narratives: The Sociocultural Basis of Understanding Reasons* (Cambridge, MA: MIT Press, 2008), esp. pp. 5–12.

65. For some discussion of the historical Jerome and Paula, and Paula's daughter Julia, as well as my reasons for using them—instead of the more customary faceless Smith and Jones—as characters in examples, see the Preface.

66. Insofar as consciousness comes in degrees, there is some vagueness in this condition. I mean to rule out only cases in which a person lacks sufficient consciousness to function as a person. Drowsiness is not ruled out; certain drugged states, such as the so-called twilight sleep, are. There are grey areas here. I am inclined to say that a mother has second-person experience of her newborn infant, but that a condition such as advanced Alzheimer's precludes second-person experience. My intuitions are not strong as regards those cases, though. (I am grateful to Kathleen Brennan for calling my attention to the need to address these issues.)

67. I will discuss the question of the degrees of knowledge of persons in more detail in Chapter 6.

68. For some discussion of the role of attention in conscious awareness of something being perceived, see Campbell, *Reference and Consciousness*.

69. It is hard to know how to make this element of condition (1) precise. It is possible for two persons to make some sort of mind-to-mind contact even if neither of them has sensory perception of the other; Paula's having contact with Jerome through sensory perception of Jerome is not necessary for her having a second-person experience of Jerome. On the other hand, Paula's just thinking of Jerome in Jerome's absence does not count as Paula's having a second-person experience of Jerome even if in thinking about Jerome Paula is conscious of Jerome as a person in some sense. Second-person experience requires conscious awareness of another person considered as a person; contact of that sort does not need perception, but it does take more than an image or a memory of a person. It might also be helpful to have a gloss on the phrase "as a person." The requirement that Paula be aware of Jerome as a person rules out cases of the sort made familiar to us from the literature on agnosia, where the agnosia patient is conscious and one of the objects of her consciousness is another person, but because of her agnosia she does not recognize the other person as a person; she takes him instead to be, say, a hat on a hat stand. (See the case that gives the title to Oliver Sacks's book *The Man who Mistook his Wife for a Hat*.) This requirement also rules out cases in which Paula has conscious awareness only of some sub-personal part (say, a brain) or sub-personal system (say, the circulatory system) of Jerome.

70. The scientific descriptions of the mirror neuron system quoted above make it plain that the primary perceptual modality used in conjunction with the mirror neuron system is vision. Nonetheless, it must also be the case that the mirror neuron system can be engaged in conjunction with other perceptual modalities as well. If that were not the case, then congenitally blind children would be autistic. Although there is in fact a significant incidence of autism-like disorder among the congenitally blind, there are also many congenitally blind children who are not autistic. (See, e.g., Rachel Brown et al., "Are there 'Autistic-Like' Features in Congenitally Blind Children?," *Journal of Child Psychology and Psychiatry*, 38 (1997).) Insofar as defects in the mirror neuron system are now thought to be implicated in autism, it must be the case that the mirror neuron system can be employed even in the absence of vision, through the sense of hearing, for example. And, insofar as, for those who can read, written language can stand in for spoken language, it is possible that a second-person experience based on written communication can also be facilitated by the mirror neuron system.

71. In the case of visual perception, it is not unreasonable to take a perception of an object O as mediated in case the perceiver P sees O only in virtue of seeing some other object M. This way of construing unmediated visual perception explains

why a person's seeing a cup through his glasses is not a mediated perception of the cup, but his seeing the cup on television is mediated. The cup itself is seen only in virtue of the perceiver's seeing the image of the cup on the television screen. That image is *what* is seen; the glasses are only the *means* by which the cup is seen. As a first approximation of a general rule, then, we might say that an instance of a use of a cognitive faculty aimed at something S_1 in the world is mediated when S_1 is cognized only in virtue of that very cognitive faculty's apprehension of something else S_2. In the case of the neural system responsible for the knowledge of persons, on this understanding of the notion of mediated cognition, an instance of the use of that system will count as mediated when there is an intermediary which itself requires the use of that very neural system for the knowledge of persons. That is why intermediaries that are machines do not render the cognition mediated in the case of knowledge of persons, but intermediaries that are persons do. On this way of thinking about direct and unmediated cognition, Paula's seeing Jerome on a video screen counts as mediated *visual* cognition on Paula's part, because Paula *sees* Jerome only in virtue of seeing the image on the video screen. But Paula's knowing Jerome by means of video-conferencing with him is not mediated *second-personal* cognition, because the video screen itself is not an object of cognition for the mirror neuron system subserving knowledge of persons. The complicating cases are those in which it is hard to say whether the intermediary is what is cognized or only the means by which something is cognized. For visual perception, glasses are clearly only the means; a television image is clearly what is cognized. But what is seen with the aid of an electron microscope is hard to categorize. Analogous things can be said about the boundary cases for knowledge of persons discussed in the text and the notes below. I am grateful to Charity Anderson for calling my attention to the need to make these points clear.

72. Although Paula does not have sensory perception of Jerome in the process of emailing him (she does not see, hear, touch, taste, or smell Jerome in email communication), that fact does not rule out email contact from counting as second-person experience, provided only that it really is Jerome with whom Paula is in email contact. If someone other than Jerome is emailing Paula in the persona of Jerome, then the email communication does not count as Paula's having a second-person experience of Jerome. There are grey areas here, too. If it really is Jerome who is emailing Paula but Jerome is systematically deceiving Paula on all points about himself, it is considerably less clear whether the email communication counts as a second-person experience of Jerome for Paula. I am grateful to John Kavanaugh for pointing out these complexities to me.

73. There are complications here. If Paula reads a letter sent to her by Jerome, Paula counts as having a second-person experience of Jerome on the conditions I have given. That remains the case, even if Jerome dictated the letter to his secretary, since, when Paula reads the letter, Paula does not have any personal interaction with the secretary. When she reads the letter, Paula is not aware of the secretary;

or, even if she is, it is not the case that she is aware of Jerome as a person only in virtue of being aware of Jerome's secretary. (Of course, if the secretary has written what Jerome dictated but then added voluminous editorial glosses of his own, disguised as Jerome's own words, it becomes less clear whether this communication counts as Paula's having second-person experience of Jerome. I am grateful to John Kavanaugh for making me attentive to this point.) On the other hand, if the same message from Jerome to Paula were delivered to Paula orally by Jerome's secretary, then Paula would not count as having a second-person experience of Jerome, because in that case Paula's awareness of the secretary mediates her awareness of Jerome. This seems to me intuitively the right result. Suppose, however, that Jerome's secretary delivers orally a message to Monica, who gives the secretary a response, which the secretary delivers to Jerome, who in turn gives the secretary a message to deliver to Monica, and so on. In such a case, is it still true to say that Paula does not have a second-person experience of Jerome because condition (2) is violated? And there are many other complicated cases here. Suppose that Paula is not aware of Jerome himself but finds a stack of highly revealing love letters written by Jerome to someone else (that is, to someone who is not Monica). (I am grateful to Adam Peterson for calling my attention to the need to address this point.) Does Paula's reading these letters constitute a second-person experience of Jerome? My intuitions are less clear in these cases. There may be boundary cases where adjudication regarding second-person experience could equally well go either way.

74. I am indebted to John Kavanaugh and Adam Peterson for helping me to see that there are complexities here, too. If Jerome sends Paula email communication but then dies in the period between when he sent it and when Paula reads it, so that he is no longer conscious at the time Paula reads his message, does that communication count as Paula's having second-person experience of Jerome? And, if it does, is the third of my conditions on second-person experience violated in such a case? I am inclined to say that Paula *does* have second-person experience in such a case but that the third condition is not violated. It is possible for the presentation of a conscious person Jerome to reach another person Paula after some delay, as the email example makes clear. Nonetheless, the Jerome with whom Paula is in contact by this means is a conscious Jerome, not the Jerome who is unconscious at the time of Paula's receipt of Jerome's message. And in this way the third condition is not violated by this example.

75. I will return to the subject of second-person experience in Chapter 6, where I argue that second-person experience is a component of joint attention. It is for that reason that the characterization of second-person experience includes the requirement that Paula be attending to Jerome in being aware of him.

76. In Chapter 6, I show that a second-person experience is a matter of one person's being in a position to share attention with another person; it is a necessary but not sufficient condition for joint attention.

77. Annette Baier has suggested to me that one can mind-read the mind of a person who is sleeping, to some limited extent, but the experience one has of a sleeping person is not a second-person experience, as I have described second-person experience. It may also be the case that the mirror neuron system enables us to have a quasi-personal experience of things which are not persons, as when one has a sense of the personality of a robot, for example, or even when one has a sense of the personality of a building. But such experiences would not count as second-person experiences on my account. So there may be a broad genus of experiences of persons and quasi-personal things which is facilitated by the mirror neuron system and which enables a person in such experience to mind-read, and second-person experience may be only one species within this genus. If so, second-person experience nonetheless seems to be the exemplar on the basis of which the other species within the genus can be understood. I am indebted to Alan Musgrave for calling my attention to the need to make this point.

78. In his blog *Certain Doubts* (Friday, Nov. 7, 2008), Jon Kvanvig calls such knowledge 'knowledge de te,' by analogy with knowledge de re and knowledge de se. In a comment on that blog posted Nov. 10, 2008, Pavel Davydov asks whether there might also be knowledge of persons which is in the second-person plural, knowledge de vos, as one might call it. I am sure that there is such plural second-personal knowledge, and there are some suggestive psychological studies that might be relevant to the issue, such as studies of group hysteria. But, in my view, we do not currently have enough information to make speculation on this subject profitable, and I am leaving it out of account in this project.

79. It is no part of my distinctions among first-person, second-person, and third-person experiences, points of view, and accounts to suggest that there is opposition among these so that an agent who adopts one of these about something is thereby precluded from adopting any of the others. So, for example, someone who has first-person experiences of beliefs and desires might also consider even his own beliefs and desires from a third-person point of view, as a neurologist would. It is also possible to combine first-person, second-person, and third-person perspectives in an iterative fashion. For example, I might tell you about my introspective experiences of listening to music; then you would have a second-person experience of me which included my first-person account. Or I might introspect reflectively on my second-person experience of you, considering how I really felt about what you said. Then I would have a first-person point of view about a second-person experience. Religious believers can consider religion from a first-person point of view, where that point of view includes reflection on what they take to be their own second-person experiences connecting them in some fashion with the person of God. I am indebted to Al Plantinga for prompting me to consider this issue.

80. I am not here violating the explanation of first-person accounts given above, because, insofar as what is at issue is my conscious states, these are states I could have had during a hallucination of another person, when no other person was

present. So the experience being reported in this first-person account is one I could have had by myself.

81. For purposes of this chapter, I take 'expository prose' to mean prose which does not constitute a story and which does not fall into some other genre of literature (such as poetry) that is story-like in its artistry. I will describe accounts that are formulated in terms of knowing that something or other is the case as presented in expository prose. I am therefore using 'expository prose' as a term of art, *faute de mieux*.

82. In this respect, a second-person experience differs from a first-person experience of the sort we have in perception. There is no way for me to convey to someone who has never seen colors what I know when I know what it is like to see red.

83. I am not here implying that the only function, or even the main function, of narratives (in one medium or another) is to convey real or imagined second-person experiences. My claim is just that much less is lost of a second-person experience in a narrative account than in a third-person account, *ceteris paribus*.

84. Someone might object here that any information which could be captured and conveyed by a story could also be conveyed by an expository account. I have no good argument against this claim, for the very reasons I have been urging—namely, that we cannot give an expository description of what *else* is contained in a story; but I think the claim is false. Consider, for example, some excellent and current biography of Samuel Johnson, such as Robert DeMaria's *The Life of Samuel Johnson: A Critical Biography* (Oxford: Blackwell, 1993), and compare it to the pastiche of stories in Boswell's *Life of Johnson*, and you see the point. There is a great deal to be learned about Johnson from DeMaria's *The Life of Samuel Johnson*, but Boswell's stories give you the man as the biography cannot.

85. The degree will be a function not only of the narrative excellence of the story but also of the sensitivity and intelligence of the story-hearer or reader as well.

86. I do not mean to say that the storyteller or artist does not contribute something of her own in the narrative presentation. On the contrary, part of the importance of narrative is that its artistry enables us to see what we might well have missed without the help of the narrative, even if we had been present as bystanders in the events recounted in the narrative. It is for this reason that the quality of the artistry in a narrative makes a difference to what there is to know on the basis of it.

87. For very brief discussion of the possibility of combining knowledge *that* with knowledge of persons, see Chapter 3.

88. Someone might suppose that we could turn any story into expository propositional form just by prefixing to the story the words 'It is true in this story that' and then filling out the remainder of the sentence with a conjunction formed from all the sentences in the story. But this swollen sentence would not constitute an example of expository prose, since it would contain a story within it. And, in any case, it

would not be true that all the knowledge in the story was conveyed by means of propositions *that*. The story would be embedded in a proposition *that*, but the distinctively Franciscan knowledge of the story would be conveyed by the story itself.

89. I cannot, of course, specify what that knowledge is, since to do so would be to translate it into terms of knowledge *that*.

90. I am grateful to Minghe Li for calling my attention to the need to make this point clear.

91. It is clear that film belongs on this list, and yet it is also clear that film is a special category. In the first place, unlike narrative mediated only orally or in writing, film allows its audience visual perception of the events of the story being told. On the other hand, unlike drama presented live in a theatre, film does not allow its audience direct sensory perception of human beings themselves; it gives access to human beings only through what the film captures of the actors' performances. And so it may be that the mirror neuron system is activated by the perception of the actors in film; or it may be that the mediation of film somehow also undermines or diminishes what the mirror neuron system can do.

   In this connection, it is perhaps worth pointing out that the great Puritans of all cultures, from Plato to Mao, have had considerable concern about the moral effects of theater; and some Puritans have worried about the moral effects of acting on the actors themselves. (Some wit has said that a Puritan is a person who is worried that somewhere in the world some human being is enjoying himself. I think that wit was ill-informed about Puritans. For my part, I think a Puritan is a person who thinks that nothing is good unless it is useful, and that everything useful must ultimately serve the moral good.) The mirror neuron system helps to explain the concern about the effects of acting on actors. If mimicking an emotion uses the mirror neuron system, for example, then acting out a great evil will leave an actor (to one extent or another) with some intimate internal access to the emotions he would have had if he had done that evil in person; and that experience may have damaging psychological effects on the actor. Reporting on his observations of Robert De Niro portraying an autistic man in the filming of a movie based on his book *Awakenings*, Oliver Sacks says that watching De Niro

   was amazing ... it was like overhearing a man *thinking*—but thinking with his body, experimenting, thinking in action ... I started to wonder how deep, with [De Niro], acting might go. I knew how deeply he might identify with the characters he portrayed, but I had to wonder ... how *neurologically deep he might go*—*whether he might actually, in his acting*, become Parkinsonian, or at least (in an astoundingly controlled fashion) somehow duplicate the neurological state of the patient. Does acting like this, I wondered, actually alter the nervous system? (Oliver Sacks, *Awakenings* (New York: Harper Perennial, 1990), 382–3).

92. For the thought experiment involving Mary, see Chapter 3.

93. I do not mean to imply that knowledge gained through literature is equivalent to knowledge gained through second-person experience, or that, if Mary had only had access to great literature, nothing in her first encounter with her mother would have surprised her. I mean only what I say here: access to great literature would have lessened the surprise for Mary by some degree, however small it might have been.

94. In recent years some philosophers have considered the hypothesis that it can be explained by simulation. For an attempt to capture audience reaction to fiction in terms of simulation, see Kendall Walton, "Spelunking, Simulation, and Slime: On Being Moved by Fiction," in Mette Hjorte and Sue Laver (eds.), *Emotion and the Arts* (New York: Oxford University Press, 1997). For a helpful discussion of the positions of Walton and others in connection with simulation, see Alvin Goldman, "Imagination and Simulation in Audience Responses to Fiction," in Shaun Nichols (ed.), *The Architecture of the Imagination: New Essays on Pretence, Possibility, and Fiction* (Oxford: Clarendon Press, 2006), 41–56. For a discussion of the issue in connection with biblical narratives, see my "Second Person Accounts and the Problem of Evil," in Timo Koistinen and Tommi Lehtonen (eds.), *Perspectives in Contemporary Philosophy of Religion* (Schriften der Luther-Agricola-Gesellschaft 46; Helsinki: Luther-Agricola-Society, 2000), 88–113; repr. (among other places) in Keith Yandell (ed.), *Faith and Narrative* (Oxford: Oxford University Press, 2001), 86–103. (The original version of this paper was originally presented in my Stob Lectures, which appeared together with subsequent Stob Lectures in *Seeking Understanding: The Stob Lectures 1986–1998* (Grand Rapids, MI: Eerdmans, 2001), 497–529.)

95. See, e.g., Stephen Kosslyn, *Image and Brain: The Resolution of the Imagery Debate* (Cambridge, MA: MIT Press, 1994).

96. This is an empirical hypothesis, of course; and, since I first framed it, it has occurred to scientists working in this area also. A recent scientific study confirms that the mirror neuron system used in the actual experience of something disgusting to a person is *also* used when that person hears and understands a story about something disgusting. See Mbemba Jabbi et al., "A Common Anterior Insula Representation of Disgust Observation, Experience and Imagination Shows Divergent Functional Connectivity Pathways," www.plosone.org/article/info:doi/10.1371/journal.pone.0002939.

97. It can also help us understand the importance of pretend play in children. The predilection of children to engage in such play has been a puzzle to some philosophers and psychologists (see, e.g., Peter Carruthers, "Why Pretend?," in Nichols (ed.), *The Architecture of the Imagination*, 89–110). But pretend play can be seen as the exercise of the mirror neuron system taken offline, as simulation theorists say. In that case, the predilection for pretend play would be on a par with a predilection for ball-playing. It is a kind of play which trains the brain in a kind

of coordination useful in adult activities. But, of course, this is simply a speculative suggestion.

98. It may be that this claim needs nuancing. Maybe, for example, a person steeped in the biographies and diaries of Joseph Goebbels does begin to have some second-person experience of Goebbels. Or, to take a very different example, maybe some readers of the Gospels come to have some second-person experience of Christ. If, in fact, my claim in the text needs to be nuanced to allow for this possibility, the general point about narratives relevant to my project will remain the same, whatever else might need to be adjusted—namely, that narratives convey a knowledge of persons that is difficult or impossible to convey in propositional terms and that is philosophically useful. I am grateful to Susan Brower-Toland for calling my attention to the need to address this issue.

99. Philosophers have puzzled over the experience of emotion in engagement with fiction. (For some recent discussion of issues involving fiction and emotion, see, e.g., Nichols (ed.), *The Architecture of the Imagination*, and Jenefer Robinson, *Deeper than Reason: Emotion and its Role in Literature, Music, and Art* (Oxford: Clarendon Press, 2007).) Why does the monster in the movie, for example, inspire fear, or something like fear, in the audience, when the audience knows that the monster is not real? If the mirror neuron system is like the perceptual system with regard to its links to emotion, however, then it helps to resolve this puzzle as regards emotional reactions to fiction. The mirror neuron system is like the perceptual system in being engaged by external stimuli. You just see the sadness in someone else's face, in the same way that you just see the face. If the same system used for real second-person experience is used in the appropriation of fiction, then it will be similarly engaged by the fiction, too. Now the visual system retains its connection to feelings and emotions whether it is used in vision or in imagery. That is why the feeling of thirst can arise both from the sight and from the conjured visual image of a cool beer on a hot day. In the same way, it is entirely possible that the mirror neuron system retains its connections to feelings and emotions, whether it is used in real second-person experience or in the appropriation of fiction. Just as an object seen in imagination can prompt emotions analogous to those which would be prompted by the actual sight of such an object, so the second-person system engaged by fiction can prompt the emotions which would be elicited by an actual second-person experience of the same sort. On this hypothesis, we would not need to wonder that a person feels fear at the sight of a monster he knows to be unreal. We have no analogous surprise at finding that a person feels thirst in response to the image of a beer he knows he himself has conjured up.

Furthermore, there is an explanation of the cognitive condition of the movie-goer who feels fear of the monster he knows to be fictional. On the hypothesis I am suggesting here, the movie-watcher's mirror neuron system is engaged by the movie, so that he knows the monster and the monster's hostile intent; and it is this which gives rise to his fear of the monster. That is why, if we ask someone why he feels fear while watching the monster in the movie, he will explain himself by saying that the monster is frightening. There is a cognitive component to his emotion of fear, then, but it is the non-propositional second-person knowledge mediated by the mirror neuron system. If the mirror neuron system can be engaged by fiction as well as by actual second-person experience, as I am suggesting, then the movie-watcher can know the monster's hostile intent even though he also knows *that* the monster is not real.

For a good recent collection exploring these and other related issues pertinent to the question of knowledge conveyed by literature, see, e.g., John Gibson et al. (eds.), *A Sense of the World: Essays on Fiction, Narrative, and Knowledge* (London: Routledge, 2007).

100. And, of course, some poems, such as Homer's *Iliad* and *Odyssey* or Milton's *Paradise Lost*, are or at least include stories in an artistically complicated form.

Chapter 5

1. See, e.g., Gabriele Taylor, "Love," *Proceedings of the Aristotelian Society*, 76 (1976), 157: "If x loves y then x wants to benefit and be with y etc., and he has these wants (or at least some of them) because he believes y has some determinate characteristics . . . in virtue of which he thinks it worth while to benefit and be with y." For a more complicated exemplar, see J. David Velleman, "Love as a Moral Emotion," *Ethics*, 109 (1999), 361: "The responses unleashed by love for a person tend to be favorable because they have been unleashed by an awareness of value in him . . ."

2. Strictly speaking, this claim should be put not in terms of intrinsic characteristics of the beloved, but in terms of intrinsic characteristics which the lover perceives or believes are in the beloved, since it is plain that a lover can be mistaken about intrinsic characteristics of the beloved. But, for ease of exposition, and for tracking the current debate which does not highlight this complication, I am leaving it out of account here.

3. J. David Velleman, for example, attempts to explain love as a response just to the beloved's personhood and rational capacities. See "Love as a Moral Emotion," 338–74.

4. Robert Kraut, "Love *De Re*," *Midwest Studies in Philosophy*, 10 (1986), 425.

5. Richard of St Victor, *De Quatuor Gradibus Violentiae Charitatis*, PL 196 c. 1213, 1207; cited in Ann Astell, *The Song of Songs in the Middle Ages* (Ithaca, NY: Cornell University Press, 1990), 19.

6. Harry Frankfurt, *The Reasons of Love* (Princeton: Princeton University Press, 2004), 39.

7. Kraut, "Love *De Re*," 425.

8. Amelie Rorty, "The Historicity of Psychological Attitudes: Love is not Love which Alters not When It Alteration Finds," *Midwest Studies in Philosophy*, 10 (1986), 402–3.

9. Frankfurt, *The Reasons of Love*, 39–40.

10. Frankfurt, *The Reasons of Love*, 39.

11. Frankfurt, *The Reasons of Love*, 40.

12. Frankfurt, *The Reasons of Love*, 40.

13. See Chapter 1 for the distinction between the subjective and the objective elements in what one cares about.

14. Niko Kolodny, "Love as Valuing a Relationship," *Philosophical Review*, 112 (2003), 35.

15. For ease of exposition, in considering Kolodny's account, I will use the term 'relationship' in his sense. But I will abandon his sense in the subsequent discussion, because Kolodny's usage is too restrictive, in my view. Even as regards "attitude-dependent relationships," we typically use the term 'relationship' more broadly to refer to a connection between persons whether or not it is characterized by shared activities or a history of interaction. So, for example, we might say that Dante had a love/hate relationship with Boniface VIII, whom Dante never met, or that Dante saw his relationship to Virgil in ways complimentary to himself, although, of course, Dante was separated from Virgil by more than a millennium. So, apart from considerations of Kolodny's account, I will let the term 'relationship' range more broadly over varying kinds of significant personal connection between two or more persons.

16. Kolodny, "Love as Valuing a Relationship," 148–9.

17. Kolodny, "Love as Valuing a Relationship," 148.

18. Kolodny, "Love as Valuing a Relationship," 149.

19. Kolodny, "Love as Valuing a Relationship," 149.

20. Kolodny, "Love as Valuing a Relationship," 136.

21. For Kolodny, "this is what explains *constancy*: the fact that love . . . does not alter as alteration (in qualities) it finds. The relationship remains, even as qualities change" ("Love as Valuing a Relationship," 147).

22. Kolodny, "Love as Valuing a Relationship," 136.

23. Kolodny, "Love as Valuing a Relationship," 150. Kolodny makes this general rendering more precise in a series of six conditions on p. 151; the passage I have cited is his own summary of those conditions.

24. Kolodny, "Love as Valuing a Relationship," 141.

25. Kolodny, "Love as Valuing a Relationship," 147.

26. Kolodny himself raises and attempts to disarm a number of objections to his account. It would take me too far afield to comment on those objections, but

one of them merits some consideration in connection with my project, because someone might suppose that the objection in question also affects Aquinas's position. If relationship is a reason for love, then there seems to be a problem of "relationship doubles." If someone other than the beloved holds the same relationship to the lover as the beloved, then it seems as if the lover is bound to love that other person as he loves the beloved. Kolodny's response to this objection is simply to accept its conclusion: if the other person holds the same relationship, then the lover ought also to love that other person. If a mother loves her child Jane, and if James is also her child, then she should love James for the same reason that she loves Jane: she is the mother of each of them. Aquinas's account gives this same result, but it has the resources to explain what Kolodny's account cannot—namely, that there may be great variations in the extent and character of the love across similar relationships. On Aquinas's account, love is a response to intrinsic as well as relational characteristics of the beloved. And so Aquinas's account can explain the common fact that a lover may have differing attitudes toward relationship doubles. In the extreme case, the intrinsic characteristics of James may alienate his mother to such a degree that the alienation overrides the love consequent on the relation of parent to child. On Aquinas's view, then, but not on Kolodny's, the mother may have very different attitudes toward James and Jane, even though they are relationship doubles with respect to her.

27. Someone might suppose that the courtly-love tradition establishes a relationship between a lover and his lady. But the kind of relationship at issue in the courtly-love tradition is different from the kind of relationship at issue for Kolodny. It is possible for a lover to have a courtly-love relationship with a woman he has not met or with a woman, such as Mary, the mother of Jesus, who has the status for the lover of a spiritual, religious, or mythological figure. The thing that Kolodny picks out as central to relationship, shared history, need not be present in courtly-love relationships.

28. See Dante's arch comments on the courtly-love tradition in the story of Paolo and Francesca (*Inferno*, canto V, ll. 121–35).

29. Kolodny, "Love as Valuing a Relationship," 146. When he addresses the issue of unrequited love directly, however, Kolodny seems to claim that it is love but that it is not worthwhile (p. 171). It is not clear to me that he can hold this position consistently with his other views discussed in the text here.

30. There are also other cases that raise the same problem. So, for example, there is the case of love at first sight, where a person experiences intense love for someone whom he is seeing for the first time. (Dante's case may also include love at first sight, if such a thing could be attributed to a mere boy. On Dante's own account, he was not yet a teenager when he first saw and loved Beatrice.) There is also the sort of case represented by responses to a celebrity, such as the late Pope John Paul II. Many young people felt a great love for that Pope and traveled long distances in

the hope of meeting him and starting a relationship with him. But, plainly, in such cases the person who loves is not in a relationship with the beloved at the time he first loves, and he knows that he is not in such a relationship. Rather, in these cases, the person who loves attempts to establish a relationship because he already loves. On Kolodny's account, however, what we have to say is that in these cases it is not true that the people in question really do love, just because it is not true that they are or believe themselves to be in a relationship with the person they take to be their beloved. But this claim goes counter to what such people themselves say and what others believe about them. And so Kolodny's account of love gives counter-intuitive results in these cases as well.

31. It is part of Kolodny's account that the relationship of love has to be valued as a final end ("Love as Valuing a Relationship," 150–1). For the sake of the argument, we can add here, then, that Dante valued his relationship to his wife as a final end. His valuing of her as the sister of his friend and the mother of his children can be understood as a consequence of his valuing of his marriage relationship as a final end.

32. Apparently, at the end of his life, Gemma did come to live with Dante, but only after this long absence. If an expert in Dante's biography has evidence which I have missed that Gemma Donati came to visit Dante regularly in this period, we can take my example here as fictional. Since what is at issue is Kolodny's account of the concept of love, it clearly does not matter whether my counter-example is historical or fictional.

33. If the case of Dante and Beatrice shows that the elements constituent of love on Kolodny's account are not necessary for love, the case of Dante and Gemma Donati shows that they are not sufficient either.

34. Cf. ST I-II q.26 a.3.

35. Cf. ST I-II q.26 a.1.

36. For discussion of the scholarly debates about Aquinas's views and a survey of some of the recent literature, see, e.g., Michael Sherwin, *By Knowledge and by Love: Charity and Knowledge in the Moral Theology of St Thomas Aquinas* (Washington: Catholic University Press, 2005).

37. Cf. ST I-II q.26 a.1.

38. For some attempt to explain the metaphysics of goodness and being in Aquinas's thought, see the chapters on simplicity and goodness in my *Aquinas* (London and New York: Routledge, 2003).

39. See, e.g., ST I-II q.27 a.1 s.c., where Aquinas cites approvingly Augustine's line that the good alone is loved, and the body of article where Aquinas argues that the good alone is the proper object and the cause of love. Cf. also ST II-II q.23 a.4, where Aquinas says that the proper object of love is the good.

40. I am not sure what Aquinas would say about the love of a pet. But, given the typical kind of relationship between a human person and the pet she loves, perhaps

this kind of love can simply be subsumed within the genus of love of persons. For the typical pet lover, the beloved pet is a person or a quasi-person, so to speak.

41. ST II-II, q.23 aa.4–5. Cf. also ST I-II q.26 a.4, where Aquinas describes the love a person has to non-personal things (wine is his example) as the love of concupiscence, which is love not *simpliciter*, in his view, but only *secundum quid*.

42. ST I-II q.26 a.4 s.c.

43. So, for example, Harry Frankfurt says: "Love is, most centrally, a *disinterested* concern for the existence of what is loved, and for what is good for it" (*The Reasons of Love*, 42).

44. See, e.g., ST II-II q.27 a.2, where Aquinas distinguishes love from goodwill, which he takes to be the willing of good to another.

45. ST II-II q.25, a.3.

46. Cf. ST I-II q.26 a.4, where Aquinas says that to love is to will good to someone. Cf. also ST I-II q.28 a.4, where Aquinas explains the zeal or intensity of love in terms of the strength of a lover's desire for the good of the beloved.

47. Cf., e.g., ST I-II q.26 a.2 ad 2, and q.28 a.1 s.c., where Aquinas quotes approvingly Dionysius's line that love is the unitive force. Cf. also ST I-II q.66 a.6, where Aquinas explains the superiority of charity to the other virtues by saying that every lover is drawn by desire to union with the beloved, and ST I-II q.70 a.3, where Aquinas explains the connection between joy and love by saying that every lover rejoices at being united to the beloved. For an interesting recent attempt to defend a position that has some resemblance to Aquinas's, see Robert Adams, "Pure Love," *Journal of Religious Ethics*, 8 (1980), 83–99. Adams says: "It is a striking fact that while benevolence (the desire for another person's well-being) and *Eros*, as a desire for relationship with another person, seem to be quite distinct desires, we use a single name, 'love' or '*Agape*', for an attitude that includes both of them, at least in typical cases" (p. 97).

48. For Aquinas's views on the nature of this union, cf., e.g., ST I-II q.28 a.1, where real union is described as a matter of presence between lover and beloved. I examine the nature of union and its connection to personal presence in detail in the next chapter.

49. Velleman, "Love as a Moral Emotion," 353.

50. Cf., e.g., ST II-II q.28 a.1.

51. Because the desires of love can vary in intensity and because a person can be internally divided, there are complicated issues involving degrees of desire that cannot be addressed in passing here. For present purposes, I would say that, if a person has the desires of love in any degree, then he also has some degree of love. But that love might be faint enough and sufficiently overridden by opposed desires that it is more appropriate to describe him as characterized by the desires opposed to love.

52. For a detailed exposition of Aquinas's philosophical psychology, see my *Aquinas*, ch. 8, on the mechanisms of cognition, and ch. 9, on the will.

53. Someone might wonder whether the source of the desires does not also have to be specified. For example, would a person count as loving if his desires of love had their source in something external to him, such as a neurosurgical intervention? On the account of love given here, there is an assumption that the desires of love are the lover's own; but they would not count as the lover's own if they were implanted in the lover by an external agent. For some discussion of what makes a desire an agent's own, see my "Persons: Identification and Freedom," *Philosophical Topics*, 24 (1996), 183–214.

54. But cf., e.g., ST I-II q.32 a.6, where Aquinas discusses the pleasure that arises from doing good to another person, and ST I-II q.32 a.7, where he discusses the pleasure consequent on becoming united with another person.

55. For a fuller exposition of Aquinas's theology and philosophical psychology of love, cf. Sherwin, *By Knowledge and by Love*.

56. Cf. ST I-II q.27 a.1.

57. In my view, Aquinas's account of love has great strength because of this understanding of the reasons of love, but it is also incomplete. I will go on to argue that there need to be *two* answers to the questions about reasons for the desires of love. The first is the one Aquinas's account gives: because it's good. But the second is and ought to be "because it's *you*"—that is, because I have set my heart on you. For a discussion of the way in which Aquinas's account can be developed to incorporate this much of the volitional account of love, see Chapter 14. For further discussion of the nature of the desire for union with the beloved, in particular its character as a desire for a person rather than a desire *that* something or other be the case, see Chapters 6 and 7.

58. It is good in the sense that, among the things that could be listed as good-making characteristics of the world, this is one. Union between any two people is good in this sense, as discord between people is not good. But this is not the same as saying that union with this particular lover in the particular mode of union that this lover wants is a good for this particular beloved. It might, for example, be the case that two people (Anthony and Bernard) wish to marry the same beloved (Cecilia), but Cecilia wishes to marry Bernard and not Anthony. Then, given Cecilia's desires, union in marriage with Anthony is not a good for her, even if union between two people, considered in the abstract, is a good thing. Reasons of this sort help explain why the second desire of love on the part of a particular lover with regard to a particular beloved does not immediately collapse into the first.

59. The two desires of any love are therefore included under the more general heading of the desire for goodness, as Aquinas understands it. For detailed discussion of Aquinas's views of goodness, understood in this broad sense, see my *Aquinas*, ch. 2, on goodness.

60. The claim that the good desired for the beloved is an objective good therefore results from Aquinas's analysis of the nature of love together with his meta-ethics. It is not itself implied by Aquinas's analysis of love. I am grateful to Ish Haji for calling my attention to the need to make this point clear.

61. Since union with God is the ultimate good for each and every human person, union with God is a shareable good. A person who is in union with God is also in union with the other persons in union with God.

62. There are circumstances in which this claim would have to be modified or retracted. In the text below, I distinguish derived from intrinsic desires. It is possible to imagine a mother who has a powerful loathing of the very idea of beating her child but who has been convinced by authorities in her community that unless she beats her child she will do him serious damage. In consequence, she desires to beat her child at the times and in the ways specified by those authorities, but with a great sorrow or grief over having to do so (as she supposes). Her desire to beat her child is thus only a derived, not an intrinsic one. She would immediately lose that desire if she understood that the authorities in her community who prescribe the beating of children are mistaken. In the case of this mother, the desire to beat her child is not unloving, because it is not an intrinsic desire.

63. I am grateful to John Cottingham and Ish Haji for making me aware of the need for a distinction here, and I am grateful to John Foley for helping me see how to draw the needed distinction.

64. For a discussion of intrinsic desires, see Robert Audi, *The Architecture of Reason* (Oxford: Oxford University Press, 2001), 81–3. I am grateful to Audi for calling to my attention the usefulness of this discussion in this context.

65. A *ceteris paribus* clause is obviously needed as a qualifier on 'other' here: any other means equally good as regards correction and at least as good as regards not inflicting harm on the student—and, no doubt, other qualifying clauses as well.

66. In theory, it is also possible that a person really love someone whom she believes she does not love. Suppose, for example, that Paula has moved out of the apartment she shares with Jerome because he is sporadically violent toward her; and suppose that Jerome succeeds in making Paula feel guilty about doing so. In these circumstances, Paula can become confused enough to suppose that her moving out shows that she is unloving toward Jerome because he is unhappy (and so apparently does not have what is good for him) and apart from Paula (and so apparently not united with her). In this case, Paula's guilt and confusion could lead her to suppose that she is unloving toward Jerome in moving out. But she would be mistaken on this score. It is better for a sporadically violent person—better for *him*—if he is separated from the person he has picked as his victim, so that in moving out Paula is choosing what is good for Jerome. And by preventing Jerome from destroying their relationship (and her) through his violence, Paula is choosing as much union with Jerome as his current state of character allows. Such

relationship as she has with him is preserved better by distance than by proximity. See also the discussion of hatred in n. 74.

67. By 'final good' here, I mean the good for the sake of which all other goods are desirable. I do not mean to imply that this final good is the only good or that all other goods are only apparent goods.

68. Union with God will also join them with all the human persons who, in their own true good, are united with God, so that shared union with God is inclusive.

69. In Chapter 7, I return to this claim and discuss it in detail.

70. To see the point of the qualifier "to this extent," see n. 58.

71. Seeing this implication of Aquinas's views helps us understand his claim that the primary object of love is goodness. The lover desires the good for the beloved and union with the beloved because each of these things is good, in the sense that each of them conduces to the one true goodness which (on the doctrine of simplicity) God is.

72. For Sartre's presentation of this case, see *Existentialism and Human Emotions* (New York: Philosophical Library, 1957), 24–8.

73. To say this is not to imply that always and in every case the two desires of love collapse into one—namely, the desire for the good of the beloved. For reasons for this claim, see n. 58.

74. Aquinas's account of love also gives us insight into the nature of hatred. Insofar as hatred is the opposite of love, hatred will consist in desiring the bad for the other, or desiring not to be united with the other, or both. But now consider a person sunk in serious moral wrongdoing; consider, for example, Hitler. A contemporary of Hitler's in 1933 who desired that Hitler not come to power then would have been desiring something which is in one sense bad for Hitler and in another sense good. It is bad for a person when he loses something he wants very much. On the other hand, if what he wants is very bad, then it is good, all things considered, that he suffer the bad of not getting what he wants. It would have been better *for Hitler* if he had not come to power; that is, it would have been better for Hitler himself if he had died as someone other than the moral monster he was enabled to become in consequence of the power he gained. Something analogous can be said as regards union. Someone contemporary with Hitler who wanted to be united with Hitler, to join him in his evil, would have been wanting what is in effect not good for Hitler. Hitler is much better off being opposed than being joined, given that his actions and desires are so evil.

   And so we have to recognize that hatred comes in two varieties, one of which is opposed to love and one of which is not. Desiring the bad for someone and desiring not to be united with that person *can* be the desires of love *if* the person in question is bad enough that the bad of losing what he wants and having people alienated from him is the best thing for him in the circumstances. The difference between the two varieties of hatred consists primarily in the ultimate desire encompassing the desires for the bad and for alienation. So consider one person Paula who wants the bad (in one sense) for Jerome and who desires to be at a distance from Jerome, when Jerome is engaged in serious moral wrongdoing. If Paula's ultimate desire for Jerome is that Jerome have as much of flourishing and shared union with Paula and with God as Jerome can, then the variety of hatred she has for Jerome is in effect a species of love. It consists in the two desires of love, for the kind of good and the kind of union possible to desire for a person engaged in serious moral wrong. On the other hand, if Paula's ultimate desire for Jerome is that Jerome be increasingly worse, increasingly distant from his own flourishing and shared union with God, then the hatred Paula has for Jerome is incompatible with love. When the biblical texts (Mal. 1: 2 and Rom. 9: 13) say that God loved Jacob and hated Esau, the hatred in question can be understood as the variety which is a species of love.

It is interesting to note in this connection the line with which Jesus expresses his attitude toward those whose own inner dispositions keep them from salvation. Jesus maintains that on judgment day he will say to such people, "I never knew you. Depart from me, you who do evil" (Matt.7: 23; cf. Luke 13: 27). The knowledge in question in his line is undoubtedly the knowledge of persons, not knowledge *that*. When Jesus says to the people in question that he never knew them, the missing knowledge is personal knowledge and personal relationship between him and them. Furthermore, the result of this lack of personal relationship is a desire on Jesus' part that these people go away—the opposite of a desire for union. And the reason Jesus gives for this attitude on his part is the commitment on the part of the dismissed people to moral wrongdoing. The implication of Jesus' line to them is that their unwillingness to be internally integrated around the good keeps them in a condition where hatred which is one of the species of love is the only kind of love with which they can be loved. For further discussion of these issues, see Chapters 8 and 13.

75. I do not mean that the desire for the good of the beloved does not have to take into account intrinsic and relational characteristics of the beloved in the process of discerning what the good for the beloved is. I mean only that the desire for the good of the beloved need not be a *response* to anything in the beloved. One can desire the good for a particular third-world child whom one has been given to support by an international charitable organization without knowing anything about that particular child, beyond the fact that he is a human child in some need of basic goods necessary for generic human flourishing.

76. Another way to put this point is that one can simply set one's heart on a particular person. I discuss the issue of the desires of the heart in detail in Chapter 14.

77. If there is a relationship between persons in which it is not appropriate for one person to desire the good for and union with the other, then the relationship is not a relationship of love. Insofar as it is possible to have a general love of humankind,

however, then there may also be no connection between persons which is not also in effect a relationship for which some species of love is appropriate. In other words, it may be that there is an obligation of love toward all human persons. If this is right, then there is also an obligation of forgiveness, even if there is no *right* to forgiveness. Paula may have an obligation to forgive any person who injures her, even if that person has no right to Paula's forgiveness. (This is one reason among others for supposing that obligations and rights are not correlative. For discussion of this point, see my "God's Obligations," in James Tomberlin (ed.), *Philosophical Perspectives*, 6 (Atascadero, CA: Ridgeview Publishing, 1992), 475–92.

78. ST II-II q.26 a.6.

79. Kolodny makes a related point about relationships and their effect on the character of love; see "Love as Valuing a Relationship," 139.

80. While the kind of union appropriate to a relationship is fixed, the kind of relationship appropriate between two people is not. Two people who were at first friends rather than lovers can fall in love and marry, for example; and when they do, the nature of the relationship of love and the union appropriate for them to desire changes.

81. I am grateful to Bas van Fraassen for raising insightful questions about the account of the offices of love in an earlier draft of this chapter.

82. What I am calling 'the offices of love' may be the same or at least similar to what Niko Kolodny calls 'the modes of love.' He says: "Heather's mother and Heather's teenage friend may both love her, but they love her, or at least they ought to love her, in different ways" ("Love as Valuing a Relationship," 139). See also Kraut, "Love *De Re*," for the same or a similar use of the term 'office.' I myself was made familiar with this usage of the term 'office' by Milton; see his *Paradise Lost*, X, ll. 958–60. For exquisite exploration of what happens when the offices of love are violated, consider Shakespeare's *King Lear*. To take just one example of many in the play, at the outset of the play, Shakespeare's Lear pushes his daughters to violate the office of love between father and daughter by confessing an uncircumscribed or non-delimited love for him. By the end of the play, it has become clear that the only daughter who really loves Lear is the daughter who refused to break the boundaries of her office of love with him at the outset of the play.

83. I accept the implication of this claim that a casual sexual encounter between relative strangers does not by itself constitute union between them.

84. Because of the possibility of internal division in the will, the desire in this case needs to be understood as an effective desire—that is, a desire that would be translated into action if nothing outside the will impeded it. There clearly are cases in which a lover has ineffective desires—desires that are overridden by opposed desires—for an inappropriate kind of union with the beloved. Adjudication of these complicated cases has to be left to one side here. I am grateful to Jonathan Reibsamen for calling my attention to the need to address this point.

85. 'Failing to desire the good of the beloved' is ambiguous as between two things:

    (1) with regard to what is actually a good for the beloved, failing to have a desire for *that*; or with regard to what is actually not a good for the beloved, having a desire for *that*;

and

    (2) failing to have a desire the content of which is that the beloved have what is good for her; or having a desire the content of which is that the beloved have what is bad for her.

That is, 'the good of the beloved' can be taken referentially or descriptively. In this context, I mean the phrase only in the first, referential sense. A pedophile priest may claim that he desired only the good for the child he molested, and he may in fact be sincere in this claim. But he fails to have a desire for the good of the child anyway, in the first sense at issue here.

86. Cf. ST I-II q.27 a.3, where Aquinas talks about the different sorts of similarity, actual and potential, of intrinsic characteristics which connect two people in a relationship of love.

87. Cf. ST I-II q.27 a.3, where Aquinas discusses ways in which a person can be one with himself, and ST II-II q.25 a.4, where Aquinas explains union with oneself in terms of desiring for oneself the good which makes for union with God, including the good pertaining to the perfection of reason.

88. Cf., e.g., ST II-II q.29 a.3, where Aquinas says that, when a person's desires are unified, then there is internal union and peace in that person. It is clear that Aquinas supposes such internal unification is possible only around the good; see, e.g., ST II-II q.29 a.2 ad 3.

89. Among contemporary philosophers, Harry Frankfurt has done more than anyone else to illumine the role between a person's internal integration and her flourishing as a person. See his collections of essays, *The Importance of What We Care About* (Cambridge: Cambridge University Press, 1988); *Necessity, Volition, and Love* (Cambridge: Cambridge University Press, 1999); and *The Reasons of Love*.

90. ST II-II q.29 a. 1.

91. Cf. ST I-II q.28 a.4, where Aquinas explains a particularly strong or zealous love of God as including a person's striving for God's good by trying to ward off things incompatible with God's will.

92. In virtue of the preceding discussion of the offices of love, it might occur to someone to wonder what the offices of love are in these special cases of a person's love for himself or his love for God. For my purposes in this chapter, the offices are sufficiently characterized by the descriptions of the relationships in question. The first office is the office of self-love, and the second is the office of love between the Creator and one of the persons created by God for union with God. But, for further thought about the notion of offices of love between a human person and God, see Chapter 14.

93. For helpful discussion of this strand of thought, see Adams, "Pure Love," and Stephen Munzer, "Self-Abandonment and Self-Denial: Quietism, Calvinism, and the Prospect of Hell," *Journal of Religious Ethics*, 33 (2005), 747–81. A moving anecdote showing the view opposed to Aquinas's can be found in George Marsden, *Jonathan Edwards: A Life* (New Haven: Yale University Press, 2003), 326. Jonathan Edwards's teenage daughter Jerusha and David Brainerd were in love when Brainerd fell gravely ill with a sickness from which he did not recover. As his parting speech to Jerusha, Brainerd is reported to have said: "Dear Jerusha, are you willing to part with me? I am quite willing to part with you; I am willing to part with all my friends; I am willing to part with my dear brother John; although I love him the best of any creature living. I have committed him and all my friends to God, and can leave them with God." Marsden comments on the rank-ordering of Brainerd's loves: "David loved [his brother] John 'best of any creature living' in part because he was his co-worker and successor in his all-important mission work with the Indians in New Jersey. Jerusha, who was 'of much the same spirit with Mr Brainerd,' would understand such kingdom priorities." (It is true that, although Brainerd's speech begins in this vein, denying the power and validity of the love between him and Jerusha, it does not finish without some humanity. He concludes his dying address to her by saying: "Though, if I thought I should not see you and be happy with you in another world, I could not bear to part with you.") Aquinas would not have supposed that human love is in competition with a desire to obey and serve God or that human loves are in competition with each other in the way presupposed by Brainerd's speech.

94. For more discussion of this claim, see Chapter 7.

95. For a different interpretation of Aquinas on this issue, see Thomas Osborne, "The Augustinianism of Thomas Aquinas's Moral Theory," *Thomist*, 67 (2003), 279–305; see also his *Love of Self and Love of God in Thirteenth Century Ethics* (Notre Dame, IN: University of Notre Dame Press, 2005). My reasons for disagreeing with Osborne's position are in effect given in this chapter.

96. There is, however, this difference between God's love and human love. Whereas human love, at least in its desire for union, is responsive to good in the beloved, God's love produces good in the beloved, by enabling the beloved to have that integration of character requisite for union with God. How much God gives of this good to any one person depends on how much of it that person fails to reject. I discuss this issue at length in Chapter 8; and the general theological issue here, the nature and conditions of divine grace, is examined in detail in my *Aquinas*, ch. 13.

97. This is not the only case which Aquinas's account handles better than Kolodny's. To take one more example, consider what Kolodny says about a stalker's love for his victim. On Kolodny's account ("Love as Valuing a Relationship," 146), the inappropriate love of a stalker stems from the stalker's having a false belief that he has a relationship with his victim which renders his love appropriate. But it seems clear that a stalker might have no belief about his love's appropriateness given

his relationship to his victim. In fact, the stalker may not believe that he has any relationship to the person he is stalking; he may be hoping to establish a relationship which he himself knows is as yet non-existent. On Aquinas's account, the problem with the stalker is that he is seeking a sort of union which is inappropriate for him to desire in his circumstances; and this inappropriateness is sufficient to explain the inappropriateness of the stalker's behavior and attitudes.

98. My claim that forgiveness includes love of a Thomistic sort does, though, imply that some accounts of forgiveness (such as the account of forgiveness as the forswearing of resentment) are ruled out as too restricted. For excellent discussions of forgiveness, see Jeffrie Murphy and Jean Hampton, *Forgiveness and Mercy* (Cambridge: Cambridge University Press, 1988); Jeffrie Murphy and Sharon Lamb, *Before Forgiveness* (Oxford: Oxford University Press, 2002); Jeffrie Murphy, *Getting Even: Forgiveness and its Limits* (Oxford: Oxford University Press, 2003); and Trudy Govier, *Forgiveness and Revenge* (London: Routledge, 2002). Helpful discussions of topics related to the issues in this section on forgiveness can also be found in David Novitz, "Forgiveness and Self-Respect," *Philosophy and Phenomenological Research*, 58 (1998), 299–315; Pamela Hieronymi, "Articulating an Uncompromising Forgiveness," *Philosophy and Phenomenological Research*, 62 (2001), 529–55; Glen Pettigrove, "Unapologetic Forgiveness," *American Philosophical Quarterly*, 41 (2004), 187–204; and Glen Pettigrove, "Understanding, Excusing, Forgiving," *Philosophy and Phenomenological Research*, 74 (2007), 156–75. I am grateful to Jeffrie Murphy for helpful comments on an earlier draft of this section on forgiveness.

99. See n. 74 for some discussion of the way in which this claim needs to be nuanced to take account of cases in which the beloved is in some morally deplorable condition.

100. I am simplifying here for the sake of brevity. In fact, more than genuine, trustworthy, whole-hearted repentance on Jerome's part may be needed in order for it to be appropriate for Paula to restore Jerome to their former habits of companionship. For example, if Paula has been traumatized by Jerome's wrongdoing, then something more than just genuine and trustworthy repentance on Jerome's part may be necessary for the resumption of their former relations. For a detailed discussion of the additional element requisite in some cases, especially those involving very great wrongdoing, see my "Personal Relations and Moral Residue," in Paul Roth and Mark S. Peacock (eds.), *History of the Human Sciences: Theorizing from the Holocaust: What is to be Learned?*, 17/2–3 (2004), 33–57. Cf. also Eve Garrard and David McNaughton, "In Defence of Unconditional Forgiveness," *Proceedings of the Aristotelian Society* (2002–3), 39–60, for a discussion of the nature of unconditional forgiveness.

101. Cases in which someone suffers at the hands of a conglomerate such as a corporation or a political group are too complicated to be dealt with adequately in passing, but roughly analogous claims will hold, on Aquinas's account. Employing legislative means against Shell Oil, for example, or boycotting the company in return for injustices it has committed will be compatible with forgiveness of those injustices,

on Aquinas's views. (As far as that goes, Aquinas is not a pacifist; he thinks that violence is compatible with love in some cases. See, for example, his view of tyrannicide as compatible with love of God; cf., e.g., *In II Sent.* 44.2.2 ad 5.) On the other hand, it is clearly also possible to be vengeful toward a conglomerate or to desire to exclude a whole group from the civilized society of humankind, as happens in long-standing nationalist battles. But such attitudes are incompatible with love and forgiveness, on Aquinas's account.

102. I am grateful to Ish Haji for his comments on an earlier draft of this chapter, which helped me to see that this case needed fuller attention than I gave it in an earlier draft.

103. In my view, part of the point of the old medieval idea of penance is that it gives a wrongdoer a chance to become a different and more admirable person than he became in consequence of his wrongdoing. For discussion of this idea, see my "Personal Relations and Moral Residue."

104. See, e.g., Avishai Margalit, *The Ethics of Memory* (Cambridge, MA: Harvard University Press, 2002).

105. Cf. Richard Swinburne, *Responsibility and Atonement* (Oxford: Clarendon Press, 1989), 81–5, for an argument that forgiveness requires repentance and penance on the part of the perpetrator of the wrong being forgiven.

Chapter 6

1. There obviously can be a kind of friendship between lovers or between family members, for example, but there are additional elements in such relationships that complicate the case. For that reason, it is simpler to consider friendship between persons who have neither a family tie nor an involvement in a romantic or erotic relationship. This paradigmatic case can be extended, *mutatis mutandis*, to friendship in the broader sense as well as to other sorts of union in loving relationships, in ways I explain very briefly at the end of the chapter.

2. It may be that these things are also required for friendship between human persons one or more of whom is not adult or not mentally fully functioning or both; but in the interest of brevity I am concentrating on the simplest case of friendship.

3. For an excellent study of the nature of presence as it relates to the presence of God, see Ingolf Dalferth, *Becoming Present: An Inquiry into the Christian Sense of the Presence of God* (Leeuven: Peeters, 2006). I am in agreement with many, but not all, of the elements of Dalferth's understanding of the nature of presence in general and God's presence in particular. The ways in which my position differs from his and the reasons for those differences are in effect set out in this chapter.

4. As I explain later in this chapter, it is not possible to specify with any precision the degree of closeness needed, so 'sufficient' here is ineluctably vague.

5. Augustine, *Confessions*, V.2.

6. Cf. Augustine, *Confessions*, VII.17. In a recent lecture, "The Presence of God" (work in progress), Scott MacDonald discussed Augustine's understanding in the *Confessions* of the presence of God and called attention to Augustine's puzzling over the point of invoking the presence of an omnipresent God. I am grateful to MacDonald for sharing this lecture with me.

7. Eleonore Stump and Norman Kretzmann, "Eternity, Awareness, and Action," *Faith and Philosophy*, 9 (1992), 463–82. Dalferth has found a similar position in an eighteenth-century scholar, who defines presence as "a state in which a person by his own substance, without any intermediate moral causes and indeed without the help of any instruments or tools, can act in a place" (J. Chr. Adelung, *Versuch eines vollstaendigen grammatisch-kritischen Woerterbuches der hochdeutschen Mundart*, ii (Leipzig, 1755), 483; the translation is Dalferth's and is cited in *Becoming Present*, 57). On Dalferth's own view, the heart of the doctrine of divine omnipresence is that "there never was or will be a presence to which God is not present: *God is present to every presence*" (*Becoming Present*, 164.)

8. By 'direct and unmediated' in this context, I mean only that the cognitive access or the causal connection does not have as an intermediate step the agency of another person; I do not mean that there is no intermediary of any sort. In this sense of 'direct and unmediated,' if I am wearing my glasses when I see a person, I still have direct and unmediated cognitive access to him; and if I am on the phone with him when I cause him grief by telling him that his mother has died, I am still exercising direct and unmediated causality on him. For further discussion of the implications of this use of the phrase 'direct and unmediated,' see the section on second-person experience in Chapter 4.

9. For a detailed discussion of second-person experience, see Chapter 4.

10. In the limiting cases of minimal personal presence, someone can count as minimally personally present who is not even conscious. And so the limiting cases of minimal personal presence can be thought of as defective versions of the species, like a sub-group of elephants genetically modified to be deaf. Something good and suitable to the species is missing. In the rest of the chapter, I will omit the qualifying phrase 'in all but the limiting cases,' but it should be understood throughout.

11. On Aquinas's views, God is eternal and so outside of time. William Hasker has argued that it is not possible for an atemporal God to be present to temporal persons. See his *God, Time, and Knowledge* (Ithaca, NY, and London: Cornell University Press, 1989); see especially p. 169. For discussion of Hasker's argument in this paper, see my *Aquinas* (London and New York: Routledge, 2003), ch. 4, on eternity. In later work, Hasker has tried to deepen his support for this position; see "The Absence of a Timeless God," in Greg Ganssle and David Woodruff (eds.), *God and Time: Essays on the Divine Nature* (New York: Oxford University Press, 2002), 182–206. But Hasker's argument in that later paper is effectively refuted

in my view by Thomas Senor, "The Real Presence of an Eternal God," in Kevin
Timpe (ed.), *Metaphysics and God* (New York: Routledge, 2009), 39–59; and so I
will not deal with it further here.

12. In that chapter, I described contemporary research on mirror neurons. As I
    suggested there, it may be that the mirror neuron system underlies the capacity for
    joint attention, but the neurological basis for joint attention is outside the scope of
    this book.

13. Vasudevi Reddy, "Before the 'Third Element': Understanding Attention to Self,"
    in Naomi Eilan et al. (eds.), *Joint Attention: Communication and Other Minds: Issues
    in Philosophy and Psychology* (Oxford: Clarendon Press, 2005), 85. I will refer to this
    anthology as *JA* hereafter.

14. R. Peter Hobson, "What Puts the Jointness into Joint Attention?," in *JA* 188.

15. Naomi Eilan, "Joint Attention, Communication, and Mind," in *JA* 5.

16. Hobson, "What Puts the Jointness into Joint Attention?," 185.

17. Fabia Franco, "Infant Pointing: Harlequin, Servant of Two Masters," in *JA* 129.

18. Franco, "Infant Pointing: Harlequin, Servant of Two Masters," 129.

19. Hobson, "What Puts the Jointness into Joint Attention?," 195.

20. Sue Leekam, "Why do Children with Autism have a Joint Attention Impairment?,"
    in *JA* 210. See also Gerrit Loots et al., "The Interaction between Mothers and their
    Visually Impaired Infants: An Intersubjective Developmental Perspective," *Journal
    of Visual Impairment and Blindness*, 97 (2003), 407.

21. Loots et al., "The Interaction between Mothers and their Visually Impaired
    Infants," 407.

22. Reddy, "Before the 'Third Element'," 100–1.

23. Reddy, "Before the 'Third Element'," 97.

24. Tiffany Field and Nathan Fox (eds.), *Social Perception in Infants* (Norwood, NJ: Ablex
    Publishing Corporation, 1985), 179, 193. See also the discussion of infant mimicry
    in Chapter 4.

25. Reddy, "Before the 'Third Element'," 85.

26. Leekam, "Why do Children with Autism have a Joint Attention Impairment?,"
    207.

27. See, e.g., Loots et al., "The Interaction between Mothers and their Visually
    Impaired Infants," 403–17. Since it is in principle possible to develop shared
    attention by means of a perceptual modality other than vision, it is not surprising
    that there are also congenitally blind children who do not develop autistic-like
    syndromes. The story of Helen Keller is an excellent example of a person for whom
    shared attention was mediated by something other than vision. In his preface to
    her autobiography, Helen Keller's Radcliffe teacher Ralph Perry says of Helen and
    her companion Annie Sullivan, who translated his lectures into her hand:

What I remember best [about her in class] is the expression of her face—her smile or look of understanding—when my point or pleasantry reached her mind through the ears and the hand of Miss Sullivan. It was a delayed reaction, but all the more evident owing to its occurring by itself at a distinct interval after that of the rest of the class. (Helen Keller, *The Story of my Life* (New York: Dell Publishing, 1961), 15.)

28. Rachel Brown et al., "Are there 'Autistic-Like' Features in Congenitally Blind Children?," *Journal of Child Psychology and Psychiatry*, 38 (1997), 702.

29. Brown et al., "Are there 'Autistic-Like' Features in Congenitally Blind Children?," 694.

30. Peter Hobson, *The Cradle of Thought: Exploring the Origins of Thinking* (Oxford: Oxford University Press, 2004), 195.

31. Leekam, "Why do Children with Autism have a Joint Attention Impairment?," 212.

32. Leekam, "Why do Children with Autism have a Joint Attention Impairment?," 212.

33. Leekam, "Why do Children with Autism have a Joint Attention Impairment?," 220.

34. Cf. also Claire Hughes and James Russell, "Autistic Children's Difficulty with Mental Disengagement from an Object: Its Implications for Theories of Autism," *Developmental Psychology*, 29 (1993), 498–510.

35. Leekam, "Why do Children with Autism have a Joint Attention Impairment?," 221.

36. Leekam, "Why do Children with Autism have a Joint Attention Impairment?," 220.

37. Because philosophers take knowledge to be a matter of knowledge *that*, a more common philosophical formulation of mutual knowledge would be in terms of knowing *that*: Paula knows that Jerome knows that Paula knows that Jerome knows, and so on. In the case of infants, of course, shared attention cannot be a matter of knowing *that* in this way. And the adult phenomenon that is also shared attention is, in my view, more a matter of awareness of a person than a matter of knowing *that*. So I have formulated the description of mutual knowledge in such a way that it applies to knowledge of persons as well as knowledge that something or other is the case. For an interesting study of mutual knowledge in connection with joint attention, see Christopher Peacocke, "Joint Attention: Its Nature, Reflexivity, and Relation to Common Knowledge," in *JA* 298–324.

38. Except for the limiting cases of minimal presence, which, as I explained earlier, I am leaving to one side.

39. As I know from experience, some people will object that this is not a position compatible with Catholicism because Catholicism takes God's presence to be mediated through the Scriptures, through the agency of a priest, and through the

sacraments. In my view, this is a mistaken objection that rests on a confusion about the notion of mediation. If I see the coffee cup in front of me, is my cognition direct and unmediated? Most of us would say 'yes,' even though we know the story about the neurobiological processing necessary for vision. What makes the cognition of the cup direct and unmediated is that I do not cognize the cup by means of *visually cognizing* something else, even if there is considerable processing of visual data in the brain in order for me to see the cup. In the same way, on the Catholic doctrine of the Eucharist, for example, although the real presence of Christ in the Eucharist is mediated by a priest, Christ is directly present to those participating appropriately in the sacrament. That is because Christ is not present to those participating only in virtue of the priest's being present to them, even if on Catholic doctrine the agency of the priest is a means by which the bread and wine become the real body and blood of Christ. Something similar applies also to the other cases, where there is a means which enables the presence of God to a person without its being the case that that means makes the presence of God mediated to such a person. Just as my seeing by means of my contact lenses does not imply that I see other things in virtue of first seeing my contact lenses, so also the agency of priests, the sacraments, and the Scriptures are means by which one may have direct and unmediated presence of God. That Aquinas holds such a position is made overwhelmingly clear in his biblical commentaries (among many other places) and in his explanation of the gifts and fruits of the Holy Spirit, in my view; but this is not a subject that can be canvassed in detail in passing here. I am grateful to Paul Weithman for calling to my attention the need to address this issue.

40. Johannes Roessler, "Joint Attention and the Problem of Other Minds," in *JA* 239. Roessler is here reporting work by Michael Tomasello. See also Joseph Call and Michael Tomasello, "What Chimpanzees Know about Seeing, Revisited: An Explanation of the Third Kind," in *JA* 45–64.

41. In conversation and in correspondence, John Foley has raised a series of difficult questions about my claims regarding closeness and need. His pressing questions have made me see the importance of detailed examination of the complexities of these issues, and some of what follows in the text was worked out in conversation with him.

42. Aquinas himself speaks not of mutual closeness but of mutual indwelling, in the cognitive and appetitive parts of the soul. On his way of putting the general point, the lover is not satisfied with a superficial relationship to the beloved but seeks to gain so intimate a connection with the beloved that the lover enters into the very soul of the beloved (see ST I-II q.28 a.2). This is a wonderful way of putting the idea at issue here, but an exposition of Aquinas's formulation would take me too far afield in this chapter. So I only note it and reluctantly leave to one side any further consideration of it. See also ST I-II q.28 a.3, where Aquinas explains the sense in which love leads to ecstasy, and ST I-II q.28 a.5, where Aquinas explains that love melts the frozen or hardened heart so that the beloved is able to enter into it.

43. I accept the implication that the mere physical act of copulation, by itself or with the minimal conversation the movies often associate with it, is not sufficient for closeness either.

44. I am grateful to Anja Jauernig for calling my attention to the need to make this point explicit.

45. There is an ineluctable lack of precision here, because closeness manifestly comes in degrees; and there is no precise degree of the sharing of thoughts and feelings that is necessary for a minimal degree of closeness. It is also not possible to specify just how important to Jerome the shared thoughts and feelings have to be. The lack of precision here should be neither surprising nor worrisome, however. It is not likely that there are sharp boundaries to the relation *being close to*.

46. Precision is obviously not possible here either. It is not possible, for example, to specify how much of Jerome Paula has to be able to understand to count as close to him.

47. In an earlier version of this chapter, I attempted to capture this intuition by claiming that Paula is close to Jerome only in case Jerome has needs and desires that depend on Paula for their fulfillment. John Foley has persuaded me that, as I originally explained it, this is at least misleading, if not actually false, because in the context 'need' conjures up the notion of dependence of a self-interested sort. But one person can be close to another without being dependent on that other in a self-interested way. Worse yet, Foley has made me see, it ought to be the case that, just as God can be close to a human person, so a human person can be close to God; but, if the relation *being close to* is defined in terms of needs in the way I originally suggested, then a human person could not be close to the God of traditional Christianity, who is not dependent on anything. I am grateful to Foley for calling my attention to these problems. My attempt to handle them is sketched out in what follows.

48. The notion of mattering in this context also needs clarification. We might try to gloss mattering in terms of desires, so that something M matters greatly to a person Jerome in case Jerome desires M greatly. But this gloss would be at best inaccurate. It matters greatly to Jerome whether or not there is iodine in his diet, and this is so whether or not Jerome knows anything about iodine or the effects of iodine deficiency on a human body. For present purposes, it seems to me better to understand mattering in this context in terms related to what we care about, as I explained what we care about in the first chapter. Something M matters greatly to a person Jerome in case M contributes greatly to Jerome's being what he ought to be (in the sense that it contributes greatly to Jerome's flourishing as the best he can be) or to Jerome's having what he has his heart set on or both.

49. For an interesting discussion of mutual vulnerability in love, see Bruce Langtry, *God, the Best, and Evil* (Oxford: Oxford University Press, 2008), 168–70.

50. We might wonder whether it does not also have to be the case that Paula's willingness has as at least part of its motivation her desire for Jerome's good; but,

in my view, this desire is not necessary for closeness. That is because it is possible for Paula to manage to get close to Jerome in order to prey on Jerome. Exploitative relations, as well as loving relations, can include closeness. In a case where Paula is close to Jerome in order to exploit Jerome, it will not be true that Jerome is close to Paula, however, since Paula will be hiding at least some parts of herself from Jerome. Furthermore, although in such a case Paula will be close to Jerome, it will not be true that Paula loves Jerome.

51. I am grateful to John Foley for pointing out to me the need to address explicitly the issues in this section.

52. In fact, even unfulfilled desires of a certain sort can be attributable to God as traditionally understood. That very traditional theologian Thomas Aquinas accepts the biblical text "God will have all men to be saved" (1 Tim. 2: 4) as describing an unfulfilled state of God's will; he explains the text in terms of what he calls 'God's antecedent will' (see, e.g., *De veritate* q.23 a.2). Aquinas thinks of God's antecedent will not as a volition on God's part but as an inclination; it is, as it were, the volition God would have had if everything in creation had been up to him and nothing at all had been up to the will of human beings. For further discussion of the distinction between God's antecedent and consequent wills, see Chapters 13 and 14.

53. Cf. these two well-known poems by Catullus:

> I hate, and I love.
> Why do I do this, you might ask.
> I don't know.
> But this is what I feel,
> and it tortures me. (85)
> You are the cause of this destruction, Lesbia,
> that has fallen upon my mind;
> this mind that has ruined itself
> by fatal constancy.
> And now it cannot rise from its own misery
> to wish that you become
> best of women, nor can it fail
> to love you even though all is lost and you destroy
> all hope. (75)

(*The Norton Anthology of World Masterpieces*, ed. Maynard Mack (New York: W. W. Norton and Company, 1995), i. 995.) I have used my own translation for the first poem. The Latin is this:

> Odi et amo. quare id faciam, fortasse requiris?
> nescio, sed fieri sentio et excrucior.   (Carmen lxxxv).

54. It is worth pointing out that this case indicates the possibility of higher-order desires when the first-order desire is a desire for a person and not a desire *that*.

Catullus has a desire for Lesbia. But he loathes himself because of this desire, and so he is not impartially balanced between his desire for Lesbia and his repulsion from her. On the contrary, he is alienated from his desire for her. What Catullus lacks, therefore, is a desire for a desire for Lesbia.

55. See, e.g., my "Persons: Identification and Freedom," *Philosophical Topics*, 24 (1996), 183–214, for some introduction to the issues and the literature on them.

56. Cf., e.g., ST I-II q.27 a.3.

57. I am not sure if Frankfurt would accept the claim that an agent could be whole-hearted as regards subjective evil. But, for my purposes here, the interesting point has to do with what is objectively morally wrong, whether or not an agent would acknowledge it as wrong.

58. ST I-II q.69 a.2 ad 2.

59. He might also be confused, irrational, self-deceived, or have other impairments of this sort.

60. See, e.g., ST II-II q.45 a.4 and a.6. The biblical claim can be found in Isa. 48: 22.

61. For discussion of the details of this sort of division in the self, see my "Augustine on Free Will," in Norman Kretzmann and Eleonore Stump (eds.), *The Cambridge Companion to Augustine* (Cambridge: Cambridge University Press, 2001), 124–47.

62. I note that when in the Gospels Jesus wants to portray those people most given to moral wrongdoing, he describes himself addressing them in second-person terms and saying to them, "I never knew you" (cf., e.g., Matt. 7: 23). What is at issue here is not his knowledge of facts about these people; rather, the focus is on the knowledge of persons. For Jesus to say that he does not know these evildoers is to presuppose a connection between internal integration on their part and their ability to be known by another person. Their evildoing prevents Jesus' knowing *them*. The consequence is also clear. One cannot be close to a person one does not know. The point of the claim in that passage, then, seems to be that, in virtue of their lack of integration in goodness, Jesus cannot be close to these people or united with them.

63. It is obviously possible for there to be connections between people that are ephemeral and that can be called 'union' in some extended sense. It is possible, for example, for there to be an intense sexual encounter between people who are relative strangers to each other but who find some memorable, if transient, psychological intimacy by means of that encounter. In such a case, there is no history of relationship, so that the closeness between the persons involved is of a very limited sort. The memorability of the event thus seems more a function of the sexual excitement than of the union between the persons. We can talk about such an encounter as an ephemeral union, then, but only by taking union in some analogical way.

Chapter 7

1. In the previous chapter, I explained that lack of internal integration can be found either in the will or in the intellect. But, given the connection between intellect and will, internal division in one will be correlated with internal division in the other. So to focus on internal division in the will, as I am doing here, is not to ignore internal division in the intellect but only to presuppose it.

2. For a discussion of the hierarchical nature of the will in connection with Frankfurt's account and conceptions of freedom, see my "Sanctification, Hardening of the Heart, and Frankfurt's Concept of Free Will," *Journal of Philosophy*, 85 (1988), 395–420; repr. in John Martin Fischer and Mark Ravizza (eds.), *Perspectives on Moral Responsibility* (Ithaca, NY: Cornell University Press, 1993), 211–34; also repr. in *Free Will: Free Agency, Moral Responsibility, and Skepticism*, vol. iv of John Martin Fischer (ed.), *Free Will: Critical Concepts in Philosophy* (London: Routledge, 2005), 395–420. For a discussion of these issues in connection with Aquinas's philosophical psychology, see my *Aquinas* (London and New York: Routledge, 2003), ch. 9, on freedom of the will and action theory.

3. Of course, to the extent to which she is divided within herself, it may also be true that she *does* desire union with those others, insofar as one part of her divided self may desire what the other part does not.

4. Harry Frankfurt has done more than any other contemporary philosopher to call our attention to the importance of internal integration for human wellbeing, and I am indebted to his views, although my own views on the subject differ from his in significant ways. For a summary of his views on the subject, see Harry Frankfurt, *The Reasons of Love* (Princeton: Princeton University Press, 2004). For insightful criticism of Frankfurt's position, see Richard Moran, "Review Essay on *The Reasons of Love*", *Philosophy and Phenomenological Research*, 74 (2007), 463–75.

5. I am grateful to Marilyn McCord Adams for insightful questions that prompted some of the development of this section.

6. In "Sanctification, Hardening of the Heart, and Frankfurt's Concept of Free Will," I explained and defended a use of the terms 'desire' and 'volition' informed by, but slightly different from, Frankfurt's usage. I take a volition to be a desire that would be effective in bringing about what it desires if no obstacle external to the will prevented it. *Desire* is therefore a genus within which *volition* is a species.

7. See Harry Frankfurt, "Freedom of the Will and the Concept of a Person," *Journal of Philosophy*, 68 (1971), 13; repr. in Harry Frankfurt, *The Importance of What We Care About* (Cambridge: Cambridge University Press, 1988), 11–25.

8. See, e.g., Frankfurt, "Freedom of the Will and the Concept of a Person": "It is not true that a person is morally responsible for what he has done only if his will was

free when he did it. He may be morally responsible for having done it even though his will was not free at all" (pp. 23–4).

9. See my "Persons: Identification and Freedom," *Philosophical Topics*, 24 (1996), 183–214.

10. By 'rational' here is meant not what is without passion and without love but in accordance with a cheese-paring calculation regarding narrowly conceived prudential goods only for oneself (as some academics sometimes seem to think of 'rational'). What is meant is a capacity for responding to reasons or reasons-responsiveness. It should also be noted that a person can be reasons-responsive by seeing reasons and ignoring them.

11. *Mentally non-functional* is a vague notion that I do not know how to make more precise. The amount of dysfunction in neurotic people is not sufficient for it; the amount of dysfunction in people with multiple personality disorder probably is.

12. It probably goes without saying that Frankfurt would not accept such an explanation or such a defense of the view that an agent is to be identified with his higher-order desires and volitions.

13. It is, of course, possible that an agent might be internally divided at the second-order level of the will, and that her intellect might be correspondingly ambivalent. In that case, her second-order volitions would not be authoritative for her; third-order volitions would be required. And here the unpleasant possibility of an infinite regress seems to reappear.

    If, however, we connect acts of will to acts of intellect, as Aquinas does, then third-order volitions will be rare. They will arise, for example, in an agent who is ambivalent between whole worldviews. Consider an agent raised in the milieu of the religious right but in the process of rejecting his upbringing and adopting Marxist attitudes toward religion and politics. As he considers how to vote in the upcoming presidential election, sometimes he feels the pull of his roots. He looks back at the views of his family, and his mind is once again drawn in that direction. He thinks that he should accept again the worldview that he had when he was raised. Then he thinks that it would be good for him to have a will that wills to vote for a presidential candidate on the extreme right of the political spectrum, and he wants to have such a second-order volition. At other times, however, he rejoices in what he takes to be his progress away from the misguided and constricting worldview of his childhood, and he thinks that he should be intellectively liberated from it entirely. At such times, he thinks it would be good for him to have a will that wills not to vote for right-wing candidates, and he wants to have a second-order volition of that sort. In cases of this sort, it is a person's third-order volitions, rather than his second-order ones, that are authoritative for him.

    But it is hard to know what a fourth-order volition would be. Such a volition would reflect the intellect's determination that, for example, it would be good for the agent to have the will for the second-order volitions appropriate to right-wingers. But what would such a view be except an approval of his childhood culture and an acceptance of the religious views he originally held? In that case, the putative fourth-order volition would in fact just be a third-order volition for a will reflecting those right-wing beliefs. An act of will on an agent's part stems from considerations on the part of the agent's intellect, but the intellect's reflections on what it would be good to will are connected to what the intellect takes to be good in the circumstances or in general. An agent wobbling between completely different worldviews might generate reflections on his own standards of what counts as good in general, and so he might produce third-order volitions in himself. But reflections on his reflections on his standards of goodness seem to collapse into reflections on his standards of goodness. So, while it is possible to construct a case in which it is plausible to assign third-order volitions to an agent, higher-order volitions will collapse into third-order, or even second-order, volitions.

14. Libertarians may add here "and that is not causally determined."

15. Helga Schneider, *Let Me Go* (New York: Walker & Company, 2001).

16. Schneider, *Let Me Go*, 160.

17. Someone might object that the conclusion I am arguing for here holds only in these extreme cases. Two sorts of cases can seem to be counter-examples to my claim here. (1) The moral wrongdoing seems small and marginal to the relationship of love. (2) The objectively wrong moral acts a wrongdoer engages in are accepted as morally right by the entire community of the wrongdoer, and the wrongdoer also believes them to be right.

    In connection with (1), consider someone who habitually engages in an apparently trivial morally wrong act. Suppose, for example, that a mother compulsively steals paper clips, in small numbers, when she is able to do so without being observed. The putative objector supposes that this moral wrongdoing will make no difference to the mother's relations of love with her daughter, for example. But here the objector seems to me to be mistaken. There will be some things that the mother wants to hide from her daughter. She will not want her daughter to know that she steals paper clips. In fact, she will not want her daughter to know that she is hiding anything from her daughter. She will feel some anxiety about the fact that she wants to hide things from her daughter, and possibly also some shame. And these—the anxiety and the shame—will also be things she wants to hide from her daughter. To me, it seems clear that a mother in such a condition will be less close to her daughter than she would otherwise be and that she will suffer some willed loneliness where her daughter is concerned.

    (2) Consider the case of a slaveholder in the Antebellum South who is convinced of the moral correctness of slavery and who lives in a community that shares his convictions. On Aquinas's views, which seem to me right, it is not possible to engage in the evils of slave-owning without some recognition somewhere in the structure of a divided mind that slave-owning is morally repulsive and without some desire on the part of a divided will not to do to other human beings the hurtful things accompanying slave-owning. In order to persist in being a slave-owner, on

Aquinas's views, it is necessary to hide a great many things from oneself. But a person who has hidden a great many things from himself is accordingly also impaired in his ability to be close to other people.

So for these reasons, I think that the conclusion that can be seen clearly in the extreme cases involving Nazis and other moral monsters is one that applies also in other cases of the sort envisaged by the objection at issue in this note. I am grateful to Ron Belgau for calling my attention to the need to address this point.

18. For more discussion of this sort of case, see Chapter 13.

19. Someone might suppose that for Aquinas this claim has to be qualified with the clause "except for those in Hell," but this would be a mistaken supposition. On Aquinas's views, the doctrine of divine omnipresence has no such exception. For further discussion, see Chapter 13; see also the discussion of God's relations to Satan in Chapters 9 and 15.

20. For exploration of these views on Aquinas's part and defense of this interpretation of his position, see my *Aquinas*, ch. 9, on providence and suffering.

21. I am grateful to Paul Weithman for calling my attention to the need to make this point explicit.

22. I am not sure whether or not Frankfurt would think an agent could be whole-hearted as regards subjective evil. But, for my purposes here, the interesting point has to do with what is objectively morally wrong, whether or not an agent would acknowledge it as wrong.

23. For a discussion of Aquinas's views on these issues, see my *Aquinas*, ch. 2, on goodness.

24. He might also be confused, irrational, self-deceived, or have other impairments of this sort.

25. For a detailed discussion of this part of Aquinas's moral psychology, see my *Aquinas*, ch. 9, on freedom.

26. For some discussion of why slavishness and servility are incompatible with closeness, see the sections on closeness in Chapter 6.

27. Heinz Hoehne, *The Order of the Death's Head* (1969; repr. New York: Penguin, 2000), 162. It should be added that Himmler explained what he saw in Heydrich with the erroneous theory that Heydrich had Jewish blood somewhere in his family tree.

28. Quoted in David Cesarani, *Becoming Eichmann* (Cambridge, MA: Da Capo Press, 2004), 301.

29. Michael Bloch, *Ribbentrop* (1992; repr. London: Abacus Books, 2003), 125.

30. Richard Overy, *Goering* (1984; repr. New York: Barnes and Noble Books, 2003), 15–16.

31. Mao was enslaved to his own bad habits even when they were detrimental to the things he himself wanted for himself, and his later years were marked by distrust, strife, and isolation where the people around him were concerned. See, e.g., Li

Zhisui, *The Private Life of Chairman Mao*, trans. Tai Hung-Chao (New York: Random House, 1994).

32. Marilyn McCord Adams, *Horrendous Evils and the Goodness of God* (Ithaca, NY: Cornell University Press, 1999), 86.

33. Adams, *Horrendous Evils and the Goodness of God*, 124.

34. For the quotation and for a strong case against Benedict's position built on an examination of ancient Greek culture, see Douglas Cairns, *Aidos: The Psychology and Ethics of Honour and Shame in Ancient Greek Literature* (Oxford: Oxford University Press, 2002), 27 ff.

35. Martha Nussbaum, *Hiding from Humanity: Disgust, Shame, and the Law* (Princeton: Princeton University Press, 2004), 207.

36. Cairns, *Aidos*, 23 (footnote omitted).

37. Cairns, *Aidos*, 45.

38. Claudia Card, *The Atrocity Paradigm: A Theory of Evil* (Oxford: Oxford University Press, 2002), 206 (footnote omitted).

39. Moshe Halberthal, *Concealment and Revelation: Esotericism in Jewish Thought and its Philosophical Implications*, trans. Jackie Feldman (Princeton: Princeton University Press, 2007), 143. Halberthal is interested in the causes of shame. On his view, "Improper exposure, contrary to a person's will, results in shame" (Halberthal, *Concealment and Revelation*, 143), and he makes a helpful distinction between what he calls 'primary shame' and 'secondary shame,' depending on whether the exposure is shaming solely in virtue of being involuntary or also in virtue of revealing something deficient in the person exposed. I find Halberthal's explanation of the causes of shame insightful; my own focus, however, is on the nature of shame, rather than on its causes.

40. Nussbaum, *Hiding from Humanity*, 209.

41. For a discussion of this possibility, see Simon Wiesenthal, *The Sunflower* (New York: Random House, 1998).

42. For a discussion of hatred, see Ch. 5, n. 74.

43. Perhaps the most famous case of someone anxious about rejection by a person he knows not to be among the living is Dante. As Dante writes the reunion between him and Beatrice in his *Purgatorio*, it opens with Beatrice excoriating Dante mercilessly for his faults. Even an entirely imaginary character can serve the same role. A person who never knew his father or anything about his father might have imagined a father for himself, and he could come to feel shamed in the eyes of this imaginary father.

44. See Chapter 3 for further discussion.

45. In an insightful psychological study of shame and the problem of evil, Gerrit Glas says: "The prototypical case of shame is a situation in which the person

feels exposed and embarrassed by the look of a critical or devaluing other . . . The typical inclination of the shameful person is to hide and to avoid the look of others . . . Shame may be related to actual looks and remarks, but also to what one expects others might think or remark . . . in cases of shame, [depersonalization] denotes the incapacity to reconcile the intensely humiliating look of the internalized other with one's basic sense of self" ("Elements of a Phenomenology of Evil and Forgiveness," in Nancy Nyquist Potter (ed.), *Trauma, Truth, and Reconciliation: Healing Damaged Relationships* (Oxford: Oxford University Press, 2006), 182–3).

46. Or, to put it more precisely but more clumsily, in actively rejecting a desire for him.

47. Sylvia Nasar, *A Beautiful Mind* (New York: Simon and Schuster, 1998).

48. Jean Vanier, *Becoming Human* (Mahwah, NJ: Paulist Press, 1998), 54.

49. The connection may also hold the other way around. If Paula refuses or repudiates a desire for Jerome, then, if Jerome finds Paula's reaction to him appropriate, he will be shamed by it, because he will see his own ugliness in her rejection of him.

50. See, e.g., Vanier, *Becoming Human*, 67.

51. Thomas More makes a similar point. Speaking of a person suicidal in consequence of having been shamed, More says:

it would be a charitable thing if some good, virtuous folk . . . will sometimes go see him . . . to get advice and counsel from him on their own matters of conscience . . . This would be, in my opinion, a good way to restore his courage and lift him out of the peril of that desperate shame. (Thomas More, *A Dialogue of Comfort against Tribulation*, ed. Mary Gottschalk (Princeton: Scepter Press, 1998), 148)

52. Vanier, *Becoming Human*, 6.

53. Quoted in Ashley Montagu, *The Elephant Man: A Study in Human Dignity* (Lafayette, LA: Acadian House, 2001), 46.

54. For some discussion of Sophie Scholl and the actions of her small group, see, e.g., Annette Dumbach and Jud Newborn, *Sophie Scholl and the White Rose* (Oxford, Oneworld Publications, 2006). The widely used Internet resource Wikipedia says about Sophie Scholl:

Sophia Magdalena Scholl (May 9, 1921–February 22, 1943) was a member of the White Rose non-violent resistance movement in Nazi Germany. She was convicted of treason after having been found distributing anti-war leaflets at the University of Munich with her brother Hans. As a result, they were both executed by guillotine. Since the 1970s, Scholl has been celebrated as one of the great German heroes who actively opposed the Third Reich during the Second World War . . . The White Rose's legacy has, for many commentators, an intangible quality. Playwright Lillian Garrett-Groag stated in *Newsday* on February 22, 1993, that "It is possibly the most spectacular moment of resistance that I can think of in the 20th century . . . The fact that five little kids, in the mouth of the wolf, where it really counted, had the tremendous courage to do what they did, is spectacular to me. I know that the world is better for them having been there, but I do not know why." In the same issue of *Newsday*, Holocaust historian Jud Newborn noted that "You cannot really measure the effect of this kind of resistance in whether or not X number of bridges were blown up or a regime fell . . . The White Rose really has a more symbolic value, but that's a very important value." Posthumously, Sophie Scholl has been given many honors, and the recent movie of her life, *The Final Days*, has been widely acclaimed.

See also the discussion of Sophie Scholl in Chapters 12 and 15.

55. This possibility is explored further in Chapters 8, 12, and 13.

56. Some readers will suppose that, on Aquinas's views, the doctrine of simplicity rules out responsiveness on God's part, so that the responsiveness of God has no place in a presentation of a Thomistic worldview. For arguments that this is a mistaken understanding of the implications of the doctrine of simplicity as Aquinas understands it, see my *Aquinas*, ch. 3, on simplicity.

Chapter 8

1. Margaret Urban Walker, *Moral Repair: Reconstructing Moral Relations after Wrongdoing* (Cambridge: Cambridge University Press, 2006), 188–9.

2. In his webpage, "The Mongols," www.uwgb.edu/dutchs/WestTech/xmongol .htm, Steve Dutch says:

   The original source of this quote is hard to track. Howorth (1876, p. 404) [Henry Hoyle Howorth, *History of the Mongols, from the 9th to the 19th Century* (London: Longman, Green, and Co, 1876)] quotes it and attributes it to an early 19th century history in French by Baron d'Ohsson. The possibility it's a fabrication can't be wholly ruled out.

   If it is a fabrication, it is one based on human experience of the depth of human evil; if it is fiction, it is, like all very good fiction, veridical.

3. I am grateful to Richard Swinburne for persuading me that this objection needed to be addressed in detail.

4. Richard Swinburne, *Providence and the Problem of Evil* (Oxford: Oxford University Press, 1998), 86–7.

5. It could be argued that, *mutatis mutandis*, Anselm's account of the will is also in this tradition. In Anselm's case, the inbuilt propensity is *not* itself a propensity for moral wrongdoing, but only a propensity for what is advantageous whether or not what is advantageous is morally good. For Anselm, as for Aquinas, a propensity for moral wrongdoing comes into the world only with the Fall. But, like Kant and Swinburne, Anselm thinks that, without some force counterbalancing the tendency of reason toward the good, real free will and real moral agency would be impossible. For Anselm's discussion of these issues, see his treatises *De libertate arbitrii* and *De casu diaboli*.

6. For a detailed argument to this effect, see Alvin Plantinga, "Religion and Science," in Edward N. Zalta (ed.), *Stanford Encyclopedia of Philosophy* (2007).

7. By 'guilt' in this connection, I do not mean the *feeling* of guilt but the condition of having done what is morally wrong or the disposition to do what is morally wrong.

8. Because of the close connection Aquinas accepts between the intellect and the will, any defect in the will has a correlate of some sort in the intellect as well. But, because the defect in question is primarily in the will, I will leave to one side any consideration of the concomitant state of the intellect. For further discussion of these issues, see my *Aquinas* (London and New York: Routledge, 2003), ch. 9, on freedom.

9. It is a universal condition only for post-Fall human people; because Aquinas accepts the doctrine of original sin, he also supposes that in its original condition humankind was free of this propensity. It is clumsy to keep adding the qualifier 'post-Fall,' and so I will omit it hereafter; but it should be understood throughout in the discussion that follows.

10. Thomas Aquinas, *Super ad Hebraeos*, ch. 12, lect. 2.

11. Thomas Aquinas, *Expositio super Job*, ch. 9, sects. 24–30; trans. in *The Literal Exposition on Job: A Scriptural Commentary Concerning Providence*, trans. Anthony Damico, interpretive essay and notes Martin D. Yaffe (Atlanta, GA: Scholars' Press, 1989), 179.

12. That is why it is a mistake to take the dividing line between heaven and hell as an arbitrary cut in a continuum of moral quality, as Ted Sider does (see his "Hell and Vagueness," *Faith and Philosophy*, 19 (2002), 58–68). On the Thomistic doctrine of hell, those in hell are not those whom God elects not to forgive; they are those whose wills refuse God's love. Insofar as heaven is or necessarily requires a state of union with God, those who are in hell are not those whom God has refused to forgive but those with whom even God is not able to be united because they have refused his love. But to refuse love is an all-or-nothing thing. Even if there are degrees of acceptance of love, there is an all-or-nothing distinction between a will that elects to accept love to any degree and a will that elects to refuse it.

13. Some theologically literate readers who care about the doctrine of simplicity will balk at the idea of God's being responsive to things in the human will. For a detailed argument to show that divine simplicity does not rule out such responsiveness, see my *Aquinas*, ch. 3, on simplicity.

14. The qualifier 'invariable' is necessary in this context because, as I explained in the preceding chapter, there are complicated relations between guilt and shame; and it is possible, for example, for a person to be shamed in consequence of some great moral wrong that he has done. For an interesting discussion of shame as a result of moral guilt, see Jeffrie Murphy, *Getting Even: Forgiveness and its Limits* (Oxford: Oxford University Press, 2003).

15. For a discussion of this case, see the preceding chapter. As the rest of this chapter will make clear, this point still holds even if the shame in question has guilt over moral evil as its source.

16. Homer, *Iliad*, trans. Richard Lattimore (Chicago: University of Chicago Press, 1951), bk. IX, ll. 432, 600–10:

> at long last Phoinix the aged horseman spoke out
>
> . . . . .
>
> 'Listen then; do not have such a thought in your mind; let not
> the spirit within you turn you that way, dear friend. It would be worse
> to defend the ships after they are burning. No, with gifts promised
> go forth. The Achaians will honour you as they would an immortal.
> But if without gifts you go into the fighting where men perish,
> your honour will no longer be as great, though you drive back the battle.'
>
> Then in answer to him spoke Achilleus of the swift feet:
> 'Phoinix my father, aged, illustrious, such honour is a thing
> I need not. I think I am honoured already in Zeus' ordinance
> which will hold me here beside my curved ships as long as life's wind
> stays in my breast, as long as my knees have their spring beneath me.'

17. For those who might be inclined to raise an eyebrow at the use of 'men,' it is worth noting that that noun is the only one appropriate to the case. What is at issue for Achilles is the honor garnered in his society by males who kill and maim other males in hand-to-hand combat. It is hard not to think that, as regards this honor accorded by human beings to each other, Achilles had it right when he said to the embassy that it is not worth having.

18. I owe any understanding or insight I have into this part of the Iliad to the late John Crossett, whose superb, self-sacrificial undergraduate teaching gave me the basic furniture of my mind, and much more besides. I have tried to express my debt of gratitude to him in my eulogy for him in Donald Stump, Eleonore Stump, James Alexander Arieti, and Lloyd Gerson, (eds.), *Hamartia: The Concept of Error in the Western Tradition: Essays in Honor of John Crossett*, (Lewiston, NY: Edwin Mellen Press, 1983).

19. Augustine, *Confessions*, VIII.9. I like and have therefore used (with slight modifications) the translation by William Watts (Cambridge, MA: Harvard University Press, 1968).

20. Both Aquinas's account and his terminology are more complicated than can be presented in short space here. The presentation of justification and sanctification that follow, and the very terms themselves, are my own abbreviation of Aquinas's own position and terminology. For a fuller exposition of Aquinas's views on this score, see chs 12 and 13, on faith and grace, in my *Aquinas*.

21. In putting the point this way, I am leaving out of account everything having to do with Christ. Christ's incarnation, passion, death, and resurrection are ordinarily

taken to be central to the remedy for the post-Fall human condition, by Aquinas as well as most other Christian thinkers in the history of the Christian tradition. In my *Aquinas*, ch. 12, on faith, and ch. 15, on atonement, I have tried to show the way in which the account of justification and sanctification, as I have summarized it here, is connected to Aquinas's account of Christ's life and salvific work. On my interpretation of Aquinas's views, these two accounts are two sides of one coin: justification and sanctification are the story as regards human beings; the theological correlate is the incarnation, passion, death, and resurrection of Christ. In focusing here on justification and sanctification, I am giving an accurate portrayal of Aquinas's views, but I am omitting the Christology that is part of those views. My reason for this omission is the sensible recognition that one cannot do everything in one book.

22. Augustine, *De libero arbitrio*, III.xix.

23. The desire in the petition is itself a second-order desire. There is something mildly puzzling about the description of the act of will at issue as a person's desire that God strengthen her will since the proper objects of the will seem to be only those things that are within the scope of the will's ability to command. God's actions are not included in that scope. At any rate, as second-order desires and volitions are generally understood, they are a matter of the will's commanding itself; and so a desire that God do something does not seem to be a second-order desire. But, in fact, a will which desires that God strengthen it is a will that is trying to command itself; it is just reaching for something outside itself as a means to that end.

24. As I will explain below, this is a culmination that occurs after death, on Christian doctrine.

25. I have adapted slightly Harry Frankfurt's use of the terms 'desire' and 'volition,' for reasons explained in my "Sanctification, Hardening of the Heart, and Frankfurt's Concept of Free Will," *Journal of Philosophy*, 85 (1988), 395–420. As I am using the terms, a volition is a desire that is effective enough in its strength to produce action if nothing outside the will impedes it.

26. See my *Aquinas*, ch. 9, on freedom, and ch. 13, on grace and free will, for further discussion of these issues. Cf. also, e.g., SCG III.148 and ST I-II q.111 a.2 ad 1, in which Aquinas says that grace operates on the will in the manner of a formal cause, rather than in the manner of an efficient cause.

27. Cf. my "Augustine on Free Will," in Norman Kretzmann and Eleonore Stump (eds.), *The Cambridge Companion to Augustine* (Cambridge: Cambridge University Press, 2001), 124–47, which gives detailed argument for a similar position held by Augustine.

28. Augustine, *Confessions*, VIII.

29. The sudden conversion of the apostle Paul in a religious vision on the road to Damascus is an example.

30. By the same token, people become moral monsters slowly; see my *Aquinas*, ch. 11, on wisdom.

31. Pelagianism comes in different varieties, but all the varieties share this claim: it is possible for there to be some good in a human will without divine help or grace. The rejection of Pelagianism is essentially a rejection of this claim. For a discussion of the anti-Pelagian cast of Aquinas's thought, see ch. 12, on faith, in my *Aquinas*.

32. The phrase 'moral and spiritual' is my attempt to find some brief way of indicating that the regeneration in question has to do not only with intrinsic qualities of a human person but also with that person's closeness to God and second-personal connection to God.

33. The contention over the right way to understand this doctrine, or even the right way to understand Aquinas's understanding of this doctrine, has prompted not only books but pitched political battles. Elsewhere I have defended a particular interpretation of the doctrine and Aquinas's construal of it; in this context, unfortunately, it is possible to give only the briefest summary of that interpretation. For more detailed discussion, see my *Aquinas*, ch. 12, on faith, ch. 13, on grace, and ch. 15, on atonement.

34. For a detailed discussion of this claim, see my *Aquinas*, ch. 12, on faith.

35. ST I-II q. 113 a. 5; cf. also I-II a. 113 q. 6–7. A person does not have to remember and detest each sin he has ever committed in order to be justified, Aquinas says; rather he has to detest those sins of which he is conscious and be disposed to detest any other sin of his if he should remember it.

36. In Chapter 11, I explore in detail the narrative of Abraham's binding of Isaac; and I explain that, in the tradition Aquinas accepts, Abraham becomes the father of faith in consequence of his willingness to offer Isaac to God. In that chapter, I focus on the way in which Abraham comes to understand the goodness of God and to trust in it, and I take that trust and that understanding to be Abraham's exemplar faith. The story of Abraham's faith therefore illuminates the details of the intellectual and volitional attitude toward God's goodness necessary for faith. It is in effect an illustrative enlargement of a telescoped part of faith, as Aquinas understands faith.

37. See, e.g., ST II-II q. 2 a. 5–7.

38. For a discussion of Aquinas's position on this distinction, see my "Eternity, Simplicity, and Presence," in Gregory T. Doolan (ed.), *The Science of Metaphysics: Historical and Philosophical Investigations* (Washington: Catholic University of America Press, 2010).

39. See, e.g., ST II-II q. 2 a. 7 ad 3.

40. Aquinas's position here is illustrated vividly by an incident related in Colin Turnbull's study of Pygmies. The Pygmy serving as Turnbull's aid and guide was introduced to a Catholic priest, Father Longo, who took the opportunity to try to evangelize him. According to Turnbull, the Pygmies have a religion of their

own; without much in the way of theology or established religious institutions, they believe in a god of the forest in which they live and whose children they hold themselves to be. In general, apart from this one contact with a Catholic priest, the Pygmies Turnbull knew were entirely insulated from contact with Christian beliefs. Nonetheless, Turnbull recounts that, after the encounter with the priest, his Pygmy guide told him, "Pere Longo was right, this God must be the same as our God in the forest" (Colin Turnbull, *The Forest People* (1961; repr. New York: Simon and Schuster, 1968), 258).

41. See, e.g., my *Aquinas*, ch. 3, on simplicity.

42. See, e.g., ST I-II a.9 q. 1.

43. I say "in theory" because, on theological doctrine accepted since Augustine's time, the will of a post-Fall human being is blocked in one of these moves—namely, that from rejecting to accepting grace. For a discussion of Augustine's position and its historical influence, see my "Augustine on Free Will," 124–47.

44. The double-minded attitude of a person in such a condition has a good Franciscan-type illustration in the two voices of this poem "The Sea":

> *How is it to swim in the sea?*
> The sea? Where is it?
> I seek the sea.
> I swim, I swim, no bottom, no shore, no reason
> at all.
> Nothing to reach for.
> Where is it?
> *What is that all around you?*
> Wet, ever wet.
> Yet I thirst. I thirst, I crave.
> I cannot reach it,
> I crave it.
> *Have you gone to land for it?*
> There is no land.
> This is a fable made by fools
> to keep us bounding forward always,
> swimming, swimming, reaching out, thirsting.
> Land? Idiots believe in it. The wise know better.
> *Are you one of the wise?*
> Here is what we say.
> "We swim, we swim, we tickle the tide.
> Thirsting, bursting, barely alive.
> Living, living, alive till we die,
> until the oceans are dry."
> *Is this wisdom?*
> It is crap.
> The stuff that keeps us captive.

But how is it to swim in the sea?
To tell the truth, I love the sea.
I think it was made for me,
if it was made at all.
Good.
Yet why does it ignore my thirst?
Dry, slap-hard dryness,
gluing my tongue,
shriveling cells.
Yet strangely,
I love it.
I love it.
Do you love the thirst?
Was I was made to thirst?
Or to find thirst's answer in this world of wet?
Let it in.
Let what in?
You swim through God.
All is nothing except for this sea.
Never far away.
Always quenching your urge.
Have you not noticed?
No.
Open and see.

(I am grateful to John Foley for allowing me to use this text.)

45. See Augustine, *Confessions*, VIII.12.

46. She has alternative possibilities because she can reject grace or she can be quiescent with respect to grace. For an argument that neither option is Pelagian, see my *Aquinas*, ch. 13, on grace and free will.

47. As I was at pains to show in an earlier chapter, desiring a person is not reducible to desiring that something-or-other be done or be the case. (See the discussion of Odysseus and Kalypso in Chapter 3.)

48. Aquinas thinks that in his initial prayer in the garden of Gethsemane Christ is an example of someone who desires union with God (and is in fact in such union) but whose desires are (non-culpably) discordant from God's. In that prayer —"Father, let this cup pass from me"—Christ desires what in fact God does not desire and he desires that God should desire what Christ desires. And yet in making this prayer Christ is not in rebellion from God but in union with him. (See, e.g., ST III q.18 a.5.)

49. ST II-II q.19 a.4.

50. For more discussion of the nature of the true self, see Chapter 7.

51. Harry Frankfurt, "The Faintest Passion," *Proceedings and Addresses of the American Philosophical Association,* 66/3 (1992), 8.

52. Harry Frankfurt, "Autonomy, Necessity, and Love," in Hans Friedrick Fulda and Rolf-Peter Horstmann (eds.), *Vernunftbegriffe in der Moderne: Veröffentlichungen der internationalen Hegel-Vereinigung* (Stuttgart: Klett-Cotta, 1994), 437.

53. Harry Frankfurt, "On the Necessity of Ideals," in Gil Noam and Thomas Wren (eds.), *The Moral Self* (Cambridge, MA: MIT Press, 1993), 20.

54. Harry Frankfurt, *The Importance of What We Care About* (Cambridge: Cambridge University Press, 1988), 83.

55. Frankfurt's emphasis on activity as central to the true self is to be distinguished from his insistence on passivity as regards the objects of love. For Frankfurt, there are "volitional necessities" of love: we cannot choose what to love. See, e.g., Harry Frankfurt, *The Reasons of Love* (Princeton: Princeton University Press, 2004).

56. For the distinction between a metaphysical and a psychological sense of 'the true self,' see Chapter 7.

57. This point was made in conversation by Richard Moran. In conversation, Frankfurt has maintained that the human ideal of activity, and activity as control, can be seen in Aristotle's notion of God, as thinking about thinking, not acted upon by anything outside itself. But not all religions see the divine as isolated within itself in this way. Judaism, for example, takes God to be not only related to everything in the world as its creator but also specially related to a particular people whom he loves and to whom he reacts. Christianity puts loving interpersonal relations into the deity itself with the doctrine of the Trinity. But, as I argue below, any person who enters into loving relations with another must be passive as well as active, since being in a loving relationship includes being the recipient of another person's activity and responding to it. (In my view, nothing in this claim is incompatible with the medieval theological doctrine that God is impassible or that God is *actus purus*, but it is not possible to explain and defend this view in passing in a note. For further discussion of this point, see my *Aquinas*, ch. 3, on simplicity. See also my "God's Simplicity," in Brian Davies and Eleonore Stump (eds.), *The Oxford Handbook to Thomas Aquinas* (Oxford: Oxford University Press, 2011), and "Eternity, Simplicity, and Presence."

58. For an excellent study of the importance of passivity in human life, see also Ingolf Dalferth, *Becoming Present: An Inquiry into the Christian Sense of the Presence of God* (Leeuven: Peeters, 2006), esp. pp. 198–203.

59. See, e.g., Harry Frankfurt, "On the Usefulness of Final Ends," in Harry Frankfurt, *Necessity, Volition, and Love* (Princeton: Princeton University Press, 1998), 82–94.

60. Edmund Burke, *A Philosophical Enquiry into the Origin of our Ideas of the Sublime and Beautiful,* ed. Adam Phillips (Oxford: Oxford University Press, 1990). For an interesting contemporary philosophical discussion of the nature of human reactions to what is great in nature, art, and religion, see Howard Wettstein, "Awe and the

Religious Life: A Naturalistic Approach," *Midwest Studies in Philosophy*, 21 (Notre Dame, IN: University of Notre Dame Press, 1997), 257–80. Wettstein brings out clearly the passive element in such reactions.

61. Teresa of Avila, *The Collected Works*, vol. i, trans. Kieran Kavanaugh and Otilio Rodriguez (Washington: Institute of Carmelite Studies, ICS Publications, 1976), ch.18, p. 121.

62. Teresa of Avila, *The Collected Works*, i, ch. 19, p. 122.

63. See, e.g., Frankfurt, "Autonomy, Necessity and Love," 443: "The authority for the lover of the claims that are made upon him by his love is the authority of his own essential nature as a person. It is . . . the authority over him of the essential nature of his own individual will."

64. Frankfurt, "Autonomy, Necessity and Love," 438.

65. If we take the desire for being the recipient of someone else's desires as itself an active desire, then unrequited love—unsatisfied or unfulfilled love, love that never achieves its goal—might be construed as just an active state. But full-fledged love, which reaches its goal of being united with another person, could not be so construed; to be in a mutual loving relationship includes certain sorts of passivity.

66. If, as I argued in Chapters 6 and 7, in the discussion of closeness and of shame, there can be a desire for a person or a rejection of a person, then there can also be resistance to a person.

67. See Chapter 5 in this connection. Cf. also Job 14: 15, where Job attributes to God a desire for Job.

68. Song of Songs 1: 8, 5: 9, 6: 1.

69. Matt. 25: 40.

Chapter 9

1. The translation by Barrows and Macy is frequently very free, but in this case I am not sure that I myself could do better than they have done. The German, which can be found in *Rilke. Das Stunden Buch* (Frankfurt am Main: Insel Verlag, 1902; repr. 1972), 91, is as follows:

> Vielleicht, dass ich durch schwere Berge gehe
> in harten Adern, wie ein Erz allein;
> und bin so tief, dass ich kein Ende sehe
> und keine Ferne: alles wurde Nähe
> und alle Nähe wurde Stein.
> Ich bin ja noch kein Wissender im Wehe,—
> so macht mich dieses grosse Dunkel klein;
> bist *Du* es aber: mach dich schwer, brich ein:
> dass deine ganze Hand an mir geschehe
> und ich an dir mit meinem ganzen Schrein.

2. See Chapter 2 for further discussion of this issue.

3. See Eric Auerbach, *Mimesis* (Princeton: Princeton University Press, 1953), ch. 1.

4. See Robert Alter, *The Art of Biblical Poetry* (New York: Basic Books, 1985), ch. 4.

5. See *The Book of Theodicy: Translation and Commentary on the Book of Job* by Saadiah Ben Joseph Al-Fayyumi, trans. L. E. Goodman (New Haven: Yale University Press, 1988). For my interpretation of Saadya's theodicy, see my "Saadya Gaon and the Problem of Evil," *Faith and Philosophy*, 14 (1997), 523–49.

6. It is my hope to explore the topic of Elihu's speeches in subsequent work. In my view, we can understand Elihu as holding a divine-command theory of ethics and as coming down on the opposite side of the Euthyphro dilemma from that which God presupposes in the divine speeches. On this view, the first line of God's speech to Job is a wholesale rejection of Elihu and his position.

7. I am not here taking back my claim that I am omitting considerations of defense from this chapter and deferring them till all the narratives have been examined. To excavate and illuminate the narrative's explanation for Job's suffering is not the same thing as reflecting on whether or not that explanation constitutes a morally sufficient reason for God to allow Job to suffer.

8. For lack of a better expression, I will distinguish these kinds of suffering as external and internal, although I mean these terms in an analogical rather than a literal sense. Ordinarily, the loss of a house in a flood will produce what I am calling an external suffering. For some women, the loss of a breast to breast cancer can cause internal suffering.

9. Marvin Pope (ed. and trans.), *Job* (The Anchor Bible; 3rd edn.; New York: Doubleday, 1973).

10. Pope (ed. and trans.), *Job*, p. lxxiii (footnote omitted).

11. Pope (ed. and trans.), *Job*, p. xv.

12. Pope (ed. and trans.), *Job*, p. xxiii.

13. Pope (ed. and trans.), *Job*, p. lxxv.

14. Cf., e.g., Pope (ed. and trans.), *Job*, p. lxxx.

15. Pope (ed. and trans.), *Job*, pp. xvii–xxii.

16. Pope (ed. and trans.), *Job*, p. xviii.

17. Pope (ed. and trans.), *Job*, p. xix.

18. Throughout this book, I use the masculine pronoun to refer to the Deity, although I realize that in the current climate this usage is controverted. But it is not possible to explore and adjudicate every controversy tangentially raised by the texts and the subject matter I am discussing in this book; and, in the narratives I explore, the masculine pronoun is routinely applied to God.

19. Pope (ed. and trans.), *Job*, p. lxxx.

20. Pope (ed. and trans.), *Job*, p. lxxxi.

21. Pope (ed. and trans.), *Job*, p. 291, n. 3b; cf. also p. 318, n. 9b.

22. Pope (ed. and trans.), *Job*, p. xxii.

23. Pope (ed. and trans.), *Job*, p. lxxx.

24. The Anchor Bible translates this line as "Lo, I am small;" but the root meaning of the Hebrew word is to be contemptible or to be disgraced, so 'vile' seems better than 'small.'

25. Pope (ed. and trans.), *Job*, p. xxii.

26. Perhaps it is true that no translation can reproduce exactly the information conveyed by the original text being translated. Nonetheless, linguistic utterances typically convey a great deal of information—nuances and shadings of meanings, affect, implicit imagery—which can be utterly lost even in translations made by those competent at the original languages. To translate well requires not just competence at the syntax and semantics of another language but also a great deal of sensitivity to language in general and considerable expertise at the language *into which* one is translating. Insofar as a translation fails to convey the information a contemporaneous reader of the text in its original language would have gotten from the text or renders the original in such a way as to alter significantly the affective implications of the original text, the translation is not faithful to the original and does not portray it accurately. The flat-footedness of this Anchor Bible translation, evidently dead to the rhythm and nuances of English prose, and prone to a roller-coaster effect in its styles of diction, is concerning in this regard. But because I mean to use the Anchor Bible commentary as a foil, it seemed to me mandatory to use the Anchor Bible translation here. (I make this same apology for my use of the Anchor Bible translation also in Chapter 12, although I recognize that there are two different translators at issue in these two different chapters. As subsequent notes will make clear, the worry about translation I raise here is not my only concern about the Anchor Bible translations, but it is not possible to deal in detail with these worries in passing in the notes.)

27. I have used the Anchor Bible translation throughout except where noted, for the sake of fairness, since I am disputing its interpretation of the text. In this case, I have departed from the Anchor Bible translation at two points. The Anchor Bible commentator translates as 'gods' a Hebrew phrase which it acknowledges to mean literally 'sons of God.' Since the Anchor Bible translation thus obscures just what I think is interesting about this phrase, I have translated it more literally. (See also n. 28 for further discussion of the Hebrew at issue here.) I have also translated as 'rejoiced' what the Anchor Bible translator renders 'exulted,' but just because 'exult' can carry an array of connotations, such as gloating, for example, which do not seem warranted by the Hebrew. Finally, the Anchor Bible translator prints the text as if it were English poetry, in short broken lines beginning with words

that are capitalized; but since there is no warrant in the Hebrew text for any such arrangement, I have simply omitted it.

28. I am aware that the Hebrew locution translated 'the sons of God' is idiomatic and has extended meanings. Nonetheless, although the Hebrew expression is undoubtedly formulaic, formulas, like cold metaphors, carry the resonance of their literal meaning with them. Even a term that has become an idiom and has in consequence been distanced from its original concrete meaning retains some of the flavor of that meaning, in my view—and this claim is sufficient for the point I am making in the text. Interestingly, Saadya Gaon's interpretation of this expression is idiosyncratic, but its idiosyncratic character confirms my point. Saadya departs from the interpretation customary by his time, which takes the phrase to refer to angels. Instead, he takes the phrase to refer to a community of human persons who are somehow specially close to God and specially to be considered God's beloved; for Saadya, they are an as-it-were human family of God. Robert Eisen says of Saadya's interpretation that

Saadiah offers a novel interpretation of these figures [the sons of God] by suggesting that they are not angels, as is commonly understood, but human beings who live in the land of Uz along with Job. The *beney elohim* [sons of God] are rendered by Saadiah as "God's beloved" in accordance with the translation of the term *ben* as "beloved," even though it is usually understood as "child" . . . (*The Book of Job in Medieval Jewish Philosophy* (Oxford: Oxford University Press, 2004), 24)

(Even though it is innovative, as Eisen says, Saadya's interpretation of 'the sons of God' is still conservative by comparison with the radical interpretation of Maimonides. On Maimonides's Aristotelian views, the expression 'the sons of God' has to be interpreted allegorically to mean something like the forms of matter or the forces of nature.) Finally, it is perhaps worth remarking in this context that the biblical texts focused on sons and God's relations to sons are extensive. For an excellent study of sonship in the Hebrew Bible, see Jon Levenson, *The Death and Resurrection of the Beloved Son* (New Haven and London: Yale University Press, 1993). I am grateful to Yehuda Gellman for calling my attention to the need to address this issue explicitly.

29. These interactions do not count as second-personal, strictly speaking, on the explanation of second-person experience I gave in an earlier chapter, because they are interactions between God and creatures which are not themselves persons. But, insofar as these non-human creatures are portrayed in personal terms in the divine speeches, God's relations with them are also portrayed as personal interactions.

30. I am, of course, alluding here to Martin Buber's insistence that human beings have to say 'thou' to God in order to be rightly related to him. (See Martin Buber, *I and Thou*, trans. Walter Kaufman (New York: Touchstone Books, 1970).) It is worth noting that, in God's speeches to Job, God says 'thou' to his creatures,

including to those of his creatures which are inanimate. The metaphysical and theological implications of this part of this divine speech are worth examining for their suggestion that every creature participates not only in being, as the classical theologians maintained, but also in the personhood of a three-personed God. But this particularly rich, not to say outrageous, idea is outside the scope of this book. I am grateful to John Foley, who first helped me understand the question "Can one say 'thou' to the universe?" and then showed me how to see both the question and an affirmative answer to it on analogy with classical medieval doctrines of participated being.

31. For those who cannot resist asking why a good God would deprive an ostrich of wisdom, perhaps the answer is that, if the ostrich had wisdom, it would not be an ostrich. Perhaps in choosing to create an ostrich, God is choosing to create a creature deprived of wisdom—but still very much worth having in the world.

32. The Anchor Bible translates the Hebrew word as 'heedless' rather than as 'forgets,' but its standard and root meaning is 'forgets.'

33. The Anchor Bible translation is marked by a tone-deafness to the nuances of English that requires patience in the reader, but here the problem extends to grammar. I have changed the Anchor Bible's "Play with him like a bird" to "play with him as with a bird."

34. See Chapters 3 and 4 for discussion of these issues.

35. Not everyone accepts this condition on morally sufficient reasons for allowing the suffering of unwilling innocents. For a discussion of the controversy, see William Alston, "The Inductive Argument from Evil and the Human Cognitive Condition," in Daniel Howard-Snyder (ed.), *The Evidential Argument from Evil* (Bloomington, IN: Indiana University Press, 1996), 111–14. Since this condition clearly makes the enterprise of theodicy harder, in Part 4, on theodicy and defense I simply note that Aquinas accepts it and leave to one side any consideration of the controversy over it. For further discussion of this issue, see Chapter 13.

36. This point is restricted to innocent, *unwilling* sufferers. In Chapter 13, I discuss in detail the difference it makes to this issue if the sufferer in question has explicitly or implicitly given consent to the suffering. See also my "Providence and the Problem of Evil," in Thomas Flint (ed.), *Christian Theism and the Problems of Philosophy* (Notre Dame, IN: University of Notre Dame Press, 1990), 51–91. I am grateful to Alvin Plantinga for calling my attention to the need to make this point clear in this connection.

37. The *ceteris paribus* clause is necessary here because a good mother might be stuck with a choice only of evils, and the lesser of two evils might require letting her child suffer with no benefit accruing to him at all. For example, the mother might have to choose between alleviating a small suffering of her child's or a life-threatening suffering of some third person. In that case, she might let her child suffer without

there being a benefit for the child. Whether this sort of dilemma results from the limits on human power or whether an omnipotent deity might also be in such a position is an issue that arises in connection with some attempts at theodicy.

38. Aquinas explicitly endorses such a view of God's providence in various places. See, e.g., SCG III.112.

39. There is, of course, an additional complication in the case of Job, because there God is at least actively collaborating in Job's suffering, not just allowing it. But I am reserving questions of theodicy, to which this issue belongs, to the last part of this book. See also my "Saadya Gaon and the Problem of Evil," *Faith and Philosophy*, 14 (1997), 523–49.

40. I have rendered the Hebrew literally; the Anchor Bible has "I had heard of you by hearsay."

41. In this encounter between God and Job, there is dyadic shared attention, as the nature of God's address to Job and Job's response to God makes clear. God is also engaged in making revelations about himself, his actions, and his desires; for his part, Job has previously made his own thoughts and desires known to God, who is reacting to those desires in his speech to Job. So the major components of significant personal presence are here. For a discussion of personal presence, see Chapter 6.

42. For explanation and defense of this claim, see Chapter 4.

43. The mystical literature is full of cases in which human beings report themselves able to intuit an emotion in a supernatural person who cannot be cognized by means of the visual system. I have no idea what neural system would facilitate such a cognition. But it is worth noticing that the mirror neuron system, which facilitates such cognition in cases where the visual system gives information about the face of another person, is not ruled out. See the discussion of the use of the mirror neuron system in the appropriation of stories in Chapter 4.

44. For discussion of veridicality instead of truth in connection with knowledge of persons and related concepts, see Chapter 4.

45. I am grateful to Kelly Clark for calling my attention to the need to address this puzzle.

46. I have this information from the whiteboard at my gym, which is not a reliable source of information about anything; but the truth or falsity of this particular claim about Tums does not matter, since the point at issue for this chapter is about bio-availability, analogously understood, and not about the nutritiousness of Tums.

47. For another example of this sort of indignation or expostulation, consider, in Chapter 12, the speech Jesus makes to Martha when she finds him wanting in care toward her.

48. It is perhaps worth noting in this regard one element in the biblical book Habbakuk. In that book, the prophet issues a string of passionate accusations against God,

which seem to come straight from the heart. But he finishes the apparent outburst by saying, as it were, to himself that now he will wait to see if God will come to him to remonstrate with him and reprove him. In Habbakuk, the prophet is hoping for himself just the sort of reaction on God's part that seems, at first, hard to understand in Job's case.

49. See my *Aquinas* (London and New York: Routledge, 2003), ch. 16, for Aquinas's interpretation of the book of Job.

50. Genre criticism is, of course, often brought to bear on this text; and the judgment that this text is folkloric might be thought to preclude the sort of analysis I give of it. But scholars such as Alter and Auerbach have made us aware not only of the density of the biblical texts but also of the reward for unfolding that density. It would be a mistake, in my view, to prohibit at the outset such unfolding of the text of Job solely on the untested grounds that such unfolding is impossible for folkloric texts. I am grateful to Frank Burch Brown for calling my attention to the need to spell out this point.

51. It should perhaps be added that for those, such as Aquinas, who accept the doctrine that God is perfectly loving (or the more theologically complicated doctrine that God is love), it is also true that God hates nothing he has made. That *nothing* will include even the most alienated of his creatures; it will include even Satan, on any construal of Satan.

52. For those who have episodic bouts of wanderlust, it is probably good to point out that there is a difference between being restless, on the one hand, and loving to travel, on the other. A person who loves to travel has one settled spot which is home but has some desires or needs for some things not found at home. By contrast, a person who is restless cannot find any spot which counts as home. Any spot in which he is meets too few of his needs and desires for him to be willing to stay there for long. I am grateful to Colleen McCluskey for calling to my attention the need to make this point explicit.

53. For further discussion of the problems of love and internal division in the psyche, in connection with Catullus's attitude toward Lesbia, and for the poem from which the line is taken, see Chapter 6.

54. One might also suppose that, if there were no more than this to God's motivation, God would have called another son of God to Satan's attention, since (one would suppose) the comparison would be even more to Satan's detriment if the other person compared were more nearly a peer of Satan's than Job is.

55. Even if the final form of the book were being dictated by political or religious considerations, the ends sought could not be advanced by aesthetically incompetent work; and so a reasonably competent redactor should have been able to achieve those ends with a coherent story. We might, of course, in the end assess the book of Job as an aesthetic failure anyway; but that ought to be an interpretative strategy of last resort, forced on us when the attempt to understand the book as a product of intelligence and competence has failed.

56. Timothy Williamson, *The Philosophy of Philosophy* (Oxford: Blackwell, 2008), ch. 2. For a discussion of Williamson's point in connection with a consideration of the methodology of this book, see Chapter 2 above.

57. Where *eisegesis*—reading in—is the opposite of the more ordinary *exegesis*. For an example of 'eisegesis' used as a term of dismissal for an interpretation, see (as one example of many that might be given) Joseph Fitzmyer (ed. and trans.), *The Gospel According to Luke* (The Anchor Bible; New York: Doubleday, 1981), i. 623.

58. For further discussion of this kind of possibility, see Chapter 13.

59. For further discussion of this position, see Chapter 13.

60. For further discussion of this point, see Chapter 13.

61. In this connection, it is significant that the outcome Satan is hoping and working for, that Job will curse God to his face, has an echo in the description of the way Satan's leaving God to attack Job is described: Satan went out from the face of God. Complete distance from the face of God seems worse than face-to-face angry confrontation, since confrontation is still amenable to reconciliation, in a way at least much harder in complete absence.

62. Satan means it to undermine trust in Job's goodness on God's part, and the narrative's presentation of Satan's answer invites the narrative's audience to share in the questioning of Job's goodness.

63. Defenders of Molinism will suppose that an omniscient God does know the things I here claim are not known to anyone. For a discussion of this objection and some response to it, see Chapter 13.

64. Thomas More, *A Dialogue of Comfort against Tribulation*, trans. Mary Gottschalk (Princeton: Scepter Publishing, 1998), 82.

65. Some philosophers would suppose that it is not possible for God to take risks, because God has middle knowledge—that is, knowledge of what a person would freely do in any particular set of circumstances. Aquinas's theology does not include middle knowledge, and so in this book I am not presupposing middle knowledge on God's part. For discussion of middle knowledge and Aquinas's theodicy, see Chapter 13.

66. Someone might suppose that it makes no sense to talk about God's reasons for believing what Job will do, given that God has omniscient foreknowledge, so that this story cannot be read in the way I am interpreting it by anyone who accepts the story as describing (in any sense) the thoughts and actions of an omniscient deity. In my view, this objection is mistaken, because it misses the way in which what Job does is logically dependent on God's decision in this case. God cannot base his choice to remove his protection from Job on what Job will choose to do when his steadfastness is tested, since, unless God does choose to remove his protection from Job, Job's steadfastness will not be tested. Because Job's being in a condition to chose steadfastness under testing is logically dependent on God's

choice about protecting him, God's choice cannot also be logically dependent on God's knowledge of what Job will do in such circumstances. Someone might object here that an omniscient God knows what a human person *would* do in any given circumstances and so would also know whether Job would curse him if he were afflicted. Consequently, the putative objector will say, God's decision can be based on his middle knowledge, rather than his foreknowledge. But there are good reasons for rejecting the claim that middle knowledge is possible; and, if it is not possible, then it also is not part of God's knowledge. In any event, Aquinas does not accept middle knowledge on God's part; and so it is not part of his theodicy, or the defense of this book.

67. Someone might be inclined to rejoin that middle knowledge is unnecessary to support the objection's conclusion; God's foreknowledge is sufficient to rule out trust. Job does indeed go on to bless God, rather than cursing him, and so God can foreknow that Job will remain steadfast in his affliction. Therefore, there can be no question of trust or distrust in Job on God's part. But this rejoinder is confused. However exactly we are to understand the temporal (or eternal) relations between what God decides in his dealings with Satan and what Job does in his affliction, it is clear that there is a logical order between God's decision and Job's actions. Which of the possible futures will be actual depends on God's decision; if God decides not to remove his protection from Job, then there will be no affliction for Job and consequently also no steadfastness on Job's part. Since there is this logical order, God cannot use knowledge of the actual future in choosing to give or refuse permission to Satan. (See n. 66 for the same point on a somewhat different issue.)

68. There are many other obvious questions that I am not addressing here. At the end of the chapter, I will have something to say about some of them, such as those raised by the death of Job's children; but the most important obvious questions, such as the question whether there is a morally sufficient reason for God to permit Job's suffering, I am postponing till Chapter 13, for the reasons I gave at the outset of this chapter.

69. Someone might suppose that, if God complies with Satan's malice, then God is malicious, too. But this objection is mistaken. Malice is a matter of motive, and the same effect can be brought about by agents acting with very different motives. Both Hamlet and Polonius operate to bring Hamlet into contact with Ophelia, but their motives are radically different.

70. There is some slight variation in the pattern, and that variation might well be significant, given the other subtleties of the text. But I will leave the variation to one side, in the interest of pursuing the main thread of the episode.

71. As far as that goes, if pleasure in repetition had a part in crafting the final form of the book of Job, it would have been easy enough to expand the opening episodes with Satan, since there is a natural partition into three. Job's possessions, Job's family, and Job's person might have been attacked seriatim, thereby yielding material for

three reiterations of the scene, instead of the two with which we are currently provided.

72. The question whether God is thereby using Job simply as a means to a good for Satan obviously arises here. The answer to the question will emerge by the end of the chapter.

73. For helpful discussion of Olympias, see J. N. D. Kelly, *Golden Mouth: The Story of John Chrysostom, Ascetic, Preacher, Bishop* (Ithaca, NY: Cornell University Press, 1995). For Paula, see J. N. D. Kelly, *Jerome: His Life, Writings and Controversies* (London: Duckworth, 1975; repr. 1998). The role of Joanna of Naples in the formative years of the Franciscan order is discussed in John Moorman, *A History of the Franciscan Order from its Origins to the Year 1517* (Oxford: Clarendon Press, 1968). For Glueckel of Hamlyn, see *The Memoirs of Glueckel of Hamlyn*, trans. Marvin Lowenthal (New York: Schocken Books, 1977). There is a helpful discussion of Abigail Williams in George Marsden, *Jonathan Edwards: A Life* (New Haven: Yale University Press, 2003).

74. When Sojourner Truth died, Frederick Douglas wrote about her:

In the death of Sojourner Truth, a marked figure has disappeared from the earth. Venerable for age, distinguished for insight into human nature, remarkable for independence and courageous self-assertion, devoted to the welfare of her race, she has been for the last forty years an object of respect and admiration to social reformers everywhere. (Quoted in Nell Irvin Painter (ed.), *Narrative of Sojourner Truth* (New York: Penguin Books, 1998), 232.)

The record of her funeral says: "Sojourner Truth was this day honored as none but the great are honored ... from the mud and slime of basest enslavement, [Sojourner Truth] sought and found her level among the purest and the best" (Painter (ed.), *Narrative*, 230).

75. I am not here assuming that Job was a historical person, and my point does not depend on such an assumption. The question at issue here is a question of interpretation about a narrative. Why, in the narrative, would God do something that is so apparently purposeless and bad as complying with Satan's desire to try to drive Job into hatred of God? The answer about the motivations of God in the story has to do with the changes in Job in the story, and these changes in Job in the story are such as to make Job in the story into the kind of person who could serve as a historical exemplar epitomizing the ideals of the West.

76. In Chapter 14, on the desires of the heart, I revisit this issue and discuss in detail the philosophical and theological underpinnings of the claims I make here.

77. In Chapter 13, I examine further the notion of glory in a human life and consider the scale on which it is measured. Here I rely just on our intuitive understanding of the idea.

78. Because this is not a book on the book of Job but rather only a chapter in a book on the problem of suffering, I have had to leave to one side many features of the story

worth commenting on. In particular, I have omitted consideration of the relations between Satan and Job. Satan's fervent wish that Job should be alienated from God and his manifest desire for Job's suffering shows that Satan is alienated from Job as well as from God; and it seems reasonable to see that alienation as made worse by God's allowing Satan to attack Job. To the extent to which God cares for Satan and cares for Job, the relationship between the two of them will also be a concern for him, so that something worth having from God's point of view is diminished or lost by God's giving Satan permission to harm Job. It is not possible to explore this point adequately in a note; for present purposes, it seems to me sufficient to see that, as Satan is sketched in the story, it may be that he would hate Job only more if he were refused permission to afflict Job.

79. In this context, by saying that a person is the primary beneficiary of something God does with or to that person, I mean that God would have done otherwise if that particular person had not been a beneficiary, no matter what other good things might have resulted.

80. It is true that the story of Satan is incomplete, in the sense that we are told nothing further about Satan's condition or relations with God after the second episode brings about Job's second experience of suffering. But the end of Job's own story does give us some information about Satan. Insofar as Job's prosperity is restored to him, God's hedge about Job is also restored, and Satan's malice is effectively kept out again. It may be that the narrative gives us no further information about Satan, because the story about Satan has served its function in the narrative when it has shown us the larger context within which the story of Job is to be understood. I am grateful to John Kavanaugh for calling to my attention the need for this note.

81. In other respects, the two cases are mirror images of each other. Satan's suffering comes from his refusal of goodness, and it would be alleviated if he were to cooperate with God in integrating himself around a love of goodness and God. In his suffering, Job *is* integrated in this way, and his face-to-face encounter with God produces closeness between him and God. Satan's suffering and his coming into God's presence prompt in him only a strengthened malice.

82. It is as if the narrative were an argument against Richard Swinburne's attempted theodicy. (See his *Providence and the Problem of Evil* (Oxford: Oxford University Press, 1998).) Swinburne argues that the suffering of unwilling innocents can be justified by the use others can make of their suffering. The narrative shows the way in which suffering, justified only by the benefits it brings to the sufferer, can be used to benefit others, who are also final ends in their own right.

83. It is possible that this point could be extended even to animal suffering. As I explained in the introductory chapter, the defense presented in this book is limited; for the reasons I gave there, it does not include the suffering of animals. Nonetheless, it may be that the interpretation I have been presenting here may also give some help in thinking about the general problem of the suffering of

animals. Although in his description of his relations with the animals, God portrays himself, in general, as concerned with the welfare of each of the animals directly, there are occasional notes that may seem to undermine that general picture. So, for example, God says he hunts the prey for the lions. But then the prey seems simply instrumental to the well-being of the lions. If the story of Job presents divine providence as operating in the fractal sort of way I have argued for here, however, then it may be that the same sort of approach will explain God's relations with the lions and their prey. Perhaps even in his relations with animals God operates in the fractal way. But I mean only to gesture in this direction as a possibility. Insofar as the suffering of animals is outside the scope of my project, I raise the suggestion only to leave it to one side.

84. For more discussion of this issue, see Chapter 13.

85. Saadya Gaon accepts a similar idea and builds it into a general point about one kind of suffering. As Robert Eisen puts it, on Saadya's view "when an individual experiences suffering as a trial, God will offer him no explanation [of his suffering] because it would spoil one of the purposes of the trial . . . " (*The Book of Job in Medieval Jewish Philosophy* (Oxford: Oxford University Press, 2004), 19).

86. It is helpful to see this point about the story here, but a discussion and defense of it have to wait till Chapter 13.

Chapter 10

1. Marilyn McCord Adams, *Horrendous Evils and the Goodness of God* (Ithaca, NY: Cornell University Press, 1999), 26.

2. Adams's emphasis in her discussion of horrendous evils can leave some readers with the mistaken impression that, on her definition of 'horrendous evil,' a horrendous evil is an evil such that the life of the sufferer of that evil is in actual fact not a good for him. But this impression is just a confusion. Nothing in Adams's definition of horrendous evils rules out the possibility that the horrendous evil suffered by a person is redeemed for that person, so that the sufferer does have, even so, a life that is a great good for her. To ward off gratuitous trouble, however, I note here that I am using the expressions 'horrifying evil' or 'horrifying suffering' where I mean to call attention to the atrociousness of the evil or suffering without implying that the life of the person involved in the evil or suffering is in fact not a good for him.

3. *Oedipus at Colonus*, ll. 104–5.

4. *Oedipus at Colonus*, ll. 577–8.

5. There are two ways of thinking about brokenness and healing. In the claims I am making about Oedipus here, I am taking brokenness to be a matter of (1a) the loss of those goods whose loss does not by itself make a person morally or spiritually

worse; and I am taking healing to be a matter of (1*b*) the restoration of those goods. But, of course, it is possible to focus only on (2*a*) the loss of those goods whose loss does make a person morally or spiritually worse, and to think of healing as a matter of (2*b*) the restoration of only *those* goods. In the period when Oedipus is sovereign in his city, there are things in him that need healing, because he is unwittingly married to his mother and is unaware that he is a parricide. When the story of Oedipus's life ends, he is healed as regards those moral or spiritual things. It is characteristic of some Greek tragedy that there is a chiastic movement for the protagonist of the tragedy. At the start of the play, the protagonist is in an enviable position as regards goods in sense (1) and a lamentable position as regards goods in sense (2); by the end of the play, his condition is just the reverse. Insofar as Milton means *Samson Agonistes* to be modeled on a Greek tragedy, the same chiastic structure can be found in his play with regard to Samson. Once Samson has been captured, blinded, exiled, imprisoned, and crushed into humiliation, it is not possible for him to return to his earlier state, in which he was a sighted, triumphant conqueror in hand-to-hand combat with the enemies of his people. *This* brokenness is irremediable. But the spiritual or moral brokenness sketched in his prayer at Lehi and fully virulent in his affair with Delilah *is* curable, as his poignant last prayer in the temple shows. Milton himself calls attention to the last glorious state of Samson in his death in the Philistine temple, as I will make clear later in this chapter. I owe my understanding of the nature and structure of Greek tragedy to John Crossett, who gave me my basic understanding of classical Greek thought and much more besides.

6. Aeschylus is also well known for the view that suffering leads to wisdom, but whether Aeschylus meant that the wisdom always comes to the sufferer is disputed. So, for example, Denniston and Page write:

   His [Agamemnon's] mathos . . . what he learns from all this, is hard to see. Nobody supposes that he was morally improved by the divinely thrust-on killing of his daughter; or that, even if he had emerged from that experience a wiser and better man, his ultimate doom would have been different. Of course others may learn from the example of his fate: this is how Zeus puts mankind in general on the road to understanding, PHRONEIN BROUTOUS HODWSANTA; only the sinner himself is excluded from the company of learners. Yet this explanation—that Aeschylus meant that the rest of the world should mark the sinner's doom and accordingly mend its ways—is plainly unsatisfactory, for 179ff. strongly suggest that it is the sinner himself who is 'to learn through suffering.' (Aeschylus, *Agamemnon*, ed. John Dewar Denniston and Denys Page (Oxford: Clarendon Press, 1957), 86.)

   I am grateful to James Alexander Arieti for calling this point to my attention and for providing this reference.

7. See also in this connection the quotation from Aeschylus's *Agamemnon* given in the conclusion to Chapter 15.

8. There is a sufficient connection between intellect and will that the qualifier 'primary' is needed. For an explication of a Thomistic theory of the relation

between intellect and will, which I take to be substantially correct, see my *Aquinas* (London and New York: Routledge, 2003), ch. 13, on free will. I am grateful to James Alexander Arieti for calling my attention to the need to address this point.

9. *Oedipus at Colonus*, ll. 266–7.

10. Because I am focusing on the brokenness and ruin of the life of a perpetrator of great evil, I am concerned with a somewhat different problem from that discussed by Ian Boyd in his excellent paper "The Problem of Self-Destroying Sin in John Milton's *Samson Agonistes*," *Faith and Philosophy*, 13 (1996), 487–507. Boyd puts the problem that concerns him this way:

> Self-destroying sin is evil, the doing of which gives a Christian *prima facie* reason to doubt whether her life could be counted a great good to her on the whole. That is, most people would agree that her doing this sort of evil constitutes a *prima facie* reason to doubt whether, given the inclusion of such evil action, her life can be a great good to her on the whole. (p. 489)

I am concerned not with the way in which the inclusion of a serious sin by itself mars a life; rather, I am concerned with the broken and ruined lives, felt as broken and ruined by the sufferer, where the culpability for the suffering lies with the sufferer. Furthermore, as I now see the case of Samson, my evaluation of his case differs from Boyd's, which I at one time shared. Boyd says: "it would, of course, have been better if Samson could have attained all of the goods he did and fulfilled God's promise without sinning. But, given the choices Samson made, his suffering at his sin (and God's response to it) is sufficient for the attainment of the goods that defeat his evil" (p. 498).

On Boyd's evaluation, although the combination of the moral evil of Samson's actions and the subsequent good of Samson's heroism constitute a good life for Samson, it is not clear that there would not have been a better life for Samson if God had brought about Samson's death before he began the process of wrecking his life by moral wrongdoing. And so, on Boyd's evaluation the problem that concerns me here remains. There seems no answer to the question why an omniscient, omnipotent, perfectly good God would allow Samson to live long enough to engage in the serious moral wrongdoing that ruins his life. There is an answer to this question only in case there is some good for Samson that would not have been attainable without the wrongdoing and the ruined life that it yields. That is, there has to be some Christian analogue to the view of the Greek tragedians that there is some great good that cannot be gotten without suffering.

11. I do not mean to suggest, and nothing I say here implies, that the problem of suffering is not raised in a formidable way by the problem of the suffering of unwilling innocent sufferers. I have already examined one case of that sort in the preceding chapter on Job, and the succeeding chapters will consider further cases of the same sort.

12. A question of this sort is raised also by Al-Ghazali. He says:

Let us imagine a child and a grown-up in Heaven who both died in the True Faith, but the grown-up has a higher place than the child. And the child will ask God, Why did you give that man a higher place? And God will answer, He has done many good works. Then the child will say, Why did you let me die so soon that I was prevented from doing good? God will answer, I knew you would grow up to be a sinner; therefore it was better that you should die as a child. Then a cry goes up from the damned in the depths of hell, Why O Lord, did you not let us die before we became sinners? (*Averroes, Tahafut Al-Tahafut*, trans. S. Van Den Bergh (London: Gibb Memorial Trust, 1978), p. x)

I owe this reference to James Alexander Arieti.

13. Daniel Jonah Goldhagen, *Hitler's Willing Executioners* (New York: Knopf, 1996).

14. It should be clear that there is nothing about this view that is reducible to the position of Job's comforters. Sometimes a person who has contracted cancer is healthy for all practical purposes, because the disease is in remission; and an analogous point applies to Job. On Christian doctrine, the problem is that the disease is there, even when it is asymptomatic; and it will sooner or later kill its victim if it is not cured. Furthermore, even if we grant that, like all other human beings, innocent Job has the potential for great moral evil in him, it is as wrong-headed to think of his suffering as punishment for that condition as it is to think of the suffering attendant on treatment of an asymptomatic cancer as punishment inflicted on the patient by the patient's doctor. Suffering can come because of a disease without its being the case that the suffering is a punishment for the disease. To infer from the fact that a person suffers that the sufferer is guilty of some wrong act for which the suffering is punishment is as disgusting as it is mistaken. It seems to me quite right that in the story of Job this position evokes the wrath of God. For further discussion of this issue, see Chapter 8 on the human tendency to moral wrongdoing and Chapter 9 on Job's moral status.

15. For detailed exposition of such claims, see my *Aquinas,* ch. 12 on faith, and ch. 13, on grace. See also Chapter 8, for a discussion of these claims as they affect the problem of suffering.

16. Those literate in the history of philosophical theology will recognize the problem presented in this paragraph as a version of Augustine's puzzle over grace and free will. For my own attempt at a solution to this puzzle, see "Augustine on Free Will," in Eleonore Stump and Norman Kretzmann (eds.), *The Cambridge Companion to Augustine* (Cambridge: Cambridge University Press, 2001), 124–47, as well as my *Aquinas,* ch. 13, on grace and free will. The point at issue in the text here remains the same even if my attempted solution to Augustine's puzzle is correct. If it were better for a moral monster to have died at birth, why would God not bring about the death of such a person at birth or at any rate before that person's perpetration of great evil?

17. I put the point in terms of the availability of such benefits, rather than their possession, in order to leave room for perpetrators of great evil who have such

benefits available to them but do not possess them. I will take up this sort of case in Chapter 13.

18. *Paradise Lost*, bk. I, ll. 25–6.

19. I am also not the only person to think that Milton's *Samson Agonistes* is useful for understanding the story of Samson. In addition to Boyd, "The Problem of Self-Destroying Sin," see also, for example, James Crenshaw, *Samson* (Atlanta: John Knox Press, 1978), 143–8.

20. Horace, *Ars Poetica*, 137–9: 'parturient montes, nascetur ridiculus mus.' I am grateful to James Alexander Arieti for helping me with this reference.

21. *The Complete Poetical Works of John Milton*, ed. Douglas Bush (Boston: Houghton Mifflin Co., 1965), 513.

22. For a sensitive account of the suffering entailed by blindness, there is nothing comparable to John M. Hull's *Touching the Rock: An Experience of Blindness* (New York: Pantheon Books, 1990).

23. For the biblical rules regarding Nazirites, see Num. 6: 2–8.

24. There is, of course, also a prophecy in Oedipus's story—namely, the prophecy that sets the tragedy in motion, that Oedipus will kill his father and marry his mother. But, although this prophecy could be interpreted as an indication that the gods have ordained Oedipus for the course his life takes, it would take a particularly tendentious person to consider a destiny to parricide and matricide as a vocation.

25. In the story, both the Philistines and the Israelites share this view. After Samson attacks the Philistines, they come up against Judah with an army. The men of Judah are indignant against Samson for endangering the whole community by his attack, and they resolve to turn Samson over to the Philistines to ward off attack on the whole community. See Judg. 15: 9–13.

26. I have translated 'Yahweh' as 'Lord' here and throughout in this chapter, in order to conform more to ordinary usage than to academic practice only recently become customary in some circles.

27. Judg. 13: 8.

28. See Judg. 14: 5–6, 14: 19, 15: 14–15.

29. Judg. 16: 20 says of Samson that he did not know that the Lord had departed from him.

30. Milton has Samson say of God,

> I was his nursling once and choice delight,
> His destined from the womb,
>
> . . . .
>
> He led me on to mightiest deeds
> Above the nerve of mortal arm
> Against the uncircumcised, our enemies.
> But now hath cast me off as never known . . .   (ll. 633–41)

This is not nearly good enough, in my view.

31. *Paradise Lost*, bk. IV, ll. 71–4.

32. *Paradise Lost*, bk. IV, ll. 508–11.

33. I say 'in the genus' since, obviously, there are much worse tortures than those Samson endures. That there are much worse things to suffer, however, does not alter the generic classification of Samson's pains as difficult to endure without going mad.

34. As will shortly become clear, I disagree with Milton's assessment that Samson is the sole cause of his suffering —the sole author perhaps, if by 'author' we mean the one ultimately responsible, but not the sole cause.

35. Contemporary interpreters tend also to read the story in this way. For example, see Robert G. Boling's commentary in *Judges* (The Anchor Bible; New York: Doubleday, 1975), 249: "[Samson's] treason is the betrayal of state secrets and the tragic squandering of his great strength . . . "

36. It would undoubtedly be good to have some explanation of Delilah's motives and character. But insofar as this narrative is the story of Samson's life and not of hers, the narrative does not give us enough information to understand her in the same way we can grasp something of Samson.

37. I do not mean to imply that Samson is wholehearted in his refusal to trust Delilah or that he does not trust her for anything or that he has for her none of the warmth and affection for which, as we usually suppose, trust is requisite. Some of Samson's behavior, such as his willingness to go to sleep in Delilah's presence or to lie in her lap, makes it clear that he is affectionate toward her and he supposes he is safe in her presence in some circumstances, to some degree, no doubt for reasons that have only partly to do with *her*. Nonetheless, it is manifest that he lies to Delilah about the source of his strength because he knows that she cannot be trusted to keep his secret, even if the price of revealing it is his death. That Samson is often internally divided against himself and complicated in his reactions is evident in the story, in my view.

38. Though this is how some contemporary interpreters read the story at this point. So, for example, Boling (*Judges*, 249) says: "[Samson] could not believe, as in the wedding story, that the woman would betray him."

39. Another way to think about this point is to ask whether Samson thinks that God will give Samson whatever he needs no matter what Samson does. The episode with Delilah strongly suggests that this is indeed exactly what Samson thinks. I am grateful to Scott Macdonald for this point.

40. It is true that, insofar as Samson is called by God to fulfill a particular mission, then his doing anything which might conduce to his failure to fulfill his mission is prohibited to him. But the mere revelation of his Nazirite status is not sufficient to undermine his ability to fulfill his mission. And so secrecy does not seem obligatory

on Samson in consequence of his divinely appointed mission. I am grateful to Scott MacDonald for calling my attention to this point.

41. For a particularly post-modernist expression of outraged sensibilities as regards both Milton and Samson, see D. D. Guttenplan's "THINK TANK: Is Reading Milton Unsafe at Any Speed?," *New York Times*, Dec. 28, 2002, 9(B).

42. Actually, the text says so twice: 15: 20 and 16: 31. Contemporary scholars see in this doubling an indication of an editorial hand that has combined two different accounts of Samson (Boling (ed. and trans.), *Judges*, 240). The first occurrence comes in the text that describes Samson's single-handed defeat of the Philistine army that has come to take him and God's provision of water for him afterwards, and the second occurrence comes after the text that describes Samson's death. So another possibility is that the first occurrence is meant as a sort of articulate ellipsis, indicating the ordinary more routine activities of judging that followed this spectacular warlike beginning. At any rate, the narrative records no more great battles or stunning military victories for Samson after the first occurrence of the line in question.

43. Boling (ed. and trans.), *Judges*, 240. For various scholarly views on the connection between Samson's hair and his strength, see, for example, Victor Matthews, *Judges and Ruth* (Cambridge: Cambridge University Press, 2004), 163–4, and Yairah Amit, *The Book of Judges: The Art of Editing*, trans. Jonathan Chipman (Boston and Leiden: Brill, 1999), 305–6.

44. In a different context and for a different purpose, Thomas More makes a similar point. He says, "though [Samson's] strength failed him when he did not have his hair, he does not seem to have had strength always at hand when he did have his hair, but only at such times as it pleased God to give it to him" (Thomas More, *A Dialogue of Comfort against Tribulation*, ed. Mary Gottschalk (Princeton: Scepter Press, 1998), 143.

45. For a different view that nonetheless sees Samson's culpability as related to his lack of care for his Nazirite vow, see Amit, *The Book of Judges*, 287.

46. Someone might wonder whether God should not have failed to provide water for Samson at Lehi, thereby teaching Samson not to presume on God or to suppose that God is somehow in Samson's service. On this objection, it should have been possible for God to have taught Samson from the beginning how to be rightly related to God. This objection supposes that Samson's main defect is a failing that can be cured by divine teaching or, perhaps, divine displays of power. But to see the story in this way is to fail to grasp the importance of personal relationships, both for human flourishing in general and for the interpretation of this narrative. Even God cannot establish or sustain a relationship with another person unilaterally. Samson's problem is not that he is insufficiently virtuous in one way or another—though he *is* insufficiently virtuous. His main defect is that he closes himself off, in self-protective loneliness, and thereby makes it impossible

even for God to be close to him. In this condition, he is impervious to love in the strenuous mode.

47. For further discussion of this claim, see Chapter 6.

48. For the difference between the ordinary and the strenuous senses of 'love,' see Chapter 7.

49. On the account of love I give in Chapter 5, love includes the desire for union; but that desire is compatible not only with the absence of the union desired but also with the contrary desire, for the absence of closeness, as well. The complexity of human beings stems from their ability to be double-minded and half-hearted.

50. For the notion of a desire for a person, see Chapter 3 and the discussion of Odysseus and Kalypso.

51. For the connection between shame and desire of a person, see Chapter 7.

52. Contumely can be thought of as a correlative of humiliation. If Paula is (or ought to be) humiliated by actions of Jerome's intended to have this effect on her, then Jerome is contumelious toward Paula. A shaming attitude toward a person is similar enough to an attitude that humiliates her that a shaming attitude can be classed with the contumelious, in my view.

53. As far as this issue goes, it may be that earlier episodes in Samson's story should be construed as containing an element of providential warning, for example, in those cases where the Lord's spirit fails to come on Samson. It may be that God's departure from Samson at the crucial moment has been foreshadowed for Samson at earlier times, so that, contrary to appearances, God's departure from Samson does not occur out of the blue, as it were. On the other hand, of course, in those other cases Samson was strong even though God's spirit did not rush into him then. I am grateful to Michael Barber for calling my attention to the reading on which God's departing from Samson is a last resort on God's part, something God reaches for reluctantly, rather than a first move.

54. Readers familiar with the novel will know that there is more to this part of the story of Darcy and Elizabeth than is captured in my brief sketch here. But the point of my remarks remains the same even when all the details of the episode are filled in: Elizabeth would not have accepted Darcy if he had renewed his suit in the same complacent conviction that she could not conceivably reject him.

55. Heb. 11: 31.

56. I recognize that different thinkers have different conceptions of the nature of faith and also that the element in Samson's story that seems to someone most to exemplify faith is a function of that person's conception of faith. For discussion of the Thomistic account of faith, see Chapter 8. For a detailed examination of the Thomistic conception of faith, see my *Aquinas*, ch. 12, on faith, and ch. 13, on grace and free will.

57. Dan. 9: 4–19.

58. See, e.g., 1 Sam. 23: 2, 23: 10–12, 30: 8; 2 Sam. 2: 1, 5: 19, 5: 23–4.

59. I am not failing to notice that many other people died in the collapse of that temple in addition to Samson. But, on the theory of providence implied by the story of Job, each of those people is the protagonist of his or her own story; and *this* is an interpretation only of Samson's story. Reflection on the deaths of each of those victims of Samson's violence in the Philistine temple has to be included in the interpretations of the stories of the lives of those victims, by those interpreters who know those stories.

60. In Chapter 13, I consider in detail the scale of value for human beings and the nature of a flourishing human life, which, on the worldview of Aquinas, are to be included in the description of the possible world of the defense at issue in this book.

61. I am grateful to Scott MacDonald for calling my attention to the need to clarify this point.

62. For further discussion of this example, see Chapter 8.

63. There are those who argue that it is, in fact, quite the contrary. See John Carey, "A Work in Praise of Terrorism? September 11 and *Samson Agonistes*," *Times Literary Supplement*, Sept. 6, 2002, pp. 15–16. As this chapter makes plain, I do not share Carey's attitude.

64. This way of seeing Samson's expectant waiting for God, in blindness in the Philistine temple, is reminiscent of Milton's attitude toward his own apparently useless condition, rendered the more helpless by blindness. Milton concludes the sonnet in which he laments his failures and powerlessness by saying, "They also serve who only stand and wait" (Sonnet XIX; I am grateful to Michael Barber for calling my attention to the aptness of this sonnet of Milton's in this context). And it helps us to understand cases of deathbed repentance—not putative cases, but real ones—on the part of perpetrators of great moral evil. Such a person may not change the world in the process of dying, as Samson did. But, by opening to God in repentance, the perpetrator enables God to be close to him. Someone who dies in closeness to God has not lost his chance at some kind of greatness.

65. On this view, Samson's suffering would have been redeemed in relationship with God even if he had not fulfilled his mission by bringing down the Philistine temple; and it is also not an impossible stretch of the imagination to conceive of Samson's achieving a similar victory over the Philistines without dying himself. Fulfilling his mission and dying in the process is thus not necessary for Samson's flourishing, but it is important to him and part of his heart's desire, as his final prayer to God makes clear. In Chapter 14, I discuss the importance of distinguishing between flourishing and fulfilling one's heart's desires in the context of the problem of suffering.

66. There are many other people whose lives are impacted by Samson's, of course, and so it will occur to someone to wonder whether or not other lives would have been better if Samson had died before the episode with Delilah. Insofar as the narrative

in question is about Samson primarily, and about those others only secondarily, the story does not give us the information needed to evaluate the impact of Samson's actions on them. Of course, insofar as Samson's story includes his being glorious in some sense, then all those who care about Samson or whose welfare depends on Samson are also the beneficiaries of the good that comes to Samson. (I am grateful to Michael Barber for calling my attention to this point.) But, in the end, this narrative is only the story of Samson; to understand the suffering of others impacted by Samson's actions, we would need to have the narratives of their lives.

67. In saying this, I dissent from the claim Richard Kraut makes in his book *What is Good and Why* (Cambridge, MA: Harvard University Press, 2007): "If you say of a human being that he is flourishing, your statement is thrown into doubt if he is correctly described as either *psychologically* or as *physically* unhealthy, weak, damaged, and stunted. Certainly, if he suffers from both kinds of disabilities, the claim that he is flourishing, or that he is doing well, is impossible to sustain" (p. 133). For reasons for my dissent, see Chapters 1 and 13.

68. Cf. the discussion in Chapter 13 of those whose suffering is not successful in moving them closer to God.

69. Some people believe that Albert Speer was such a case, though there is reason to doubt that view of Speer. (In his book *The Good Nazi: The Life and Lies of Albert Speer* (Boston and New York: Houghton Mifflin Co., 1997), Dan van der Vat presents the evidence that Speer's public penitence was a mask for a lack of true repentance.) It is harder to doubt the evidence for as-it-were deathbed repentance on the part of Franz Stangl, the commandant of Treblinka. For excellent biographies of both men, see Gitta Sereny, *Albert Speer: His Battle with Truth* (New York: Albert Knopf, 1995), and *In That Darkness* (New York: Vintage Books, 1974). In this latter book, which is Sereny's biography of Stangl, Sereny reports a speech of Stangl's to her in which, after endless denial and evasion in his earlier conversations with her, he seems finally to have come to true acknowledgment of his evil and true contrition for it. Stangl died of a massive heart attack in the night after this speech.

Chapter 11

1. Victor Klemperer, *I Will Bear Witness: A Diary of the Nazi Years. 1942–1945*, trans. Martin Chalmers (New York: The Modern Library, 2001); see esp. p. 286 and p. 313. See Chapters 1, 14, and 15 for other discussion of Klemperer.

2. In Chapter 14, I try to give some precision to the notion of the desires of the heart; here, as before, I will rely just on an intuitive understanding of the idea.

3. Norman Kretzmann's insightful analysis of the binding of Isaac can be found in his "Abraham, Isaac, and Euthyphro: God and the Basis of Morality," in Donald Stump et al. (eds.), *Hamartia: The Concept of Error in the Western Tradition: Essays*

in Honor of John Crossett (Lewiston, NY: Edwin Mellen Press, 1983), 27–50. I am indebted to this article of his and to him.

4. See John Hick, *Evil and the God of Love* (New York: Harper and Row, 1966). For Hick's defense of his solutions against objections, see, e.g., "God, Evil and Mystery," *Religious Studies*, 3 (1968), 539–46; and "The Problem of Evil in the First and Last Things," *Journal of Theological Studies*, 19 (1968), 591–602. See also Richard Swinburne, *Providence and the Problem of Evil* (Oxford: Oxford University Press, 1998).

5. In Chapter 14, I will show that the desires of the heart in fact do figure in the stories of Job and Samson, and I will say something further about this feature of both stories.

6. See Rom. 4: 11 and Gal. 3: 7; but cf. also Acts 3: 25, Heb. 6: 13–19, and Jas. 2: 20–23. Cf. also certain parts of the Gospel of Luke that take on an independent life in liturgy and music—the Magnificat (Luke 1: 55) and the Benedictus (Luke 1: 73)—and that refer to God's promises to Abraham as being fulfilled in salvation for Israel in those times.

7. In certain Christian traditions, 'detachment' is the name given to a particular theological or spiritual excellence consisting in ordering one's desires for the good correctly, so that one loves everything one loves for the sake of love of God. This is not the sense of 'detachment' at issue here. (In Chapter 14, I discuss an ordering of the desires of the heart that has at least a family resemblance to this sense of 'detachment.') Rather, in this connection, by 'detachment' I mean an alienation, or an attempt at alienation, of oneself from one's own desires of the heart for the good or for what one believes to be the good for oneself.

8. For a recent book that helps orient readers to the Jewish tradition, see Jerome (Yehuda) Gellman, *The Fear, the Trembling, and the Fire: Kierkegaard and Hasidic Masters on the Binding of Isaac* (Lanham, MD: University Press of America, 1994); see also his *Abraham! Abraham! Kierkegaard and the Hasidim on the Binding of Isaac* (Burlington, VT: Ashgate Publishing Co.,2003).

9. I say nothing here about Islamic commentary on the story only because my own expertise does not cover the Islamic tradition of commentary on biblical stories or themes.

10. It continues to be the subject of insightful commentary today, too. A rich, sophisticated commentary, with much reference to the Jewish commentary tradition, can be found in Jon Levenson, *The Death and Resurrection of the Beloved Son* (New Haven: Yale University Press, 1993). There is a sensitive literary study of the text in Robert Alter, *Genesis* (New York and London: Norton and Norton, 1996). Besides these, there are many other helpful contemporary studies of the story, too numerous to be listed individually here; I will cite some of them subsequently in this chapter.

11. A helpful survey of ancient Jewish and Christian commentary on the story is included in Edward Kessler, *Bound by the Bible: Jews, Christians, and the Sacrifice of Isaac* (Cambridge: Cambridge University Press, 2004).

12. I am grateful to Stephen Evans for showing me the care needed in the interpretation of Kierkegaard's views on this subject and for correcting my first attempts to summarize Kierkegaard's views.

13. Commentators differ in the status they attribute to Hagar and Keturah. Midrashic commentary takes Hagar, for example, to be a wife of Abraham, not a concubine. (See *Midrash Rabbah: Genesis*, trans. H. Freedman, i (London and New York: Soncino Press, 1983), 381.) My own sense of the text is that Hagar and Keturah were each a concubine, not a wife, and I will refer to them as concubines in what follows.

14. Continual insertion of the qualifier 'in the story' would render the prose clumsy, and so I am in general omitting it after this point. But readers should take it as understood that what is being assessed here are the actions, motivations, and relationships of characters in the narrative.

15. Søren Kierkegaard, *Fear and Trembling*, trans. Walter Lowrie (Princeton: Princeton University Press, 1968), 55.

16. Kierkegaard, *Fear and Trembling*, 57.

17. Kierkegaard, *Fear and Trembling*, 57.

18. Heb. 11: 17–19.

19. Kierkegaard, *Fear and Trembling*, 69.

20. Kierkegaard, *Fear and Trembling*, 69.

21. Kierkegaard, *Fear and Trembling*, 70.

22. In recent years, philosophers have become interested in the story of the binding of Isaac as an example of a tragic dilemma. On this way of reading the story, which Philip Quinn tentatively considers Kierkegaard's real view, God's command to Abraham to sacrifice his son puts Abraham in a tragic dilemma, between the religious requirement to obey God's command, on the one hand, and the moral prohibition against murder, on the other. Quinn argues that this dilemma is irresoluble and that that fact constitutes a reason for rejecting the veridicality of the story, because it is incompatible with the goodness of God to force anyone into an irresoluble dilemma. See Philip Quinn, "Moral Obligation, Religious Demand, and Practical Conflict," in Robert Audi and William Wainwright (eds.), *Rationality, Religious Belief, and Moral Commitment*, (Ithaca, NY: Cornell University Press, 1986), 194–212, and "Agamemnon and Abraham: The Tragic Dilemma of Kierkegaard's Knight of Faith," *Journal of Literature and Theology*, 4 (1990), 181–93. It is not clear how plausible Quinn's line is as a reading of Kierkegaard. On Quinn's interpretation of Kierkegaard, as far as I can see, the special characteristics of Kierkegaard's knight

of faith and the absurdity that characterizes his beliefs are not found in the Abraham of the story.

23. At any rate, the biblical text (Judg. 11: 39) says that Jephthah fulfilled his vow, and the tradition commonly (but not invariably) supposes that he fulfilled his vow by sacrificing his daughter.

24. It is not clear to me how Kierkegaard's explanation of the story in terms of the teleological suspension of the ethical is supposed to cohere with what he says about Abraham as a knight of faith. The Abraham of the teleological suspension looks unlike the knight of faith and more like someone engaged only in infinite resignation. He recognizes and accepts that his religious requirements override his moral obligations, and so he prepares to kill his son. The element of the absurd that characterized the knight of faith seems to have dropped out.

25. Gen. 11: 30.

26. Not all his children, of course. By his last wife or concubine, Keturah, he has six other sons.

27. Gen. 25: 8–9.

28. See Gen. 12: 1–4. I say "first recorded speech" because the text can seem to imply that there was in fact an earlier, unrecorded speech of God to Abraham. The recorded speech of God to Abraham comes when Abraham is in Haran; in that speech, God tells Abraham to go to the land of Canaan. But Abraham is in Haran precisely because he and his whole family had left their home in Chaldean Ur in order to travel to Canaan (Gen. 11: 31). They get as far as Haran, when Abraham's father Terah decides to end the journey and stay there, in Haran. So it is possible that God spoke to Abraham (or to Terah) when Abraham was still in Ur and that the divine command to go to Canaan came on that occasion. If so, then that implied part of the story helps to explain why the divine command that comes to Abraham in *Haran* includes the command to leave his father's house. It may be that, although Terah's original purpose in leaving Ur was to get to Canaan because God had commanded him to do so, by the time Terah has reached Haran he is unwilling to go any further. The interpretation of the narrative given by Stephen in the book of Acts (Acts 7: 2–8) reads the story of Abraham in this way, except that in Acts a different reason is assigned for Abraham's leaving Haran.

29. The estimate of Abraham's age at the time of God's last visitation to him is based on the estimate of Isaac's age at that time. For reasons that Isaac was probably adolescent then, see below.

30. The eight are: (1) Gen. 12: 1; (2) Gen. 12: 7; (3) Gen. 13: 14–17; (4) Gen. 15: 1–16; (5) Gen. 17: 1–21; (6) Gen. 18: 10–32; (7) Gen. 21: 12–13; (8) Gen. 22: 1–18.

31. Although the divine speeches are not made by using illocutionary verbs of promising, the context makes it plain that God is promising. For some basic discussion of the nature of promising and the linguistic forms of promising, see the entries "Promising" and "Performatives" in the *Routledge Encyclopedia of Philosophy*.

32. For a helpful summary of the contemporary philosophical literature on promising and a useful corrective to the prevailing accounts of the normativity of promises, see Seana Valentine Shiffrin, "Promising, Intimate Relationships, and Conventionalism," *Philosophical Review*, 117 (2008), 481–524. Among other things, Shiffrin is concerned to undermine the claim that the normativity of promises has to do with the expectation of the person to whom the promise is made that the promise will be fulfilled. I share Shiffrin's position on this score. My point in the text here does not have to do with the normativity of promises, but only with the customary reactions of the person to whom the promise is made. My point has to do with ordinary psychology, not with the normativity of promises.

33. Of course, there are also promises that have to do with the present rather than the future, as in 'I promise you I am telling you the truth.' Here the promise functions as an oath confirming the truth of the utterance in doubt for someone else. Promises as oaths are outside the scope of the discussion here. I am grateful to John Foley for calling my attention to the need to address this issue.

34. Some people will take objection to this example on the grounds that one cannot be obligated to love someone, either because love is not the sort of thing that can be obligatory or because love is not the sort of thing over which one has control and one cannot be obligated to do something if that something is not under one's voluntary control. This objection may apply to conditions on being in love, but they do not apply to love on the Thomistic conception of love defended in Chapter 5. As presented there, the two desires of love are within the power of the will, *ceteris paribus*; and, at least in some circumstances, they are also obligatory, as the discussion of offices of love in that chapter makes clear.

35. I am leaving to one side here complications having to do with the defeasibility of obligations engendered by promises.

36. For an excellent discussion of the difference between a person's first-person and third-person expressions of his intentions, that is to say, between promises and self-predictions, see Richard Moran, *Authority and Estrangement: An Essay on Self-Knowledge* (Princeton: Princeton University Press, 2001).

37. It is immaterial to my point to consider why anyone would lend on the promise of swift return when he is unwilling or unable to trust the promise or the promise-keeper, but it is very easy to imagine circumstances that make such action understandable. Imagine, for example, that Paula is Jerome's boss and that Jerome is very worried about his job.

38. The story includes a name change for Abraham and for Sarah midway through the events leading to Isaac's birth; but I will refer to both of Isaac's parents with the names that are familiar to us: 'Abraham' and 'Sarah.'

39. Robert Alter argues that the Hebrew word translated 'family' here is better translated as 'birthplace,' but I am not persuaded by the arguments he gives for this reason. (See *Genesis*, 50.) If, however, his translation is the better one, it would not undermine the interpretation of the passage I am concerned to bring out here.

40. It is possible that Terah also took with him Nahor and Nahor's family. The text that mentions those Terah took with him omit Nahor from the list, but there is some indication in other texts that the audience is meant to suppose that Nahor's family was in Haran. Isaac's wife Rebecca is a member of Nahor's family and seems to come from Haran; at any rate, her brother Laban is in Haran (cf. Gen. 27: 43). It is possible, then, that the group Abraham leaves behind includes Nahor's household as well as Terah.

41. Gen. 12: 5.

42. Midrashic commentary makes a related point: "R. Nehemiah said: There was anger [in heaven] against the Patriarch Abraham when Lot his brother's son *went* with him. 'I promised him, *Unto thy seed have I given this land'*. . . said God, 'yet he attaches Lot to himself'" (*Midrash Rabbah: Genesis*, i. 338).

43. It is in fact not an uncommon way of understanding Abraham's attitude. So, for example, the edition of the Pentateuch by J. H. Hertz (in *The Soncino Edition of the Pentateuch and Haftorahs* (2nd edn.; London: Soncino Press, 1967)) comments on God's coming to talk to Abraham after Lot departed from him this way: "God chose that moment to renew His assurance to Abram, because he may then have been depressed by the departure of his nephew, whom, in default of a son, he had regarded as his probable heir, through whom the Divine promise was to be fulfilled" (p. 49).

44. Of course, there are some things that Abraham does have to do to cooperate with the divine promises, on any ordinary understanding of them. So, for example, when God tells Abraham that the promised child will be the child of Abraham's own loins, then presumably sexual intercourse on Abraham's part is necessary for the fulfillment of the promise. The difference between that sort of cooperation on Abraham's part and the other things Abraham does to try to make the promises true is that the other things, unlike sexual activity on Abraham's part, are not necessary if the divine promises are to be fulfilled, including the promise that the child in question will come from Abraham's loins.

45. And whatever is necessary for their fulfillment. Cf. n. 44.

46. Double-mindedness is one sort of division in the self, and there are others as well. For a discussion of divisions in the self, see Chapters 6 and 7.

47. Robert Alter points out that, on the preceding occasions when God has come to Abraham, Abraham has said nothing; Abraham's first speech to God in the narrative is one expressing doubt about God's promises (*Genesis*, 63).

48. The Hebrew word used to describe Abraham's righteousness (*tsedaqah*) is derived from the same root as the word *tsadiq*, which Abraham uses to designate the righteous in Sodom and Gomorrah, when he urges God not to destroy the righteous with the wicked. The narrative's comment implies that, in virtue of believing in God's reliability as a promise-keeper and thus in God's goodness, Abraham becomes good or righteous himself, at least in God's eyes. Exploring

the complicated implications of this comment would require more analysis than is possible in passing in a note. For discussion of some of the issues involved, see Chapter 8.

49. Of course, reiteration of a promise or other expression of commitment can serve multiple functions. The tone with which the promise is reiterated, for example, can convey useful or comforting information about the current state of the person making the promise. And yet it remains the case that, if the recipient of the promise were fully persuaded of the truth of the promise and thus entirely trusting of the promise-maker, he would not have a desire for the reiteration of the promise. The request for the reiteration or confirmation of a promise betrays some anxiety on the part of the person making that request.

50. For a discussion of the appropriateness of attributing trust to God, see Ch. 9, nn. 65, 66, and 67.

51. *Midrash Rabbah: Genesis*, i. 482–3. The Rabbis are here commenting on the text that says that God tried Abraham, but the point is applicable in general.

52. It is not possible to do justice to the whole narrative of Abraham's life in one chapter, even a very long chapter, and so many details relevant to a full consideration of the points of the narrative at interest in this chapter have had to be left out. The details of the story of Hagar are one such case. Hagar is identified as an Egyptian (Gen. 16: 1). Shortly before the part of the narrative in which Hagar appears for the first time, there is an episode detailing Abraham's journeying into Egypt. That episode involves Sarah centrally, because she draws the desire of the Egyptian ruler. By the end of the episode, the Egyptian ruler has loaded Abraham with many costly presents, including maid servants (Gen. 12: 16). So it may be that Hagar is introduced into Abraham's family on this occasion. If so, then the details of Abraham's dealings with the Egyptian ruler are significant for the events that result in the birth of Ishmael and all the rest of Abraham's story. With reluctance, for reasons of space, I am leaving these details unremarked.

53. Besides the gender issues raised by the treatment of Hagar, there are also issues of race, since Hagar is an Egyptian. Some readers of the story of Hagar and Ishmael suppose that Abraham treats Hagar and Ishmael differently from the way he treats Isaac because Hagar is an Egyptian. I have some sympathy with this point of view, but I would add that, if this interpretation of Abraham's conduct is right, then God has yet another reason for disliking Abraham's attitude toward the expulsion of Hagar and Ishmael.

54. To say this is not, of course, to give a theodicy or defense for Hagar's suffering or even to suggest a benefit that might redeem that suffering for Hagar. There is no indication in the story that Hagar has a heart's desire for matriarchal status; in this narrative, we are given too little information about Hagar to have any clear idea about what the desires of her heart are. This narrative is Abraham's story, not Hagar's. On the other hand, of course, given the nature of this society

and Abraham's hunger for descendants, it clearly conduces to Hagar's objective well-being to have an angel of the Lord promise that Hagar will be the mother of descendants by Abraham.

55. It is noteworthy that Hagar's story is believed without question or doubt. Perhaps Hagar's willingness to return to Sarah in the circumstances is, at least for Abraham, powerful confirmation of the truth of Hagar's story about the angel.

56. Gen. 16: 15.

57. There is evidence of a maternal and filial bond between Hagar and her son not only in her great grief for *him* when she thinks that they will both die in the wilderness but also in his acceptance of the wife that she finds for him.

58. I am keenly aware of the fact that in the narrative God has allowed Hagar to suffer the evils of being enslaved and taken as concubine. If this chapter were exploring Hagar's story rather than Abraham's, then this suffering of Hagar's would be its chief concern. Since, however, this chapter is about Abraham, as he is presented in the narrative in which he is the main character, Hagar's story and Hagar's suffering have to be left to one side. In this connection, though, it is worth noticing that the only character other than Abraham with whom God talks and to whom God gives promises and consolation is Hagar. Although the person doing the talking to Hagar is, in the narrative, an angel of the Lord, when the angel speaks to Hagar, the angel says God's lines to her; the first-person pronoun in the promise to make of Ishmael a great nation refers to God, not to the angel. In this respect, Hagar's contact with God is different from that of Lot or from that of Sarah. The angels visiting Lot speak to him only in their own voices, not in God's. And, although God does make a remark concerned about Sarah in a context in which God and Sarah are listening to each other, God's remark is not addressed directly to Sarah; and its point is only to let Sarah know that God knows she has lied about her laughing when she overheard God's conversation with Abraham.

59. Many details of the narrative have implications relevant for understanding why God does not prevent Abraham's errors in interpreting the divine promises. So, for example, if Abraham had not taken Lot with him when he left his home at God's command, Lot would never have been in Sodom. And, if Lot had not settled in Sodom, he would not have fled to the hills after the destruction of Sodom. In that case, his daughters would not have committed incest with him, and their children by Lot would not have been born. But, then, as the narrative tells the story, there would not have been the nation of Moab, which is descended from Lot by one of his daughters. Without Moab, there would not have been Ruth the Moabitess, who is the mother of Obed, the grandfather of David. Midrashic commentary also makes this point: "R. Isaac commented: *I have found David My servant* (Px. LXXXIX, 21): where did I find him? In Sodom" (*Midrash Rabbah: Genesis*, i. 335). By taking Lot with him, contrary to God's directive, Abraham thus starts a chain of events that leads to suffering, since Moab is one of the enemies of Israel, but that

also results in the birth of David, the great king of Israel and the founder of the Davidic line of kings. In this case, as in many others, the details of the narrative have ramifications worth further reflection and analysis. But I point this case out only to leave it to one side, with regret, in the interest of concentrating on the main threads of the story.

60. This interpretation is therefore also an answer to a question that might occur to someone: why does God not allow his promises to be fulfilled through Hagar? If Abraham could suppose that the divine promises have their fulfillment in Ishmael, why doesn't God give up his original plan to produce children for Abraham through Sarah and let Ishmael be the appointed and promised seed? The answer to these questions is that doing so will not contribute to producing in Abraham that trust in God and in God's goodness that God has been laboring to bring about.

61. There is much more to be said on the subject of Hagar's pregnancy than I can address in passing here, but it is important to see that God's allowing Hagar to conceive has long-term implications in the narrative, many of which will result in suffering for Abraham's descendants, as the genealogy of Ishmael (Gen. 25: 13–15) and the subsequent history of the Ishmaelites make clear (cf., e.g., Judg. 8: 22, 24).

62. It can seem as if Hagar has to return. On the interpretation I have been developing, Abraham supposes that the child Hagar is carrying is the promised seed from which his posterity will grow into a great nation. The narrative makes clear that Abraham has his heart fixed on having posterity and being the patriarch of a people; and the story makes it equally evident that Abraham is a man of determination and daring, as witness, for example, the story of Abraham's recovery of the people taken from him in tribal warfare. It seems highly likely, therefore, that Abraham would have found Hagar and brought her back to his tent in case there had not been an angel to send her back. But this consideration is not decisive. The angel that sent Hagar back could presumably also have hidden her from Abraham if Abraham had sought her.

63. Robert Alter points out that "a covenant sealed on the organ of generation may connect circumcision with fertility—and the threat against fertility—which is repeatedly stressed in the immediately preceding and following passages" (*Genesis*, 73).

64. See, e.g., Hertz (ed.), *The Soncino Edition of the Pentateuch and Haftorahs*, 58.

65. Abraham's laughter is recorded in Gen. 17: 17 in connection with the divine visitation when God institutes a covenant with Abraham. Sarah's laughter is mentioned in Gen. 18: 12 in connection with the three angelic visitors before the destruction of Sodom and Gomorrah.

66. As commentators are quick to point out, the Hebrew word transliterated 'Isaac' is cognate with the Hebrew word for laughter. It is worth considering why this promised and much desired child should take his name from the skeptical laughter

that greets the announcement of his conception and birth. To me, the name seems to enshrine the problem with trust that is one of the dominant themes of the story.

67. It is good to highlight the fact that the petition for Ishmael is Abraham's response to the expression of the divine promise, and that the petition is not so much for Ishmael as for Abraham: Abraham is asking to be patriarch through Ishmael's line. If Abraham had somewhat later in this episode tried to make sure that God gave good gifts to Ishmael as well as to the child to come, then this episode in the story would look different to us.

68. It is noteworthy in this connection that God does not bring about the conception of Isaac until Ishmael is a teenager, although, obviously, the entire story surrounding the conception and birth of Isaac could have taken place while Ishmael was still a baby. The delay in the birth of Isaac allows Ishmael to be Abraham's son, his only son, the son whom he loves, for years. The delay in the birth of Isaac allows Ishmael to grow through his most formative years without having to compete with Sarah's son. It is at least worth wondering whether Abraham would have had to wait so long for Isaac if there had not been Ishmael in his life. At any rate, there is certainly some good for Ishmael in the delay in the birth of Isaac, and so some divine care also.

69. Gen. 17: 20.

70. Sarah dies when Abraham is 137 years old, and the narrative specifies that Abraham takes Keturah as his wife or concubine after Sarah dies.

71. Cf. *Midrash Rabbah: Genesis*, i. 400.

72. Sarah dies when Isaac is 37 years old, and Hagar was expelled in the aftermath of the feast celebrating the weaning of Isaac.

73. There is, of course, also the question whether at this time Hagar would have been fertile enough to bear six more sons. But, since this is a narrative in which the ordinary expectations about the age of fertility for women are completely overthrown, this consideration alone is not sufficient to rule out the possibility that Keturah is Hagar.

74. Commentators have regularly noted that Abraham's age and the implications of Abraham's age are one of the reasons Sarah laughs. Part of the evidence cited by these commentators is the fact that, in the narrative when God repeats to Abraham what Sarah said to herself when she laughed, God omits the part of Sarah's line that has to do with Abraham.

75. We might wonder whether Keturah did not have daughters also, who are left unmentioned by the narrative. But, since these narratives care enough about daughters to mention the one daughter Jacob had, it seems not unreasonable to suppose that this narrative would have mentioned daughters of Abraham's, too, if there had been any.

76. There is, therefore, a certain appropriateness in Abraham's coming to be considered in Christian tradition the *father* of faith and the ancestor of all those who believe. Later in the chapter, this issue will arise again.

77. Commentators sometimes remark on the inappropriate placement in the narrative of the story of Keturah here in the middle of the story about Isaac and Rebecca. (See Alter, *Genesis*, 124.) But, to me, the story of Keturah in fact coheres remarkably well with the story of Isaac's marriage to Rebecca, once we reflect on Abraham's stake in that marriage.

78. Some people will find this part of the narrative disappointing; they would prefer that the high point of the story of Abraham's life, the binding of Isaac, is also the point at which Abraham's double-mindedness ends. But to me the narrative seems better as it stands. Abraham does not become a fairy-tale hero after the binding of Isaac. He stays human. He is the father of faith as the human being he is, with all his struggles for trust and double-minded attitude toward the divine promises. His exemplary faith is embedded in his very real human character.

79. She does, in fact, have only one conception, resulting in the birth of the twins.

80. Obviously, the expulsion of Keturah's sons has a strong resonance with the expulsion of Ishmael, as well as some significant differences. It is noteworthy, for example, that there is no mention of sending Keturah away. But I simply note this connection between the two episodes in the narrative and add it, reluctantly, to the heap of things that have to be left to one side in this chapter.

81. As Sarah puts it when she explains why she wants Ishmael and Hagar to be expelled. Like Abraham's other attempts to guarantee the fulfillment of the divine promises, his having sons by Keturah has significant ramifications for the subsequent history of Abraham's descendants, as the narrative makes clear in the genealogy of these sons (Gen. 25: 2–4). (In this connection, see also n. 84.) It is not possible to explore this side of the story in passing here, but it is noteworthy that the narrative does not record the presence of any of Keturah's sons at Abraham's burial.

82. In fact, if Abraham's taking Keturah as his concubine occurs as late as a decade into Isaac's marriage to Rebecca, then there is a second explanation of Abraham's sending Keturah's sons away when he does. If Abraham supposed that his death was near, then he might well have made sure to send Keturah's sons away from home to protect Isaac's position. If the question of inheritance seemed imminent to Abraham, then it makes sense to suppose he acted as he did in order to give all he had to his son Isaac (as the text says). (For other Genesis narratives in which the protagonist has a sense of his impending death, cf. Gen. 48: 21 and 29, where Jacob expresses his awareness that he will die shortly, and Gen. 50: 24, where Joseph expresses his recognition that his death is imminent.)

83. Gen. 25: 5.

84. The narrative of Abraham's life is embedded in a much larger narrative, and in that larger narrative Abraham's sons by women other than Sarah play a great role. So, for example, one of the sons of Keturah is Midian, the father of a tribe that is often at war with Israel; but it is also part of the larger narrative that Moses flees into Midian, marries a daughter of a priest of Midian, and has children by her, so that the descendants of Keturah and the descendants of Sarah are rejoined in Moses's children. The larger narrative might be thought of as the story of peoples, in which the stories of individuals are embedded. It would undoubtedly be profitable for considerations of the problem of suffering as regards whole communities and nations to examine that larger narrative with the methodology I am employing here on the smaller-scale narrative, but doing so is outside the scope of this book.

85. Gen. 18: 14.

86. In summarizing the nature of the encounter and the nature of the part on which I mean to concentrate in the way I have just done, I am already passing over complications well worth careful attention, because Abraham's interlocutor in this encounter is, by turns, three human or angelic visitors and God himself. For the sake of brevity, I am leaving this complication and many others to one side; and so in what follows I will simply concentrate on the part of the conversation between God and Abraham about the impending destruction of the two cities. It is not possible in one chapter, even one long chapter, to attend adequately to everything that is worth consideration in this dense narrative.

87. See, e.g., Robert Alter's gloss on this passage (*Genesis*, 80).

88. Gen. 18: 25.

89. Midrashic commentary records the opinion that Abraham stopped at ten righteous people, because he remembered that there were eight righteous people in Noah's ark, but that that number had not been sufficient to keep God from destroying everything with a flood. Cf. *Midrash Rabbah: Genesis*, i. 432.

90. So, for example, Robert Alter says that Abraham is "surprisingly audacious in the cause of justice" (*Genesis*, 81). For an interesting interpretation of this episode different from my own, see Jon Levenson, *Creation and the Persistence of Evil: The Jewish Drama of Divine Omnipotence* (Princeton: Princeton University Press, 1988). Although I have learned a great deal from Levenson's interpretations of the story of Abraham in this and in other works, in the end I read the story differently from the way in which he does. Nonetheless, my interpretation shares some things at the heart of Levenson's own views, including, not least, an emphasis on relationship as central to an acceptable account of God and the suffering of human beings.

91. Those saved are Lot, his wife, and his daughters; and, although the text does not explicitly identify them as righteous or innocent, it does make plain that Lot and his family do not share the prevailing sinful customs of their adopted city.

92. Lot, Lot's wife, and Lot's two daughters set out for Zoar, which God has agreed to spare for their sake; but only Lot and his two daughters make it there.

93. Gen. 19: 18–21.

94. Those who suppose that it is ever acceptable for non-combatants to be exposed to the perils of war presumably think that it is at least sometimes acceptable for the innocent to perish with the guilty.

95. It is not the preservation of particular righteous people beloved by Abraham either. I am thinking here of Lot and his family, of course, but there is no indication at all in the narrative that Lot and his family are uppermost in Abraham's mind as he bargains with God.

96. In the interest of brevity, I have omitted the intervening episode involving Abimelech and Sarah, although that episode is not irrelevant to my central purposes here, involving, as it does, the possibility of someone else's impregnating Sarah, so that the son Sarah gives birth to is not Abraham's. Miraculous intervention by God, recognized by Abraham, keeps Sarah chaste in Abimelech's household. Clearly, this episode is also important in the tale of Abraham's developing trust in God to keep his promises, and I omit consideration of it here with regret.

97. At this point the Anchor Bible abandons the Masoretic text and reads with the Septuagint; on that reading Ishmael is playing with Isaac.

98. I am aware, of course, that this is not the usual interpretation of Sarah's stance in this part of the story. Chrysostom, for example, thinks that Sarah's stance is not only right and appropriate but even rational, and he cites as evidence for this evaluation the fact that God himself agrees with Sarah. It is puzzling to me that a theologian of Chrysostom's stature would have supposed that there is a valid inference from God's concurring with a human person's action to the goodness of that action. Certainly, Chrysostom must have known that the same act can be done out of very different motives for very different ends, as witness his different moral evaluation of the human and the divine intention to put Christ to death. For the discussion of Sarah, see John Chrysostom, *Homilies on Genesis*, trans. Robert C. Hill (Washington: Catholic University of America Press, 1992), homily 46, 3–13.

99. Gen. 21: 11. (In this chapter, I have sometimes, as here, used the translation of Genesis in Hertz (ed.), *The Soncino Edition of the Pentateuch and Haftorahs,* but I have modernized the English slightly.) The omissions in the line about Abraham here are noteworthy. The narrative does not include Hagar in the reasons for Abraham's distress over the contemplated expulsion. And, even when it comes to Ishmael, the line 'on account of his son' does not make clear what Abraham was worrying about with regard to Ishmael. Was it Ishmael's safety in the wilderness? Was it the pain or the moral wrong of acting in such a way as to betray Ishmael's trust in his father? Or was it jeopardizing his connection to the posterity promised him through Ishmael, his son?

100. It is notable that there are other occasions on which God does *not* come to guide Abraham's action when God's guidance would have made a difference to the unfolding events. For example, God does not come to talk to Abraham to tell him

not to listen to Sarah's plan for Abraham to have sex with Hagar. What makes this occasion different from the other occasions on which God does not guide Abraham has to do with the nature of the divisions in Abraham. On this occasion, and only on this occasion, if Abraham acts on his better self, he will be acting in opposition to God's plans. That is, if in the goodness of his heart Abraham cannot bring himself to expel Hagar and Ishmael, then the result will not be in accordance with God's plan that Isaac have a special status in Abraham's lineage. When God intervenes on this occasion to add his moral authority to Sarah's demands, God brings it about that Abraham can accede to Sarah and still be acting in accordance with his better self. What God's guidance to Abraham on this occasion brings about, then, is that Abraham can further God's plan without thereby incurring serious moral failure. So God does not intervene to keep Abraham from moral failure. But he *does* intervene to keep Abraham from helping to bring about God's ends through moral failure. It is helpful to see this point by contrast with Kierkegaard's interpretation of the binding of Isaac, on which God seems to be requiring Abraham to disdain morality in the interests of furthering God's purposes.

101. Gen. 21: 12.

102. To be clear about this claim, one has only to notice that God could have come to talk to Abraham to prohibit his having sexual relations with Hagar. Insofar as God could have prevented Ishmael's birth in this way (or in any of a number of other ways including rendering Hagar infertile) but did not do so, God has a share of responsibility for the birth of Ishmael.

103. There is also the question, of course, about God's relations to Sarah. Insofar as he sides with Sarah when she is so thoroughly in the wrong, it might seem that God is failing her. Would it not have been better for Sarah if God had opposed her, rebuked her, or commanded her to do better? God's relations with Sarah, however, and the details of Sarah's role in the story of Abraham and Isaac are outside the scope of this chapter. It is certainly worthwhile considering Sarah's acts, Sarah's beliefs and emotions, and Sarah's responses in the stories of Ishmael and of the binding of Isaac; but it is not possible to examine everything in this short space. What is at issue in this chapter is just Abraham's story, not Sarah's.

104. Gen. 21: 13; see also 17: 20 and 21: 18, where the promise is to make of Ishmael a great nation.

105. Of course, there is also the injustice of the entire institution of slavery, which enables Hagar's fate to be decided entirely without her input or consent. But what is at issue here is only Abraham's expulsion of Hagar and Ishmael within the cultural context in which slavery is accepted.

106. I qualify the point in this way because there is also the issue of Ishmael's living with his father. No matter what good comes to Ishmael in consequence of God's promise, the plan still deprives Ishmael of the company of his father. If this chapter were examining Ishmael's story rather than Abraham's, I would focus on this point

and examine it in detail. As it is, I leave it to one side. The best that can be said about it as a part of Abraham's story is that perhaps Abraham feels the loss of his son's company as a great pain, which he can communicate to Ishmael to mitigate at least a little Ishmael's (quite correct) sense of abandonment.

107. For the sake of brevity, I am leaving the dreadful injustice to Hagar to one side; but this much should probably be said. Given the nature of the society in the narrative, insofar as God guarantees Ishmael's safety and flourishing, much of what constitutes Hagar's well-being is also safeguarded.

108. Chrysostom seems to think that Sarah mandated this harsh treatment for Hagar and Ishmael and that Abraham executed her mandate because God had told him to do everything Sarah said in this regard. Consequently, Chrysostom thinks, the moral appropriateness of Abraham's failure to provide adequately for his concubine and his son demonstrates Abraham's moral and religious virtuousness in this case. (See John Chrysostom, *Homilies on Genesis*, homily 46.) I myself would take as true the denial of Chrysostom's conclusion and use it to support the denial of his premiss.

109. I hope that it goes without saying that it is especially distressing given Hagar's powerless condition in this story. She is used to breed a child; and when that child ceases to occupy the role of heir, she is, in effect, thrown away.

110. There is, of course, an obvious question here: why does God not intervene earlier? Why, for example, does God not send his angel to Hagar as soon as she is out of Abraham's house, in order to guide her to just the right place for her to live and to raise Ishmael to adulthood? For the reasons I made clear in Chapter 9 on Job, I do not think that this text gives us evidence on which to begin trying to answer this question. This narrative is the story of Abraham; but to answer the question, we would need the narrative of Hagar, and that we do not get here. I would say, however, that the narrative makes clear that God is aware of Hagar and attentive to her throughout the story.

111. Gen. 21: 18.

112. For more discussion of this sort of case, see Chapter 9 and the discussion of the analogous problem as regards Job.

113. And, *pace* the Molinists, this is something not even God can know if the separation of morality and self-interest remains a permanently unactualized possibility. For a more positive appraisal of Molinism, see, e.g., Thomas Flint, *Divine Providence: The Molinist Account* (Ithaca, NY: Cornell University Press, 1998). For further discussion of Molinism, see Chapter 13.

114. Walter Brueggeman points out that Abraham says "Behold, here I am" three times in this narrative. In addition to this passage in 22: 1, there is the place in 22: 7 where Abraham responds to Isaac's address to him, and the place in 22: 11, where Abraham responds to the angel's call to him not to slay Isaac. (See Walter Brueggeman, *Genesis*, (Atlanta: John Knox Press, 1982), 187.) My own

interpretation of the narrative of Abraham is different from Brueggeman's, but I have found his interpretation helpful nonetheless.

115. It is worth noting that the same thing happens at the crucial point in the binding of Isaac (Gen. 22: 11), and perhaps for similar reasons. The angel of the Lord prevents Abraham from bringing the knife down on Isaac just by uttering his name. Only when Abraham has responded with recognition of the messenger of the Lord does the angel of the Lord deliver God's message halting the sacrifice. In that case, too, it is essential that Abraham know that it is God who is halting the sacrifice. Presumably, when the angel is speaking as a mouthpiece of God's, Abraham recognizes the voice of God, as it were, in the voice of the angel.

116. Gen. 14: 1–16.

117. See Gen. 14: 21–4, 20: 9–14.

118. It has, in fact, occurred to me to wonder whether the episode of Abraham's bargaining with Sodom and Gomorrah has as one of its main purposes in the narrative making this very point clear. Abraham is not afraid of standing up to God and talking back to God.

119. Kierkegaard devotes considerable attention to this question and focuses on Abraham's inability to make his action intelligible or rationally understandable (*Fear and Trembling*, 124).

120. Gen. 22: 1. "These things" includes more than just the expulsion of Ishmael, but I am leaving the others to one side to focus on Ishmael.

121. There is a rabbinic tradition that Sarah died when she learned of Abraham's binding of Isaac. Cf. *Midrash Rabbah: Genesis*, i. 497, where the commentators derive Isaac's age at the time of the binding from Sarah's age at her death. This is a very human interpretation of a mother's reaction to learning that her husband set off to sacrifice her only child; but there is no tangible evidence for it, and in my view it assigns an age to Isaac at the time of the binding that is improbable as the narrative portrays him in that episode.

122. Many commentators have remarked on the way in which God's identification of Isaac heightens the pathos for Abraham, but they have generally failed to notice the way in which God's identification of Isaac calls Ishmael to mind. The *Midrash Rabbah*, for example, takes the point of this complicated identification of Isaac just as a way of highlighting in Abraham's own mind how much he loves Isaac. (See *Midrash Rabbah: Genesis*, i. 486–7.)

123. I am not forgetting that Hagar was also sent away. But this part of the narrative is not about her, and so I am leaving comment on Hagar to one side here. But we should also remember that, at least to some extent, what protects Ishmael and conduces to his survival is also a protection for Hagar.

124. Cf. Gen. 15: 4–5, 15: 18, 17: 4–16.

125. It is, of course, possible to interpret God's identification of Isaac as Abraham's only son as God's acknowledgment that he has failed to keep his promise regarding

Ishmael, so that Ishmael is no longer living. But to interpret God's words in that way in the narrative is to fail totally in trust of God; and the narrative gives no indication that we should ascribe such a total failure to Abraham.

126. Cf. Gen. 22: 4.

127. There are many other textual resonances between the episode of the expulsion of Ishmael and the binding of Isaac. Cf. Alter, *Genesis*, 107.

128. It is worth asking what the rewards and punishments are where this test is concerned. The promises God makes to Abraham after the binding of Isaac are very similar to God's previous promises, except that God adds a promise that Abraham's seed will triumph over their enemies. And, in the visitation involving the destruction of Sodom and Gomorrah, God makes plain that his fulfillment of his promises to Abraham is contingent on righteousness on Abraham's side. So perhaps Abraham's passing of this test was requisite for the fulfillment of the divine promises. But it is not possible to do justice to these issues in passing here; I raise them only to set them aside in the interest of brevity.

129. Kierkegaard himself canvasses the ways in which damage to the relationship between God and Abraham or God and Isaac could occur in consequence of a wrong attitude on Abraham's part in connection with his acceptance of God's demand to sacrifice Isaac.

130. I include Kierkegaard in this group. Kierkegaard thinks that the knight of faith, such as Abraham, has a "double movement" in his soul (*Fear and Trembling*, 128). That is because Abraham "did not renounce his claim upon Isaac" (p. 59) but was "willing nevertheless to sacrifice [Isaac] if it was required" (p. 46). For Kierkegaard, Abraham was willing to kill his son if God required him to do so as a proof of his faith.

131. For an apparently similar interpretation, see Heb. 11: 17–19.

132. Gen. 18: 14.

133. It is worth pointing out in this connection that Abraham binds Isaac. If Isaac had not willingly cooperated in that process, how would Abraham have done so? At this point in the story, he is an old man, and Isaac is strong enough to carry up a mountain a very big load of wood. If Isaac had been terrified at what Abraham was trying to do to him, or if Isaac had found it evil, would he have tamely submitted to being bound by Abraham?

134. I am grateful to Philip Quinn for having helped me to sort out this point.

135. Gen. 22: 5.

136. Gen. 22: 8.

137. Chrysostom supposes that he has to read God's claim to know now as a figurative way of claiming that God has succeeded in revealing Abraham's faith to all people who will hear the story about the binding of Isaac. Chrysostom distorts the text in this way because he thinks he has to do so in order to avoid impugning God's

omniscience. He fails to see that there is no impugning of omniscience if God fails to know what is not there to be known. See John Chrysostom, *Homilies on Genesis*, homily 47.

138. Gen. 22: 15–18.

139. For the same reasons, it is also true, on the interpretation I am arguing for here, that God is not asking him to kill his son.

140. In fact, the Abraham who accepts the teleological suspension of the ethical is hard to square with Kierkegaard's own interpretation of Abraham as the knight of faith. If Abraham is willing to let God suspend the ordinary rules of morality, so that killing his son becomes acceptable, in what sense is he believing something absurd or expecting to have the very thing he gives up? He seems rather just to be resigning himself to losing Isaac at God's command. Furthermore, the moral prohibition against a father's killing his own child is morally indefeasible, as Kierkegaard recognizes, so that, if Abraham were willing to murder Isaac at God's command, he would be doing a grave moral evil. A God who would require a person to contravene an indefeasible moral obligation would be immoral himself, and it is hard to see why Abraham would be admirable for engaging in the teleological suspension of the ethical to obey him.

141. Kierkegaard makes much of the idea that a pedestrian reader of the story could confuse himself into thinking that he too could be an Abraham, a hero of faith, if he would only kill his own child as an offering to God. As should be clear, on the interpretation of the story I have argued for here, a person who sacrificed his child in hopes of winning favor with God would be the anti-type of Abraham.

142. One could wonder if Sarah, too, at some point knew the story of the binding of Isaac. There are some slight suggestions in the story that the reader is to suppose she did. Isaac knows that they are on their way to make a burnt offering to God. If Isaac knows that, surely Sarah does also. Furthermore, although it takes Isaac some time to get up his courage to ask where the lamb for the offering is, astute and bold Sarah surely would have noticed and asked immediately. What would Abraham have done if she had asked? Tried to fob her off with the line he gives his son? Would that line have had any chance of satisfying Sarah? These are just speculations, of course. But it seems hard to believe that at some point Sarah did not know the whole story. I prefer to think that she knew it before they set out for Mount Moriah. There is a Jewish tradition that Sarah knew it and the knowledge killed her (see n. 121 above), but that is going further in search of hermeneutical satisfaction than I am willing to go myself.

143. For a discussion of the story of the binding of Isaac in connection with the Euthyphro dilemma, see Kretzmann, "Abraham, Isaac, and Euthyphro."

144. It is true that Abraham does not live long enough to see the growth of his biological family, or his family of faith, beyond his grandchildren. In this respect, Abraham is analogous to Moses, who sees the promised land in the distance but dies without

entering it. But Abraham must himself understand that his desire for the status of patriarch can be fulfilled only partially while he lives. The status of patriarch requires many more generations of descendants than could be crowded into the lifetime even of the long-lived characters of the narrative. I am grateful to Scott MacDonald for calling to my attention the need to make this point explicit.

145. Or at least not obviously present. In Chapter 14, I examine the last part of the book of Job in which Job's wealth and community status are restored, to show that there is a way in which the book of Job does raise the issue of the desires of the heart for Job.

146. In Chapter 14, I will have much more to say about the way in which the desires of a person's heart are to be valued and weighed against that person's flourishing; I also consider in detail the way in which a theodicy or defense needs to take the desires of the heart into consideration.

Chapter 12

1. I am not introducing a new technical term here. I am using 'redemption' in this connection just as a synonym for 'defeat'. A benefit that redeems a person's suffering is just a benefit that defeats that suffering for that person. For some discussion of the notion of the defeat of suffering, see Chapters 1 and 13.

2. For further discussion of this claim and the complexities that attend it, see Chapter 14.

3. In Chapter 14, I will return to this point to consider it in much greater detail.

4. Cf. Abraham's rescue of Lot (Gen. 14: 1–16).

5. Cf. Abraham's being sent out of Egypt with many gifts by the ruler of that territory (Gen. 12: 10–20).

6. For some explanation of the basis for distinguishing varieties of shame, see Chapter 7.

7. Although the story at issue in this chapter suggests an answer to this question, a full consideration of a possible answer to it has to wait for the discussion of theodicy in Part 4. See Chapter 13 for further reflection on it.

8. Marilyn McCord Adams, *Christ and Horrors: The Coherence of Christology* (Cambridge: Cambridge University Press, 2006), 35.

9. Adams, *Christ and Horrors*, 35.

10. C. S. Lewis, *A Grief Observed* (New York: Bantam Books, 1960), 40–1.

11. Lewis, *A Grief Observed*, 3–4.

12. I am grateful to Theodore Vitali for calling my attention to the need to make these points explicit here.

13. Matt. 5: 1.

14. Luke 6: 17.

15. Cf., e.g., Augustine, *Harmony of the Gospels*, in *Nicene and Post-Nicene Fathers*, ed. Philip Schaff, vi (Grand Rapids, MI: Eerdmans, 1956; repr. 1996), bk. II, ch. 19.45, pp. 124–5. Aquinas also accepts this position. See, e.g., ST I-II q.69 a.1 ad 1, where he assumes it.

16. Cf., e.g., Augustine, *Harmony of the Gospels*, ed. Schaff, vol. vi, bk. II, ch. 79.155, p. 174, where Augustine explicitly affirms the methodological principle underlying this method of harmonization.

17. Joseph Fitzmyer (ed. and trans.), *The Gospel According to Luke* (The Anchor Bible; New York: Doubleday, 1981), i. 623 and 622, respectively.

18. So, for example, faced with what seems to be a discrepancy in the description of the location of a village named 'Bethany' in the Gospel of John, Raymond Brown says of the first mention of Bethany in the Gospel, "This is not the town near Jerusalem ([mentioned in John] xi 18), but a site in the Transjordan of which no trace remains." Here Brown is resolving a tension in the text by accepting the existence of *two* villages each of which was named 'Bethany'. See Raymond E. Brown (ed. and trans.), *The Gospel According to John* (The Anchor Bible; New York: Doubleday and Co., 1966), i. 44.

19. Although the context calls for it, I am omitting discussion of the methodological principles of historical biblical scholarship because the subject is too complicated for brief summary here. For one recent debate regarding these issues on the part of historical biblical scholars themselves, see, e.g., John Collins, "The Exodus and Biblical Theology," *Biblical Theology Bulletin*, 25 (1995), 152–60, and Jon Levenson, "The Exodus and Biblical Theology: A Rejoinder to John J. Collins," *Biblical Theology Bulletin*, 26/1 (Spring 1996), 4–10; repr. in Alice Ogden Bellis and Joel S. Kaminsky (eds.), *Jews, Christians, and the Theology of the Hebrew Scriptures* (Atlanta: Society of Biblical Literature, 2000), 247–61. For a detailed assessment of the issues with respect to Judaism, see, e.g., Jon Levenson, *The Hebrew Bible, the Old Testament, and Historical Criticism: Jews and Christians in Biblical Studies* (Louisville: Westminster/John Knox, 1993).

20. Cf., e.g., Brown (ed. and trans.), *The Gospel According to John*, i. 972, for the expression of such a charge.

21. Augustine notes that, in the various Gospel stories describing a woman's anointing Jesus, the woman is said in one story to anoint his feet and in another to anoint his head. Commenting on this discrepancy in the stories, Augustine says:

It is true that some person may possibly be found absurd and artful enough to argue, that because Mark states that the ointment was poured out after the alabaster vase was broken, there could not have remained in the shattered vessel anything with which she could anoint His feet. But while a person of that character, in his endeavours to disprove the veracity of the Gospel, may contend that the vase was broken, in a manner making it impossible that any portion of the contents could have been left in it, how much better and more accordant with piety must the position of a very different individual appear, whose aim will be to uphold the truthfulness of the Gospel, and who may therefore contend that the vessel was not broken in a manner involving the total outpouring of the ointment! Moreover, if that calumniator is so persistently blinded as to attempt to shatter the harmony of the evangelists on this subject of the shattering of the vase, he should rather accept the alternative, that the [Lord's] feet were anointed before the vessel itself was broken, and that it thus remained whole, and filled with ointment sufficient for the anointing also of the head, when, by the breakage referred to, the entire contents were discharged. (Augustine, *Harmony of the Gospels*, ed. Schaff, vol. vi, bk. II, ch. 79.155, p. 174)

22. I have addressed some of the issues at length in my "Revelation and Biblical Exegesis: Augustine, Aquinas, and Swinburne," in Alan G. Padgett (ed.), *Reason and the Christian Religion: Essays in Honor of Richard Swinburne* (Oxford: Clarendon Press, 1994), 161–97, and "Visits to the Sepulcher and Biblical Exegesis," *Faith and Philosophy*, 6 (1989), 353–77.

23. John Chrysostom, *Commentary on Saint John the Apostle and Evangelist* (Homilies 48–88), trans. Sister Thomas Aquinas Goggin (Washington: Catholic University Press, 1959; repr. 1977), 165–6.

24. Cf. Augustine, *Homilies on the Gospel of John*, trans. John Gibb and James Innes, in *Nicene and Post-Nicene Fathers*, ed. Philip Schaff, vi (Grand Rapids, MI: Eerdmans, 1956; repr. 1996), Tractate 69.3.

25. Cf. Matt. 26: 6–13 and Mark 14: 3–9.

26. For a discussion of second-person experiences and accounts, see Chapters 3 and 4.

27. Perhaps it is true that no translation can reproduce exactly the information conveyed by the original text being translated. Nonetheless, linguistic utterances typically convey a great deal of information—nuances and shadings of meanings, affect, implicit imagery—which can be utterly lost even in translations made by those competent at the original languages. To translate well requires not just competence at the syntax and semantics of another language but also a great deal of sensitivity to language in general and considerable expertise at the language *into which* one is translating. Insofar as a translation fails to convey the information a contemporaneous reader of the text in its original language would have gotten from the text or renders the original in such a way as to alter significantly the affective implications of the original text, the translation is not faithful to the original and does not portray it accurately. The flat-footedness of this Anchor Bible translation, evidently dead to the rhythm and nuances of English prose, and prone to a roller-coaster effect in its levels of diction, is concerning in this regard. But, because I mean to use the Anchor Bible commentary as a foil, it seemed to me mandatory to use the Anchor Bible translation here. (I make this same apology for my use of the Anchor Bible translation also in Chapter 9, although I recognize that there are two different translators at issue in these two different chapters. I need to add that the worry about translation I raise here is not my only concern about the

Anchor Bible translations, but it is the only one that can be addressed in passing in a note.)

28. Brown (ed. and trans.), *The Gospel According to John*, i. 420–2.

29. Brown (ed. and trans.), *The Gospel According to John*, i. 447.

30. Brown (ed. and trans.), *The Gospel According to John*, i. 429.

31. Brown (ed. and trans.), *The Gospel According to John*, i. 431.

32. Brown (ed. and trans.), *The Gospel According to John*, i. 423.

33. Brown (ed. and trans.), *The Gospel According to John*, i. 432–3.

34. Brown (ed. and trans.), *The Gospel According to John*, i. 435.

35. Brown (ed. and trans.), *The Gospel According to John*, i. 435.

36. Luke 10: 38–42.

37. I am here quoting from the Anchor Bible commentary on Luke, in the interest of having something of the same spirit in all the translations. See Fitzmyer (ed. and trans.), *The Gospel According to Luke*, i. 891.

38. Brown (ed. and trans.), *The Gospel According to John*, i. 433.

39. Brown (ed. and trans.), *The Gospel According to John*, i. 429, 430.

40. Cf., for example, his citing with approval the "critical judgment that both stories [involving the women], first Mary, then Martha, were added" (Brown (ed. and trans.), *The Gospel According to John*, i. 433).

41. Brown (ed. and trans.), *The Gospel According to John*, i. 433.

42. Brown (ed. and trans.), *The Gospel According to John*, i. 453. See also i. 447.

43. Brown (ed. and trans.), *The Gospel According to John*, i. 433.

44. Brown (ed. and trans.), *The Gospel According to John*, i. 449–52.

45. Brown (ed. and trans.), *The Gospel According to John*, i. 454.

46. Brown (ed. and trans.), *The Gospel According to John*, i. 435–6.

47. Brown (ed. and trans.), *The Gospel According to John*, i. 429.

48. Brown (ed. and trans.), *The Gospel According to John*, i. 426.

49. Brown (ed. and trans.), *The Gospel According to John*, i. 435.

50. Brown (ed. and trans.), *The Gospel According to John*, i. 426.

51. Brown (ed. and trans.), *The Gospel According to John*, i. 435.

52. Brown (ed. and trans.), *The Gospel According to John*, i. 435.

53. Brown (ed. and trans.), *The Gospel According to John*, i. 428.

54. Brown (ed. and trans.), *The Gospel According to John*, i. 429.

55. Brown (ed. and trans.), *The Gospel According to John*, i. 430.

56. John 19: 25.

57. If in fact the unidentified woman who anoints Jesus in the stories in Matthew and Mark can be identified as Mary of Bethany, as seems reasonable to many

scholars, then Mary of Bethany figures in all four Gospels, these two in which she is not mentioned by name, and Luke (10: 38–42) and John, where she is explicitly identified. Martha, by contrast, is mentioned only in Luke (in the same story as Mary) and in this story in John.

58. John 19: 19.

59. John 19: 25.

60. See Jean Vanier, *Drawn into the Mystery of Jesus through the Gospel of John* (Mahwah, NJ: Paulist Press, 2004), 195–6. It is noteworthy in this connection that, when Mary and Martha send their message to Jesus, they do not give the name of the person who is sick. They say only, "the one you love is sick." If Lazarus had been to that point a completely healthy person, it is a bit harder to explain why the sisters would not have added the name and identity of the sick person in their message to Jesus. Without some context, it is hard to know how they think Jesus could identify the unnamed sick person; the content of the message itself is compatible with its being even one of the sisters who is sick. And, if the message is being sent orally by someone who is being entrusted with identifying the sick person, then it is even more perplexing why the content of the message sent does not identify Lazarus as the sick person. If a messenger is going to explain the identity of the sick person, then the point in leaving the name of the sick person out of the content of the message is clearly something complicated.

61. Brown explains that the name 'Lazarus' is a shortened form of 'Eleazar,' and he explains that it is apparently a common name in this period (Brown (ed. and trans.), *The Gospel According to John*, i. 422). No doubt, he is entirely right on this score. But it is also interesting that, in another Gospel, when Jesus wants a name for a sick and impoverished person in a parable he is constructing about social justice, the name that it occurs to him to pick for the sick and impoverished person is 'Lazarus' (see Luke 16: 19–31).

62. For some discussion of whether the second phrase 'of God' should be included here, see Brown (ed. and trans.), *The Gospel According to John*, i. 423.

63. The text as Brown gives it omits the name of Mary in the list of the three Jesus is said to love and instead identifies her just as the sister of Martha. The Vulgate does include her name, but nonetheless identifies her as the sister of Martha. Without wanting to put too much weight on it, I note just that there are various ways to understand the two different highlightings of the sisters. To give just one example, it may be that of the two sisters Mary is the more well known to the narrative's audience for her anointing of Jesus, but Martha is the one with whom the narrative expects the audience to believe that Jesus is especially at home.

64. The Greek word translated 'glory' is *doxa*. Although 'glory' and *doxa* have different etymological roots and somewhat different ranges of meaning, they capture roughly the same idea. For purposes of this chapter, I will take the terms to be more or less equivalent.

65. In the Gospel of Luke, for example, Jesus is portrayed as having raised two people before the time in his life at issue in this story in the Gospel of John (Luke 7: 11–15, 8: 49–56). If this story in John were to be read in combination with those stories in Luke, then one might favor the idea that Jesus had formed a plan in advance and was waiting for the right moment at which to put it into action. But I mention this possibility only to leave it to one side in this chapter.

66. There is controversy over how to interpret Jesus' understanding of his relation to God; but this controversy is not relevant to my purposes, and nothing in my claims in this chapter should be taken as implying a certain position with regard to this controversy.

67. Brown (ed. and trans.), *The Gospel According to John*, i. 423.

68. For further discussion of glory understood in this way, see Chapter 13.

69. For other discussion of Sophie Scholl, see Chapter 7 and Chapter 15.

70. For further discussion of the standard of value underlying these brief remarks, see Chapter 13.

71. John 12: 9.

72. John 11: 27.

73. John 11: 15.

74. John 11: 42. The word for 'faith' is a grammatical form of the same word used in John 11: 15 about the faith of the disciples.

75. For more general discussion of this point, see Chapter 13.

76. Cf. John 12: 9, where the story says that many people came to Bethany not just because Jesus was there, but also because they wanted to see Lazarus, whom Jesus had raised.

77. Someone might suppose that, even if Jesus could not reveal the full plan to them, he might have helped them in some other way, say, by sending a message back to them reminding them that he loved them. Even if we suppose that there is some message of this sort that Jesus could send the sisters that would not constitute a very broad hint alerting them to his plan, it nonetheless seems to me that there are other reasons militating against the idea. When John Chrysostom is exiled by the Empress and his much beloved Olympias falls to pieces in consequence, he counts on her to know that he loves her, and he expects her to pull herself together in that knowledge. The power of the love between the two of them is trivialized if he has to shore it up with reminders. If their past history of shared love and companionship is not enough to make her know, in the great crisis of their lives, that he loves her, then how could a billet-doux possibly do it? I am grateful to Susan Brower-Toland for calling my attention to the need to address this issue.

78. John 11: 11.

79. It is worth asking why they do not send him a second message, reiterating their request and asking for an explanation of his absence. On the hypothesis discussed

below that Mary of Bethany is the woman in the story in Luke, there is a ready explanation of this otherwise puzzling fact. Shamed people do not stand up for themselves or make demands about what is due them in friendship.

80. For this story, see Luke 2: 42–50.

81. The things that would have to be changed include, for example, the explanation of Jesus' pausing on the way to Bethany. As I explain that pausing below, Jesus is stymied because of the sisters' reaction, which he did not foresee. If in fact he did foresee their reaction, then his pausing can still be explained in terms of it, but it will not then be true that he is stymied by it, since he will have known about it in advance. In this case, his pausing will be solely for the sake of dealing with the sisters' reaction to him.

82. For discussion of personal presence and joint attention, see Chapter 6.

83. John 11: 8–16. In the interest of brevity, I omitted this part of the text from the presentation of the story above.

84. In this sense, and just to this extent, in this suffering Mary and maybe Martha also exemplify the phenomenon John of the Cross calls 'the dark night of the soul.' In this phenomenon, a person feels psychically or spiritually cut off from God, in a way that is very painful but that is also recognized, even by the sufferer in the end, as a providentially ordered means designed to bring the sufferer closer to God.

85. For example, speaking of this line as uttered by both the women, John Chrysostom says:

> Mary . . . declared, at once, with faith: "Master, if thou hadst been here, my brother would not have died." Do you perceive how much true wisdom the women possessed, even if their understanding was weak? For on seeing Christ they did not immediately begin to lament or to cry or moan, as we are accustomed to do when we see some of our close friends coming to us in time of sorrow. On the contrary, they at once expressed admiration of their Master. And so they both believed in Christ, but not as was fitting. For they did not yet understand clearly . . . that He was God . . . (*Homilies on St John*, 171)

Aquinas adopts and elaborates the sort of line Chrysostom takes; see *Super Evangelium S. Ioannis Lectura*, ed. P. Raphaelis Cai (Rome: Marietti, 1952), [1511], p. 282.

86. See, for example, Aquinas in the passage cited in the preceding note. For other examples, see John Calvin, *The Gospel According to St John* (Grand Rapids, MI: Eerdmans, 1959; repr. 1979), 10; and John Wesley, *Explanatory Notes upon the New Testament* (London: Epworth Press, 1950; repr. 1959), 352.

87. Someone might suppose that withdrawal as a response to hurt caused in a personal relationship is peculiar to modern European culture, and that therefore this interpretation of Mary is anachronistic. Such a supposition seems to me itself parochial and plainly mistaken. To take just one example among many that might be given, it is possible to find such a withdrawing response to interpersonal trouble

among the Yanomama Indians in the Peruvian Amazon, at a time when they were still a people who were virtually completely isolated from Western culture; for a vivid description of such a case, see Kenneth Good, *Into the Heart* (New York: Simon and Schuster, 1990).

88. Luke 10: 38–42.

89. For some concern about whether the words 'and the life' should be omitted from the text, see Brown (ed. and trans.), *The Gospel According to John*, i. 424–5.

90. As my presentation of Brown's translation above indicates, Brown translates the Greek to say that Martha whispered to Mary. The Greek term being translated here, however, has 'secretly' as its ordinary meaning.

91. Augustine, *Homilies on the Gospel of John*, 275.

92. Calvin, *The Gospel According to St John*, 7, 10.

93. Calvin, *The Gospel According to St John*, 11.

94. For a discussion of this position on the part of some commentators, including Bultmann, see Brown (ed. and trans.), *The Gospel According to John*, i. 435.

95. For Brown's acceptance of this position, see *The Gospel According to John*, i. 435.

96. At any rate, he makes no answer consisting of words addressed to her. Insofar as he groans and weeps and looks as troubled as he is, he conveys to Mary a response to her line to him and to her weeping that will communicate in significant ways to Mary things of great concern to her.

97. Calvin, *The Gospel According to St John*, 11.

98. To attribute discouragement to Jesus shares certain features with attributing to him a non-culpable mistake. As I explained above, such an attribution is without theological implications for all positions willing to attribute a human nature to Jesus.

99. See Matt. 23: 37 and Luke 13: 34.

100. Consider in this connection the sort of discouragement expressed by the first voice in this quasi-dialogue recorded in Isaiah:

    Then I said, I have laboured in vain. I have spent my strength for nothing, and in vain; yet surely my judgment is with the Lord, and my work with my God. And now, saith the Lord that formed me from the womb to be his servant, to bring Jacob again to him, though Israel be not gathered, yet shall I be glorious in the eyes of the Lord, and my God shall be my strength. And he said, it is a light thing that you should be my servant to raise up the tribes of Jacob and to restore the preserved of Israel. I will also give you for a light to the Gentiles, that you may be my salvation to the end of the earth.   (Isa. 49: 4–6 KJV)

101. There is some suggestion in the text that this dinner is in the home of someone who would not ordinarily have had someone like Lazarus as a dinner guest. The fact that Lazarus's status as a guest is worthy of mention gives this impression, as does the fact that Martha is among those who serve the dinner. Even in a

patriarchal society, there is something noteworthy about having the sister of one of the dinner guests be among the servants.

102. One might wonder if the cost of the ointment is an argument against my characterization of Mary and her sister and brother as at the lower end of the social scale. That they are in fact in that condition is made clear, in my view, by the fact that Martha is among the servants at the dinner where Lazarus is a guest. It is hard to imagine a wealthy woman agreeing to work with the servants, especially in a culture dependent on servants. (In the story about the two sisters in Luke, where Martha wants Mary to help her with meal preparations, it also seems that the sisters do not have servants to help them.) As for the question how a woman who was not wealthy could own something as expensive as Mary's ointment, various answers are possible. Someone who liked Mary very much might have given her this as a gift. Alternatively, she might have taken what she had for necessary purposes and used it prodigally to buy ointment.

103. Brown finds it hard to understand why anyone would first anoint feet and then wipe off what one had used to anoint the feet (*The Gospel According to John*, i. 435, 451). But, of course, there are any number of reasons for taking off from a body part a substance one has just put on it. No doubt, it is infradig to mention soap. But even if the substance is not one that is meant to be removed immediately after having been put on, one can still imagine that it might be good to remove from feet the excess of a substance such as ointment.

104. Although it is not necessary for my purposes in this section, it is worth pointing out that the reason Jesus is close to Mary at the end of the story lies in Jesus as well as in Mary. He is willing to tolerate a weepy woman making a spectacle of herself at a dinner party and touching him in public in a highly emotional, socially inappropriate way. One has only to imagine a woman from the local parish treating her priest in this way in public at the parish fish fry to see the point. In the story, Jesus does not ask her to control herself or give her to understand that he will make sure to keep her at a distance after this or even jump up to offer her pastoral concern and benevolent care. On the contrary, he is willing to receive care from her. In his love for her, he is willing to let her love him in the passionate and unruly way in which that love wells up in her. Great-souledness is required on both sides of a relationship for love to be present with power.

105. I recognize, of course, that, on the Chalcedonian formula of the incarnation, which takes Jesus to be one person in two natures, fully human and fully divine, this outcome for Mary will have been part of the plan formulated by Jesus in his divine nature at the outset. On *this* complicated way of thinking about the plan, there is one plan in the human mind of Jesus; that plan in that mind rests on a mistake about the way in which the sisters will react to Jesus' failure to come to them. But there is also a different plan, this one in the mind of Jesus operating in his divine nature. This plan has no mistake in it. But part of this divine plan is for Jesus to operate on a human plan with a mistake in it. On the Chalcedonian doctrine of the

incarnation, Mary's anointing of Jesus would not have occurred if Jesus operating in his divine mind had not planned to operate on the plan containing the mistake formulated by his human mind. The Chalcedonian formula of the incarnation implies two minds and two wills in the incarnate Christ, and so it allows for this sort of complexity in the actions and intentions of Jesus.

106. To take just one example, Augustine, speaking of the episode of the anointing of Jesus in the Gospel of Luke and comparing it to the episode of the anointing of Jesus by Mary of Bethany in the Gospel of John, says, "my theory is, that it was the same Mary who did this deed on two separate occasions, the one being that which Luke has put on record, when she approached Him first of all in that remarkable humility, and with those tears, and obtained forgiveness of her sins" (*Harmony of the Gospels*, ed. Schaff, vol. vi, bk. II, ch. 79.154, p. 173).

107. If this hypothesis is true and if it were acceptable to combine all three stories in Matthew, Mark, and John into one larger narrative, as Patristic and medieval commentators tend to do, then there would be a wealth of detail that could be added to the story of the anointing in the Gospel of John. In my view, that added detail only enriches the interpretation I have given of the Johannine story. Because the combination of Gospel stories into one larger narrative raises the methodological issues that I said at the outset of this chapter I would foreswear, I have omitted here using the anointing stories in Matthew and Mark in my interpretation of the story in John. It is worth noticing, however, that, in each of the anointing stories in Matthew and Mark, Jesus is said to claim that the story of the woman's anointing him will be told wherever the gospel is preached (Matt. 26: 13; Mark 14: 9). If the current scholarly view is correct that takes the anointing stories in Matthew, Mark, and John to be describing the same episode, then all the canonical Gospels contain this woman's story except Luke, unless the anointing story in Luke should turn out to be about the same woman, even if not about the same episode. In that case, every canonical Gospel would contain a story of her anointing him, even if the stories were not all about the same episode. But I mention this point only to set it to one side and eschew further consideration of it, in order not to labor at the extensive literature, in the history of interpretation and in current scholarship, on the identity of the woman anointing Jesus in the Lucan story.

108. Brown (ed. and trans.), *The Gospel According to John*, i. 435, 449.

109. Fitzmyer (ed. and trans.), *The Gospel According to Luke*, i. 683.

110. For two different discussions of such cases, see Claudia Card, *The Atrocity Paradigm: A Theory of Evil* (Oxford: Oxford University Press, 2002), and Martha Nussbaum, *Hiding from Humanity: Disgust, Shame, and the Law* (Princeton: Princeton University Press, 2004).

111. For a discussion of the case of the Elephant Man in connection with shame, see Chapter 7.

112. For a detailed examination of the claims about social ostracism of those whose guilt is relieved by repentance and reform, see my "Personal Relations and Moral Residue," in Paul Roth and Mark S. Peacock (eds.), *History of the Human Sciences: Theorizing from the Holocaust: What is to be Learned?*, 17/2–3 (Aug. 2004), 33–57.

113. Augustine says about her that the story lets its audience see her "force her way into the feast . . . and with a holy shamelessness seek for health" (Augustine, *Sermons on New Testament Lessons*, in *Nicene and Post-Nicene Fathers*, vi, ed. Philip Schaff (Grand Rapids, MI: Eerdmans, 1956; repr. 1996), sermon 49, p. 416). Although my own views diverge from his, I have learned from Augustine's various commentaries on the anointing stories in the Gospels. In the case of the anointing story in Luke, Augustine seems to me focused on the problem of Sinner's guilt to the exclusion of any recognition of the problem of shame for her.

114. In his own expression of a similar thought, Augustine says: "had such a woman [as Sinner] approached that Pharisee's feet, he would have been sure to say what Isaiah says of such, 'Depart from me, touch me not, for I am clean' " (Augustine, *Sermons on New Testament Lessons*, vi. 416).

115. Augustine comments that, in treating Simon in this way, Jesus is concerned for Simon's welfare as well as for Sinner's. On Augustine's view, Jesus is trying to heal Simon of the sort of proud disdain that his attitude toward Sinner expresses; the same point applies also to the other guests at the dinner who are participants in the scene. See Augustine, *Sermons on New Testament Lessons*, vi. 416.

116. For further discussion of the nature of shame and its remedies, see Chapter 7.

117. There are, of course, interpreters who do affirm it. As I have already indicated, Augustine is one of them.

118. From this point on, I will simply let this supposition govern the interpretation, and so I will substitute 'Mary of Bethany' for 'Sinner.' I will not continue to call the reader's attention to the conditional nature of the interpretation being developed, but the reader should take its conditional nature as understood.

119. Luke 10: 38–42.

120. See John 12: 9.

121. Besides the two stories in John and Luke, one of which is uncontroversially about Mary of Bethany and one of which is in dispute, in the history of biblical interpretation there is yet a third set of stories that some Patristic and medieval commentators have also taken to be about Mary of Bethany. This third set of stories consist in the texts that are also about a Mary: Mary *Magdalene*. Aquinas, who supposes that Mary of Bethany is to be identified with Sinner, also maintains that Mary of Bethany is to be identified with Mary Magdalene; and he cites Augustine for support in this connection. (See *Super Evangelium S. Ioannis Lectura*, ed. Cai, [2472], p. 459.) Those contemporary reference books that still mention this view regularly cite it as a confusion. For example, in the entry on Mary in Carol Meyers (ed.), and

Toni Craven and Ross S. Kraemer (assoc. eds.), *Women in Scripture: A Dictionary of Named and Unnamed Women in the Hebrew Bible, the Apocryphal/Deuterocanonical Books, and the New Testament* (Grand Rapids, MI: Eeerdmans, 2000), 122, the following claims are made: "In spite of a total lack of evidence in the canonical Scriptures or early church tradition, Mary [Magdalene] became identified with the woman who 'was a sinner' in Luke 7: 36–50, who washed the feet of Jesus with her tears and dried them with her hair . . . She then became conflated with Mary of Bethany, sister of Martha and Lazarus."

I have no interest in treating the stories of Mary Magdalene at the tomb of Christ in the way I treat the story of the unidentified woman in Luke. I do *not* want to weave a conditional narrative of Mary of Bethany that takes the stories of Mary Magdalene as part of a larger narrative of Mary of Bethany. I explicitly reject this aim not because I think that the identification of Mary of Bethany with Mary Magdalene is mistaken. On the contrary, my own notion of what makes sense of personal relations and what makes literary sense strongly inclines me to accept the identification. But I have neither the space nor the inclination to present, examine, and adjudicate the large historical and contemporary literature on this controversy. And so in this chapter I am simply accepting the prevailing view that takes Mary Magdalene and Mary of Bethany to be two different women. Nonetheless, it should be noticed that the stories of Mary Magdalene at the tomb are stories about a heartbroken woman, insignificant in the eyes of the men named in the story, weeping and determined to get to Jesus, anxious to anoint him. For a discussion of this story in contemporary and medieval interpretations, see my "Visits to the Sepulcher and Biblical Exegesis."

Chapter 13

1. Although, in my view, the story of the raising of Lazarus has both Martha and Mary as protagonists, it complicates the discussion considerably to discuss both of them. For my purposes here, Mary's role in the story and her suffering are the most interesting. And so, for the sake of simplicity, I am leaving Martha to one side and focusing just on Mary as the story's protagonist.

2. This is an odd list of suffering, of course, since the items on the list are related to one another in different ways. Some are species of others, for example. The list is not meant as a Porphyrian tree of suffering but only as a catalogue of the kinds of suffering found among the protagonists of the biblical narratives examined in Part 3. (Readers interested in Porphyrian trees as devices for categorization can consult my *Boethius's De topicis differentiis* (Ithaca, NY: Cornell University Press, 1978; repr. 1989).)

3. This is a particular claim about the particular sufferers focused on in Part 3 on narratives, and it needs to be distinguished from the following two general claims

that resemble it but that are false, both in my view and in the Thomistic worldview at issue in this book.

(1) For every sufferer, if he only understood the nature of the benefits provided by his suffering, he would be willing to trade his suffering for the benefits his suffering enables him to receive.

On this claim, knowledge of the benefits of suffering would be sufficient to cause every sufferer to accept his suffering for the sake of the benefits provided by the suffering. But this claim is not true, for the reasons I gave in Chapter 8. Human beings are perfectly capable of preferring their own power and pleasure over greater goods, even if they understand the nature of those greater goods and the means necessary for acquiring them.

(2) For every sufferer, if that sufferer were in certain circumstances, which include his understanding the benefits provided by his suffering, he would freely will to accept suffering for the sake of those benefits.

This claim is a counterfactual of freedom. On Aquinas's worldview, and also on mine, there are no true counterfactuals of freedom. But if there were, there is no reason for supposing that this one would be true, for the reasons given in Chapter 8.

The claim in the text is then just a particular claim about Job, Samson, Abraham, and Mary of Bethany. It can be generalized, but only to those people who are like Job and the others in surrendering to the love of God.

4. In addition to the account of love discussed and developed earlier in this book, Aquinas's theodicy also presupposes many other parts of his ethics, metaphysics, epistemology, action theory, and moral psychology. It is not possible in one book on the problem of suffering to excavate and examine every such philosophical position; but I have explained and defended many of the relevant parts of his philosophical worldview in my *Aquinas* (London and New York: Routledge, 2003). Readers concerned with some of the broader philosophical context within which Aquinas's theodicy is embedded should feel free to consult my general study of his thought.

5. In the popular imagination, hell is God's torture chamber, where those who have failed to be good enough for heaven go, where God takes unjust retribution throughout an unending period of time for wrongdoing committed during a short period of time, and where repentance is unavailing because God will not forgive. There is very little in common between this popular idea of hell and the idea of hell accepted by Aquinas. I have explained and defended Aquinas's interpretation of the doctrine of hell elsewhere. (See particularly "The Problem of Evil," *Faith and Philosophy*, 2 (1985), 392–423 and "Dante's Hell, Aquinas's Theory of Morality, and the Love of God," *Canadian Journal of Philosophy*, 16 (1986), 181–98; repr. in Patricia A. Athay et al. (eds.), *The Philosophers' Annual* (Atascadero, CA: Ridgeview

Publishing Company, 1988), 236–53). I am grateful to John Greco for calling my attention to the need to make this point explicit.

6. For some discussion of the difficulty involved in trying to make such an argument, see Chapter 8.

7. Some people will suppose that the appropriate explanation involves the theory of evolution and that that theory is incompatible with the existence of God. In my view, the supposition that the theory of evolution is incompatible with the existence of God is false. For some discussion of this issue, see Ernan McMullin (ed.), *Evolution and Creation* (Notre Dame, IN: University of Notre Dame Press, 1985).

8. Cf., e.g., Richard Swinburne, *Providence and the Problem of Evil* (Oxford: Clarendon Press, 1998), 196–201.

9. Origen's name is associated with the belief that all human beings are saved, sooner or later, although some human beings are saved only after extensive periods of purgation in an afterlife.

10. There are other variations on the Thomistic interpretation of the doctrine of hell as well. For example, on the Thomistic interpretation, no one in hell is ever taken to heaven. In his work *The Great Divorce* (New York: HarperCollins, 1973; rev. edn., 2001) C. S. Lewis suggests that there might be a regular bus line, as it were, from hell to heaven, available for anyone in hell who does want heaven, as distinct from simply not wanting hell. As far as I can see, nothing of importance to my project would be lost if Lewis's view rather than Aquinas's view of hell were the right one. I am grateful to John Greco for calling my attention to the need to make this point explicit.

11. The point of the phrase 'in the circumstances' is to limit the class of worlds with respect to which the comparison of the availability of the benefit is made. For example, the circumstances include the choices of the human persons involved, not only those of the sufferer but also those of others suitably related to the sufferer.

12. See, e.g., William Rowe, "The Empirical Argument from Evil," in Robert Audi and William Wainwright (eds.), *Rationality, Religious Belief and Moral Commitment: New Essays in the Philosophy of Religion* (Ithaca, NY: Cornell University Press, 1986).

13. For a discussion of the controversy, see William Alston, "The Inductive Argument from Evil and the Human Cognitive Condition," in Daniel Howard-Snyder (ed.), *The Evidential Argument from Evil* (Bloomington, IN: Indiana University Press, 1996), 111–14.

14. The sense of 'primarily' at issue here can be explained by saying that, if this benefit did not come to the sufferer, then God would not have allowed the suffering.

15. In "The Magnitude, Duration, and Distribution of Evil: A Theodicy", in Michael Beaty (ed.), *Philosophical Topics*, 16/2 (Fall 1988), 161–87, Van Inwagen argues that this moral principle is false, and he gives the following counter-examples: the state

quarantines someone with a contagious disease; the state employs the right of eminent domain to force the removal of a person's house that stands in the way of a desperately needed irrigation canal. In both these examples, he argues, we have instances that violate the principle at issue here because a person is rightly made to suffer when the benefits accrue only to someone other than the sufferer.

But I think that neither of these cases is a counter-example to the principle in question, because that principle has to do with suffering that is both non-voluntary and undeserved. If a person knows he has a serious disease that he can easily pass on to others by moving around and if he does not voluntarily limit his movements in the way required to keep from spreading the disease, he will be guilty of an act violating commutative justice, because he will be taking something from others (namely, their health) without giving anything commensurate in return, when nothing in the case warrants his considering his victims in any way other than as his equals. In such a case the state may with justice inflict on him the suffering of involuntary quarantine. That the sufferer endures some restriction in his movements is a consequence of the constraints entailed by having a serious and contagious disease. That he bears this suffering involuntarily may be chalked up to his fair deserts, given that he would otherwise engage in movement significantly endangering the health of others. So this apparent counter-example to the principle is not a real counter-example, because the suffering in the example does not meet one of the conditions in the principle—namely, that the suffering in question be undeserved.

The second apparent counter-example seems to be analyzable in exactly the same way, except that in that case the injustice the sufferer is trying to engage in violates distributive (rather than commutative) justice. I am grateful to Van Inwagen for many helpful discussions on this subject.

16. For detailed textual support for the interpretation of Aquinas given in this paragraph, see my *Aquinas*, ch. 16. For the view that the benefit has to go primarily to the sufferer, see, e.g., Aquinas, *Super ad Romanos*, ch. 8, lect. 6: "God takes care of [human beings] in such a way that he doesn't allow any evil for them that he doesn't turn into their good."

17. As I explained in Chapter 1, I am operating only with a rough characterization of the mentally fully functional. If an adult human being is appropriately held morally responsible for his actions and is appropriately the subject of the reactive attitudes, then he is within the bounds of the mentally fully functional. For explanation of why the suffering of Samson is included in the description of the involuntary suffering of innocents, see the rest of Part 4.

18. Various texts suggest that Aquinas supposes the good of animals is somehow subordinated to the good of human beings or to the good of the animal species or even to the good of the whole world. (For one example, see text ending in the designation for n. 38 below.) Interpreters who take these passages as evidence that Aquinas accepts as moral anything done to animals as long as it benefits human beings would be mistaken, however. On Aquinas's equation of being and

goodness, it is always wrong to undermine or destroy the being of any creature unless that diminishment of being is necessary for the production of even greater being. As far as I can see, for example, on Aquinas's views eating meat is morally acceptable only in case there is no other, equally good route to necessary nutrition for human beings. For further discussion of this issue, see my Aquinas, ch. 2, on goodness.

19. Else Poulsen, *Smiling Bears* (Berkeley, CA: Greystone Books, D&M Publishers, 2009), 4–5. I am grateful to Adam Green for calling this book to my attention.

20. Poulsen, *Smiling Bears*, 25.

21. Detailed reflection on the cognitive and affective capacities of such sentient beings would need to include consideration of the large scientific literature exploring such capacities on the part of particular animal species. To take just one example at random, what sort of suffering is a songbird capable of experiencing? Does a songbird have the capacity for relationship to other sentient beings? Could the good of songbirds fall somewhere within the genus of relationship, as the good of human beings does? These and similar questions are important for considering the problem of suffering as regards songbirds, but I doubt that we understand enough of the neurology of songbirds to give any reasonably informed answers. Current research has discovered that a songbird can use mirror neurons to sing in concert with another songbird (see Greg Miller, "Mirror Neurons May Help Songbirds Stay in Tune," *Science*, 319/5861 (Jan. 18, 2008), 269). The surprise this finding has occasioned is a sign of how little we understand about the sentience of non-human sentient creatures. And similar points apply to human beings who are not adult or who lack normal adult cognitive capacities. But, without such understanding, how reasonable are our discussions of possible morally sufficient reasons for God to allow the suffering of such beings? In this connection, see, for example, the many suggestive and insightful articles in the section "Imitation in Animals," in Susan Hurley and Nick Chater (eds.), *Perspectives on Imitation: From Neuroscience to Social Science* (Cambridge, MA: MIT Press, 2005), i. 223–302. See also the notes to the brief discussion of this same issue in Chapter 1 above.

22. I say 'entirely voluntary' to distinguish this kind of suffering from the kind often endured by those pressured to volunteer for it by their cultures and communities. It is hard to suppose, for example, that in every case the suffering of suttee was entirely voluntary for those women who chose it.

23. For a discussion of reasons why entirely voluntarily endured pains do not raise the problem of suffering, see Chapter 1.

24. If, as Plato, Aquinas, and others thought, punishment (that is, punishment that is just and that is in all other ways appropriate for the wrongdoing it punishes) is medicinal for a person, then punishment does not undermine the flourishing of the person punished; but it might nonetheless go contrary to the heart's desires of the person punished. Its doing so would be sufficient for it to count as suffering, on the exposition of the nature of suffering I gave in Chapter 1.

25. This claim does not entail that God is not justified in allowing Samson's suffering. The suffering consequent on ill-health that a person suffers as a direct consequence of knowingly choosing to live an unhealthy lifestyle is not ordinarily thought to be punishment for that person. And yet no one could reasonably accuse that person's doctors of injustice because they cause him suffering he does not deserve in the course of their medical treatments on him.

26. Cf. Matt. 26: 24.

27. Aquinas himself is willing to go still further in this direction. He thinks that even moral wrongdoing can be a kind of evil that human beings suffer against their will. He does not mean to deny that any given morally wrong action that a person does is one which that person's will has chosen. If it were otherwise, the action in question would not count as a *moral wrong* on that person's part. Rather, Aquinas supposes that the condition of being a moral wrongdoer can go against the will of a person who nonetheless wills to do what is morally wrong. This is in effect one of the many ways in which a person's will can be divided against itself.

    And so Aquinas includes sin on his list of the things that human beings suffer and for which they need God's consolation. For example, when Aquinas is explicating the Pauline claim that all things work together for good for those who love God, he argues that God permits only those sufferings he can turn into goods for the sufferers. And, he says, this claim is "plainly true when it comes to the painful evils that [created persons] suffer. That is why it says in the gloss that the humility [of those who love God] is stimulated by their weakness, their patience by affliction, their wisdom by opposition, and their benevolence by animosity" (*In Rom.* 8.6).

    But, Aquinas goes on to say, this claim is true even with regard to sin. He says:

    Some people say that sins are not included under 'all things' [in the biblical passage]. . . . But against this is the passage in the gloss . . . if some among the saints go astray and turn aside, even this God makes efficacious for good for them . . . such people rise again [from their fall] with greater charity, since the good of human beings is charity . . . They return more humble and better instructed.   (*In Rom.* 8.6)

    And so Aquinas thinks that God needs to give consolation to human beings even for their sins. On his view:

    People need to be supported in the evils that happen to them. And this is what consolation is, strictly speaking. Because if a person didn't have something in which his heart could rest when he is overcome with evils, he couldn't bear up [under them]. And so one person consoles another when he offers him some relief, in which he can rest in the midst of evils. And although in some evils one human being can take consolation and rest and support in another, nonetheless it is only God who consoles us in all [our] evils. (*In II Cor.* 1.2; see also *In II Cor.* 12.3, where Aquinas explicitly includes mortal sins in the list of things that work for the good to those who love God.)

    Even for our sins, Aquinas holds, we need to be and we are consoled by God. That is why, Aquinas says, Paul calls God 'the God of *all* consolation' (*In II Cor.* 1.2. See also *In Rom.* 8.7).

As Aquinas sees it, then, at least for some people, the condition of being a moral wrongdoer is a suffering for the wrongdoer, in virtue of the fact that the higher-order will of such a person is at odds with the first-order will on which the person acts when he does morally wrong acts. As a result, to some limited extent, the moral wrong he does is *also* against his will. Because his will is divided against itself, there is a certain involuntary character to the morally wrong acts he does. To this extent, his being a wrongdoer constitutes a kind of involuntary suffering for him.

And so, on these views of Aquinas's, not only the effects of Samson's wrong-doing—the ruin of his life and the blighting of his vocation—but even the very condition of his being a moral wrongdoer is a suffering that falls within the scope of my project.

I have considerable sympathy with this position of Aquinas's. At any rate, it is certainly true that for some people a sense of their own sinfulness is a great suffering. (For a classic, moving description of this sort of suffering, see John Bunyan's *Grace Abounding to the Chief of Sinners* (New York: Penguin Books, 1987).) Nonetheless, I will leave out of my account suffering correlated just with the condition and sense of being a moral wrongdoer. Since Aquinas himself seems to relegate it to the genus of suffering within which I take Samson's suffering to fall, to include it here, as a separate species of suffering, would be to add complication without altering the lineaments of Aquinas's theodicy; and there are complications enough in his account as it is.

28. I am grateful to Li Yong for calling my attention to the need to make this point clear.

29. It is true that, in coercive circumstances, a person may agree to engage in activities that she knows will result in her shaming. But it is the external circumstances that press her into this agreement; and, if it were up to her will alone, she would not be in these circumstances.

30. This idea is clearly central to those religions or worldviews that recommend trying to give up desire as much as possible in the interest of warding off suffering. The recognition of a connection between desire and suffering is behind the Stoic recommendation of *apatheia*, for example, as well as the Buddhist approach to nirvana.

31. Someone might suppose that, even if Job had not cared about his children and so had not felt pain over their deaths, their deaths would still have counted as suffering for him, on the understanding of suffering I argued for in Chapter 1, in virtue of the fact that their deaths undermine his flourishing. I think that this position rests on an unwarranted interpretation of flourishing; for arguments to this effect, see Chapter 14.

32. He might still have endured injuries in combat, of course, if his remote place had been invaded by marauders. It remains true, however, that, in virtue of his

ability to remove himself from the scene of warfare, Samson has some control over the suffering of battlefield injuries, as Job does not have over the suffering of disease.

33. For arguments that we do not have voluntary control over what we care about, see Harry Frankfurt's discussion of volitional necessities, especially in *The Reasons of Love* (Princeton: Princeton University Press, 2004).

34. For discussion of justification and faith, see Chapter 8.

35. For a discussion of implicit faith, see Chapter 8. For some further discussion of this issue, see also my "Providence and the Problem of Evil," in Thomas Flint (ed.), *Christian Philosophy* (Notre Dame, IN: University of Notre Dame Press, 1990), 51–91.

36. For some further discussions of the issues in this section, see my "The Problem of Evil," in Robert Pasnau (ed.), *The Cambridge History of Medieval Philosophy* (Cambridge: Cambridge University Press, 2009).

37. For a general discussion of this Augustinian position in later medieval philosophy, see, e.g., Scott MacDonald (ed.), *Being and Goodness: The Concept of the Good in Metaphysics and Philosophical Theology* (Ithaca, NY: Cornell University Press, 1991). For Aquinas's views, see my *Aquinas*, ch. 2, on goodness.

38. Aquinas, *In Rom.* 8.6.

39. This is not the same as the doctrine of original sin; that is because, on traditional doctrines Aquinas accepts, the very first sin in the created world is on the part of one of the angels. I note this point only to leave it to one side. If one rejects the idea of angels, then one can take the first sin as the sin of a human being. In that case, the point in the text would in fact be part of the doctrine of original sin.

40. For further discussion of this distinction, see Chapter 14 on the desires of the heart.

41. Putting the point in this way does not attribute to God change over time. For discussion of responsiveness on the part of a simple, eternal, immutable God, see my *Aquinas*, ch. 3, on simplicity, and ch. 4, on eternity.

42. Marilyn McCord Adams has been influential in calling to our attention the fact that religious believers have different standards of value from those of non-believers, and that this fact needs to be kept in mind in discussions of the problem of suffering. She says, "Insofar as the highest human happiness is usually conceived of as involving some relation to the best good(s), and moral precepts direct humans to their individual and collective ends, different ontologies will produce different accounts of the human good and varying moral precepts" (Marilyn McCord Adams, *Horrendous Evils and the Goodness of God* (Ithaca, NY: Cornell University Press, 1999), 12). And, as she goes on to point out, these different standards significantly affect our evaluation of whether or not the existence of evil in the world is compatible with the existence of an omniscient, omnipotent, perfectly good God. The different standards of moral good and the different understandings of a good human life

will give us greatly varying views of whether or not there is a morally sufficient reason for God to allow suffering. Insofar as the problem of suffering is a challenge to the consistency of the beliefs of religious believers, however, it is obviously the standards and values of the religious believer that need to be taken into account in discussions of the problem. (Cf. also Adams, *Horrendous Evils*, 13.)

43. There is a distinction between the worst thing that can happen to a person and the hardest thing for theodicy to justify. I am asking about the former here in the interest of sketching a standard of value for human beings. I am not here attempting to rank cases of suffering in order of difficulty for theodicy. I am grateful to Scott MacDonald for calling my attention to the need to clarify this point.

44. For an explanation of Aquinas's kind of libertarianism, see my *Aquinas*, ch. 13, on free will.

45. There is more to hell than simply the loss of God's presence, on Aquinas's views, because there is also penalty or punishment; but Aquinas supposes that the loss of God's presence is sufficient for hell.

46. For explanation and defense of the Thomistic claim that all true union even with human persons is possible only in union with God, see Chapter 5.

47. For discussion of Aquinas's views that union is possible only in integration around goodness, see Chapters 6 and 7.

48. In my view, one important difference between Christianity and ancient Greek worldviews lies in this standard of value. By way of illustration, there is among the sayings on the oracle of Delphi the exhortation "Know thyself." But, for a view such as Aquinas's, the enterprise of trying to know yourself is likely to be marked more by self-deception and isolation than by anything that could count as success even at self-knowledge. It is better, and also more likely to be successful for self-knowledge, to try to know others, God most signally, and to be known by others in return. The African proverb that a person is a person through other persons is more nearly like Aquinas's view than is the Delphic saying. (For the proverb, see M. K. Asante and A. Mazama (eds.), *Encyclopedia of African Religions* (Thousand Oaks, CA: Sage Publications, 2009), 143. I am indebted to Monica Green for the proverb and the reference.)

49. In Aquinas's terms, the point has to be put differently, of course; on the doctrine of the Trinity, in medieval terms, there are three persons in one God. But this is a technical sense of 'person,' derived from Boethius's formulation, with substance taken analogically: a person is an individual substance of a rational nature. Nonetheless, the technical sense as it is used in the doctrine of the Trinity is compatible with the claim that God is a person, in our sense of the word 'person.' There is just one will and one intellect in the triune God, on the traditional doctrines Aquinas accepts. Insofar as, in our sense of 'person,' something having one mind and one will is a person, it is true to say that for Aquinas God is a person

in our sense of that word. Some readers will also want to object to the claim that for Aquinas God has a will and a mind, on the grounds that for Aquinas God is simple and therefore has no parts that can be distinguished from one another as mind is distinguished from will. But, although it is true that Aquinas's God is simple, Aquinas himself talks about the intellect and the will of God. Formulating claims about God in order to bring the doctrine of simplicity to the fore requires so much clumsiness in locution that Aquinas himself regularly omits it. For defense of these and the other claims about Aquinas's views that I make in this part, see my *Aquinas*.

50. The correlation between goodness and being that Aquinas accepts also provides a metaphysical foundation for this view of his. For this part of Aquinas's theory of value, see my *Aquinas*, ch. 2, on goodness.

51. Because of the connection he accepts between the intellect and the will, Aquinas thinks that there is no major change of heart possible after a person has his first experience of the afterlife and sees whatever of God he can see. For explanation of Aquinas's moral psychology, see my *Aquinas* ch. 9, on freedom, and ch. 11, on wisdom.

52. It is for these reasons that it is a mistake to try to find a boundary line in the continuum of goodness that separates those allowed into heaven from those relegated to hell. (See, e.g., Ted Sider, "Hell and Vagueness," *Faith and Philosophy*, 19 (2002), 58–68.) Those in heaven are not those whose lives have summed to a certain degree of goodness on the continuum. They are those who at the time of death have the desires of love for God. This condition is not degreed, as Sider's argument supposes, but all-or-nothing.

53. On Aquinas's views, this is true of persons in hell as well as persons in heaven. Aquinas does not share the view, popular among some preachers, of hell as God's torture chamber; but he does suppose that there is suffering in hell. On his views, part of the point of that suffering is to keep persons in hell from becoming worse than they otherwise might be. For discussion of these and other issues related to Aquinas's account of hell, see my "Dante's Hell, Aquinas's Theory of Morality, and the Love of God."

54. Aquinas supposes that there is no traffic between heaven and hell; that is, no person who was really in heaven ever goes to hell, and no person who was really in hell ever goes to heaven. (The qualifier 'really' is needed to handle some theological complexities, such as the harrowing of hell, which are not relevant to the project of this book.) It is clear enough why the inability to lose heaven would be essential to peace and joy in heaven. But it is less easy to see why it is not possible for a person in hell to repent and come to heaven. The reasons Aquinas gives for his view that it is not possible have to do with his understanding of the conditions needed for changing one's mind.

55. Aquinas, *In I Cor.* 15.2.

56. In the context of Judaism and Christianity, the belief in the existence of suffering in the world is also one of the central beliefs of the religion. Think of the rescue of the Israelites from slavery in Egypt for Judaism and the passion and death of Christ for Christianity, to take just two of the obvious cases.

57. Peter van Inwagen, "The Problem of Evil, the Problem of Air, and the Problem of Silence," in Daniel Howard-Snyder (ed.), *The Evidential Argument from Evil* (Bloomington, IN: Indiana University Press, 1996), 156.

58. The closest thing to such an argument that I know is the attempt to show that bodily resurrection is impossible. But, in my view, the best arguments attempting to demonstrate this claim are based on a misunderstanding of the nature of the doctrine of bodily resurrection. For defense of this position, see my *Aquinas*, ch. 6, on the soul, and also my "Resurrection, Reassembly, and Reconstitution: Aquinas on the Soul," in Bruno Niederberger and Edmund Runggaldier (eds.), *Die menschliche Seele: Brauchen wir den Dualismus?* (Frankfurt: Ontos Verlag, 2006), 153–74.

59. By speaking of this point as an extrinsic limit on loving relationship, I do not mean to imply that absence of personal relationship with God does not come in degrees. Zero is the extrinsic limit on the continuum of the positive integers, but there is a continuum of integers below zero. For Aquinas, although there is no mutual loving relationship between God and any persons in hell, some people in hell are more distant from that love than others. See also note 62 below.

60. I say 'shared' here because, strictly speaking, the intrinsic limit is the loving personal relationship with God that is shared with all the other human beings who each have their own shared loving personal relationship to God, in the community of shared love that constitutes heaven. In this life, however, there are limits on the sharing of such love among human beings, and extreme circumstances, such as solitary confinement, may make any sharing practically impossible. Nonetheless, even solitary confinement does not make impossible the very great good of loving personal relationship with God.

61. It is necessary to add 'ultimately' or 'finally' because until the very end of the earthly portion of a human life it is always possible to alter the final condition of a human person.

62. For Aquinas, the extrinsic lower limit on flourishing also comes in degrees. The state of everlasting distance from God is a degreed state too, on his views. As far as I can see, this part of his worldview makes no significant difference to the lineaments of his theodicy, and so I am leaving it out of account here, for the sake of keeping complications to a minimum. But if in fact someone supposes that this part of Aquinas's worldview does make a difference to his theodicy, it can be added to the account of this chapter at no cost except that of complexity. In that case, the lower limit of flourishing would have to be dealt with in the same way as the upper limit.

63. For more discussion of glory, see Chapter 12.

64. In her book, *Adam's Task: Calling Animals by Name* (New York: Knopf, 1986; Skyhorse Publishing, 2007), Vicki Hearne puts a related point in a somewhat different way. She emphasizes the importance of what she calls 'the heroic' to human flourishing. She says: "We, too, are noble animals. I mean that we are born to it, born to the demands of the heroic, of a pleasure earlier than love and nearer to heaven ... Hence an ethics ... that makes no attempt to trick out the syntax and the semantics of the heroic as a certain mode of being human, is not an ethic ... " (p. 153).

65. Someone might suppose that a person in heaven could want more excellence for herself than she has without wanting more openness to God. But, since these two things are in reality the same, according to Aquinas, to want one of them without the other is to be divided in oneself. Given that union with God in heaven requires being integrated within oneself, an internally divided state of this sort is not compatible with being one of the redeemed in heaven.

66. Dante, *Paradiso*, III. 64–87.

67. Some readers will suppose that by speaking of a morally sufficient reason for God to allow evil, I am attributing moral obligations to God, and they will resist such attribution. I myself think that it is a mistake not to attribute moral obligations to God, and I have argued elsewhere for this position. (See my "God's Obligations," in James Tomberlin (ed.), *Philosophical Perspectives*, 6 (Atascadero, CA: Ridgeview Publishing, 1992), 475–92.) But it is important to recognize that this position as regards God's obligations is not entailed by a theodicy; a theodicy does not require anyone to posit moral obligations for God. A morally sufficient reason for God to allow suffering is only a reason that, by objective moral standards, is sufficient for God to be justified for his permission of human suffering.

68. I say 'both' because, even for a person whose suffering is involuntary *secundum quid*, the suffering can be defeated by the warding-off of a greater harm as well as by the providing of a greater good. It is perfectly possible for some suffering to contribute both to warding off a greater harm and to providing a greater good. As regards the benefits of justification and sanctification, discussed at greater length in the text below, it is possible for suffering to play a role simultaneously in justification and sanctification if the internal integration of the sufferer increases sufficiently in consequence of the suffering.

69. In his commentary on the book of Job, Gregory the Great, who is the schoolteacher of the later Middle Ages in this as in many other things, lists four reasons for God to allow *any* suffering. On Gregory's view, God allows suffering if it constitutes (1) punishment that does not eventuate in correction, (2) punishment that does eventuate in correction, (3) the shaping of a psyche in a way which wards off future sin, or (4) the shaping of a psyche in a way which leads to greater love of God and greater union with God. It is clear that not all of these are mutually exclusive.

Furthermore, which of them is the result justifying a particular case of suffering will be a function of the response of the sufferer to that suffering. Of Gregory's four cases, the first is outside the scope of the discussion in this book, which is confined to the suffering of unwilling innocents. But the remaining three can be mapped onto the two reasons I attribute to Aquinas, insofar as the benefit Gregory assigns to suffering contributes either to redemption or to glory. See Gregory, *Moralia in Job*, V.12.

70. Of course, the same person at one time might not be a person of faith and at another time might be a person of faith (or vice versa). So the benefit defeating suffering has to be relativized not only to a person but also to the condition of that person at a particular time.

71. This example therefore shows that, for a benefit to defeat an instance of suffering, more is needed than the fact that the benefit outweighs the suffering and could not be gotten without the suffering. The issues here are complicated and cannot be dealt with adequately in passing. But, in my view, the heart of the matter has to do with what a person cares about. Without obtaining Jerome's consent, Paula can use suffering to provide a benefit for Jerome that outweighs the suffering and could not be gotten without the suffering, *provided that* it is appropriate to suppose Jerome would have given his consent if he had known what Paula knows about the suffering and the benefit. That is, Paula is justified provided that she has good reason to think that Jerome would care to have this benefit at the cost of his suffering if he were to understand the facts of the case. Where the benefit is a matter of warding off harm to Jerome that is greater than the suffering he endures and that could not be warded off without the suffering, the supposition is appropriate. But, where the benefit is a good, it may be that no one could appropriately suppose, in the absence of any actual willing on Jerome's part, that Jerome would care enough about the benefit to accept it at the cost of his suffering. What Jerome would care about in such circumstances may be an indeterminate matter. So, for example, it is reasonable to suppose that Jerome would care to avoid death even at the cost of suffering; it is not reasonable to suppose that he would care to have enhanced enjoyment at the cost of suffering. He might or he might not; and, in advance of Jerome's actually reaching a decision, there might be no determinate truth regarding what he would care about on this score. This line of reasoning is a sketch of an explanation of the asymmetry of our intuitions about the cases involving warding off harm and providing greater good. Of course, if there are true counterfactuals of freedom, then some other explanation will have to be found if these intuitions are to be validated.

72. Not much ingenuity or imagination is needed to explain how a person could incur cost and risk in such a case, and so I leave rounding out the details of the case, in one way or another, to the reader.

73. No doubt, some readers will suppose that my example is not representative and that parents often do subject their children to involuntary suffering for the sake of

greater goods. The suffering of dental work and piano lessons might be offered as examples of this claim. But, in my view, the suffering of dental work is justified by its warding off greater harm, not by its providing a greater good; and this is the case even for dental work that seems to have a cosmetic component, such as straightening teeth by means of braces. Given the social stigma attached in industrialized countries to crooked teeth, braces ward off a social harm, even if they do not ward off a physical threat. As for cases such as piano lessons, it is hard to imagine forcing a child to endure piano lessons with the kind of suffering that is involuntary *simpliciter*. But if a child could be forced into piano lessons totally against his will, then most of us would suppose the parent was not justified in producing that suffering for that child. We expect that a child taking piano lessons has given some general consent to cooperate with the parent in the child's nurture.

74. In putting the point so baldly, I am eliding more than one qualifying clause that would be required if the point were to apply to human beings. If what were at issue were one human person's allowing the suffering of another human person, we would have to consider what the cost would be of the rescue, what the degree of relationship is between the sufferer and the possible rescuer, and so on. But it is not necessary to consider these details here, because the question has to do with morally sufficient reasons for *God's* allowing suffering, and all the otherwise necessary qualifications are obviated in God's case. For example, God incurs no cost to himself in preventing any human suffering.

75. This attitude toward Job's suffering and this understanding of the benefits defeating suffering, argued for in a very different way, can be found also in medieval Jewish thought. So, for example, Saadia Gaon says: "the tribulations [of a person such as Job] are not on account of some past sin on the servant's part. They are spontaneously initiated by God. Their purpose, therefore, lies in the future . . ." (Saadia Gaon, *The Book of Theodicy: Translation and Commentary on the Book of Job*, trans. Len Goodman (New Haven: Yale University Press, 1988), 127). I have discussed Saadia's theodicy in "Saadya Gaon and the Problem of Evil", *Faith and Philosophy*, 14 (1997), 523–49.

76. There is also a problem about the connection between the benefits so understood and the desires of the heart. I will return to that problem later in this chapter.

77. Strictly speaking, this claim needs to be slightly qualified for reasons having to do with the incarnation.

78. Aquinas, *Super ad Hebraeos*, ch. 12, lect. 2.

79. To say that this is the only obstacle is not to say that a human being can achieve this union on her own without help from God. But since, on Aquinas's views, the apostle Paul is correct in claiming that God desires to save all human beings, the *obstacle* to union with God comes only from human beings.

80. In fact, the full story, which lies outside the scope of this project, includes not only grace but also the incarnation, passion, death, and resurrection of Christ. To

stay within the bounds of this project, whose subject is the problem of suffering and not the atonement, it is enough to consider justification and sanctification in the human persons undergoing these processes without including the theological story of divine provision of these goods for human beings. I have discussed grace and the atonement in my *Aquinas*. In a subsequent project, I hope also to examine at more length the biblical narratives of the passion and death of Christ.

81. Aquinas thinks of this as the volitional component of the act of faith.

82. Augustine has made famous the stormy internal conflicts that can exist in a person when his will is divided within itself. In his *Confessions*, he records his struggle to accept a life of celibacy, and he notes his surprise that a will can command itself to a particular good course of action and also disobey its own command. Cf. *Confessions*, VIII.7, 9.

83. Given this role for suffering in Aquinas's theodicy, someone might wonder whether the suffering of those who die very quickly as a result of their sufferings has to be added to the list of things outside the bounds of this project. Because such sufferers die and die quickly, the time needed for the beneficial effects of the suffering, as Aquinas construes it, appears to be missing for them.

   This objection is confused, however, about the process of death, even on secular views but especially on Aquinas's account. Recent neurobiological discoveries have made us aware of the stunning speed of some brain processing; and, as many people have testified after traumatic events, it is possible for there to be stretched-out psychological time even in very short physical time. (For a brief popular summary of the relevant neurobiology, see Pascal Wallisch, "An Odd Sense of Timing," *Scientific American Mind*, 19/1 (Feb.–Mar. 2008), 36–43.) So there is psychological space for insight and desire even in the short time of the process that is swift death. Furthermore, on Aquinas's account, death is not an end but a transition; and everything depends on the way in which one makes that transition. So, for Aquinas, what happens in the process even of swift death can make a great and lasting difference to the person in that process.

   Dante, who is an excellent Thomist, gives vivid expression to this idea. Among the redeemed in the *Purgatorio* is a notorious sinner who died suddenly on the field of battle in the midst of his sins. Dante the traveler expresses astonishment at finding that sinner in purgatory, which is technically a part of heaven, since instant death leaves no time for deathbed repentance. "Ah," the redeemed person tells Dante, "while those around me took me for dead, I longed for God and shed an inner tear for what I had become." In that inwardness, Dante implies, is the explanation of the sinner's redemption (*Purgatorio*, V.69–135).

   If thoroughgoing repentance in the process of sudden death is possible, as Dante, and Aquinas think it is, then other serious psychological alterations are possible as well. Nothing about swift death therefore rules out the application to its suffering of the theodicy Aquinas defends.

84. *St Augustine: Commentary on the Lord's Sermon on the Mount*, trans. Denis Kavanagh (The Fathers of the Church, vol. 11; Washington: Catholic University of America Press, 1951), 168–9.

85. For an annotated translation of the text, see Nicholas Ayo (trans.), *The Sermon-Conferences of St Thomas Aquinas on the Apostles' Creed* (Notre Dame, IN: University of Notre Dame Press, 1988). Although I have preferred to use my own translation, I found Ayo's helpful, and for this work I give citations both to the Latin and to Ayo's translation. Thomas Aquinas, *Collationes Credo in Deum*, sect. III; Ayo (trans.), *The Sermon-Conferences*, 40–2.

86. There is a translation of this commentary: *Commentary on Saint Paul's First Letter to the Thessalonians and the Letter to the Philippians by St Thomas Aquinas*, trans. F. R. Larcher and Michael Duffy (Albany, NY: Magi Books, 1969). Although I have preferred to use my own translations, I found the Larcher and Duffy translation helpful, and I will give citations for this work and for the commentary on Philippians both to the Latin and to this translation. Thomas Aquinas, *Super ad Thessalonicenses I*, prologue; *Commentary on Saint Paul's First Letter*, trans. Larcher and Duffy, 3.

87. Aquinas, *Super ad Hebraeos*, ch. 12, lect. 1.

88. Aquinas, *Super ad Hebraeos*, ch. 12, lect.2.

89. Aquinas, *Expositio super Job*, ch. 1, sects. 20–1; trans. in *The Literal Exposition on Job: A Scriptural Commentary Concerning Providence*, trans. Anthony Damico, interpretive essay and notes Martin D. Yaffe (Atlanta, GA: Scholars' Press, 1989), 89.

90. Aquinas, *Expositio super Job*, ch. 9, sects. 15–21; *The Literal Exposition on Job*, trans. and ed. Damico and Yaffe, 174.

91. Only one of the two metaphors is in the text translated in the Revised Standard Version, the King James, and the Anchor Bible.

92. Aquinas, *Expositio super Job*, ch. 7 sect. 1; *The Literal Exposition on Job*, trans. and ed. Damico and Yaffe, 146.

93. The view persists for some time after Aquinas as well. Cf., e.g., Thomas More, *A Dialogue of Comfort against Tribulation*, ed. and trans. Mary Gottschalk (Princeton: Scepter Publishers, 1998), 53: "if we cannot, as Saint Paul says we cannot, get to heaven except by many tribulations, then how will they get there who never have any at all? Thus we see clearly . . . how true are the words of the saints of old. With one voice . . . they all say the same thing: that we shall not have continual prosperity both in this world and in the next."

94. *St John Chrysostom: On Wealth and Poverty*, trans. Catharine P. Roth (Crestwood, NY: St Vladimir's Seminary Press, 1984), 66–7.

95. *St John Chrysostom: On Wealth and Poverty*, 68.

96. Aquinas, *Super ad Hebraeos*, ch.12, lect. 2.

97. Aquinas, *Super ad Thessalonicenses* I, ch. 4, lect. 2; *Commentary on Saint Paul's First Letter*, trans. Larcher and Duffy, 39.

98. Aquinas, *Super ad Philippenses*, ch. 3, lect. 2; *Commentary on Saint Paul's First Letter*, trans. Larcher and Duffy, 102.

99. Aquinas, *Super ad Romanos*, ch. 5, lect. 1.

100. For an excellent recent exposition and defense of Molinism and middle knowledge, see Thomas Flint, *Divine Providence: The Molinist Account* (Ithaca, NY: Cornell University Press, 1998).

101. It should be clear that substituting foreknowledge for middle knowledge will not give us an argument to the same conclusion. Foreknowledge of what a person will freely do in certain circumstances is possible only in case the future holds those circumstances and that person's freely willed choices in those circumstances. If there is divine foreknowledge of what a person will do in those circumstances, that knowledge cannot be used as a basis for a divine decision about whether or not to bring about those circumstances. The foreknowledge is correlative with the obtaining of those circumstances.

102. Someone might object that without middle knowledge God could not know that without suffering a person might become even worse than he currently is, so that my attempt to sidestep the Molinist objection in fact presupposes the truth of Molinism. But this putative objection seems to me mistaken. Most people would be willing to grant the point that a high-ranking Nazi such as Speer or Goebbels would have been worse without the suffering endured in Germany's loss of the Second World War. But middle knowledge is not needed to explain this attitude toward the Nazis; a certain experience of human character and behavior, an ability to make an inductive generalization, is sufficient to account for it.

103. The analogous point seems to me uncontroversial when it comes to medicine and biological health. Even for those who are suffering from some terminal disease, hospitals are careful to maintain sanitary conditions and provide other sorts of care that keep the dying from further diseases. There is a good in warding off further disease even for those who cannot be made healthy.

104. For detailed discussion of the nature of forgiveness that supports this claim, see Chapter 5.

105. It is also important to add that, even for those human persons most alienated from God or from themselves, there is always a non-negligible chance of redemption while they are still living. Even if this chance comes to nothing, it is still good for the person to have had it.

106. To say this is not to blame a sufferer for rejecting the benefit that the suffering might have brought to him. A person can be responsible for something that is bad on some scale of value without being culpable for it. So, for example, at a

certain period of Chinese history, some mothers bound the feet of their daughters, thereby causing pain and other suffering to their daughters; but we do not blame these mothers for doing so at that time in that cultural context. Analogously, the fact that a person freely rejects a good made possible through suffering does not entail that he is to blame for that rejection.

107. The case made familiar in the newspapers has to do with the infectious agent responsible for bovine spongiform encephalopathy, or mad cow disease. The *prion protein* is an ordinary, important constituent of healthy neurons in very many animal species. If it refolds in a certain way, it becomes a *prion*, a sort of vampire molecule that destroys neurons and turns good prion proteins into prions destructive like itself.

108. Internal divisions in the self are not the only kind of psychic brokenness possible for human beings. A person who is irremediably psychologically broken in some way can nonetheless have one or another degree of the internal integration needed for openness to love. The sorts of cases Jean Vanier has made famous illustrate the point. For further discussion of Vanier's work, see Chapter 7.

109. No doubt, there will be divergent views about the best exemplars of this class. But one such case already discussed in earlier chapters is that of the so-called Elephant Man. See Chapter 7 for this example.

110. I am grateful to John Greco, whose questions helped me to see that this point needed to be made explicit.

111. For more detailed discussion of presence and omnipresence, see Chapter 6.

112. It is clear that there are degrees of such experience. For human beings in this life, the religious experience of mystics no doubt is an upper bound. At the lower bound, it seems to me that it is possible to receive something of the consolation of God's presence and love without recognizing it as such. The consolation of love, and its opposites, need not operate at the level of full consciousness. We know now that even those rendered unconscious by anesthetics apprehend comments made by their surgeons and nurses, so that healing is hindered by crude or demeaning conversation on the part of medical personnel during the course of an operation. Analogously, a person sufficiently sick might not know that her daughter was with her; but, somewhat below the level of her consciousness, her daughter's presence might nonetheless produce psychic ease and peace. In the same way, perhaps it is possible even for a person who believes of himself that he is alienated from God, or that he is an atheist, to receive some kind of consolation from God's presence, provided that, contrary to what he believes of himself, he has not closed God out entirely. There is a poignant description of such a complicated psychic state in the autobiographical work *Grace Abounding to the Chief of Sinners*, by the seventeenth-century Puritan writer John Bunyan. So perhaps there are people who believe of themselves that they have no religious experiences but who are wrong in that claim.

113. The notable exception to this claim has to do with the dark night of the soul, discussed in the body of the text below.

114. There is an English translation of this work: *Commentary on Saint Paul's Epistle to the Galatians by St Thomas Aquinas*, trans. F. R. Larcher and Richard Murphy (Albany, NY: Magi Books, 1966). Although I have preferred to use my own translations, I found the Larcher and Murphy translation helpful, and I will give citations for this work both to the Latin and to the Larcher and Murphy translation. Aquinas, *Super ad Galatas*, ch. 5, lect. 6; *Commentary on Saint Paul's Epistle*, trans. Larcher and Murphy, 179–80.

115. Aquinas, *Super ad Philippenses*, ch. 4, lect. 1; *Commentary on Saint Paul's First Letter*, trans. Larcher and Duffy, 113.

116. Joy is one of the fruits of the Holy Spirit; and it is a state resulting from the gifts of the Holy Spirit, which are necessary to salvation, on Aquinas's views.

117. *Super ad Philippenses*, ch. 4, lect. 1; *Commentary on Saint Paul's First Letter*, trans. Larcher and Duffy, 112.

118. See, e.g., Aquinas's discussion of the suffering of Christ in his commentary on the Gospel of John.

119. We ourselves share this view when it comes to relationships between human persons. That is why we do not leave a person in pain to himself. We suppose that there is some great consolation for him, which even pain cannot take away, in having someone who loves him near him in his suffering. It is worth noting in this connection that we have this attitude even toward infants. We suppose that even a neonate benefits from being cuddled by his mother when he is in pain.

120. Job 42: 5.

121. Christ's cry of dereliction on the cross is the most dramatic expression of this condition.

122. See Mother Teresa, *Come Be My Light: The Private Writings of the 'Saint of Calcutta'*, ed. Brian Kolodiejchuk (New York: Doubleday, 2007).

123. For more discussion of skeptical theism, see Chapter 1. Aquinas would agree with skeptical theism that a limited human mind cannot comprehend the infinite mind of God. But Aquinas accepts the idea that God can communicate his purposes to human beings through revelation. So, even if skeptical theism is right about what unaided human intellects can understand, Aquinas would suppose that human intellects are not always unaided.

124. Aquinas, *Super ad Hebraeos*, ch. 4, lect. 2.

125. I say 'specific' in this context because, of course, Aquinas's theodicy provides a general answer that applies in an abstract way to every case of human suffering.

126. For further discussion of shared attention and closeness, see Chapter 6.

127. James Patterson and Hal Friedman, *Against Medical Advice* (New York: Little, Brown, and Co, 2008), 192–3.

128. For a fervent formulation of this complaint, see William Hasker, *The Triumph of God over Evil* (Downers Grove, IL: IVP Academic, 2008), 189–91.

129. As late as the end of the nineteenth century, even *Scientific American* was publishing diatribes against anesthetics (see the quotation in *Scientific American* (Aug. 1991), 14); and the lamentable nineteenth-century animus against anesthetics, particularly in connection with childbirth, often had a religious basis. For a detailed discussion of nineteenth-century attitudes toward anesthetics, see Martin S. Pernick, *A Calculus of Suffering: Pain, Professionalism, and Anesthesia in Nineteenth Century America* (New York: Columbia University Press, 1985).

130. The point of this *ceteris paribus* clause is to leave unspecified and to one side other conditions that would have to be met for the claim to be true but that are not germane to the discussion here. These include, for example, the cost to the agent of helping the sufferer, the relationship (if any) that the agent holds with respect to the sufferer, and so on.

131. The exception to this claim might be thought to be pain, where we tend to think a person is in pain if and only if she knows that she is in pain. But Timothy Williamson has recently argued that even pain is not transparent (see his *Knowledge and its Limits* (Oxford: Oxford University Press, 2000), 24–5).

132. Esther 4: 14 (KJV modified).

133. It may also be that Paula's trying to prevent Jerome's suffering alters the context of that suffering. Paula's care for Jerome and the connection that her trying to prevent his suffering makes between the two of them, however attenuated it might be, change the circumstances of Jerome's suffering. It is possible that the change of circumstances is itself a reason for God's willing not to allow a suffering for Jerome that God would have allowed if Paula had failed to try to help Jerome. This idea or something similar underlies the practice of petitionary prayer. For a discussion of this point, see my "Petitionary Prayer," *American Philosophical Quarterly*, 16 (1979), 81–91.

134. For a detailed examination of a kind of psychic state in which a person both believes that suffering is allowed by God for the good of the sufferer and still feels grief over the suffering, see Chapter 14.

135. For discussion of Aquinas's views on this subject, see Norman Kretzmann, "A General Problem of Creation: Why Would God Create Anything At All?" and "A Particular Problem of Creation: Why Would God Create This World," in Scott MacDonald (ed.), *Being and Goodness* (Ithaca, NY: Cornell University Press, 1988), 208–49.

Chapter 14

1. In Chapter 1, I explained that 'a desire of the heart' and related expressions are ambiguous as between (i) a person's desire for a thing and (ii) the thing desired. We say, for example, that (i) his heart's desire was to marry her and that (ii) he lost his heart's desire when she died. I am relying on context alone to disambiguate the phrase in order to avoid clumsy circumlocutions.

2. For more discussion of this analogy, see Chapter 1.

3. I am grateful to John Foley for persistent questioning of my earlier attempts to sidestep this question and for many helpful suggestions, drawn from Jesuit spirituality, about how to answer it. This chapter would not have been written or taken the shape it currently has without his determined sheep-dogging of my earlier efforts to produce the defense of this book without this chapter.

4. Except for conceptions of flourishing that make flourishing identical to the satisfaction of desires. But equating flourishing just with desire satisfaction is problematic enough that it can be left to one side here.

5. Jean Vanier, *Becoming Human* (Mahwah, NJ: Paulist Press, 1998), 158–9.

6. Jonathan Hull, *Touching the Rock: An Experience of Blindness* (New York: Vintage Books, 1991), 205–6.

7. I have great admiration for Vanier, and for Hull, and I have sympathy for the views they express in the passages I cite from their work. In citing them for the purpose I do in this chapter, I am *not* trying to distance my position, or Aquinas's, from theirs or so much as suggest that they are to be allied with the position I attribute to Cassian in the section below. My point is only to support the claim that flourishing is compatible with heartbreak, in order to show that heartbreak needs to be addressed apart from flourishing in any consideration of the problem of suffering.

8. For a persuasive statement of a case for such a view, see Marilyn McCord Adams, *Horrendous Evils and the Goodness of God* (Ithaca, NY: Cornell University Press, 1999).

9. Although the following text from Cassian illustrates beautifully a position I want to repudiate, I do not want to repudiate Cassian. In other parts of his writing, he shows great insight into many philosophical and theological doctrines. His treatment of *acedia*, to take just one example, is particularly good and can be read with profit today.

10. John Cassian, *The Monastic Institutes*, trans. Jerome Bertram (London: Saint Austin Press, 1999), 55–6.

11. I understand that many people take the story of Abraham's binding of Isaac to be of exactly this sort. On my interpretation of the story, however, it cannot be read as analogous to Patermutus's story, with God playing the role of the abbot. On

the interpretation I defended in Chapter 11, unlike Patermutus, Abraham is not willing to end the life of his son when he goes to obey God's command.

12. Teresa of Avila, *The Interior Castle* (Mahwah, NJ: Paulist Press, 1979), 98, 99, 100.

13. Augustine, *Confessions*, IX.12.

14. Cited in Ann Astell, *The Song of Songs in the Middle Ages* (Ithaca, NY: Cornell University Press, 1990), 126.

15. Cited in Astell, *The Song of Songs*, 130.

16. Cited in Astell, *The Song of Songs*, 133.

17. *Super Evangelium S. Ioannis Lectura*, John 12: 24–5, lect. IV.7 [1643–4].

18. *Super Evangelium S. Ioannis Lectura*, John 14: 27–31, lect. VIII.1 [1966].

19. Quoted in R. W. Southern, *Saint Anselm: A Portrait in a Landscape* (Cambridge: Cambridge University Press, 1995), 165.

20. Quoted in Southern, *Saint Anselm*, 155–6.

21. Quoted in Southern, *Saint Anselm*, 160.

22. For Aquinas's beautifully argued and carefully nuanced explanation of this point, see ST I-II q.19 a.10.

23. 'The commander of the armed forces' is used referentially when it refers to the particular person who is the President; it is used attributively when it refers to anyone who holds the office of commander without reference to a particular person who in fact currently holds the office.

24. And Aquinas certainly does. On his view, goodness is a function of God's nature, not God's will. For further discussion of the issue, see my *Aquinas* (London and New York: Routledge, 2003), ch. 2, on goodness.

25. It is important to put the point in terms of what *happens* to her father, rather than in terms of any action on her father's part, since there are certainly things her father might do that would cause Teresa a grief she would approve of having.

26. The official formula was "Whatever policy Chairman Mao decided upon, we shall resolutely defend; whatever directives Chairman Mao issued, we shall steadfastly obey." See Roderick MacFarquhar, "The Succession to Mao and the End of Maoism," in *The Cambridge History of China*, xv. *The People's Republic, pt. 2: Revolutions within the Chinese Revolution: 1966–1982* (Cambridge: Cambridge University Press, 1991), 372.

27. Cited in Astell, *The Song of Songs*, 133.

28. Cited in Astell, *The Song of Songs*, 130.

29. For this distinction, see Chapter 13. Roughly put, God's *antecedent* will is what God would have willed if things in the world had been up to God alone. God's *consequent* will is what God in fact wills, given what God's creatures will. God's

consequent will is his will for the greatest good available in the circumstances, where at least some of the circumstances are generated through creaturely free will.

30. Or try to accept—a distinction illustrated by Teresa's own description of herself.

31. For more detailed discussion of this claim, see Chapter 5.

32. C. S. Lewis, *The Problem of Pain* (New York: Macmillan, 1962), 113.

33. The last clause is a necessary caveat because, presumably, even an adherent to the no-self position would be distressed at finding sin in himself (and maybe even at finding sin in others), since sin cannot be considered in accordance with God's will.

34. For a good philosophical explanation of the way in which Christ's will was opposed to God's will but without culpability, see Aquinas's discussion of the issue in ST III. q.18. a.5.

35. Lewis, *The Problem of Pain*, 113.

36. Harry Frankfurt, "On the Usefulness of Final Ends," in Harry Frankfurt, *Necessity, Volition, and Love* (Princeton: Princeton University Press, 1998), 82–94.

37. In this respect, the desires of the heart are to human flourishing what accidents are to a primary substance, on Aquinas's Aristotelian hylomorphism. Any particular accident is not necessary to a material substance, but it is necessary to such a substance that it have accidents. Analogously, no particular desire of the heart is necessary for a person's flourishing, but it is necessary for her flourishing that she have desires of the heart.

38. The qualification in the parenthetical phrase is meant to remind the reader of the fractal character of providence and stories of suffering, so that no one might get confused and suppose that on my view (or Aquinas's) the benefit for the suffering of Lazarus's death goes primarily to his sister.

39. Cf. in this connection Job 29: 1–25.

40. There is a further complication in the case of Job that I note but, with regret, leave undeveloped. In the course of his suffering, Job develops an additional heart's desire. He yearns for his words to be written in a book and preserved for all time (19:23–24); he fervently desires that God would answer him and that a book would be written about his case (31:35; cf. also 13:3, 14:15, and 23:3–4). This heart's desire of Job's is also fulfilled, but in a complicated way. Although God does answer Job, the complete fulfillment of this heart's desire of Job's is not accomplished in Job's sight. It is accomplished, but in a way that only readers of the story can see, through the very existence of the book of Job. Furthermore, in this case not only the fulfillment but the heart's desire itself is dependent on Job's suffering. These features of the story continue the story's pattern of revealing some things to readers of the story that are not revealed to the characters within the story, and they also preserve in a particularly rich way the story's commitment to the

connection between suffering and the greatness of the sufferer. Because this is a book on the problem of evil and not on the story of Job, I note these things only to leave their development to one side.

41. I am not forgetting that exercise can also be pleasurable, social, community-building, and otherwise beneficial. But if exercise were not conducive to health, it is hard not to suppose that it would lose most of its value, and that other ways of seeking pleasure, social interaction, and the rest would be preferred.

42. As I argued in Chapter 3, a person can be the object of a desire. On the Thomistic account of love I defended in Chapter 5, to love a person includes having a desire for union with him; and, as I argued in Chapter 7, this desire is not a desire *that* but rather a desire for a person. So, a desire for union with a person is a desire for that person. *Mutatis mutandis*, the same point applies to God. There is something pleonastic about the formulation 'God and union with God' in this context, therefore. But pleonasm is sometimes clarifying and therefore helpful. Furthermore, there is at least some conceptual difference between union with God and shared union with God. So I will use the somewhat pleonastic phrase 'God and shared union with God' throughout this chapter in speaking about the deepest desire of the heart on the view held by Augustine and Aquinas.

43. That is, although Aquinas makes a strong connection between God and morality, he is not a divine command theorist. He ties goodness to God's nature, over which even God does not have control.

44. For Aquinas, then, things correctly valued as objectively good are commensurable and compatible. This is a controversial position, which cannot be dealt with adequately in passing here. Readers not antecedently inclined to accept it can add it to the list of things characterizing the possible world of the defense at issue here.

45. Earlier, I tried to explain the desires of the heart by analogy with the more familiar idea of a web of belief. I suggested that there is a web of desire, too, and that the heart's desires are at the center of the web. That is why, when a person is heartbroken in virtue of losing the desires of his heart, he has no heart for anything else. The reflections in this paragraph suggest that there is something not quite right about the image of a web. If one could stand a pyramid on its apex and support the rest of the pyramid on the apex, then one might have a better image for the ordering among the desires of the heart. Dropping certain things from the web of belief requires a rearranging of the web. Losing the apex of an inverted pyramid just crashes the pyramid. At least at the beginning of sorrow, heartbreak is more nearly like a crashed pyramid than like a rearranged web.

46. In addition to the reasons for rejecting it given below, there are also in effect arguments against it given in Chapter 5, in the discussion of the nature of the offices of love and the responsiveness of love to the beloved. For my purposes in

this chapter, however, there are other, more important reasons for rejecting the quodlibet view, which I turn to in the subsequent sections of the chapter.

47. I am indebted to conversation with John Foley for the focus on this question and for some of the ideas about how to answer it given in the text below. His comments and objections regarding earlier attempts of mine to answer this question made a great difference to the final shape of this chapter.

48. Stacey O'Brien, *Wesley the Owl* (New York: Free Press, 2008).

49. O'Brien, *Wesley the Owl*, 218.

50. For Aquinas's views of the nature of human beings and for his understanding of the human soul, see my *Aquinas*, ch. 6, on the soul.

51. This is a point the medieval tradition was clear about; see, e.g., Aelred of Rievaulx, *On Spiritual Friendship*, trans. Mary Eugenia Laker (Kalamazoo, MI: Cistercian Publications, 1977). Aelred says:

not all whom we love should be received into friendship, for not all are found worthy of it. For since your friend is the companion of your soul, to whose spirit you join and attach yours, and so associate yourself that you wish to become one instead of two, since he is one to whom you entrust yourself as to another self, from whom you hide nothing, from whom you fear nothing, you should, in the first place surely choose one who is considered fitted for all this.   (pp. 92–3)

The animus against particular friendships among those devoted to religious life, common in the modern period, would have seemed strange to Aelred.

52. For a defense of the notion that union in love can come in degrees, see Chapter 13.

53. Here, as in the discussion in Chapter 1 of what a person ought to be, I am not making a claim about a person's moral duties by talking about what ought to be. There may be a true moral claim in the neighborhood of the claim that persons ought to be the deepest desire of one's heart; but the normativity in the claim as I am intending it here has to do with the way the world would be if the world were optimal.

54. On this view, the deepest desire of the heart cannot be reduced to propositional form. For earlier discussion of the relevant philosophical claims, see Chapters 3 and 7.

55. I am grateful to John Foley for two sets of comments on earlier drafts of this chapter that called this line of Augustine's to my attention in this connection and that helped me see how to bring the issues here into focus.

56. Someone might suppose that this claim has to be false because hunger is a kind of pain, and all pain is translucent. The claim that all pain is translucent is currently not uncontroversial, however (see Chapter 1 for a discussion of this issue). Furthermore, even if all physical pain were translucent, the kind of pain involved in psychic hunger is psychic pain, not physical pain. If either the fact or the

object of psychic pain were translucent, a good deal of the practice of counselors and pastors would be obviated.

57. For an explanation of this claim and defense of it, see my *Aquinas*, ch. 5, on knowledge, and ch. 8, on the mechanisms of cognition. By saying that cognition is innate, I do not mean to deny the influence of the environment on its emergence. The capacity to learn a language is innate, but without a certain environmental influence language learning can become permanently impossible for a human being.

58. That awareness, like consciousness itself, comes in degrees is well attested in a large literature in philosophy, psychology, and neurobiology; it is also a staple of the counseling profession.

59. There is no way to explain or defend this view in passing here; and so, for those not antecedently inclined to accept it, it needs to be taken as another part of the description of the possible world at issue for the defense of this book. The basis of the view is the doctrine of divine simplicity, which makes a very strong connection between goodness and God's nature. Since I wrote the chapter on simplicity in my *Aquinas*, in consequence of my team-teaching and conversation with John Foley my view of simplicity has developed. My most recent attempts to present and defend it can be found in "God's Simplicity," in Brian Davies and Eleonore Stump (eds.), *The Oxford Handbook on Thomas Aquinas* (Oxford: Oxford University Press, 2011), and "Eternity, Simplicity, and Presence," in Gregory T. Doolan (ed.), *The Science of Metaphysics: Historical and Philosophical Investigations* (Washington: Catholic University of America Press, 2010).

60. O'Brien, *Wesley the Owl*, 177.

61. O'Brien, *Wesley the Owl*, 211.

62. O'Brien, *Wesley the Owl*, 211.

63. The poem exists in two versions. The first is the written version, as the poet Michael Dennis Browne originally produced it. It reads:

> Light upon the Water
>
> Like the light upon the water,
>   Summer in the swaying trees,
> Radiance of the woken flower,
>   You are these and more to me.
>
> From this hour, from this moment,
>   Where we make our holy vow,
> No more distant, no more hidden,
>   We are undivided now.
>
> Life before us, love within us
>   More than we can sing or say,
> Everything is grace, is given,
> All our dreams begin this day.

("Light upon the Water", in *Things I Can't Tell You* (Pittsburgh, PA: Carnegie Mellon University Press, 2005), 80.)

The second is the version as revised and set to music by John Foley in collaboration with Michael Dennis Browne. It reads:

Light upon the Water

1. Like the light upon the water,
    Like the summer in the trees,
    like the radiance of the flower,
    You are these and more to me.

2. Life before us, love within us,
    more than we can sing or say;
    every thing is grace, is given,
    all our years begin this day.

3. From this hour from this moment,
    where we mark our holy vow,
    no more hidden, no more distant,
    we are undivided now.

The song is forthcoming in a collection now in progress.

64. John Greco has pointed out to me that there is a distinction between everything's having the property *being a gift*, and a particular thing's having the property of being a particular gift to a particular person. It is the latter that is at issue here. I am grateful to Greco for calling my attention to the need to ward off potential misunderstanding here.

65. Cf., e.g., John Locke, *Some Thoughts Concerning Education* (New York: P. F. Collier & Son Company, 1909–14; repr. New York: Bartleby.com, 2001), sect. 36: "For if the child must have grapes or sugar-plums when he has a mind to them, rather than make the poor baby cry or be out of humor; why, when he is grown up, must he not be satisfy'd too, if his desires carry him to wine or women?" I am grateful to Steve Chanderbhan for the reference.

66. Here, for the missing definition of the notion of heart's desire and the omitted analysis of the individuation of heart's desires, I am substituting typology. As in Chapter 3, I am relying on a type to do the work ordinarily done in philosophy by analysis. In this case, the type is not a person in a fictional or historical story, as it was in Chapter 3, but a protein in a biochemical story told by biologists. And so I am proceeding Franciscanly, rather than Dominicanly, typologically speaking.

67. I am aware of the large literature discussing the nature of a gift and the impossibility of a gift, but I cannot address it in passing here. In my view, that literature suffers because it neglects or misunderstands the second-personal character that is part of the nature of a gift.

68. To me, it seems that this point holds even when the gift-giver is anonymous. That is why, for example, anonymous gift-giving can be a form of flirtation. But I do not

have the space here to argue this point; those who are not willing to accept it can bracket anonymous gift-giving from the claims made in this section.

69. See Chapter 8 for the discussion of these processes and their connection to union with God in love.

70. For explanation of this claim and for the distinction between surrender and submission, see Chapter 8.

71. For a presentation and defense of the view presupposed here—that union is possible only in case the persons in that union of love are each integrated around the good—see Chapters 6 and 7.

72. In fact, although it is not necessary to my argument here, it seems to me arguable that the value of a heart's desire for a person is enhanced, not diminished, when the desire for it is woven into the deepest desire of her heart. On the scale for subjective value for a person, a thing will only gain in value for her if it is also desired as part of the giving and receiving of love with God.

Chapter 15

1. Some people will feel inclined to suppose that if the claim I am making here is right, it shows nothing more than the irrationality of ordinary human people who do not care sufficiently about the things that are intrinsically valuable. This sort of objection has been addressed in Chapter 14 in the discussion of the stern-minded attitude.

2. By 'enable' here, I mean something like 'give the power to.' At any rate, the question cannot be formulated without some qualification of this sort, since, as I explained in earlier chapters, Aquinas takes human beings to have libertarian free will, so that they can reject love as well as accept it.

3. The qualification 'in the circumstances' has to be included here because what constitutes the necessary or best possible means to an end depends on the context in which the means and end are situated. The necessary or best possible means to harmony between a mother and her son is one thing for Gertrude and Hamlet while Hamlet's father is still living and another entirely after she has participated in his murder.

4. The phrase 'to be able to' has to be added because, since human beings have free will, God's allowing suffering cannot be guaranteed to have only one particular effect on the sufferer.

5. See the discussion of this idea in Chapter 10.

6. Annick Shaw et al., "Religion, Spirituality, and Posttraumatic Growth: A Systematic Review," *Mental Health, Religion & Culture*, 8 (Mar. 2005), 1–2. I am grateful to Monica Green for calling my attention to this topic and for providing me with a

plethora of resources, not only the articles cited in this and the following notes, but also many other relevant works, too many to cite in their entirety here.

7. Sean Ransom et al., "Actual Change and Inaccurate Recall Contribute to Posttraumatic Growth following Radiotherapy," *Journal of Consulting and Clinical Psychology*, 76 (2008), 811.

8. P. Alex Linley and Stephen Joseph, "Positive Change Following Trauma and Adversity: A Review," *Journal of Traumatic Stress*, 17 (2004), 11–21. Shaw, Joseph, and Linley cite studies documenting posttraumatic growth after bereavement, bone-marrow transplantation, breast cancer, childhood sexual abuse, chronic illness, disaster, HIV infection, military combat, myocardial infarction, parenting a child with leukemia, political imprisonment, refugee displacement following war, sexual assault, and shipwreck (see Shaw et al., "Religion, Spirituality, and Posttraumatic Growth," 2).

9. Crystal L. Park and Vicki S. Helgeson, "Introduction to the Special Section: Growth Following Highly Stressful Life Events—Current Status and Future Directions," *Journal of Consulting and Clinical Psychology*, 74 (2006), 791. See also Vicki S. Helgeson et al., "A Meta-Analytic Review of Benefit Finding and Growth," *Journal of Consulting and Clinical Psychology*, 74 (2006), 797–816.

10. Sirko Rabe et al., "Neural Correlates of Posttraumatic Growth after Severe Motor Vehicle Accidents," *Journal of Consulting and Clinical Psychology*, 74 (2006), 880.

11. William R. Miller and Janet C'De Baca, *Quantum Change: When Epiphanies and Sudden Insights Transform Ordinary Lives* (New York and London: Guilford Press, 2001), 157.

12. Shaw et al., "Religion, Spirituality, and Posttraumatic Growth," 6, 8.

13. Here are just two. Berit Gangstad et al., "Cognitive Processing and Posttraumatic Growth after Stroke," *Rehabilitation Psychology*, 54 (2009), 69–75. Crystal L. Park et al., "Pathways to Posttraumatic Growth following Posttraumatic Stress: Coping and Emotional Reactions following the September 11, 2001, Terrorist Attacks," *American Journal of Orthopsychiatry*, 78 (2008), 300–12.

14. Miller and C'De Baca, *Quantum Change*, 158.

15. Miller and C'De Baca, *Quantum Change*, 157.

16. See my *Aquinas* (London and New York: Routledge, 2003), ch. 13, on grace and free will.

17. In this sense, and just to this extent, Mary exemplifies the phenomenon John of the Cross calls 'the dark night of the soul,' in which a person is psychically or spiritually cut off from the deity, in a providentially ordered way that is designed to bring her much closer to God at the end of the process, but that is also very painful for her.

18. Even for heartbreak over animals, something roughly analogous to these lines can be said. C. S. Lewis says:

I am now going to suggest—though with great readiness to be set right by real theologians—that there may be a sense . . . in which those beasts that attain a real self are in their masters. That is to say, you must not think of a beast by itself, and call that a personality and then inquire whether God will raise and bless *that*. You must take the whole context in which the beast acquires its selfhood . . . In this way it seems to me possible that certain animals may have an immortality, not in themselves, but in the immortality of their masters . . . In other words, the man will know his dog; the dog will know its master and, in knowing him, will *be* itself. (*The Problem of Pain* (New York: Macmillan, 1962), 139–40.)

Reflecting on her grief over the death of her owl, Stacey O'Brien says: "He was amazing, curious, joyful, strong willed, full of life, a huge soul . . . My last prayer is that we be reunited in the afterlife . . . " (*Wesley the Owl* (New York: Free Press, 2008), 218).

19. For the notion of freedom here, see Chapter 7; see also my *Aquinas*, ch. 9, on freedom.

20. Clara Claiborne Park, *The Siege: A Family's Journey into the World of an Autistic Child* (rev. edn.; New York: Little, Brown, and Co., 1995), 15, 16, 29.

21. Claiborne Park, *The Siege*, 29.

22. Claiborne Park, *The Siege*, 320.

23. For a discussion of the story of Cory Friedman, see Chapter 13.

24. Victor Klemperer, *I Will Bear Witness: A Diary of the Nazi Years. 1942–1945*, trans. Martin Chalmers (New York: Modern Library, 2001), 433–4:

Brief morning reflection arisen from great love. In fact, the main point after all is that for forty years we have so much loved one another and do love one another; in fact, I am not at all sure at all that all this is going to come to an end. For certain, nothingness—en tant que individual consciousness, and that is the true nothingness—is altogether probable, anything else highly improbable. But have we not continually experienced, since 1914 and even more since 1933 and with ever greater frequency in recent weeks, the most utterly improbable, the most monstrously fantastic things? Has not what was formerly completely unimaginable to us become commonplace and a matter of course? If I have lived through the persecutions in Dresden, if I have lived through February 13 and these weeks as a refugee—why should I not just as well live (or rather die) to find the two of us somewhere, Eva and I, with angel wings or in some other droll form? It's not only the word "impossible" that has gone out of circulation, "unimaginable" also has no validity anymore.

For further discussion of Victor Klemperer's diaries, see Chapter 1.

25. See also the discussion of Sophie Scholl in Chapter 7 and Chapter 12.

26. I am taking 'luminous' as roughly equivalent to 'glorious' in this context. For a discussion of the notion of glory at issue here, see Chapter 13.

27. Cf. in this connection Isa. 56: 3–5, where God, through the prophet, promises a eunuch, who trusts in God but who grieves for himself as "a dry tree," that God will give him a name better than that of sons and daughters, an everlasting name.

28. See Chapter 14 for discussion of John Hull.

29. Susan Neiman, *Evil in Modern Thought: An Alternative History of Philosophy* (Princeton: Princeton University Press, 2002), 114.

30. I am not claiming that, on such a view, a sufferer of horrifying evil must think that his life is not a good for him, or must wish to die, or must fail to value his life. It is possible to have a life not worth living and to be keenly aware of that dreadful fact; but it is also possible that a person might value and wish to prolong a life that is in fact not worth living. The issue here is not the sufferer's evaluation of his life, but rather the quality of that life itself.

31. Well, in the view of her sister Martha. I extrapolate from the text in supposing that Martha's view is Mary's; but the extrapolation is not implausible, in my view.

32. I put the point in this way to ward off the objection that suffering is itself an accident of fortune. It is possible for any person to give his time, energy, and other resources for the well-being of others; to the extent to which he does so, there will be suffering in his life.

33. Aeschylus, *Agamemnon*, 177–83. I am grateful to my friend James Alexander Arieti, who helped me to see how to translate these lines.

34. For this hymn, see Joseph Connelly (ed.), *Hymns of the Roman Liturgy* (Westminster, MD: Newman Press, 1957), 62.

SELECT BIBLIOGRAPHY

For bibliography regarding the works and the thought of Aquinas, see my *Aquinas* (New York and London: Routledge, 2003).

Achebe, Chinua, *Hopes and Impediments* (New York: Anchor Books, Doubleday, 1989).

Adams, Marilyn McCord, *Horrendous Evils and the Goodness of God* (Ithaca, NY: Cornell University Press, 1999).

—— *Christ and Horrors: The Coherence of Christology* (Cambridge: Cambridge University Press, 2006).

Adams, Robert, "Pure Love," *Journal of Religious Ethics*, 8 (1980), 83–99.

Aelred of Rievaulx, *On Spiritual Friendship*, trans. Mary Eugenia Laker (Kalamazoo, MI: Cistercian Publications, 1977).

Aeschylus, *Agamemnon*, ed. John Dewar Denniston and Denys Page (Oxford: Clarendon Press, 1957).

Al-Ghazali, *Averroes, Tahafut Al-Tahafut*, trans. S. van den Bergh (London: Gibb Memorial Trust, 1978).

Alston, William, "Does God Have Beliefs," in William Alston (ed.), *Divine Nature and Human Language: Essays in Philosophical Theology* (Ithaca, NY: Cornell University Press, 1989), 178–96.

—— *The Reliability of Sense Perception* (Ithaca, NY: Cornell University Press, 1993).

—— "The Inductive Argument from Evil and the Human Cognitive Condition," in Daniel Howard-Snyder (ed.), *The Evidential Argument from Evil* (Bloomington, IN: Indiana University Press, 1996), 97–125.

Alter, Robert, *The Art of Biblical Narrative* (New York: Basic Books, 1981).

—— *The Art of Biblical Poetry* (New York: Basic Books, 1985).

—— *The World of Biblical Literature* (New York: Basic Books, 1992).

—— *Genesis* (New York and London: W. W. Norton, 1996).

Amit, Yairah, *The Book of Judges: The Art of Editing*, trans. Jonathan Chipman (Boston and Leiden: Brill, 1999).

Aquinas, Thomas, *Super Evangelium S. Ioannis Lectura*, ed. P. Raphaelis Cai (Rome: Marietti, 1952).

—— *Commentary on Saint Paul's Epistle to the Galatians by St Thomas Aquinas*, trans. F. R. Larcher and Richard Murphy (Albany, NY: Magi Books, 1966).

—— *Commentary on Saint Paul's First Letter to the Thessalonians and the Letter to the Philippians by St Thomas Aquinas*, trans. F. R. Larcher and Michael Duffy (Albany, NY: Magi Books, 1969).

—— *The Literal Exposition on Job: A Scriptural Commentary Concerning Providence*, trans. Anthony Damico, interpretive essay and notes Martin D. Yaffe (Atlanta, GA: Scholars' Press, 1989).

Arieti, James Alexander, *Interpreting Plato: The Dialogues as Drama* (Savage, MD: Rowman and Littlefield, 1991).

Armstrong, Regis, and Ignatius Brady (eds.), *Francis and Clare* (New York: Paulist Press, 1982).

Armstrong, Regis, J. A. Wayne Hellman, and William Short (eds.), *Francis of Assisi: The Early Documents*, i. *The Saint* (New York: New City Press, 1999).

—— *Francis of Assisi: The Early Documents*, ii. *The Founder* (New York: New City Press, 2000).

Asante, M. K., and A. Mazama (eds.), *Encyclopedia of African Religions* (Thousand Oaks, CA: Sage Publications, 2009).

Astell, Ann, *The Song of Songs in the Middle Ages* (Ithaca, NY: Cornell University Press, 1990).

Audi, Robert, *The Architecture of Reason* (Oxford: Oxford University Press, 2001).

Auerbach, Eric, *Mimesis* (Princeton: Princeton University Press, 1953).

Augustine, *St Augustine: Commentary on the Lord's Sermon on the Mount*, trans. Denis Kavanagh (The Fathers of the Church, vol. 11; Washington: Catholic University of America Press, 1951).

——— *Confessions*, trans. William Watts (Cambridge, MA: Harvard University Press, 1968).

——— *Harmony of the Gospels*, in *Nicene and Post-Nicene Fathers*, ed. Philip Schaff, vi (Grand Rapids, MI: Eerdmans, 1956; repr. 1996).

——— *Homilies on the Gospel of John*, trans. John Gibb and James Innes, in *Nicene and Post-Nicene Fathers*, ed. Philip Schaff, vi (Grand Rapids, MI: Eerdmans, 1956; repr. 1996).

——— *Sermons on New Testament Lessons*, in *Nicene and Post-Nicene Fathers*, ed. Philip Schaff, vi (Grand Rapids, MI: Eerdmans, 1956; repr. 1996).

Ayo, Nicholas (trans.), *The Sermon-Conferences of St Thomas Aquinas on the Apostles' Creed* (Notre Dame, IN: University of Notre Dame Press, 1988).

Baldwin, Thomas, "From Knowledge by Acquaintance to Knowledge by Causation," in Nicholas Griffin (ed.), *The Cambridge Companion to Bertrand Russell* (Cambridge: Cambridge University Press, 2003), 420–48.

Benowitz, Larry, Seth Finkelstein, David Levine, and Kenneth Moya, "The Role of the Right Cerebral Hemisphere in Evaluating Configurations," in Colywyn Trevarthen (ed.), *Brain Circuits and Functions of the Mind: Essays in Honor of Roger W. Sperry* (Cambridge: Cambridge University Press, 1990), 320–33.

Bermudez, Jose Luis, and Sebastian Gardner (eds.), *Art and Morality* (London: Routledge, 2003).

Bernier, Raphael, and Geraldine Dawson, "The Role of Mirror Neuron Dysfunction in Autism," in Jamie Pineda (ed.), *Mirror Neuron Systems: The Role of Mirroring Processes in Social Cognition* (New York: Springer, 2009), 261–86.

Blackburn, Simon, "An Unbeautiful Mind," *New Republic*, 5 and 12 (Aug. 2002), 29–33.

Blakeslee, Sandra, and Vilayandur Ramachandran, *Phantoms in the Brain* (London: Harper Perennial, 2005).

Bloch, Michael, *Ribbentrop* (1992; repr, London: Abacus Books, 2003).

Boling, Robert G. (ed. and trans.), *Judges* (The Anchor Bible: Garden City, NY: Doubleday, 1975).

Bonjour, Laurence, and Ernest Sosa, *Epistemic Justification: Internalism vs. Externalism. Foundations vs. Virtues* (Oxford: Blackwell, 2003).

Boyd, Ian, "The Problem of Self-Destroying Sin in John Milton's *Samson Agonistes*," *Faith and Philosophy*, 13 (1996), 487–507.

Brettler, Marc Zvi, *The Book of Judges* (London and New York: Routledge, 2002).

Brown, Frank Burch, *Good Taste, Bad Taste and Christian Taste: Aesthetics in Religious Life* (Oxford: Oxford University Press, 2000).

Brown, Rachel, Peter Hobson, and Anthony Lee, "Are there 'Autistic-Like' Features in Congenitally Blind Children?," *Journal of Child Psychology and Psychiatry*, 38 (1997), 693–703.

Brown, Raymond (ed. and trans.), *The Gospel According to John* (The Anchor Bible; 2 vols.; New York: Doubleday and Company, 1970).

Browne, Michael Dennis, "Light upon the Water," in *Things I Can't Tell You* (Pittsburgh, PA: Carnegie Mellon University Press, 2005), 80.

Brueggeman, Walter, *Genesis* (Atlanta: John Knox Press, 1982).

Buber, Martin, *I and Thou*, trans. Walter Kaufman (New York: Touchstone Books, 1970).

Bunyan, John, *Grace Abounding to the Chief of Sinners* (New York: Penguin Books, 1987).

Burke, Edmund, *A Philosophical Enquiry into the Origin of our Ideas of the Sublime and Beautiful*, ed. Adam Phillips (Oxford: Oxford University Press, 1990).

Burkett, Elinor, "God Created Me to Be a Slave," *New York Times Magazine*, Oct. 12, 1997, pp. 56–60.

Cairns, Douglas, *Aidos: The Psychology and Ethics of Honour and Shame in Ancient Greek Literature* (Oxford: Oxford University Press, 2002).

Call, Joseph, and Michael Tomasello, "What Chimpanzees Know about Seeing, Revisited: An Explanation of the Third Kind," in Naomi Eilan, Christoph Hoerl, Teresa McCormack, and Johannes Roessler (eds.), *Joint Attention: Communication and Other Minds: Issues in Philosophy and Psychology* (Oxford: Clarendon Press, 2005), 45–64.

Calvin, John, *The Gospel According to St John* (Grand Rapids, MI: Eerdmans, 1959; repr. 1979).

Campbell, John, *Reference and Consciousness* (Oxford: Oxford University Press, 2002).

Card, Claudia, *The Atrocity Paradigm: A Theory of Evil* (Oxford: Oxford University Press, 2002).

Carey, John, "A Work in Praise of Terrorism? September 11 and *Samson Agonistes*," *Times Literary Supplement*, Sept. 6, 2002, pp. 15–16.

Carruthers, Peter, "Why Pretend?," in Shaun Nichols (ed.), *The Architecture of Imagination: New Essays on Pretence, Possibility, and Fiction* (Oxford: Clarendon Press, 2006), 89–110.

Cassian, John, *The Monastic Institutes*, trans. Jerome Bertram (London: Saint Austin Press, 1999).

Catullus, "Odi et amo," in *The Norton Anthology of World Masterpieces*, ed. Maynard Mack (New York: W. W. Norton and Company, 1995), i. 995.

Cesarani, David, *Becoming Eichmann* (Cambridge, MA: Da Capo Press, 2004).

Chrysostom, John, *Commentary on Saint John the Apostle and Evangelist* (Homilies 48–88), trans. Sister Thomas Aquinas Goggin (Washington: Catholic University Press, 1959; repr. 1977).

——*St John Chrysostom: On Wealth and Poverty*, trans. Catharine P. Roth (Crestwood, NY: St Vladimir's Seminary Press, 1984).

——*Homilies on Genesis*, trans. Robert C. Hill (Washington: Catholic University of America Press, 1992).

Collins, John, "The Exodus and Biblical Theology," *Biblical Theology Bulletin*, 25 (1995), 152–60.

Connelly, Joseph (ed.), *Hymns of the Roman Liturgy* (Westminster, MD: Newman Press, 1957).

Crenshaw, James, *Samson* (Atlanta: John Knox Press, 1978).

Dalferth, Ingolf, *Becoming Present: An Inquiry into the Christian Sense of the Presence of God* (Leeuven: Peeters, 2006).

Damasio, Antonio, *The Feeling of What Happens* (New York: Harcourt, 1999).

Darwall, Stephen, "Fichte and the Second-Person Standpoint," *Internationales Jahrbuch des deutschen Idealismus*, 3 (2005), 91–113.

——*The Second-Person Standpoint: Morality, Respect, and Accountability* (Cambridge, MA: Harvard University Press, 2006).

Davies, Brian, *The Reality of God and the Problem of Evil* (London and New York: Continuum, 2006).

Davies, Martin, and Tony Stone (eds.), *Mental Simulation* (Oxford: Blackwell, 1995).

DeMaria, Robert, *The Life of Samuel Johnson: A Critical Biography* (Oxford: Blackwell, 1993).

Dissanayake, Ellen, "Antecedents of the Temporal Arts in Early Mother–Infant Interaction," in Nils Wallin, Bjoern Merker, and Steven Brown (eds.), *The Origins of Music* (Cambridge, MA: MIT Press, 2000), 389–410

Draper, Paul, "The Skeptical Theist," in Daniel Howard-Snyder (ed.), *The Evidential Argument from Evil* (Bloomington, IN: Indiana University Press, 1996), 175–92.

Dumbach, Annette, and Jud Newborn, *Sophie Scholl and the White Rose* (Oxford, Oneworld Publications, 2006).

Eco, Umberto, *Art and Beauty in the Middle Ages* (New Haven: Yale University Press, 1986).

Eilan, Naomi, "Joint Attention, Communication, and Mind," in Naomi Eilan, Christoph Hoerl, Teresa McCormack, and Johannes Roessler (eds.), *Joint Attention: Communication and Other Minds: Issues in Philosophy and Psychology* (Oxford: Clarendon Press, 2005), 1–33.

Eilan, Naomi, Christoph Hoerl, Teresa McCormack, and Johannes Roessler (eds.), *Joint Attention: Communication and Other Minds: Issues in Philosophy and Psychology* (Oxford: Clarendon Press, 2005).

Eisen, Robert, *The Book of Job in Medieval Jewish Philosophy* (Oxford: Oxford University Press, 2004).

Evans, Richard J., *The Third Reich at War* (New York: Penguin Press, 2009).

Farah, Martha J., *Visual Agnosia* (Cambridge, MA: MIT Press, 1990).

Feinberg, Todd, John DeLuca, Joseph T. Giacino, David Roane, and Mark Solms, "Right-Hemisphere Pathology and the Self: Delusional Misidentification and Reduplication," in Todd Feinberg and Julian Paul Keenan (eds.), *The Lost Self: Pathologies of the Brain and Identity* (Oxford: Oxford University Press, 2005), 100–30.

Felder, Cain Hope, *Stony the Road We Trod* (Minneapolis: Fortress Press, 1991).

—— *Troubling Biblical Waters* (Maryknoll, NY: Orbis Books, 1993).

Feynman, Richard, *"Surely You're Joking, Mr Feynman!"* (New York: Bantam Books, 1985).

Field, Tiffany, and Nathan Fox (eds.), *Social Perception in Infants* (Norwood, NJ: Ablex Publishing Corporation, 1985).

Fitzmyer, Joseph (ed. and trans.), *The Gospel According to Luke* (The Anchor Bible; 2 vols.; New York: Doubleday, 1981).

Flint, Thomas, *Divine Providence: The Molinist Account* (Ithaca, NY: Cornell University Press, 1998).

Fogassi, Leonardo, Pier Francesco Ferrari, Bennor Gesierich, Stefano Rozzi, Fabian Chersi, and Giacomo Rizzolatti, "Parietal Lobe: From Action Organization to Intention Understanding," *Science*, 308, Apr. 29, 2005, pp. 662–7.

Fokkelman, J. P., *Narrative Art in Genesis* (Assen: Van Gorcum, 1975).

Franco, Fabia, "Infant Pointing: Harlequin, Servant of Two Masters," in Naomi Eilan, Christoph Hoerl, Teresa McCormack, and Johannes Roessler (eds.), *Joint Attention: Communication and Other Minds: Issues in Philosophy and Psychology* (Oxford: Clarendon Press, 2005), 129–64.

Frankfurt, Harry, "Freedom of the Will and the Concept of a Person," *Journal of Philosophy*, 68 (1971), 5–20; repr. in Harry Frankfurt, *The Importance of What We Care About* (Cambridge: Cambridge University Press, 1988).

—— *The Importance of What We Care About* (Cambridge: Cambridge University Press, 1988).

—— "The Faintest Passion," *Proceedings and Addresses of the American Philosophical Association*, 66/3 (1992), 5–16.

—— "On the Necessity of Ideals," in Gil Noam and Thomas Wren (eds.), *The Moral Self* (Cambridge, MA: MIT Press, 1993), 16–27.

—— "Autonomy, Necessity, and Love," in Hans Friedrick Fulda and Rolf-Peter Horstmann (eds.), *Vernunftbegriffe in der Moderne: Veroffentlichungen der internationalen Hegel-Vereinigung* (Stuttgart: Klett-Cotta, 1994).

—— "On the Usefulness of Final Ends," in Harry Frankfurt, *Necessity, Volition, and Love* (Cambridge: Cambridge University Press, 1999), 82–94.

—— *Necessity, Volition, and Love* (Cambridge: Cambridge University Press, 1999).

—— *The Reasons of Love* (Princeton: Princeton University Press, 2004).

—— *Taking Ourselves Seriously and Getting It Right* (Stanford, CA: Stanford University Press, 2006).

Frith, Chris, and Daniel Wolpert (eds.), *The Neuroscience of Social Interaction: Decoding, Imitating, and Influencing the Actions of Others* (Oxford: Oxford University Press, 2004).

Gale, Mike, *The St Louis Jesuits: Thirty Years* (Portland, OR: Oregon Catholic Press, 2006).

Gallagher, Shaun, "The Practice of Mind," in Evan Thompson (ed.), *Between Ourselves: Second-Person Issues in the Study of Consciousness* (Charlottesville, VA: Imprint Academic, 2001), 83–108.

—— *How the Body Shapes the Mind* (Oxford: Clarendon Press, 2005).

—— "Neural Simulation and Social Cognition," in Jamie Pineda (ed.), *Mirror Neuron Systems: The Role of Mirroring Processes in Social Cognition* (New York: Springer, 2009), 355–71.

Gallese, Vittorio, "The 'Shared Manifold' Hypothesis: From Mirror Neurons to Empathy," in Evan Thompson (ed.), *Between Ourselves: Second-Person Issues in the Study of Consciousness* (Charlottesville, VA: Imprint Academic, 2001), 33–50.

—— " 'Being Like Me': Self–Other Identity, Mirror Neurons, and Empathy," in Susan Hurley and Nick Chater (eds.), *Perspectives on Imitation: From Neuroscience to Social Science* (Cambridge, MA: MIT Press, 2005), i. 101–18.

Gallese, Vittorio, Christian Keysers, and Giacomo Rizzolatti, "A Unifying View of the Basis of Social Cognition," *Trends in Cognitive Science*, 8 (2004), 396–403.

Gangstad, Berit, Paul Norman, and Jane Barton. "Cognitive Processing and Posttraumatic Growth after Stroke," *Rehabilitation Psychology*, 54 (2009), 69–75.

Garrard, Eve, and David McNaughton. "In Defence of Unconditional Forgiveness," *Proceedings of the Aristotelian Society* (2002–3), 39–60.

Gay, Peter, "Inside the Third Reich," *New York Times Book Review*, Nov. 22, 1998.

Gellman, Jerome (Yehuda), *The Fear, the Trembling, and the Fire: Kierkegaard and Hasidic Masters on the Binding of Isaac* (Lanham, MD: University Press of America, 1994).

—— *Abraham! Abraham! Kierkegaard and the Hasidim on the Binding of Isaac* (Burlington, VT: Ashgate Publishing Co., 2003).

Gendler, Tamar, "Thought Experiment," in *Encyclopedia of Cognitive Science* (New York: Nature Publishing Group, 2002).

Genovese, Eugene, *The World the Slaves Made* (New York: Vintage Books, 1976).

Geschwind, Norman, and Albert M. Galaburda, *Cerebral Lateralization* (Cambridge, MA: MIT Press, 1989).

Gibson, John, Wolfgang Huemer, and Luca Pocci (eds.), *A Sense of the World: Essays on Fiction, Narrative, and Knowledge* (London: Routledge, 2007).

Girard, Shelly, "Why Have Natural Childbirth?" (http://pregnancyandbaby.com/pregnancy/baby/Why-have-natural-childbirth-606.htm).

Glas, Gerrit, "Elements of a Phenomenology of Evil and Forgiveness," in Nancy Nyquist Potter (ed.), *Trauma, Truth, and Reconciliation: Healing Damaged Relationships* (Oxford: Oxford University Press, 2006), 182–3.

Glueckel of Hamlyn, *The Memoirs of Glueckel of Hamlyn*, trans. Marvin Lowenthal (New York: Schocken Books, 1977).

Goldhagen, Daniel Jonah, *Hitler's Willing Executioners* (New York: Knopf, 1996).

Goldman, Alvin, "Imagination and Simulation in Audience Responses to Fiction," in Shaun Nichols (ed.), *The Architecture of the Imagination: New Essays on Pretence, Possibility, and Fiction* (Oxford: Clarendon Press, 2006), 41–56.

—— "Mirroring, Mindreading, and Simulation," in Jamie Pineda (ed.), *Mirror Neuron Systems: The Role of Mirroring Processes in Social Cognition* (New York: Springer, 2009), 311–30.

Good, Kenneth, *Into the Heart* (New York: Simon and Schuster, 1990).

Govier, Trudy, *Forgiveness and Revenge* (London: Routledge, 2002).

Grahek, Nikola, *Feeling Pain and Being in Pain* (Cambridge, MA: MIT Press, 2007).

Greenslade, S. L. (ed.), *The Cambridge History of the Bible* (Cambridge: Cambridge University Press, 1963; repr. 1988).

Guillaume de Tocco, *Ystoria sancti Thome de Aquino de Guillaume de Tocco* (1323), ed. Claire le Brun-Gouanvic (Toronto: Pontifical Institute of Mediaeval Studies, 1996).

Guttenplan, D. D., "THINK TANK: Is Reading Milton Unsafe at Any Speed?" *New York Times*, Dec. 28, 2002, p. 9(B).

Halberthal, Moshe, *Concealment and Revelation: Esotericism in Jewish Thought and its Philosophical Implications*, trans. Jackie Feldman (Princeton: Princeton University Press, 2007).

Hasker, William, *God, Time, and Knowledge* (Ithaca, NY, and London: Cornell University Press, 1989).

—— "The Absence of a Timeless God," in Greg Ganssle and David Woodruff (eds.), *God and Time: Essays on the Divine Nature* (New York: Oxford University Press, 2002), 182–206.

—— *The Triumph of God over Evil* (Downers Grove, IL: IVP Academic, 2008).

Hearne, Vicki, *Adam's Task: Calling Animals by Name* (New York: Knopf, 1986; Skyhorse Publishing, 2007).

Helgeson, Vicki S., Kerry A. Reynolds, and Patricia L. Tomich, "A Meta-Analytic Review of Benefit Finding and Growth," *Journal of Consulting and Clinical Psychology*, 74 (2006), 797–816.

Hellige, Joseph B., *Hemispheric Asymmetry: What's Right and What's Left* (Cambridge, MA: Harvard University Press, 1993).

Hertz, J. H. (ed.), *The Soncino Edition of the Pentateuch and Haftorahs* (2nd edn.; London: Soncino Press, 1967).

Hick, John, *Evil and the God of Love* (New York: Harper and Row, 1966).

—— "God, Evil and Mystery," *Religious Studies*, 3 (1968), 539–46.

—— "The Problem of Evil in the First and Last Things," *Journal of Theological Studies*, 19 (1968), 591–602.

Hieronymi, Pamela, "Articulating an Uncompromising Forgiveness," *Philosophy and Phenomenological Research*, 62 (2001), 529–55.

Hobson, Peter, *The Cradle of Thought: Exploring the Origins of Thinking* (Oxford: Oxford University Press, 2004).

Hobson, R. Peter, "What Puts the Jointness into Joint Attention?," in Naomi Eilan, Christoph Hoerl, Teresa McCormack, and Johannes Roessler (eds.), *Joint Attention: Communication and Other Minds: Issues in Philosophy and Psychology* (Oxford: Clarendon Press, 2005), 185–204.

Hoehne, Heinz, *The Order of the Death's Head* (1969; repr. New York: Penguin, 2000).

Homer, *Iliad*, trans. Richard Lattimore (Chicago: University of Chicago Press, 1951).

Hopkins, Dwight, and George Cummings, *Cut Loose Your Stammering Tongue* (Maryknoll, NY: Orbis Books, 1991).

Hughes, Claire, and James Russell, "Autistic Children's Difficulty with Mental Disengagement from an Object: Its Implications for Theories of Autism," *Developmental Psychology*, 29 (1993), 498–510.

Hull, John M., *Touching the Rock: An Experience of Blindness* (New York: Pantheon Books, 1990).

Hurley, Susan, and Nick Chater, "Imitation in Animals," in Susan Hurley and Nick Chater, *Perspectives on Imitation: From Neuroscience to Social Science* (Cambridge, MA: MIT Press, 2005), i. 223–4.

Hutto, Daniel, *Folk Psychological Narrative: The Sociocultural Basis of Understanding Reasons* (Cambridge, MA: MIT Press, 2008).

Iacoboni, Marco, Istvan Molnar-Szakacs, Vittorio Gallese, Giovanni Bucciono, John C. Mazziotta, and Giacomo Rizzolatti, "Grasping the Intentions of Others with One's Own Mirror Neuron System," *PloS Biology*, 3/3 (2005).

Iverson, Jana, and Susan Goldin-Meadow, "What's Communication Got to Do with It? Gesture in Children Blind from Birth," *Developmental Psychology* 33 (1997), 453–67.

Jabbi, Mbemba, Jojanneke Bastiaansen, and Christian Keypers, "A Common Anterior Insula Representation of Disgust Observation, Experience and Imagination Shows Divergent Functional Connectivity Pathways," www.plosone.org/article/info:doi/10.1371/journal.pone.0002939.

Jackson, Frank, "Epiphenomenal Qualia," *Philosophical Quarterly*, 32 (1982), 127–36.

John, Eileen, and Dominic McIver Lopes, *Philosophy of Literature* (Oxford: Blackwell, 2004).

Kandel, Eric R., James Schwartz, and Thomas Jessell, *Principles of Neural Science* (4th edn.; New York: McGraw Hill, 2000).

Keller, Evelyn Fox, *Reflections on Gender and Science* (New Haven and London: Yale University Press, 1985).

Keller, Helen, *The Story of My Life* (New York: Dell Publishing, 1961).

Kelly, J. N. D., *Jerome: His Life, Writings and Controversies* (London: Duckworth, 1975; repr. 1998).

——*Golden Mouth: The Story of John Chrysostom, Ascetic, Preacher, Bishop* (Ithaca, NY: Cornell University Press, 1995).

Kessler, Edward, *Bound by the Bible: Jews, Christians, and the Sacrifice of Isaac* (Cambridge: Cambridge University Press, 2004).

Kieran, Matthew, and Dominic McIver Lopes (eds.), *Imagination, Philosophy, and the Arts* (London: Routledge, 2003).

Kierkegaard, Søren, *Fear and Trembling*, trans. Walter Lowrie (Princeton: Princeton University Press, 1968).

Kirmayer, Laurence J., "On the Cultural Mediation of Pain," in "When Is Pain Not Suffering and Suffering Not Pain," in Sarah Coakley and Kay Kaufman Shelemay (eds.), *Pain and its Transformations: The Interface of Biology and Culture* (Cambridge, MA: Harvard University Press, 2007), 363–401.

Klein, Peter, "Epistemology," in *Routledge Encyclopedia of Philosophy* (London: Routledge, 1999).

——"Knowledge, Concept of," in *Routledge Encyclopedia of Philosophy* (London: Routledge, 1999).

Klemperer, Victor, *I Will Bear Witness: A Diary of the Nazi Years. 1942–1945*, trans. Martin Chalmers (New York: The Modern Library, 2001).

Kolodny, Niko, "Love as Valuing a Relationship," *Philosophical Review*, 112 (2003), 135–89.

Kosslyn, Stephen, *Image and Brain: The Resolution of the Imagery Debate* (Cambridge, MA: MIT Press, 1994).

Kraut, Richard, *What is Good and Why* (Cambridge, MA: Harvard University Press, 2007).

Kraut, Robert, "Love *De Re*," *Midwest Studies in Philosophy*, 10 (1986), 413–30.

Kretzmann, Norman, "Abraham, Isaac, and Euthyphro: God and the Basis of Morality," in Donald Stump, James Arieti, Lloyd Gerson, and Eleonore Stump (eds.), *Hamartia: The Concept of Error in the Western Tradition: Essays in Honor of John Crossett* (Lewiston, NY: Edwin Mellen Press, 1983), 27–50.

——"A General Problem of Creation: Why Would God Create Anything At All?," in Scott MacDonald (ed.), *Being and Goodness* (Ithaca, NY: Cornell University Press, 1988), 208–28.

——"A Particular Problem of Creation: Why Would God Create this World?," in Scott MacDonald (ed.), *Being and Goodness* (Ithaca, NY: Cornell University Press, 1988), 229–49.

Lamarque, Peter, and Stein Haugom Olsen, "Literature, Truth, and Philosophy," in Eileen John and Dominic McIver Lopes (eds.), *Philosophy of Literature, Contemporary and Classic Readings* (Oxford: Blackwell, 2004), 341–54.

Lane, Harlan, *The Wild Boy of Aveyron* (Cambridge, MA: Harvard University Press, 1976).

Langtry, Bruce, *God, the Best, and Evil* (Oxford: Oxford University Press, 2008).

Leekam, Sue, "Why do Children with Autism have a Joint Attention Impairment?," in Naomi Eilan, Christoph Hoerl, Teresa McCormack, and Johannes Roessler (eds.), *Joint Attention: Communication and Other Minds: Issues in Philosophy and Psychology* (Oxford: Clarendon Press, 2005), 205–29.

Levenson, Jon, *Creation and the Persistence of Evil: The Jewish Drama of Divine Omnipotence* (Princeton: Princeton University Press, 1988).

——"The Eighth Principle of Judaism and the Literary Simultaneity of Scripture," *Journal of Religion*, 68 (1988), 205–25.

—— *The Death and Resurrection of the Beloved Son* (New Haven: Yale University Press, 1993).

—— *The Hebrew Bible, the Old Testament, and Historical Criticism: Jews and Christians in Biblical Studies* (Louisville, KY: Westminster/John Knox, 1993).

——"The Exodus and Biblical Theology: A Rejoinder to John J. Collins," *Biblical Theology Bulletin*, 26/1 (Spring 1996), 4–10; repr. in Alice Ogden Bellis and Joel S. Kaminsky (eds.), *Jews, Christians, and the Theology of the Hebrew Scriptures* (Atlanta: Society of Biblical Literature, 2000), 247–61.

Levitin, Daniel, *This is Your Brain on Music* (New York: Dutton, 2006).

Lewis, C. S., *A Grief Observed* (New York: Bantam Books, 1960).

—— *The Problem of Pain* (New York: Macmillan, 1962).

—— *The Great Divorce* (New York: HarperCollins, 1973; rev. edn., 2001).

Linley, P. Alex, and Stephen Joseph, "Positive Change following Trauma and Adversity: A Review," *Journal of Traumatic Stress*, 17 (2004), 11–21.

Locke, John, *Some Thoughts Concerning Education* (New York: P. F. Collier & Son Company, 1909–14; repr. New York: Bartleby.com, 2001),

Loots, Gerrit, Isabel Devise, and Jasmina Sermijn, "The Interaction between Mothers and their Visually Impaired Infants: An Intersubjective Developmental Perspective," *Journal of Visual Impairment and Blindness*, 97 (2003), 403–17.

Lopes, Dominic McIver, *Sight and Sensibility: Evaluating Pictures* (Oxford: Clarendon Press, 2005).

Lowe, E. J., *Personal Agency: The Metaphysics of Mind and Action* (Oxford: Oxford University Press, 2008).

Ludlow, Peter, Yujin Nagasawa, and Daniel Stoljar (eds.), *There is Something about Mary: Essays on Phenomenal Consciousness and Frank Jackson's Knowledge Argument* (Cambridge, MA: MIT Press, 2004).

MacDonald, Scott (ed.), *Being and Goodness: The Concept of the Good in Metaphysics and Philosophical Theology* (Ithaca, NY: Cornell University Press, 1991).

MacFarquhar, Roderick, "The Succession to Mao and the End of Maoism," in *The Cambridge History of China*, xv. *The People's Republic, pt. 2: Revolutions within the Chinese Revolution: 1966–1982* (Cambridge: Cambridge University Press, 1991).

McMullin, Ernan (ed.), *Evolution and Creation* (Notre Dame, IN: University of Notre Dame Press, 1985).

Margalit, Avishai, *The Ethics of Memory* (Cambridge, MA: Harvard University Press, 2002).

Marsden, George, *Jonathan Edwards: A Life* (New Haven: Yale University Press, 2003).

Matthews, Victor, *Judges and Ruth* (Cambridge: Cambridge University Press, 2004).

Meyers, Carol, Toni Craven, and Ross S. Kraemer (eds.), *Women in Scripture: A Dictionary of Named and Unnamed Women in the Hebrew Bible, the Apocryphal/Deuterocanonical Books, and the New Testament* (Grand Rapids, MI: Eeerdmans, 2000).

Midrash Rabbah: Genesis, trans. H. Freedman, i (London and New York: Soncino Press, 1983).

Miller, Greg, "Mirror Neurons May Help Songbirds Stay in Tune," *Science*, 319/5861, Jan. 18, 2008, p. 269.

Miller, William R., and Janet C'De Baca, *Quantum Change: When Epiphanies and Sudden Insights Transform Ordinary Lives* (New York and London: Guilford Press, 2001).

Milton, John, *The Complete Poetical Works of John Milton*, ed. Douglas Bush (Boston: Houghton Mifflin Co., 1965).

Mithen, Steven, *The Singing Neanderthals: The Origin of Music, Language, Mind and Body* (London: Phoenix Books, 2006).

Montagu, Ashley, *The Elephant Man: A Study in Human Dignity* (Lafayette, LA: Acadian House, 2001).

Moore, Derek, Peter Hobson, and Anthony Lee, "Components of Person Perception: An Investigation with Autistic, Non-Autistic Retarded and Typically Developing Children and Adolescents," *British Journal of Developmental Psychology*, 15 (1997), 401–23.

Moorman, John, *A History of the Franciscan Order from its Origins to the Year 1517* (Oxford: Clarendon Press, 1968).

Moran, Richard, *Authority and Estrangement: An Essay on Self-Knowledge* (Princeton: Princeton University Press, 2001).

—— "Review Essay on *The Reasons of Love*," *Philosophy and Phenomenological Research*, 74 (2007), 463–75.

More, Thomas, *A Dialogue of Comfort against Tribulation*, ed. and trans. Mary Gottschalk (Princeton: Scepter Press, 1998).

Mother Teresa, *Come Be My Light: The Private Writings of the 'Saint of Calcutta'*, ed. Brian Kolodiejchuk (New York: Doubleday, 2007).

Munzer, Stephen, "Self-Abandonment and Self-Denial: Quietism, Calvinism, and the Prospect of Hell," *Journal of Religious Ethics*, 33 (2005), 747–81.

Murphy, Jeffrie, *Getting Even: Forgiveness and its Limits* (Oxford: Oxford University Press, 2003).

Murphy, Jeffrie, and Jean Hampton, *Forgiveness and Mercy* (Cambridge: Cambridge University Press, 1988).

Murphy, Jeffrie, and Sharon Lamb, *Before Forgiveness* (Oxford: Oxford University Press, 2002).

Nasar, Sylvia, *A Beautiful Mind* (New York: Simon and Schuster, 1998).

Neiman, Susan, *Evil in Modern Thought: An Alternative History of Philosophy* (Princeton: Princeton University Press, 2002).

Nemirow, Laurence, "Physicalism and the Cognitive Role of Acquaintance," in William Lycan (ed.), *Mind and Cognition* (Oxford: Blackwell, 1990), 490–9.

Nichols, Shaun (ed.), *The Architecture of Imagination. New Essays on Pretence, Possibility, and Fiction* (Oxford: Clarendon Press, 2006).

Nichols, Shaun, and Stephen Stich, *Mindreading: An Integrated Account of Pretence, Self-Awareness, and Understanding Other Minds* (Oxford: Clarendon Press, 2003).

Novitz, David, "Forgiveness and Self-Respect," *Philosophy and Phenomenological Research*, 58 (1998), 299–315.

Nussbaum, Martha, *The Fragility of Goodness: Luck and Ethics in Greek Tragedy and Philosophy* (Cambridge: Cambridge University Press, 1986).

—— *Hiding from Humanity: Disgust, Shame, and the Law* (Princeton: Princeton University Press, 2004).

O'Brien, Stacey, *Wesley the Owl* (New York: Free Press, 2008).

O'Neill, Onora, "The Power of Example," *Philosophy*, 61 (1986), 5–29.

Oberman, Lindsay M., and V. S. Ramachandran, "Reflections on the Mirror Neuron System: Their Evolutionary Functions beyond Motor Representation," in Jamie Pineda (ed.), *Mirror Neuron Systems: The Role of Mirroring Processes in Social Cognition* (New York: Springer, 2009), 39–59.

Oppy, Graham, "Propositional Attitudes," in *Routledge Encyclopedia of Philosophy* (London: Routledge, 1999).

Osborne, Thomas, "The Augustinianism of Thomas Aquinas's Moral Theory," *Thomist*, 67 (2003), 279–305.

—— *Love of Self and Love of God in Thirteenth Century Ethics* (Notre Dame, IN: University of Notre Dame Press, 2005).

Overy, Richard, *Goering* (1984; repr. New York: Barnes and Noble Books, 2003).

Owen, Adrian M., et al., "Detecting Awareness in the Vegetative State," *Science*, 313, 9 Sept. 8, 2006, p. 1402.

Painter, Nell Irvin (ed.), *Narrative of Sojourner Truth* (New York: Penguin Books, 1998).

Park, Clara Claiborne, *The Siege: A Family's Journey into the World of an Autistic Child* (rev. edn.; New York: Little, Brown and Company, 1995).

Park, Crystal L., Carolyn M. Aldwin, Juliane R. Fenster and Leslie B. Snyder, "Pathways to Posttraumatic Growth following Posttraumatic Stress: Coping and Emotional Reactions following the September 11, 2001, Terrorist Attacks," *American Journal of Orthopsychiatry*, 78 (2008), 300–12

Park, Crystal L., and Vicki S. Helgeson, "Introduction to the Special Section: Growth following Highly Stressful Life Events—Current Status and Future Directions," *Journal of Consulting and Clinical Psychology*, 74 (2006), 791–6.

Parker, DeWitt. "Knowledge by Acquaintance," *Philosophical Review*, 54 (1945), 1–18.

Patterson, James, and Hal Friedman, *Against Medical Advice* (New York: Little, Brown, and Co., 2008).

Peacocke, Christopher, "Joint Attention: Its Nature, Reflexivity, and Relation to Common Knowledge," in Naomi Eilan, Christoph Hoerl, Teresa McCormack, and Johannes Roessler (eds.), in *Joint Attention: Communication and Other Minds: Issues in Philosophy and Psychology* (Oxford: Clarendon Press, 2005), 298–324.

Pernick, Martin S., *A Calculus of Suffering: Pain, Professionalism, and Anesthesia in Nineteenth Century America* (New York: Columbia University Press, 1985).

Pettigrove, Glen, "Unapologetic Forgiveness," *American Philosophical Quarterly*, 41 (2004), 187–204.

——"Understanding, Excusing, Forgiving," *Philosophy and Phenomenological Research*, 74 (2007), 156–75.

Plantinga, Alvin, *Warrant and Proper Function* (Oxford: Oxford University Press, 1993).

——"Religion and Science," in Edward N. Zalta (ed.), *Stanford Encyclopedia of Philosophy* (2007).

Polzin, Robert, *Samuel and the Deuteronomist* (New York: Harper and Row, 1989).

Pope, Marvin (ed. and trans.), *Job* (The Anchor Bible; 3rd edn.; New York: Doubleday, 1973).

Poulsen, Else, *Smiling Bears* (Berkeley, CA: Greystone Books, D & M Publishers, 2009).

Quinn, Philip, "Moral Obligation, Religious Demand, and Practical Conflict," in Robert Audi and William Wainwright (eds.), *Rationality, Religious Belief, and Moral Commitment* (Ithaca, NY: Cornell University Press, 1986), 194–212.

——"Agamemnon and Abraham: The Tragic Dilemma of Kierkegaard's Knight of Faith," *Journal of Literature and Theology*, 4 (1990), 181–93.

Rabe, Sirko, Andreas Maercher, Tanja Zoellner, and Anke Karl, "Neural Correlates of Post-traumatic Growth after Severe Motor Vehicle Accidents," *Journal of Consulting and Clinical Psychology*, 74 (2006), 880–6.

Ramachandran, Vilayanur S., and Lindsay M. Oberman, "Broken Mirrors: A Theory of Autism," *Scientific American* (Nov. 2006), 62–9.

Ransom, Sean, Kennon Sheldon, and Paul B. Jacobsen, "Actual Change and Inaccurate Recall Contribute to Posttraumatic Growth following Radiotherapy," *Journal of Consulting and Clinical Psychology*, 76 (2008), 811–19.

Reddy, Vasudevi, "Before the 'Third Element': Understanding Attention to Self," in Naomi Eilan, Christoph Hoerl, Teresa McCormack, and Johannes Roessler (eds.), *Joint Attention: Communication and Other Minds: Issues in Philosophy and Psychology* (Oxford: Clarendon Press, 2005), 85–109.

Rilke, Rainer Maria, *Letters to a Young Poet*, trans. M. D. Herter (New York: Norton, 1993).

——*Rilke's Book of Hours*, trans. Anita Barrows and Joanna Macy (New York: Riverhead Books, 1996).

Rizzolatti, Giacomo, Leonardo Fogassi, and Vittorio Gallese, "Mirrors in the Mind," *Scientific American*, 295/5 (Nov. 2006), 54–61.

Robinson, Jenefer, *Deeper than Reason: Emotion and its Role in Literature, Music, and Art* (Oxford: Clarendon Press, 2007).

Roessler, Johannes, "Joint Attention and the Problem of Other Minds," in Naomi Eilan, Christoph Hoerl, Teresa McCormack, and Johannes Roessler (eds.), in *Joint Attention: Communication and Other Minds: Issues in Philosophy and Psychology* (Oxford: Clarendon Press, 2005), 230–59.

Rorty, Amelie, "The Historicity of Psychological Attitudes: Love is not Love which Alters not When It Alteration Finds," *Midwest Studies in Philosophy*, 10 (1986), 399–412.

Rowe, William, "The Empirical Argument from Evil," in Robert Audi and William Wainwright (eds.), *Rationality, Religious Belief and Moral Commitment: New Essays in the Philosophy of Religion* (Ithaca, NY: Cornell University Press, 1986), 227–47.

—— "The Problem of Evil and Some Varieties of Atheism," *American Philosophical Quarterly*, 16 (1979), 335–41; repr. in Daniel Howard-Snyder (ed.), *The Evidential Argument from Evil* (Bloomington, IN: Indiana University Press, 1996), 1–11.

Saadia, Gaon, *The Book of Theodicy: Translation and Commentary on the Book of Job*, trans. Len Goodman (New Haven: Yale University Press, 1988).

Sacks, Oliver, *The Man who Mistook his Wife for a Hat* (New York: Summit Books, 1985).

—— *Awakenings* (New York: Harper Perennial, 1990).

Sartre, Jean-Paul, *Existentialism and Human Emotions* (New York: Philosophical Library, 1957).

Schneider, Helga, *Let Me Go* (New York: Walker & Company, 2001).

Schroeder, Timothy, *The Three Faces of Desire* (Oxford: Oxford University Press, 2004).

Senor, Thomas, "The Real Presence of an Eternal God," in Kevin Timpe (ed.), *Metaphysics and God* (New York: Routledge, 2009), 39–59.

Sereny, Gitta, *In That Darkness* (New York: Vintage Books, 1974).

—— *Albert Speer: His Battle with Truth* (New York: Albert Knopf, 1995).

Shattuck, Roger, *The Forbidden Experiment: The Story of the Wild Boy of Aveyron* (Tokyo: Kodansha International, 1994).

Shaw, Annick, Stephen Joseph, and P. Alex Linley, "Religion, Spirituality, and Posttraumatic Growth: A Systematic Review," *Mental Health, Religion & Culture*, 8 (Mar. 2005), 1–11.

Sherwin, Michael, *By Knowledge and by Love: Charity and Knowledge in the Moral Theology of St Thomas Aquinas* (Washington: Catholic University Press, 2005).

Shiffrin, Seana Valentine, "Promising, Intimate Relationships, and Conventionalism," *Philosophical Review*, 117 (2008), 481–524.

Sider, Ted, "Hell and Vagueness," *Faith and Philosophy*, 19 (2002), 58–68.

Smuts, Barbara, "Encounters with Animal Minds," in Evan Thompson (ed.), *Between Ourselves: Second-Person Issues in the Study of Consciousness* (Charlottesville, VA: Imprint Academic, 2001), 292–309.

Sophocles, *The Oedipus Cycle*, trans. Robert Fitzgerald (New York: Harcourt Brace Jovanovich, 1977).

Southern, R. W., *Saint Anselm: A Portrait in a Landscape* (Cambridge: Cambridge University Press, 1995).

Stanley, Jason, and Timothy Williamson, "Knowing How," *Journal of Philosophy*, 98 (2001), 411–44.

Stocker, Margarita, "Biblical Story and the Heroine," in Martin Warner (ed.), *The Bible as Rhetoric: Studies in Biblical Persuasion and Credibility* (New York: Routledge, 1990), 81–102.

Stump, Eleonore, *Boethius's De topicis differentiis* (Ithaca, NY: Cornell University Press, 1978; repr. 1989).

—— "Petitionary Prayer," *American Philosophical Quarterly*, 16 (1979), 81–91.

—— "The Problem of Evil," *Faith and Philosophy*, 2 (1985), 392–423.

—— "Dante's Hell, Aquinas's Theory of Morality, and the Love of God," *Canadian Journal of Philosophy*, 16 (1986), 181–98; repr. in Patricia A. Athay, Patrick Grimm, and Michael Simon (eds.), *The Philosophers' Annual* (Atascadero, CA: Ridgeview Publishing Company, 1988), 236–53.

——"Sanctification, Hardening of the Heart, and Frankfurt's Concept of Free Will," *Journal of Philosophy*, 85 (1988), 395–420; repr. in John Martin Fischer and Mark Ravizza (eds.), *Perspectives on Moral Responsibility* (Ithaca, NY: Cornell University Press, 1993), 211–34; also repr. in *Free Will: Free Agency, Moral Responsibility, and Skepticism*, vol. iv of John Martin Fischer (ed.), *Free Will: Critical Concepts in Philosophy* (London: Routledge, 2005), 395–420.

——"Visits to the Sepulcher and Biblical Exegesis," *Faith and Philosophy*, 6 (1989), 353–77.

——"Providence and the Problem of Evil," in Thomas Flint (ed.), *Christian Philosophy* (Notre Dame, IN: University of Notre Dame Press, 1990), 51–91.

——"God's Obligations," in James Tomberlin (ed.), *Philosophical Perspectives*, 6 (Atascadero, CA: Ridgeview Publishing, 1992), 475–92.

——"Revelation and Biblical Exegesis: Augustine, Aquinas, and Swinburne," in Alan G. Padgett (ed.), *Reason and the Christian Religion: Essays in Honor of Richard Swinburne* (Oxford: Clarendon Press, 1994), 161–97.

——"Persons: Identification and Freedom," *Philosophical Topics*, 24 (1996), 183–214.

——"Saadya Gaon and the Problem of Evil," *Faith and Philosophy*, 14 (1997), 523–49.

——"Francis and Dominic: Persons, Patterns, and Trinity," *American Catholic Philosophical Quarterly* (Proceedings of the American Catholic Philosophical Association), 74 (2000), 1–25.

——"Second Person Accounts and the Problem of Evil," in Timo Koistinen and Tommi Lehtonen (eds.), *Perspectives in Contemporary Philosophy of Religion* (Schriften der Luther-Agricola-Gesellschaft 46; Helsinki: Luther-Agricola-Society, 2000), 88–113; repr. (among other places) in Keith Yandell (ed.), *Faith and Narrative* (Oxford: Oxford University Press, 2001), 86–103. (The original version of this paper was originally presented in my Stob Lectures, which appeared together with subsequent Stob Lectures in *Seeking Understanding: The Stob Lectures 1986–1998* (Grand Rapids, MI: Eerdmans, 2001), 497–529.)

——"Augustine on Free Will," in Eleonore Stump and Norman Kretzmann (eds.), *The Cambridge Companion to Augustine* (Cambridge: Cambridge University Press, 2001), 124–47.

——*Aquinas* (London and New York: Routledge, 2003).

——"Personal Relations and Moral Residue," in Paul Roth and Mark S. Peacock (eds.), *History of the Human Sciences: Theorizing from the Holocaust: What is to be Learned?*, 17/2–3 (Aug. 2004), 33–57.

——"Resurrection, Reassembly, and Reconstitution: Aquinas on the Soul," in Bruno Niederberger and Edmund Runggaldier (eds.), *Die menschliche Seele: Brauchen wir den Dualismus?* (Frankfurt: Ontos Verlag, 2006), 153–74.

——"Saint Louis Jesuits and Sacred Music: Beauty as a Road to God," *Sacred Music*, 134/4 (Fall 2007), 11–24.

——"Eternity, Simplicity, and Presence," in Gregory T. Doolan (ed.), *The Science of Metaphysics: Historical and Philosophical Investigations* (Washington: Catholic University of America Press, 2010).

——"The Problem of Evil," in Robert Pasnau (ed.), *The Cambridge History of Medieval Philosophy* (Cambridge: Cambridge University Press, 2009).

——"God's Simplicity," in Brian Davies and Eleonore Stump (eds.), *The Oxford Handbook to Thomas Aquinas* (Oxford: Oxford University Press, 2011).

—— and Norman Kretzmann, "Eternity, Awareness, and Action," *Faith and Philosophy*, 9 (1992), 463–82.

Stump, Eleonore, Donald Stump, James Alexander Arieti, and Lloyd Gerson (eds.), *Hamartia: The Concept of Error in the Western Tradition: Essays in Honor of John Crosset* (Lewiston, NY: Edwin Mellen Press, 1983).

Surin, Kenneth, *Theology and the Problem of Evil* (Oxford: Blackwell, 1986).

Swinburne, Richard, *Responsibility and Atonement* (Oxford: Clarendon Press, 1989).

—— *Providence and the Problem of Evil* (Oxford: Oxford University Press, 1998).

Taylor, Gabriele, "Love," *Proceedings of the Aristotelian Society*, 76 (1976), 147–64.

Teichman, Jenny, "Henry James among the Philosophers (A Review of *Love's Knowledge: Essays on Philosophy and Literature* by Martha Nussbaum)," *New York Times Book Review*, Feb. 10, 1991, p. 24.

Teresa of Avila, *The Collected Works*, vol. i, trans. Kieran Kavanaugh and Otilio Rodriguez (Washington: Institute of Carmelite Studies, ICS Publications, 1976).

—— *The Interior Castle*, trans. Kieran Kavanaugh and Otilio Rodriguez (The Classics of Western Spirituality; Mahwah, NJ: Paulist Press, 1979).

Thiele, Leslie Paul, *The Heart of Judgment: Practical Wisdom, Neuroscience, and Narrative* (Cambridge: Cambridge University Press, 2006).

Thompson, Evan, "Empathy and Consciousness," in Evan Thompson (ed.), *Between Ourselves: Second-Person Issues in the Study of Consciousness* (Charlottesville, VA: Imprint Academic, 2001), 1–32.

Tilley, Terrence, *The Evils of Theodicy* (Washington: Georgetown University Press, 1991).

Tomberlin, James, and Peter van Inwagen (eds.), *Alvin Plantinga* (Dordrecht: Reidel, 1985).

Tugwell, Simon (ed.), *Early Dominicans* (New York: Paulist Press, 1982).

Turnbull, Colin, *The Forest People* (1961; repr. New York: Simon and Schuster, 1968).

Van der Vat, Dan, *The Good Nazi: The Life and Lies of Albert Speer* (Boston and New York: Houghton Mifflin Co., 1997).

Van Fraassen, Bas, *The Empirical Stance* (New Haven: Yale University Press, 2002).

Van Inwagen, Peter, "The Magnitude, Duration, and Distribution of Evil: A Theodicy," in Michael Beaty (ed.), *Philosophical Topics*, 16/2 (Fall 1988), 161–87.

—— "Critical Studies of the New Testament and the User of the New Testament," in Eleonore Stump and Thomas Flint (eds.), *Hermes and Athena: Biblical Exegesis and Philosophical Theology* (Notre Dame, IN: University of Notre Dame Press, 1993), 159–90.

—— "The Problem of Evil, the Problem of Air, and the Problem of Silence," in Daniel Howard-Snyder (ed.), *The Evidential Argument from Evil* (Bloomington, IN: Indiana University Press, 1996), 151–74.

—— "Reflections on the Chapters by Draper, Russell, and Gale," in Daniel Howard-Snyder (ed.), *The Evidential Argument from Evil* (Bloomington, IN: Indiana University Press, 1996), 219–43.

Vanier, Jean, *Becoming Human* (Mahwah, NJ: Paulist Press, 1998).

—— *Drawn into the Mystery of Jesus through the Gospel of John* (Mahwah, NJ: Paulist Press, 2004).

Velleman, J. David, "Love as a Moral Emotion," *Ethics*, 109 (1999), 338–74.

—— "Narrative Explanation," *Philosophical Review*, 112 (2003), 1–25.

Walker, Margaret Urban, *Moral Repair: Reconstructing Moral Relations after Wrongdoing* (Cambridge: Cambridge University Press, 2006).

Wallin, Nils, Bjoern Merker, and Steven Brown, *The Origins of Music* (Cambridge, MA: MIT Press, 2000).

Wallisch, Pascal, "An Odd Sense of Timing," *Scientific American Mind*, 19/1 (Feb.–Mar. 2008), 36–43.

Walton, Kendall, "Spelunking, Simulation, and Slime: On Being Moved by Fiction," in Mette Hjorte and Sue Laver (eds.), *Emotion and the Arts* (New York: Oxford University Press, 1997), 37–49.

Walton, Kendall, "On the (So-Called) Puzzle of Imaginative Resistance," in Shaun Nichols (ed.), *The Architecture of the Imagination: New Essays on Pretence, Possibility, and Fiction* (Oxford: Clarendon Press, 2006), 137–48

Wesley, John, *Explanatory Notes upon the New Testament* (London: Epworth Press, 1950; repr. 1959).

Wettstein, Howard, "Awe and the Religious Life: A Naturalistic Approach," *Midwest Studies in Philosophy*, 21 (Notre Dame, IN: University of Notre Dame Press, 1997), 257–80.

Wiesenthal, Simon, *The Sunflower* (New York: Random House, 1998).

Williams, Bernard, *Shame and Necessity* (Berkeley and Los Angeles: University of California Press, 1993).

Williamson, Timothy, *Vagueness* (London: Routledge, 1994).

—— *Knowledge and its Limits* (Oxford: Oxford University Press, 2000).

—— *The Philosophy of Philosophy* (Oxford: Blackwell, 2008).

Wilson, Catharine, "Literature and Knowledge," in Eileen John and Dominic McIver Lopes (eds.), *Philosophy of Literature: Contemporary and Classic Readings* (Oxford: Blackwell, 2004), 324–8.

Wykstra, Stephen, "Rowe's Noseeum Arguments from Evil," in Daniel Howard-Snyder (ed.), *The Evidential Argument from Evil* (Bloomington, IN: Indiana University Press, 1996), 126–50.

Yee, Gale (ed.), *Judges and Method: New Approaches in Biblical Studies* (Minneapolis: Fortress Press, 1995).

Zhisui, Li, *The Private Life of Chairman Mao*, trans. Tai Hung-Chao (New York: Random House, 1994).

INDEX